An Ia Story

One Thread in the Tapestry of Consciousness

Cover Art:

Teresa Baken's

Literary Support:

    B.L. Burke
       M.M. Sweet
          C.R. Williams

An Ia Story

One Thread in the Tapestry of Consciousness

s. 'a. stanley

© Copyright 2002 S. A. Stanley. All rights reserved. First edition.

No part of this publication may be reproduced, stored in a retrieval system, or transmitted, in any form or by any means, electronic, mechanical, photocopying, recording, or otherwise, without the written prior permission of the author.

Printed in Victoria, Canada

```
National Library of Canada Cataloguing in Publication Data

Stanley, S. A. (Sharon A.)
  An Ia story : one thread in the tapestry of consciousness
ISBN 1-55369-025-7
  1. Self-realization.   I. Title.
BF637.S4S72 2001                    158.1         C2001-903428-8
```

TRAFFORD

This book was published *on-demand* in cooperation with Trafford Publishing.
On-demand publishing is a unique process and service of making a book available for retail sale to the public taking advantage of on-demand manufacturing and Internet marketing.
On-demand publishing includes promotions, retail sales, manufacturing, order fulfilment, accounting and collecting royalties on behalf of the author.

Suite 6E, 2333 Government St., Victoria, B.C. V8T 4P4, CANADA
Phone   250-383-6864   Toll-free   1-888-232-4444 (Canada & US)
Fax   250-383-6804   E-mail   sales@trafford.com
Web site   www.trafford.com   TRAFFORD PUBLISHING IS A DIVISION OF TRAFFORD HOLDINGS LTD.
Trafford Catalogue #01-0427   www.trafford.com/robots/01-0427.html

10   9   8   7   6   5

Contents

Acknowledgement
Introduction

1. Setting the Stage for the Final Earthly Performance 1
2. Tangles in the Thread of My Existence 28
3. Strangling in the Tangles 42
4. Examining the Tangles 75
5. Disentangling Myself 120
6. Inspecting Conventional Reality 142
7. Spiritual Boot Camp 165
8. Crash Course in Confusion 180
9. Walking Through the Threshold 223
10. Dying to Live 250
11. Lessons in Gender Reality 267
12. Reflections on Limitation 288
13. Scrutinizing the Nature of Human Relationship ... 297
14. A Race for Understanding 320
15. Believing in Me 338
16. Illness: A Gift Supporting Awakening 354
17. Winds of Change 366

An Invitation 403

Acknowledgement

Whom do I acknowledge in regard to the support I have received in bringing forth this story?

Considering that we are all threads composing the tapestry of consciousness, and therefore intricately connected, the real question is: whom can I *not* acknowledge?
Who has not supported this venture?

Ultimately, we are all supporting each other coming to an understanding of the truth of our deeper connection to each other, and to something greater.

Experience has shown me that gratitude is an all-encompassing, miraculous force that flows through us when we are able to live from the center of our hearts.

My acknowledgement and gratitude are as all-inclusive as the tapestry of consciousness.

Introduction

When I was no longer able to hold onto the illusion I called my life, I made a commitment to discover who I really am and to live my life as I had an inkling it was meant to be lived—as a gift. I perceived my commitment as the beginning of a journey. Actually it was the beginning of the end of my reality as I was living it and the beginning of my recognition that I was but a thread woven into the tapestry of consciousness. This awareness would inevitably lead to the understanding that if I am one thread, I am all the threads. Indeed, I am the tapestry itself.

To travel the distance, I was repeatedly required to release that which prevented me from taking a further step. Step by step, I was freeing myself from the limits of a personal self and moving into the whole: I was dying; I was coming to life; I was becoming life. My journey home is your journey home. Woven together, we all compose the tapestry of consciousness—of life. It is not enough to have ideas about this journey. It must be lived. We must experience the journey to assimilate the truth and embody home.

All of us are encoded to embark (experience the awakening process) at a certain time. If it is not your time, what lies before you will be of little or no value to you. If it is your time, you will find these words to be a valuable tool, one that can support your first step, strengthen your sense of trust in the process, and create greater momentum. All will take this journey sooner or later, for in our hearts we all yearn, knowingly or not, to return from where we came—home.

Like climbing to the summit of Mt. Everest, we reach home by taking one step at a time. Surprisingly, however, this journey does not belong to us. We belong to the journey. The journey will define itself, as mine has. It will show us what we need to understand and do to walk out of our own fear. It will rip us from our attachments, jerk us free from the limiting hold that our history has on us and break us down until nothing is left but pure potential. Then we will understand the meaning of God.

Reaching home is not the end of the journey. Rather, to reach home is to be home—*to be the home*. Being the home shifts awareness from being the thread to being the tapestry. Life is no longer personal, but impersonal. It is no longer about me but about something much larger than me. The impersonal journey requires us to become support for others so they too can make their way home. No one is truly home (free) until we are all home.

You will not commit to go the distance because it brings fulfillment, or importance, or anything else. That is personal. You will commit to go the distance because of what you have become...what you have always been...*a gift to the world.*

1

Setting the Stage for the Final Earthly Performance

In the tapestry of consciousness, "I" am one thread, consisting of uncountable and amazingly varied fibers, all of which act as a memory bank. All the experiences that I have ever encountered during my existence—my history—are held within this thread and influence, if not define, the nature of each and every embodiment. No two threads are exactly alike, although there are innumerable similarities. This is why revealing myself as one thread of consciousness may be of relevance to you. Detailed examination of one thread inevitably and naturally leads to the examination and greater understanding of other threads (yours). When viewed collectively, they provide a true understanding of the dynamic expansiveness of the Whole—the entire tapestry of consciousness. In this context, this story is your story also, for there is only one true story of how we make the journey home…

As with all of us, when we enter onto the earthly stage, props must be established and other "actors" involved in the designated performance must take their places. Through many embodiments, the same actors gravitate to the same stage, acting out the same dramas, over and over again…before long, rehearsal is unnecessary. In fact, the roles the performers take on become so fixed and automatic that they no longer recognize themselves outside of their roles. In essence, we lose sight of who we really are. As such, it is important to note, there are no "good" roles or "bad" roles. There are no victims or perpetrators, only actors adeptly playing their parts. (Only off the stage can we recognize the truth of who we are.) Our biological families play invaluable roles to us for they support us stepping initially into the Earthly lessons waiting to be experienced…

It was an auto accident that set the stage for the beings who agreed to play the role of my parents to be brought together. My mother, age twenty-one, was involved in the collision. My father, age twenty-nine, stopped to give assistance. Marriage followed quickly.

Shortly after the birth of their first child, my parents moved from a nearby town to the second floor of my maternal grandmother's Victorian home. Grandmother and two young aunts occupied the first floor. The move had been precipitated by Mother's homesickness—having never before lived away from home. Also, she was in poor health, stressed from the rigors of being a new mother and pregnant once again, this time with me. "I" (the first aspect of more to come) was born in the confines of my grandmother's bed, assisted by the local doctor who then still made house calls.

My maternal grandfather had been sickly for a considerable time and his death shortly before my birth was upheaval enough for the family. I was told that Grandfather was a large man of German descent. Most revealing was his habit of starting off each day with a half-pint of whiskey drunk down in the bathroom of the local tavern. Grandmother's ways I would come to know firsthand. Underneath she was gentle and kind. However, her maintaining a stern, controlling matriarchal position over the entire family overshadowed her positive attributes.

Mother was thirteen when the youngest of her three sisters was born. Because she was saddled with helping in their mothering, her philosophy about child-rearing became "just have 'em and get it over with." Accordingly, it was exactly ten months after my older brother's entrance that I appeared on the scene, and another ten months later that my younger brother stepped onto the stage. Although Mother was hell-bent on having a fourth child in like fashion, her doctor cautioned her that she would not survive another pregnancy unless she gave her body a couple of years rest. Hence, her plans of further family expansion were jettisoned.

Father was of Irish/English descent, also the eldest of four children and the only son. Like my mother, he too was the offspring of a hard-drinking father. Except for a brief family effort at homesteading in Wyoming, Father spent his youth in a nearby farming community among extended family, much poorer than my mother's circumstances. Seeking employment through government opportunities during the Depression had provided him with a host of travel opportunities that would have otherwise been unavailable. He also spent four years in the service and had been a military policeman during the Second World War, first landing on Omaha Beach. He never uttered a word about what atrocities he had witnessed. Instead, he lived at the edge of his experiences: bragging about having driven around celebrities and high-ranking officials; proudly displaying to visitors his confiscated Nazi dress sword and German cigarettes; and dutifully participating in every patriotic event in our community. His military years would be the only meaningful punctuation in his life. It had given him a sense of home and family. Nostalgically, he would remain frozen in this raw era for his entire life.

Being hard-working country folk, my family (parents, maternal grandmother, aunts and uncles) lived a simple, make-do existence. Collective efforts were taken to grow and preserve garden produce, to gather hickory and black walnuts from my great-uncle's woods, and to pick and dry morels and berries for the winter. Geese and chickens were butchered and dressed in the backyard, the down saved to stuff pillows. Summer sausage was made by hand and hung from the attic rafters to age. Fat drippings became the basis for homemade soap. Clothes were scrubbed on washboards and hung out to dry. Outgrown clothes were handed down to the next in line and those that could no longer be passed on were recycled into rag rugs.

Father's occupation, a lineman for the railroad, took him on the road for days or sometimes a week at a time. He also tended bar part-time at the Veteran's Club, the social hub of my parents' life. In public, like his father, he carried himself as a jocose and engaging character who was quick with a quip or embellished story. This facade kept others at a comfortable distance.

His personal life was the antithesis of his public figure. He would sit taciturn with a newspaper spread in front of his face during meals. After dinner, he would retreat to his chair absorbed in watching television or reading a book. Even without something to distract him, it was rare for him to engage in conversation, let alone make eye contact. Neither contributing to household responsibilities nor spending time with his wife and children lured his attention, nor was such within his capacity. When he did engage, he lived life in a state of harried urgency and impatience. Late for any function was being at least a half-hour early, and the goal, once there, (except for the bar or club) was to get back home as quickly as possible. His formula for expediting family excursions was to sit in the car and honk the horn. It was an understood rule that we never, under any circumstances, kept Father waiting.

My mother was a garrulous conversationalist, having a reputation for being able to talk off, not just your ear, but also your arm and leg. Gossiping with neighbors was a primary focus in her life. Around us children she was more likely to be withdrawn, complaining about her health or how hard she had to work, and caught in crying spells. She was plagued by migraines and regularly spent entire days with the curtains drawn, lying on the couch, cold compresses covering her face, resolute on suffering and living her life in the clutches of depression. Fortunately for her, as well as for my brothers and me, her two younger sisters and mother came to her aid during our preschool years.

Once we began school, my mother spent a great deal of time as a dressmaker. Her occupation was a way to supplement the family income. More importantly, it provided her with money she could call her own as well as facilitated her contact with people outside the immediate neighborhood. Thereby, her need to stay abreast of community gossip was even more greatly fulfilled. Her busybody behavior embarrassed me even at an early age and from it, I adopted the belief that beyond petty inquisitiveness, people had no concern for each other.

My parents' marriage functioned within a context of mutual antagonism and general unhappiness. Father regularly demeaned my mother reducing her to tears, while she nagged him enough that he was left feeling as incompetent as she felt demoralized. Unlike Father, Mother needed affection. However, not even her compulsive attending to him or pleading brought her the caring she sought. In bed at night, I would hear her begging him to hold her, only to hear him annoyingly tell her to leave him alone and go to sleep. My childish impression left me to believe that my mother must be smelly or have bad breath to be ignored like that—a feeling that I readily transferred onto myself.

Seldom did my parents ever physically strike us. Yet we were repeatedly reproached for something or another. For example, coming from Father in the form of an impersonal, collective reprimand habitually punctuated with profanity, I often heard such things as: "These goddamn kids!" or "Who's making all that goddamn noise?" or "Jesus Christ, all of you get in bed! Now!" Even when he was not openly castigating, his body language indicated his irritation. I was too young to understand that his reactions were more the product of his disposition or of having his isolation disturbed than any flagrant misconduct on our part.

Mother's discontent over our childish behavior often fixed us in a beady-eyed stare that penetrated right through me as if I didn't exist. Her constant reprimand was, "I'm going to have to tell your father that you've been bad," or "Your father will be upset when he finds out about this." Since the nature of our misconduct was infrequently explained, I deliberately positioned myself within proximity of my parents' conversations hoping to overhear the cause of their disapproval. Father would question Mother, "Did *she* give you trouble today?" And she would respond with an overtaxed sigh, "Well, she's her usual self." I wanted to scream at them, "What's wrong with being my usual self?" I didn't; I was not supposed to be listening. Eavesdropping was not born in my childhood, only activated there. It had been born somewhere long before and would continue to be a survival tool for years to come.

As very young children, my brothers and I routinely sat on our parents' bed with Mother who would converse with Father while he changed his clothes at the end of his workday. One time, he turned to Mother and impatiently demanded, "Does *she* have to be here?" From then on, I was excluded from that ritual. This incident helped to cement my sense of being bad and therefore unworthy. It also taught me that there was something wrong with viewing a person unclothed, something shameful about the body. In addition, continually being referred to as "she," anchored my belief that I did not deserve to belong—that I was a nobody.

Father hated conflict. His rule, "If you can't say anything nice, then keep quiet," was his means to keep the illusion of peace in a tension-saturated environment. No one was allowed to argue or yell except him. No one else was allowed to voice an opinion or a perspective. While we were required to stuff our emotions, his negativity had free expression. His standard approach to coping with disputes was telling us, as well as Mother, to shut up. When the patriarch was in residence, survival was dependent on keeping him accommodated, remaining silent or keeping a wide circle. It took little time to learn that sarcasm disguised as humor was a viable avenue to vent frustrations and animosity.

My terror of criticism, rejection and punishment as well as my belief that I was a despicable person, all now infused into my role, kept me in a state of all-encompassing self-constraint. For example, once our mother found out that my brothers had stolen some candy from a local store. She phoned the owner to explain what my brothers had done, then made them walk to town all alone to pay for it and deliver an apology. I was traumatized by their punishment and felt guilty-by-association to the degree that I thought everyone would hate me for my brothers' bad behavior.

On another occasion when I was about four, while all the adults were outside, I pulled a chair up to my Grandmother's china cupboard and took a couple of lemon drops that she kept in a candy dish. I felt so immediately conscience-stricken by my actions that I slipped away to the garden and hurriedly buried the lemon drops in the dirt instead of eating them. Thereafter, I spent hours obsessing over my actions. It was the karmic grip that my past had on me even as a small child that left me believing that my needs could not or would not be supported simply through asking, or that I was worthy of having my needs met at all.

Then there was the time I was playing with a friend's china tea set when I bumped a cup and the handle broke off. Terrified of my friend's rejection or either of our mothers' reprimands, I hid the broken cup and skedaddled home. Unable to cope with my wrongdoing, I avoided going to my friend's house. Thereafter, my belief that I was a bungler and could only do bad things festered more intensely, another belief that had been born in ancient times and kept alive and reinforced through many earthly performances.

Once, I became lost in a department store while on a family shopping trip to the city. I sat hunkered down in a chair in the store office waiting to be claimed, convinced that my punishment for straying was never to see my family again. When Mother finally appeared, rather than extending the comfort I needed, she apologized to store officials for my behavior and then turned away leaving me to follow her out the door. The incident triggered a cascading array of deeply-established, interconnected Hansel-and-Gretel-type fears: becoming lost; wandering alone in the unknown; never being able to find my way back home once I had taken that one fatal step beyond a point of no return; and not being able to survive outside of the familiar.

On a different occasion, I locked myself in the bathroom with the intention of exploring the medicine cabinet. Before I could proceed with my curious mischief, I sliced my finger on a razor blade. My fear of being punished for my wrongdoing outweighed my need for help to the degree that I refused to obey Mother's imperative to unlock the door. Consequently, she was forced to phone a neighbor who placed a ladder to the second-floor window, cut the screen, and crawled through to retrieve me.

After the incident, Mother dispensed her most common admonishment, "What's wrong with you?" Indeed, I would spend a great deal of my life trying to understand exactly that. The experience taught me that I had to be more circumspect; being truthful was unsafe, and exploring my world was all-around perilous. With my misbehavior seldom explained to me, my perception of it was exponentially more extreme than my "crime" actually warranted. Anxiety became a natural state. So did pulling on my hair and clenching my jaws. Anticipation of a reprimand consistently triggered the same thought, "Now I'm dead!" My innate sense of fear of my own perceived wickedness, as much as my fear of being despised, punished, and rejected, were tightly intertwined around me like a cocoon, restricting my vision of a greater reality. I was my own judge and jury. I knew nothing about dismissal or acquittal, only guilt.

Paradoxically, I had an intensely inquisitive and serious nature, which produced a need to explore my world, know what made it tick, as well as explore, expound on, and articulate my many thoughts and feelings. With no safe outlet for self-expression and with no one to assure me that my thoughts and feelings were not bad, those same thoughts and feelings became over-charged and all-consuming: a monster that had to be controlled at any cost. Self-revelation came with the risk of being rejected, which left me to have to face my feelings of badness. The only safety for me was in silence and invisibility.

One day, after returning from a week's absence, Father put his arm around my shoulder (or maybe rested his arm on my shoulder) as he entered into a living room full of relatives. His touch felt like a hot poker searing my skin. Confusion swiftly muddled my thoughts, "What is he trying to do? Impress my relatives? Maybe he doesn't actually know he's touching me! Or maybe he thinks I'm someone else." My first reaction was to break contact. Yet I desperately needed his attention. If I pulled away, I might upset him and then he might get angry; then I would feel terrible. Between a need to be validated and a fear of rejection, I was immobilized.

Despite our parents seldom having time for us, Father was never short on promises. If we kept quiet in the car, then he would buy us candy when we reached our destination. If we behaved all week, he would take us somewhere on the weekend. If we played outside until the football game was over, then we could watch television. When he got paid, then he would give us our allowance. If, then; if, then; if, then. The problem was that even when the "ifs" were fulfilled, he consistently reneged on the promise of the "then." Still, I used his promises to convince myself that he cared about me and tried to behave in a way that assured that he would fulfill them, even while experience taught me to distrust his sincerity. I was incapable of comprehending that his behavior was simply his way of keeping his children under control and out of his way.

There was one family custom in particular that supported my conditioned belief that I had to be helpful or at least available to others regardless of whether or not I was actually needed, and mostly, at the expense of my own needs and desires. After a Sunday family dinner, the men would move to the yard to talk men-talk, and my brothers and boy cousin would go out to play. The women, on the other hand, would move to the kitchen to clean up. Invariably, rather than be allowed to play, my girl cousin and I would be expected to remain with the women "to do our share," which meant that I would be handed a towel to dry dishes. I was never able to see any point in this since the person doing the washing couldn't wash fast enough to keep busy the two or three others who were also waiting, towel in hand. I hated being in the confines of the kitchen with the chatter—which even then I considered senseless—and the waiting, waiting, waiting to be useful. I wanted to be outdoors and free. But if I voiced my discontent, I would be flatly reminded that everyone had to do "her" share. I wanted to scream, "What about the boys?" But I never did.

Sexuality was a matter that further frightened me and made me feel dirty. My uncle sometimes joked about his wife's "grass patch" and such, causing my brothers and male cousin to snicker. Although I was barely old enough to understand the nature of my uncle's remarks, I was sufficiently embarrassed to want to run and hide. Once on a family drive, my younger brother asked my parents about a mule he observed with an erection. Flustered silence in the front seat told me this was not a subject open for discussion. (I was approaching thirty before I could say the word penis, breast or vagina without turning red in the face.) Even so, my female cousin and I would sometimes play having a baby. Intuitively, I knew that anything having to do with genitals would bring strong disapproval. Nevertheless, I was inclined to press my genitalia against a pillow or the corner of a chair. I was too young to know that this was masturbation or that my behavior was a means to release the stress that accompanies embodiment. I saw, however, that my actions produced a disapproving glare from Mother, resulting in my learning also to be secretive about my sexuality.

My deep-seated fears took other forms as well. I was enthralled by every aspect of a storm: the kaboom of thunder, the streaks of light brightening the night sky, raindrops falling from somewhere far away, and especially the rainbows. Hardly before a storm's passing, I would be outside barefoot playing and splashing in the refreshing aftermath. But to step into one of the same puddles at night in which I had splashed during the day? That I couldn't do. Even when my childish logic told me that it was impossible to drown in a puddle, nothing could compel me to step into a puddle after dark when I was unable to determine the depth of the water. This same fear was transferred to larger bodies of water, and I refused to swim with my face submerged or where I couldn't see the bottom.

Fear of disappearing manifested in a myriad of other contexts. The pasture across the fence from the school playground was riveted with gopher holes. I spent much time hanging on the fence studying these holes, fascinated by them. I puzzled over how they could have possibly gotten there and curiosity made me want to examine them more closely. Yet I was fearful that if I stepped over the fence some horrible creatures hiding in those holes would reach out and grab me and suck me in, *never again to be seen*. When a blacktopped portion of the playground cracked and sunk, I was convinced that it was not safe to play there either. Whatever was lurking below ground might be able to reach me through the cracks, *never again to be seen*. Also, in bed I would frequently lay awake listening to the sounds of the night—like mice playing with hickory nuts left in the attic to season—thinking someone was coming to drag me off, *never again to be seen*. Nightmares carried a similar theme. I would often awaken in panic certain that angry, scruffy-looking men, even aliens from another planet, were staring at me through my bedroom windows. Whatever the nature of my fears, I dealt with them alone.

In contrast, I loved heights. I was naturally inclined to climb to the top of hills, or trees, or rooftops. As high as I could elevate myself, I never felt as if I was able to see enough. I wanted to know what was over the rise, or the next bluff, or beyond the horizon. I wanted to climb mountains to obtain a bird's eye view of the world. I wanted to know where every road ended, where every rainbow led. I wanted to know what existed beyond my field of vision.

My family neither embraced a formal religion nor any apparent sense of spirituality, so I was left to develop my own beliefs. I saw God as a big, powerful man who lurked behind the clouds waiting to identify and punish bad people down on Earth. Wary of my existence becoming known to him and of being snatched away for being a bad girl (never again to be seen) tempered my love for lying in the sun-warmed grass watching clouds drift across the sky.

Riding on the rope swing attached to a high limb of a Methuselah maple tree in Grandmother's yard, revealed my unconscious desire to escape my earthly experience. At the height of its arc, I felt as if I could fly clear of the swing and keep moving forever into the vastness of the sky way beyond even God's reach. I particularly liked swinging after dark when the stars were so close I was certain I could simply reach out and touch them. When traveling in the car at night, I chose to lie in the back window where my unobstructed view of the celestial world transported my awareness to a state of wondering, the state in which my attention naturally gravitated when I was less anxiety-ridden. It was in this wondering state—wondering from where I came and how I got to Earth—that I unconsciously connected to a self outside of the human role I was playing and thus to my origin. However, because childhood is formidable enough, simply becoming familiar with the physical dimension, it is an inopportune time to be recollecting our true nature or our beginnings.

My cat, Baby Tiger, who came into my life when I was four, was to play an important role to me throughout my growing-up years. She was my constant companion during the day and mollified my nighttime fears. She followed me wherever I went to the extent that when I started school, she had to be shut in the house. I spent many winter hours sitting on a warm, blanket-covered radiator in my bedroom with her curled in my lap. Together we would watch birds fussing about in the old, gnarly apple tree outside my window while I sang to my heart's content. I was certain that she liked my songs as much as I did. I was also certain that she never tired of listening to me talk to her.

Although I had no understanding of it, out-of-body experiences were a common facet of my childhood. They frequently occurred in Grandmother's sitting room where the women would gather after Sunday dishes were done, and where I appeared to be napping. I could see my body asleep on Grandmother's woolen couch, feel my heavy breathing, and clearly hear the conversations being carried on around me. It always amazed me that I could be sleeping but not sleeping, yet, unbeknownst to the adults, privy to all.

My cousins, brothers, and I were allowed to run freely on Grandmother's farm. Thus, nature came to provide a sense of safety, solace, and belonging that I never felt anywhere else. I spent much time wandering across the meadows, smelling wild flowers, observing butterflies, listening to birds, and filling my pockets with objects found along the way: smooth stones, twigs and feathers—anything to touch and feel. I loved the warmth of the sun touching my freckled skin as much as the breeze rumpling my copper hair. It was during this childhood roaming that my deep-seated, all-consuming affinity for trees developed and flourished. It was here that something working through nature began to speak to me.

By conventional observation, it would have appeared that I was in the habit of talking to myself, but this trait was much more than a childish imagination. I had conversations with a voice that spoke to me from somewhere inside of myself. This was not the voice in my head that made me feel bad, but a quieter voice, one that drew me unknowingly out of my physical reality and into another dimension. I knew that people who talked to themselves were considered daft, so I took precautions to have these conversations only when my solitude was assured.

Losing myself in daydreams was another of my pastimes. In one repetitive reverie, I was absorbed in collecting gold rocks (nuggets) scattered everywhere in the grass like Easter eggs and putting them in a woven basket that I carried with me for just such occasions. Regardless of the presence of others, they never took notice of the gold nuggets or of me for that matter. While picking up these nuggets remained my never-ending goal, I wondered why others were unable to see the value that I saw in the rocks or even to see them at all. Another common daydream was being able to fly. By simply lifting my arms, elbows up, and hands pressed to my chest, I could navigate to wherever I placed my focus. Most importantly, I was able to fly high enough off the ground to be safely out of everyone's reach.

At the age of eight, my life took a painful turn when we moved from Grandmother's home to a larger town a hundred miles away, only to move twice more within two years, ending back in the town where we had first moved. I missed my rural surroundings: the trees, flowers, birds, meadows, and wanderings. I was terrified of going to unfamiliar schools as well as making new friends. My fear of saying something that would bring disapproval or rejection from peers and elders escalated. I was devastated by the slightest criticism or reproach. Father was absent more often and Mother was increasingly more distant and depressed. My brothers and I were never close, particularly my older brother and me. He was an antagonistic bully. I used my long fingernails and a spray bottle of perfume, both of which I kept ready to use, to keep him at bay. However, my defenses proved to only trigger his amusement. Like Dorothy in **The Wizard Of Oz**, I just wanted to take Baby Tiger and go home: back to Grandmother's and the beautiful countryside where I was free to ramble—back to safety.

A year after we moved, a girl, slightly younger than I, disappeared from our community one summer evening. This was a time when children played safely outside until their parents called them to come in at dark. Officials knocked on doors, questioned residents and looked down wells, cisterns and other places that might conceal the little girl's body. My bedroom was a large closet in an old Victorian house made into a duplex. The door to the attic was in my bedroom. In bed at night, I listened for telltale sounds, which would confirm my belief that the kidnappers were hiding directly over my head. I was convinced that if I went to sleep I too would disappear, *never again to be seen.* My parents' bedroom was adjacent to mine, but it would have been a remote thought to seek comfort from them. The following spring, morel hunters found the girl's small body in a wooded area a few miles from where Grandmother lived. It was devastating to believe that the beloved area to which I yearned to return was as unsafe as any other was.

Father, his parents, and his three sisters were noted for being avid readers, which I equated to being intelligent. They often reminisced about their education in a one-room country school and perfecting their spelling skills to win spelling bees. Although I readily mastered my weekly spelling assignment, I would wait for an opportune moment and then cautiously bring Father my word list to have him quiz me. My efforts were a further attempt to attain validation and to assuage my insatiable need for him to acknowledge my intelligence as well as to own his relationship with me. His aggravation, along with a reinforced assurance that he did not really care about me, was the most I ever received. For him to recognize me, he would have to explore deep within his own history; he would have to move through his guilt, fear, and misguided deeds. For me to recognize myself, I would have to do the same.

Despite my reserve and self-doubt, I did well academically. My interests and achievements set me apart from my brothers who were much less academically successful, and my teachers' positive attention offset the lack of praise I received from my parents.

As I became proficient at reading, books became an avenue of escape. **Little House On the Prairie** and **Little Women** were two of many books in that genre that allowed me to vicariously experience emotions as well as a sense of a caring family. Of the sisters in **Little Women**, Beth was the character with whom I most identified. Her awareness of her impending death, as much as the fact that she had never been able to imagine or dream of her future, left me with a peculiar sense of fascination. I also identified with **Ann of Green Gables**. I was impressed by Ann's overt expression of willfulness despite the fact that it continually left her facing some sort of dire consequences. **The Diary of Ann Frank** left me with an eerie push-pull sense of intrigue and horror (evoking memories from my most recent prior embodiment). In time, I would move on to exploring the great classics, fervidly attempting to grasp the nature of the human dilemma. The worst aspect of reading, annoying, as much as disappointing, was that the end of a book inevitably signaled my return to the mundane.

Money was a critical concern with my parents. Consequently, they translated every aspect of life into dollars and cents. Father continually "stewed" about ending up in the poorhouse and relentlessly complained about whatever he could, from the lights, gas, and phone being overused (or used at all) to too much food being consumed. Meanwhile, Mother pinched, scraped, and hoarded her own earnings for herself. When we received the obligatory Christmas and birthday presents, which were consistently quite practical, they came weighed and measured and rationalized, "You got two presents and your brothers got three, but your two cost as much as their three so no one has a right to complain." I grew up fearing being a burden to them, as much as hating their too pragmatic approach to "gift-giving."

My parents used to tell us, "If you make your bed, you have to lie in it," which translated, whatever you do, it's your problem. Don't ask us for help. This philosophy further supported my fear of being a burden to them and guaranteed that I became financially self-sufficient at an early age. By age ten I was making potholders and selling them to Mother's sewing customers. From there I graduated to raking leaves and mowing lawns and was soon housecleaning, ironing, and babysitting. At fifteen, I acquired a work permit that exposed me to a variety of jobs. Making money became a way to acquire a sense of parental approval, and along with it a semblance of security, self-worth and independence. It did not lessen my fear of ineptness, criticism, and social anxiety, but the positives outweighed the negatives. Within this context, I learned that the only things that I could rightfully call mine were those for which I worked extremely hard. However, I was terrified of making wrong decisions—making mistakes—and being stuck with them, which left me tending to avoid decision-making altogether. Conditions were ripe for me to be stuck in a deprivation mentality and the struggles that accompany it.

During adolescence I was taken under the spiritual wing of a middle-aged spinster who brought sewing for my mother. She took me with her to Sunday morning church services where I would sit very properly on the hard, wooden pew trying to still my wayward mind to the pastor's sermon just as attentively as the other parishioners appeared to do. Upon being baptized, she became my godmother, and more than that, she was what I imagined a loving mother would be like. It was easy to be on my best behavior with her, but I still feared sparking her disapproval.

Through grade school and most of high school, I continued to participate in church activities but felt publicly shamed having been as old as I was when I was baptized. I worried that the congregation considered me a heathen for all those years. I saw my confirmation as an opportunity to fall into good graces with the congregation as well as prove my intelligence and worth to my father. The final step to confirmation was an oral exam in front of the Sunday morning congregation, stating the definitions of spiritual concepts, verbatim. Although I was unable to comprehend the definitions, I obsessively memorized them, terrified that a single error would expose me as an impostor. Except for one other girl, I was the only candidate who gave perfect responses. My sense of pride withered to feelings of utter abandonment, however, when afterward, my father stood in line with the other parishioners and merely shook my hand as he passed rather than stand proudly by my side as the other parents did. The struggle to contain my tears and subdue the urge to run and hide in shame had never before been so difficult.

The church remained my substitute family for a while. Yet a growing sense of distrust—an inner agitation—haunted my relationship to formal religion. As conscience-stricken as doing so made me, by my teenage years, I had begun to question established beliefs. People damned to hell merely because they were unfamiliar with church regulations? Having to be baptized to be saved? Was this God's justice? The idea that I was made in God's image was disconcerting: I was female; God was male. Further, I could not understand why worship had to be carried out in a designated building when I felt my best and greatest closeness to a sense of God when I was in nature. In church, I felt stifled as if I had to continually monitor my behavior and conform it to the norm, or I would be judged. There was too much emphasis on sin, damnation, and repentance. Being involved in religion and feeling positive about myself felt mutually exclusive.

It was the relationship between church and money where I found my greatest confusion. Men from the church came knocking at our door one day requesting pledges to tithe. I felt the pressure behind their courteousness as I sat across from them in our shabby-looking living room. Without any agreement on my part, they handed me a year's supply of envelopes in which to place my weekly offering. I wanted to tell them to get lost, that my money was hard-earned and my security, and I was not inclined to have it strong-armed from me. But my mind was stuck on a singular thought: "These men will kill me if I fail to agree." So I accepted the envelopes. Sunday after Sunday rolled around, and whether or not I went to church, I felt guilty about my anger, about negotiating with myself over how much money to give, and in the end, I felt selfish about not giving as much as I thought I should. Despite my issues with the church, stepping away from it proved difficult for it was another way by which I attempted to obtain a sense of family.

My feeling that I was not truly a member of my biological family intensified as I grew older. As my need to feel a part of a family also continued to intensify, I developed a habit of secretly watching from an upstairs window the activities of the next-door neighbors who had become like foster parents to me. I would observe them interact with their four children imagining the meaningful conversation taking place and what it would feel like to be part of a devoted family and in a real home.

Whenever I visited Grandmother, I would retreat to a second floor hallway closet where decades of **National Geographic** magazines were stacked in piles along one wall. My greatest interest was in the articles depicting so-called primitive cultures. My intrigue viewing naked bodies clashed against my sense of propriety. I did not know that the real enticement involved the nature of the culture: the mutual support, the cooperation and acceptance, the interdependence, the family/community bonding, and living unhampered and intimately attuned to nature. I wondered if God really did condemn these people for not being baptized. The thought left me fired up inside. I told myself that when I grew up I would become a missionary, not so much to convert "heathens," but rather to help people understand something else, something that I could not explain.

Despite the degree that my maternal grandmother maintained her rule over her daughters, my connection with her was through our mutual love of flowers. Whenever we visited her and the season allowed, I would examine the native perennial beds along the sides of the house as well as under the apple tree. Then I would meander among the rows of zinnias, snapdragons, gladiolus, dahlias, and such in her garden. The multitude of color alone was like being in a rainbow wonderland. I never picked or asked for any, although I yearned to do so. Instead, I would anticipate my departure when Grandmother would pick an armful for us to take home.

Mother had little success growing plants. First, she disliked being outdoors. The weather—wind, sun, heat, cold—she believed, was "mean" to her. Her houseplants regularly succumbed to neglect. The unnurtured child in me, who identified with her plants, was intensely disturbed that Mother failed to recognize or meet their needs and could simply let them die. During adolescence, I took to digging up a corner of the yard to grow flowers for myself. It would become ingrained that I assessed others' sensitivity to life by the quantity and condition of plants in their environment.

My intuitive awareness was as acute as my fears. I could feel my parents' strong estrangement from each other as much as from life itself. And, my entire family's superficiality was apparent to me at an early age. In particular, I readily sensed my paternal family's dislike for my mother. I could feel my mother's sense of rejection, which I also owned for myself. Butting against my intuition, adding to my confusion and distrust, was my paternal relatives' claim, "We love you so much," whenever our family departed from a visit. Many times, I had wanted to yell at them to stop lying to me, that they could not fool me. At the same time, I was afraid of being wrong. It was easier to doubt myself than to doubt them. I could feel skeletons in the family closet, and the shame clothing them, though I could not label them. I also sensed the lack of anyone being really present at family gatherings where there was much talk but little communication. Playing poker and drinking, the meat of get-togethers, provided the means for family members to avoid deeper interactions. Within whatever dynamics the family functioned, everyone seemed to know them well. Yet, whether I tried to be myself or the person I thought they wanted me to be, I felt as if I threatened everyone.

I greatly anticipated my paternal grandparents' visits, especially when errands took my parents away. It was then that I could engage in genuine dialogue with my grandparents. These rare moments of being seen and heard, the feeling of being acknowledged for who I really was, were like a high that I wanted to hang onto forever. The moment my parents returned, however, my grandparents directed their attention to the superficial, where the rest of the family resided, leaving me feeling bewildered, frustrated, and betrayed.

Clairvoyance was not a prerequisite to picking up Mother's resentment toward me. She was privately, as much as publicly, critical. In conversation with others and in my presence, yet as if I was absent, she would embarrass me by saying: "Well, there must just be something wrong with her. She's fourteen and hasn't gotten her period!" Or, "She's just like her Aunt Dolores" (whom my mother disliked). Or, "As much as I've sacrificed for her, she has no appreciation of anything." When I expressed a desire to be a flight attendant, she claimed I was too fat. My appeal for help in sewing a dress was ignored, but after I completed the dress, she criticized my work. She returned to the clothes basket items to which she felt I had not given proper attention, "to be ironed correctly this time." Armature against her criticism, coupled with my stubborn determination to figure things out by myself, amplified.

The notion that I could do nothing "right" was again more inexorably etched into my belief system.

The conflict between my mother and me escalated in direct relation to her increasing hypochondria and increasing demands on me. In my escalating sense of helplessness and anger, I more deeply resented my brothers who, I felt, were required to do so little. For example, on sunny summer afternoons, they played baseball while I hung out laundry. More than ever, it seemed that to be a boy was to be safe and free; to be a girl was to be at least at the service, if not the mercy, of others. By now my negative feelings were crystallizing, and I was becoming mouthy and blatantly hostile toward Mother. There was nothing she could do to make any situation right, even if she tried. I was beyond the point of no return and now my own worst enemy. Her standard response to any outburst became a flat, "This is my house and if you don't like it, you know what you can do." Already damaged from feeling like the outsider, her position hurt me all the more deeply. Helpless and angry, I put more effort into convincing myself that it was I who was wrong, unappreciative, and contrary. I tried to be obedient, but doing so only brought more torment.

In my anger toward Father for not acknowledging me as his daughter and Mother for not loving me as her child, I became vindictive, conjuring up scenarios of what might happen to me that would leave them remorseful. My favorite was my being killed in a car accident, whereby they would be forced to attend my funeral. There, they would finally recognize my beauty and innocence, as well as my value, as they viewed me lifeless in my casket. Tearfully, they would proclaim, "We're so sorry for not loving you. Please forgive us." Then I would forgive them, but they would never know this. Therefore, they would be eternally locked in their guilt, and I would feel that they'd gotten what they deserved.

Further, to satiate my sense of revenge and because my circumstances reinforced my belief that the only way to get something for myself was simply to take it, I would sometimes sneak into Mother's room and steal change from her purse. A greater fear of Father prevented me from ever taking anything from him, although the desire was there. My behavior, like my anger, left me horribly ashamed of myself but I was unable to control it.

An encounter during adolescence bolstered my negative feelings about being a female. My two cousins and my brothers and I were playing in the pasture during a Sunday afternoon family gathering. The boy cousin, a few years older than I and whom I had always feared, helped me over a barbed wire fence. As I turned to help him, he confronted me with his erect penis. My first horrified thoughts were, "How ugly! How awful!" In panic, I quickly closed my eyes, only to lose my balance and stumble into a pile of fresh cow manure. I got myself back to Grandmother's and hid in the shed to assess what I would do next. Truth did not feel like a safe option, but my soiled clothes would not go unnoticed. I decided I would sneak to the bathroom, wash my clothes, and just put them back on wet. I was spotted before I even entered the front door. My only recourse was to fabricate a lie. No one ever questioned my story or guessed the truth, and my cousin and I never spoke about the incident, but thereafter I kept a wide circle of him. Doing the same with my shame was more difficult.

Compounding my discomfort around sexual matters was an uncle's habit of pulling my shirt out and blowing down the back of my neck. Whenever he did this, he would profusely laugh while I would freeze up, not knowing what to do or say, although my stifled inclination was to smash him in the face. This uncle had taken an interest in my brothers and me that my father never had. It confused me to think that keeping my distance from him brought the possibility of missing out on horseback riding and other fun outings. I blamed my negative thoughts, and once again obscured my intuitive awareness by trying to convince myself that he was simply amusing himself (not really trying to look down my blouse).

Even without having to deal with my uncle's weird behavior, I felt embarrassed, frightened, and betrayed by my body as it began its pubescent changes. Denial was my only way to deal with what was happening. My mother continually complained to our neighbor about my habit of discarding my suffocating beginner bra and dress for tomboy attire as soon as I came home from school. This was the woman for whom I babysat, so I was embarrassed all the more. I did not want to be a girl, let alone a woman. I felt even more suffocated when I reached high school and by social dictates, was required to wear a girdle, garter belt and hose. I often watched boys intentionally walk up the stairs behind one brazen, young teacher who clearly never wore a girdle. I was embarrassed for her. Yet I respected the courage she had to be comfortable with herself regardless of the opprobrious attention she received. I could not understand why I had to be strapped into clothing, why I could not go bare-breasted like men and have it bring no attention, or why women did not have the freedom to be comfortable with their own bodies.

Mother was too inhibited to discuss coming of age with me, and I was relieved. What I knew about the topic came from a lecture given by the physical education teacher and from secretly having read material in the community library. I could never imagine any of this actually happening to me. My life was complicated enough just coping with my budding breasts. When the first sign of my menses came, I believed that there could be no greater humiliation, no greater loss of control over my body, or greater betrayal by it. Now, I certainly was dirty and impure. The thought of my mother discovering my predicament horrified me. My only recourse was to deal with the situation on my own. I felt as if everyone on Main Street was watching as I ventured to town the first time. It took forever to even muster enough courage to walk into the drug store, but the greatest challenge came with having to face a male cashier. Mother found evidence of my rite-of-passage, she claimed by coincidence, however I noticed signs that she had been snooping in my bedroom. I was resentful of her knowing anything about my sexuality and was uncontrollably, helplessly outraged and betrayed when I heard her divulging my condition to my father.

I talked to myself more and more as I grew older. Without question, I considered my behavior abnormal and feared that if I were discovered I would be condemned.

But again, my need overrode my fear, for this monologue I carried on provided me a sense of relief and comfort that only otherwise came from being with Baby Tiger or in nature. Nevertheless, during adolescence, whenever I sought to connect and communicate with my quiet inner voice, I found myself instead being drawn into an inexplicably horrifying, silent, empty nothingness like a deep, endless black hole. All sense of my own identity was obliterated as this force drew me ever deeper into itself. My only protection was a panic-activated soundless inner scream, which invariably jolted me free from wherever I was being pulled. After a number of these occurrences, cautious restraint kept me within the limit of how deeply inward I could travel before tapping into this tormenting void. Thus, I became further distanced from my own inner communication.

As I entered high school, my feelings of estrangement grew into a sense that my life had more control of me than I did. I was clueless as how to take charge. Who was I? I would compulsively stare and stare in my bedroom mirror prying deeply into the eyes staring back at me. The reflection did not convince me that I was seeing myself. I would look closer and more intently. I still could not see myself, only a frightening endless nothingness staring back at me. My repeated sessions before the mirror consistently ended in impotent confusion. Unknown, my real self remained hidden behind the character presented, like an actor on stage. I confused "who I am" with the role I assumed as part of the human performance.

High school proved to be a trying situation all around. During my first year, my English teacher, in collaboration with the librarian, claimed that the Dickens novel I had chosen to read was too difficult and refused to allow me to check it out. (I was still trying to understand the human dilemma.) I swallowed my hurt over being perceived as dumb and accepted a book that was considered more at my level. A week later, I was called into the office and interrogated by the principal along with the librarian about swear words directed at the English teacher that had been found in the Dickens book. They ignored the fact that the handwriting was dissimilar to mine and that I had not been allowed to even check out the book. "Someone could have written this for you," I was told. I struggled to contain my tears. Once dismissed, I walked away utterly deflated. Worse, I was sure, as gossip goes, that every teacher in the school would shortly have me condemned.

At the end of the grading period, I received a "D" in English. I was shocked and furious that I had done nothing to deserve it. The best I could do was arm myself with pertinent graded homework and test papers and then approach the teacher in an attempt to explain that she must have made a mistake—confused me with a not-so-bright girl whose name, similar to mine, alphabetically came directly before mine. The teacher refused to so much as open her grade book or even respond to my defense. Instead, she firmly dismissed me with, "No mistake has been made." My hurt transmuted to self-righteous indignation. The educational system, on which I had relied for a sense of acknowledgment, could no longer be trusted. Worse, I resigned to the belief that I was stupid.

From this incident, I learned on a smaller scale a lesson I had experienced during innumerable embodiments and which fed my deep sense of fear—innocence does not protect me from persecution. I became intensely more wary of anyone in authority and everyone in general. At fifteen, the responsible, capable student part of me withdrew from school. This was not an easy position to maintain considering my desperate fear of criticism. Yet my resistance was spontaneous and self-perpetuating.

I spent the remainder of my high school years drifting from class to class feeling increasingly more inept and unsure of myself. The minute I walked into a class some part of me invariably became captive to a reality outside of class activities. I could gaze out of the window for an entire period and not remember where I had been when I returned my attention to the class. Other times, wondering how a fly on the window was affected by direct sunlight or about the origin of a particular word that the teacher used in a sentence, carried me off into my own cascading reflection. Despite every effort to stay present, the part of me that was captive to its own wondering only returned when the class bell rang. It was my innate intelligence that allowed me to slide through my academic experiences.

This listening deficiency, this inability to remain present, also existed in a larger social context. I would say, "Aha, aha, aha," as I made myself appear to be in conversation, while my mind was far away in some undefinable other reality. When it was my turn to speak or I was asked a question, I had little idea where to pick up the conversation. I would never have thought to explain that my mind had wandered for a moment and that I therefore needed a statement repeated. I was too ashamed of my shortcoming.

Besides my listening difficulties, I endlessly obsessed over saying something offensive. For instance, while trying to explain to a friend about my Aunt's surgery, I found myself wondering if using the word "scab" would be appropriate. I told myself that it was silly to be afraid to say "scab," but I couldn't shake my belief that the word was akin to swearing. The more I thought about how to communicate my thoughts safely and properly in a given situation, the more nervous and hesitant I became. When I did speak, it would be accompanied with stammering, perspiring, or blushing. Under pressure, my thoughts would habitually come forth upside down, inside out, backward, or compulsively as if my life depended on explaining myself. Magnifying this shortcoming, I was even unable to manage making eye contact.

My inability to pay attention in conversation stood in stark contrast to a deeper listening capacity. Whether it was a bird singing from a distant perch, an insect chirping in the night, raindrops tapping vegetation or wind rustling the leaves of trees, whenever I was in nature, my listening took on a radar-like quality. I could actually feel an adjustment, an expansion in my ears as they tuned into these comforting sounds. At home, my ears were also hypersensitive, but here I was listening for trouble.

The peers, with whom I had begun to associate in junior high, molded a more tightly-knit circle in high school. It was understood that outsiders were unwelcome in our clique. We were a composite of bright girls. However, with the common handicap of dysfunctional families, we were unable to apply ourselves to anything of much self-benefit.

Casey, a girl my age who had moved next door to me in adolescence, was also a member of the clique. Our relationship had a sisterly closeness as well as a healthy infusion of mutual antagonism. Of all I found curious about her, most striking was that her mother required absolutely nothing of her. She was free to do whatever she wanted whenever she wanted and was provided the money to do so. She often spent time at my house while I scrubbed floors, made beds, or baked cookies. Her articulating her belief that my mother was unfairly demanding of me and that my brothers received preferential treatment provided an unprecedented perspective. We spent many a summer night sleeping on her front porch, exploring our beliefs about the nature of God, the possibility of ghosts, or life on other planets.

My sense of belonging was tested in high school when a new student enrolled. She was the brunt of ridicule with her unkempt appearance and outdated attire. With curiosity toward her, as well as discomposure, I watched her diverse but fruitless attempts to interact with various classmates. One blustery, snowy day, as a joke, a group of students, some of whom were clique members, plotted to take her coat from her locker and hide it. She asked around for its whereabouts when she discovered it missing, but no one would reveal the truth. Since she had not found it by dismissal time, she went home without it. The next day she returned to school wearing a more pathetic substitute. By then I had learned where her coat had been stashed. So as not to be seen as the squealer, I clandestinely disclosed to her the game in which she was unknowingly caught. I was aware that in speaking to her, she would attempt to attach herself to me. I also knew the tacit clique rules well enough to understand that I was jeopardizing my position by associating with this new girl. I would have had to step out of my sense of belonging to be friends with her. However ashamed I was of my behavior, I was unable to sacrifice my secure position in the clique for a position of integrity.

In grievous need of attention, I turned to the opposite sex. Nonetheless, I was intimidated by boys and terrified of anything with sexual overtones: an off-colored joke, **Playboy** magazine, or a public display of affection. At fifteen I had my first date. I felt important to be asked out. In contrast, I remained fully traumatized by the one time my father ever made physical contact with me; memories of his touch searing my skin were now seared into my psyche. The impact was evident by my apprehensively clinging to the passenger door, minimizing the opportunity for my date to reach over and take my hand. At the same time, I had an even greater apprehension of having to deal with his potential anger or rejection should I have to rebuff his advances. Unwilling to say yes, but afraid to say no would become a theme in my life.

I had been having a recurring dream about a gallant, tall, thin cowboy riding up on his great steed, rescuing me from my mundane life, and carrying me off to a wonderful land where our life would be filled with romance and adventure. I could even smell his English Leather, a brand of men's cologne that I liked well enough that I carried a sample bottle around with me to smell. Meanwhile, I grew all the more confused about my identity. Although I feared my sexuality, as well as losing my virginity and becoming pregnant, my body began to take on a mind of its own. It wanted to explore the burgeoning sexual energy I had suddenly found myself having to labor so tenaciously to contain. Supporting my intensifying confusion was a growing inexplicable sense of being wicked and shameful, as I was betraying myself by having an interest in exploring my sexuality.

Making matters worse, Mother became increasingly suspicious as I entered my dating years. Both my parents had always shown great concern for their reputation, and now it seemed that my mother believed that whom I dated reflected on their position in the community. Habitually positioned by the front door or a window, she would scrutinize my comings and goings from dates. I was certain that her only concern was the possibility of my becoming pregnant. When she was not giving me the silent treatment, she was attempting to define or control my experiences. "You can't go on a date with Ron. Gertrude's neighbor told her that his family is southern trash," she would declare. My suggestion that she might want to meet Ron and decide his credibility for herself never worked. Heresay was enough. I hated her being a killjoy. However, her prohibition never prevented me dating whomever I chose, although I was never brave enough to be openly defiant.

Sometimes when no one was at home, I would lock the doors, pull the shades, dim the lights, and then strip free of all my restrictive clothing. Thus, I would begin to dance to an inner passion impossible to subdue. I would move, lithe and free flowing, like the wind, free of emotional, parental or social constraints, ostentatiously pirouetting from room to room, only stopping when I became dizzy or breathless. Nonetheless, while I abandoned to dance, some inner guard stood sentinel, fearful of being unexpectedly discovered, especially by Mother, whom I would never allow to see me in such a vulnerable condition.

Teen dances were the antithesis of my secret dancing. My body simply could not move to the rhythm of the music. At worst, it felt like a dead weight. At best, I had a problem getting the right and left halves of my body to work together, or simply move my feet from one spot to another. It was like being on a scooter. The left leg attempted to maintain movement and direction, while the right just stayed rooted in one spot. (This carried over into other activities, like skating and swimming.) I watched how others effortlessly moved their arms, legs, and torso in synchronized motion to the music, simultaneously conversing with each other and having a good time while I felt like a fool. I was convinced that there was a faulty connection between my brain and body parts.

My singing fell into the same genre as my dancing. As much as I loved and needed to sing, I was incapable of hitting or holding a note or following a tune. My voice gave out before it even came out. In junior high I had earnestly wanted to be a member of the girls' chorus and had found the courage to audition. To my horror, I was rejected. Fortunately or not, Mother, who had been hired to make the dresses for the chorus members, pulled clout and I was invited to join after all. I loved to sing at the old people's home, mental hospitals, and other places where we toured. I loved the sophisticated Broadway tunes we performed. But I knew I could not sing, and I felt dishonest, ashamed that I had not been selected on my own merit.

I was already aware that I was more of a handicap than an asset as a member of my church choir. Oftentimes, I would mouth the words to the chosen hymn so as not to stand out from the whole or ruin the Sunday service. I often wondered what good I was if I could not dance or sing, but like my dancing, I could hear from deep inside of me, a different music. There I could hear myself perfectly attuned to it.

At fifteen, I took my last vacation with my parents. It began typically enough, but ended up having a deep impact on me. We went to visit Father's family in Michigan. During the stay, my cousins, my brothers, and I were invited to go boating with some friends. For me the outing was punctuated by an incident during a swim near shore. While my younger brother and I were roughhousing in the water, I was knocked unconscious by an unintentional blow from his knee. I landed stomach down in the water with my head twisted to the side. Thinking I was feigning injury, my brother moved on to other distractions. I heard my voice saying, "If you don't get up, you'll drown." But some part of me, feeling peacefully attuned to the movement of the waves, desired to stay in this position. I was unable to force myself to move. The waves rhythmically rocked my body back and forth gradually pulling my face below the surface. Meanwhile my voice continually repeated, "If you don't get up, you'll drown." Suddenly I was aware of my brother yelling at me, and my body being jerked out of the water. The part of me connecting to the water gave a silent plea, "Please, don't bring me back!" Following this incident, I felt heavier, my body more foreign, my feelings more oppressive, and my view of myself more negative.

The following Christmas, a boy I met during that vacation sent me a card with ten dollars in it. I was taken aback and felt unworthy of his generosity. Besides, he was two years older than I was, which alone, left me frightened of him. What if I should keep the money and then happen to see him again the next summer? That would obligate me to date him, perhaps alone, where he might try something. But I did want the money. When a normal teenage girl might have felt flattered, I was on the verge of hating him for making me feel trapped. Caught in my own predicament, I wrote to the boy, thanked him for his generosity, and then explained that since I did not feel comfortable taking the money, I had donated it to the Salvation Army. In fact, I had kept the money for my personal use. And as if that was not enough for God to strike me dead, I then proceeded to use the lie to impress my grandparents. Years to come, I would still be shaming myself for my behavior. This incident was the first pronounced sign of a deeply ingrained patterning: self-worth, money, and men, coupled with fear of obligatory sex were sticky strands of a deadly web in which I remained trapped.

Sliding from my adolescent to my teenage years, my conflict with Mother became unbearable. Now, she resented my being anywhere but home or with anyone but her, and she used her poor health as a means to keep me corralled. At the moment of walking out of the door to join waiting friends, she would only then say in her subdued, whiney voice, "You know how poorly I'm feeling and how much work I have to do. I was sure you were going to stay home and help me today." If I ignored her and went out with my friends, I felt guilty; stay home to appease her, and my anger flared. I hated her for not letting me have my own life; and worse, I hated myself for hating her.

It had become routine that I go along as the neighbor's babysitter on their two-week summer camping trip. When I accepted their annual invitation, Mother did not come right out and say that I could not participate. Instead, she declared, "I can't get along without you for that long." A heated argument ensued. I took the position that my brothers could help out for once, but she would not sway. In the end, and not without a greater sense of helplessness and rage, I surrendered to her wishes. The neighbor suggested that I ignore my mother's manipulation and go anyway. The thought of being that defiant or selfish scared me. Unknowingly, I was now fully anchored in the belief that I was indispensable to my mother. Further fueling my negative feelings toward myself was the fact that this neighbor woman, who did her best to be a positive influence in my life, could hear me yelling at my mother during our constant battles.

I was ashamed of our living conditions. Our home was unkempt and cluttered from Mother's obsessive hoarding and Father's slovenly ways. Our furniture was old, mismatched and dilapidated, the carpet was threadbare, and the walls were adorned with essentially paint-by-number pictures. Sewing paraphernalia was characteristically strewn from the dining room, my mother's central work location, throughout the house. To sit down anywhere, required first moving her materials somewhere else then checking for pins or needles that could otherwise take one by surprise. My cubbyhole of a bedroom on the first floor was used as a changing room for Mother's customers. Therefore, she required me to keep it presentable. On the other hand, the rest of the house was put in order only when company was expected. Then it became a massive production to stuff the chaos out of sight and scrub the area of entertainment spotlessly clean. I could not understand why everything was about show, why no one in the family wanted to live within a permanent context of orderliness, or why I had to live by rules that applied to no one else but me.

Beyond the embarrassment at having friends see the state of my family environment, I bought into my parents' continual laments over their state of poverty enough that pity left me obliged to aid them. Rallying my brothers' participation, we would cooperatively buy our parents "gifts"—furniture, lamps and various other household items that they would not otherwise have provided for themselves. Besides pity and obligation, my actions were founded on a need to make my living situation more tolerable, to assuage my obsessive sense of selfishness as well as a means to buy my parents' acceptance. Struggling to not empty my pockets to anyone who cried poor would reach addictive proportions.

By age sixteen, I was largely financially independent of my parents. Beyond my schooling, I supplied all my personal needs, particularly my clothes. What I chose and what I wanted to wear replaced the hand-me-downs and homemade clothes that had defined my wardrobe for most of my life. Having nice clothes became extremely important to me. With great effort, I attempted to create a sense of identity—which I desperately needed—from my wardrobe. I worked too hard for my money to be extravagant, but with store-bought clothes, Mother viewed me as uppity which exacerbated my feelings of shame and self-centeredness. Consequently, my efforts to feel positive about myself were sabotaged.

By the time I became old enough to obtain a drivers license, I had saved enough money to purchase and maintain my own car, which more than a vehicle of transportation, became a vehicle to escape my familial situation. Father tainted my freedom, however, when he habitually checked my odometer and then would mutter something like, "Jesus Christ, you put a lot of miles on that car last night!" Why did I continually have to prove my innocence or feel guilty for whatever I did? Whatever I tried to do or have for myself, I felt as if it was always being taken away underhandedly. In moments like this, I wanted to scream at him, to the entire world, "To hell with you, I haven't done anything wrong!" But it was a foreign notion to challenge him. He remained too unapproachable; I had learned well to say nothing to him unless it was "nice." In simple recourse, I unhooked the odometer cable when leaving home and engaged it again before returning.

The independence that my car afforded was further impaired by Mother's expectation that I, at her convenience, chauffeur her on errands and shopping trips. My annoyance over waiting while she gossiped with most everyone she met habitually turned to exasperation, which repeatedly precipitated arguments between us. I would thunder at her that I was not her servant, that she had no right to take up more of my time than necessary, and that I was unwilling to sit in the car waiting endlessly for her when she was just dilly-dallying. As a matter of course, I would remind myself that I was her only option and that I was acting just as badly toward her as my father did. Also, I would then condemn myself both for hurting her feelings and being so thoroughly reactive. Through greater awareness I would eventually understand that I had, in fact, agreed to come into embodiment to take on the role of servant, which was about responsibility, not obligation or sacrifice.

With her sharp tongued, busybody, self-pitying nature, Mother readily alienated herself from others as much as she did from me. There was no question that I felt bad about her not being liked. The one way I found to temper my own animosity and pity toward her and also to bolster her self-confidence was to help her whenever she went out by putting an outfit together, assisting her with her makeup, and finally styling her hair. Somewhere, somehow, I also knew that my need to make her look and feel attractive was an attempt to neutralize her apparent jealousy toward me.

Although one part of me was caught between feeling attractive and fearing it, another part of me was overly-critical of my looks—one more of my innumerable contradictions. I hated my freckles which lemon juice would not fade. I hated my eyebrows, my facial hair, and the warts on my left knee, and my fat thighs. But my red hair, of which I was discreetly proud, was like a banner setting me apart from all the rest. Throughout my youth, it afforded me a degree of attention even from male peers who taunted, "I'd rather be dead than red in the head."

The seed of my eating disorder was carried with me into this lifetime and cultivated in my childhood. When Mother made a dessert—a pie or pudding—she would divide it into five portions, one for each member of the family. Having a meager appetite, I seldom had room to eat mine at dinner. I would ask to save my portion for later, to which she would respond, "If you don't eat it now, it's going to one of your brothers. I'm not having food sit around." This resulted in me stuffing myself rather than being deprived of "my share." My eating disorder mushroomed during my teen years. I ate when I was anxious, angry, or sad. I ate to fill the emptiness inside. I ate when I needed to jump out of my skin. I ate when I felt as if I was suffocating. I hated my self-indulgence, and regardless of my weight being normal, I could only see myself as grossly overweight. It took little effort to convince Mother to obtain prescription diet pills for me. Taking only a fragment of a pill kept me wired for hours. I would go for days eating crumbs of food. At least, I had control over my body if nothing else in my life. I had no idea that I was taking uppers, but intuitively I knew that I was abusing my body.

At this time, Father, having suffered for many years from severe bleeding ulcers, finally agreed to surgery. Witnessing him overcome with pain, day after day, moaning and groaning and saturating the house with the weight of his suffering had greatly impacted me, especially since there was nothing I could do to help him. He drew up a will before entering the hospital certain that he would not survive the surgery. I anticipated that without the pain (as much as his witnessing his own recovery), he would return home with a new disposition. Instead, he remained as irritable, impatient, and brooding as ever. His obsessive worrying particularly bewildered me. I failed to comprehend how his negativity could have so tenacious a hold on him or what it would take for him to change. As much as I desired to understand what supported his worry and negativity, I was blind to the degree that these characteristics had become part of my own mentality.

During my teenage years, I began having my first conscious premonitions of death. The one most horrifying instance began during a visit to my maternal grandmother's with my parents. Prior to arriving, I felt inexplicably anxious—much more than usual. When we arrived, Grandmother informed us that an elderly neighbor had passed away that morning. He had been a kindly gent, wheelchair bound by polio, but always free with funny stories, candy, or a little wooden trinket of some sort whenever my brothers and I had found our way across the street to visit him in his workshop. Home here among the hills of my childhood hardly felt the same knowing that he was no longer part of it. During the entire visit, I could scarcely think of anything other than him (his energy). Compounding my confusion, I felt my inner voice was telling me that there were more deaths to come.

Immediately after arriving home, a friend stopped by with the news. A friend, with whom I had developed an uncommon rapport and who had recently departed for college, had been killed that morning when he fell beneath the wheels of a train on which he had been hitching a ride. Between the sense of personal loss and questioning my being personally responsible due to my premonitions, I felt a devastation that would haunt me for years to come. Mother tried to comfort me as I stood in the hallway fighting back my tears, but her touch burned as much as my father's had so long ago. Unfamiliar with this kind of overture from her and furious that it took death for her to respond to my needs, I recoiled. Simultaneously, I hated myself for making her feel rejected. With no one to support me in a greater understanding of my premonitions, I locked my voice along with my knowing as far away inside as possible. Still, periodically they would creep out, making me feel further out of control and more terrified of myself.

Throughout my teenage years, it had become a routine to deal with my burdensome feelings through nocturnal visits to the neighborhood cemetery. Even my fear of being seen frequenting such a place never overshadowed my need to be there. I would covertly enter this ghostly sanctuary through a rusty, wrought-iron gate which was hidden deep in shadows, created by a corner street light penetrating through the foliage of nearby trees. Then I would wander the tree-lined lanes winding through the crumbling, turn-of-the-century tombstones absorbing comfort from the energy I found there. Characteristically, my visits ended by my sitting under an old oak tree secretly crying, freeing my deeply agonizing pent-up emotions. I could not have realized that the sense of relief I experienced there was much more than an emotional release; the consolation I was feeling was coming from unearthly intervention.

During my last years of high school, I sank deeper into despondency. I desperately needed someone to listen to me, someone with whom I could safely share my thoughts and feelings, as much as someone who would assist me in finding answers to my endless questions. I needed someone to support me in seeing and understanding myself, someone to help soften my horrible loneliness. However, I had difficulty convincing myself that I was even comfortable with clique relationships. Friendship with Casey proved trying if not confusing. Sometimes we were best friends. Sometimes she turned her back on me, at which time I felt utterly abandoned. She was highly intelligent and with no effort ended up in the advanced classes, which confounded me, for otherwise, except when we were alone together, she mostly acted like a buffoon. In my hurt and envy I took advantage of this. At the same time, something about her—her masculine energy—frightened me. I wanted to blame her for the friction between us, but mostly I blamed myself.

Worse, I was unable to make sense of dating. The boys I attracted wanted sex. The thought of sexual intercourse reduced me to terror. Becoming pregnant felt like a fate worse than death. As far as my dread of my sexuality allowed me to experiment, I merely felt that if my conduct became public, I would be automatically despised. One boy, who was a couple years older than I, smart but running with the wild, reckless, and hard-drinking crowd, specifically challenged my gender relationship fears. (This was a boy whom Mother held in good standing because he was involved with church activities, and his father was a teacher at the high school.) He asked me out on dates, and although he was casual about me, I accepted. When he came home during his first semester at college, he bragged about his sexual prowess, like screwing girls in closets at parties. He claimed that his goal was to take my virginity also. Fear of rejection left me unable to tell him flat out that he was wasting his time, while an apprehension of an indefinable something else left me struggling to defend my virginity. When a mutual friend, and unknowingly an admirer, informed me that my college interest considered me a "tight box," my fathomless fear of being the subject of public ridicule flared. Outside of this situation, a dateless senior year brought closure to my high school gender experiences. I was convinced that something was wrong with me. The words to a favorite song, "Following dreams I'm not sure of, I chase the bright, elusive butterfly of love," epitomized my confusion about love and gender relationships.

Love aside, life in general felt illusive—way too complicated. I was merely fumbling my way through, trying to make sense of where I was as much as trying to figure out how to play a game without knowing the rules. I had a hint of awareness that there was more to life than what I was experiencing. Whatever it was that I was looking for seemed to be somewhere else, somewhere beyond my reach. When I was where I thought I needed or wanted to be, a certain, insidious restlessness pervaded my awareness. I had a notion that if I could comprehend my parents' unhappiness, I would have a key to relieve myself of mine. More importantly, if I could understand another's nature, I could understand who I am. Thus, I continued to question. Between such a backward approach and having an overly serious nature, I only succeeded in threatening others and frustrating myself. Eventually, I would discover the route to awareness as well as have the strength to uncover personally the issues that supported my overwhelming discontent. Consequently, I would then be able to understand the nature of the human dilemma in general. Ultimately, inexorably, my insatiable wondering and profound inner frustration were bearing me in the direction I was destined to travel.

The summer I graduated from high school, my grandmother and aunt took my cousin and me on a vacation to Colorado. On one occasion, my co-travelers stopped to explore a gift shop in Rocky Mountain National Park while I conducted my own exploring outside. Setting aside a twinge of hesitation, I began to follow a trail that I discovered to the side of the gift shop. It was shortly clear that the trail was leading to higher elevations, possibly to the top of a nearby mountain peak. I was unaware that it was more than simple curiosity moving me as I continued to trek along. The happening was, in fact, much greater than my ability to conceive at the time; it was actually my path that was finding me. I was being set up by unseen forces to enter into my awakening process.

The farther I moved along this trail, the stronger the urge to follow it became. At one point, I sat under an evergreen to catch my breath. Although I was confident my relatives were already irritated by my disappearance, my uncontrollable need was to continue ascending until I stood on top of the mountain and observed whatever there was to see from there. I resisted common sense long enough to climb a bit farther, but finally protocol overrode my need and I returned to the gift shop to face whatever my aberrant behavior had produced. I wanted to beg my relatives to wait for a while in order for me to further explore. I dismissed my urges by reminding myself that there was an agenda that had to be maintained and that my companions were girly females who quite properly and easily contented themselves driving along observing the scenery from the car: not tomboys like me who needed to be out exploring. Deeper awareness left me sensing that I was also different in other ways, although I was uncertain as to their nature. I silently took my place in the back seat trying not to be sullen or act disappointed, but something to do with the mountain left me feeling frenzied inside.

Upon our return, my aunt informed Mother that she thought I had not had a good time. My fevered reaction was, "There, I've caused trouble again." I was sure my traveling partners would hate me and never want to have anything further to do with me. How could I explain that I had not meant to cause trouble? That I had tried to monitor my attitude? I swore that someday I would return to the mountains, and when I did, I would climb to the top and know for myself what it was that had left me so unsettled.

I was stepping into my adult life with no sense of self other than a sense of ineptness, shame, worthlessness and wickedness. I felt connected to nothing. The sixty's enticements did little for me. Because of an odd, undefinable discomfort of having my senses dulled and my physical intolerance of alcohol, involvement in the drinking scene was short-lived. There was talk in school about kids using drugs but I personally knew of no one who used them and believed that only degenerates like Chicago gangsters engaged in such activities. Occasionally I smoked cigarettes, mostly because of peer pressure and also to rebel against my parents, although I never smoked openly. With the need to brush my teeth after each smoke to rid myself of the unpleasant taste, as well as the painful effect smoking had on my chronic tonsillitis, smoking never became a habit. The clique had been head-over-heals obsessed with the Beatles. I related better to classical music. And although I was stepping into the era of rock concerts and free love, I felt distant from all that. A male classmate had bet me that I would be the first girl to reach the altar. Marriage and childbearing were beyond my imagination; I did not feel worthy of either. At this point, just thoughts of attending church services threw me into a panic. I was on my way to entering college despite my fear of doing so, mostly, because I did not know what else to do with my life.

A number of clique members were volunteering their time and services to political campaign activities. Politics, as well as causes, especially the Vietnam War, confused me. To me, one candidate's speech sounded no different than any other: simply a lot of words. Additionally, I never could understand the difference between Democrat and Republican. I was clueless as to why I had no ideals, no beliefs, no dreams, no ambitions, and no sense of a personal future—nothing of value in which to put my faith or to do with my life.

Unable to engage myself in anything meaningful, I found avenues of escape. I worked a great deal. I watched television. I slept even more. I ate. I clung to a few clique members, although I was intuitively aware that insecurity was the most prevalent element that kept us together and that I was selling my soul to avoid my own loneliness. I felt abandoned by Baby Tiger who had suffered a stroke that had left her partially paralyzed. Worse, I was horrified that her condition sickened me and that I pushed her away when she attempted to be close to me.

The negativity of my family environment would be far-reaching. I was walking into my future with my thoughts convoluted, encrusted in cynicism, and my mind closed off from the opportunities and adventures that life had to offer. I knew how to be accountable to everyone but to myself. It was my karmic death-hold on fear of persecution that left my human self struggling within the confines of a safe zone—fight or flight—and maintaining a parochial reality while guaranteeing invisibility to my real self, who I am outside of the role I was playing in the human performance.

Yet there was a bare flicker of knowing that left me feeling that somewhere there was a reality that worked for me. In fact, my greater knowing was intact but buried in an all-but-forgotten place deep within me, a place that could only be reached by journeying inward, stepping, one-by-one, through the incalculable layers of fear camouflaging it. I had not embodied to have a great childhood or an easy life. My purpose for embodiment was about merging with my knowing; thus enabling me to accomplish the purpose my life was to serve. Viewing my childhood from a spiritual vantage, owning it for what it was—a gift—would be an integral part of the process. Only through accessing my greater awareness would I be able to acknowledge and express the gratitude due to my parents and others who had come to play a role to my awakening process. Ultimately, my inner restlessness—a deep yearning for a reliable reality—would be the motivation to examining the thread of my existence (my consciousness) all the way to its core, and thus understanding how it is interwoven into the fabric of collective existence (consciousness). There was no visible evidence at this stage in my life that I was actually on my way home or that I was preparing the way for others to follow.

2

Tangles in the Thread of My Existence

A tall, blue-eyed, blond boy two years older than I, who lived in a neighboring town, entered into my life shortly following my high school graduation. He was gentle, caring and supportive, dire contrast to any of my prior dating experiences. While I valued those traits, part of me found him lacking confidence, and especially since he had already flunked out of college, also lacking intelligence. In a word, I found him uninteresting. (The greater truth was that I did not know how to handle a relationship that came without struggle.) I continued to date him anyway. After a few months, he declared his love for me. Between my inability to receive (his love) without feeling obligated to reciprocate and my active hormones, I surrendered my virginity to him in the front seat of his car, parked in front of my parents' house. We were both quite shy in regard to our sexuality, and I trusted that he did not think less of me for being sexual. He was certainly not the kind of boy who would consider me a conquest or casually talk about our personal interactions with his friends. Still, some part of me felt tarnished even shamed over my encounter with "intimacy." In contrast, another part of me felt a sense of justified revenge toward my mother who had continued to communicate in her own underhanded way that I was sluttish.

Since it was the Vietnam War era, it was inevitable that my boyfriend would be drafted. Before he left for boot camp, he proposed marriage. I did not know how to say no and was scared of facing life on my own. Further, I was entrenched in the "dessert routine": if I did not grab onto something, whether or not I wanted it, I would get nothing at all. I accepted his offer. Yet, when I contemplated the future marriage and everything that came with it, it felt claustrophobic. But when I looked into my future outside of that, I felt like Beth in **Little Women**: there was nothing there. Unable to let go or even be honest with myself, I convinced myself that I loved this decent, gentle man. Our life together, as we were planning it, would work out. I would make it work.

Between a state scholarship and a couple of part-time jobs, I was able to attend a nearby university. Entering college was more a product of not knowing what else to do—a sign of resignation—than having taken charge of my life. I was surprised that I had even been accepted considering the nature of my high school grades as well as my view of my aptitude. I felt swallowed up by the enormity of the institution and overwhelmingly isolated and insecure interacting with or even being amidst so many strangers. Nonetheless, I had made my bed and quitting equaled failure.

Choosing a major was a problem since I was unable to decide what I wanted "to be." There were my grandmother's **National Geographic** magazines that as a youth had instilled in me an intense curiosity about how people from other cultures and past times lived and interacted. I contemplated a major in sociology, archeology, or anthropology. However, I did not feel competent enough. Besides, the possibility of having to travel to far-off places frightened me. I also was interested in art, but I never considered myself creative enough to be a successful artist. I nevertheless decided to take a number of art classes, partly to fulfill a creative need and partly to create a diversion from the required curriculum. I finally settled on teaching the mentally handicapped—which was how I unconsciously perceived myself—and a minor in philosophy.

Besides feeling inhibited in public and with no better means of applying myself to higher academia than I'd had in high school, I found the classes pretentious, empty and wearisome. If educational concepts confused me, philosophical ones were worse. I drifted through lectures unable to pay attention or even to remain awake. Studying produced similar results. I was unable to memorize material well enough to master exams, which was my definition of education at the time. Rather than question the value of the system, I deemed my ineptitude the problem.

Although not perceived consciously at the time, my real frustration lay in my innate awareness that knowledge is a function of a greater dimension of reality not accessible by the intellect. Knowledge is not something that can be taught to us, not something that is necessary to expound upon, analyze, or prove, nor is it something to be spoon-fed or swallowed whole. Knowledge comes to us when we have prepared ourselves to receive it.

One evening when my brothers and I were sitting around talking, our conversation turned to never having felt loved by our parents. Circumstances soon led us to a mutual decision to confront them about the matter. I was chosen to be the spokesperson. Shortly thereafter, we took them by surprise. I knew, since I was the one initiating the discussion, that I would be viewed as the ringleader. Both parents sat in their customary spots, father crying and withdrawn, appearing as if he was clueless as to what we were communicating. Mother cried as well, but she also repeatedly, defensively proclaimed in her God-awful whiney voice, "I guess I just can't do anything right!" In the end, we departed without having received the validation that we had been seeking. I didn't understand that expecting my parents to provide something they were incapable of giving demonstrated my ignorance of a greater awareness: getting what I was wanting—love—starts with me, and no one else. My actions, viewed from a greater perspective, were not right or wrong, nor good or bad. Humanly, I was playing out my own disconnection.

Sometime after my older brother enlisted in the army, he and his girlfriend decided to marry. The girl was a classmate of mine whom my parents appraised as southern white trash. I was certain that if my parents had left well enough alone, the idea of marriage would have withered away as fast as it was born. With great bitterness, they participated in the wedding. They were aware when my brother left for Vietnam that his new wife was pregnant. Mother was all the more embittered which made the door all the more tightly shut on this new family member. Admittedly, I did not like this girl either. She was not very bright and ran with the wild crowd. Also, there was something hard about her and callous, almost masculine. She intimidated me as if she could and would chew me up and spit me out if I crossed her. Regardless of my inhibitions or my parents' reaction, I felt obligated to make an effort to embrace her. Furthermore, I enjoyed children and was excited about being an aunt. Shortly after she gave birth, I mustered enough courage to pay her a visit. She came to the door with an air between suspicion and indifference. I gave the best greeting I could, and then quickly offered up a baby gift, which turned out to look more like a peace offering. Icily, she informed me that if I wanted to see the baby, I would find him at the babysitter's. After obtaining directions, I drove away. My heart was pounding as if I had narrowly escaped death. No attempt at calming myself proved effective. I only wished that I could forget about all of this, say that I gave it my best effort, and go home before my parents discovered what I was doing behind their backs.

Instead, I proceeded to the babysitter's house where I awkwardly introduced myself when she answered the door. Without any question, she invited me in and immediately led me to a crib. One glance at the baby revealed, beyond a doubt, beyond any doubts my parents had, that this was my brother's progeny. For me it was love at first sight—love so strong I struggled to contain my tears. There was little room for reaction, however, for the sitter suddenly divulged that my sister-in-law had failed to pick up her son the previous day as agreed. She further conveyed that this was not a novel situation, but the first time she had not at least phoned to check in. The sitter finished her revelation by conveying her certainty that my sister-in-law had no intention of returning for her child this time. My shock turned to disbelief, when she just as suddenly asked me to take the baby. I held my nephew for a while, sick at heart and no longer able to contain my tears. I could not understand why a mother would ever consider abandoning her baby. Yet I did not want to judge her. One thought pressing against all the others was, "Oh my God! What will my parents say?" I gathered the baby up and sat in the car with him for a while trying to figure out what to do. A certain strong fear that the mother might accuse me of stealing her baby wrapped itself around my efforts to sort this problem out. Not knowing what else to do, I returned to my sister-in-law's with the baby in my arms. Standing above me in the doorway, giving her son no notice, she announced in no uncertain terms that she no longer wanted him. (I was unaware that she was already involved with another man.) My only recourse, under these circumstances, was to bring this beautiful little bundle home with me.

My parents were highly agitated—angry over my actions, and as cold toward their grandson as his mother was. I wanted to scream at them, "He's an innocent baby! Don't pass your judgment of his mother onto him!" If they thought my brother's marriage put a dent in their reputation, this situation thoroughly tarnished it. I felt sorry for them, sorry for their attitude, but somehow, and much to my dismay, I was embarrassed myself.

With much to-do and a great sense of self-sacrifice, my parents came full circle, finally exchanging their animosity for a sense of purpose. They then set out to obtain temporary legal custody of my nephew until my brother returned from service. Their endeavor had the combined benefit of saving face in the community *and* assuring that their daughter-in-law have nothing further to do with the family. They even spied on her, sitting in their car at night across the street from her apartment, documenting her comings and goings with men to build a case against her if the need arose. It was, without question, rough for me to understand my sister-in-law's behavior, but my parents' behavior sickened me.

It was during this family ordeal that I first became acutely aware of my parents' chemical dependence, especially my father's. He seemed inebriated more often than sober. My judgment of their condition separated me from a larger reality. It would be years before I realized that alcoholism, like any other addiction, in and of itself, is not good or bad, nor right or wrong. Rather, understanding that addictions are merely manifestations of profoundly deeper issues is what is relevant to dissolving them. It would also be years before I realized the significance of being an adult child of alcoholic parents. I was the product of a toxic family and my own addictions, although less obvious, were equally debilitating and separating me from my greater awareness. My family legacy of intrigue and conflict, having been snowballing from prior embodiments into this one, was about to overtake me in more ways than stars in the sky. It was all set up to happen, my struggle to avoid strangling myself in the knotted threads of my karmic family.

Once my fiancé departed for service, I braced myself to deal with my loneliness. Working a couple of jobs, caring for my nephew, and writing endless tearful letters saved me from complete depression. Keeping busy would overall become my choice survival tool. It would also to be the major means to avoid honestly facing my life. Assigning definition to my relationship with my fiancé made it impossible for me to realize that the relationship itself had been merely a lesson and that upon his departure that lesson had ended. I was already being moved onto further lessons—all gender-imbedded.

The new lesson came in the form of a young man five and a half years my senior, a philosophy major recently graduated from the same university I was attending. I first met Carl at a restaurant where I was hostessing and where he had been recently hired as a dishwasher. The moment I laid eyes on him, an odd, bewildering force awakened deep within me, entirely engrossing my sensibility. I had no idea what was happening, but I thought he was the most handsome man I had ever seen. I took much effort to be near him. When not at work, my thoughts ran wild with anticipation. My uncontrollable attraction to him confounded whatever emotional equilibrium I had, but not even guilt over straying from my fiancé, could steer my attention away from Carl. My guilt changed to remorse when my fiancé returned on leave and I, without serious deliberation, broke off our engagement. I cried myself weak believing that I had broken his heart and that he would never recover. Yet I could not reenter the relationship. I was driven, instead, to returning to this sweet man everything he had given me as if I was clearing out all evidence of him ever having been in my life.

Regardless of having some awareness that I was on a perilous path, the magnetism between Carl and me had a life, an agenda of its own. My earlier anxieties over the conventionality of a sweet marriage paled in comparison to the turmoil I would soon experience on this roller coaster ride of a relationship into which I was stumbling. Much more than playing out the unhealed parts of my childhood, this attraction, regardless of what either of us labeled it, was founded on unfinished business from prior embodiments demanding to be outplayed. Our becoming involved with each other was as inevitable as it was unavoidable.

The immediate sexual tension between us took only a little time to be acted out. Disclosing nothing significant about his own experiences, he pervasively queried me about mine. The way he carried on, I expected a demonstration of exceptional prowess during our first sexual encounter. While voicing his regrets that I was not a virgin, the ensuing awkward exercise left me missing the clues that he was. Even so, my guilt flared as well as my feeling of being sluttish. Further sexual encounters came at his whim, at which time, he would hastily pull into a parking lot for me to provide him with a blow job or plop himself on top of me on a friend's living room couch whenever opportunity allowed. The lack of a hallowed sense of safety as much as a lack of fulfillment from these initial encounters quickly dowsed whatever romantic fantasies I may have had. Unknowingly, my fears of either being a disappointment or rejected, coupled with an odd, slightly discernable belief that I was responsible for his sexual satisfaction, left me open to sexual exploitation. As long as I interpreted our interaction "love," I remained separate from a greater truth.

At first I was overwhelmed by the high degree of Carl's intelligence. He could go on and on about, what then seemed to me to be, the most sapient of considerations. Soon enough, I learned that he unabashedly inflicted his beliefs onto others. In fact, his intelligence equaled his insolence, and he brandished both in ways that spared no one. When not immersed in raillery, seductively charming his way from one situation to another, he was operating on the offensive—openly belittling others, backing them into a corner, controlling conversations, prying deeply into their thoughts and feelings, and then leaving them confused and defenseless. Other times he epitomized sanctimoniousness. The few friends I had began to recede from my life as he entered it. Most often his behavior thoroughly embarrassed me, yet I was sequacious, regardless of the cost.

When he and my parents met it was instant animosity: he was a bum; they were miserly and obsessed with money. Worst, he used my parents' not loving me as a means to deepen the wedge already existing between us. No one could love me like he could, so he assured me. For him to love me as much as he professed he did, surely I owed him something. My obedience? Trapped between Carl and my parents, but not able to give up either, I became all-around evasive in order to make our relationship work.

One incident in particular illustrates the degree of Carl's obsessive need to control. He considered himself an accomplished artist (he mostly replicated the masters) and asked me to obtain permission for him to join me with his drawings when I was scheduled to have assignments critiqued at the end of the grading period. Given the affirmative, together we carried our sketchpads into class. He waited in the background while my professor examined my sketches, one page after another, giving feedback as she went. After she gave me her final comment, she turned to address Carl's work. He laid his sketchpad on the table, and ignoring standard protocol, turned to the first page himself and began to elaborate in detail about the nature of his efforts, leaving no room for the instructor to reply. Initially, she attempted to establish her professional leverage, but these efforts left the two of them wrestling over the pages. She finally backed off as he continued page after page, blabbering on and on, self-absorbed and seemingly unaware of how tense and awkward the atmosphere had become. Although I was thoroughly humiliated by his behavior and certain that it would affect my grade, I never mentioned a word to him. I had learned well to say nothing at all if I was unable to say something "nice."

Creating grandiose dreams of adventure, reminiscent of my father's unfulfilled promises to which I had clung as a child, was Carl's greatest skill. He insisted we take a secret vow of marriage and then save all our money for a year-long trip west, which he asserted must also remain secret. To add to the seriousness of the venture, he planned to borrow money from his mother for a down payment on a new Volkswagen van. As daring and romantic as our plans were compared to my ordinary and tiresome existence, I was confused about being left out of the decision-making process, disconcerted over the secrecy he insisted upon, and felt painfully dishonest keeping our plans hidden from my parents. I was caught in a deepening fear of disappointing Carl or missing out on something not to mention how I craved returning to the mountains once again. I held my doubts in check.

When Carl was laid off from his most recent job, working in a factory, he returned to Chicago and holed up at his mother's cramped apartment where his older brother also resided. Since he had not yet purchased the van, it became my routine to drive into the city to visit him. I soon discovered that our so-called dates were spent solely at the racetrack where he absorbed himself in betting on horses while I attended to finding safety from the hoards of people, the stench, and the tobacco smoke.

Winning money, as opposed to earning it for a living, was an alien concept that frightened and confused me. There would be ample opportunity for me to become familiar with that condition, as Carl could not stop betting so long as there was any money left in one of our pockets. Realizing my intuitive capacity, he often encouraged me to choose horses for him. I understood neither the nature of my knowing then nor how it manifested, but I was committed to pleasing him. Still, using my knowing to be successful at gambling frightened me, exacerbating my fear of failing. Doubt threw me into my intellect and left me in an even more confused relationship with my knowing. Besides this, I learned that as much as Carl requested my input in choosing a horse, he rarely acted on it. I made many attempts to convey my feelings of discomfort with his gambling, but he professed to go to the racetrack only to win money for his mother or for my schooling. He claimed that I was too insecure to take the kind of risks he could. Beside his purported selflessness, I perceived myself as the epitome of self-centeredness. The part of me that clung to my father's promises (lies), my mother's "desserts" and my fear of Carl labeling me selfish were what kept me supporting his gambling habit, even while I felt cheated.

By the end of my first year of college, my mediocre grades reflected my mental state. The classes I didn't drop, I only sporadically attended. Not knowing what else to do, I decided to quit college, move to Chicago, and live with Casey, my surrogate sister, who, with a couple of other clique members and another girl, had rented a large apartment in a trendy, uptown neighborhood. My parents were extremely upset over my plans, baffling, since heretofore they had been indifferent to my educational pursuits. The escalating friction between my mother and me, however, made leaving inevitable. My beloved cat died during this time frame. I was devastated by the loss, as much as by my rejection of her after her stroke. I was unable to recognize her gift—her death was facilitating my move from home. Another difficulty in leaving home was the mutual attachment between my nephew and me. Once I was out the door, my nephew was the strongest incentive to visit my parents. In fact, I continued to come home on weekends both to be with him and give my mother relief from childcare. My close relationship with my nephew would end with my brother's return from Viet Nam and subsequent marriage.

I felt no less trapped in my new circumstance than the one that I left. Carl's abrasive humor and condescending opinions threatened everyone. Casey became jealous over my closeness to the roommate with whom I shared a bedroom. Rules were formulated with regard to how the apartment was to be maintained, but someone was continually disgruntled with someone else's slacking off. Boyfriends and neighborhood acquaintances regularly gathered in the living room to listen to music, drink and smoke marijuana. I desperately wanted to fit in, but for all my attempts I felt yet more ill at ease. Casey claimed that marijuana produced the ultimate in heightened awareness. She persuaded me to give it a try, but rather than reaching a heightened awareness, my chronic tonsillitis just got worse. Also, I felt as if my senses were uncomfortably, if not dangerously, stifled. Furthermore, I was terrified of a police raid and of being arrested simply by association with what took place in our apartment; I was terrified of my parents' killing me if they got wind of my lifestyle. These considerations, along with everyone's dislike of Carl, entangled me in a quagmire with which I was ill-equipped to deal. Despite being unable to fit in or have fun like everyone else, I was too afraid to simply walk out the door and face life on my own.

Living in a metropolitan environment was a foreign experience in relation to my small town upbringing: houses close enough together for neighbors to shake hands out their windows; tiny yards fenced to keep people out; children playing in the streets. The extent of ethnic enclaves in Chicago, as well as the degree to which people identified with them, was alien to me. The only such enclave in my town was a black community located on the north side of the railroad tracks. "What are you?" a curious Chicagoan would query. It took a number of such situations before I realized I was being asked to define my ethnicity. Then there was, "What do you do?" Again, it took a number of incidents to realize that I was being asked to reveal my occupation. I did not actually know what it meant to have a sense of identity, but I didn't like to think of myself by my ethnicity or what I did to support myself or that that was the limit of interest others had in me.

Seeking a job in Chicago was as oppressive as the city itself. I first tried an employment agency, where my only professional skill, typing, opened few doors. Still, I managed to land an office job. Restraining my body at a desk lined up with dozens of others in a large, windowless room under artificial lights for eight hours, processing data while fearing I would bumble in some way and have to face my supervisor's disapproval, was suffocating. I perpetually struggled with an overwhelming desire to race out the door, strip myself of my business garb, and find sanctuary in a secluded, sunny spot.

I found a job suitable to my temperament when a roommate introduced me to waiting tables at a downtown restaurant. I was still not out-of-doors, but at least I was free to physically move around, and my hours were less restrictive. The tips, which symbolized approval and appreciation, provided a sense of immediate gratification as well as security. The more effort I put into being efficient and hard working, the more I was rewarded, and the more empowered I felt. I was unaware that I felt comfortable in a public situation only because I was able to conceal myself behind the role I assumed. I was further unaware that I was using my job to create my identity.

Moving to the city and closer to Carl did not leave me more satisfied with the relationship; I felt more used and defiled. If we met at his place, I had to travel across town to see him. If he came to my place, it was only because he was on his way to the racetrack and needed a quick sex-fix (which was awkwardly provided in the hallway) or money (with the promise of winning big).

As the summer wore on, I got increasingly nervous about Carl controlling our trip fund. I had been giving him money to set aside and he was supposedly setting aside his own money as well. I felt guilty about my skepticism. Finally, three months later than our planned departure date, I confronted him about our savings. He expertly tried to avoid revealing that he had gambled away both his and my money. Now, rather than a year traveling the country as "we" had planned (and as I had bragged about to my friends and family), we were only able to travel through the west for a month.

The trip did provide the means for me to return to the mountains, but since I was consumed with trying to please Carl or prove myself to him, I had no time or room for the personal experience with nature I had been seeking. The antithesis to my sedate female relatives, he was a maniacal drill sergeant who dictated every moment's experience and whose sole purpose for hikes was to guarantee that we fell into our sleeping bags every night exhausted. I returned from our trip no closer to understanding my enticement to the mountains than when I had been with my grandmother, aunt, and cousin. Regardless of how I approached viewing the trip, it did not feel like a shared experience. It certainly had no tones of the romantic adventure that I had presented to friends and family. Carl swore that we would soon embark on another camping trip; this one for the year "we" had initially planned. And what he promised, I was obliged to believe.

Upon our return to Chicago, Carl holed up again at his mother's where he continued to weasel money from whomever he could to play the horses while I returned to my parents' intent on returning to college. They made a show of supporting me, but my mother and I were immediately at odds. When she slapped me with her standard line about it being her house and if I did not like her rules I should get out, I took my leave and rented a sleeping room with a private bath on the second floor of an old Victorian house. I found a job waiting tables and enrolled in school again full-time. To avoid taking classes I didn't like and to fulfill my personal creative bent, I decided to change my major to art. However, I still had too little confidence in myself to be successful: memorizing key art history facts and sketching live nudes (which thoroughly embarrassed me) only momentarily held my interest, and I felt more lost, lonely, and depressed than ever.

I continued to direct my energy into living in a relationship the way I thought I was supposed to, with someone I thought I loved, while my interactions with Carl became more and more warped. Resisting his strong-arming money from me, I habitually bought him "gifts"—like new clothes to replace the shabby ones he habitually wore or a camera to make it possible for him to fulfill the creativity aptitude he claimed to have. I even took out a loan—burying my burgeoning shame—in order to bail him out of financial predicament. He was unpredictable or, better stated, predictably unpredictable. It was the same kind of walking-on-eggshells dance that I did with my parents to try to win (buy) their approval, except Carl was more complicated. When he was not aloof, he was endlessly expounding on philosophical principles by which he thought I could benefit. He gave me a copy of Buber's **I and Thou** claiming that I would profit from it, if I could comprehend it. I certainly tried, and somehow I felt I did, but my doubt left me convinced that females, particularly me, were not intellectually designed to decipher such arcane facts. Nevertheless, I pretended to understand his esoteric discourses and earnestly attempted to mold his beliefs into my own expression, but I merely sounded like his clone.

With me even more than with others, Carl ferreted out my thoughts and feelings. "A penny for your thoughts," was his least threatening approach. Invariably, I found myself spilling my guts as if tricked into a confession. He would then wrench my thoughts and feelings, masticate and half-digest them, and finally spew them back at me, unrecognizable and worthless. I would be more befuddled than ever. His most used lines were, "What's wrong with you?" or "You have no understanding," or "If I were you, I would think..." or "would have done..." or "would have said..." It became commonplace that any confrontation between us resulted in me becoming frustrated and confused, reducing me to tears and apologies, and finally surrendering to his sexual desires. When confrontation failed to accomplish this sequence, his silent treatment was as effective as my mother's was in bringing me to blame myself and grovel to make amends. As a last resort, he would use his violent temper.

In rare moments of conscious self-honesty, and then only minimally, I questioned whether the relationship would survive without my effort. Once when I was disheartened enough to take action, I informed Carl that I needed to be separate from him for a week to decide whether I wanted to continue with him. But before the week ended, I was knocking on his door. He smugly informed me that he had known I would be unable to stay away. It had yet to dawn on me that he needed me as much as I needed him.

My maternal grandmother was diagnosed with lung cancer, so Carl drove with me across the state to visit her. She lay incapacitated in bed as he brazenly assured her that she was fortunate to be in so little pain in her death experience. It was remarkable that despite her being able to maintain a tyrannical hold on her four daughters, Carl could so readily and swiftly bring her to her knees. I was humiliated that he would ignore family protocol as much as horrified that he could be so insensitive to the distress his conversation was causing her. Between not knowing how to deal with the situation and having already experienced being ripped apart by him when I had confronted him about his behavior, I stood silently beside him. Finished with his dissertation and ignoring my family gathering for dinner, he walked straight out the door and got into my car where he waited for me to join him. I handed my aunt a lame excuse and made my exit. (Father had taught me well to never keep a man waiting.) My aunt phoned the following day requesting that if Carl came with me for another visit, he refrain from talking about death. Feeling further humiliated and rejected by my family, I never visited Grandmother again.

When she died, Carl refused to come to her funeral. I was glad, relieved. As much as I was uncomfortable attending the funeral alone, I was tired of continually dealing with the public embarrassment of his unpredictable and aberrant behavior. I sat dry-eyed in a pew behind my mother and her three sisters, curiously watching their reactions and hashing around in my mind the family dynamics, the conflict between generations of females. I thought perhaps that I had no feelings toward Grandmother because I could not cry at her funeral. On one hand, Grandmother's cold and removed demeanor had always frightened me, but on the other, I felt a certain kindness, a certain generosity about her. Only recently, my aunt had given to me—my cousin also—items for our hope chests that our grandmother had been accumulating over the years—hand-crocheted pillow covers, towels, and such. What most stuck in my mind was a gift Grandmother had given to me when I graduated from high school. It was a blue ceramic bowl with a lid to which she had added bath powder as well as a personally written poem. Contrary to the usual "gift-giving" in my family, this had felt uncalculated and unfamiliarly personal, touching an obscure cord inside me. Then I knew that she was much softer than she had ever allowed herself to be seen, and though unable to mourn her demise, deep within me, I could feel a certain connection to her.

Carl made an unexpected visit one night. I was prohibited from having male visitors in my rented room so we retreated to his van to talk. Being the end of the month, it was evident that his visit was more about money than me; he was in the habit of gambling away the money his mother set aside to pay the rent. Then, unable to replace it before she discovered it missing, he looked to me to cover his tracks. This time, I found the courage to ask him if he came for my money or for me. Consistent with his character, instead of giving me a direct response, he demanded to know what I thought. Slipping from courage to defensiveness, I considerably softened my position before I was able to articulate it. I failed to see his insecurity behind his claim that I had misjudged him or his insecurity behind his abrupt insistence to be sexual.

After the encounter, I sat, dazed, in a bathtub of water nearly hot enough to sterilize myself. I did not know what was happening to me other than it felt as if his sperm was contaminating my insides. I wanted to reach into my vagina, by whatever means necessary, to destroy all evidence of his invasion. Intuitively, I was aware that having surrendered to his sexual demands this time had left me in the position I had dreaded for so long. I succeeded in dismissing my awareness until I missed my period. At the age of twenty-two, on the floor of Carl's van, I had become pregnant.

Carl told me matter-of-factly that he was not ready to be a father. He was neither interested in working nor in supporting a family. I was terrified about not being able to support myself. The amount of time I could work as a waitress was obviously limited, and I was unwilling to face the condemnation I could expect by seeking aid from my parents. I had made my bed, now I must lie in it. My already floundering sense of self-reliance took a plunge, when one night at work, I retaliated against my supervisor (who had been a high school classmate) for what I considered an act of maltreatment toward me and ended up fired. I was now completely demoralized and panicky, but I continued to look to Carl for my cues. Being an unwed mother felt like a fate worse than death. Yet somewhere deep within me, I held a knowing that this pregnancy did not occur by chance, and I had no choice but to bring it to fruition regardless of my circumstances. Feeling the miraculous first movement of new life confirmed this.

Abortion was illegal in the United States, and the voice of the back alley abortionist Carl encouraged me to contact terrified me. I was unable to dismiss the thought that if I used his services, I would become a statistic. Carl assured me that if I gave him my recent savings, he would multiply it at the racetrack enough to afford me a safe abortion in England where Casey was presently living. Instead, he came home with empty pockets. Another clique member, whom I had secretly supported when she had become pregnant at age fifteen—she was sent away to have her baby and then gave it up for adoption—agreed to help me get the money. In the end, that too fell through. As a last resort, Carl, in a gesture he considered generous, sold his van; this was the van on which *I* was making current and back payments to avoid repossession. He turned over to me the amount of money he considered I needed for the trip, putting the greater portion in his pocket. Then I turned my car over to him.

After the doctor in London examined me, he informed me that I would have to be admitted to the hospital for a more complicated abortion procedure because my pregnancy was beyond the first trimester. I breathed a silent sigh of relief. Carl had not given me enough money for this contingency. I would not have had the abortion anyway, because away from his influence, I had the courage to follow my own inclinations and was more able to make contact with a growing determination to bring this baby into the world. Nonetheless, I remained apprehensive of the imminent repercussions.

My pregnancy was no exception to Carl's compulsion to maintain absolute secrecy about his life. He had therefore created a code by which we would communicate, whether by phone or letter, how the procedure had gone. However, he had not left me with a code to communicate any other scenario, and I did my best to communicate the circumstances using his code as it was. Not until my return home did either of us realize that he had misconstrued my message.

Initially, "we" had planned to go to England together, but as the time to go grew near, he claimed that there was insufficient money. Notwithstanding, he had impressed upon me, before my departure, to see as much as I could while abroad.

Budgeting the money initially set aside for the abortion, I managed a trip to Europe and also to Scotland and helped make it possible for Casey to join me. I had read much about Stonehenge and had a strong urge to see it. Now, that the opportunity was upon me, Casey was unable to free herself from work. I found that, although Stonehenge was only a day trip from London, I was fearful of becoming lost and never finding my way back on my own or at least without having to ask someone for help. I was thoroughly annoyed, not to mention perplexed by my insecurity, but the best I could do was sidestep it. Adding to this irony, upon my return, Carl accused me of misusing his money. He, himself, had squandered the entire portion he had kept for himself at the racetrack. Surrendering my remaining forty dollars, I was virtually penniless.

Of all her five children, Carl was his mother's darling, and in her eyes, could do no wrong. She chastised him as if he was a naughty boy when she learned about our predicament. She was quite fond of me, but more because she was a compulsive caregiver, she opened her door to me. This did not mean that I was obtaining anything for free. As much as I was grateful, Carl's mother was a Jekyll and Hyde, one moment hee-haw laughing about something and just as suddenly, seemingly without provocation, uninhibitedly raging, both emotionally and physically. Just as swiftly, she could revert back to her prior state, as if someone had pulled a switch. Although such behavior frightened me, Carl and his brother most often were indifferent to her raging, if not amused. I would soon learn just how exactly Carl modeled his mother's behavior patterns.

As a member of Carl's mother's household, I found myself in a situation foreign to the rigid work ethic in which I had been raised. Among them, no one had much interest in working. Through tardiness and absenteeism, Carl's mother was terminated from her factory job; neighborhood loan sharks regularly hassled her over non-payment of borrowed money. She spent her time frequenting local taverns and bringing male acquaintances home for the night. Carl's and his brother's lives evolved around reading newspapers, watching sports events on the television or listening to them on the radio, as well as, playing golf and studying racetrack programs. I was aware of the welfare system, however my parents had taught me well. Accepting anything without having earned it was unfamiliar and shameful. But in the end, I had no choice but to have my baby at the county hospital.

Carl's youngest sister, Carmen, who had dealt with the stigma of being pregnant and unwed, gave me much encouragement and communicated her belief that her brother would always be there for me like her husband now was for her. I needed to believe her, but simply the fact that I slept on the couch while Carl shared the second bedroom with his brother told me I was unimportant.

My entire pregnancy was punctuated with nightmares of losing my unborn child in some dreadful way. I most commonly saw various family members slicing away at my protruding belly, like a hunk of Jell-O with my baby curled safely inside, each slice bringing him closer to death and me closer to panic. I often awoke to a silent scream, "No! You can't have him. I'm keeping him alive this time." I tried to convince myself that my fears that my parents would only want my baby dead if they learned of my pregnancy were irrational, but I was helpless to think otherwise.

Despite the nightmares, experiencing the wonders of pregnancy, along with the spectacle of a beautiful autumn—my favorite, the season I considered magical—created a bright ray in my trying situation. Without greater awareness, I was unable to see the synchronicity to the circumstances in my life. Even if an angel presented itself to me and proclaimed that my life was much more than appearances allowed me to see, that outside of my judgment, my life had a purpose greater than my linear mind could imagine, and I was being divinely guided, I would have hidden from the message, denied it, felt unworthy, too afraid to even examine its significance.

Convincing myself that my protruding belly would go unnoticed, I decided to drive to my parents' to retrieve belongings I had stored there. When Carl and I arrived, I learned from a neighbor that they were out of town. Securing a key from her, I collected my possessions anyway. In a moment of inexplicable panic that I would be unable to provide for the child or myself, I took some canned goods from the cupboard. I also took some outgrown infant clothes and a baby blanket that I had gotten for my nephew: items that my mother had stashed away. As irrational as my behavior was and as certain as I was that my mother would discover my actions, I had no control over them or the shame that followed. I was unaware that my pregnancy as well as all of the major characteristics of my life at that time subconsciously triggered unhealed past life memories, which in turn supported my behavior. I would have to explore those memories to free myself of the remorse that would maintain a grip on me until then.

Carl was convinced that our child was a girl and had chosen a name for her, allowing me to decide on a boy's name, just in case. I was, in fact, terrified of having a baby girl. I feared that hating female offspring was a genetic curse of which no generation was exempt.

3

Strangling in the Tangles

My fear of having a daughter was ready to be laid to rest very early one morning when my water breaking woke me from a sound sleep. Only hours before, we had arrived home from an out-of-state camping trip. On our last night of camping, when a need to urinate dragged me from the tent to find relief, I unexpectedly stumbled in the dark and fell. I was certain that the fall had shaken something, however I silently returned to my sleeping bag. I was relieved late the following day when Carl suddenly decided to return home. I cautiously pulled myself to my feet, made sure I left no mess, and then proceeded to take a quiet, warm bath before anyone else arose. Except for the fear of bungling the birth and having to face Carl's wrath, I would have secretly taken care of the situation myself, as I had done with my initial menstrual experience. Now, as then, I wanted no one to know or have anything to do with my body. My peace was interrupted when Carl's mother suddenly banged on the bathroom door. Minutes later, she had Carl up and ready to take me to the hospital.

After pulling into the hospital parking lot, we walked the seemingly endless distance to the admittance entrance. I wanted Carl to hold my hand, embrace me, or even tell me how excited he was like I imagined an expectant father would be with his wife. I wanted him to help me deal with my dread of doctors and medical facilities. The humiliation of going to the county hospital was demanding enough. Carl, instead, walked along beside me chatting on about something or another, which made me feel all the more isolated. Shuffling through the abundance of colorful leaves in the first light of dawn, smelling autumn in the air, and knowing that it was going to be one spectacular Indian summer day gave me a degree of consolation.

The experience was no less humiliating than I had anticipated. It began after sign-in when Carl departed, and I sat alone waiting to be wheeled off to the maternity ward. Total immersion into degradation followed when I was required to surrender my body, assembly line fashion, to being stripped, shaved and subjected to an enema. Then I was rolled into a room full of women all in various stages of deliver many of them screaming in pain, while nurses periodically came by to check if my cervix had dilated any farther. It had been a long stretch since I had eaten, and I was starved. All I was allowed was ice chips to suck on. Labor was induced, an episiotomy performed, and my feet were anchored in stirrups until circulation was cut off in my legs. Minutes into the next day, with an array of interns circling me (curious and surely judging me as a hopeless unwed mother!), the doctor on duty, forceps in hand, pulled my son, Adam, into the world. I didn't get so much as a glimpse of him before he was whisked away while I was told to focus on delivering the afterbirth. Thereafter, the doctor walked out, leaving an intern to sew me up. I finally found the nerve to explain that the circulation was cut off in my legs and then asked him to please consider releasing my legs from the stirrups so I could have some relief. He responded that he would do so if I promised not to bother him any further. I knew then not to ask him when I could see Adam. Instead, I lay there feeling the pressure of the needle poking in and out of my perineum as he completed the stitching and feeling the needles-and-pins running up and down my legs as circulation slowly returned. I was angry about not seeing my son and feeling more disgraced and worthless than I could ever imagine.

Hours later, as unreal as it seemed, I had my very own child in my arms. I checked him over from head to foot. He was perfect except for the forceps sores branding both sides of his head. The sores made me feel guilty, as if I had done something wrong during delivery. Gazing deeply into his eyes for the first time, however, confirmed what I had been feeling throughout my pregnancy: I already knew my baby and had a responsibility to bring him safely into this life. The stirring I felt in my heart was as painful as it was incredible. After nine months of waiting and a troublesome, prolonged labor, my singular desire was to keep him close to me.

My moment of bonding was quickly tainted by a nurse who insisted, not once, but persistently, that I would never successfully nurse my baby because my nipples were inverted. "If you know what's best for him," she claimed, "you'll agree to have him bottle-fed." I was angry. Angry that she did not support me, angry that her opinion made me doubt myself, and angry that she made me feel inept and flawed and as helpless as I thought only my mother could make me feel. I wanted to scream at her to get away from me, even scratch her eyes out or kick her. Struggling to contain my tears, I found the strength to politely ask her to leave me alone, as well as to assert that neither she nor anyone else had my permission to bottle-feed my baby. Familiarizing ourselves with each other was all the two of us needed.

When she finally departed, my tears sprung forth. I desperately wanted someone's support, someone to assure me that I was not doing anything wrong. Despite my extensive baby-sitting experience, I was suddenly terrified of harming my son—if not through my ignorance, then through my willfulness, my carelessness, or something unforeseen. As accustomed as I was to fending for myself, I felt overwhelmed by the thought of having to fend for Adam also, but there was no point in my feeling helpless or sorry for myself. I had made my bed; now I had to lie in it. It was time to buckle up and be accountable. I set aside my tears, set aside my discouragement, as well as everyone else's, and set myself to the task of mastering the secrets of breast-feeding. My commitment to the moment, however, never deterred my desire to disappear with my child out the nearest door and into the solitude of the warm, nurturing embrace of the lingering Indian summer day.

Despite the fact that Carl had never been supportive and had remained openly uncommitted and indifferent about being a father throughout my entire pregnancy, I pretended that he was supportive and portrayed him as such to those who were aware of my condition. Part of me remained hopeful that he would own his relationship with his son. Yet I incessantly worried about what I would do if he maintained his indifference after our baby came. I had told myself that my pregnancy was my problem, and I should not burden Carl with the product of my carelessness. I could not, or perhaps did not want to see that whether or not he remained physically present, he was incapable of taking responsibility. As difficult a person as his mother was, I was grateful for her involvement. Particularly because, between their mutual attachment and her excitement over her favorite son producing an offspring, it was impossible for Carl to walk completely away from the situation.

Hospital regulations had excluded Carl from the delivery experience, so when I was in a position to do so, I called him from a pay phone. Right then, he told me not to have any expectations of him, for he did not know yet how he felt about the situation. When I hung up the receiver, I once again choked back my tears. I was learning that his noncommittal attitude was a form of control. As with my father previously, I was more fully learning to expect nothing from him despite my hopefulness. With prompting from his mother, he eventually came to the hospital to sign the legal papers. Still, being an unwed mother left me feeling demoralized, as if I was wearing a scarlet letter. I was at least grateful to Carl for making it possible for our son to carry his name because, for reasons beyond my capacity to understand, I was horrified by the thought of my son being stuck with my family's name. In the end, and much to my surprise, Carl's initial reaction to Adam, was an unexpected, instantaneous adoration.

The weather continued to be extraordinary after I brought Adam home from the hospital. Carl's sister, Carmen, to whom I was most grateful, lent us, among many essentials, a buggy. Even without it, I would have been unable to keep my son or myself indoors. Carmen had warned me about post-partum depression. I was, knowingly or not, relying on nature to see me through the transition as well as to assuage my overwhelming sense of isolation. The elderly European women who lived up and down the street wagged their fingers at me and now and then commented on the foolishness of my taking a newborn outside. Again, as with the nurse of the breast-feeding incident, but not without a degree of doubt, my feelings overrode others' opinions. I knew only that I had to be in nature, and I was unwilling to leave my son behind. I reasoned that fresh air and sunshine could only be healthful for both of us compared to being in the confines of a smelly, stuffy apartment.

Adam was a voracious feeder, and although Carl's sister had also warned me about nursing for nourishment versus nursing for comfort and the possibility of getting sore nipples from over-nursing, I was unable to ignore his fussing and continually put him to my breast. Within a short time, I was raw and tender and temporarily reduced to pumping my milk and bottle-feeding him. This only added to my conflicting emotions. Sometimes I felt sucked so dry of personal energy that

I wanted to rip my baby from my breast and run away. Other times I felt as if nursing brought us so close that our hearts beat as one. Despite this sweet bundle of a gift, some shadowed but unrelenting part of me would not be convinced that what I was living was my life and would remain bent on following my insatiable yearning for a reliable reality.

Shortly after Adam was born, I received a phone call from my father; it was the first that I had ever received. He claimed to want to visit me, but I suspected that the neighbor, whom I had asked to borrow the key to my parents' house, had informed my parents of my delicate condition. Clearly, my father was chiefly attempting to look good in the eyes of the extended family by bringing the stray lamb back into the fold. Beyond my animosity and distrust, I saw the degree of courage that it took for him to make this trip. After all, I had now fulfilled my parents' fear of social humiliation. He was nervous yet cordial during his brief visit. For a man who could not function outside of perfunctory interaction, he was doing his best. He even appeared to accept the idea of having a grandson when I finally found the courage to present Adam to him. The charades came to an end, however, when an instant before he departed, he took me aside and declared, "This is a hell hole! Why don't you pack up your child and come home with me?"

He was correct about the hell hole. Carl's mother was a compulsive shopper who had little inclination toward housework. His brother was a pack rat who routinely scoured the alleys, as well as neighborhood garbage bins, and stored his finds throughout the apartment to the degree that just climbing the stairs was like maneuvering through an obstacle course. The walls were covered with grime and the windows might not have been washed for a decade. Carl pointed his finger at his family's behavior, but could not own that he was a chip off the old block. I hated living in such uncleanness and disorder and had taken as much effort as my status allowed to shape up the situation.

Regardless of my circumstance, there was no way that I would ever return to my parents' home and submit myself to living by their rules. I would never let them take pride in saving me from my wayward existence. My father's comment left me viewing him as my adversary and Carl my ally. Yet, despite the nature of events and my willful position, after my father's visit, I did my best to maintain contact with my parents. My mother's disdain over my having an illegitimate child caused her to treat Adam as she had initially treated my nephew: he did not exist. My father only cared that the discord stay hidden. As for Carl, he fed the situation by continually addressing my parents as Mr. and Mrs., contending that he did this because of their deplorable attitude toward me. I believed that he was disguising his condescension, and not well. I needed my parents to accept my child. And, I still needed them to accept me. Consequently, I could not help but support my further disappointment.

During an initial visit to them, Mother convinced me to see the family doctor for a sinus infection I had been unable to shake. To my amazement, she even made the appointment for me for that afternoon. The doctor, taking the opportunity to third-degree me about what I was going to do about being an unwed mother, revealed the truth. Mother was actually using him to do her dirty work. None of this was about her concern for me. It was too humiliating to explain to the doctor that Carl had absolutely no interest in marriage. I wanted to scream at him, scream loud enough for my mother to hear, to tell him that living outside of convention did not make me bad. But I had been taught to remain silent if I had nothing "nice" to say. I walked out the door uncertain of how I had responded; the experience was already a blur. It felt as if the entire world were judging me. Mother had taught me well about bitterness. Knowingly or not, it was becoming a force that would continue to deeply contaminate every aspect of my life. After one more disastrous visit, exacerbated by Carl's continued haranguing lectures about my parents' lack of concern for me, and I quit trying to reconcile differences and instead kept a safe distance.

Psychologically, that distance increased when my brother informed me that our parents had added a codicil to their will stating that if they died I would be unable to inherit my allotment until I was fifty years old. They surmised that Carl was using me to get to their money. Their actions equated to my being disinherited. I needed their love and acceptance, which due to my upbringing, was in my mind analogous with money. Having stolen those cans of food and clothes for my baby, now felt like I had a noose around my neck. I had no clear evidence that they were aware I had taken anything, for it was not family custom to directly accuse or confront anyone of anything. Yet I knew that they knew, and surely this was their way of punishing me. One part of me attempted to rationalize that I was overreacting, especially since I had given so much to them throughout my life. Another part of me felt like the most abominable character that had ever walked the face of the earth. In an effort to manage my shame, I told myself that their conduct was not my problem; furthermore, I could care less about their money. In reality, this was the best I could do to protect myself from my pain.

My mind went round and round as I appraised additional issues that fed my escalating confusion. First, my parents had convinced my brothers and me to take out life insurance policies when we were teenagers by offering to pay the first year's premium, which amounted to a dollar apiece. Naturally, they were listed as the beneficiaries. It took little intelligence to realize that they were unwilling to pay for our funeral costs should such circumstances arise. Carl had already pointed out to me the fruitlessness of maintaining the policy. Once again, being precariously wedged between Carl and my parents, I had convinced myself that Carl knew best. After all, he claimed to have only my best interest in mind; also, he expected me to cancel the policy. Therefore, I hoped that I would not suddenly meet with death. Since Carl had no means to foot funeral costs, and most certainly no inclination, the weight of the burden would undoubtedly fall on my parents. They would pay for my funeral expenses, but not without making themselves look like martyrs and me a scoundrel.

Second, due to my brothers and my upbringing, and the degree that we had supported our parents and ourselves, I would have never guessed they had any assets to protect. All we had ever heard from them, one way or another, was how poor they were. Further, it was inconceivable how they thought that Carl could get their money. Was he going to steal a check, forge their name, and then go to the bank to cash it? Really, how could he possibly pocket their assets? I was incensed. When I heard a short time later that they had built an addition onto their house and also bought a mobile home in Florida with a cash payment, I was even more convinced that I had been duped. Feeling disowned became complete when I heard that photographs of me had been removed from the family photo display. My fear of being an outcast was now a reality, and I mostly blamed myself. I had a long way to go before a key embodiment would reveal the exact nature of what we were all once again replaying. Until then, I was reduced to collecting, sorting, sifting, examining, and obsessing over fact upon fact, then weighing and measuring, further trying to convince myself that I was not as bad as my parents believed me to be.

Since Carl remained disinclined to seek employment, even under the present circumstances, I was forced to return to waiting tables a few weeks after Adam's birth. Before departing, I would pump my breasts, always hoping there would be sufficient milk to last him during my absence. Besides cash, work provided a sense of relief from the repressive situation at home. Working, however, did little to diminish my guilt over leaving Adam, especially when I most often returned home to find him wailing in Carl's arms.

I chose not to reveal that I was an unwed mother when I applied for my first job. I told myself that, if the facts were known, my chances of being hired would be reduced. Underneath my rationale was a sense of unshakable shame. When I wanted to proudly show my son to the world, I hid him in order to avoid being judged, or worse, condemned. Adding one more deception to the growing list made managing the charades that I called my life all the more complicated. I did not know why I was so sensitive to my condition, why I kept my son in the closet, or why I lived my life as a lie. I desperately did not want to be this way, but I had no idea how to be any different. Then there was Carl. Openly or not, he clearly communicated his expectation that I maintain our complex secrecy game.

My first waitress job proved to be all around disastrous. First, I was required to invest money I did not have in uniforms. Then one of the cooks, a Chinese man, I soon realized, had an uncontrollable crush on me. His attention half-frightened, half-embarrassed me. When he first gave me a Chinese tea pot as a gift, protocol left me to say "thank you," while at the same time, I had no idea how I would explain the situation to Carl. He had not yet shown any overt signs of jealousy. Instinctively, I knew differently. Still, I liked the teapot and somehow, in some way, was flattered to be given something by anyone, regardless of who it was. Instinctively, I also knew that accepting anything from a man always came with a big price.

To both my astonishment and dismay, shortly after accepting the "gift," I found the cook waiting in his car at the curb in front of my apartment as I left to go to work one afternoon. Instantaneously, the fear of Carl looking out the window struck me with terror. There was no way this man could know anything about my situation. I had told no one. But how did he find out where I lived? He must have discovered that I had an illegitimate child and therefore thought that I was a loose woman. Why else would he be seeking me out? I was certain I could lose my job over this. Worse, Carl could kill me. Fearful of upsetting him along with a host of other confusing, conflicting thoughts and feelings, I accepted the ride. I had to admit to myself that it was nice being driven to work instead of waiting for a bus. (Being dependent on Carl's brother for transportation when he was around was embarrassing enough in and of itself.) Still, I pressed myself to the passenger door fearful of him reaching over and taking my hand. Risking gossip being seen by co-workers upon arrival wiped away any possible sense of benefit. Day after day, his attention increased while I did my best to avoid him. I wanted him to simply recognize how uncomfortable he made me and then cease and desist. Clearly, I had no tools whatsoever to sensibly deal with the situation. And I could not see that my resistance only fueled his interest. I was deep into living out my history, exactly where I needed to be to eventually regain sight of who I really am.

I was freed from having to deal directly with the situation when I came to work one evening only to be fired on the spot. Allegedly, I had failed to properly wait on a party of people the prior evening. To me, it made no sense; I had been found guilty without a chance to defend myself. I had been very busy, yes, but I had pulled my load. No customer had voiced discontent to me. Nothing they were telling me was true. I was stuck with, besides my deepening sense of humiliation and ineptness, three new, expensive uniforms that I had just managed to pay for. Willfully, I contained my tears, my sense of hurt and my anger. I dismissed my pain, my throbbing, milk-laden breasts and headed out the door.

The following day, a fellow waitress phoned wanting to buy my uniforms. Before the conversation ended, she divulged that the owner had actually fired me to make room for a relative who needed a job. The information afforded no sense of relief from my hurt. Although it took little time to find another job, this time I kept my life more of a secret; I kept my distance from any possibility of another attraction occurring. I worked harder making sure that no owner could ever again fire me for failing to do my share. More than ever, a willful determination fueled my life and unknowingly locked me more fully into a survival mode as well as into greater isolation.

Nothing became easier. In particular, my fear of attracting men's attention was more greatly reinforced by an incident shortly after entering my second waitress situation. Standing on a street corner late at night waiting to catch a bus home from work, I had guardedly drawn myself near the entrance of a closed store to avoid attention. I never felt safe being out alone in the city especially after dark and especially because we lived in an unstable neighborhood. Feeling even more threatened when a car full of men stopped at the red light, I nevertheless stepped forward to see if the approaching headlights belonged to the bus. It was, in fact, yet another car full of young men. Before I could retreat into the shadows, I had caught their attention. Consequently, they ogled me to the point of distraction and rear-ended the car already stopped at the intersection. I was in a panic and only wanted to disappear. My thoughts that I was somehow responsible were reinforced when the drivers of both vehicles, getting out to assess the damage, turned on me yelling that the accident was my fault. Unable to respond, I cowered more closely in the entrance of the building. To my relief, when the light turned red, the two drivers abruptly jumped in their respective vehicles and drove off. This incident transpired so quickly that only my pounding heart was evidence that it had not been my imagination. Now more vulnerable in public situations and less inclined to go out, I learned to keep an even wider circle between men and me.

Life on the home front was no easier. Returning from work one night, I discovered that Carl's mother (or so I thought) had rummaged through my personal space, doubtless in an attempt to locate money. I approached Carl, who conceded that it was certainly probable. She had already been visiting the pawnshop in order to maintain her lifestyle, which was totally foreign to my straight-laced upbringing. I was, for the most part, presently supporting the household, and my money was my security—and now I had another person trying to relieve me of it—I was provoked. When I confronted her, she burst into one of her rages, knocking me to the floor and yanking at my hair. Carl curtailed her assault, after which he proceeded to blame me for instigating the fracas. As usual, once his mother's rage was spent, for her it had never happened. For me, it was the impetus—the gift—I needed to move beyond my fear of change and out of that situation. Working extra hours, I soon secured enough money to rent a three-room attic apartment three doors down the street, which was the farthest Carl was willing to move from his mother. With a fresh coat of paint and a sparse, hodgepodge array of furnishings, I had a place to call my own as well as a fragile sense of self-reliance. I thought that I would feel as if I had a real relationship with Carl now that we were living together on our own, even sleeping in the same bed for the first time, but this was not to be.

Carl swallowed his animosity toward members of his extended family enough to attend his paternal grandfather's wake, which was located in his grandparent's Ukrainian neighborhood. Carl's paternal grandparents had never accepted his mother because she came from a Jewish family—they were Catholic—and because they believed that her first child was not their son's. As we pulled up to a curb on a side street, Carl suddenly claimed that due to the fact that he had such unpleasant relatives, I would be more comfortable waiting with Adam in the car. Before I could respond, he assured me that his visit would be brief. True to character, my feelings of rejection left me silent and sulky, but nonetheless obedient. Two hours later, I wanted to march into the funeral parlor and voice my feelings over his insensitivity, scream at him if necessary, regardless of the riot it might cause. Instead, I continued to wait, brought to a fuller awareness of my shame over being an unwed mother; I was more than ever aware that being unmarried bothered me more than I had been willing to admit. Now, I explicitly understood that underneath Carl's purported indifference to the opinions of others, especially his relatives', he was also ashamed. I could have owned this truth, but when he finally returned and I broached the subject, he argued that he was sick and tired of my insecurity and the impact it had on him. As usual, in order to keep peace, I allowed his rationale to overshadow my truth.

Habitually surrendering to Carl's insatiable sexual demands, I soon became pregnant a second time. I obsessed over how I could support a toddler, as well as a man who refused to take responsibility for much of anything, and be pregnant. When I cautiously suggested to him to consider employment, he turned wild, shouting, "You didn't fucking need me working when you had your first kid! Why would you use me as an excuse now?" As always, his words left me helplessly confused. What did I have to complain about? I had gotten through that experience despite his attitude and behavior. And what right did I have to place expectations on him? But now my responsibilities went way beyond myself. Besides the added obligations, having gone to work immediately after giving birth the first time had taken its toll on me, both physically and mentally. He never knew, or at least he had been indifferent if he did. How could I go through a pregnancy, again turn over my newborn, and go right back to work? I tried to convince myself that I could manage if I tried harder. Regardless how I hashed over the situation, however, the only way out seemed to be to end the pregnancy. The thought of doing so, on the other hand, made me feel like a coward! Immoral! Lazy! A no good! A quitter! If I had only been taking birth control pills. Still, the thought of manipulating my body with drugs remained as traumatic as ever. Anaesthetizing my feelings enough to rationalize my actions, this time I had an abortion, which was now legal. In doing so, I vehemently swore that this would be the last time that Carl ever impregnated me. In fact, this would be the last time that any man ever would. I hated Carl for the choice I felt I had to make. I blamed him, but I never told him I did. As I had learned to do during my upbringing, I simply pretended everything was fine, and I had my life fully under control.

Nonetheless, a deep inner feeling that I was meant to have and would have a large family remained like a thorn in my consciousness. Further, I felt as deep a connection with this child I was about to abort as I had with Adam prior to his birth. Behind my confusion was a greater truth. My deeper knowing supported that truth. Eventually, I would remember that I had already populated the world, and my family was waiting for me to help them remember who they are. First, I had to remember who I am.

My life fell into a predictable routine. At work I was a super employee, appearance-wise strong and staid. I never took sick days and I was never late. I was competent, reliable, organized and focused enough to work circles around other waitresses. Managers regularly relied on me to fill in the gaps on busy days or during emergencies. I made myself indispensable—survival mode at its best. At work I felt as if I had charge of my life. Besides being able to make significant amounts of money, being the best was a means of being noticed. One price I paid for being the best was competing with others to hold that position. I could be manipulative, even aggressive, in regard to getting my share of customers—my "dessert," although I preferred to ignore this fact.

I struggled with my inability to have a positive relationship with money. This struggle was played out to perfection with Carl's aid. He continually drilled into me that I was self-centered, greedy and obsessed with money. Primarily to prove to him that his belief was untrue, I turned over my entire earnings to him daily. However, appearances made it look as if we divided responsibilities; it was "agreed" that he would handle buying groceries and paying the bills, and I would get a small portion to keep for my own use. I wanted and needed to trust him, even while experiences proved that he was incapable of keeping his end of the bargain. He continually gambled my hard-earned money at the racetrack, and I continually relinquished my last fragment of income to save us from being evicted or having the utilities shut off. When my stifled anger and disappointment finally fully erupted, he coolly suggested I manage the money myself, since I lacked trust in him. Frustrations over being penniless overrode my guilt for distrusting him, and I did just that. After giving him his daily quota with which to gamble, I hoarded the rest away for living expenses, emergencies, vacations and the like. Still, relieving him of "responsibilities" did not remove me from the hide-and-seek money game we played. He had a way of sniffing out my stash regardless of my creative efforts to hide it. He prided himself that he never took it all; whatever my reserve, he would at least leave me with a five or ten dollar bill. To add to my frustration, I spent so much time and energy finding new hiding places that, more often than not, I would forget the most recent, leaving me frantically searching the house for my own money. After a few more years of having my efforts to survive sabotaged, I found the courage to open a savings account with only my name on it. This maneuver brought me face to face with the fact that Carl and I did not have a shared relationship.

My life centered on Adam when I was not working. I was more than competent in the mechanics of his upbringing, but raising a child took its toll on me as much as other facets of my life, especially because he was a mama's boy. If I stepped out of his sight, panicky screams commanded me back into his view. His naps were brief, and he was awake, bright-eyed at the drop of a pin. Seldom sleeping through the night, I surrendered to bringing him into my bed, then laid awake anyway, fearful that if I went to sleep I would roll over and suffocate him.

Notwithstanding, I adored him and marveled as if watching a miracle in progress, as he advanced from one stage of development to another, learning to walk and talk and express himself. I thought that there could be no other child in the world more beautiful and precocious than mine. Whatever he was doing, I always had my camera poised. But our greatest closeness evolved around my reading to him. From his toddler years, until he started high school, we explored the world through books. Regardless of the hour, he habitually resisted sleep until I returned from work and read him a story—or two—or three.

My deep apprehension of losing Adam never slackened, even after his birth. This was epitomized by an incident during a camping trip to Canada when he was almost two years old. I awoke at sunrise one morning to walk in solitude along the high bluffs of a river that dropped as a waterfall through an abysmal gorge straight into Lake Superior. The beauty of the moment was energizing, and I was disinclined to return straightaway to camp. When at last I did return, I found Carl sleeping soundly and Adam nowhere to be seen. Instantly alarmed, I imagined his little body smashed on a boulder, deep within the gorge, while another part of me avowed it was impossible to bring him this far into the world only to lose him. When I woke Carl, he defended that Adam was too smart to wander off, but as the panicky part of me took control, I snapped, "He's a baby!" Down the trail I tore, screaming his name against the roar of the falls, positive that he had come looking for me when I was on my walk. I ran from place to place, straining to peer over the edge of the cliff and into the gorge below me, screaming myself dizzy and hating Carl all at once. Without success, I returned to camp exhausted and weighing down my fear with the hope that Carl had found Adam. I could see Carl as I approached our site, but no Adam. Nonetheless, as I neared, Adam appeared seemingly from nowhere, still dressed in his bright blue sleeper, setting off his cherubic smile and wondrous, huge brown eyes. With tears of relief streaming down my face, I drew him into my arms, simultaneously feeling horrified for having been so out of control. I assured myself that under the circumstances, I had a right to be frenzied. Carl was amused at my plight and admonished me for my lack of faith, leaving me filled with contempt. He further infuriated me when he calmly explained the situation to a park ranger who was sent to investigate the report of a woman heard screaming in the woods. There would be other situations triggering my obsessive fear of losing Adam, but never again would I allow hysteria to consume me.

Tainting my relationship with Adam and my sense of motherly confidence was Carl's view of my mothering skills. He maintained that without his intervention Adam would not have even survived his infancy, that due to my inability to pay attention to the moment, I would have dropped him on his head or drowned him in his bath water. His position readily fueled my already existing fear of inadvertently harming or causing Adam's death in some way or another.

Further, he criticized that I was incapable of really playing with Adam as he could and claimed that I distanced myself from him by maintaining a parental position. My argument was that I was the mother. As much as I worked to shore up my belief that I was not a bad mother, Carl worked to undermine it. On the other hand, the two of them played rough and competitively, and more often than not, I felt as if I was raising two children rather than one. I disliked the manner in which Carl interacted with Adam and blistered with anger whenever one of them came out of a bout of "play" with a bump, scrape or bloody nose. My familiar response (unknowingly a premonition) was, "One of these days one of you is going to really get hurt if you continue to carry on this way!"

While Carl derided my mothering skills, signs of discord between Adam and him were evident from the beginning. Adam had never been cooperative in letting Carl change his diapers, and as a toddler, Adam would struggle so fiercely that Carl would have to pin him to the floor with a knee to his chest. Adam would immediately surrender the struggle if I took over, which made Carl all the more upset. Another show of strife between them manifested when Adam began dropping his bottle in Carl's face when Carl was lying down on the couch or floor. Approaching Carl and holding the bottle in position as if he wanted to be sure that Carl was taking notice, and even as Carl warned him not to drop the bottle, Adam would let go and just as fast, turn and run, with Carl on his heels. The scenarios became more sophisticated as Adam grew older, and it all appeared to be in jest, but their behavior consistently left me feeling agitated.

When Adam was two, Carl discovered four kittens dumped in a trash can in the alley. I was already resistant to the situation, having been evicted from one apartment as a result of Carl bringing home one dog and then another against our landlord's wishes. We successfully nursed all four of them to health. By then they had become part of the family. Through work I found homes for two and the remaining two, Amiga and Amigo, became to Adam what Baby Tiger had been to me. They exclusively bonded with him. The three of them slept wound around each other at night and otherwise were hardly ever out of sight of each other. To locate the feline siblings, we only had to look into the plethora of houses Adam was perpetually building for them out of boxes, furniture and blankets. It was delightful to observe the relationship, partly because it reminded me of my relationship with Baby Tiger.

At the age of four, Adam came in from play one day seriously querying me about a conversation that he had just had with two older friends who were from Catholic families. "Mommy, Frankie and Jimmy say that a man called God lives up in the sky, and he is really powerful, and he can punish us if we do something bad, and send us to hell!" He then asked me about God and hell. Caught off guard, I responded that people have many different beliefs about who God is and, as he grew up and gained more experience, he could decide for himself what he wanted to believe. I then told him that he was too innocent to ever have to give much attention to hell. Last of all, he asked me if everyone believed in God. I then exposed him to the concepts: Christian, atheist and agnostic. While I explained that I would probably label myself an agnostic—although personally I believed that God could be found in nature, I did not count that—he firmly decided that he wanted to be an atheist.

I had already felt guilty for failing to formally introduce Adam to religion. After all, I reflected, real parents take responsibility for such matters: my parents had "sent" their children to church, but had refused to go themselves. Carl's Catholic siblings and the Jewish side of his family certainly had with their offspring. I had examined various eastern religions a bit, but whether Buddhism, Hinduism or Islam, as with political parties, I continually got them confused. To me it was all rhetoric. Carl's scorn toward religious matters, while inculcating that his philosophical dogma had great value, added to my perplexed state. All considered, I was more bewildered about God than I had ever been in my youth. Hence, the explanations I gave Adam at that time were the very best I could provide.

From the moment of our discussion, Adam adopted the unabashed habit of openly announcing himself an atheist. As a youngster, people were taken by surprise, yet found his behavior cute. I explained to him that it was not customary to advertise one's religious beliefs, especially when of this nature, but he was little deterred. At the same time, I asked myself why it should be any more shameful to be an atheist than a Catholic or a Muslim. Adam would maintain this behavior into his teenage years, and I would eventually realize that he was shrouding his own fears of formal religion.

Seven years after our original trip west, we were finally heading on the extended trip that Carl had so long ago promised. My perpetual pinching and saving were what was making this trip possible. Most assuredly, after my many years with Carl, I had few illusions of romance or adventure left. Still I set my sights on having a fulfilling experience. As with our previous trip, I had built this trip up enough to others that I feared appearing a braggart or a failure if I did not make the most of it.

Carl set the tone by endlessly talking about how much he could be winning at the racetrack, insisting that he was participating in this trip solely to please me. Without question, this left me feeling responsible for his discontent. My only relief from him, my job, was gone. I struggled to circumvent my immediate sense of loneliness and homesickness. Homesickness? I literally had no home. Returning to Chicago at this point was not an option; that would have left me to face my sense of failure, and given Carl free rein to gamble the remaining trip money.

Maintaining a positive attitude about the trip and a sense of control over my life were deeply undermined by an incident shortly into our venture. Contrary to morning plans, Carl had turned the day into a marathon drive, unrealistically bent on reaching a new destination by dark. Instead, we landed in a small city park immediately off the interstate well after sunset. I was disturbed by the situation, concerned for our pets' welfare. Both dogs and especially the two cats were skittish creatures. From the start of the journey, the two cats had taken to hiding in their carrier in the back seat or beneath the seat and only came out after dark or by significant coaxing. As had become the routine, we set up camp and then pulled the cats out of the car and into the tent where they proceeded to bury themselves at the bottom of the sleeping bags. At some point, they would rouse themselves from their safe haven and one of us would zip open the door, giving them their freedom to roam. The first hint of sunrise would always bring them scurrying back to the security that the sleeping bags provided.

This particular time, both had returned as usual, only Amigo had unexpectedly wanted out again. Equivocating for a moment over making a "wrong" decision, I finally unzipped the door and tried to return to sleep. By the time we were rising to start the day, Amigo had not returned. Any effort I made to convince myself that all would turn out fine was overshadowed by an overwhelming sense of knowing; a sense of death ripped at my consciousness, my gut and my solar plexus. I hated myself for having given in to Amigo's meow to leave the tent and was waiting for some comment from Carl. My sense of relief, when he came charging back into our campsite, was dashed when he lapped down a full dish of water.

By the time we were packed, it was clear to me that Amigo was ill. Having seen warning signs when I had been out searching for him about the placement of rat poison in the alley exacerbated my dread. As we merged onto the interstate, I found myself continually turning around to check on Amigo as well as to assure Adam that all was fine, but trying without success to persuade Carl to find a vet immediately instead of visiting Teddy Roosevelt National Monument.

The historic site was unquestionably interesting, but my concern remained on Amigo, and how I would deal with Adam if the cat died. My relief was shortly arrested when before we exited the site, Carl announced that he wanted to hike across a prairie trail before moving on. Frustrated, I declared that he could go and take Adam and the dogs; I was staying with Amigo. I waited until they were out of sight, then I moved to the back seat and gently drew Amigo from his cage. He was limp and panting severely. Feeling totally helpless, I made him comfortable in my lap and gently stroked him while my tears dampened his fur.

When I saw Carl and Adam approaching, I placed Amigo back into the cage with his sister and returned to the front seat. As we drove along, Adam questioned me about Amigo's sickness. I did not exactly lie to him; I simply wanted to be in the best of circumstance to deal with this. Upon reaching the campsite, we presented to Adam the truth of the situation. Then we wrapped Amigo in a towel and buried him. I took comfort that he was laid to rest high in the mountains beneath the evergreens, not left in the backroom of a veterinary clinic.

I played the incidents over and over in my mind, sick with guilt and self-condemnation—caught in my I-did-it-wrong-again syndrome. If this were not bad enough, Carl, as only Carl could do, distinctly accused me, without accusing me, of being responsible for Amigo's death. Rationally, I knew that circumstances were circumstances, decisions were decisions, and that was that. But no other pain—one I would carry for many years to come—could bear harder on me than feeling responsible for the death of one of Adam's beloved pets.

The next time this trip would feel like a horrible burden would be when Amiga was critically injured, caught beneath the hood of the car when Carl started the engine. Since Carl fainted at the sight of blood, I would be the one to make the decisions, moment by moment—driving her a hundred miles through the mountains to a vet to save her life. Regardless, I would remain unable to acknowledge that I had been the one who produced a favorable outcome, that I was not an incompetent failure. Neither would Carl give me any credit.

When my thoughts and emotions were not out of control, I concentrated on making the most of circumstances, if not for myself, at least for Adam. The indomitable explorer in me maintained enough energy to center my attention on investigating the various areas of the country we traversed, from the desert, to the mountains, to the Pacific coastline. National parks, preserves, interpretive sites and centers, as well as historic markers were a must-see. Within me lay an aching to follow every trail I came to, to see where it would take me. I carried my binoculars and field guides wherever we hiked in order to study the birds, trees and plants along the way. Characteristic of my childhood patterning, my collection of pine cones, feathers, stones, shells and other odd bits of nature's beauty were carefully stored in a box or knapsack.

When the weather became too cold to camp in the southwest, Carl decided to drive to Florida to visit his brother who had recently moved there. He had lived with us for the previous year, mostly depressed and doing little but sleeping until noon, reading the newspaper or watching television, that is until Carl had finally kicked him out. Since Carl himself did little more than his brother did, I had found his rationale, as well as his actions, interesting. I had felt uncomfortable with his brother living with us, not so much that he was there, but that he was always there, to the point I felt my privacy was compromised. I was also threatened by the feeling, one I did my best to dismiss, that he was attracted to me. Nevertheless, he was exceedingly attached to Adam and vice versa, and he had helped put food on the table when I was pregnant, when Carl had had no concern for doing so. I felt eternally indebted to him for that. Despite his brother having recently entered a new relationship, Carl had no reluctance whatsoever to simply drop in on him. He welcomed our surprise arrival as best he could. His partner did not. As if this was not awkward enough, Carl being Carl was unable to keep his opinions to himself to the point that the situation was soon reduced to a verbal skirmish between his brother's partner and him. Thus our visit ended shortly after we arrived.

Overall, I was grateful for the way the situation transpired because Carl was now ready to return to Chicago. We stayed with his mother and her new husband, an alcoholic, as long as I could handle, which was only long enough to find an apartment. Without jobs and having three pets, I was certain our chances were next to none. Unable to see my Divine support, I labeled our immediate success "luck." The second floor apartment was rundown and came without a yard. On the other hand, I loved the challenge of making the most out of little. Besides, the apartment came with a huge deck area that provided plenty of room for planters, hanging laundry and eating outdoors.

Carl immediately fell into his old betting routine regardless of our depleted financial state. I didn't expect anything different of him, nor was I any more able than before to resist his strong-arm tactics. Out of necessity, my full attention fell on finding a job, to reestablish my sense of security and self-reliance. I was as obsessed with working as Carl was with gambling. Oddly, I calculated my approach, making out a list of downtown restaurants where I thought I could make the greatest amount of money, regardless of whether or not these restaurants were advertising for help. Then I set out to make the rounds. If I had to do this, it was going to be my way for once.

Upon entering the first restaurant on my list, the cashier claimed that they were doing no hiring at the time, but I could fill out an application. I surprised myself by boldly following through with my plan, which was to simply explain that I was intent on immediately landing a job, and if someone were seriously interested in hiring me, only then would I consider filling out an application. Otherwise, I was unwilling to waste my time or unnecessarily give out personal information about myself. It was the beginning of the lunch hour, and customers were already streaming through the door. Yet I could see that the cashier was taken aback by my position as well as equivocating in regard to how to deal with me. Just as I thought she was going to tell me to get lost, she requested that I sit in a corner room to wait for an interview. I would soon learn that she was the owner's aunt.

While I waited, I examined the operation. It appeared to be well-managed. The waitresses wore more dignified uniforms than I had often been required to wear in previous situations. It was the room in which I was waiting that most caught my attention. It had ten tables and windows looking onto the street. Although it was a hike to the kitchen area, I was never bothered with how hard I had to work, as long as benefits matched output. I wondered what kind of seniority a waitress would need to obtain such an ideal situation as a large station separate and all to herself. No doubt, whoever had this station would have to be efficient and fast.

When the interview was over, I had a job that began the following day. Later, however, I was embarrassed to learn that other waitresses were being given days off in order to make room for me. After a couple of weeks, I was offered the charming, little room that I could never have imagined getting. I also acquired a host of regular customers as well as the means to make a significant income. Only retrospect could reveal that this job was about much more than creating financial security. My lessons were upon me. A good share of my clientele came from nearby City Hall, and the state and judicial buildings, guaranteeing a steady diet of politically-minded, power-flaunting male customers.

Carl had refused to enroll Adam in kindergarten the year before, so I expected a battle when I informed him that it was time that he attend school. Carl's cynical view of the Chicago public schools remained tainted by his own childhood experiences, especially one, whereby he had flunked a grade. He claimed that this was because his father, in a state of drunkenness, had shit in the hallway of his teacher's apartment building. If he had his way, Adam would never go to school. While I questioned my decision to enroll him, a part of me was determined to override Carl's position regardless of the cost. I knew that with Adam in school Carl would have to find another excuse for being unemployed. Beyond knowing that Adam needed to learn to develop relationships outside of his family, I felt that it was time he was away from his father as well.

Adam had never gone anywhere without us without making a fuss. Going to school was no exception. My doubts flared as every day for months Adam cried his way to school. My heart ached for him, but the determined part of me remained unwaveringly adamant about his attending. His teacher reported that once he was on his own, Adam soon dried his tears, and that, regardless of what topic arose for discussion, he consistently had something valuable to contribute—these reports reassured me that I was doing the best for my son.

Our apartment was only a short, safe block from Adam's school. Even so, Carl walked him there every morning, and then to and from lunch, as well as home again every day after school, engaging him in conversation and clowning around with his classmates along the way. This routine became like a cause for him, as if he was his son's protector or bodyguard. While his behavior might have been seen as devotion, I labeled it manipulative and unhealthy. He also insisted on driving me, as he had in the past, to and from work, except if it was evening and doing so interfered with his gambling schedule; then I took public transportation. It was easy to admit to myself that I hated him using me as an excuse to avoid his life. On the other hand, it was tough to admit that I was using him as an excuse to avoid my life. I was also somehow attached to the convenience of being chauffeured; it was impossible to accept that being chauffeured was the main avenue to obtain any kind of attention from Carl. In addition, it was tough to accept that I was replicating my parents' behavior—my mother depending on being chauffeured by my father as an avenue to obtain attention from him.

My life was filled with addictions, phobias and obsessive-compulsive behavior. Eating was the foremost. Genetics left me two inches over five feet, muscular and at an average weight of 120 pounds. Anger flaring as Carl walked out of the door to gamble, I habitually stepped to the refrigerator and binged. Then to whip my body back into obedience, I would rigidly count calories, compulsively exercise or "fast" for a day or two. Other times I would chew food until I got the flavor out of it and then spit it in the garbage instead of swallowing. Outside of bingeing, I preferred picking at food rather than sitting down to a meal, mainly, because I was unable to tolerate my stomach feeling full. Snacking entailed eating crumbs of cookies or pieces of broken chips in the bottom of the bag, leftovers or items ready to spoil. However, in social situations, I had to stuff myself. I seldom ate openly on these occasions but would grab food and quickly consume it out of sight of others, as if I was stealing. Since my teenage years I had been hooked on Coca Cola (only with ice), and there was little I wouldn't do to have my one Coke a day, that was despite being otherwise obsessed with eating healthfully, which meant only fresh and homemade food.

Clothes shopping also took on compulsive overtones. Buying something for myself helped fill my emptiness, but I only allowed myself seconds, closeout or clearance items, and even then felt guilty for being self-indulgent. Being a garage sale junkie came naturally. It was an affordable means, in my circumstances, to give myself "crumbs" and reinforce my sense of unworthiness. Making do could be an absorbing challenge, yet over time, it became tedious and disheartening.

Another of my obsessions was watching other families interact. Whether at the zoo, in shopping centers or walking through the neighborhood, I energetically poked, prodded and peered into backyards and through unclosed curtains, trying to see beyond surface appearances, still trying to get a deeper understanding of the dynamics that composed family. My efforts consistently produced nothing but frustration. I reminded myself that I had my son. Yet, as important as Adam was to me, there was still something missing. I thought it was that Carl was seldom physically or emotionally available. However I recognized that that was not it either, because when he did take time for us, I did not like being with him.

At the top of the weird behavior list was my fixation with trees. Whether I was walking, riding in the car or on public transportation, I was unable to abstain from studying them or the conditions in which they were able to take root and grow. Whether in cracks in the sidewalk, along the narrow strip of soil between garages, in alleys or gangways, abandoned lots used as dumps, or the shadowed side of billboards, their tenacity, their ability to adjust and survive in extremely alien situations never ceased to amaze me. I accepted my behavior as obsessive when riding on the elevated transit, I would crane my head around or even get up to stand in the aisle to get a better view of how a particular tree was managing to adapt to its particular circumstance.

Never able to sit down and relax until my abode was organized and comfortably clean was yet another obsession. Maintaining household order was like a second occupation, considering I had a child, enough pets to feel like a zookeeper, and a slovenly hoarder for a partner as well. I resented coming home from work and finding a sink full of dishes to clean before I could begin making the evening meal, only to have to clean up the kitchen again after the meal, before moving on to other chores. Requesting assistance from Carl produced little more than lame excuses, aggravating my exasperation and resentment. He only helped if it suited his needs—like fix the car when it broke down in order to not miss going to the racetrack.

I also compulsively rearranged the furniture. Whenever a certain undefinable frustration beset me, I would push and shove our odd collection of dressers, chairs and tables back and forth until my back went out or I was utterly exhausted. Regardless of the arrangement, it never felt balanced or comfortable.

My fear of being thought abominable warped my adult behavior as much as it had in my childhood. I incessantly obsessed over situations where I had no control or that were a waste of time. Negativity constantly permeated my thoughts and molded my sour attitude and defensive behavior. My insecurities manifested in idiosyncratic behaviors such as flushing the toilet as I entered a stall in a public facility so as to avoid the embarrassment of someone hearing me urinate. I was sure to feel like an idiot if I happened to be corrected in conversation. If a policeman stopped me for a traffic violation, I went to pieces. Called to my boss' office, my bowels would go berserk, activating the same dreaded "I'm dead" response that I had as a child when I worried over my father's disapproval. Safety only existed in how effectively I could get others' approval.

Yet my fear of being judged never prevented me (in moments of anger, frustration, deprivation or injustice) from pocketing a pen that did not belong to me, wolfing down a piece of food out of sight or altering a check in a way that left me with an extra fifty cents. Although Carl infrequently returned from the racetrack with money, my impulse when he did was to sneak in his drawer and take some for myself. My behavior was an extension of my childhood habit of filching money from my mother's purse when I was angry at her, feeling deprived or vengeful. It was easy to rationalize that everyone in the restaurant stole, from the owner in his own insidious ways, to the managers, cooks and busboys. Carl himself was continually stealing. Even so, any attempt at palliating my compulsive pilfering never blunted my extreme sense of shame over failing to live a deeper integrity.

There were other phobias. My childhood fear of disappearing in water where I could not see the bottom remained active. I had a bizarre obsession over obtaining too little sleep. Another persistent terror was causing an auto accident or striking a pedestrian, exacerbated by my inability to pay attention in the moment; I was either lagging along slowing traffic or had the pedal to the metal. I would drive, comatose, miles beyond my intended destination or suddenly realize that I had momentarily forgotten where I was going. Being in a car was like being in a time warp.

Whether it was winter or summer, being indoors left me claustrophobic. This state intensified when nightfall necessitated drawing the curtains or blinds shut. The only way for me to create a sense of comfort being indoors was to have all of the windows and doors open, allowing for the flow of fresh air, or be in a position where I could see the out of doors. Ironically, I also feared being locked out or burning down my dwelling. Leaving to go somewhere, I often circled the block a number of times, each time returning just to make sure I had shut off the iron or the oven or closed the door to the wood stove. If I repressed this ritual, during my entire absence, I would agonize over my negligence or the possibility of having no home which to return. Obsessive/compulsive disorder was as of yet a foreign concept; still, I knew my behavior was abnormal.

My sense of deprivation was a chronic and acute issue: I was terrified of not having enough money to pay the bills, buy food or meet other essential needs. I hoarded away as much as possible, paradoxically perpetually anticipating some dilemma taking me by surprise, and when my savings account was diminished somehow, I would rivet my energy on not simply replenishing, but increasing it. Honesty would eventually reveal that I actually hoarded money to appease my insecurity more than to meet emergencies. Only as I was moved into a reality of abundance, would I be able to understand that my securities and insecurities were actually one and the same.

Another aberrant pattern occurred when I was going out. Whether it was a vacation or an afternoon walk, I would be overcome by a feeling that I would not return and thus be thrown into putting my house in order and grabbing something to eat before departing. At the same time, I would make sure that I had everything necessary to meet my anticipated needs, as if I was to be absent for an undetermined period of time rather than just an afternoon, a day or a weekend. I brought numerous extra wraps as well as shoes and socks to replace my sandals in case the weather turned cold. I brought shorts and a sleeveless top in case the weather turned warm. Then there was an umbrella or rain gear in case the weather turned foul. I had to make sure I had water, snacks, lip balm, sunscreen, pens, writing paper, a number of choices of books to read and other "essentials" stashed in the car. Regardless of my efforts, I never felt comfortably prepared to go anywhere.

I felt panicky and unworthy of eating at a fine dining restaurant or staying in a motel—even an inexpensive one. Camping was all I deserved. I believed that I was of the lowest social class, a non-existent, undeserving, nothing nobody. Really, only beautiful, intelligent, educated or wealthy people deserved to walk on the prestigious side of the tracks, not me. Even with my beliefs having a life of their own, I could stand outside of them and see them as disturbing if not disgusting.

As an adult my compulsive behavior carried over from my teenage years, going to a mirror, any and all mirrors, looking at myself, always looking hard, seeking, searching, but never finding a reflection that I felt was mine. What was reflected back to me in the mirror persistently appeared as nothing more than a stranger. I was unable to find "me" in the mirror, reinforcing my terror that I did not exist. I would laugh at my own absurd thoughts, but at the same time, frustrated, I would continue staring, staring until I was pulled into the depths of my own pupils. As in my youth, all I ever found was a frightening expansive void, followed by a deeper sense of agitation. As with all of us, it would take much more than a mirror to obtain a true reflection.

Nightmares plagued my slumber. A common theme was my being on the run, hunted down with nowhere to hide. Another was never being able to find a sense of home. For instance, I would rent a spacious, bright apartment with many windows, a huge, open porch and mature shade trees in the yard. However, when I proceeded to move in, I would find the apartment windowless, full of filth and debris left from previous tenants or full of mindless strangers, rooms that turned into mazes or the yard barren of life. Then there was the dream where I was a student unable to master the curriculum enough to graduate and get on with life. The most common dream, however, had to do with being a waitress: as quickly and effectively as I served my customers, that many more were waiting, which left me perpetually overwhelmed and exhausted. I would silently scream, "I can't serve all of you! There are too many of you!" Regardless of my sense of futility, I would never quit trying. Someday I would realize that these dreams were keys to understanding myself. Eventually, I would understand fully that all of my behavior was governed by experiences initiated in prior life times.

Fully conditioned from childhood that idleness was unacceptable, but more assuredly to avoid being quiescent long enough to look deeply into my issues, I moved through life at full speed, juggling as many activities as I could. Soon after Adam came along, yoga became my tool to manage tension, quiet my restlessness and provide a sense of control over my own body. I started out following a televised program, then found the courage to move on to a park district class. I practiced yoga to the point of obsession and became so accomplished as to even impress fellow class members.

My deeply ingrained connection with nature remained another prime survival tool. During my annual two-week vacation, I was free to isolate myself in nature long enough to be sustained for the duration of another year. In between, caring for my jungle of houseplants, cultivating a community gardening plot and frequenting city parks and forest preserves were proximate substitutions for sustaining that connection. There was truth in Carl's jealous accusations that I spent more time in the woods than at home.

The state of my affairs took a variety of physical forms. I carried pain in most every part of my body. I ground my teeth during sleep while cramps overtook my legs; varicose veins ached during the day. Allergies to a mélange of substances produced headaches, sinus infections and skin irritations. Menorrhagia caused anemia and exhaustion. Because sexual intercourse produced urinary tract infections, I took antibiotics prophylactically. I compulsively twisted and pulled on my hair; clenched my thumbs inside fisted hands; tensed my jaws, and constantly chewed on ice cubes to quench a seemingly unquenchable thirst. Cuts and bruises revealed my proneness to accidents. I nervously perspired to excess and was obsessively self-conscious about being thought dirty or smelly (or because my body was either too cold or too hot), therefore, often showering two or three times a day.

These health issues frightened me and made me feel as weak and helpless as I viewed my hypochondriacal mother. An exceptionally high pain threshold made it possible for me to endure my own physical discomfort, and an unidentifiable drive kept me from giving up. No health insurance, plus my instinctive distrust of the medical system, left me only seeing doctors when situations seemed beyond my perceived control. The mere contemplation of allowing a doctor to examine my body would have me in a cold sweat as well as breaking out in a rash on my neck and chest. I believed I should be able to create my own wellness, especially considering I exercised, had educated myself on nutrition and had become a vegetarian. But I was not able to manifest that reality—nor did I know how to nurture the rest of me: my emotional, mental and spiritual bodies. My physical state was not the problem, but the symptom; it was only an accumulated manifestation of deeper issues, all of which would eventually have to be addressed in order to create true wellness. Dis-ease does not begin in the physical; it is where it ends up if left unaddressed.

Due to my continued fear of anything having to do with sex, along with an intrinsic sense of fidelity, I remained prudishly faithful. Nonetheless, sexual advances, even proclamations of love remained the norm. One critical incident, prior to quitting my job to go on our camping trip caused me to recoil even more deeply into my protective state. On a Friday evening during cocktail hour, a drunken customer grabbed me right in public as I was exiting the washroom. Before I could react, he harshly forced his lips onto mine and thrusting my lips apart, plunged his tongue deeply into my mouth. My immediate impulse was to bite his tongue off and spit it right back in his face, and then escape to the washroom to sterilize my mouth in some way. Instead, completely rattled, I pushed him away as best I could, while simultaneously fearing repercussions. Finally he had released me and walked away gloating, leaving me feeling angry, confused, helpless, and violated. Somehow, this man had always frightened me, not just his large size, something else. And, somehow, I had known that my aloofness had been a challenge. I never mentioned a word of this "kiss" to anyone, not even my boss. I was too ashamed. Besides, I knew my boss wouldn't have supported me anyway, since I had repeatedly rejected his sexual advances as well. I hated them both, but my livelihood, my survival, remained dependent on them in one way or another.

Only recently was I beginning to be able to let go of the plain Jane look—hiding my feminine self (my beauty) at all cost—that I had clung onto as a shield against men's advances. I was even beginning to have my hair smartly styled for the first time since having met Carl. I still hung onto my guarded demeanor, but not quite so obsessively, even while it remained common for my bosses, male co-workers and customers—all those uncles still blowing down the back of my blouse—to make sexual advances toward me. I was learning to take their behavior less personally. What I wanted to do was master the art of telling them to back off, to laugh at their infantile, self-demeaning behavior, to not take them or myself so seriously.

Fellow waitresses often shared reports of their sexual adventures: nude photographs of themselves, partner swapping, kinky sex, promiscuity and sexually transmitted diseases. Their experiences were not only foreign and confusing to me, but thoroughly embarrassing, even an off-color joke was enough to turn my face beet-red. I regarded my position about sexuality as prudish, if not anachronistic. Just the same, I thought that these waitresses, who shared their adventures, had gone too far; to me they were as crude and opportunistic as men were. The differences between their lifestyles and mine were certainly obvious; yet I failed to see that I gave myself away sexually to no less a degree than they did.

I never shared my sexual harassment issues with Carl, but he was nevertheless innately suspicious of whatever I did. He had an uncanny way of undermining my fragile sense of self. My approach to him about anything was very carefully calculated to allay his mistrust, yet my efforts were invariably wasted. In simply sharing thoughts about something as innocuous as accepting an invitation to a party, he would strike, "If you really need to go to the birthday party, then you go ahead, but I just can't understand why you think you need to be with other people." As with my mother, his position was sharply double-edged. First, he wanted me only at home taking care of his needs. And, if I did go out, he acted as if I was going to be "fucking" every man I ran into.

Ironically, Carl had never been above getting his sexual needs met outside of our relationship. He kept his encounters close to home, however, first starting with Casey back when we shared an apartment. Later he had a dalliance with a college friend's wife. Then he moved on to the mother of one of Adam's classmates. He audaciously asked me for money to take her on dates, and I, having been trained to keep peace at all cost, struggled to subdue my rage at this direct humiliation. With each affair he had voluntarily divulged the circumstances, going to the extent that he gave explicit detail, and enumerating by comparison my sexual inadequacies. He excused his conduct by alleging that I was incapable of meeting his needs. At the same time, these disclosures were followed by an insistence of having sex with me. I was becoming aware that the rock-hard wall I put around myself for protection was becoming denser, and I was becoming more stone cold and petrified by my own anger. Worse yet, I was unable to do anything about my condition.

With some awareness of how my childhood had affected me, I worried over how our dysfunctional family environment was damaging Adam. He was extremely bright and sensitive. Carl's and my unrestrained conflict was impacting him. He got caught in my anger toward Carl, plus his and his father's antagonistic relationship was intensifying year by year. I knew that I was often unavailable for him in the way he needed me to be and that I was unnecessarily controlling. To some extent, I realized that living my life from a context of fear reduced my intentions to be a good mother into some vague form of warped manipulation. To a fuller extent, I realized that I was not honoring the commitment I had made to never do to my son what my parents had done to me.

From the moment of Adam's birth, a part of me contemplated when and how I could leave Carl. I had rationalized that it would be when Adam was toilet trained, when he started school or when I no longer had to concern myself over childcare. The truth was: Carl would never let me leave with Adam; I did not have the courage to stand up to him; and I remained afraid of being on my own. I would tell myself that I was still young and had plenty of time to get my life right. But I was near panic as I approached thirty and saw my life slipping away. The intriguing theme, "Can man rise above his environment?" from the American classic, **Ethan Frome**, remained a nagging question in my mind from the time I had read it. The main characters had attempted to escape their circumstances through the only means they saw viable, suicide; but instead, their failed attempt left them completely dependent on the people and situation they had attempted to escape. My parents' philosophy—when you make your bed you must lie in it—epitomized their fate. Lacking a greater awareness, I was unable to identify the nature of the characters' failure to get out of their bed: that is, only a greater understanding leads to freedom.

A message from the novel, **Death Comes to the Archbishop**, left another dreadful impression on me. A novice patronizingly commented to the dying Archbishop that a cold does not kill a person. The Archbishop, amused with this naiveté replied, "I shall not die of a cold, my son. I shall die of having lived." In the words the Archbishop spoke, I heard that I was wasting my life. I did not even know what it meant to live. Regardless of having a deep sense that life must be lived as nothing less than a gift, I was certain that I was wasting mine. The undercurrent produced by this thought was unnerving. The best I could do at the time was think that if I worked on being a better person—a perfect person—my life would not be a waste. The greater truth is "not wasting my life" has nothing to do with "being a better person." Not wasting my life has to do with seeing beyond my *illusions* of who I am in order to know how to live who I *truly* am; understanding that my perfection is present and intact—virginal, immaculate. Simply "being" instead of "trying."

Still believing that I was the disgrace of the family, I continued to avoid contact with my parents. On occasion, our paths crossed at my younger brother's place (he played the role of keeper of the family ties). Then, as customary, my mother, with her stony stare, behaved as if Adam did not exist, while my father nervously carried on a perfunctory conversation. Regardless the flavor of the situation, they continued to send the obligatory Christmas gifts, until finally I wrote to them saying that sending seasonal presents to my son did not make a relationship. I stifled my hurt and continued to nurse a sense of responsibility for the failed relationship. Carl continued to support my estrangement from my family by continually drilling into me that my parents were self-absorbed and they had no honest concern for me the way his mother did.

When my brother informed me that my paternal grandfather had died, I dismissed my insecurities enough to attend the funeral rites. The night of the wake, I entered the funeral home and first noticed my father standing with two unfamiliar men near the casket. I had not seen him in almost three years. The farther I walked the length of red carpet toward them, the stronger the adrenaline rushed through my body. I felt as if I was facing a firing squad. My father nervously shook my hand while the two men jokingly queried why he was not introducing someone so attractive. A stunned expression washed across their faces as he awkwardly introduced me as his daughter. Recovering, they questioned why, as long as they had been friends and co-workers, he had never mentioned that he had a daughter. My father was speechless. Quickly, I excused myself before my tears took over. I found a secluded place to lick my old wounds, which had been momentarily split open: the memory of my father waiting in the receiving line to shake my hand instead of standing proudly beside me when I had passed my confirmation test. While one part of me wanted to cry out, "I haven't done anything to deserve this!" another wondered why my parents' behavior still had a hold over me.

The number in attendance at my grandfather's funeral was testimony to how well he was thought of in the community. I did not know what to think or feel, and I shed no tears. Instead, I observed. I wondered if my grandfather had really earned the seemingly deep regard that his family held toward him. I blamed myself for never having been able to get close to him.

The following day, I wanted to probe my grandmother about her life, her fifty-plus years of marriage and, especially, how she felt in regard to facing the future on her own. But prior experience had taught me what I would create if I stepped over the lines of family protocol with this line of inquiry. Since I had never mastered the art of superficiality, I once again surrendered to my most reliable survival tool: aloof detachment, which predictably merely fed the tension my presence spawned. The outcome of the experience was for me to touch that part of myself that craved acceptance by these people. If I could just explore the family's history, if someone would only open up, I was convinced I would be able to free myself of my sense of rejection and confusion.

A conversation with my mother's sister shed a ray of light on my understanding. She asked me why I thought that my parents never mentioned or celebrated their wedding anniversary. I recognized immediately what she was implying. And, although society had become more tolerant of pre-marital sex and unwed mothers, I knew this had not been the case during my mother's youth. Eureka! I could see that her denigration of me, viewing me as a slut, distrusting me as a teen, as well as her rejection of my son, were her projections onto me of her own unresolved guilt and shame. My poor mother! Armed with a certain sense of clarity, I now craved to identify every remaining skeleton in that closet, to satiate that yearning within me to make sense of who I am, my life, and everyone in it. Eventually I would make sense of my life, but only by tapping into my inner source of knowledge, my own library of information, not by interrogating my biological family.

Premonitions had remained a part of my reality despite my continued efforts to deny them. When I "knew something," I knew it. Waiting for the lunch hour to begin, I knew prior to their arrival which of my regular customers would be in. I often knew when the phone was about to ring and who was calling. I sensed objects falling and breaking before the happening occurred. Out with Carl one day, I found myself clutching the armrest of the car door anticipating an accident. I wanted him to pull off the expressway, but I was afraid that my feelings were wrong and my request would result in him belittling me. Moments after he exited, however, the rear axle of the car broke causing a wheel to fall off. Even with experiences like this, I tried to convince myself that I could not take my knowing seriously because I was mostly only able to realize it in retrospect, like, "Oh, yes. I remember having a certain strong sense three days ago that the one of our dogs was going to need medical attention."

When I turned thirty, Carl threw a surprise birthday party for me. I felt honored that he would be so thoughtful as to offset my dread over this punctuation mark in my life. Usually the most I ever received from him was a description of what he would have gotten me if he'd had the money. Occasionally he had borrowed money from me to buy me a present, which he would then present with a magnanimous flair, promising that he would reimburse me when he made a big win. However, my flattery over my surprise party shifted to a familiar sense of worthlessness as the celebration wound down, and in the presence of our guests, he asked me for money to reimburse his sister for the cost of the cake and other expenses.

He was certain that the only reason he was unsuccessful at gambling was because I never gave him as much money as he needed (and asked for) to enable him to play the horses effectively. Beyond what I gave him on a daily basis, he perpetually ensnared me in agreements. If I gave him fifty dollars extra, then he could recoup what he had lost the night before. If I gave him three hundred dollars, then he would stay home the entire following month regardless of whether he lost or won. It was the same "if, then" kind of game that my dad used to play, repeating itself, only I failed to realize this. Ultimately he would smash my fragile sense of self to nothing one way or another if I pushed my own position too far. My survival was dependent on grafting myself to others' beliefs: a manifestation of my fear of persecution, a patterning so deep that it controlled my body, emotions and thoughts. Nonetheless, I had made the agreement that during this present and final embodiment I would step out of my fear of persecution. Any gods up there taking wagers would undoubtedly be taking bets on my failure, not success, for they alone knew what I was up against.

My only requirement regarding vacations was to be far removed from civilization. Routinely camping in an untrammeled corner of Yellowstone National Park (sometimes Appalachia) made this possible. Our annual camping trips had allowed me to become more connected to what had taken place during my first trip to the mountains at eighteen. I could only fully experience this inexplicable phenomenon when I went off alone. Doing this without betraying the nature of my clandestine quest to Carl necessitated stealing whatever time I could after a day's outing when he and Adam were building a fire or early in the morning before they had arisen. But once alone in a secluded spot, I shed as many clothes as the situation permitted, surrendered myself to absorbing the rays of the sun and the warm breeze scanning my skin, breathing the scent of the pines and firs embrace. I could feel a transformation taking place, as if I was being fed or filled with something which allowed me to come alive inside, to dance, spiraling free of the limitations of this body, and this world. Outside of this connectedness, life felt overwhelmingly meaningless. Thus, my yearly two-week vacation sustained me through another unendurable year.

One summer as we were pulling out of the campground for the day, I noticed an array of sleeping gear hanging over a clothesline at a campsite down the road from us. Huge, black clouds marching across the sky made it clear that someone was in for a miserably wet night's sleep. It occurred to me to put the gear away, but my fear of getting into trouble for intruding on someone else's personal space caused me to hesitate. Carl's position, that someone who was stupid enough to leave his sleeping gear unattended got what he deserved, intensified my conflict. Before he pulled onto the main road, however, an inner force overrode my habit of conceding to him and prompted me to jump out of the car and secure their gear. A teddy bear and a couple of dolls inside the tent confirmed my actions. So did the storm, which shortly blanketed the entire valley.

That evening, I watched as a woman with two little girls moved from one campsite to the next, engaging campers in conversation as she went. When she approached our site and asked Carl if he was the one who had put her sleeping gear away, he pointed to me. She proceeded to explain that she was newly divorced and a novice camper, but had taken on the challenge of giving her two daughters an outdoor experience. She knew how different their experience would have been had I refrained from taking action. The message in her gratitude was unavoidable; it was time for me to listen, as well as to have confidence in myself. I had no idea how to do either, but the incident rattled something inside of me, and left me knowing it was time to begin.

As I sat on a mountain peak catching my breath during an arduous hike a few days later, I viewed the vastness of a snow-capped mountain range spreading out in all directions as far as I could see. This sight further awakened something inside of me and quickened a pervading urge to soar like an eagle across the expansiveness before me. My need to be free to explore whatever was out there stood in stark, harsh contrast to my monotonous, depressing existence.

After returning to camp, I sought out my familiar place of solitude, a tiny waterfall formed in an isolated section of the creek that ran through the campground, to further reflect on what I had been feeling sitting on top of the world. I felt simultaneously quiet and frenzied inside. I watched the wild flowers dance in the breeze as thoughts danced in and out of my mind: if I could make sense of my behavior and everyone else's, even the world's, I could be okay. Carl was the philosopher. As much as he had pushed Buber's **I and Thou** on me, and as much as I had contemplated and stretched my brain to absorb it, I had only ever been discouraged by my inability to comprehend such seemingly important concepts. While I sat there troubling over my incapability, I failed to realize that the understanding I was seeking does not come from literature or from the establishment's pontifical, ideological rhetoric. It comes from my knowing. I already had what I was seeking. I already knew God.

Prior to leaving for this vacation, a fellow waitress, who worked part-time in order to support herself through college, had declared that her waitressing was different from mine: I was a professional. Although it was not her intent to be judgmental, her comment had impacted me like a good dousing of cold water. For years I had clung to the security that waiting tables provided, but the thought of my occupation being my identity—my life—was oddly terrifying. This incident got me to thinking that I had to get out of the restaurant business, and soon. Although I had no understanding what "getting out" looked like or how to initiate it, I was already overwhelmed and exhausted by my responsibilities. Nonetheless, on the mountaintop, communing with the vastness engulfing me, I understood that I would be returning to school, I thought, to complete my education. Actually I was taking the initial step in removing myself from my own disconnection.

I had difficulty choosing a major, so I tried thinking in terms of what interested me. My need to be creative had not diminished. Though I had never really explored what being creative actually meant, I assumed that it meant simply being artistic. Unable to dance or sing, I had chosen art as a channel of expression, continually dabbling with various media: charcoal, pastels, watercolor and oils. I had tried carding and drop spinning raw wool to knit. I had then taught myself to knit. Following this, I moved on to macramé, basket-weaving, drying flowers for arranging, photography and working with clay. I wanted to feel accomplished in some venue, not merely a dilettante, but sooner or later, except for growing plants and gardening (which I didn't consider a talent), I lost interest. By this process of elimination, I soon could see that what truly interested me was all around me, as it had always been. I would study nature.

I could not comprehend how returning to school would be possible, any more than I could grasp that a force beyond my awareness was moving me into action, overriding my overwhelming fear of stepping out from behind the role I hid behind into the vastness of the unknown. Furthermore, I was incapable of knowing that finishing my education was only the first step in the initial preparation for me to free myself from the karmic bed in which I was laying. I attributed it to plain luck when I discovered that I was within two months of the ten-year grace period allowed for college credits to be transferred (I would start out with fifty credit hours already behind me). Only after traveling a considerable distance on my path, and then only in hindsight, would I be able to recognize that all along the way it had been and was Divine guidance supporting my endeavors: miracle upon miracles falling around me.

When Carl's family got wind of my venture, his aunt boldly announced that she saw a breakup in the process of happening. I already felt guilty fastening my attention on myself to the degree that my undertaking required. Consequently I dismissed the ring of truth in her words and instead labeled her meddlesome. Yet, like a sliver in my knowing, I was unable to completely ignore her comment.

Rearranging my work schedule—conveniently, a waitress retiring after twenty years made this possible—and maintaining sufficient trust that my reduced hours would still provide the income we needed to financially survive, I enrolled in a state university environmental science program. Wiser from prior experience and much less inhibited, I sought out a counselor rather than trying to make sense of my academic program on my own. My counselor, with whom I felt oddly comfortable, proved to be reliable and interested in me as an individual. When I felt handicapped due to my age, he saw it as an asset. He worked with me, not making allowances, but making circumstance function to my advantage. He acknowledged my intelligence and expected me to be a role model in whatever classes of his I was enrolled. He assigned journaling in my internship classes, which required me to be expressive. Then he provided detailed response to my thoughts and feelings. All of this was new to me.

My fear of being in social situations was my first major test. I still went into a state of agitation or bladder nervousness, if not a cold sweat in public, and while I worked on developing the ability to be with others, I missed the fact that I only had to learn how to *be*. It was becoming clear, however, just how strong my need was, not simply to be listened to, but to be heard and certainly noticed. I began to more carefully observe how people in conversation seldom listened to each other, but instead, anticipated the moment in which they could articulate what was on their mind, even when it necessitated interjecting, interrupting or changing the subject. What I saw was a reflection of myself. When I was not hiding behind reticence, my need to articulate an incident in my life or an idea would be all but waiting to explode. Meeting my needs to express myself, however, came with the price of failing to acknowledge what the other person was momentarily conveying, rudely changing the subject or disrupting the flow of conversation, and certainly leaving myself feeling disheartened over my own behavior. The irrefutable truth was that I was a horrible listener, just as horrible as almost everyone else. I was humiliated to acknowledge my deficiency. Yet I would be unable to overcome it through denial or struggle. The best I could momentarily do was accept my shortcoming. I didn't recognize it at the time, but this was the first step to moving out of it.

Schooling also provided me with the opportunity to examine the nature of my competitiveness. During my earlier attempt at higher education, I sat in the back of the classroom; this was to avoid being called on, horrified of the potential repercussions of giving incorrect answers. Uncharacteristically, I now sat in the front row where I believed the smart students sat. There I could be seen and heard and called on if the professor required a response. Now I was willing to take the risk of attempting to be seen as smart and even willing to compete with others to be acknowledged. Still, my logic told me that my seating habits were the means to compensate for my listening deficiencies.

Regardless of my attempts to pay attention, my mind still wandered; but, because I was so interested in the subject matter, it was less of a problem. I unabashedly used rote memorization to study and became an expert at regurgitating, almost verbatim, text material on exams. My perfect grade point average reflected an obsession to succeed more than my commitment. I thought that I was mainly acquiring a degree as a means to prove to myself that I was not stupid. Little did I know that I had stepped onto the path that would eventually lead me far beyond the sense of self that I so dearly desired.

Added to the list of my many idiosyncrasies was my inability to sit down to study without first making a huge bowl of popcorn. Any attempt to study without the popcorn fix would consistently prove fruitless. Even concern over gaining weight had no influence. I finally gave up the struggle, although without reaching peace of mind.

My behavior would be understandable—at least when once viewed from an expanded level of awareness. In an Anasazi embodiment, my husband and I had been shamans. It was a time of drought and starvation, when climatic conditions threatened the survival of our civilization. I had lived from a place of empowerment, despite being in a malnourished state. In the process of reclaiming that power (returning to academia), the Anasazi memory was being awakened on a cellular level, bypassing my conscious mind. Its imprint was that to be empowered is to be in a physically weakened state. This memory manifested via a food allergy to corn. Ironically, a symptom of food allergies is fatigue. The force of this memory would be akin to a cocaine addiction: the more I began to live the power that lay dormant within me, the more the body would crave corn products, thereby seeking to manifest fatigue and malnourishment.

Going to school meant having less time to spend with Adam. This regret was added to the guilt I already carried over knowing that for many years I had worked more hours than actually necessary. If I had succeeded at anything, it was to further support my son's sense of abandonment.

During the time I was returning to school, Carl had suddenly and unexpectedly renewed his relationship with a great aunt with whom he had had considerable conflict. This was particularly surprising because, up until Adam's birth, he had taken great effort to have no contact with her. Auntie was childless, approaching ninety, financially secure, but excessively miserly. Insinuating that she was leaving her money to various family members, she presently managed and manipulated them freely to get her needs met. At one point, a niece, with whom Auntie had lived for a couple of years, ousted her when she could no longer deal with her. Then a great-niece helped her move into an apartment adjacent to hers with the promise that she would look after her, but the niece moved to another part of the city a few months later. Subsequently, Auntie's care fell into our hands. A year later, with her physical and mental health rapidly deteriorating to a point that she could no longer live alone, she and Carl made a deal. She would provide a down payment on a house where we would all live; in exchange we would provide the care she needed, as well as take responsibility for the mortgage and household expenses. When I queried Carl about not being privy to the plan, yet a vital part in its implementation, he ripped into me, "You always have a way of sabotaging everything!" Essentially, I needed a sense of home as much as Carl or I would not have yielded to a situation in which I had no input or that was beyond my means to support financially.

After several months of searching, he decided to place a bid on a house he found to his liking. I was uncomfortable with his choice and simply could not imagine us living there. I failed to see that he had actually gotten cold feet when, at the last moment, he declined completing the contract, and instead, informed me that he wanted to see one other house.

Having previously written an environmental assessment of the neighborhood for a college assignment, I was familiar with the area where the other house was located. The property was minutes away from the university I attended and a mere block from a forest preserve that ran for miles as a green belt along a river. Additionally, three beautiful, old cemeteries abutted the preserve. The neighborhood was void of apartment buildings, isolated, secure and dotted with incredibly beautiful ancient oaks. Regardless of feeling unworthy or being able to picture what it would be like living in such a picturesque and elite neighborhood, a feeling of anticipation overtook my sensibility. My mind was in a cloud as Carl pulled along the curb in front of the for sale sign. Even before we entered this dwelling a deep sense of knowing instantly overtook any doubts I had. Literally, I saw us living there. I saw the yard planted with an abundance of flowers and trees and bird feeders hanging from every window. I saw the forest preserve becoming my personal haunt. I saw myself able to be outdoors more than I could ever imagine. And I saw Adam going to a decent school. With an inexplicable urgency moving me and obscuring my anticipation of Carl scoffing at my request, I stepped behind him and whispered, "Tell the realtor you want to put a bid on this property." A few months later we were living in an environment that was beyond anything I felt I deserved.

However much I wanted a home, this would prove to be no idyllic state. Since there were only two bedrooms and neither Carl nor I would consider having Adam sleep in the basement, we ourselves took it. Besides, I needed to believe that Auntie's relatives would be less likely to think that Carl and I were taking advantage of her by knowing of our sleeping arrangements. We learned after we moved in that the basement flooded during heavy rainfall, although we had been informed when we bought the house that the problem had been solved. We also learned that sufficiently heating the house in winter was nearly impossible, for the house was minimally insulated, the windows had no storms and the furnace was antiquated.

Besides these and other concerns, caring for Auntie was a substantial challenge. She was cantankerous and overly critical about everything. For years she had lived on the likes of soup made from chicken necks and day-old bread. Yet, when I served her a decent meal, she claimed it was not kosher or else "shit" and would indignantly push it away. At the same time she accused me of needlessly spending money. There was a continual tug-of-war with her to get her to use the toilet rather than urinating in her clothes, which left me with an endless amount of laundry as well as continually spot-cleaning the furniture and carpet. When I finally thought the problem was at least half-resolved by getting her to wear diaper-type protection, she proceeded to hide the soiled ones in her dresser drawers or bed in an effort to reuse them, soiled or not, when they dried out. We battled in the morning when I insisted she put on clean clothes. We battled when I made her bathe regularly and clean her false teeth in the sink instead of picking them clean with a fork at the table. When I put her to bed and thought I was free until the next morning, she would wake in the middle of the night screaming that she was being starved and demanding her lunch. Feelings of utter entrapment left me yelling at her proportionate to the degree that she criticized me. Knowing the neighbors were privy to the discord left me feeling like a raging teenager again, but even more helpless. Carl had no patience in the situation and yelled at her even more than I did, that was when he was home. With this escalating tension, Adam took refuge in his bedroom. I was quickly realizing the actual cost of acquiring this house. However, even while I thought I was doing everything all wrong, there was still a greater truth in operation.

Adam finished his grade school years in a school where his teachers reasonably inspired and challenged him. His friends were bright, first-generation Americans whose parents pushed them intently to be successful academically. On the surface he appeared sound, but when he and I went camping in the Appalachians the summer before he entered high school, I discovered he was obsessed about failing. He worried to the extent that his trip was spoiled. My suggestion that unless he set aside his worry we might as well return home was ineffective. He had been a precocious child and impeccably well behaved—a teacher's dream. It was impossible for him to fail. Coming from another angle, I asked him to imagine what failing looked like. He responded, "My teachers won't like me." When I asked him what else, he added, "Carl and Grandma won't like me." Finally he added, "You won't like me." Both Carl and his mother had rewarded him with money for obtaining good grades since he first started school. I believed encouragement was much more appropriate than bribery. The support I had given him was the support I had never received from my parents. Now, I had to own that I had overstepped the fine line between supporting him and using him vicariously to demonstrate my own aptitude. Also, I had used him for validation, if not much more. I was no different than the parents of his Asian friends whom I readily judged as being overbearing. I was disgusted to see how I had negatively impacted him and angry that it had taken circumstances to escalate to this point before I was moved to action. Now, I had to learn how to step back and appropriately support him. This meant identifying my own needs and refraining from using him to get them met.

Our talk temporarily curtailed Adam's fear of failure, but once he started school it sprang alive again and I watched him pour extreme effort into his studies. Late at night I would tell him to put his books away to get some sleep. His position within the top ten best students in school was never enough. He aimed to be number one. Carl, too, was an overtly competitive person and even in conversation had to have the last word. Whether basketball or Monopoly, they each played against the other with a vengeance. I would have preferred to blame Carl for his son's overheated need to be on top, but my own obsession to maintain a perfect grade point average gave me another perspective.

It had been years since I had allowed Carl to drive me to and from work. I thought if he wanted to be useful, he should be useful—become employed—not merely create a show of it. Taking public transportation allowed me time to be alone with my feelings. The route I took to complete the last leg of my return afforded me a walk through the forest preserve and more time alone. The woods had continued to be a safe haven for me to release my increasingly uncontainable emotions. As a daily ritual, the first step into the woods was like opening an emotional floodgate. Tears of helplessness and pain routinely overwhelmed me as I tromped along the familiar path. Stepping out of the woods produced a reverse action. By the time I was at my front door, my stoic mask was in place and nothing in my composure revealed my inner state.

Regardless, the weight of my world was becoming more and more impossible to endure, to the degree that I began to experience unexpected breakdowns at the restaurant. The manager, for whom I was the epitome of composure, was flabbergasted when I fell apart in his office, adamantly responding to his sincere overtures of concern that nothing was wrong with me. Playing out the same scene a number of times, in exasperation, he declared, "You don't have to talk to me, but you have to talk to someone and by the looks of it, soon." Talking about my problems necessitated breaking the rules that had been inculcated throughout my childhood. Having made my bed meant that I had to lie in it, but did I have to lie in it forever? My relationship with Carl was deeply humiliating; the sense of secrecy and deception that Carl had demanded and I had maintained since its inception had gradually become all-consuming. Neither did I know how to be truthful about my personal life, nor how to ask for help. Even with it becoming exceedingly more rigorous to maintain the fraudulent cloak around my life, doing so appeared easier than allowing my lifestyle to become public and facing the possibility of being condemned, or having to face my own shame. Beyond food for gossip, I was unable to fathom anyone being interested in my problems. I saw no alternative except to continue more strenuously to maintain my life as it existed, but change, like a lava flow, was already beginning to consume it.

4

Examining the Tangles

Carl habitually flaunted his infrequent "winnings" by making frivolous purchases, sometimes for himself, sometimes for Adam or me, but he rarely contributed to monthly expenses or repairs on our antiquated car. The part of me that waited for promises, nonetheless, nursed expectations of someday being rewarded for my tenacity. When he suddenly, as well as regularly, began to supply expensive amenities, suspicions began to overshadow my eager excitement. One night while he was at the racetrack, I went through his drawers. There I found the true source of his affluence: his aunt's savings account book recording withdrawals amounting to thousands of dollars, testimony to his pilfering. I was enraged and humiliated, enough so as to confront him squarely upon his return. I walked away with a wrenched neck and bruises. A few days later he extended an apology and a promise that he would never steal from his aunt again. I desperately wanted to believe him—if he changed I was free from having to take appropriate accountability, like removing myself from our imbroglio—but this was becoming increasingly trickier to do.

His behavior left my own lack of integrity staring me in the face. Although whatever I had ever stolen was nominal, intuitively I knew that honesty functions as an absolute. I held the position that until I became a perfect person I had no right to object to his behavior. Ultimately this stance was just another way for me to avoid addressing the situation at hand.

I took the same "safe" position in regard to accepting his increasingly violent temper and physical abuse toward me. This was because once, when he had egged me to the point of breaking, I had thrown a frozen chicken that I was taking out of the freezer for dinner at him. As he had with his mother in similar circumstances, he laughed at me, riling me all the more and from that time on often made reference to my nasty nature: his means to camouflage his own violent tendencies. He was as prone to spontaneous outbursts as much as his mother was. Likewise, I had learned to stay clear of them, as clear as I had of my father's vociferous eruptions.

At the same time, some part of me was markedly more ready and willing to do battle with him, as well as every other domineering male I knew. This especially included the owner of the restaurant in which I was employed. He was a shrewd businessman and therefore valued my exceptional competence and dependability. Yet, over the years that I had been employed there, I had never given him the full obedience that he expected of his waitresses. He had initially requested, through his hostess, that I wear makeup. Rather than state that I would not allow him to use my looks to maximize his profits, I claimed that I was allergic to makeup. I had never participated in employee parties or contributed to the purchase of expensive birthday and Christmas gifts for him. I had never gone bar hopping with him and other employees after hours. I no longer hovered over his table like the other waitresses when he and his friends sat down to eat, sacrificing service to my paying customers to support what I considered his "lord of the harem" mentality. He presented proposed policy changes as if benefits to his employees, but I could never refrain from questioning his actions. Many of the waitresses thought I had guts to test him, but I thought if I genuinely had guts, I would not compromise myself even as much as I did simply to maintain my financial security. Push came to shove when it was time for the latest Christmas bonus. It had been rumored that bonuses would be sufficiently reduced because of a poor financial year, but when I saw how much less mine was compared to previous years, as well as to how much less it was than a novice waitress' bonus, I knew that the owner was making a statement to me personally. A shot at my pocket was the worst kind of wound. I told myself that I deserved what I got, but some part of me was becoming more intensely defiant, while my job performance remained impeccable. My growing indifference to the possibility of losing my job amazed me as much as frightened me. Nonetheless, when it would come time to step out of that environment, the part of me that feared losing its "dessert," would struggle to keep the door open enough to run back if necessary, as it did whenever it was time to move on to new circumstances.

Shortly before I exited the world of waiting tables, one of the owner's three uncles, all of whom worked at the restaurant, unexpectedly died. Since I had been fond of him, I was compelled to send a sympathy card to his sister, the woman who had initially been instrumental in my being hired (and whom I had used as an ally while she used me as a confidant). In the card, I wrote a note, which came forth from what felt oddly like my heart. It was a foreign experience to be so expressive, and I felt vulnerable and inhibited actually passing the letter on to her, especially having little doubt that she would share it with the rest of the family. Besides being too insecure to attend the wake, I felt that my writing the note was what was necessary to bring closure to my relationship with the man. However, the following day, the sister informed me that the family had read my card and mutually decided that it would be used as part of the eulogy. I was taken aback—half-flattered and half-embarrassed, and further, in disbelief that anyone would value my expression. (In truth, I had been intuitively aware that my expression would be used in the manner it was.) Nevertheless, the event nudged a deeper part of myself, a part that would have preferred to remain undisturbed.

Despite the distracting conditions of my personal and professional life, I obtained my undergraduate degree. Then, because I only knew how to be busy, and because I thought I should be doing something worthwhile with my life, I half-heartedly enrolled in a masters program. I was only slightly saddened that I received no recognition from anyone for my accomplishment; I was more concerned about the limited prospects of finding employment in my field, and further, having a job that allowed me to be outside. Before I had hardly begun to consider resumes and interviews, however, a fellow student approached me about a job opportunity. Kerry had gained the confidence of the site manager of the city-run nature center where she was in the process of completing her internship as a prerequisite to graduating. She explained that the manager had forced the most recent naturalist to resign, eliminating his position and dividing his salary to support two new positions. Kerry was to take the higher salaried position and, since the site manager knew nothing about naturalist work, she was leaving it to Kerry to find someone else to take the lesser salaried position. I was presently being offered that position. As an enticement, Kerry stated that she planned to stay only through the summer—although I should not disclose this to the site manager—and then I would automatically be moved into the higher paid position when she left. She further asserted that, although there was a difference in our titles, as far as she was concerned we would be working as equals. My first impression was that the site manager and Kerry were each using the other to fulfill personal agendas and the most recent naturalist had been ousted only because of personality conflicts. Regardless of the situation feeling amiss and sensing trouble ahead, I put my integrity aside, along with my fear of surviving on a substantially decreased income and grabbed eagerly for the "dessert," while convincing myself that I was engaging in worthwhile enterprises.

I watched my great need for the site manager to acknowledge how qualified and committed I was to the position, even while I felt incompetent. She showed no personal interest in me at all. She simply and matter-of-factly explained the procedure that I was to follow at City Hall to get hired and then dismissed me. For fear of winning her disapproval, I followed her directions exactly, yet somehow the process went awry. A week later she called me into her office and underhandedly accused me of failing to follow her instructions—a setting that would become all too familiar. The second time around I was finally placed on the payroll.

I was soon to learn how profoundly the nature center was a captive of city politics. This was a much faster track than the restaurant world and I was inexperienced. Survival appeared dependent on learning the game. I studied how Kerry fraternized and humored the site manager. They both had aggressive, masculine dispositions, which intimidated me. My serious nature, deep insights and commitment to being a competent naturalist, conflicted with the site manager's aim of making a political name for herself. Never quite knowing what she wanted to hear or how to fit in, I was either on the sidelines or tripping over my own attempts to be noticed.

Worse, I soon determined that despite how Kerry had initially presented our working relationship, she aimed at being top dog, whatever it took. This became evident when she asked me to develop and teach an after-school program, which I did, but which she then took credit for in the quarterly programming publication. When I approached her, she nonchalantly claimed to have forgotten to mention that the classes were to be a cooperative effort. I walked away in a raging silence, my "if you can't say something nice, don't say anything at all" patterning restraining me from blasting her. I continually bristled with indignation at her constant pretense of asking me for input about matters for which she had already made decisions. Similarly, I watched her entice a procession of volunteers with promises in order to get her bidding done and make herself look important. I watched her take credit for any and all successes and blame others when something went wrong. I did not think that anyone could be as manipulative or deceptive as Carl, until I met her. At the same time, I struggled with an inner awareness that I was not exempt from this sort of behavior, although I would have liked to excuse myself by taking the position that my behavior was not as extreme.

At the end of the summer and concerned about finances, I sounded Kerry out about quitting and my assuming her position. She was again nonchalant saying that she had changed her mind about attending graduate school and had forgotten to mention it to me. In fact, it was clear that I had allowed myself to be duped from the beginning. (It was the only way I could get where my lessons were waiting.) I would never get much beyond either walking away from her manipulations, licking my wounds and choking my rage, or unscrupulously fighting back. I felt as if I was standing outside myself watching myself caught in yet another ridiculous struggle from which I was unable to extricate myself. It would be beyond my imagination that someday I would be profoundly grateful for the valuable lessons the situation provided.

My impeccably neat and tidy nature became an advantage in relationship to Kerry's habitual unkempt appearance. Without being straightforward, the site manager was reduced to using numerous strategies to get Kerry to clean up her act, all of which in the end proved futile. What most disturbed me about my co-worker's undignified image was her habit of wearing a tee shirt with a quote, "life is a bitch and then you die," written across the back. My first impression was that she had nerve to so openly advertise her feelings. Then I took to wondering if she truly did feel this way about life. From there, I was forced to examine my own attitude. I certainly did think that life was tough; at least it had been so far. But a bitch? Clearly, this position struck undeniable fear in me. Further, it seemed irreverent, even dangerous, too self-fulfilling. It also triggered a deep inner pain. Could I afford to take on this kind of attitude? I felt stuck between the novel **Ethan Frome** (life is about hopelessness) and **Death Comes to The Archbishop** (life is meant to be lived to the fullest). The situation prompted me to reread Pearl Buck's novels starting with **The Good Earth**. It was obvious that I was looking for something, some understanding not available in my current reality.

During the course of my four years in that job, I unsuccessfully applied for the few other naturalist positions that came available in the area. Each failed effort left me feeling more inferior and more trapped, although I knew hiring decisions were primarily political. Further, whether I wanted to be or not, I intuitively knew that I was right where I was meant to be to live the lessons at hand and my efforts to seek other employment were mostly about seeking relief from the discomfort of these lessons.

In the meantime, my employment plight deteriorated. Caught in a conspicuously unprincipled, cutthroat, big-league arena, I fell deeper into my survival mode. I was competitive and resistant. I sabotaged, deceived, or was actively over-committed. I pilfered in a petty manner. I felt swallowed up. On some level, I could see that my struggle was the harvest of my attempts to get a sense of identity (a sense of self) from my circumstances, and regardless of the political hierarchy and pecking order, everyone there was reflecting everyone else's insecurities. And I was no exception.

Critical to my growth, the job brought me out of the isolation and safety I found in waitressing. Those years that I endured at the nature center provided me with the opportunity to study the psychological nature of the volunteers and other people that the center attracted. Regardless of my belief that I was being my usual, judgmental self, I could see a host of stray souls looking to attach themselves to something, to acquire validation and to gain recognition—a sense of importance. And regardless of the way in which they presented themselves, their involvement was a means to get their individual needs met more than to provide a service to the center or the community. Again, I did not see myself as an exception to this observation, although I would have preferred to do so.

Working as a naturalist further provided opportunity for me to meet other "professionals" in the field and gave me exposure to various philosophies about our natural environment and efforts to save it. I found curious the degree of commitment and enthusiasm that these supposedly dedicated people put forth to support their causes. As much as I tried and thought I should, I was unable to manufacture their vigorous commitment. Meanwhile, I participated in animal rehabilitation and reforestation projects, Audubon education programs and prairie restorations while I questioned—sometimes only to myself, sometimes otherwise. I could not see that reclaiming abandoned farmland and planting a variety of seeds constituted a prairie; or planting saplings to an area stripped of trees constituted reforestation. I did not see nature as a formula—soil, seeds, a few trees and animals—that could be humanly duplicated. I viewed the Earth as a living entity, with an essence of such magnitude it made our fumbling, egoistic intentions to "save her" laughable. Again, what I saw and felt left me feeling judgmental and standing alone outside of the status quo, or in conflict. I could not understand why I was unable to believe as other people did: why was I powerless to simply shut off my mind and all of its questioning; or why was I condescending toward those who held contrary beliefs? Why couldn't I simply fit in? I would soon learn more about this characteristic.

The site manager put into operation her idea of having a haunted Halloween event, by which she would turn the nature preserve into a trail of frightening scenes, including costumed people jumping from behind bushes and trees and taking participants by surprise. She was skilled at implementing such public events and loved to do so. Her rationale for this event was to raise money to support the nature center. I thought it contradictory to attempt, on one hand, to provide city children, many of whom had never been in nature, a positive experience through school field trips, then, on the other hand, use the same facility as a means to scare them witless (which I observed happen). I also thought it farcical that, since this was a city-run facility, the city could not generate the revenue to maintain its functioning. Mostly, I simply felt the deep violation of nature taking place. Any attempt I made at articulating my view was conspicuously unwelcome. Year by year the event became a greater success. Planning began months in advance. Publicity increased. Scenes became more elaborate necessitating an ever-greater volunteer force. The days the event ran were extended. Consequently, much of the nature center programming was set aside while time and energy were directed into preparations. Besides the nature center being financially supported, the proceeds padded the pockets of many involved. The amount that I got paid under the table kept me silent but also corroded my sense of integrity. Each year I felt more entrapped by my collaboration in the event, as by my involvement in my situation in general.

What fed my frustration was a deeper need to create. I did not want to war or compete with Kerry, or with anyone. I did not want to be the boss. That frightened me. I wanted to work together, to share an experience, to share a mutually created success. I wanted to be a part of something of greater importance. Intuitively, I understood that to do so was in alignment with an inherent need to co-create. Yet, what I needed to accomplish could not be attained within the context of my present reality, for my present reality was not in alignment with my inherent nature. My present reality was what supported my endless struggles. To be in alignment with my inherent nature, I would have to simply walk out the door and face my waiting isolation.

Aside from my issues with politics, policies and philosophies, teaching about nature came instinctively. Kerry's greatest gift to me was that eventually she left me alone to develop and instruct whatever classes and workshops I chose. Consequently, I became adept at taking concepts and translating them to levels geared for preschoolers, college students, handicapped or teacher training classes. Visitors to the center sometimes sought me out to converse about nature on a more personal level. I was yet unaware of the real skills I was obtaining or of the real importance they would be serving. I was also unaware that I was learning to teach from my heart.

On the other hand, some annoying character in me continually obsessed over giving misinformation or being asked a question that I was incapable of answering and subsequently being perceived as an imposter. Therefore, I went through obsessive gyrations to be prepared and perform as perfectly as possible. In retrospect, I began to recognize that, regardless of my obsession to be prepared, sooner or later I would invariably, even spontaneously, abandon my lengthy notes and other aids. I never thought to do this. It simply happened—or so I thought. Most surprising, beyond my self-doubt, every situation turned out to be a natural success.

Living adjacent to a forest preserve, as well as now working as a naturalist, allowed me to spend an almost endless amount of time in nature—the amount of time for which I craved. Without question, I invariably felt profoundly different when there. Something was happening. The experiences that had once been unique to my two-week vacation were becoming an increasingly regular occurrence. Whatever it was to which I was connecting when in nature seemed to ever more intensely permeate my mind, my breath, my listening, my sight, as much as every pore in my skin. These contacts left me vibrating in such a way that my body no longer felt solid and the high with which I was left was like no drug I could imagine. This high stole me away from my pain and moved me to a different reality. This was sweet nectar in a bitter existence—a form of relief without which I could no longer manage my life.

Guilt aside, I began to conjure ways to spend more of my work hours outdoors. When off-duty I gravitated to the forest preserve adjacent to my house, which I had begun to label "my woods." Every tree became "my tree." All the birds were "my birds." All the flowers belonged to me. I was possessed with being possessive. It could be risky business going to the forest preserve. There were vagrants, men, teenagers bent on partying and an occasional exhibitionist. Sporadic sounds of gunshots and evidence of target practice were common. Having intruders in "my woods" sometimes made it difficult for me to make the connection I sought and otherwise left me cautiously fearful. Every violation to the woods—girdled, hacked or burned out trees, bullet casings, beer cans or broken bottles scattered around, off-road-vehicle related erosion—felt like a personal desecration. I vehemently desired all who came with such destructive intent to simply vanish. Still, their presence never deterred me from seeking the communion, especially with the grand old oaks, seemingly necessary to keep myself alive.

Another phenomenon that began to occur during this period was an obsessive need to listen to music—not any kind of music, only certain songs. These songs I played to excess. I played them until I had them memorized, until I had absorbed their essence, until they tore at me from the inside out, ripping at my guts. I played them until I was in an agonized state, and until the pain inside of me was momentarily wept free and I collapsed in exhaustion. As overwhelming as these occurrences were, I was unable to refrain from listening. Carl, even with only a glimpse of my affliction, became convinced that I was going mad, and I was beginning to agree with him for once.

As a graduate student, my department paid for one class a semester. This arrangement fit perfectly into my schedule, as well as into the level of enthusiasm that I was able to muster toward continuing my education. However, my feelings changed when my advisor offered me six hours of graduate credit for a seven-day field study trip that he and another professor were leading through the southern Appalachian mountains, studying the area from a cultural, historical, political, social and environmental perspectives. My advisor was considered an expert on the area and I had learned, through taking a number of related classes from him, that I had a deep historical interest in the area as well. Carl, Adam and I had been there camping a couple of times, but this trip itinerary included meetings with a variety of local experts, including a spokesperson from the Cherokee tribe. I was excited enough to overlook my discomfort of having to be in a van full of students for a drive that would not stop until we met our destination.

I soon discovered that the itinerary held less interest for me than something else. The fact that I mainly wanted to be off by myself in the woods did not go unnoticed. My advisor joked that I continually appeared to be lost in nostalgia. His observation was correct. Whatever it was that was haunting me left me feeling unsettled and distracted, looking for something that was lost in memory—a memory hidden on one back trail or another, all of which I had an obsession to explore. It had always been problem enough to quell the urge to explore every trail I came upon, to follow every path to the very end in order to discover what treasure, what secret something or another might be waiting to be claimed. One student brought his dulcimer along and played it at night when formal matters were complete. His music fed my inexplicable preoccupation; I wanted him to play continually.

When we were on our own, and when I wasn't fixated on exploring back trails, I spent my time studying plants, sometimes with another student, though he and I had entirely different approaches. He relied on his field guides, identifying the plants botanically, systematically moving from one to another. I had no patience with technical names or scientific approaches. My madcap desire was to touch, taste and smell them, absorb their medicinal qualities, feel their essence, lie among them, examine how they moved in the wind, explore them in relation to their habitat, or else press their leaves and flowers between the pages of my journal to study at a later date. Overall, the trip ended with my usual frustrations over my aberrant behavior.

Since I was unable to settle on a topic for the required paper, the second professor suggested that I write about the history of the development of transportation routes in the area. Though this sounded too technical for my nature, oddly, I agreed anyway. After studying the literature I had gathered, I attempted to manifest something concrete, but I was powerless to even organize my thoughts. As the semester drew to a close, I realized that I was going to have to accept an incomplete. It was against my nature to either rush to complete an assignment, or be tardy with handing it in. Leaving anything I started unfinished was completely foreign to my nature. I contained my anxiety by telling myself that I had an entire year to complete the paper and receive credit for the class.

Considering my inability to support the family on my present salary, I suggested to Carl that he seek employment. I thought he could start by obtaining a real estate license since his lack of a work history made applying for conventional jobs tough. His refusal enraged me enough that I ended up obtaining the license myself. I used Kerry's guilt over my financial quandary, due to her change of mind about quitting, as leverage to step out whenever I needed to show property.

I rationalized that now that I was selling real estate I needed my own car. The truth was that having my own vehicle was a beginning step in reclaiming my freedom. During the course of my years with Carl, we had gone through numerous vehicles. I had paid for them, as well as their upkeep, although the titles were invariably in Carl's name and their predominant use was for his travel to and from the racetrack. If I had use of the car, it was only around his track schedule. I had long since realized that, like my mother, allowing him to chauffeur me was a means of getting some attention from him. Further, I realized that him chauffeuring me was fulfilling his need to be needed. I was determined, once I purchased my car, that he was not going to turn it into a run-down, mobile dumpster, as he did with all of our other cars (those he did not sell to have gambling money). In fact, it became tacitly understood that he stay clear of my vehicle. Having the means to come and go as I pleased left me feeling stupid and ashamed over having sacrificed my freedom to the degree and for as long as I had. I also realized that without using real estate as an excuse, it would have been next to impossible for me to directly meet my own needs. Further, it was impossible to deny that, with my own vehicle, Carl and I were left to live more separate lives. It was awkward to admit, however, that I felt quite comfortable with this arrangement.

I managed to juggle the two jobs for two years. This included working evenings and weekends and also falling into conflict with an aggressive, seasoned saleswoman who openly wrangled clients from me and left me feeling victimized. Besides this, I had to deal with the stigma of working for a company whose owner had recently been found guilty of criminal charges and faced serving time (the story making headlines). On top of all this, I was trying to keep my masters program alive. I finally admitted that I no longer had an interest, the energy, or whatever else was required to be in sales. Indeed, my negativity was undermining my success. Giving that up, I remained unable to refrain from keeping my plate loaded. Consequently, I began to teach outdoor education classes to home-schooled children, and various other programs to other educational facilities and church groups, as well as yoga classes in my spare time. Again, I rationalized it was to make ends meet. A deeper motivation was my need to receive validation, as well as a sense of identity, to find a place where I could feel as if I belonged. Of yet greater significance: keeping myself on overload was a viable means to avoid directly dealing with personal issues.

Due to a series of circumstances, I was handed sole responsibility of the nature center's honeybee operation when Kent, the volunteer beekeeper who had initiated and maintained it, decided to relinquish his responsibilities. He had already taught me the fundamentals of beekeeping. From the beginning, the more I learned, the more intrigued I became. Looking into the hive was like viewing a complicated machine or organism in its entirety. At the same time, all of the individual components and how they functioned to support the whole could also be recognized. It appeared that the queen was the figure of rule; but it was the collective consciousness that provided order to the whole. One thought about this superbly synchronized, complex society habitually led to another until my head would spin from wondering. I began to acquire a reputation as a knowledgeable speaker on honeybees and consequently received requests from various organizations to give talks or training programs. Being in this position provided me the opportunity to have something that Kerry couldn't undermine and also gave me a comfortable sense of identity. Further, I valued the personal friendship that Kent and I had formed. I gradually came to feel at ease talking with him. He listened to me and appeared to appreciate what I had to say. He also became a confidant, someone with whom I could air my frustrations, especially with my job situation. While I valued our one-on-one relationship, in social circumstances I found him to be annoyingly garrulous and jocose enough to be almost nonsensical.

Through the Audubon society, I had been given a scholarship to a weeklong seminar at one of their field locations in Minnesota. Being temporarily free of responsibility and on my own was a new experience. Nonetheless, my gaucheness remained alive, while aloofness proved to be the only reliable means to manage it. One facilitator, an entomology specialist, had an obvious attraction to me, and I to him, which suddenly brought all of my gender issues to the surface. Under the circumstances, I knew that many women would simply take the opportunity to indulge in a good time. In fact, one woman was trying to do just that with him. I kept a safe distance. Yet some part of me was interested in pursuing what was waiting to happen. This facilitator spent the first few days attempting to draw me out, whether in class or otherwise. Finally he cornered me and proceeded to drill me with questions: "Why are you so unwilling to share your expertise on honeybees with the group? Why are you so aloof? Why do you always look so sad? Why do you avoid me? Why can't you relax and have fun? Do you realize how attractive you are?" I couldn't tell him how awkward I felt around others, how unskilled I was with chitchat, how whatever I said more often than not was misconstrued or caused offense. I could not tell him that the fear surrounding these issues had a life of its own. Neither could I believe that if this man got to know me that he would see me as anything more than wicked or dirty. Just the same, at some other level, I needed him to be attracted to me; even while I was terrified that he would say he loved me, and then I would have to resist giving myself to him. My initial reaction was to confess the shadiness of my secret lifestyle—display my scarlet letter—to give him a clearer perspective, to aid him in rejecting me. Ironically, I did begin to relax. I even began to reveal aspects of myself. He seemed to take my disclosures in stride, while my tendency to condemn myself before anyone else got the chance, stared me in the face.

The last evening of our stay, I saw him go off with the woman who had been attracted to him. I ignored my hurt feelings and instead asked myself how I could make the most of my last night in this beautiful environment. I was disinclined and too intimidated to participate in the final formal evening function taking place. I was pulled instead to slip away to the lake both to find comfort in the night and to open to the transformation that was suddenly waiting to commence. I had learned not to struggle with these unearthly phenomena. I knew I couldn't. I didn't want to. Everything about the nocturnal moment was mystically alive and humming. From the inside out, I could feel myself coming alive too. Like a stone dropped in a pool, rings of energy were expanding outwardly through every level of my being. I was becoming the night, as light as the night was dark. Clearly, something was about to happen. Thus, I was little surprised when this man suddenly appeared from nowhere. Somehow, I knew he would come. I knew he was meant to be part of the impending experience.

While he assisted me in my final efforts to slide a canoe in the water, he explained that the other woman had solicited him to spend the night together. Wanting to be discreet about his disinterest, he felt the necessity to take some time with her. Then he asked if he could join me. For an instant, I found myself trying to attempt to project Carl's reaction onto the situation. Just as suddenly I was imagining what my fellow bunkmates would think about my being absent all night. My impulse was to return to the meeting hall where other participants were gathered for the evening. Instead, I stepped to the front of the canoe.

We paddled around the lake listening to bullfrogs, reveling at the night sky and eventually exchanging our personal stories. It amazed me how he uninhibitedly revealed even the pit marks in his past. I queried further, but I would not have thought to judge him. For me the encounter was enlightening, magical and carefree, one of the few times in which I felt a deep sense of connecting to another person—particularly a man. My fear was far removed from the experience. (More accurately stated, I had brought a deeper connection to the moment.) As the first rays of light began to expose our rendezvous, to my amazement, I initiated a discussion about engaging in sex. Without the cover of the night, it was too late for such activity, overall too late, which had made discussing the matter safe for me. We mutually agreed that such an encounter would diminish a perfect evening. I was curious, however, to know what having such an experience would have been like. I wondered if I would have been able to have an orgasm, which would have been, for the most part, a novel experience. Like Cinderella at the ball, I so wanted the magic of the night to endure.

The tittering glances we received as we entered the dining hall for breakfast clouded the beauty and innocence of our nocturnal encounter and left me scurrying to depart. My prince was at my car unabashedly asking for my address and giving me his as I finished packing. He wanted to stay in touch. I did not know how to do this and be with Carl. All the innocence of the prior evening seemed to have instantly vanished, and I felt once again trapped. Since I had to stop a number of times on the way home to nap, I obsessed about how I could explain my tardiness to Carl. The irony was whether or not I was truthful, he never believed me anyway. Arriving home exhausted and distant, and with his rapid-fire questions shooting holes in my composure, he successfully proceeded to wrench my experience out of me. He then twisted and dirtied it until its true significance was shattered, and I was collapsed in the driveway tearfully apologizing for my dreadful behavior. I despised him for what he could reduce me to, as much as I despised myself for repeatedly falling into his snare. I wanted to scream at him that I did not belong to him, that I was not chattel. Instead, I proceeded to clean up the mess that had been created during my absence.

I received a number of friendly letters from this man, as well as a copy of **The Little Prince**, a favorite book of his and one he wanted me to read, significantly a story of a character that explored many different worlds. Guilt, as much as fear of further reaction from Carl, left me unable to muster much of a response. Still I felt tones of a forlorn lover, a Juliet. I could not see that my experience, in and of itself, was of little significance as Carl contended. On the contrary, its relevance lay in the many and varied reference points it provided, in the taste of freedom I had had, as well as it being a stepping stone leading me into profoundly new experiences.

One day a young woman who volunteered at the nature center approached me to discuss her interest in joining the Peace Corps. I became excited and even envious thinking of the possibility of adventure and helping others and thus, greatly encouraged her. However, the more I presented inducements for her to embark on this adventure, the more she produced reasons to the reverse, none of which to me seemed legitimate. It was clear that fear was her only obstacle and that was what she was really asking me to support. She was nonplused by my final comment, which I delivered with surprising passion, "If I had no responsibility other than to myself, I wouldn't hesitate to embrace such an opportunity." She would remain unable to step out of her fear zone. She had not really been seeking feedback from me anyway. Actually, I had been set up. Not by her, but by something greater, something that functions beyond our linear reality. In a short time I would be required to own my statement.

Soon after this conversation I heard, as an inner knowing, that I had to set aside my languishing masters program to obtain teaching credentials. Although I had little enthusiasm for furthering my education or the energy to take on added responsibility, I did not question what was being asked of me. On one hand, I thought this made sense since it would provide a greater opportunity to acquire a better paying job in the environmental education field. In fact, I felt an immense sense of urgency to get this undertaking completed as soon as possible in order to get on with my life.

A fellow classmate suggested that I seek funds from the financial aid office. Asking for help? Asking for money? Somehow, beyond my conventional ideas of what seeking aid was about, I knew that I had to pursue and accept help in order to successfully overcome this handicap. In the end, I followed through on her suggestion. Even as I walked in the door, I felt complete confidence that this enterprise was going to bear fruit. Further, I enjoyed my interaction with the young man who interviewed me and who would prove supportive for the two years of intense work necessary to reach my goal. With financial aid and the money I had banked from selling real estate, I was able to feel a semblance of financial security.

The last issue was the conflict between my work hours and my class schedule. When I approached Kerry with my plan, she claimed that she was already overworked and could not manage without me. I countered by enumerating the ways she already effectively excluded me from participation in all decision-making, and most important activities. Hitting harder, I informed her that when I wanted to know what was going on, I best found out through her bevy of favorite volunteers, and further, that she was aware of this. I realized that her being a one-person operation would be a valuable reference point in obtaining the permission I needed from the site manager. My manipulations proved effective, but Kerry was livid; and I was taken aback, shocked in fact, by my own lack of integrity, using Kerry's game against her to get what I needed.

I was rapidly approaching burn out with academia, as with every other aspect of my life. I had little patience with inept professors and the time and gyrations necessary to acquire a piece of paper giving sanction to do what I was compelled to do. This time, I was unwilling to spend hours memorizing material that I forgot the day after an exam. Instead of impressing instructors and obsessing about grades, I planned to use academia more efficiently. I calculated an agenda whereby I would meet with a new professor, ask a few pertinent questions, and then ask to see a number of papers written by prior students. The responses from the professor, as well as the quality of the papers revealed the standard he set, and the amount of energy required to get the token "A." With that established, I could decide what I wanted to obtain from the class for myself. I learned that I was able to absorb text assignments subconsciously—feel the essential information rather than read text over again and again—while "I" was somewhere else. This enabled me, when taking tests, to shut off my brain and let the answers simply flow out of the part of me that had retained the information. Required to role-play in methods-of-teaching classes, I captivated professors and fellow students by drawing from my environmental teaching experiences—bringing live bees to class and such—to create lessons. Once, undaunted by napping kindergarten children whom I was required to observe in order to apply their behavior to educational principles, I simply made up the behaviors. I found this challenging and creative and not at all deceitful: the fact that I could create scenarios demonstrated my understanding of the principles. My unexpected approach to academia was rewarding and empowering. I was defining my own learning but an insecure part of me still contained enough power to regularly undermine my confidence.

I had to declare a minor to obtain teaching credentials, so I automatically chose art. However, during the first semester, I ascertained that this choice would not be the quickest avenue to accomplish the goal. Besides this, I soon realized that, although my need to be creative remained active, my actual interest in art classes was minimal. Instead, I felt frustrated and isolated, unable to resonate to the group dynamics. Therefore, I headed straight for an advisor's office and asked her to assess my credits to see what minor I could declare that would require taking the fewest classes. To my chagrin, she claimed that I only needed two classes to acquire a history minor, one of which, American history, was required for a teaching degree.

Since first attending college at age eighteen, I had twice dropped the class and then had successfully avoided taking it until now. The idea of having to take two history classes unnerved me, but knowing that I had to take five art classes to achieve the same end, I succumbed. I did not exactly understand my aversion to history. I did know that I detested memorizing names of so-called important men—presidents, generals and politicians, along with dates of wars and other purported important events. I saw no value in keeping alive or glorifying memories of socially-sanctioned violence and killing, where one side was always the good guys, the other the bad guys. I hated having to remember whether an important political figure was a Democrat or a Republican. I could literally feel my mind shutting down even at the thought of being subjected to digesting a time line of mindless historical events.

Much to my amazement, Doctor Jennings, from whom I would take both classes, approached history from a social perspective—a position that captivated my interest and left me having no problem listening to his lectures. He delved into the why's and how's of social consciousness. Further, he not only encouraged but also insisted that his students contemplate, take positions, question and even challenge his beliefs. His exams were never about regurgitating memorized material. He also required us to critique professional articles. My first reaction was, "Who am I to question experts?" As I let go of my limiting thoughts, I realized that not only were there weaknesses in authors' theories, it was relatively easy for me to identify them. And I was not being critical or judgmental; I was simply examining more deeply. Perhaps most importantly, I was also learning that there is a fine line between being the critic and being the observer. How I approach and use my perceptions determines which state I am in.

As I came to know Professor Jennings, he divulged that he was a recovered alcoholic, a compulsive eater and had difficulty in creating healthy relationships. He never appeared to be uncomfortable sharing this information about his life. Beyond what he taught in the classroom, I learned from him that being an effective teacher was not contingent on first being a perfect person or having all the answers. I valued the depth our discussions took us. I also valued the deep connection between us. Much like my Audubon experience, I was acquiring a more positive attitude toward men. I felt comfortable stopping by his office for a chat, although I watched my neediness, my tendency to latch onto someone with whom I could engage in meaningful conversation.

I had also given thought to what it would be like to have sex with this man. I was learning that this was not a sick or unnatural behavior. In fact, it was very human. (Honesty was revealing that I had wondered what it would be like to have sex with other men too.) Becoming comfortable with my burgeoning interest in sexuality was a prerequisite for my real studies: understanding the nature of sexuality and how it supports unconsciousness.

School and my naturalist job provided opportunities to develop personal interactions with others for the first time since my involvement with Carl. Although I felt I was learning how to have friendships, at least one-on-one, I remained caught in my phobia of being in social situations. If I was teaching, I was fine because my role to the situation was defined. But at functions where I was required to mingle, I would move from one group to another, never quite sure where or how to fit into a conversation, hoping for an invitation or at least a signal to join in. Ironically, when included in the conversation, I became tongue-tied, ridiculously pretentious, or most often bored beyond belief. I had begun to realize that I looked too hard at people, too deeply into their eyes for too long a time. This was not my intent. I simply got lost somewhere in the moment and appeared to be staring, triggering their discomfort. I tried to correct my behavior but merely became more confused about where exactly to look at a person when in conversation. I habitually took note of alternative emergency "escape routes." If escaping out the door was not an option, I typically sought refuge in the kitchen where I could find safety in being useful.

Obtaining the naturalist job allowed me to have health insurance for the first time ever, but I was unable to carry Carl on my policy because we were not married. When the secretary unexpectedly asked me why I had only placed my son on my insurance policy, a sudden, irrational fear of my co-workers discovering that I was "living in sin" activated an uncontainable necessity to wed. In some weird way, it actually felt as if my life depended on it, and my obsession to survive held sway over any rational thinking. Persuading Carl into such a radical move was an interesting challenge considering that he, a devout non-conformist, held only contempt for matrimony. I obsessed for days as to how to approach him. When not obsessing, I was examining my own sanity. I could barely tolerate being around the man, and we had not regularly slept in the same bed for years. Finally, I carefully presented marriage as a tool to vitalize our relationship, as well as a means for him to have health insurance in case he should need it. Miraculously, he readily agreed! I failed to see that his agreement was based on his own fear of losing me, or that in fact, he was already losing me...or that I had already let him go.

I had often wondered what marriage would feel like, but held no romantic illusions about my upcoming experience. Besides, the thought of my actions drawing attention from family and friends embarrassed me, especially since over the years I had compensated for my shame over being unwed with so many scenarios that I no longer could keep straight whom I had told what. I informed Carl that the silver band that I had bought in England while pregnant with Adam would do for a ring. After all, my purpose for having purchased it had been to give the appearance of being married. The real rationale for my attitude was that I felt unworthy of having anything better.

Carl presented me with a diamond necklace, and for a moment I thought that something meaningful was taking place. But when I saw the impressive gold necklace that he had bought for his mother at the same time, my warmth cooled; it felt as if his gift to her was a form of apology, or as if he was letting her know that his marriage to me made her no less important. I had often thought that his relationship with his mother was beyond just mother and son, especially with the visible competition he and his brother historically engaged in over her, as well as, his habit of visiting her on an almost daily basis. I did not know how I could have such awareness and remain so determined to go through with it, but something had a hold on me from which I was unable to free myself. Ultimately, as I suspected, marriage provided little more than a deeper sense of entanglement.

Having health insurance at this time turned out to be an asset, for if it was not one nagging ailment, it was another that fed into my escalating exhaustion and deteriorating health. Besides the weight of the world on my shoulders, I felt as if I was being buried beneath the weight of my own life, my own pain. My ability to contain my emotions and keep my life together was diminishing and I felt myself sinking into utter helplessness. This was despite and in contrast to my profoundly spiritual encounters.

The thought of phoning Gambler's Anonymous had been creeping into my jumbled thoughts for some time, but I had managed to keep it at bay. One blustery, snowy Saturday when I was alone at work, however, I fell completely apart. After a morning of panicked deliberation, I finally picked up the phone and dialed the number. I was shaking from head to foot with fear, sure that the wrath of God would be upon me for betraying Carl and asking for help when I should have been helping myself. Nonetheless, as soon as I heard a voice on the other end, a surge of tears broke through my resistance and left me hysterically divulging my secret life.

When I hung up the phone, I undeniably felt that a weight had been lifted off me. At the same time, I felt a sense of panic at the thought of Carl discovering my actions: Our secret life was no longer a secret. Beneath all of this some part of me was saying, "There's nothing wrong. You're just a fake trying to get sympathy." A kinder part of me seemed to be saying, "It's okay. You needed to do this, but this isn't really who you are." In trying to comprehend all these reference points I only became more confused.

Not visible to me then, this overt admission had been a hairpin turn in my life in terms of taking positive personal responsibility for myself; it had been a first fragile but firm step in freeing myself from my shame. Even so, participation in Gananon meetings bewildered me. I found that the group, all women, spent too much time reviewing what they could and should have had if their husbands had not been gamblers. Shoulda, Woulda, Coulda. I was not looking for mutually supported pity; I was looking for understanding, for resolve. Carl believed (and had convinced me through the years) that he couldn't possibly be a compulsive gambler since he only played the horses. Needless to say, when he discovered the nature of my weekly outing, he was furious about my attending "something that was such a waste of time," but I was moving out of reach of his influence. One enlightening fact that I gained from the meetings was that gamblers do not gamble to win; they gamble for the thrill. According to the Gananon philosophy, being involved in the program was essential for maintaining my own sobriety. In contrast, an inner knowing revealed that Gananon was a stepping-stone, nothing more. Even my insecurity—my inane preponderance of "shoulds," my paralyzing need to have something onto which to grasp—could not keep me attending more than a few meetings.

Auntie was now lost in infantile senility. She required assistance in being fed and could hardly be left alone. Further, her kidneys were failing to the degree that water-filled blisters were erupting on her legs. The raw skin left from the broken blisters required regular changes of dressings. Her reality, if it was present at all, centered on the past. She became a greater burden of care than I could have ever imagined, but feeling her death imminent, I put aside my annoyance, as much as my impatience, and focused on drawing on a sense of compassion for her. (A few years earlier I had failed to be compassionate to a cantankerous, old neighbor who had relied on Carl and me for both physical and emotional support during the time prior to her death. I felt Auntie was a second chance to get it right.) Carl believed that Auntie was simply more contrary than ever and, therefore, had less patience with her than normal.

My attitude toward my intuition was catapulted into a new realm when Christa McAuliffe was selected as the first non-astronaut for a space-shuttle flight. I watched her explain to a television reporter that her young daughter was afraid she was not returning. I heard a voice from inside say, "She should be afraid. You aren't coming back." Horrified, I quickly buried this message, but my stomach began to feel as if it was twisted in knots, and I felt a horrible pressure, intense and frenzied. A few days later, Carl and I took a drive to an appliance store to purchase a new stove. On a wall lined with televisions, all tuned to the launch, I watched the space shuttle Columbia explode.

Panic consumed me as I realized what had happened. My impulse was to run. Whatever it was, rooted there in front of dozens of television sets, I continued to watch the story unfold. I was unaware that something was shifting. This time, however, rather than burying the horror I was feeling, rather than burying the guilt or sense of responsibility, and despite wanting to, I remained right there with the situation. Could Christa's life have been saved if I had phoned someone? Could the whole tragedy have been prevented? Who would have believed me? I'm a nobody. I'm not important. It seemed absurd to actually phone an official to convey my premonition. My mind raced in many different directions. I wanted to talk to someone about this; yet, as in my youth, the thought of being condemned terrified me. I lacked the awareness to know how to act on my premonitions, or to understand if the responsibility to do so was even mine. I was thoroughly confused. Confusion was as close to understanding as I could get, but consciousness was about to be forced on me in a more personal way.

Adam was fifteen when he decided to commit suicide. In view of his chaotic and unstable family environment, his decision was understandable. I had been watching his withdrawal into himself for quite a while, but unable to deal with my own issues, I was unable to support him with his. One morning as I drove him to school, he handed me a paper that he had written. In it he explained that the only constraint from taking his life was the belief that it would disturb me, as well as his favorite teacher. Terrified, I went at once to talk to this teacher who expressed serious concern over recent and dramatic changes he also had been observing in Adam's behavior. I wanted to scream, "It's all my fault. I did this to him because I'm too cowardly to address any real issues." Instead, we discussed viable ways to support

Adam in whatever he was going through and agreed to maintain contact. Carl's position to Adam's behavior was that he was just trying to get attention. I could not believe that Carl would take so cavalier a position. I desperately needed his support. So did Adam. How could he be so overly concerned for his mother's welfare and ignore his son's? I was unable in my own insecurity to understand that Carl was terrified of dealing with this crisis.

Meanwhile, Adam continued to isolate himself in his room, coming out only to go to school or eat. He told me that he needed to cry, but could not because his feelings were frozen inside. Never before had I felt so desperate or frightened. My son was of vital importance to me; now I was faced with losing him. Some part of me believed that I was getting what I deserved: if I had been a better mother, if I had not been caught up in my own life, even if I had taken timely action, this would not be occurring. One day, nearly frantic, I picked him up at school. Refusing to take him home only for him to shut himself in his bedroom, we ended up sitting in a booth at a Long John Silver's restaurant. Quelling the tears welling up inside, I divulged that I was afraid even to open his bedroom door for fear of finding him dead; I lay awake at night straining to stay alert to any telltale sounds of trouble. I told him that being in this position was killing me. Further, I impressed upon him that if he chose to die, he needed to go ahead with it; but if he chose to live, he needed to do so for his own reasons, not for my sake or his teacher's.

I listened to my words, which simply spilled out of me. I was horrified! It sounded as if I was telling Adam to go ahead and kill himself. But, as I concluded my appeal, I watched a tear form in both of his deep, brown eyes and roll down his youthful cheeks. Continuing on, I added that his feelings were not so abnormal and for confirmation, he should talk to his friends. The next day he acted on my suggestion and came home excitedly sharing his discovery with me. With relief, I saw that he had relinquished his thoughts of suicide. For many years afterward, Adam's and my most intimate conversations would be carried out in our Long John Silver's discussion booth. Troubles were not over however. They had only begun.

The incident with Adam left me assessing my own situation. My life had often been punctuated with thoughts of committing suicide. My greatest deterrent had always been a fear of bungling the deed and leaving myself crippled and therefore dependent in some way or another. Thereby, like the characters in **Ethan Frome,** I would become a lifelong burden to those whom I was attempting to escape (my mother and father who had conditioned me to be self-reliant above all else). I had felt that the most definitive and responsible way out was to lay myself across the railroad tracks and wait for an oncoming train. In brooding over Adam's issues, I discerned that I had not found an adequate reason for living either. Moreover, the situation displayed how I had inflicted my own fears onto him—using and abusing him—projecting upon him my own monstrous, unresolved issues. I was sick. My life was sick. This family was sick. Morbidity was everywhere, and I hated myself for my participation. Whether active or passive, I was as guilty as Carl in bringing my son to this state. If I were to be instrumental in his healing, it was essential that

I examine as deeply as necessary the part I played in the family dilemma. My determined effort would eventually draw me into manifold past life memories revealing our psychological and emotional snarl so convoluted as to be almost impossible to untangle.

Overall, I was beginning to unravel and appreciate just how debilitating my existence was. Like an antiquated dam, my life was buttressing years of accumulated emotional sediment, full of cracks and unquestionably stressed to the breaking point. Denial, the method I had used to shore up the leaks, was no longer viable. The force of the emotional backlog was becoming greater than my capacity to keep it under control. With the dam giving way, I was beginning to recognize that I was drowning in my own fear, anger, sadness, resentment, illusion and self-deceit. My dysfunctional behavior had so many avenues that my life looked like a merry-go-round, with me in the middle. My circumstances were killing me, *a different kind of suicide,* and there was nothing I could do to save myself.

It was excruciating to acknowledge that I had been living my life from an unconscious state; beyond that, I had never been living at all. I had been avoiding life. Whatever the cost, I wanted my life to be worth something. On the other hand, I could not conceive what a worthwhile life looked like. My limited awareness left me to believe that it might mean being a nice person, kind and generous; not just presenting myself that way; and surely it required releasing cynicism, sadness and a gamut of other deplorable emotions. I swore that I would pull myself out of my bottomless pit. I would find out who I really am. I would get control of my life and live it as a gift, whatever that meant. This was the promise I made to myself. And unlike my father or Carl, who never kept their promises, I would keep mine. Although daunted, I would fulfill my promise.

I had no concept where or how to begin to discover who I am. My first step was to head to the bookstore and purchase some self-help books. One that initially impacted me was, **The Road Less Traveled.** However, while I was trying to find a road map or a guideline through reading the latest popular philosophies, I failed to see that where I had to start was right where I was. In fact, honoring and understanding where I was at was the essential ingredient required to move forward. When I made the commitment to find out who I really am, to live my life as a gift, I had no idea that finding my true self and living life as a gift were really one and the same. Nor did I have a true idea of the magnitude of the work I had taken on or an understanding that what I was doing for myself, I was doing for everyone. Neither could I comprehend the force aligned against me. It was not that I was on a road less traveled; I had committed myself to traveling uncharted territory.

My long-time struggle to still the voice inside me diminished as I sought to take responsibility for my life. Actually, the voice was becoming a complex connection to something unfathomably deep, which I would soon find unimaginable to live without. Yet I was a novice at understanding this communication. Sometimes messages came like a thought suddenly placed in my head that I knew was not mine because it stood apart—sometimes subtly and sometimes distinctly—from my own clutter of thoughts. Sometimes messages came as images in my mind or even audibly. They came disjointed, given to me a piece at a time, testing my patience. Other times a strange feeling akin to pressure would suddenly envelop my body or mind. Sometimes I was certain that I was experiencing shock treatment. When the messages were cryptic or untranslatable I felt as if I was the hub of someone's humor. Most often I felt as if I was in the throes of learning a new language or operating in a different kind of reality to which I needed to be constantly alert.

One message, "Heal thyself," was a resounding command that had been coming for many months. I had ideas of what it meant, for I certainly had health issues, and my emotional state was definitely in need of alteration, but I had been addressing both as best as I could for some time. While I strengthened my commitment to upend my life, the message continued remarkably more strongly.

Late one evening, as Adam watched television and I ironed freshly laundered curtains, the thump I heard from Auntie's room signaled that she had fallen out of bed. Since Carl was at the racetrack and I was not strong enough to lift her back into bed by myself, I made her as comfortable on the floor as possible and returned to my ironing. Death energy suddenly swept through the house revealing that Auntie's departure was close at hand. Simultaneously, I felt an outer hypertension and an inner calmness as I concentrated on completing my task. Upon Carl's midnight return, he dragged Auntie to her feet, harrying her to hold on to her walker so he could get her to the bathroom. Intervening, I beseeched him to realize that she was incapable of meeting his demands. He scoffed me out of the room and continued his badgering. I could already feel her dropping dead in Carl's arms, and felt sorry that this would be his final memory of his relationship with his aunt. Seconds later he was calling to me. I found him pale and faint, standing over what was now a corpse, his remorse visible only for that moment.

My mind meandering in all directions kept me awake most of the night. The entire experience with Auntie had been utterly humiliating, and one that I thought I had completely failed. At the same time, it was impossible to conceive that this burden of responsibility, my 24-hour-a-day duty, was over and that my time was actually mine to do with as I pleased. I swore bitterly that I would never again play nurse to another octogenarian. I did not understand that where my resistance lies was where my lessons would be lived (and learned). Time would eventually reveal that this entire episode with Auntie had nothing to do with failure. In truth, it was an initial preparation to playing an even more personal role to yet another octogenarian.

With the word of Auntie's death out, relatives who still clung to her promises appeared for the funeral. Disappointment was in order, for she had long since closed any joint accounts that had other relatives' names on them except for Carl's, and after his number of years of leeching, there was not enough immediately available money to pay for her funeral costs. Consequently, he was again forced to turn to me for rescue. Once again, my compulsive sense of obligation, my inability to say no, and my fear of causing trouble and being rejected outweighed my fury over feeling used.

Auntie's assets at her death were a mortgaged house that went to probate, $100,000 that would shortly end up in Carl's pocket, and enough money in a trust for Adam to get him started in college. Professing to not want to be on file for taxes, Carl opened a joint bank account with me as the primary holder. Week after week, I watched the money dwindle—$700 one day, $300 the next, and $1,100 a week later. Without enough money left to pay off the $40,000 mortgage when the house came out of probate, we would lose it. Any attempt to address the issue with Carl only produced a confrontational, "You have to be really insecure to think that I would gamble our home." I carefully deliberated how to act appropriately on this situation. Was I going to immobilize myself with doubt, take a typical passive position or believe in myself for once?

An unshakable inner force overriding my fear, one day I took the account book from Carl's drawer, went to the bank, and transferred enough money to pay off the mortgage and lawyer's fees into a personal account, as well as enough to replace our malfunctioning furnace. Then I went home, returned the account book to its original place and waited for the hurricane to hit. And hit it did with a hundred-fifty-mile-an-hour gale force. Both his accusation that I had stolen his money and his rage over my actions sickeningly amused me, but I remained rooted. After he completely drained the original account, he turned on me with even greater force. As many times as he struck out at me, I caved in only enough to surrender the $5,000 that I had relegated for the new furnace, the same inner force that had initially overridden my fear and sense of guilt holding fast to the rest. If everything else went to feed his addiction, our home would not. He could knock me flat, but I would not take a backward step—not under any circumstance. Besides bringing Adam into the world, this felt like the toughest moment of believing in myself in my entire life.

With Auntie gone, Carl and I were able to move from the basement into our own bedroom. After years of sleeping on the most makeshift of beds imaginable, I finally gave myself permission to purchase a quality mattress set. Afterward, I wondered why it had taken me so long to support such a practical need as getting a good night's sleep. My sense of satisfaction was short-lived, however, by Carl's claim that he had known at the time we made the purchase that the bed was too soft for him to be comfortable. He professed to have said nothing then, as he felt it was more important for my needs to be met, despite the expense to him. Consequently, he had a legitimate excuse to continue sleeping on the couch, and despite being put off by his fake show of self-sacrifice, I was content with the way the situation evolved. First, I was free of sleeping with him. Second, I had a tidy space that I could essentially call my own. I accepted the luxury without feeling overwhelmingly self-centered, not realizing that, beyond personal comfort, forces intent on initiating training me in my sleep were orchestrating the whole incident.

One day I returned from work to find the bed stripped to the mattress and all of the bedding lying on the floor. Carl quickly explained that the dog had urinated in the middle of the bed. In disbelief, I asked him what he had done to clean the spot? He admitted that, since he did not know what to do, he had done nothing. His words instantly sent me into an all-consuming rage. I screamed at him; why he had not phoned me rather than leaving the urine to dry in the mattress? I blustered that he never hesitated to phone me otherwise. Why, when he had an opinion about how to handle everything else, not this? I wanted to smash him; I wanted to smash the dog for what they had done to me. The dog was already showing signs of stress from my behavior. Even Carl was taken by surprise. Finally, I yelled at him to just get away from me. He did not challenge me for once. He did not even laugh. Meanwhile, I grabbed a pail of water, a scrub brush and began to scrub.

I watched myself scrub until the mattress was half-soaked, asking myself the entire time why I was so reactive, and why was I feeling so helpless? Carl was only being Carl! The dog was not at fault; he had a close attachment to me and was probably only responding to the odors of my menstrual cycle. I loved this dog, but Carl was another matter. It felt as if by not cleaning the mattress he had, in some way, violated me personally. The entire incident left me feeling violated. The more I scrubbed the more violated I felt. I valued this bed. Not only for the quality of sleep it afforded, but also for the sense of peace and safety. Now, it was all gone: my sanctuary dirtied. The harder I scrubbed, the more loudly I protested, "This is not funny, and I cannot laugh about it. Tomorrow I won't be able to laugh, nor the next day. Not even next week or next month. Maybe, just perhaps next year it will be funny. Then I can laugh." I found an odd sense of comfort from my words, as if I was giving myself permission not to feel ashamed over my behavior. I clearly understood that someday I would find this situation amusing. The greater truth was, regardless of the nature of any of my experiences, at some point in time, when far enough removed from them, I would be able to find, not just this one, but all of them amusing. What I was being shown was not to condemn my behavior or take myself overly seriously.

My long-held premonition of Carl and Adam's antagonistic play manifested during this time frame. Carl phoned me at work one day, stony-voiced and clearly ready to faint, as he always did at the sight of blood, "Come home quickly, Adam's been hurt." Controlling my surging panic, I raced out the door to my car, praying all the way that Carl, before he fainted, think to get Adam to our neighbor, a retired doctor. Arriving home, I found that Carl had done just that. When I walked in the neighbor's house, father and son were laid out side by side on the floor. The doctor was applying a pressure bandage to Adam's arm while his wife soaked up blood from the carpet. Our German Shepherd jumped around adding to the confusion. The doctor informed me that Adam had to be taken to the hospital where he be directly admitted to emergency surgery. The neighbor claimed that from what he could determine, serious nerve damage had been sustained. Adam and Carl had been "roughhousing." When Adam had taken a swing at his father, his arm had come down on the open blade of a tiny knife Carl had been holding. Leaving Carl to recover, I took the dog home and then took Adam to the hospital, setting aside the details of what, when, who, where and how for later.

In the emergency room, I informed the attending physician of my neighbor's diagnosis. Blustering that he was the doctor, not me, he proceeded to treat Adam's wound only superficially—and indicating in no uncertain terms that his authority was not to be challenged. At the same time, he questioned me in regard to the nature of the circumstance. I knew it was his duty. Decidedly, this was an accident. Then why didn't it feel like an accident? Why did I feel guilty? Why did I feel overwhelmingly responsible? My apprehension intensified when Adam was unable to respond to the doctor's instruction to push on his hand. "Adam, you're a baby. You can't handle pain," the doctor accused. Adam retorted, "I don't feel any pain. I don't feel anything!" My confusion escalated as I struggled to ignore our neighbor's diagnosis—now resounding in my head—in favor of the belief that it was the attending physician who was most competent and a good thing that our neighbor had retired.

Adam maintained his normal routine as I strived to ignore the misgivings increasingly holding my nerves in tense distraction. I tried to convince myself that I was simply being my negative self but what I perceived as doubt would not diminish. After the second day, Adam phoned me at work beseeching, "If you don't take me to the doctor immediately, I'm going to punch holes in the wall!" In other words his pain was unbearable. When our regular doctor examined the wound, she quickly redressed it, gave him a tetanus shot, and then rushed us off to see a specialist across town. After the specialist cut the stitches out of his arm, he went inside the wound to pull out blood clots between his muscles caused from internal hemorrhaging. As far removed as I was from panic, I nevertheless had to galvanize my attention to avoid fainting as the doctor directed me how to help Adam endure the pain. Subsequently, he was admitted to the hospital. Next, he was pumped with antibiotics in preparation for surgery. Two days later, a specialist set about repairing a severed ulnar nerve, a lacerated tendon and lacerated muscles, which from the point of the wound to the end of his fingers, had already significantly atrophied leaving his hand shriveled into a tightened fist. Only time would reveal if Adam regained full use of his hand. Recalling the dreams during my pregnancy of trying to keep him alive, I vacillated between empathy for Adam and a sense of helpless rage toward Carl springing from an unfathomable depth inside me.

Adam valiantly weathered the experience. After the cast was removed and he completed rehabilitation, he concentrated on further rebuilding his weakened muscles and began to seriously weight train. I never questioned Carl about how he felt about the situation, for he would never leave himself vulnerable enough to be honest, but the tension between father and son was palpable. I questioned Adam one day, when he asked me to take note of the size of his muscles, whether or not he was still afraid of his father's temper. His response was, "No, now I'm lifting weights, I know I'm stronger than he is. If he comes after me, I can beat the shit out of him." (A number of times when Carl's anger toward me had taken form, Adam had attempted to intervene. Then when Carl had turned on him, he had just as quickly turned and high-tailed it to safety as he had done as a child.) Worse, Adam purchased a hunting knife from a friend and then proceeded to hone his throwing skills, certain he would use the knife if necessary. If anything, his behavior was completely out of character. He was a gentle being through and through. And as angry as I was, I knew the same was true about myself.

On another occasion, Adam again presented me with an opportunity for a greater understanding. In a conversation, he divulged, "Mom, you know I can start talking to Carl about my favorite author or sports team or whatever, but by the end of the conversation, my views end up being exactly the same as his." (Adam had called his father by his given name from the time he was about six or seven.) I could certainly identify with his position. Carl never let anyone have a say in any conversation or hold onto any personal perspective for long. Even more interesting was the fact that I had never modeled for Adam an effective or positive way to deal with his father's overpowering personality.

Carl's approach to Adam's coming of age concerned me. Adam had grown up with Carl's "tits and ass" attitude toward women, to the extent that Carl had habitually pointed out a good-looking specimen to Adam—and me—even when he was a youngster. Carl's derogatory opinion of females had perpetually been a point of contention between us during the entire course of Adam's upbringing. He was incapable of seeing that Adam did not adhere to his ribald behavior. I knew of no "right way" in terms of supporting Adam through his sexual passage, but I did know that I wanted him to feel safe to explore his sexuality, as well as all other aspect of himself; I wanted him to feel safer than I had ever had the opportunity to feel.

During the time that Carl's and my conflict was increasing, Adam began hanging with a group of troubled boys. One day he asked permission to spend a weekend in Indiana with these friends, one of whose parents owned a trailer there. He had already shared with me that his friends drank and some did drugs. Although I knew how troubled he was, and despite my concerns, I realized that I trusted—I had to trust—that he could take care of himself. I could not do to him what my mother did to me. I had to let him have his experiences. Upon each return from a weekend there, he would share with me what had taken place. The first time he and his friends had been drinking and playing volleyball, he discovered that after just one beer he was unable to hit the ball. He did not like that. Consequently, the remainder of the trips involved him taking care of his friends when they became inebriated. I had taught him well to be a caretaker. How could he be any different? Knowing the full extent of what he had working against him, I was proud of his square handling of himself. I was also proud of myself for standing back and appropriately supporting him in his own experiences, rather than being controlling or manipulative, as I was prone to be.

Almost a year after Auntie died, and with the house ready to come out of probate, Carl spent considerable time articulating his indecision as to whether to place my name on the deed. He contended that I really deserved nothing considering that I had stolen his money, but he felt he would add my name to the deed simply because he was that kind of person. I found it an amusing situation that neither of us actually had the house for he could not obtain the deed until he paid off the mortgage, but the money to pay off the mortgage was in my hands. I recognized that a part of me wanted the security of being included on the deed while another part just said, "Fuck you and your manipulation. You can have the house." If this was not confusing enough, I had never been quite sure if my need to get married ultimately had to do with guaranteeing a claim to the house. My guilt over that possibility imbued Carl's position with a certain sting, but to my astonishment, I managed to abstain from reacting to his manipulation. In the end, his seemingly generous gesture left me co-owner. The price either of us would pay for being homeowners was yet to be fully defined.

It was obvious that Carl was becoming threatened beyond measure by my interactions and activities outside domesticity. My personal need to move further into a new space of understanding and functioning began to eclipse my need to grovel to get Carl's approval or to prove to him that I was not self-centered or bad. In fact, I had been openly calling him on his manipulations. For example, he habitually remained non-committed and uncooperative whenever my vacation time approached. Days before my most recent vacation and irritated over this yearly game, I had informed him of the day and time that I was pulling out of the driveway and, that if he was not in the car at that time, I would assume that he had decided to stay home. The real test for me was not second-guessing myself.

The night before our departure, Carl burst into my bedroom, snapped on the overhead light, and before I could react or even fully awaken, jumped on the bed, grabbed my hands, yanked them over my head and pinned me down with his knee on my chest. Our eyes locked in a contest of wills as he pressed his knee still more firmly into my chest and I felt as if he was the boa constrictor at the nature center squeezing the life out of me. I held my breath and drew myself above the pain and fear and everything else necessary to sabotage his sense of pleasure or conquest. He continued to apply more pressure as I continued to lay stone-still, my will unremittingly pitted against his. He finally released his knee from my chest, but I continued to lay motionless, not willing to take that long-needed breath until he left. Although I was certain that he would not return, I slept fitfully for the rest of the night, my thoughts and feelings tied in knots. It was an unfamiliarly strong sense of headiness that kept me from falling to pieces.

The next morning, with the pain in my chest, I wondered if I should go to the doctor rather than on vacation. Determination kept me following through with the schedule I had set. Carl was nowhere to be seen. He was taking a timely walk with the dogs. As for me, I did not hesitate to pull out of the driveway. Adam was aware of my condition and queried me about Carl being responsible. Because I remained caught in "protecting" him, I could only fail to be honest with Adam—or myself. Carl made contact with me a few days later through his brother, where Adam and I were staying while visiting Disney World. He apologized for hurting me and admitted that he really had wanted to come with me, but did not know how to under the circumstances. I had been keenly aware that he would take my stipulations as an ultimatum triggering his attack response. Surprisingly, I had little reaction to his apology. I felt accomplished that I had stood my ground and not attempted to coax him into coming. I also felt good that I had left without him, not to be vindictive, but simply because it was my vacation; it was important to me and I was going to take charge of it for once. Of vital importance, I was validating how good it felt to have control of circumstances in my life and how enjoyable these circumstances could be without Carl's presence. Above the plethora of lessons this situation provided, the one that I was unable to readily see was that I was beginning to trust in myself and that this trust supported my making my own decisions, which were leading to positive changes in my life.

To date I had known only little more than work, responsibility, caretaking and sacrifice: happiness remained an alien reality. Seeking a therapist through my health care plan became my first attempt to bring this emotion into my life. My assigned therapist was a mousy little man who appeared to be caught in the bureaucratic red tape that accompanies the medical profession. Besides seeming to actually use the industry to "hide out," he appeared to be no happier than I.

A teacher who visited the nature center and who had pressed me to become friends had been seeing a psychiatrist twice a week for eight years. She divulged that she wanted to end therapy but was actually afraid that her therapist would be devastated. She ran errands, did shopping, and was there in many other ways for the therapist. I was amazed. If anything, their predicament was like a sick marriage. I also knew that this friend was using me as a surrogate therapist, and as much as I was willing to support her, she was that willing to suck my energy dry. The entire situation, besides being much food for thought, left me sober in terms of maintaining the appropriate client/therapist relationship.

What I initially noticed about myself in therapy was my habit of using Carl as the issue, incessantly needing to explain myself, the depth of my anger, positioning myself as the victim, as well as my need to make my therapist my ally. I recognized the inappropriateness of my behavior—to some degree, I knew that seeking blame leaves understanding unattainable—and I wanted to move beyond blame fully and immediately. I had yet to realize, however, that change, particularly breaking free of old patterns, is not instantaneous, nor does it come on demand even when facing one's life head on. It is a process that requires patience, commitment, focus and tenacity, of which the first presented the greatest challenge. I could change only as quickly as I was ready to change. Readiness occurs from moment to moment, one experience creating an impetus and foundation for the next. Step by step, I was proceeding into understanding; I was healing. Time and retrospect would reveal this.

Week after week, I continued with therapy, convincing myself that I was benefiting and would be unable to progress without it. I continued to sit in my designated seat in the corner of the tiny, windowless cubicle, sweaty and anxious, steeped in my own defensiveness, observing that my therapist sat too close, too nervous himself, for my comfort. I became aware of my habit of softening or coloring my stories—as if I was under interrogation—to avoid losing his approval. I had no intention of being deceptive—he was not challenging me. I understood that there was no gain in it, but deception simply emerged of its own accord, an ingrained survival mechanism. After my session, I would ride down the elevator exasperated as I assessed my behavior. I sensed that the therapist had no fewer problems than I did, although his problems appeared to be more attractively packaged. On some level, I understood that he was not what I needed in a therapist. However, being part of a health care plan left me no other choice, unless I wanted to pay for a therapist out of my own pocket—which I didn't. Further, if I admitted that I was bored with this therapist and had gone as far as I could with him, then I would have to face forging ahead on my own. At the time, pretending that his services were of value was easier than being honest with myself, or him. What I failed to recognize was that the therapy sessions were primarily an avenue for me to learn to trust—not him, not the situation, but myself, as all of my impending experiences would be.

Carl was once again threatened by my seeking outside support—he was still trying to keep our life a secret, much like my father had required of his family—and knew he was losing control of me. "If you need help, why don't you just come to me instead of a stranger?" he demanded. Trying a new tactic, he professed that it would be more efficacious if we attended counseling together. I was thoroughly against this, but let my "shoulds" rule out. These sessions unsurprisingly consisted of his expounding on my problems, as well as the therapist's, infuriating me and putting my therapist altogether on the defensive. Carl was correct in regard to everything he articulated, although his goal was merely to direct attention away from himself. Privately, the therapist confessed that simply knowing that Carl was in the waiting room gave him a sick feeling in the pit of his stomach. I was embarrassed by his admission and felt responsible for his discomfort, but on the other hand, this information fed my greater understanding of Carl's capacity to intimidate others, including professionally trained psychiatrists. I also felt less of a failure in regard to contending with him.

Carl continued inadvertently to assist in closing the door to our years of perpetual conflict. With our relationship dangerously strained, he decided to stay with his mother in Florida for a while, where she had recently moved to live with his brother. Any length of time he was away was a relief for me. When he returned a few weeks later, he announced that a psychic had told him that my problem with sexual frigidity was related to sexual abuse in my childhood. Although I was livid at his infringement on my personal space by talking about my sexuality to a stranger, the questions cast in my mind left me obsessed to find the truth. Carl had always been convinced that my father had sexually abused me. I found the idea of my father being physical, not to mention violating someone, absurd. Yet a strange, nagging doubt cast its shadow on the matter. At some point I realized that a definitive means to acquire the truth I was seeking was to find a hypnotherapist to take me back into my past and find out for myself what had happened. Therefore, at my next regular appointment, I informed my therapist that I had to see a hypnotherapist. Willingness to personally foot the cost revealed the degree of my commitment.

My therapist happened to have a friend who was a hypnotherapist and who worked independently from his home, which meant no health care plan procedure, regulations or restrictions. The only drawbacks were that I would have to drive thirty miles to the suburbs for the appointment and my wallet would be fifty dollars lighter. I walked out of the session with a feeling of relief. Although I was unable to openly admit to myself that this was, in fact, my last session with this therapist, intuitively I could feel the door permanently closing behind me.

I was compelled to make the appointment immediately upon arriving at home. I liked that this doctor answered the phone himself, and I liked the sound of his voice. When the appointment was made, I felt excited, even greatly anticipatory. A force of energy infiltrating my body and mind in an ever-increasing degree shortly intensified these feelings. I was soon unable to concentrate on anything but the sense of dire urgency to have a session with the hypnotherapist. The force of energy that heightened during the drive there rose to a feverish pitch as I sat waiting on a hallway bench outside his office listening to the muffled conversation and wondering which voice was his. I had no idea what was happening to me, why my jaws were so painfully clenched, why I felt so agitated, but I was relieved that the washroom was readily accessible.

The first time I looked into this doctor's watery blue eyes confusion, plus an intensification of energy, overtook me. He did not feel like a stranger. More disconcerting, my usual sense of apprehension and guardedness was minimal, although I was certainly overwhelmed as much as anxious to know what was happening to me. Whatever it was, it felt beyond my power to control. Outside of our initial greeting, I would refer to him by his first name, David. Certainty that I was to do so left me no choice.

I followed David into his office, which was built over his garage. It upset me that it was unclean, unkempt, smoke-filled and cluttered with walls of books and recording equipment—more combination bachelor pad/recording studio than a professional space. My addictive impulse was to put order to the chaos. Contrary to my rigid sense of protocol, I found myself expressing my all-around reaction. He responded that he was not into hiding himself: what I saw was who he was. Then he asked me if I kept my personal space nice and presentable while hiding my chaos in the closet. I knew he was speaking metaphorically. His bull's eye shot was embarrassing, but it set the stage for me to drop the pretenses and duplicities on the spot—or at least as best as I was able.

Without thought or forewarning, I next heard myself blurting out, "I hold myself responsible for my own learning and need to direct my own healing. I need you to support me, not tell me what's wrong with me. If this doesn't work for you, you need to say so." If he was taken by surprise, he never let on. He merely explained that the first visit routinely determined client/therapist compatibility and that he found me to be highly intelligent and would like to work with me. My sense of knowing surpassed any need to develop a comfort level between us. I wanted to get to work immediately before I strangled on my own energy. Completing the allotted hour, I asked him when he was going to hypnotize me. His amused response was that I had been in an altered state for the entire visit. It was then that I understood what had been happening to me all along, in fact, what state I was in most of the time.

What aggravated me about David was his habit of smoking his pipe during our sessions causing my eyes to become dry and itchy, leaving me with a pounding sinus headache, not to mention that I smelled horrible when I left. It frustrated me that whatever setting I was in, I had to battle someone's smoking habit. Carl's mother was a chain-smoker and despite the fact that she was aware of my allergy to tobacco smoke, she always smoked in our house. Why not be forthcoming about this, when I had been about my attitude toward his messiness? I continued to resent that. I wanted to ask him to refrain from smoking his pipe in my presence. Instead, I reasoned that this was his space, and he had the right to do what he wanted. On the other hand, I was paying him and therefore had a right to be comfortable. I would never directly address David's behavior, but I would play out this smoking issue countless times before I fully understood why I attracted people who smoked into my life.

I was greatly disconcerted when my first regression uncovered nary an incident of sexual abuse in my childhood. Why then this all-pervasive sense of sexual violation? Why this confusion, and shame and fear? I had seldom felt that Carl and I had shared a sexual experience. Rather, I had resigned myself to supplying his needs. Habitually, before going to the racetrack, he would spend an hour or two taking a bath and studying the nightly track program, after which he would insist on his usual sex fix. The signal for his readiness usually took the form of his putting his arms around me—more like a manacle than an embrace—and pushing his erect penis into my backside. With Adam usually around and acutely attuned to being shut out of these matters, meeting Carl's demands were often complicated and embarrassing. In further need, he would often wake me after his return or in the middle of the night. Since early in our relationship, providing oral gratification for him had defined our sexual encounters. He would clamp his hands onto my head in forceps fashion pushing my mouth up and down on his erection. I would hurl his hands off my head, hoping he would recognize my agitation, but he would force them back, pumping away at me until he ejaculated. While he was in the throws of self-gratification, my thoughts were generally on separating him from his member with my teeth.

Conventional sex was no picnic either, especially when penetration usually resulted in a vaginal or urinary tract infection. I was becoming more and more resistant to oral sex and sexual encounters in general. In fact, I began to notice that every part of me—more parts than I could define—resisted his invasion of me, and I had come to use my infections as an excuse to avoid penetration. When that failed, I put into effect the same infallible "tight-box trick" that I had used as a teenager. Undaunted, he would find somewhere on my body to pleasure himself. The more I avoided sex or was less willing to engage, the more persistent he was. It became impossible to even take a shower or otherwise remove my clothes without his appearing at my side—or front or back—pumping away on me as if I was a bitch in heat.

Early on, I had acquired an intellectual perspective about the nature of intimacy by reading self-help literature and had attempted to apply my thinking to my life. When our relationship was young, I had once found the nerve to ask Carl why he seldom kissed me; he claimed that I had bad breath. For many years after that, besides increasing the number of times a day I brushed my teeth, I constantly had a piece of gum in my mouth. Further, I took greater pains to maintain a higher standard of hygiene, especially paying attention to those parts used in the sexual act (a reaction to a childhood belief that my father rejected my mother because he found her dirty or smelly). I dropped my expectations of tenderness and convinced myself that I should be grateful that someone would put up with me at all. As our relationship progressed, I had made a number of futile attempts to express my need for intimacy which I thought should, for instance, begin by going on a quiet walk together or in the kitchen sharing a meal preparation, and which did not necessarily have to end in sexual gratification. The rare times that Carl did attempt to be intimate, I automatically shut down; I had no trust—in Carl, in the situation or in myself.

If I was presently unable to fully see how these issues were rooted in my childhood experiences, I was certainly unable to comprehend how deeply they were rooted in a more remote past. The greater truth was that we were both using the sexual arena to play out an ancient conflict between us. Only further significant development would lend a greater understanding of, not just the struggle between us, but also who I am/am not as a sexual being, as well as a greater truth as to the nature of intimacy, which has nothing to do with sex.

At this juncture, hypnotherapy became the tool for me to begin to effectively bypass intellectual and emotional roadblocks as well as self-limiting beliefs and social conditioning that thwarted my efforts to obtain a truer understanding of myself. It was time to get out of my head and into my heart, to look to myself rather than to Carl, in order to get that understanding.

In a subsequent session, David, like an unexpected right hook, informed me that my first move was to leave Carl. "Therapists aren't supposed to tell their clients what to do!" I furiously exclaimed. His rejoinder that he was merely reflecting back to me what he had heard me communicate to him was a further essential blow. Even while I attempted for a moment to maintain my indignant air, I knew he was speaking my truth. Carl had continually deemed himself my savior, while I had believed that he could not survive without my taking care of him. Then, too, "I had made my bed…" Also, I held onto a warped hope that someday he might change: quit gambling and become responsible and then our life would be happy. Intellectually caught off guard by having to face a deeper truth, I finally and unexpectedly confessed that I simply lacked the courage to leave Carl.

David's quick response to my lack of faith in myself was that all I had to do was look at my hands to know my strength. Again I was taken aback and, this time, thoroughly embarrassed. My hands, for the previous few years, had appeared to be responding to an inexplicable energy moving through them. I often had to concentrate or even sit on them to keep them still. Besides this, they had to touch and feel almost everything, as if picking up energy emitting from objects. Further, my fingers often thumped and tapped, even when restricted in a pocket, in a way that I had finally realized was not random. As I learned to pay attention, I recognized that my fingers were actually typing out or writing messages. Whether in my fingers alone or my entire hands, this phenomenon was intensifying whenever I was in the woods, and also now whenever I was in sessions with David.

I drove away with an image of a rabbit in my head. It took little effort to realize that I was the rabbit. Contemplating the nature of the animal, I could see how I habitually froze up during moments of confrontation, or else I darted away to safety. I wondered what a fear-free life would look and feel like. I wondered if it was possible, if anyone had ever reached this state. In the moment, the idea was incomprehensible; but the seed had been planted.

I arose one morning feeling overwhelmingly pressed to tell Carl I was leaving him. I did not feel ready. I wanted to at least prepare some sort of speech, maybe even have a go at practicing. None of my stall tactics worked. It was plain to see that some part of me would do close to anything to avoid this encounter. Nonetheless, there was again a force beyond my ability to comprehend overriding my resistance. My hands felt electrified. I stepped into our tiny kitchen where Carl was fixing breakfast for himself and told him I needed to talk to him. He turned around and eyed me suspiciously. Face to face, and with no room to back away, I felt overwhelmingly exposed. My throat was constricting, perspiration ran down my sides, my heart was pounding and my body trembling from the adrenalin rush. This felt like life or death. I watched my mind continue with its efforts to find ways to escape the situation, shut down or at least, soften the message enough to avoid his wrath. I listened while one part of me commanded, "No, you won't be a rabbit! You have to do this! You're ready to do this!" and another part countered, "I can't! I don't know how!" I was caving, ready to say "forget it" and bolt, when a sudden, unexpected surge of painfully intense energy shot up my hands (which were stuffed in my jean pockets) spontaneously delivering the words: "I am no longer willing to continue our conflict." I immediately felt the first sweet taste of freedom even as I questioned what I had done. Carl immediately began to sob! That sweet taste of freedom faded quickly as I slipped into helplessness, just as I had when faced with my father's tears as a youngster. I continued to cave as I battled justifying my action, softening my position, or getting sucked further into his pain. Carl, himself, knocked me starkly back into sobriety when he declared that he was going to wake Adam immediately to talk to him so he could be assured that he got the truth.

Next he announced—seemingly arrogantly to me—that he would give me my freedom. I heard myself vehemently respond, "You have nothing to do with my freedom! You never have! You never will!" Not knowing what to do from there, I headed for the garage to get my bicycle. I had no idea what this test was about, but I knew I was facing it full force and was terrified beyond belief, especially by all of the unknowns into which I was catapulting myself.

As I mounted my bike, Carl stepped into the yard and spat, "You never really loved me!" Instantly, I was treading deeper through my swelling guilt. I pedaled hard along the bike path trying to keep from totally "freaking out." I was unable to count the times I repeated, "How can he claim to love me when he treats me like this?" I had contemplated the meaning of love for many years, never getting farther than confusion. Sometimes, I was certain that I felt a deep sense of love toward Carl. Retrospect revealed that without Adam as a focal point, meaningful moments between us had been rare. I was finally able to admit that I disliked him and the way he treated me. (In fact, some part of me hated him, hated him as much as I hated myself.) I had been coming to the awareness that he had never owned his relationship with me, and his claim of love was his way of keeping me under his control, which it had. It was inevitable that I had to own the fact that he hated women and his unconscious motive in our relationship was to destroy me. Love was a trap. I would not allow myself to be trapped again. I believed the only way to deal with this was to stay clear of the possibility of a man making this claim. Who would anyway? Men's interest did not include divorcees—or so I thought. As I finished my bike ride, I made a point of avoiding being sidetracked by his professing his love for me. Only further experiences would reveal that I distrusted the idea of love more than I did those who claimed to love me. The truth about love was waiting for me to discover it.

I was realizing both that I had been living in a state of depression during our entire relationship and Carl had supported it. When I began to sink too far, he would take action—surprising me with an unexpected "gift" or helping me in some unanticipated way—to pull me back, but not out, only as far as he needed me to be to allow him to maintain his control. Yet Carl had not made me depressed. I had brought it to the relationship. Honesty forced me to own that I had been depressed for as long as I could remember. I had to discover why, like my mother, I fallen into depression (repression of anger). I had to understand it from the inside out. Of utmost importance, I had to see how I had gotten myself into this embroilment I called a relationship. Had I been using Carl to keep myself depressed? Had I been using depression to keep myself with Carl? Regardless, there was no longer room for it in my life.

Carl had the time, during my absence, to collect his thoughts and was waiting for my return. He emphatically demanded, "If you're going to divorce me, do it, and do it immediately. I'm not going to let you play games with me." Staying outside of his intimidations, I could see his discomfort in the defensive role and his attempt to regain his offensive position. I was not interested in being vindictive or making this a war, despite my anger, but I realized that I was going to have to maneuver through a field of land mines—some my own, some his—before I was safely out of this reality. If I could have had a wish, it would have been to have someone do this for me or at least support me. However, the reoccurring surge of energy in my hands was a comforting, albeit bewildering reminder that I had the strength and the courage to transport myself from my own bed of limitation and into a healthier state.

Oddly enough, I had been having a recurring dream that I was in prison and yearning for release. Getting out, I discovered, merely required opening the door. Once out, I realized that the only reason I had been in prison at all and for so long was because I had, without even checking, assumed the door was locked. It never had been. It was my beliefs, not the circumstances, that had kept me a prisoner my entire life. I had made myself a prisoner. Understanding the nature of my beliefs, how they manifested and how they supported my limitations would be a key to moving further into freedom—a key that would also support my traveling the length of the thread of my consciousness and back to the beginning of my creation.

Because I took Carl seriously about immediately obtaining a lawyer, I phoned one that I knew who volunteered at the nature center and invited him to meet me at a coffeehouse. Once there, I unabashedly explained my situation. During the entire time that we conversed, I was overcome with an unfamiliar sort of giddiness. At one point he even inquired as to whether or not I was on drugs. His comment only added to my amusement, as well as to my growing concern over my out-of-character behavior. He only knew one divorce lawyer whom I was able to afford, and as I had little interest in researching alternatives, I accepted his recommendation. We continued to meet after that. While I held our interactions as purely platonic, it was undeniable that he was interested in me; it was also undeniable that my fear of men's advances was well intact. He would be the first man with whom I began to deal with this issue. I would also learn that he had his life no better together than I did, personally or professionally. Of utmost importance, interaction with this man would force me to own the fact that I was no exception when it comes to failing to be honest about one's relationship with one's own life.

My appointment with the divorce lawyer required a long drive on the expressway through heavy traffic and into unfamiliar territory, which alone was enough to fry my nerves. His cold, masculine, impeccably clean and orderly office environment—the antithesis of David's space—with his sophisticated, smartly-attired receptionist set a severe, formal tone. Despite my intimidation, I set aside my sense of inferiority, as well as my humiliation over having to divulge my sordid personal life, and succinctly disclosed the nature of my relationship with Carl. The first question from the lawyer was why, seeing the nature of my intelligence, had I remained in this relationship for so long? It was a perplexing question, one that I had already posed to myself. I could only respond that I aimed to have that understanding someday.

Extricating myself from Carl's clutches, as well as from my own self-destructive tendencies, required strength and courage, as much as hard-core self-scrutiny and determination. Moreover, I had to relinquish my obsessive sense of responsibility for his welfare if I were to stay out of prison. He was well aware of all my weaknesses, especially my need to prove that I was not a bad person. Regardless of my thoughts and beliefs about our co-dependency and all it represented, the relationship was indeed in the bumpy first stage of grinding to a halt.

Self-scrutiny revealed, among other matters, that I was adept at playing the victim role. Unquestionably, I had used our relationship as a means to avoid living my life, or even examining a deeper awareness of myself: a place I was terrified to go. In keeping that part of me hidden, I supported my own state of depression. I had, in fact, created my own isolation—my own prison. Carl was the "outer" vehicle to my maintaining that isolation. It was a painful admission that I had been using him as much as he had been using me. I would have liked to contend, "Well, yeah, but he used me more," but as I was learning, using others is not to be rationalized in relation to degrees. Either we do or we don't. And as humans, who operate from needs and desires, we all use each other.

During this time I learned that Carl's sister, Carmen, was facing her husband divorcing her. Carl's reaction was that he had to advise her. Inside me I heard, "You're not getting your claws into her, too!" Carmen's husband was also a domineering man. She and I had never spent much time together, but there was a deep bond between us. Compelled to talk with her, I made an unexpected call on her one evening. Since her husband was at home and did not tolerate visitors, we took a walk in order to converse. I found myself confiding information about Carl's and my relationship that I had never before shared. Shock was my first reaction to what I heard myself saying, followed by a certainty that Carl would be furious if he got wind of this conversation. However, the flow of thoughts came of their own volition. A few weeks later, she stopped by the nature center to talk to me, something under normal circumstances she would never have done. In tears, she claimed that she could not divorce her husband because of her vows to God; that only death could dissolve the marriage. She would try to talk her husband into seeking marriage counseling. She mentioned nothing about how miserable she was in the relationship. I found myself asking her if she thought God would expect her to be unhappy and unfulfilled for the rest of her life simply to keep a vow that she had made with him. To my surprise, my words evoked a truth in Carmen that enabled her to address her ordeal more realistically. My message also provoked some thoughts for me: first, that my words could have such positive impact on someone else; and second, that I was nervy to think that I could possibly know God's thoughts.

After working overtime one Saturday, as I was regularly inclined to do, instead of driving home after work, I found myself turning onto the expressway and heading in the direction of my hometown. I was reluctant as much as unnerved about this undertaking, but an irrepressible force was in operation. Ultimately, I was aware that renewing contact with my parents was a critical step in my healing and one that could only take place by my first having had broken ties with Carl.

It was evident that they were not at home when I pulled in the driveway, but I had no doubt where to find them. When they saw me from where they were sitting at the bar in the Veteran's Club, they were noticeably taken aback. I could see them emotionally preparing themselves for an attack as they habitually did when around me, and I was also aware that they would not want to "deal" with me in public. I explained that I had simply driven out to have a talk with them, at which point they insisted that we return to their house. I knew that I was going to relate my status to them and that as a consequence they were going to be left with much food for gossip, and a well-what-can-you-expect-after-what-you've-done-with-your-life attitude that would be strenuous for them to conceal. Furthermore, I was aware that my test was to abstain from being affected by their judgment, as well as my need for their approval. Since I had never informed them that Carl and I were married, they were surprised about the divorce. With Carl removed from the picture, I figured, my mother, who seldom missed a television soap opera, would make an effort to stay in touch, out of curiosity if nothing else.

When Carl's mother learned of the situation, she was thoroughly upset and demanded that I give her son one more chance. What she was asking was for me to continue taking care of him. For many years I had been as intolerant of her as I had been of their warped devotion to each other. I had become weary of Carl visiting her on a daily basis when she lived in Chicago, but never having time to spend with me. I had become tired of bailing her out of her endless crises—the worst of which had her living with us—while she took minimal responsibility for what she created. For years, I had given him gambling rations half-rationalizing that I had been sparing him hitting on his mother for money when actually she had been freely and open-handedly giving him whatever money she had anyway. It had been humiliating to realize how well Carl had conned me, and his mother—how sick the entire situation was. It had taken me a long time to grasp that just because she had once taken me in during my time of need, I was not eternally indebted to keep her life afloat. Although her request instantly triggered my guilt, I could no longer make it my duty to please her or her son. My life was no longer about pleasing anyone. I simply had to do what I had to do; that was all that I knew, and that was what was guiding me through my own fear and out of my archaic way of managing my life. Whatever conflict Carl's mother and I had played out, I still loved her with all my heart, but I had to keep my promise to myself.

Carl's first show of resistance to my leaving was mild-mannered: he began to stay home from the racetrack at night. Next, he "borrowed" money from me to enroll in real estate school. He insisted on going for walks with me, and then attempted to hold my hand or put his arm around me. He insisted that he had the insights I needed to better understand myself. When I didn't bite at that, his approach was to share his unsolicited insights, "I'll tell you what's wrong with you and then you can tell me what's wrong with me." My response was, "I don't need your insights. I have my own. You address your own issues, and I'll take care of mine." When push came to shove, I vehemently exclaimed, "Don't ever tell me again that I have no understanding, because I do! I have a tremendous amount! And you can't take it away from me, and you can't silence me!" I further emphasized,

"And don't ever expect me to apologize to you for anything again, because I've never, ever done anything wrong. I hated being this out of control. Yet I walked away feeling relieved and lighter, as if I had reclaimed a part of myself.

When Carl completed real estate school, he was left to face obtaining a job for the first time since his college years. His typical self-assuredness had vanished, and he was openly, tearfully terrified simply of the thought of stepping out into life. Most enlightening, I observed him rationalize his conflict with almost every female that became part of his professional life as her being backstabbing and aggressive like males. Not trapping myself into feeling sorry and taking responsibility for him became a maddening test for me. I found ways to step over appropriate boundaries and call it by another name. For instance, I used his birthday as an excuse to buy him clothes suitable for a professional position. I did not give him the clothes directly; I gave them to Adam to give to him. Unconsciously, all along, I had been training Adam to be Carl's caretaker, and when I was out of the picture, he would be the one who continued to come to his father's rescue.

I was more than curious to see how we would both deal with the reality that I was no longer available to accommodate his sexual needs. Although finally admitting to myself how demoralizing my sexual experiences with Carl had been, I had to submit to his abuse one more time to know that if I surrendered again I had only myself to blame. Still, he would go out of his way to walk into the bedroom or bathroom when he was sure I was naked. Acknowledging my attempt to cover my body brought his invective, "You think I'm fucking interested in your body?"

Outside of my fear of Carl, a vindictive part of me not only knew how, but also wanted to flatten him. Moving out of the victim role and into greater insights regarding our relationship and both of our insecurities had some unsuspecting provocations. As long as I remained separated from my emotions, I could operate from a place of integrity. The moment I was caught in them I was fighting hard and dirty. Attempting to be a positive role model for Adam, I struggled to vacate the relationship with as much dignity as possible.

Carl convinced himself that the only reason I was withholding sex or leaving him was because I was having an affair. His increasing jealousy and rage over losing me led him to follow me. He would show up at the school library in the morning where I went to study before going to work. Or he would unexpectedly show up at work in the same manner. Telephone calls purportedly querying what I might want at the grocery store composed his lame excuses to check up on me at work. He even insisted on going with me shopping, on errands or for walks in the woods.

Ironically, it was an unexpected affair that facilitated wresting myself free from my self-destructive lifestyle. In the middle of confiding my deteriorating work situation to Kent, my beekeeper friend, confidant and ally at the nature center, he suddenly blurted out that he was in love with me. I was flabbergasted and felt betrayed. First, although failing, he was still in a marriage himself. And then, I needed him as a friend. Besides, I viewed being divorced as being deflowered and therefore, undesirable. In fact, the words to a song, "I'm just a second hand rose," had been running through my head since I had informed Carl of my intentions of leaving him. Somewhere locked in my confusion was a belief that men were only interested in virgins. Even a flow of men sniffing around my office door since word of my divorce had gotten out had not convinced me otherwise.

Adhering to the idea that being loved was conditional, some bewildering part of me overrode my fears, and I soon found I had sexually surrendered myself to Kent. I did not know if my actions were a neat form of revenge toward Carl, but Kent was enthralled, as if I was bird-of-paradise when he was accustomed to smelling daisies. He could not get enough of me. Neither could he hold back from dreaming about how we were going to live our life. While everything about the relationship was imminently dead-end, I was obsessively hanging onto it for dear life, trying to make it something that it could never be. Intuitively my understanding was intact. He was a means not an end. We were only steps for each other to move ourselves into a new beginning. I was way beyond him in terms of growth and understanding. Nevertheless, I convinced myself that if I tried harder the relationship could be a success. When I looked into the future, however, I could only see myself adapting to his lifestyle. I did not realize that my trying harder translated to making enough concessions to remain aboard.

Instinctively sensing a shift in me, Carl kept a more vigilant watch and even began to openly interrogate me as to my whereabouts and whether or not I was having an affair. He refused to understand that there was no longer anything he could do to me or give me to appease or keep me ensnared in his sticky web. As much as I feared the consequences, that part of me that was ready to flatten him, that felt that he was getting what he deserved, loved the cat and mouse game we played. With his heightening tendency toward violence, however, I was now walking an even more dangerous line.

Since Carl feared what I might say to others, he went to great lengths to inform anyone who had association with me that I had gone crazy. But he didn't stop there: his Florida psychic had revealed that in a previous life he had been an Indian chief, consequently, he chased disclosures about my mental instability with stories of his importance as this Indian chief character as if it was his present identity. This entire situation was a significant lesson for me in rising above his assertions, particularly facing the challenge to my new and fragile sense of self-esteem.

When I had initially reconnected with my parents, I had also found it necessary to reconnect with my paternal grandmother who was in her nineties. Prior to residing in a nursing home, she had been cared for by the oldest of my father's sisters. The first time I had gone to visit her, Carl had pressed to accompany me despite the deterioration of our relationship. When we arrived at the house, with two of my aunts present, Carl instantly took control and I watched everyone, including myself, shut down, very much reminiscent of the time years earlier when he delivered his harangue to my maternal grandmother shortly before her death. I singularly wished him invisible so that I could accomplish the purpose of my visit.

I continued periodically to visit my grandmother. Her health had been rapidly failing and already she had been rushed to the hospital by ambulance a number of times. I was certain it was nothing more than her fear of death that was keeping her alive. At one point she had been left to face having her feet amputated or having the arteries in her legs replaced. Knowing her need to present a proper appearance, it had been obvious that she would opt for the artery replacement. Her hope that she would be up and about after the surgery had been quickly dashed, and at my last visit, she had been propped in a wheel chair, smelling of urine and looking self-conscious. She pulled up her robe to show me the result of her surgery, and I had questioned the integrity of putting someone in her condition through such an ordeal. It had been clear to both of us, though unspoken, that she had sacrificed time by consenting to the artery replacement. I did not feel sorry for her. On the contrary, I had wanted to tell her that it was okay to let go, that death was not as difficult as she thought, even when I had no proof. Besides, I had not yet gotten sufficiently beyond family conditioning to be free to speak from my heart. She died a few weeks later, rushed to the hospital with heart failure for the last time. I was as distant and removed at her funeral as I had been at all funerals since attending the one of my high school friend whose death I had felt as a premonition. Instead, my attention was riveted on studying my relatives. I asked myself who I was to be the judge; it was okay to break out the cards and booze after the funeral. Mostly I was painfully aware of both my need and the impossibility of belonging. Little had changed since my childhood except that I could no longer escape from the realization that I had been no less acutely aware as a child than I was now.

One part of me had an unquenchable hunger for messages from my inner voice. At the same time, another part of me balked like a stubborn mule when I was instructed to do something that felt uncomfortable or unreasonable. Such as, "You have to make restitution for wasting your life," a message that began to surface shortly after I had received the message, "Heal thyself." While out running one day, I had heard this message once too often. I stopped; thrust my exasperation through my labored breath, "Okay! Okay! I know life is a gift! I know I've wasted my life! I know I have to make restitution! Now, just tell me what it is I have to do, and I'll do it!" The response was clear and resolute, and upon me before I had hardly completed my peevish demand: "You must let people know who you are!" Immediately, I was on my knees in the middle of the street with despair and fear surging from every cell in my body as if I had just received a death sentence. Protest was useless for I had already made the commitment to honor the promise I had made to myself.

What "letting people know who I am" entailed and why the message was so traumatic would take years to unfold. If I had known the significance of the message then, the nature of the steps involved, how strong the fear to take them would be, or the degree that "I" would have to die in order to succeed, I certainly would have attempted to go unconscious again. I had yet to understand that in reaching for growth we are only given as much as we can manage at any particular time. This meant that as long as I anchored my attention solely in the moment, I would be able to handle whatever was being required of me. Each moment I consciously lived would lead me, step-by-step, closer to wherever I was headed. I could no longer only keep busy and call that living my life.

I knew my first step was to bring my business with Carl to completion. He would not move out, and my lawyer had informed me that to avoid losing ground in the divorce proceedings, it was essential that I remain in the house until the divorce was final. This made no sense to me, but, aware of my reluctance to leave Adam during his last months of high school, and my inability to readily surrender anything to Carl, I acquiesced to my lawyer's advice.

Overshadowing my needs, insecurities and legal position was my feeling that Carl was becoming more dangerous and that we both were sucking Adam ever more deeply into the middle of our turmoil. Some noticeable part of me was beginning to push Adam out of the house, away from the tension and chaos and into a new reality, just as I had pushed him into the independence of first grade. Was I confusing his life with my plight and trying to take responsibility for saving both of us? I had no answer, but I went so far as to ask Carl to assuage Adam's fears that he would commit suicide over the divorce. Instead he used my request as leverage against me saying that he had not made a decision whether he was going to kill himself or not. I walked away too disgusted with him to react.

Adam was as frightened of leaving home as I was. I was confident that he could take charge of his own life and was capable of doing so despite the burdens that we as his parents had placed upon him. David, my therapist, had stated that if Adam were to have a chance at happiness, he had to see me happy. That comment was a grievous strike to this mother's heartstrings. In addition to owning the power in that message, I used it as a reference point in terms of how I could best support Adam. At the moment, with all of the emotions that I had stuffed for years erupting at every turn, I felt like an abysmal failure as a mother to my son.

One of the toughest aspects for Adam in facing his upcoming departure was leaving Amiga, his cat. This matter had been unexpectedly settled late the previous winter when Amiga suddenly and inexplicably quit eating. We enticed her with all of her favorite morsels, but she became less and less responsive. With my every urge to take her to the vet, I would remember how frightened of people she was and how traumatic the trip would be for her, especially in her present condition. I felt caught in a "damned if you do and damned if you don't" situation. My hope that Carl would pick up responsibility for this dilemma was in vain: he had never been able to handle death issues. Adam and I had watched day after day as Amiga became consistently weaker, but as much pain as we were experiencing, she appeared to be free of any. In fact, lying against Adam on his bed, hardly strong enough to move, she appeared very peaceful. Every effort I made to convince myself that she had to go to the vet had no force behind it.

My perspective shifted one night in early spring when I walked into Adam's room and found death energy permeating the space. I knew that Adam would not be able to handle Amiga dying in his room. Feeling as if I was in a trance, and not really understanding at that moment what I was saying, I told Adam that it was time to take her to the vet. Carl brought the car around while I wrapped her in a pillowcase. Then, to soothe her growing panic, I pressed her firmly to my heart as I carried her out to the car. Before Carl pulled away from the curb, she began to struggle simultaneously emitting a strange choking cough, after which she fell motionless in my arms while the entire time Carl yelled at me about how to handle her. I lay her precious body down on the seat and stifled my urge to scream at him to shut up as I got out of the car and returned to the house to tell Adam. It was not until then that he realized the nature of the situation. Adam, being quite intuitive, was already aware.

Overriding my sense of loss was a feeling of gratitude that Amiga had died in my arms rather than in Adam's bedroom. We buried her under a favorite old sentinel oak, close to where another of our pets had been buried a few years earlier. Nothing could cause me to doubt that Amiga willed her death in order to avoid being an obstacle in Adam's new life.

I pondered what Amiga had to do with Baby Tiger; my mind continually wandering to the time of her stroke and how I, as a teenager, had disgustedly watched her flounder in her attempts to jump on my bed or walk down the stairs. In my own fear of death, I had shunned her. I relived the pain of the morning my mother informed me of Baby Tiger's death, as well as my sense of loss and guilt for how I had treated her. I had never let go of the guilt, but perhaps being there for Amiga had been a means for me to make restitution for my previous insensitivity.

Carl was served legal notice the day before Adam's high school graduation ceremony. Overall, the incident put a damper on the occasion, especially because Carl accused me of orchestrating the timing. His reaction fed my belief that there was no end to the extent he would travel to make me the bad person.

Unrealistically, I had believed that our divorce could be amicable and had conceded to Carl that I was willing to work together without legal council to come to a financial agreement. Being unduly cooperative was a means for me to "aid" Carl since he had no money to hire a lawyer. If I had been more direct with myself, I would have admitted that I felt guilty over my belief that I had put him in this position, and that my offer was another way for me to make it acceptable to get my own needs met. Since the unfortunate timing of the arrival of the legal notice, he was openly on the offensive, leaving any of my efforts toward affability futile.

Driving Adam to the university would be the last occasion that we were together as a family. This was the first time that Adam had been away from home on his own, and it was only his age that kept his tears in check. The situation had the same flavor as when we had walked him to school for the first time, and now, as then, I kept reminding myself that I was supporting the right action. After unloading his possessions into the dorm room he would be sharing with his best friend, we went to lunch. But Adam's emotions got the best of him, and my heart ached for him. It would have taken little for him to jump in the car and call it quits. Carl tried humor while I tried reasoning, but to no avail. I kept saying to myself that there had to be a viable way to support him. When I heard, "Just get out and leave him alone," I dug a quarter from my bag and suggested that he dial his dorm number to see if he could catch his roommate. Ten minutes later his roommate was joining us for lunch. Since he had arrived the previous day, he was able to give Adam the scoop on how to make the initial adjustments. We said our goodbyes and left the two of them ready to explore the campus.

It was impossible to believe that the baby I had fought to bring into the world was now out of my life. This was one more colossal adjustment, and I was already on adjustment overload. A good cry in the woods when I arrived home helped me deal with my sense of loss; I had the faith that both Adam and I could deal with whatever was in store for us. We both had great tenacity. Without a doubt, we both were growing up. I could have been unnerved considering the disparity in our ages, but I was just grateful that I was maturing at all.

Like a gift from heaven, one final incident became a further impetus to exit my self-destructive reality. I had been telling Carl for some time that Pup, our second remaining dog, based on observing the massive amount of water he had been consuming, and then faster than I was able to respond, relieving himself in the basement, was in need of medical attention. He was well up in age and nothing could be unexpected. Carl had paid me no heed.

I came home one night to find Pup collapsed on the basement floor in the middle of a huge pool of his own urine. It was an awkward situation for no other reason than this canine had always been cantankerous enough that he never let anyone mess with him. How I could get him up the stairs and to the care he needed without him drawing blood was a serious consideration. Since it was too late to reach a vet, I phoned Carmen to ask her advice. (Her daughter had worked for a vet, and Carmen, herself, had dealt with her own menagerie.) She not only informed me of an emergency animal center, she insisted on accompanying me.

Taking a deep breath, I separated from my fear of being bitten, and then came to terms with the nausea I was experiencing from the stench of urine-soaked fur. Slowly, I approached the old fellow and softly explained what my intentions were. He lay on the cold, tile floor making no attempt to even raise his head. I gently toweled his long Collie coat of fur, accustoming him to the situation. Once reasonably dry, I ever so carefully slid my arms beneath him enough to lift him and carry him up the stairs. Clearly he had too little energy left to even growl at me. I did not need a doctor to tell me that this dear creature was close to taking his last breath. The vet's diagnosis matched mine right down to the fact that Pup was suffering kidney failure and could be either euthanized, or I could take him home only to have him die in a short time.

For me the decision was clear if only from a practical perspective: I had no time or energy or whatever else it took to deal with this situation any longer than necessary. Besides, a certain inner lucidness left me confident, as I had been with Amiga, that it was simply time for this ornery, old fella to move on. The hang-up was that he was Carl's favorite. Carmen asked me if we shouldn't wait until I contacted Carl, to give him the opportunity to participate—I thought I had already done that.

It was already after ten. There was a chance that Carl would soon be home from the racetrack, that is, if he lost his money early. It would have been easy for me to simply phone him, let him know what was occurring, and then prolong the situation until he arrived. Some part of me would not let me act on this consideration. I told myself that not attempting to phone him would come with a price, and that he had a right to be present. Buried guilt from having owned his insinuation that I had been responsible for the death of Amiga's sibling so many years before gnawed at my conscience. Yet, not once had he ever been inclined to be responsible for the health of any of our pets. In whatever struggle I was caught, ultimately I knew that I would not make a phone call. Something would not let me play out my guilt. Carmen said nothing when I informed the vet that I would have to take the body home with me and then asked to have a few moments alone with Pup.

Pup lay motionless on the cold, metal table watching me as I pulled a chair close enough to have intimate eye contact with him. Again, I took a deep breath to calm myself. This was painfully difficult: how many tearful goodbyes could I handle? As our eye contact strengthened, I connected to a deep calm within him. I softly requested that he not blame me for his death, that beyond all doubt I knew I was being guided. Like mental telepathy, I was sure I could hear him speaking to me, telling me that he understood that it was his time also to move on. I felt assured.

The vet gave a knock on the door and entered. He held in his hand the syringe of liquid that would put Pup's old body to rest. I didn't want the vet to see me cry; I wanted to hold my pain until I could get to the woods, but doing so required great an effort. Pup and I maintained unblinking eye contact while the vet searched for a vein viable enough to inject the fluid. As much he had lived like a lion, he quickly slipped away as gentle as a lamb. Afterward, I remained sitting beside him, staring into his lifeless eyes and feeling as if I was in a dream.

The vet informed me that the big pool of urine that immediately formed around him—he had had no water for considerable time—was a sure indication that his kidneys were completely shut down; this came as further reassurance that the situation was as it was meant to be. After paying for the service, the second vet stepped forward and handed me a box. Pup had been neatly secured in a blanket and placed inside.

Since it was nigh onto midnight after dropping Carmen off, there was little question that Carl would be home and, having discovered Pup missing, would have surmised what was afoot. He was out the front door hardly before I pulled to the curb. Without a word, I quickly opened the trunk, revealing the lump that had once been a member of this dysfunctional family. His contempt for me was already visible even before he shoved at me whether or not I had considered giving him a chance to be at Pup's side. He did not want an answer; he wanted me to feel remorseful. And all I wanted to do was yell at him that he had already had plenty of chances to deal with the situation, none of which he had acted on. I stifled my desire to scream at him, "Stay home and you'll be up on things!" or "Don't tell me how much you love this creature; after all, you were the one who right from the start beat him into obedience!" Instead, I remained silent, full of fear, anger and hurt, and defiantly struggling to not attack or attempt to exculpate myself. He then accused me of getting rid of his dog to get at him. Why would I expect comfort or understanding from Carl? I told myself that I was okay, I did not have to feel guilty, and I could bear up under his barrage of insults: this was only his pain speaking.

As he moved to the garage to get a shovel, he further yelled at me that he was going to phone Carmen to get to the bottom of this, to see if I were actually so insensitive that I would avoid calling him. My first impulse was to rush into the house and phone Carmen myself, to coach her as how to respond to Carl in order that it would go easier on me. Something stopped me. I had thought perhaps it was my disinclination to get her further involved.

While he carried the box containing Pup down the alley, heading for the woods to bury him, despite it being the middle of the night, I retreated to my bedroom where I lay in bed trying to give myself solace by reminding myself that Carl's anger was misplaced. He had not yet put to rest the time his mother, with her normal degree of callous indifference, had secretly put down her dog—Pup's mother and a favorite of Carl's—for no reason other than she no longer wanted to be bothered. Then when Carl had confronted her about her actions, she had claimed that the dog had been hit by a car and could not be saved. In the end, Carl had phoned the vet to "get the truth." It was one of the few times I witnessed his rage toward his mother come unleashed. If Carl had known of her plans soon enough to intervene, it would have meant that our menagerie would have been one size larger and most assuredly the demise of the mother of our first two dogs would have also come to fall on my shoulders. My final thought on the painful matter was that I was forever finished with pets.

With Adam away at college, I isolated myself in the bedroom when I was at home as a means to give Carl space and avoid confrontation. Nonetheless, he continued to walk in the bedroom under some pretense or another. He had agreed weeks before to move his belongings out of the bedroom, and recently I had told him that if he did not do so, I would. That he would take this as an ultimatum concerned me, but at the moment, I couldn't see any other way to make him leave me alone. Since I did not want to disturb his things, I decided to move the entire dresser to the extra bedroom. He came home while I was in the middle of the task. While he stood on one side of the dresser and pushed in one direction, I stood on the other side and pushed in the opposite. His rage was unconstrained; my determination was unwavering. I warned him that if he even made a move to harm me, I would phone the police. He recognized my seriousness.

It was during this confrontation that I let go of any lingering hope that I could safely remain in the house during the divorce proceedings or that he could honor me enough to move out. He was not in a financial position to make any changes. As much as we both needed a sense of home, his having yet to heal from his childhood humiliation of experiencing his family being evicted from their apartment (their belongings piled on the curb and them left with nowhere to live) made his need to stay in the house greater than mine. I had the financial means to move; it was logical that I be the one to do so. It was obvious that we could no longer live together. Further, I was exhausted from the endless struggle and unwilling to die over a house. Finally, it did not matter if my lawyer understood; the time for me to relocate had come.

Once I had shifted my mind set, what I needed to support the waiting changes in my life effortlessly followed. A few days after the "dresser" confrontation, with Carmen accompanying me, I walked into a newly carpeted, second floor apartment in an old, brick four-flat. The apartment had no porch or yard, but "my woods," along with a neighborhood park, were within walking distance. The emptiness, as well as the spaciousness of the four rooms reflected how much I needed an orderly, uncluttered, quiet space. My first thought upon seeing the adjoining living and dining room was that the space would be perfect to conduct yoga gatherings. I was delighted with the nine, large south and west facing windows, providing an abundance of sunlight, as well as a view of white ash and catalpa trees surrounding the building. I felt as if I was in a tree house. I tried using the high rent to justify avoiding the undertaking, but I was beginning to comprehend that my days of using poverty mentality to keep myself immobilized were coming to an end. The real issue was that what I knew I had to do was bumping up against my fear of doing it. A final compelling feature was that the landlord did not require a lease. I phoned David to hear his input, but only felt irritated by my own dependency. After all, this was my life and my actions could no longer be based on anyone else's sanction. Finally I put down a deposit to hold the apartment until the landlord verified my employment.

I did not inform Carl of my actions. At first I felt guilty that I could be as secretive with him as he had consistently been with me throughout our relationship. However, my plans were revealed to him when he took the message from my new landlord announcing that the apartment was mine. It was obvious that he was pleased with my decision, above all, because he could now have to himself what he most wanted.

As right as the decision felt, moving was painfully difficult. I disliked giving up the benefits of owning my own home, and caring for my flower gardens was a vital part of my life, regardless of how much time and energy they required. Already I had dug up a number of spring bulbs and replanted them at Carmen's with the expectation that I could enjoy them there. Also, the thought of being without our last remaining dog deeply saddened me. Overlooking all of this, even after securing the apartment, I was unable to forfeit my belief that if anyone should be moving, it should be Carl. Surely it was unreasonable that I should have to pay rent on an apartment, and upkeep and taxes on a house that he could not afford, while he was free of any financial responsibility. I would walk from room to room examining items and wondering what I was supposed to take, not wanting to miss out on my "dessert." (Nothing had any significant value outside of being bones of contention.) How often had my mother and I fought over what belonged to whom? My position that I had a right to take whatever I wanted sent me immediately nose-diving into the same kind of guilt and greediness I experienced in regard to her. It became apparent that I was afraid to provoke Carl by taking anything to which I knew he was attached: to give him ammunition to shoot holes in the divorce proceedings. If I took what I wanted, I'd feel guilty. If I took nothing, I'd feel angry. Clearly, physically moving was much easier than mentally and emotionally moving. If I were going to survive, however, I had to release myself from all attachments, especially my indignation, as well as desist from using him to vent my anger. If I were going to survive, I had to just get on with my life.

In the end, I took only my bed and a few odd pieces of furniture, along with my personal belongings. Except for the couple of large items, I made the shift from my old environment to my new reality completely on my own. I watched my inclination to feel sorry for myself and to wish there were someone around to aid me. Still I knew that, whatever this move was really about, I had to complete it alone. Notwithstanding, my persistent sense of injustice continued to color my thoughts. But my days of hopelessness and helplessness—my days of self-indulgent misery—were in the process of waning. The real move was from an ingrained mode of survival to a new way of being. I was rising out of my environment.

5

Disentangling Myself

I had surmised that my life would be much easier, possibly even fun, now that I had heaved myself out of "my bed" and was focused on achieving freedom. This was incorrect. Geographically relocating, in and of itself, did not translate as emancipation from my past this time any more than moving to Chicago at age nineteen had meant freedom from the quagmire with my parents. Gathering all the fragments of myself out of the old space would be a monumental, multifarious task, as well as consume considerable time. Besides having no road map for direction or guidance in how to excavate my real identity, I felt ill-equipped to deal with the unfamiliar reality into which I was being moved, or more appropriately stated, dragged toward in an ironclad grasp at such breakneck speed that I was convinced I was going mad. I was incapable of comprehending that what I was actually accomplishing was not simply removing myself from an addictive lifestyle: I was dissolving my entire karmic history. This had nothing to do with becoming perfect, but everything to do with learning to live fully centered in the present: the essential prerequisite to letting the world see me for who I really am. By trusting in this process (surrendering to the process) I ensured that my life would be more overwhelming than it had ever been. However, to live the change that was required in order to live my purpose, I had only to be right where I was in the moment.

Even before I was finished cleaning and putting order to my new abode, I was shown the real reasons that I was in my own space—the need to cry. For years, the need to cry had been besieging me, but I had carefully concealed or contained my tears until an opportune time to give them free rein. In my newly discovered solitude, my tears flowed spontaneously, erupting at all hours of the day and night. I would hysterically break down mid-thought, while reading or scrubbing the floor, or at three in the morning. Music could evoke irrepressible sobbing, especially new-age music. Even when I was not lamenting, I was on the verge. I cried so much I thought I might cry myself blind. But this crying was different from in the past. It was no longer born from self-pity or a sense of helplessness. These tears were the means to bring long buried pain to consciousness—eons of my soul's anguish—which was obscuring my greater awareness.

The same energy to which I connected in my woods was present in my apartment, but I had yet to understand that there was a relationship between crying myself empty and these para-sensory experiences. An electrifying energy would gradually engulf me, indicating an impending encounter, pulsating my senses beyond the physical world. I was powerless to explain or restrain these timeless interludes and exited them feeling exhausted and disoriented, as if I had just been returned from a UFO abduction. An uninterrupted night's sleep was rare. Part of me dreaded the impact of these episodes, while another part anticipated and welcomed them.

I handled these energy experiences—and my mushrooming sexual energy as well—by practicing diaphragmatic yogic breathing, balancing the energy inundating me. I was unaware that I was learning to profoundly center myself; indeed, every experience necessitated acquiring a new center. I was aware that I constantly took slow, deep, deep breaths. Another way to handle these energy "hits" was to take long, blistering hot baths or showers. I also used vigorous exercise.

It was a wrenching conflict taking a financial position regarding the divorce. I had invested a considerable amount of money into the house, and the majority of our personal possessions, including Carl's vehicle, had been purchased from my income. I could have dickered over everything. In contrast, the part of me that operated from guilt believed that I deserved nothing. My guilt was compounded because I knew how attached Carl was to the house and that he would be forced to sell to honor any kind of decent settlement. He hastily returned me to sobriety one day when he mentioned that he was contemplating demanding maintenance from me as part of the divorce settlement. Under no circumstances was I willing to be his provider any longer. In the end, I informed my lawyer that all I wanted in terms of property settlement was fifty percent of the value of the house and nothing more. As Adam was approaching eighteen, child custody or support were not issues. Unexpectedly, and not without trepidation, I even hid half of my savings in a friend's account just in case Carl surfaced with further surprises.

When my lawyer presented me with the initial contract he had drawn up, my fragile hope for a quick divorce evaporated. I tried to convince him that asking for seventy percent of the value of the house would leave Carl decidedly less cooperative than he already was. My lawyer defended his approach as standard procedure; that he had to leave room for negotiation, while I slid into a panic just thinking about defending my life when Carl saw that I was asking for so much. Oh well, I reflected, the entire sum of Auntie's money, except for the house and a few tokens of magnanimity had gone to the races. As much as Carl had professed to be his mother's support, he had not even given her any of the inheritance. Neither had he contributed to Adam's education. I had suggested that sharing Adam's education be part of the divorce agreement. He flatly refused. Knowing that he had also stolen money from Adam as a child infuriated me all the more. I let my lawyer know he was up for a tough fight.

Carl had hired a female lawyer, which was a conspicuous indication that he was turning power over to no one. No communication from her now forced my lawyer to take court action: she forgot her legal documents for the first court appearance and the judge was obliged to reschedule. At the second, she requested a continuance. At the third scheduled appearance, Carl cornered me while I waited in the foyer for my lawyer. With his upper lip quivering, an overt forewarning that he was losing control, I was subjected to another tirade on my flaws. My only recourse was to seek protection from a security guard. It was in the wake of this incident that my lawyer was finally beginning to awaken to the nature of the challenge we both were facing.

Admittedly, I had been fueling Carl's insecurities through my own behavior. Periodically I would drive to the house at intervals when I knew he would be away. I would then work in my flower gardens or take the dog for a run in the woods. The longer I remained, the more bitter I became over feeling like an outsider in my own home; although, from a different perspective, I knew I had outgrown being there and would never return even if given the chance. Still, I habitually took something when I left. I rationalized that I had a use for what I took or had paid for everything anyway and could take whatever I pleased. Nevertheless, I inevitably felt as if I was stealing, especially since what I took I did not necessarily want. Carl knew when I had been there and when something was missing and, although he didn't actually value what I took any more than I did, he was infuriated that he had no modicum of control over my comings and goings. He blustered about changing the locks but was aware that he was in no legal position to do so. I wrestled with my aberrant behavior, but it seemed that circumstances in my life had more control over me than I had over them.

With Kent and me both free of living with spouses and able to openly have the relationship we had been anticipating, rather than it blossoming, it was wilting before my eyes. Integrating our lives ultimately meant me molding my life to his. This might have occurred had it not been for an incident in the spring when I received a couple of bee stings directly to my eye while setting up new hives. Following treatment for an allergic reaction, I then received a warning from the emergency room doctor that if I continued to keep bees, the next sting would cost me my life. I defiantly refused to believe him or be scared to the extent that I continued to keep bees anyway. But with the precautions of suiting up, wearing a bee veil and gloves (as I should have anyway), keeping a syringe of adrenaline at hand in case of emergency, agreeing to a five-year immunotherapy program, and with the doctor's admonition constantly running through my head, the satisfaction I had gotten from beekeeping was waning. I finally asked myself if it was worth the risk, and what I was trying to prove anyway. I gave up keeping bees, but not without feeling victimized and angry: angry that I had to give up the one thing I could call my own at the nature center; angry that I had to fear for my life, especially when in nature; and angry that Kerry got a smug sense of satisfaction from my plight. The two truths, which I was reluctant to own because then I would have had to abandon feeling victimized, were that I had become bored and tired of the endless amount of time and energy beekeeping required and that, without the bees, there was little else to keep Kent and me together.

We continued to talk about sharing a future once we were both free from the constraints of marriage, but I was unable to see how I could live my life within the peculiar context it was taking and at the same time remain involved with him. Already this affair was only slightly less consuming than my life with Carl. Besides this, the sexual aspect was proving troublesome. I remained like a sweet, sexual delicacy that Kent had never before tasted and of which he could not get enough. Initially, I had freely given myself to him regardless of how clandestine, awkward, or even demeaning our meetings were, much like I initially had with Carl. At the same time, I deluded myself with rationales such as: he is a kind, generous and worthwhile man; he would never be abusive; he enjoys the outdoors as much as I do; he genuinely loves me and when he reaches the sexual saturation point, we can begin having a more shared experience; he has an interest in, if not values, my metaphysical endeavors. But I was not that patient. Instead, to tolerate being together, I began to push to bring our relationship to a "higher level." I even openly explained that I did not want to be merely a sexual object. As much as Kent tried to understand and interact in a way that would meet my needs, he was stuck in his own behavioral pattern, and we were both becoming discouraged. In an anguished attempt to come to terms with my frustrations, one day I unexpectedly blurted out that I saw our relationship as dead, but added that out of the ashes I believed we could build a new one. He responded by stepping into his vehicle and driving away.

Rather than allowing situations to work themselves out or seeing them as perfect whatever they were, my ingrained response was to "fix" them. This situation was no exception. To my bewilderment, every attempt to phone Kent resulted in my hand literally being frozen a few inches from the receiver. After several days of the same, I accepted that there was a force greater than my understanding intervening.

For "homework," I assessed my behavior with Kent and was unable to deny that I had been obsessed with the relationship. The entire situation was undignified. Sometimes, when I had been uncontrollably agitated, especially at work, I had felt as if I would go crazy if I couldn't talk to him. During these moments, I would compulsively phone him at home, hoping that he would answer and not his wife. When we were able to steal time together, he was unable to provide the comfort or understanding that I sought. I pondered more seriously the nature of so-called love and so-called relationships, along with my propensity to lose myself in them. However, I did acknowledge that, outside of the drama we shared, I held a strong sense of love for him.

Living for the first time without the distractions of a relationship afforded me greater visibility into the extent of my fear of being alone. How I loved to walk into my apartment, close the door behind me, shut my eyes, take a deep breath and absorb myself in solitude. Without warning, though, I could flip out of this peacefulness and into a feeling that my sanctuary was a prison. At such a time, I would find escape by talking on the phone or going shopping. Afterward, I would chastise myself for wasting time creating meaningless conversations or otherwise dishonoring those I used to slake my insecurities. Since I essentially enjoyed being by myself more than with someone else, I tried making sense out of this behavior but was unable to follow the meandering and confusing lines of thought to their ultimate conclusion: when I was by myself I was actually being with myself, and being with myself was about being with something much greater, finally leading to the disappearance of self. It was a path I was already relentlessly forging but simultaneously resisting. Now resurfacing for my mature examination was the preoccupation of my early childhood: the disappearance/destruction of "me" was the real crux of my fear.

Between therapy and my solitude providing further time to reflect on myself, I was more intensely recognizing the degree of my negativity and how it permeated every aspect of my life, and how my fear supported that negativity. In order to survive, my fear had procured a plethora of disguises, which resulted in me living my life in a state of defensiveness. I only wanted resolve, and I wanted to extricate myself from my self-imposed limitations. This was not about what Carl or my parents had done to me. There was no more time or room to blame anyone. I had little trust that anything positive could happen to me without my all-consuming effort, but I had to know what freedom from my own negativity felt like. And so, I put all my energy to the task.

Reading a variety of popular self-help books continued to provide me with various perspectives as to how to heal the emotions and become a positive person, but merely healing my emotions did not seem like enough. I wanted to get rid of my emotions. I had no patience for the way they disrupted my life and limited my understanding. I wanted to be a Mr. Spock of Star Trek fame. I told myself that I was crazy, that without emotions to filter experiences, there would be no way to relate to life. Nevertheless, I was beginning to notice that there was, that there had always been, a part of me—the observer self—standing outside of my struggles watching myself engage in them. That observer self had no emotions—no judgment. As much as I wanted clarity on this, I would have to be matured into it. For now my emotions were playing an essential role to moving me into a greater reality.

My work with David continued to be extremely intense, but an admittedly expedient method in examining the nature and depth of my fears and dysfunctional behaviors. I came to each session with an understanding of what I needed to address, while he provided the support I needed to work through these issues. I inevitably departed ready to move on to the next concern at hand. But the longer I was in therapy, the more I found myself having to look at certain aspects of my awareness that I would rather have avoided. This included the fact that, in some way, there was a co-dependence between David and me. We spent enough of my sessions discussing him that I knew as much about his life as he did mine; I came to realize that he had no fewer unresolved issues than I did. Sometimes I was annoyed that he spent such a large portion of my session talking about himself. When I talked, I compulsively explained my thoughts in minute detail to assure that I was fully understood. Further, there was a recognizable need in me for him to view me as special or different from his other clients. I hated being this obsessive and needy, but I had no control over my behavior. At the same time, I felt myself needing to have a more personal relationship with him: not sexual but platonic (although I had wondered what it would be like being sexual with him). I wanted to meet with him informally to explore myself outside of the limitations of professional restrictions. He had already informed me that he had once had an affair with his wife's best friend and, although it had never become sexual, he had taken responsibility for what he had created. He was ambiguous as to whether he was setting boundaries by divulging this or if he was simply sharing something further about himself.

Nonetheless, my need to have a more intimate interaction with him began to manifest in an unforeseen way. To avoid traffic, as I rationalized, I scheduled my appointment for nine at night, which made me his last client of the day. The drawback was that his schedule was, by then, considerably backed up and my appointment was most often delayed. The benefit was that my session could, and most often did, run overtime. Afterward, while I wrote out my check, he would play one of the many songs that he had composed and recorded or another piece that was relevant to the session, adding to our time together. I felt selfish taking up his time without further compensation and keeping him on duty when his day was over, but he appeared to support the situation as much as I did. Over the course of my therapy, he would expose me to many songs, many of which would play an important role in my healing. I valued this personal interaction. Meanwhile, I continued to try to convince myself that my behavior bordered inappropriate, that I was being self-centered and should know better. I even tried to persuade myself that I should verbalize my doubts to him, but something else—a greater force in operation— would not allow my lessons to be restricted by protocol and, therefore, continually overrode my doubts.

Now that my life was simplified and the one year-grace period allowed to complete my graduate paper for credit was nearing, I renewed my commitment to fulfill that responsibility. This time, however, I followed my urge to alter my original topic to embrace a more social perspective. After collecting the resources I thought I needed, I shut myself in my apartment for an entire weekend with the intent to have a finished product by Sunday night. The weekend came to a close and I had manifested nothing but frustration. A second attempt, and then a third, produced the same empty-handed results.

While going through my fruitless weekend rituals of inundating myself in the literature I had gathered, I was consistently sidetracked reading about Daniel Boone blazing the first functional trail through the Appalachian Mountains. His courage and tenacity in the face of uncountable dangers deeply impressed me. The more I read and reread about him the more my interest in writing about anything else dwindled. I viewed Daniel as a true pathfinder. He blazed a trail through the wilderness then retraced his steps, gathered his family as well as others who had interest, and led them to a new existence. Some participants lost their lives (including one of his sons) to Indian attack, some turned back before the journey had hardly begun, while others went only so far and homesteaded at that point. Nevertheless, some pioneers made it the entire distance. Those who did formed a new community. As much literature as I could find about the journey itself, there was precious little on the nature of the development of the resulting community. For me, this was like reading an adventure story with the pertinent final chapters missing. Therefore, I spent hours contemplating how they might have rallied together to make their community a success, what difficulties they actually experienced and what efforts were required to maintain a collective experience. But telling a story does not suffice as a graduate paper.

At some point, my advisor phoned to discuss my progress. After revealing that I could not find a concrete topic, he claimed that if I created an outline, I would have fewer problems. He made an appointment to see me, as well as my outline. At the appointment, after assessing the outline, he looked at me and stated, "I'm disappointed in you. This is not the level of work I expect from you." I was undisturbed by his comment, for it was not the level of work I expected from myself either. I explained that there was a block that I was unable to identify or move beyond which prevented me from writing this paper.

I returned home even more determined to fulfill my obligation, but the block remained. While I persisted with my efforts, the year ran out. To manage my mortification over my sense of failure, I told myself that I would finish the paper when the block was gone, after which I could re-enroll in the class to receive credit for my efforts. Eventually, I would write about a trail blazer who founded a new community in an unfamiliar territory, only it would be a first-hand account, and I would be living the answers to the questions I had had regarding the successful development of the Boone community. Daniel Boone had been the reference point. My discontent over my perceived failure to produce actually supported my continued movement forward.

Unexpectedly one day, I found myself walking into a new age bookstore for the first time in my life. The energy in the store overtook me and I was mesmerized by the stimulation of my senses. Altered state took on new meaning. Powerless to keep my hands off the crystal-laden trays: handling the crystals sent painful surges of energy running through my hands. The scent of incense wafting through the air coupled with the sounds of new age music vibrated my senses out of the limitations of the physical and I struggled to contain the tears taking form deep inside of me. My eyes danced from title to title on the seemingly endless display of new age books. I wanted them all. In the end, I walked out with a music tape, a package of incense and two books, one about chakras and the other, entitled **The Seat of the Soul,** which provided explanations of new age concepts. At home, I pulled out **The Seat of the Soul** and immediately devoured it. My urge was to make it my personal gospel, but I was informed that it was important for those who needed a primer. I thought that if anyone needed a primer, I was the one. On the other hand, I was vaguely aware that the material presented was only a drop of greater reality. Still, I tried to use the book to meet my personal needs. The book on chakras, in and of itself, did not entice me, being quite technical; instead it provided a foundational understanding for me to begin to further explore the dynamics of my own energy system beyond what I had learned from practicing yoga.

Despite beginning to move out of my addictive behavior, I fell into the trap of trying to define the form that my learning was to take. Hence, I collected class schedules and fliers from various places that offered spiritually oriented classes and workshops. First I attended a tai chi class offered through a local Chinese herb store. In practicing the movements, I consistently drifted out of my body and off into other realities, making it impossible to follow instruction or stay synchronized with other participants.

From tai chi, I moved to kundalini yoga. With the intense and prolonged deep breathing, I felt even more out-of-control than with Tai Chi and it took hours, if not longer, to recover. Nevertheless, I was not willing to let go of the class. Nor was I willing to release the belief that I would eventually have the deeply intense interactions with other classmates for which I yearned. This was despite my present frustration of being unable to relate to any of them.

The instructor, to whom I was inclined to give significant respect, gave much attention to group chanting, but as with singing, I was powerless to manage this. Thoroughly frustrated one day, I informed him of my difficulties. He gave a simple response, "You keep your head bowed." His message, whatever it meant, instantly tore at me. Feeling equally furious and helpless and knowing that he could not and would not say anything further, that in fact he had perfectly communicated exactly what he was meant to for me to move into a greater awareness, I asked him to explain. Being the great teacher that he was, he ignored my request. However, the following week he handed me a small, well-worn book. I recognized that he was giving the book to me, but managed to diminish the gift by insisting on returning it when I was finished with it. Learning to receive was another lesson for another time. I anticipated reading the book, believing that there was surely something important for me in it since my teacher had given it to me. The book read like a philosophical treatise on how to be a perfect yogi, and after reading the first ten pages, I could do little more than skim through it. Feeling the importance of having the book, yet being unable to discern exactly what about it was important, was acutely frustrating for my linear mind which could not comprehend that the information in the book was already intact subconsciously.

From the moment of my instructor's comment, I was continually seeing a vision of myself sitting in a perfect lotus position, except for one flaw; my head was bowed down, constricting my throat chakra. As a result of this vision, I was becoming aware of how I held my entire body: spine straight, shoulders set back and raised to a point of tenseness, and head bowed slightly forward as if an unidentifiable weight pressed on it from behind. While I told myself that it would be impossible for anyone to carry herself in this tense, unnatural manner, that it would have negative short-term as well as long-term effects, I was shown that this was, indeed, how I carried myself, both physically and energetically. Further, I began to recognize that for as long as I could remember, I had carried an intense pain in my neck, which other than having to support my head in a special way when I slept, I ignored. The message among my teacher's words, the book and the visions, but which I could not hear—partly because I was trying so hard to figure it out and partly because I wasn't ready—was that healing my throat chakra was a key to becoming an adept.

Continuing to believe that I could benefit from classes and workshops, as well as needing to become comfortable going out on my own, I registered for a couple more. I even went to a class in which participants were taught to have out-of-body experiences. Although my out-of-body experiences were common, I thought perhaps there was something further I needed to learn or that I could not consider myself proficient until I could make my experiences happen on demand. The leader, an expert/author on OBE, had created a complicated and lengthy step-by-step process. This included awakening oneself in the heart of the night just enough to maintain a subliminal state and be able to follow further instructions, which included sitting in a half-reclining position and then performing some mental maneuvers with the goal of flying around in outer space. We were then taken through a couple of exercises that I skeptically considered to be manipulated and misleading. However, participants seemed quite serious about obtaining the desired experiences, for no other reason than for the thrill or sense of accomplishment. When I asked myself why I had really attended this class, I was immediately shown the undeniable desire in me, not simply to be acknowledged, but viewed as spiritually advanced or learned. I had even been taken by surprise when I had volunteered to share a personal experience with the class. My heart had begun to race and I had begun to perspire as I habitually did when divulging anything of a personal nature. But participants had been noticeably impressed. A more important observation was how my ego had been noticeably inflated. This incident left me even more acutely aware of my need to be recognized; I hated this predicament, but I could do little about it.

I went home with the instruction book fully intending to master having out-of-body experiences on command. Instead, what I received in the process of practicing was an intense awareness that I was putting myself in danger by continuing my pursuit. With reluctance I abandoned my efforts, aggravated.

Through my educational and my naturalist activities, I had formed what I had thought I wanted and needed, and what I considered to be female friendships. I had gone so far as to dispense with publicly teaching yoga and had begun instead to teach it without financial gain to a small circle of women, including Carmen, in my apartment. It took little effort to recognize the degree of dysfunction and insecurity—considerably more than my own—of the women I attracted. Having worked on my own issues to the degree I had, others' issues were readily identifiable. (I no longer looked at myself as the only dysfunctional person in the world.) However, it was a compulsive need to help these women whenever they needed me and even when I knew that they were embroiled in their affairs to the extent that they were not going to be moving forward very quickly, if at all. Without them, I would have had to face being alone, an issue I was yet unable to fully recognize, let alone own. A greater understanding would be that these women were reflecting back to me, whatever the degree, what I needed to see about myself in order for me to move forward. While I was predisposed to judge them, they were actually a great gift to my advancement.

It was through a thoroughly disconnected woman who had latched onto me during a workshop, I received a most profound reference point in terms of how I would be required to live my life. She happened to mention one day that she had seen a quote on a friend's bathroom wall which she thought would be of interest to me. Without hesitation, I asked her to copy it for me. The quote came from an Elder Aboriginal Woman: "If you have come to help me, you are wasting your time. But if you come because you know your liberation is bound up with mine, then let us work together." As I read the quote, I could feel the meaning, whatever it was, anchor deep within the heart of my understanding. It was like reading gospel: I felt deeply moved, deeply humbled. I made a copy to keep on my refrigerator and then copied the quote onto the front cover of my journal and every new journal I started thereafter, in order to keep it fresh in my thoughts. I had an idea of the validity of the quote, but it would be years and many steps down my own path to enlightenment before I understood its full significance. Then it would only come through living it, living the knowing that freedom cannot be attained individually—where my current focus was—for no one is free until we are all free.

Also through my educational undertakings and my naturalist activities, I had greater interactions with men. I discovered that they were not in the least concerned about women being virgins. The sexual part of me, that I had kept stifled, was breaking from its shackles. It churned inside of me, erupting everywhere, butting against my insistence to keep relationships platonic and leaving me altogether distracted with the struggle to control it. A bike ride, a visit to the museum, or an unassuming conversation over a cup of tea inevitably led to that dreaded moment when I would have to deflect the inevitable advance. Even frankly prefacing interactions with, "I'm only interested in casual relationships," made little difference. Making matters worse, as if I was on my first date, it remained impossible for me to directly say no to sexual overtures. The best I could do was back away, play naive or engage in a tussle.

One incident became serious. When a young man greeted me on the street as I returned from an afternoon bike ride, I suddenly realized that he was generally around whenever I was leaving or entering my apartment. Shortly after that he virtually blocked my entry as I returned home from work one day, earnestly beseeching me to talk with him for a few minutes. Even with alarm bells going off in my head, I could feel myself being sucked into this young man's apparent pain. Not wanting him near my apartment, I walked down the street with him as we talked, hoping to pacify his need. My fear was triggered when I learned that his girlfriend, when he was a teenager, had poured boiling water on his penis. Subsequently, he had spent much time in and out of mental hospitals. He was disgruntled that the girls he singled out to be his girlfriends continually refused to "cooperate," and he lived in the garage behind his mother's house. The depth of his rage toward women felt akin to Carl's. As he pressured me to be his girlfriend, I discreetly refrained from saying I was not interested and instead equivocated that I was almost old enough to be his mother. Unrelenting in his pressure, I finally hedged that perhaps we could go for a bike ride sometime when I was free. My mistake.

My mistake became his thread of hope. He badgered me all the way home as to when we could ride. Then notes appeared on my car and he began waiting for me outside my apartment building. When I could not avoid making contact with him, I urged him to seek professional help rather than take bike rides with me. Instead, he began ringing my doorbell at all hours of the night, and otherwise hung around my car waiting for me to leave. I was terrified, and therefore helpless to know how to handle the situation, other than avoid him, which only fed his determination. I could not believe that my sense of freedom could be so suddenly eradicated and that I could, once again, feel so preyed upon and reduced to living in fear. I kept asking myself why I had to pay such a big price for such a small mistake. Why I had to hole up in my apartment or sneak out the back door hoping I could escape his persistent effort to be with me.

The situation came to a head one weekend when Adam was home from school. The rage Adam carried from his childhood, his intolerance for belligerent, aggressive men, coupled with his conditioning to protect me, exploded as he confronted the young man attempting to damage my car. The man, in return, threatened to kill Adam. When I called a relative, a captain in the police force, about the situation, he urged me to file a complaint immediately. I did not want to do that; I simply wanted the man to go away and leave me alone. Later that night, he began incessantly pressing on my doorbell. At two in the morning when he left off, I wanted to believe that he had given up, but somehow I knew he had merely changed tactics. Subsequently, an inner prompting pulled me out of bed and to the dining room window from where I could see him squatting beside my car and letting the air out of my tires. I phoned the police immediately. They cornered him, and after the skirmish that ensued, I had little choice but to file the complaint.

He came to court with his mother. In the lobby when he pointed me out to her, she approached me and proceeded to castigate me as if I was the villain. She demanded to know why I had not come to her to resolve this problem instead of the police. Her words instantly triggered my bad-person syndrome. Just as fast, I was blaming myself for the state of affairs while my helplessness unleashed my anger. To make matters worse, a male friend, who had accompanied me, and who was a reactionary person himself, was ready to take both mother and son on. What a great distraction for all the people waiting around, I thought, like a circus show. When push came to shove, I was forced to step out of my helplessness mode enough to diffuse the imminent explosion ready to occur.

In court, the judge informed my pursuer that if he ever spoke to me again, he would be arrested and put in jail. Finishing with him, the judge turned and ordered me to stay away from my pursuer. Although incensed that I had gone through such a nightmare only to be viewed as an instigator, particularly by a male, I knew deep inside that the pain that I had connected to in this man forced the outplay of this drama. I also knew that it was the same pain that my father carried, as well as Carl and almost every man whose path crossed mine. I was as responsible for this conflict as the man I viewed as the perpetrator. Seeing even as little as I did in regard to how I was a contributor in the situation, I was chagrined and certainly unwilling to openly own it. Imagining how others would view me if the truth became known shut me down all the more. Intuitively, I knew this lesson was not complete. I had, in fact, avoided the lesson. I knew this instinctively when I listened to the mother's words, "Why didn't you come to me about this problem?" I knew that I had allowed myself to be talked into calling the police. I knew it felt all wrong to go to court. I knew I had not addressed the situation from a place of strength. I had not addressed my fear. I had backed away, allowing the system to fix the problem, rather than embracing my own resolution. On the other hand, I was unaware that I would get another chance to master this lesson—as many chances as necessary to master all of my impending lessons, for this was about ultimate mastery. There would be another stalker entering into my life shortly. This time the situation would be more deadly than I could imagine.

Despite my feeling that either all the men in the world were unhealthy or else that was all I was able to attract, I realized that sooner or later I was going to have to allow this sexual character in me to express itself. However, I found no one appealing enough to get that close. The times I made attempts felt as if I was betraying some indefinable part of myself. A male friend suggested that I create a sexual liaison with a friend of his who was discontent in his marriage and was looking for non-committed sex. This friend and I made contact, which was followed by regular phone conversations, but I was compelled to go no further. The mother of one man announced that I should marry her son. She thought I would be good for him and could keep his life together for him. Resolute, I held fast to a belief that when I was healthy enough, I could then have a worthwhile relationship.

I had supported Carl, my son, various in-laws, in addition to myself for much of my life. Despite this, I had never lived beyond my means nor been in debt. I had consistently had something, regardless of how nominal the amount, hoarded away for an emergency or some unexpected need. Maintaining this position had never eased my obsessive fear of being unexpectedly caught unable to adequately support myself. This insecurity was tested when Charles, a retired man, began volunteering at the nature center. He was affable, effective working with children, and liberal with his time. I valued our friendship and our meaningful conversations, and even considered him a father figure, while I tried to deny my neediness. I had been supportive when his wife unexpectedly died and he supported me through my divorce. We occasionally went out for coffee or had dinner together, while I held on to the belief that I had finally formed a successful platonic relationship with a man. When he had first given me a potted plant, I thought little of it; he had given Kerry one also, and he was clearly a generous man. But, when I found a fifty-dollar bill in the card he gave me for my birthday, my suspicions began to rise, so I attempted to return the money. He would not hear of it.

He then began to ask me if I would like any of his wife's jewelry. I consistently responded that he should give the jewelry to his daughter, who was actually the offspring of his first marriage. One day when I stopped by on an errand, he drew me into his bedroom and pulled out a drawer full of jewelry, much of it obviously valuable. He urged me to pick whatever and as much as I wanted. Some part of me was enticed, yet I was not seduced. I claimed that I was not in the habit of wearing jewelry and could not take anything, but if my having something was important to him, he could choose the item himself. After refusing a further offer of a choice of diamond rings, I finally accepted an opal pendant and a gold chain. Afterward, I felt extremely guilty and was fearful of the repercussions should Carl find out. I took the items home and stashed them in my jewelry box.

Soon after that, he began to press what I considered large sums of money—three or five hundred dollars—on me, claiming that I worked so hard and made so little and that the cash would take the stress off of me while I finished school. I was becoming disheartened by his behavior, as well as my failing efforts to maintain a guilt-free relationship, but I suppressed my feelings by continuously reminding myself that he was a devout Catholic and a well-respected man in the community and that he was quite generous with everyone. I repeatedly explained to him that I dearly cherished our relationship, but I considered it platonic, and I did not want or need his money. Sometimes he took the money back; other times he flatly refused. I was enticed by the novelty of being taken care of as much as repulsed by the entire situation: repulsed by the idea that behind the gentleman's facade lurked a lascivious old man. The money was eventually accompanied by attempted affections and a showy proposal of marriage. I questioned myself as to why I failed to simply tell him to get lost, but the thought of doing so triggered my "you-can-only-say-something-nice" conditioning. One part of me argued that he really loved me; he was old and might die if I simply shut him out and then I would have to carry the burden of his death. Another part of me claimed vehemently that I owed him nothing. Unable to simply release the relationship, I fell instead into my typical discomfort between obligation and protecting myself.

The worst moment came when he informed me that he had added my name to his will. Although he never explained what that meant, just the idea alone sent me into extreme distress. I could not imagine the degree to which his friends and family would think that I had bamboozled him when it came time to read the will. I begged him to reverse his decision. It felt like a life and death matter that I convince him to change his mind. At the same time, I did not think that my reaction could be more over-dramatic. From whatever angle I studied the matter or tried to convince myself that inheriting money was a normal occurrence, I was thoroughly agitated by the thought of having my name in his will.

Interestingly, receiving money without having worked for it complicated rather than solved my money issues, as did having money that I was free to simply spend on myself. Carl had carried a mental list of things he promised to buy for me—as he had with Adam also—when he struck it big at the racetrack. Some part of me had clung to those promises as tenaciously as I had to my father's. Nonetheless, when Auntie's money came into his hands, and he finally had the means to fulfill his promises, he did nothing more with it than he had ever done. I was forced to look at the entire situation more honestly. The truth was anything that he ever promised me I could give directly to myself if only I hadn't given my money to him in the first place. Giving him money was the only realistic chance I had for him to keep his promises to me. I realized how much more I needed the promise (I was addicted to the thrill of those promises, much like Carl to his anticipation of his big win) than what they would bring. It was as if I wanted someone else to take care of me although I was able to take care of myself. Yet, when someone *was* willing to support me, my sense of unworthiness was triggered.

Here, juxtaposed my shame and confusion, as well as my blossoming awakening, was a longing to be given nice things and to know what it would be like to be lavish—to buy something because I wanted it as opposed to "making it do" or it being reduced enough in price to justify having it. Because it was much easier, I mostly used Charles' subsidy to aid Adam rather than myself, and I banked anything left over. As with most circumstances, I felt helplessly trapped by this one also, but whatever form my circumstances took, as I brought my greater awareness to them, layer by layer, strand by strand, I understood that each was ultimately a facet of my healing process.

My guilt over having abandoned Adam by leaving the family did not lessen after we each went our own way. Logistics of both our lifestyles made time together feel scheduled and awkward. I had never asked him if he wanted to live with me when I moved into my apartment. I rationalized that his home was in the house, and that was where he would naturally want to return when not at the university. Since I had neither an extra bedroom nor a couch, if he did stay with me, I would have to be the one sleeping on the living room floor. I was relieving him of having to choose between his father and me. I further rationalized that, in fact, he needed to be with his father because of their unresolved issues. Although there was truth to all of this, I was using my rationalizations to hide from the shame-inducing fact that I did not want Adam to live with me. I wanted to be free of his and his father's slovenly ways, free of domesticity and everything it encompassed. I wanted my maternal responsibilities to be over. It was tough to be honest with myself about my needs when I considered myself a failure as a mother. Taking care of people was an ingrained means of survival. It had been my only avenue to feel a part of my family, and now my burgeoning new sense of self was clashing against my Cinderella addiction.

I had a degree of awareness of how adept Adam and I were at manipulating each other. I believed that I had to do or give Adam something in order for him to want to have anything to do with me. True, much of his contact with me was founded on his getting his practical needs met. Without my effort, I felt there would be little interaction between us and when he did make contact outside of needing something, I felt undeserving. I was powerless to understand why it should be so difficult to abandon my guilt or why it should be so complicated to set appropriate boundaries with my son.

Through my work with David, coupled with my short-lived relationship with Kent and other male interactions, my awareness of my distrust of men and fear of losing myself sexually was gradually leading me to the awareness that my real distrust was with my own femininity, the meaning of which I had only just begun to ponder. When I envisioned a feminine woman, I saw someone with a sophisticated hairdo and makeup and who was seductively dressed—like a model. If this vision qualified femininity, then I had none: there was nothing glamorous or sophisticated about me. Exploring further, I recalled that as much as I had hated the restrictions that came from wearing clothes (bras, girdles, garter belts, hose) as I entered my teenage years, it had been important to me to look my best, as well as be noticed. I had given much attention to my hair and makeup and had spent my earnings on nice attire. Yet, when I became involved with Carl, I stopped making myself up and began to cut my own hair; I even gave away all of my dresses to a needy friend reducing my wardrobe to jeans and sweatshirts. Carl had often encouraged me to wear a dress, but I was repulsed by the thought of being sexually available for him to drool over. I detested being seen in a bathing suit or anything of a seductive nature. Even a landlord once telling Carl that I looked like a movie star filled me with humiliation and guilt that I must have done something wrong to attract his notice in that way. I could only secretly admit that there was a certain beauty about me. Nevertheless, I remained confused over the difference between being feminine and being sexually alluring.

I had no idea where all of this was leading until one day I heard that it was time to don a dress. This message was instantly followed by the same kind of horrible panic that I felt in puberty when my body had betrayed me into womanhood: the same kind of horrible panic as when in anguish I had cried out to Spirit to just tell me what I have to do and was told that I had to let people know who I really am. Emotionally prostrated, I continued to hear the same message. I discussed all of this with David. He merely suggested that I purchase a dress and see what happened from there. Even with his support, it took weeks of obsessively walking in and out of clothing shops before I was able to fulfill my instructions. I first "test-wore" my new dress, which was cut long enough to cover my legs and comfortably stretchy at the waist, to a session with David. I stood at the door and self-consciously announced, "I'm wearing a dress." With a smile, he responded, "I see." The significance of this requirement was not apparent, however, it felt like a tottering first step into something of considerable importance.

I wanted to believe that wearing my new dress to my hypnotherapy session was the extent of my lesson, but I soon heard that it was time to let the world see me in a dress. This horrified me as much as initially putting the dress on, but I was certain that I would be able to accomplish this with my panic substantially more under control. Besides, being on the threshold of entering the teaching profession required that I upgrade my wardrobe, and I could at least purchase some feminine attire. An eclectic, bohemian-looking wardrobe, along with a little eye makeup and cheek coloring, a butch haircut and newly pierced ears stated, "I'm a tough female, so don't even think you can mess with me," or so I thought. I was far from understanding that femininity had nothing to do with physical appearance, presentation or even being in a female body, but where I was at that moment was where I needed to be in order to move into a true understanding of the nature of femininity.

My apartment was situated close enough to the forest preserve for me to continue my regular woodland visits which were becoming consistently more intense and perplexing. In fact, stepping into the woods invariably brought me into an ever more-intensely altered state of consciousness. My body seemed to dissolve as the energy waiting there suffused my awareness, remaining with me more strongly each time I departed. Despite my momentary disorientation, nothing I had ever before experienced had left me feeling so real, so much a part of something vitally sustaining, so important.

I began to discern little woodland beings I labeled forest fairies, whenever I was in the woods. Most particularly I felt them when I was in the vicinity of the mature oaks, the one in particular that sheltered three of our deceased pets. I became certain that the fairies lived in the oaks, that one in particular. My perception was that they would tend to come together upon my appearance as if anticipating my arrival. Consistently, they would approach me from behind, coming closer and closer, until they were darting and dancing near me like playful hummingbirds, but keeping themselves behind, just outside my peripheral vision. Only if I was lost in thought or looking elsewhere, would they dart in front of me. The sound they made was not physically discernable, but I could sense their zooming close to my ears, around my back and especially near my heart, leaving a golden contrail as they moved. Whenever I suddenly turned—hoping to catch them by surprise and "see" them—they instantly distanced themselves, reading my thoughts, before I even began to swing my head around. However, the minute I decided to ignore them (or dismiss them as results of an overactive imagination) they instantaneously resumed or intensified their antics. I came to realize that their behavior was not indiscriminate: they were communicating with *me*, making me aware that they acknowledged my presence. I eventually surrendered my need to connect with them at a physical level. I never went into the woods expecting or hoping to see these little Tinker Bell entities, even so they were usually present and appeared to delight in my presence, as much as making their presence known to me. As accustomed to them as I became, I never took them for granted, for I considered them an extraordinary gift.

My walks had oftentimes led me through a hole in a fence that defined forest preserve from adjacent cemetery property. The most significant attraction there was a line of giant oaks running along the edge of an unused dirt road in the oldest section of the cemetery. Over the years, I had shed an incredible number of painful tears sheltered beneath their protective limbs. On my current visits, however, it felt as if these oaks were the ones in pain—in pain and weeping. My initial impulse had been to cover my ears for the sound was more than I thought I could bear. Doing so proved futile for their agony was deeply rooted inside of me, and it was from there that I was hearing them. With enough of these distressing encounters, each one impacting me more profoundly, I opened up to receive clarity. This was even while another part of me was content to be in ignorance. Whatever was happening, it felt larger than I could handle. I could only acknowledge that it had something to do with death and destruction—death and destruction of the planet, mankind destroying the planet. I took to coming here more regularly. I had no choice; I was being required. I felt as if I could not abandon the oaks; I needed to hear them weep. Their weeping was putting me in touch with something inside of me, something too deep to be able to readily access, maybe something in me that was also dying.

My ever-intensifying experiences in the woods, and more frequently in my apartment, repeatedly left me to question my own sanity. Even so, it was becoming continually more impossible to leave this reality that I had found—or that had found me—and return to "ordinary reality." Through my hypnotherapy sessions with David, I was becoming more fully aware of various characteristics of my mind. I had a clear grasp of my intellectual self where the ego was housed, and I could easily tap into my subconscious self, freely accessing emotions and memories. Until directives became ever so greatly intense, I simply believed that it was merely my inner voice giving me commands. However, I could no longer deny that there was a strange, new space into which I was beginning to tap. This new space was related to what was happening to me when I was in the woods and now, almost every other place as well. It was calling to me, and I was unable to ignore it. It evoked an energy in me that soon permeated my life and greatly tested my newly-found sense of centeredness—and my sanity. It was terrifying, but I had to go to it, whatever it was.

The price I had to pay to secure this connection was to break my ties with David. I had been seeing him regularly for well over a year and had relied on him to help me trust in myself. Presently, his responses to my current questions only added to my mounting frustrations. It was dreadful to admit that as much as I obsessively shared, I was guarding my energy experiences from him. At some point, I had even begun prefacing my thoughts with, "I know you won't believe this, but..." I was inadvertently challenging his belief system and, therefore, his comfort level. He did not have my answers, and I was recognizing my shallow need for him to listen to me in order to obtain validation and trust in my own sanity. Although it was essential that I validate my understanding on my own, I nevertheless attempted to conjure up ways to hold onto our relationship. I had a strong sense that I was to learn hypnotherapy. Yet, despite how I approached the idea, regardless of the degree that the two of us discussed the matter and the degree of his willingness, it did not seem that he was to be the one from whom I was to learn, or that it was presently the time to do so. Letting situations come to fruition in their own timing, as opposed to making them happen, was another lesson to be learned in its own time.

I said my goodbye to David one evening knowing in my heart that it was time to step into this beckoning new world. David's last words, more a warning than a farewell, "You're choosing a very lonely path, you know?" echoed intensely through my being and triggered doubts that I had not before felt. Taken utterly by surprise, I wanted to defend myself. Instead, I quietly acknowledged his comment. Where I was going could be no lonelier than where I had been for my entire life, or more exactly, for what felt like forever. I was going because, ultimately, I knew I had no choice. During the drive home I wept, partly from feeling the loss of my relationship with David, and partly because I felt so utterly alone. Taking off the training wheels was terrifying. I assured myself that I could replace them if I chose.

A message that had begun to continually replay through my mind, "The seeker is the sought," left me feeling that the path David spoke of was choosing me; I was not choosing it. Like Eve with the forbidden fruit, the allure of this new world, this place that was calling to me, soon overcame any remaining reservations about exploring it. I took the plunge, and soon learned that this new space had a language, exponentially more powerful than my own inner voice, and its messages had a profundity that left me—physically, mentally, spiritually—reeling. I was constantly overwhelmed and thrown off balance by this energy—this new world. And everyone in my life certainly felt the same about me. Thus far, I had never felt so challenged. If this were insanity, I embraced it with my heart and soul.

It was to become customary that as I closed the door on one experience—hypnotherapy— a new one would open. So it was that driving home from work one day shortly after having said goodbye to David, I felt urgently pressured to stop at the new age bookstore. Before I realized it, I was walking out of the store with a book that had been on display in the store window. I had no choice about buying it for my attention was literally fixed on it the moment it came into my sight. Upon arriving home, I randomly opened the book and in the same manner my attention was riveted on a single paragraph. The message was that when a person works intensely at personal growth, s/he can move beyond the subconscious self to an expanded level of consciousness called the super-conscious or higher self. Not understanding the dynamics of this transition can leave the person confused and fearful. Just as important, doctors and therapists, not recognizing the signs of this phenomenon as healthy and normal, misdiagnose, often prescribing medication or, in some cases, institutionalizing their patients rather than appropriately supporting them. In one paragraph, I had been provided with exactly what I needed to validate myself. This was no coincidence. The book was put in my hands because I needed and was ready for the understanding it provided. My higher self, my super-conscious (spiritual awareness), my connection to a great universal energy of which I was a part, was beckoning me. This place felt akin to that which I had connected to as a child when lost in my own inner world or out wandering in nature. I was in wonder over the incident in general as much as over the information provided. Now, I had to figure out what to do with this information—or so I thought.

Here, even as I continued to stride along even more tenaciously, using the tools I acquired along the way to open doors of awareness, fear still maintained its fixed clutch on my consciousness; and loneliness, which had been such a leprous force in my life, remained barely manageable. Even so, I was learning that beyond these was an entirely different reality. I was beginning now to understand the message, "Heal thyself." It was the key to opening up to higher levels of consciousness. I pondered if it were this universal energy that was requesting me to heal myself. The more understanding that came to me, the more I thirsted to know. I continued to search nooks and crannies of my mind, examining and releasing beliefs and behaviors that no longer served me. I was awakening to my true identity, but little did I know that I was just skimming the surface. What kept me going then was that I thought getting to where I was supposed to be, and to who I am, was just another step or two away—as when climbing a mountain, believing that just over the next ridge is the summit, only to find when going the perceived distance that there is another, and yet another ridge to traverse. I realized my obsessive desire to climb every mountain that I had ever encountered symbolized my inner hunger for the expansive panorama that only mountaintops afforded.

Between finishing my schooling, tending to my personal growth and moving further into energy transformation, not to mention the constant conflict with Kerry, I was becoming worn down. As I was seeing clearly the nature of the dysfunctional people the center attracted and how I had mirrored them, I felt a growing necessity to leave. The situation no longer reflected a changing me, and I was feeling that same old gnawing feeling that something was missing in my life. As much as I presently felt survival necessitated removing myself from this situation, and although I knew I was prostituting myself for an illusion of security by staying, I couldn't bring myself to quit.

Carl's refusal to cooperate in the divorce proceedings remained a further aggravation. With a new life opening before me, and since I had never felt married anyway, going through a legal ordeal to say I was finished when I was already finished seemed ludicrous. Despite my attachment to the house and my sense of injustice over having to leave it, for some time I had seriously been contemplating giving it to him as a means to expedite the legalities. However, I was half-sobered by the fact that those who knew of my situation thought I was being rash. I was also aware that this was about believing in my own worth and healing myself. An impending experience revealed that the entire situation was actually not in my hands.

An intense spring storm delayed my after-work respite in the woods one day. Consequently, I positioned myself on my living room radiator, watching and waiting, electrified with energy as I connected to this wondrously powerful natural phenomenon. I was antsy and willing to weather the conditions to be more a part of it. Common sense kept me subdued. Finally, the gale force winds following behind the deluge as it moved through beckoned me to delay no longer. I donned my rain gear and headed out. Without question, I would have the woods all to myself.

The intensity of energy rushing through me and blending with the force of the wind as I stepped into my damp, earthy-smelling other-world made clear that something enormous was waiting to happen. The fact that the fairies were present confirmed this sense. I wondered what was being asked of me as I moved deeper into the woods. Shortly, as the west wind increased, howling through the sylvan canopy, I found myself wrapping my arms around a sapling maple. The wind was wrenching the sapling, and me with it, back and forth. Within moments, I felt peacefully a part of this blusterous moment, albeit frozen in a locked position embracing the sapling, my inner ear tuning into what was forthcoming. This tempestuous message was important: I had to stay aligned with the movement of the greater force, whatever its dynamics, or else I would be subject to being blown to pieces. I had to maintain an inner peace despite external circumstances. As suddenly as I was frozen, I was just that suddenly released. I took this shift as meaning that I had successfully received the message.

Compelled to continue, I proceeded along the well-worn path; I knew it like the back of my hand. I paused at the mammoth oak, a tree with great out-spreading branches. Without question, it had stood sentinel there since long before the area was forested. This was where the forest fairies most often greeted me. They remained close at hand, not playful as normal, but quiet, almost solemn. Beneath the oak's protective boughs was where Adam's cat, Amiga, had recently been laid to rest. Drawn to linger there for a moment, I strongly felt her presence.

While I continued down the trail, my mind fell on mundane thoughts, and then suddenly was drawn to painful events in my past. Unexpectedly, from deep within the howl of the wind that was now moving as forcefully through me as it was around me, I heard, "You will need the money. You need to open up to it." Memories of my sordid relationship with Carl and his aunt brought tears of intense anguish. I paced up and down the trail, simultaneously surveying the rising moon and merging with my torment. Unexpectedly, I began to wail loose deeply-buried feelings of guilt and shame. Screams of helpless rage, ripped from the depth of my own inner darkness, merging with the darkness of the night. I shrieked until hoarse and exhausted, "I'm not a bad person! I'm not! I'm not! I'm leaving my shame here! I relinquish it forever! I'm not a bad person." My pain and shame were carried away with my words, purged by the roar of the howling wind.

Much later, my inner calm juxtaposed that of the trees still wrenching back and forth in the wind. I had taken a giant first step in breaking free of my obsession with being bad. The calmness was a reference point. Much more purging—the opportunities were waiting—would be required before the inner calm became a way of being. I remained in the woods, listening to the message, "Heal thyself!" over and over in my mind, until the moon rose high enough to light my way out. Healing and madness could certainly seem the same.

Whatever had happened in the woods had strengthened my courage to the point that I could do what was necessary to bring my lessons with Carl to an end. In his most recent claim, he averred that the house was a means for him to provide a home for our son; therefore, he was willing to buy me out...at ten percent of the value of the house. For me, his stance confirmed the messages I had received in the woods. My receiving a reasonable share of the assets was the means to validate my own worthiness and reclaim parts of myself that I had lost in the relationship. Contrary to my current thoughts, the money would never provide me with another house, or ever serve me personally, but eventually I would understand that it was supporting me in finding my way *home*.

Since almost a year had gone by before Carl had produced this counteroffer, it had been becoming all too clear that he was maneuvering himself into a position to obtain a loan to buy me out. The message given to me in the woods left no room for compromise. I would have to wait this out as long as it took him to come to his senses. Knowing Carl meant understanding that I was in this for the long haul. Therefore, I yielded to accepting whatever time was necessary to bring this phase of my life to completion. Leaving anything undone was not a choice.

Meanwhile, with determination, I had completed my education classes and was now obliged to student-teach. When I knew I was finished with my job and that it was time to move on, however, rather than simply walking out the door, my insecure character still got the best of me. Consequently I presented my case to the site manager in a way that left her agreeing to give me a leave-of-absence after the point that my "comp time" was used up. This was a deadly move on my part. The tension between Kerry and me was already near explosive. I walked out of the site manager's office next having to face Kerry. Without question, she would perceive my enterprise as undermining her authority. I stepped nervously into her office and requested a moment of her time. As a rule, she continued to engage in her present endeavor rather than give me her full attention. I became distracted by her activity and lost my chain of thought. Also as habit, she responded, "Go ahead, I'm listening." She said nothing to me when I finished. Instead, she excused herself and walked out. It was obvious that she was on her way to the site manager's office. It was also obvious that she would have the final word. When she returned, she informed me that the site manager was waiting to see me.

Again in the site manager's office, this time to be informed that the leave-of-absence would not work, I was handed resignation papers to sign. I never knew what had transpired between the two of them and should not have cared. Nevertheless, between my emotions and my imagination, I left feeling more rejected, more like a bad person, than I ever thought possible. I obsessed over my perceived reprehensible behavior. I obsessed over all the things I might have done "wrong" during my employment. Yet, there was nothing that either my boss or co-worker could blame me for that they had not done themselves, and many times more intensely. I hated myself and I hated the site manager. I hated Kerry for causing me to feel like an outsider. My outrageous reaction to the closing (or slamming) of this chapter in my life blinded me from seeing the gifts that it had provided.

A decade into the future, the site manager's and my paths would cross again, far removed geographically from the present location. Only then, and only after exploring our greater history, would I comprehend the karmic ties through which we were all replaying an old conflict. Only then would the emotional charge be deactivated, enabling final closure to this painful chapter of my life. The experience had never been about a job or money or anything else mundane. It had been a vehicle for me to begin cracking away the layers of the old self, in nature, where a greater, more reliable sense of self could begin to emerge.

Meanwhile, besides having to deal with my ridiculous emotional state, I was now facing my fear of being unemployed. The gift of this condition was that I had the opportunity to extricate my sense of self-worth from making an income.

6

Inspecting Conventional Reality

My work with public school teachers through my naturalist position taught me that the Chicago public school system had too many drawbacks for me to want to work there, not the least of which was the idea of having to work indoors. I was altogether unhappy about being required to student-teach. After all, I was not obtaining an education degree in order to teach but to get a better paying job in the environmental field. At least, that is what I continued to try to convince myself, despite indications to the contrary.

I had registered to student-teach in the northern suburbs, rationalizing that if I had to do so, the suburbs were preferable to the city schools. Figuring all the angles, I also thought that student-teaching in the area might be a foot in that door, if in fact I was required to formally teach. On the designated day, I sat, trance-like, in the waiting area along with three other student-teachers. I was in stark resistance to spending the next sixteen weeks within these halls. My impulse was to run while I could still get away, but I remained frozen. As I pleaded, "Not here! Not now! They're going to think I'm crazy!" I connected suddenly to the energy of a woman I could see walking toward me from the far end of the hall. It was clear that she was the teacher with whom I would be working. The moment introductions were made the pulsing energy diminished, and thankfully, I was able to ground myself. Teresa was surprised about my age, relieved that she would be working with someone mature for a change...as for me, well, I refrained from enlightening her on this matter.

This smartly dressed, affable woman and I instantly made a heart-felt bond. Faster than my reservation could arrest, we were deep into discussion. Her interest in my "metaphysicalness" even assuaged my fear that my weird nature was going to undermine my success. Before the first week was over, we had already shared histories. From the beginning, the stage was set for her to rely on me for advice, as well as for me to use her as a sounding board.

Teresa was exceptionally liberal in allowing me to work with her students and invited me to bring in my environmental expertise in any way germane to the subjects being taught. I observed her teaching techniques and how she related to her class. She was a gifted and inspired teacher, and her fourth-grade students adored her. I dismissed as judgmental my understanding that she related so well to them because a part of her operated at a fourth-grade level. I surmised I could never be as successful at teaching as she was. Among other reasons, I was unable to take pedagogy as seriously as she did.

Despite Teresa giving me free rein, I felt constrained: stifled in the conventional classroom context, not to mention the close physical space. Although Teresa encouraged me to mingle with other teachers—sit in their classrooms and hang out in the lounge during lunch—the thought of making small talk felt dreadful. As usual, I felt safer and more comfortable keeping my distance. I was sure that I had learned all I could within a matter of weeks; I did not know how I was going to endure this four-month commitment. Only the close bond between Teresa and me made my stay tolerable.

There was, inevitably, Liam, the teacher across the hall from Teresa's classroom who was preening for my attention, blatantly devising ways to interact. Except to be courteous, I ignored him. He had no appeal, and his demeanor bespoke dysfunction. I had certainly had enough of that. As much as loneliness remained a struggle, for the moment I was managing without a man in my life. Undaunted by my lack of encouragement, Liam increased his efforts to capture my attention, and just as strenuously, I continued to ignore him. With strong certainty, however, I felt something between us was waiting to happen.

One morning, Teresa and I were engaged in our usual pre-school chat as Liam conspicuously entered the classroom. He just happened to have brought with him a plaque of recognition that he had received as a Peace Corps volunteer in the early seventies. He thrust it forward for our due admiration as he proceeded to share the story that came with it. The ruse was flagrant. But, aside from being impressed, what struck me in his monologue were my words to the young girl who had asked my advice a year earlier about joining the Peace Corps: if I had no other obligations than to myself, I would not hesitate joining…now I had no obligations other than to myself. While energy pressured me from within, the message began to settle into my psyche: I was joining the Peace Corps! There was no time to be perplexed for suddenly I was hurling questions at Liam left and right—a surging impulse to pick his brain. When he walked out the door, it was clear that he felt successful in making an inroad.

As huge an undertaking as this was for someone as timid as I had once been, I was on the phone with the local Peace Corps recruiting office requesting an application as soon as I entered my apartment that afternoon. It became unimaginably difficult to stay put in the moment when my insecurities caused me to jump all over the possibilities—wondering, worrying, doubting—trying to get a clear handle, until I was a nervous wreck. If anything, knowing that this was in my future, instead of being a public school teacher, made my time student-teaching more tolerable. For now, I had to get a grip, at least if I were going to avoid being a basket case.

Within two weeks after completing the initial application, I had an interview. I had a plethora of ideas about how I needed to present myself in order to impress my recruitment officer, which I fortunately abandoned before I could sabotage myself.

She questioned me in regard to my flexibility and adaptability. I watched carefully, listening, sensing what right answers she was wanting. She went on to explain that the application process could be lengthy and, because of the number of applicants, the odds of being accepted were stiff. She added that she would be sending me more forms to complete, after which, upon evaluation, she would notify me whether or not she was forwarding my application on to Washington D.C.

I was certain that the interview went well when she handed me three sample job assignments before I walked out the door. The one that held my attention the most was one for a naturalist/interpreter/educator at an historical site, a restored fort no less, in a country of which I had never heard. Locating the country on an atlas when I returned home, I adamantly declared, "The last place I will ever consider going is to some obscure, little island in the middle of nowhere!" I wanted adventure! Leading nature safaris across the Serengeti Plains or educating Rwandan natives in order to preserve the upland gorillas! I wanted mud huts and elephants! Not telephones and tourists on some island in the Caribbean! I wanted my mettle tested, my self-reliance, my strength of spirit! I wanted to know of what I was made! I wanted the harshest of conditions! In the end, I admitted barely willingly that, if I received an invitation, I would welcome whatever assignment I was given.

My most serious impediment, as I saw it, was that in order to be accepted, I had either to be divorced or have permission from my husband to join. This really riled me. Carl would gladly go out of his way to prevent me from getting whatever I wanted. I was sure that he would refuse to give his permission, which was a moot point since I would never think of asking him anyway. Furthermore, I was sure if he got wind of my plans, he would all the more heartily sabotage the divorce to spite me. Regardless of the certainty that I was once again putting Adam in the middle of Carl's and my struggle, I went so far as to direct Adam not to tell his father anything.

Compounding my remaining inclination to obsess over my issues—perceived or otherwise—was my conviction that Peace Corps officials would consider me too unstable mentally to be accepted, especially with my being on record as having sought out counseling. I told myself that this could be viewed as positive, rather than a weakness, but fear of being thought crazy gnawed at my confidence. I considered the possibility of being deceptive if necessary, however experience was continuing to reveal that deceit, whatever its form, only complicated my life and left me feeling horribly out of tune with myself. I contained this particular concern by assuring myself that David would provide a statement of sanity when the time came. Less distracting concerns I attempted to set aside in a similar manner. Due to my conditioning, it was beyond my understanding that it was not necessary for me to expend extreme effort to make this happen; rather all I had to do was merely get myself out of the way and let the process unfold. This required trust—a concept in which I was only beginning to see value.

Liam was teaching in the same school in which he had begun some twenty-five years earlier after completing his Peace Corps stint. He was open about the fact that he hated his job and even openly carried his surly attitude around with him on the job. I was amazed that he was able to get away with this, especially in an upper-class community school. It came as little surprise when he informed me that he had definitively decided that, if he could obtain a leave-of-absence, he would join the Peace Corps again. Having found a common interest, I finally agreed to a coffee invitation.

It was immediately noticeable to me that Liam was extremely emotionally closed off and self-absorbed, as well as extremely intellectual. He was an adept conversationalist, but he shared little of his personal self. Rather, he rambled on about his many past adventures traveling abroad. His goal in life was to visit over a hundred countries. He had a bookshelf full of photos albums from his travels. Curiously, his photos had virtually no people in them—not a traveling companion, a friend, or a native. He did not particularly impress me, especially since I could see so many shades of Carl there, but I continued to meet him for coffee or dinner. After a few such interactions, I knew that his life was molded into a rigid routine.

On subsequent dates, though he was never forward, nor attempted any advances, it was clear that he was interested in taking the relationship into a sexual realm. He had finally shared—following an uncountable number of martinis and a painful release of tears—that he had broken off an engagement a year earlier with a woman with whom he had been involved for many years. However, he was not free of her, as she had become suicidal in the wake of the breakup, and he felt responsible. Whenever she was at a low point, which was frequent, she would make contact with him, but beyond that, he claimed to have no interaction with her.

During the time I was filling out further forms from my recruiting officer, I was compelled to phone Liam for answers to some questions I had; he invited me over. I could tell by the nature of the energy moving through me as I drove there that something was underway, but I did not expect him to greet me at the door with a bottle of champagne. Although I seldom drank and a sip of anything alcoholic was enough for me to feel the effects, I agreed to have a glass. From there, Liam pulled out a world map and we spent the duration of the evening sprawled on his dusty, living room floor pinpointing and discussing Peace Corps host countries. I was not sure when I realized—or let myself own the realization—that I would not be going home that night, but Liam was astonished when I made the announcement. I did not condemn myself and hardly felt embarrassed over my forwardness, that was even while I momentarily bounced between trying to convince myself that tipsiness put me in this position and thinking that I was too insecure to be without a man in my life. A knowing that I had to stay overrode an attempt to back out the door. Something was requiring me to stay—to be sexual with Liam. Without question, this carnal encounter was waiting to happen; someone had to make the move. It was strange to crawl into bed with a man under these conditions, under any conditions. I watched my inhibitions, my fears and doubts as the night progressed into dawn. Sex was better than I could ever have imagined. In the morning, Liam went off to work with a smug smile on his face, and I returned to my apartment to reflect. More than anything else, I only wished I was able to blot out the previous night's experience. I attempted to muster a sense of shame over my out-of-character behavior. Both an unidentifiable resistance and a certain sense of enticement, however, told me that I was being moved into further unexplored territory, and there was no turning back.

It took only a short time to recognize that Liam wanted me in his life, but was afraid of my being there. Insecurities, from which I thought I had freed myself, seemed to rise from nowhere. As much as I needed to be alone, I obsessed over when we would be together next; obsessed when a day passed and he did not phone; obsessed whether or not I would ever see him again. Eventually he would make contact with me, at which time I would thrash myself for worrying. Then when we were together, I was frustrated, distracted and half-wishing I was in my own space.

Actually getting close to him meant learning to operate within the framework of his unspoken rules; his comfort zone. It was understood that we never casually dropped in on each other nor was I to ask questions that were too personal. He kept me a secret from his mother because, he claimed, she was too nosey. Whenever his phone rang, he moved to the bedroom and shut the door before carrying on a conversation, concerned that it might be his ex-girlfriend. I spent a good deal of my time waiting for him to finish watching the football game or a favorite weekly mystery show before we could carry on with our plans. He pooh-poohed my spiritual inclinations, leaving me to closet that side of myself as well as my need to articulate my insights when I was with him. Nonetheless, when he was "blue," he would phone me to cheer himself. At other times, he became annoyed by my cheerfulness. His preoccupied addictions to alcohol, marijuana, caffeine, nicotine, sugar, television and books revealed the limits of how deeply he was willing to look into himself.

All the same, the nature of our sexual relationship allowed the part of me to explore that had been deadened in my relationship with Carl—and that had remained so in my relationship with Kent. When it came to sexual interaction, Liam was ready to meet my needs as much as his. I was learning about the nature of sex for pleasure, what it was like to be a full-fledged, orgasmic, sexual female, and I was thoroughly awed by my sexual appetite. Liam had no regrets. In fact, he would joke about my libidinous side and I was not embarrassed or reduced to feeling bad or dirty. I was open and willing and ready to understand the dynamics of sexuality. Mostly, I felt successful: successful that I was overcoming my own inhibitions, that I was learning to let go and feel safe, feel that I would not be devoured alive by turning my body over to a man. No one could ever call me a tight-box again. Even so, a deeper knowing made me aware that I had a long way to go before understanding what was being required of me.

Our dates settled into a routine of dinner, drinks (inebriation for Liam) and a night of sex at his place. (And as I gradually acquiesced to him smoking in my apartment, our liaisons took place there as well.) Surprisingly, I began to "flip out" during sex. Some part of me was in bed bodily engaged while "I" was gone. I imagined this to be like a drug-induced high. During a couple of encounters, I interrupted our intense sexual moments to have Liam write down messages that were coming into my mind. He always went along, but it was evident that he was displeased. I told myself that it was for Liam's sake when, at some point, I put a lid on these encounters. Most noticeable, however engaged my body was in the sexual encounter, regardless of the multitude and depth of orgasms I experienced, some part of me remained a steadfast observer.

Predictably, when morning arrived, Liam, discreetly or otherwise, showed me to the door. I was always ready to return to my personal space and sense of self. On the other hand, I felt dismissed when he did this, which ultimately led me right into clenched jaws of hurt and anger.

All too soon, I began to find the sexual aspect of Liam's and my relationship much like watching a favorite movie over and over; I was bored. Ultimately, if my body became sexually charged, which inexplicably was more often than not, I could simply masturbate, go for an exhausting run or take a hot shower. More than I could imagine, I hungered to express my heart and soul—whatever that meant. Rather than addressing my loneliness full force, however, I remained in the affair, struggling to express myself at a deeper level and accepting tidbits of attention, while abandoning newly claimed parts of myself, bit by bit, in an effort to make this situation functional. Remove sex from the relationship, and little else remained besides our instabilities.

At one point, I found the nerve to convey that my interest in our sex life was waning; therefore, it was becoming laborious for me to perform. Liam proceeded to rent a pornographic movie, suspecting that all I needed was a little new stimulation to dive deeper into the pleasures of sex. Watching the movie revealed, more than anything, the difference from where Liam and I operated. His involvement came from his genitals. In my burgeoning beliefs, intimacy was not synonymous with sex, no matter how good.

I wanted to push aside all my distractions and leave for the Peace Corps immediately. This desire was based mainly on the fact that I remained resistant to becoming a classroom teacher. I had finished student-teaching and landed a substitute-teaching job at a school for emotionally disturbed children. This school seemed well-prepared to handle the dynamics of the students, the majority of whom were medicated. If a student did become out of control, pushing a buzzer brought in a specially-trained teacher who, at the least, would talk the nonconforming student out of the room and, if required, wrestle him to the floor, place him in a straight jacket and march him off to a time-out room. Although these procedures seemed to be carried out in a kindly manner, I wondered why they had to be carried out at all. I felt as if I was living the movie, **One Flew Over the Cuckoo's Nest**. I thought that there was a better way to serve these children. However, my taking the position that I was a novice here, and had no right to judge, clashed with a deeper sense of knowing. (Even with my independent thinking experiences in Dr. Jennings' class, I was to date unable to break my pattern of doubting myself.)

The teacher who had recommended me as a substitute-teacher suggested that I consider a full-time position in the fall. I avowed that I was unqualified to meet these children's extensive needs, but withheld that these children pained my heart. Overall, I felt traumatized and drained by merely being in these surroundings, if not incompetent. He assured me that I was quite capable of handling the job. (He really wanted me there because he had a personal interest in me, and I was sure that he thought he was going to collect on the "favor.") In talking to the principal, I reiterated my feelings. Getting wind of the conversation, the teacher who had endorsed me, chastised me for my honesty, "This is not how you get a job. And now you've made *me* look bad." I owned his displeasure enough to feel guilty myself and be more cautious. Still insecure over being unemployed, I equivocated as to whether or not to try for a permanent position. In the end, I was able to choose the door.

Since my self-worth was tied to having an income, spending a summer without a job, which translated "unproductive," was formidable. It was more of a challenge to choose to just *be* as opposed to being unconscious in busyness. I was learning to slow down. In an effort to come to terms with the dread of being alone with nothing to do, I packed my camping equipment in the car and left the city. I had no itinerary, only a direction: west.

My empty loneliness sprang alive hardly before I was out of the city. It felt like a punishment having to go off to destinies unknown all by myself. Day after day, from rising to retiring, I was able to do little else but cry myself exhausted. I would watch myself drive into a town, and wander from shop to shop, looking for a chance to engage someone, anyone, in conversation. When I was successful, I would afterward condemn myself for my mindless chatter, making myself the center of my attention or making myself look important. I hated this compulsion. I hated my neediness. I hated this struggle with the elusive demon of my loneliness and had no doubt that I was falling apart. What I was yet unable to see was that the unreliable paradigm in which I lived my life was what was crumbling. To understand what was in the process of being born from my old reality, I was being required to bear witness to its demise, which included the demise of the personal self. In truth, I was actually falling together.

In exasperation one morning, I hiked up the side of a mountain and, finding a secluded spot, removed my clothes. Then I surrendered to the transformational forces of the sun and wind. Thus, my distraction shifted into the magical state that this environment invariably produced in me. Loud and clear, the message put forth was, "You can either cry your way through this trip or you can dry your tears and start living the experience waiting for you." Given in this manner, there was really no choice. With the sun penetrating the depth of my pain, and the gentle, alpine breeze giving comfort, I collected myself and then made a commitment to release my self-indulgent behavior. Accordingly, I was able to be with the obsession, rather than being its victim.

The morning also brought me to a gift shop that I came upon on a gravelly country road supposedly going to nowhere important. I ended up purchasing a book that would most likely be found nowhere else. It was an autobiography of a genteel English woman who had come to Colorado on holiday way back in the early eighteen hundreds and ended up remaining for the rest of her life. Her story proved to be ridiculously colorful, ruggedly adventuresome and profoundly touching in an odd sort of way. Night after night, snug in my two-man tent, I would read a chapter or two before I fell asleep. As I moved further into the story, I began to hear a message repeating itself in my head, "If she can do it, you can do it." Whatever the message meant, it was heartening.

The journey, which began to define itself from moment to moment, had me exploring all the Colorado back roads my over-sized, outdated car could manage. Most often, I landed in some ghost town or other, or in an old, historic mining district. I studied the bygone, as well as the surviving communities with the same scrutiny as I did the abundance of environmental wounds and scars everywhere dotting the mountainsides just beneath casual observation. I wondered how long ago the wounds had been inflicted and how long it would take for them to disappear. My mind was filled with the idea that if people would learn to listen to the Earth Mother, and realize the pain that we unnecessarily inflict upon her, it would then follow that we take responsibility for our actions. A more accurate concept, one that I was unknowingly beginning to live, was that true healing is a personal matter; once we heal ourselves, we bring that healing—our Wholeness—to the world.

An inquisitive retired couple acting as hosts in an obscure national forest campground where I stayed for a night asked if I ever got lost traveling unfamiliar back country roads alone. My response, "I can't get lost, because wherever I am, is exactly where I am supposed to be," butted suddenly against my phobia of being lost and alone and unable to find my way home—my "Hansel and Gretel" syndrome. The true significance of my words was far beyond my ability to comprehend in that moment, for I was being prepared to travel into uncharted territory, the ultimate frontier; and not only was I being required to familiarize myself with the terrain, I would be required to set up conditions for others to follow. It was too soon to realize that I *am* a pathfinder. It was not time and I was unprepared. However, I would continue to use my words as a reference point as I continued my travels (travails). Regardless the circumstances, I am never lost.

Liam had found a number of reasons to initially decline my offer to join me. I had at first felt angry and rejected, as usual, even when I had been fully aware that this was meant to be a solo experience, and that my "invitation" had been a means for me to avoid it being so. His decision actually had been a great gift in regard to further examining my neediness. However, when I made contact with him in the middle of my trip, as I had promised I would, he decided to fly to Denver to spend my final week traveling together. The insecure part of me latched onto the situation even while I questioned. Was he appeasing me? Was he afraid to lose me or was he missing me? I didn't know.

He was keen on studying history, at least those aspects relating to politics and conflict, going far afield to visit war memorials and historic battle sites: places I would never consider visiting. I could hike all day and not think of being tired or hungry; he preferred to hike long enough to say that he went on one and then quickly retreat to the nearest establishment to treat himself to a martini or dessert and coffee. Camping fell into the same category. Undeniably, my adventure was reduced to a vacation the moment Liam appeared on the scene. Regardless, I had created a reference point in terms of knowing that the meaningfulness of my journey, if not the ease with which I experienced it, was based largely on my willingness to experience it alone.

I saw very little of Adam during his school breaks. He worked for the Chicago Transit Authority for two summers, traveling the subway routes relieving tellers at various stations along the way; his hours were long and sporadic. It was a tough job. However, he made decent wages for summer employment. Above the monetary benefits, I thought that this was a great opportunity for him to acquire experience in the real world. This proved to be true. And provided a lesson for me also.

Through working different shifts, he came to know many tellers. Most astonishing to him was his discovery of the amount of graft taking place and how many people were involved. In fact, many employees openly shared, if not bragged about, their exploits, and often encouraged Adam to follow suit. So this became his test of integrity. He explained how he could abscond with enough money to pay for his upcoming school year, or how easily he could justify taking enough to buy a Coke and hot dog for lunch when he knew that some employees were stealing double or triple their salaries. One man even explained the loopholes in the chain of command: how one would refrain from squealing on their subordinates or superiors, because they too were doing the same thing at their level.

His observations took me back to my nature center experiences. The first time a city-employed carpenter openly bragged to me about regularly pilfering supplies from the city: enough to operate his moonlighting business, I was flabbergasted, not so much that he would steal, but that he was so cavalier about it. I soon learned that graft was not novel. Over time, I observed the site manager use her position to her advantage. Like the other employees working under her, I said nothing: I either acquiesced or I was out the door.

My thieving had never been the result of planning or plotting. More compulsively, it simply overtook me at unsuspecting times, but mostly when I was angry or resentful, or when I felt I had been wronged or deprived. I was even beginning to find it amusing—in a sick way—how exaggerated my response to my own puny pilfering had always been, not much different than when I had stolen lemon drops from my grandmother's cupboard as a child. Furthermore, I acknowledged that by assuring Adam that he would find his own way through his experience, I was giving myself permission to release the weight of the shame I carried. My days of maintaining this peculiar pattern, this addiction/phobia state, were coming to an end. But, again, the door could only be closed once and for all when I had fully explored the karmic patterning that produced this behavior.

Returning to Chicago left me faced with securing a job. Word in the college education department was that teaching positions were scarce. Despite having gotten my resume in too late at the district where I had student-taught to be considered for the present year, I was not overly disappointed, for I felt too inferior to attain a position in a suburban school system. My greatest hope of success was to direct my energy on schools in the Chicago district where quotas had to be met. Being Caucasian, my best chance would come from driving to black communities on the opposite side of the city, just as black teachers, to meet quotas, were forced to commute out of their communities to secure employment. I did not care what race or ethnicity my students were. I cared about minimizing the number of hoops I had to jump through to obtain a job, as much as minimizing travel time to and from work. It was annoying enough to have to sell myself—to stretch facts in ways that hopefully conformed enough to expectations set by the interviewers to entice them into hiring me. I resisted aligning myself to frustration. My aim was to teach in the vicinity where I lived, and to that end, I made a list of schools where I was willing to work and "began the rounds." I decided that if I were unable to secure an interview on the spot, I would leave no resumes, but simply move on to the next school on my list just as I had done for my last waitress job. Confidence had been the key then and also was now. I approached the secretary of the first school I entered with my request, and moments later, I was conversing with the principal. I was unsure how it happened; however, I walked out with a permanent substitute position for the fall term in hand.

My first placement was in a class of mentally disabled students. Feeling overwhelmed and inept, I berated myself losing my patience and raising my voice. Although I feared reprisal for my lack of professionalism, whenever I walked up the hallway, I could hear any number of teachers yelling at, if not belittling, their students. When the teacher for whom I was subbing returned, I was assigned to teach music to grades kindergarten through eighth at the same school for three days and a neighboring one for two. Considering my musical ignorance, this assignment felt like a punishment. Nonetheless, with little more than an old, portable record player, some records left from Adam's childhood, and some classical music of mine, an obsessive determination and a fear of failing, I rose to the challenge.

Outside of a few moments of feeling successful, I hated teaching. Liam's interpretation of teachers merely being overpaid babysitters constantly rang through my head. The teachers I relieved saw no value in my presence other than it provided them with a break. Then the students (especially the junior-high-aged ones) saw their teacher's absence as license to go wild. Most of the time I felt like an inexperienced animal tamer. I found myself intimidated by the older male students—some larger than I—who took great efforts to undermine my authority. It was a constant struggle to stay centered when I only wanted to scream, "Shut up and listen, or leave!" I was in constant fear of making an egregious blunder and being taken to task. Putting up with a full year of this felt like a death sentence. Not even the security of a regular paycheck assuaged my malcontent.

Two months into subbing, the school librarian informed me that a permanent position was open at the school where her husband worked and, if I liked, she would have him talk to the principal. I was surprised by this offer, especially since I was unable to relate to fellow teachers, so had kept mainly to myself. Besides, as a substitute, I felt that I went fairly unnoticed by the other teachers and believed that, if they did happen to notice me, it would only be because of my incompetence.

Both the principal and assistant principal were present during my interview. I felt the usual uneasiness and attempted, once again, to adapt my qualifications to whatever my interviewers were looking. I was hired immediately to start the following week. I walked away relieved to have financial stability, and I immediately committed myself to be the best teacher possible. Only in retrospect would I see that my chain of jobs had not been acquired through happenstance or luck, but provided through Divine support as vehicles to break me free of further disempowering ideas that limited my reality.

Before the first day had ended, my feeling lucky to have been hired was replaced by a wondering why every situation in my life had to be such an overwhelming challenge. The seventh-grade class, to which I was assigned, had been without a permanent teacher for two months. Because of the students' inability to properly conduct themselves, they had been banned from eating in the lunchroom as well as restricted from other activities. Their collective intrinsic calling was to break down consecutive substitute-teachers in less time than the predecessor. And so far, they had succeeded. Presently, it felt as if someone had opened a door, shoved me into a roomful of big-mouthed, smartalecky, mutually belligerent students guided by a ringleader who maintained his status by an expert use of intimidation, and then quickly locked the door behind me. While one part of me was feeling helpless and looking for support, another part of me had already rolled up her sleeves and was in the midst of assessing the situation: digging in for the long haul.

When I was able to keep myself out of the way and not take my students' behavior personally, I could see that, behind their defenses they were troubled, frightened and lacking self-esteem. First, I had to figure out how to convince them that, not only was I not the enemy, I was on their side. I had been required to spend two extra years in higher education to earn the right to stand before them. But not one of the many compulsory methods-of-teaching classes had prepared me for the real world of teaching that these students were here so well equipped to provide.

It took no time to realize that there was little support or guidance for me in this blackboard jungle. Neither were there adequate resources, nor clear understanding of the curriculum. Most of the students read from one to four grades below level, taking into account that a percentage had already been held back a grade. Overall, their limited reading skills made teaching at grade level next to impossible. In addition to homeroom, I was responsible for teaching history to two eighth-grade classes, plus my seventh-graders. I wanted to make this subject interesting, but considering the degree of their limitations, the lack of enrichment materials and my unfamiliarity with the curriculum, I was at a loss where to begin.

To make matters worse, I could not see what real principles supported the institution. The greatest emphasis appeared to be on preparing students to perform well on standardized tests for little other reason than for the school score well with the local school council and when compared to other schools across the nation. Administration, besides emphasizing high performance on standardized tests, seemed to only be bent on acquiring funds, administering discipline and administrating bureaucratic paper shuffling. Teachers themselves were expected to write grant proposals in order to obtain needed teaching materials, as well as keep minute records of student misbehavior in case of legal action against the school.

I could only wonder what mixed messages students received from the kind of role-modeling and double standards I saw imposed on them. Candy at school was against regulations, but teachers often ate it themselves while teaching or used it as a reward when students were well-behaved. While one of the two male teachers in my departmentalized team wrestled out-of-control students to the floor with maneuvers he had learned while in Vietnam, the other verbally ridiculed his students to the same humiliating position. The first-grade teacher trained her students as if they were in boot camp, while the reading teacher imposed her obsessive/compulsive psychology to the point that she, among other things, placed marks on the floor so her students would know precisely where their chairs were to be placed before they left her class. Additionally, her approach to managing her students was screaming in their faces.

The system inhibited opportunities for independent thinking and self-reliance; instead, it demanded conformity. The majority of my students were from low-income, single parent and minority backgrounds. The ones that did not fall within this category came with no less insecurity. From my own experience, I knew that with a foundation of self-esteem, my students could be productive, independent learners. Without it, their chances of rising out of this environment were grim. Statistics already predicted the girls producing babies and the boys lured into gangs within a precious few years.

The system defined my role as a teacher, but I strained to operate within that limited context. It was impossible to be pedantic and inspiring at the same time. In my job description I found nothing that I could offer them that would help them even in the slightest to lead productive lives, much less inspire them to freedom from their limited circumstances. I strived to make the classes interesting and democratic. But it was as if the students had been brought up in a straight-jacket school system. By the time they got to me, to take them out of straight jackets was like taking the lid off of a beehive after it had been given a good kick. I gave my students a modicum of freedom with an unrealistic expectation that they could handle it. When they proved me wrong, I became frustrated and angry and ended up putting them, in one way or another, right back into their straight jackets. My serious commitment, my need to achieve perfection, as well as my need to make everything alright for my students, only got me over-involved and perpetually exhausted. It was clear what did *not* work; yet I was unable to find what did. A seasoned teacher—

the Vietnam vet with whom I co-taught and saw little eye-to-eye—chucked me some sage advice, "Quit coddling these kids and just relax. They're going nowhere. Give them seatwork to do and bring yourself a novel to read. You'll make life much easier for yourself and them."

    I realized that, above all else, there could be no cohesion with the class ringleader undermining my position. With his exceptional height and being over-age, he was a misfit for seventh-grade. I had approached him in as many ways as I knew possible to convince him that his behavior was unacceptable, but he continued to be downright disrespectful. A few weeks into teaching, as he walked out of the door for the day, I informed him that when he came to school the next day, he needed to bring a parent with him to talk to the principal about being moved to another class, because I was no longer allowing him in mine. Surrounded by fellow students, and although laughing down in my face, he knew I was serious. Afterward, I left a note with the principal explaining my actions and my position.

    The night proved long and sleepless. I did not know if, as a teacher, I had the power to refuse to allow a student in my class. Being a new teacher and untenured, I told myself that I needed to get my act together, or I would soon find myself substitute-teaching again. However, there was a stubborn part of me that refused to budge. The following morning, the principal announced over the intercom that she was on her way up to my third floor classroom with my student and his mother. After introductions were made, the principal explained to me that she had just had a long talk with both mother and son, and that he understood the importance of respecting others. Speaking to them, she then added that if I gave the okay, the youngster was free to return to my classroom. But it was my decision. I instantly realized that the principal was setting me up. She expected me to say yes. "No!" the headstrong part of me adamantly exploded, "I've talked to him for weeks about his behavior, and he hasn't changed. His word means nothing to me. He cannot respect me, and I will not let him back." With the game over and knowing that he was now going to a sixth/seventh grade class with a male teacher he disliked, he begged me to take him back. "You're way too late for this," I responded. Subsequently, his pleading turned to anger. Annoyed by the unexpected twist of circumstances, the principal shuffled the mother and son out the door, while I examined what my behavior had created. I saw that I now had two strikes against me. I had not played the principal's game and, in some capacity, I would have the boy in my class the following year—if I didn't get myself terminated. Once again, I felt as if my outlandish behavior had landed me on the outside, as well as on the defensive. Nonetheless, this was all unpremeditated on my part. Of my own volition, I would have never had the nerve to be so upfront. In contrast, as afraid of reprisal as I was, I felt a sense of accomplishment, even empowerment.

    With the ringleader ousted, the class became tolerably cohesive and responsive; at least they understood that I meant business. One of my endeavors, in particular, proved successful. While I took attendance and lunch money at the start of the day, I had the students write in journals that I required them to keep. My original intention, besides giving them the opportunity to freely express themselves, was to get to know them as individuals since classroom time did not allow for this. The boys usually wrote about the weather being cold or playing football the night before, but the girls came to share themselves in a more personal way. On a bi-weekly basis, I collected their writings, took them home, and spent a Sunday reading through them and making personal comments to each student. I could not have known exactly how personal an interaction would be created, until the girls began to request feedback on family issues and other facets of their personal lives. Sometimes I felt like Ann Landers. All told, they came to anticipate reading my comments and realized that my interest in their success was more about them as individuals than academics or statistics.

Whether a conscious decision or something that happened along the way, I found myself unremittingly focusing on creating opportunities for my students to develop self-esteem. I had even written the word on the board and then provided time for an open discussion. From that point, almost every incident that took place in the classroom was examined from a place of self-esteem. I discovered that my students liked to be read to aloud. They especially enjoyed, **The Education of Little Tree** and **To Kill a Mockingbird,** which were foundational in helping them build their self-esteem, as well as vocabulary, listening and self-expression skills. As I read each chapter, I would have them draw whatever pictures came to mind. This became a means for those who were academically challenged to otherwise feel accomplished creatively and gave me a thread of hope that I was doing something right.

My self-esteem lessons were tested by a real-life situation that occurred with my students. They had a habit of doing their science homework, a subject taught by one of my two co-teachers, while in my history class. When I asked them why they did their homework for the other teacher (and on my class time), but not for me, they confided that the other teacher openly humiliated them whenever they failed to turn in their work, then they elaborated on his tactics. Angered, I asked them why they accepted being treated this way. They couldn't see that they had any choice. I asked them to think about the worse thing that could happen to them. They were certain that they would get expelled for standing up to him. I explained to them that if their behavior was within appropriate expectations, there was little he could do that he was not doing already. I gave them the example of Dorothy in **The Wizard of Oz.** She believed that the only way she could get home was to talk to the Wizard, but she had to overcome her fear of him to do so. When Toto pulled the curtain away, it became obvious that the dreaded Wizard was a fake: merely a frightened, little man with a big voice perpetuating his power by keeping others in fear.

The nature in which my students returned from science class the following day told me that something had transpired. They made sure that the door was closed and then they vented their excitement. When the science teacher started his berating routine, one student, who was a natural-born leader, raised her hand for permission to speak and then articulated that the students did not like the manner in which he spoke to them. According to the class, he was speechless. After class, the teacher then cornered the spokesperson to explain that when he talked like that, he was not referring to her. She responded that it made no difference to whom he was speaking; his approach was unappreciated.

The librarian, with whom I had shared the story and who was a friend of the science teacher's wife, informed me later that he had divulged to her that he had been quite taken aback by the students' honesty and that, in all his thirty-five years in this profession—all in the same school where he had both student taught and received his own primary education—he had used this approach because he knew it was failsafe in getting students to do homework. In essence, he was admitting that he used humiliation tactics to control them.

The sharp-edged behavior of the science teacher was diminished after this incident, and my students unquestionably became more self-confident and cohesive, but I wondered what price I would pay. Although the science teacher was part of my departmentalized team, he scoffed at my input in our departmental meetings, and otherwise, treated me as if I was nonexistent. I knew I was not alone, for the entire staff up to the principal, either backed away from or kowtowed to his abrasive cynicism. I could feel his crushing dislike for me and cringed whenever I was near him (a similar feeling as the site manager's presence at my prior job had triggered). Not only would it take a number of confrontations, but also a number of years down the path, before I understood the true nature of my reaction to him. He was merely another being with whom I had played out my persecution issues; under different circumstances, he had killed me for standing up and protecting "the children" when they were unable to protect themselves.

Another of my primary aims was to inculcate my students with the understanding that, neither national test scores, nor grades could be a reliable measurement of self-worth or true intelligence. I clarified that there are many ways that people learn, whether it is through reading, listening, observing or hands-on experience, but the educational institution does not cater to individual learning styles. I added that if a student is unable to adequately perform within the given context defined by the system, he or she is labeled as intellectually substandard. I used my older brother as an example. Although he had never been academically successful, he was brilliant at taking apart anything from a malfunctioning car engine to a furnace and putting them in working order without the aid of instructions or guidance. Further, I explained that the system required me to give them grades, but whatever they received was more a reflection of the number of assignments they completed rather than their true intelligence. I understood, to some degree, that my efforts were as much about reassuring the damaged adolescent in me as they were about encouraging them.

One student, in particular, allowed me to feel that I was making a positive impact. Aaron came with a great need for attention. He initially followed me around, submissively posturing slightly behind me, waiting for me to acknowledge him. When I did, his eyes were riveted to the floor and his voice came out in a stuttering whisper. Having little time to meet individual needs, I immediately stated that I would always address his questions but, in exchange, I required him to look me in the eyes when he talked to me and to speak in a manner that freed me from having to either guess or ask him six times what he was saying. Aaron would have to give up a lifetime of conditioning to live up to my expectations of him. Yet, by the end of the first semester, I was witnessing a small miracle. Aaron had quit his fatuous posturing, learned to project his voice in class, was being shown respect by his fellow students, and had even been voted student council representative by his classmates.

The only glitch to the success story was Aaron had put himself in a position to receive an F in art. To get the token A, I required students to turn in all of their assignments; they were not graded. Aaron turned in none. I knew that art was a form of self-expression that terrified him. I clarified with him the consequences of his choice, and he said he would think about what he was going to do. Another side to this picture, of which I was aware, was that Aaron's mother was a domineering individual whose influence spilled over into the school by way of her being on the local school council. I anticipated her reaction to Aaron's failing grade.

On parent/teacher conference day, Aaron's mother marched into the classroom, her husband and Aaron in tow. A glance at the grades, followed by a glare at Aaron, instantaneously reduced Aaron to his former posturing, reminiscent of a scene from **One Flew Over the Cuckoo's Nest** where Miss Ratched's condemnation of a young patient's behavior diminished him to ego-deflated stuttering. In spite of the high quality of Aaron's grades overall, his mother honed in on the F in art. I explained that he had been aware of the situation, had made a choice, and was willing to accept the consequences. Mrs. Lopez ignored me. Instead, she screamed at Aaron to explain himself while demanding that he get his unfinished work from his desk.

I was unwilling to allow Aaron to commit emotional suicide (or his mother to commit psychic murder) over this. Assuring him that everything would be fine, I requested that he leave the room and wait in the hall. Then I asked Mrs. Lopez to contain herself for a moment and listen. As was becoming the norm, my words came out hard and fast from a place I could not identify: "Aaron is your son, but he is my student. He and I have worked very hard over the last few months to get him where he is now. If you can't see the important product of our effort then everything we've accomplished will be undone by your condemnation of him. Don't destroy Aaron. Accept his F, as he has, so he can learn his lesson rather than be defeated by it." Even as I was speaking, I was aware that my words could cost me my job.

Taken aback by the truth in my message, she defended, "I only have my children's best interest in mind. I know I'm over-controlling, but I'm afraid of them not being successful." My response came out as a command, "I want to hear you say that Aaron's F in art is okay." She looked at me in a surprised manner, but did not question me. Instead, although only half-heartedly, she said it was okay. I demanded that she say it again, this time with conviction. Two times later, I demanded that she and her husband, who had sat silently through this entire encounter, say it together. The sixth time it was said, we all broke into laughter. That is the way Aaron found us when I requested that he rejoin us. Again, supporting Aaron was supporting the adolescent in me who had never felt supported. It also had to do with vicariously undoing, and restitution for, what I had inflicted on my own son. What I did *not* know, was from whence came my growing assertiveness, or the real extent of how these situations were allowing me to heal the damaged sides of myself.

As with the naturalist job, I looked for a place to fit in among my fellow staff members. What I found were cliques: a Jewish clique, a Spanish clique, "the-old-dinosaur-putting-in-time-until-retirement" clique, and a youngster clique. I did not fit anywhere. Once I went out after school for drinks with a group of teachers who did so on a regular basis, but doing so was more uncomfortable than operating on the outside. My patterning, my own insecurities, had trapped me again. Without having clear awareness of this, I did not realize I was recreating as much conflict as I had committed myself to resolve.

Adam was one of my greatest assets and biggest supporters during my teaching initiations. He had great insight into the nature of adolescents, and we had many fruitful conversations on the nature of teaching. At the time, he was even contemplating becoming a high school principal. My concern, one with which I was disinclined to deal, was that I was attached to having conversations with Adam—looking for validation from him as much as anyone else.

Just before Adam departed for college, he took my car to visit a friend of his who lived in a neighborhood where finding parking was difficult. When he got back to where he had parked the car after he left his friend's, he discovered that a cab driver had squeezed in to park his vehicle illegally in front of him and, consequently, Adam was unable to maneuver out of his parking spot. With help from his friend, he was able to budge the cab forward enough to make room to exit, but not before angrily punching out the cab driver's rear view mirror. He told me the story when he arrived home. Then he added, "This is a bad thing I did, isn't it, Mom?" I responded that I did not see it as bad, though he clearly wanted me to condemn him. I would not do so, but he persisted. Finally, I said, "If you did it again, under the same circumstances, it might be bad, but maybe you won't need to do it again." He got the point. The lesson for me was to be understanding with my students, never condemning them, regardless of the circumstances. It was a reference for myself also, although much more difficult to personally apply.

Adam had gotten into the habit of coming home from university every other weekend, partly because his girlfriend, Mindy, went to school in the area. He would take the bus to Chicago, but insisted that he could not spare the time to take the bus back, expecting me to drive him. This meant that I spent a full day on the road to save him a couple hours of travel time. I felt he was taking advantage of me. However, any other way, I would have gotten little or none of his time. Besides this, I still felt guilty for abandoning him and even more so once I had begun dating—to the extent that I kept Liam a secret. Further, a part of me remained angry that Carl had the home and the son, while all I had was disjointed visitations and financial responsibilities.

Besides spending time with Adam, another gift of driving him to school was the experience the return trip provided. For many years, whenever I was on the road alone, I would encounter the most bizarre, intense sensations within the confines of my car, as if I was in a weird perception-heightening capsule—like the sensory deprivation tank I had once experienced. I was never sure who was doing the driving at these times, yet I was never apprehensive about getting in an accident. If anything, I looked forward to these moments.

My social life had flourished since leaving Carl, or more aptly stated, I was having enough experiences to recognize that I was not a social being. I could manage in one-on-one interactions, while larger social interactions continued to find me tense and shut down and/or mindlessly rambling, as if my voice ran on a force apart. In spite of myself, my delving deeply into my own issues had endowed me with a burgeoning wisdom upon which others were coming to rely. (It was now easy to see in others the disconnection that I saw in myself.) Accordingly, friendships came now in the form of my being a support or counsel. I knew to some degree that helping others provided me the sense of validation I needed, regardless of the cost to myself. Most often though, these relationships were tedious and burdensome, as was the case with the computer teacher, Gertrude, who had been trying, as she claimed, to become friends with me for some time before I finally let her in.

I could not have admitted that this was also the case with Teresa. She had worried that after I finished student-teaching we would lose contact, but I was aware that this would not be so. She liked being active outdoors as much as I did, so we spent much time walking or biking and conversing. I listened to her and she listened to me, although I was aware that she could only minimally understand from whence I came or whither I went. Typically, our outings were planned around her needs or schedule. I excused this by pointing out that her life was the more complicated and it should be me, therefore, who was the more flexible.

While in therapy I had delved deeply into my childhood and healed many issues. Yet, as many as I had addressed, there seemed to be as many or more waiting on the threshold. Some part of me continued to hope that when I had healed sufficiently I would fit into my biological family. My parents had even informed me that when my divorce was finalized, they would reinstate me in their will. I assumed that they were communicating that they now felt it safe for me to be in the family.

I still found it next to impossible to simply be when I was in their space. Chitchat remained arduous to carry on, although it was hardly necessary on my part: Father, after an initial greeting, largely ignored me, and Mother talked incessantly—chiefly about her health. When it was not her health, it was inane gossip, an article she had read or the latest scoop on her favorite soap opera. Sometimes when my impatience got the better of me, I would interrupt and ask, "What is the point you are trying to make?" Awakening from her babbling for a moment, she would pause and look at me puzzled before continuing. After an hour or so, I only wanted to scream at her to shut the hell up.

Invariably, to make my stay tolerable and because I felt obligated to do something for them since I was in their home and eating their food, I compulsively took on some project or another. Working in the yard was where Mother and I found common ground. She liked plants, but she never had what it took for them to thrive. Therefore, her flowerbeds were most often as chaotic and overgrown as her house. Once we got started, we could accomplish much in a short time. This was despite my father, who at this juncture would pull himself from watching television to "supervise" the undertaking. From his lawn chair, smoking his cigar and incessantly spitting, he would sooner or later declare, "You two've been working too hard. I want you two to cut it out now." Then he would invariably demand repeatedly, "How much do I owe you?" when the work was complete. I never stopped bristling whenever he did this, especially knowing that he had no intention of paying me anything. I would never have remotely imagined that somewhere in the future I would be able to find humor in his behavior. What struck me most when I spent time with my parents, however, was the intense friction between them, as well as their alcohol dependency. What also struck me was that there was even less for me here in my family as a changed person than there was before.

Unable to accept the relationship within its limitation, I invited my mother to stay with me for a few days during spring break. She had never before gone anywhere and left her husband behind, so she was immediately dwelling more on his welfare than her own adventure. Nevertheless, I made elaborate plans to take her places that she had never been before and made sure it cost her nothing, among many reasons, to remove that as a barrier between us. We had dinner with my elder gentleman friend, Charles, at an ethnic restaurant. We went to a play and to the zoo. We went out with Teresa and her mother-in-law to an expensive jazz club for breakfast one morning. The two of them, fully made up and dressed to kill, left my mother fumbling in her purse to find her lipstick. Not wanting to cause her further uneasiness, the words to ease her discomfort, "Don't worry, Mom, you look just fine," never found expression. It was plain, at least to some degree, in this scenario, and at my mother's expense, that Teresa and I lived different realities despite my trying to adapt to her sophisticated lifestyle.

Much to my surprise, Liam agreed to go to dinner with the two of us one night. Even more to my surprise, the two of them were noticeably comfortable with each other. I wondered how different the nature of the interaction might have been without alcohol playing a role. I even noticed that I was feeling left out and a bit jealous. After dinner, Liam suggested that we take my mother to listen to a German band at his favorite restaurant. I got drunker than I had ever been in my life. This was enough of a sobering lesson in and of itself. The fact that my contacts were not in their case when I went to put them in the following morning revealed the degree of my intoxication, and drove the lesson home. This was the first time in my twenty-five plus years of wearing contacts that I had ever lost one. I had used alcohol to fit in, and in doing so I had lost my vision.

When I drove my mother home, only her yippy, little poodle acknowledged her arrival. Before I could get her bag out of the car, she was at the next-door neighbor's garage sale proclaiming how hard she had worked while in Chicago, ironing my curtains, washing my dishes, etc. With effort, I kept my reaction to myself. Above all, she made it clear that she was unable to live without her martyr identity. I stayed long enough to witness how cruel Father was to her, swearing at her, telling her to shut up. I asked her why she stayed with him, but her only rejoinder was that the wife of a couple with whom they played cards had asked her the same question. The entire episode sobered me into a closer scrutiny of my reality.

Still believing that teaching was not where I belonged, I completed my first year and accepted the same position for the following term. It had been a tough but rewarding year. I cared more about my students' overall growth than their academic achievements and I was proud of how we all had succeeded.

Notwithstanding the distractions that teaching presented, I continued to move more deeply into that world so profoundly calling to me. The deeper I went, the more separated I felt from my worldly existence. I had come to value this aspect of my life more than any other, despite being perpetually overwhelmed. I was beginning to extract that my sexual energy was not lust at all and had little to do with sexual desire, although Liam could never have agreed. *This* sexual energy was something that the greater energy moving through me was awakening. Besides interaction with Liam, frequent long, scalding showers remained the most viable avenue to keep this blazing, sexual-like energy from devouring me.

As for Liam, I was unable to convince myself that I was in love with him, although I deeply cared for him. I had put considerable effort into getting him to understand me and then tried not to trounce on him when he put up his protective barriers, exactly as I had done with Kent. I was finding this relationship stuff that I (along with everyone else) seemed to be so addicted to, rather meaningless and a waste of time and energy. We were both using each other to get our needs met. As disillusioned as I was, I felt there was a healthy way of being in relationship and if I stayed focused on healing, I would eventually find it. I was correct, but not in my present scope. Already I was being prepared to separate myself from the limitations of a sexual identity. Once done, I would find the relationship I was seeking, or that was seeking me—a relationship with something greater.

Liam and I spent nearly three weeks of our summer vacation traveling through the northeast. Our camping gear was used on only five occasions. His idea of a great trip was to drive from one winery to another sampling the local fare. When we were not imbibing, we were touring the preponderance of civil war battlefields and war memorials. I found it amusing that as a war buff he knew from memory names of important generals and dates, as well as locations of major battles. The more days that went by, the more I surrendered to him defining our agenda and the more clear it became that, instead of sharing an experience, I was on Liam's vacation. I watched how I pouted, became withdrawn or even resentful considering him to be inconsiderate of my needs. At the same time, I realized he was exactly where he needed to be; I was actually free, therefore, to be where I needed to be. Nevertheless, I wanted him to be with me. I was clueless that no one but me was going to be able to travel in the manner in which I was being required. Clueless that, in fact, I *was* on my own, whether or not others were in my presence, or I in theirs.

I started my second year of teaching and expected the previous year's successes to afford a foundation from which to continue building. This was not to be. I could have sworn that the children with the most problems were selectively chosen and assigned to room 310. Their collective energy was nothing like I had ever experienced. Any cohesiveness that I may have been able to build was sabotaged by, what I called, the "revolving door syndrome." In the course of the school year, I would have eight students leave and twelve enter. Each new student who enrolled came with more baggage than the previous. I began to phone parents for serious behavior problems, but that soon backfired. One mother informed me, after I had phoned her three times over the course of the first semester, that her husband beat her, as well as the children every time he heard that I had phoned and would I please stop. A father instructed me to not bother calling him; he wanted nothing to do with his daughter, "phone the police and have her thrown in jail." It came as no surprise that behind every student's problem is his environment—I knew that personally—but that understanding was beginning to take on a bleak, new significance.

The special reading teacher, who had gone through great pains to befriend me, tended my students during lunchroom duty and they, as well as other students, hated the way she treated them. I had frequently articulated that they should try not to take her personally. I bit my own tongue to avoid telling her off myself, until one day I witnessed her yell in the face of one of my students trying to make him stand in the corner for what she considered talking too loud. The more he stood his ground the more she screamed, until everyone in the cafeteria was watching. She was blinded to the boy's thorough demoralization, verging on tears, but when she realized that he was not going to budge from his seat, she turned to me for support. Icily, I told her that she should take responsibility for the scene she had created. Afterward, I informed the principal, adding that it was nothing novel, and further conveyed that she should not be dealing with older students when it was obvious to everyone, especially to the students themselves, that she despised them. She was no longer assigned lunch duty. Though it was no secret that she was relieved, she cornered me about my non-support and from then on acted as if I did not exist. Fortunately for me, some part of me was beyond caring about being accepted; yet it was noticeably uncomfortable to work within the context of such negative energy.

Carl's lack of cooperation in regard to concluding the divorce effectively hindered the possibility of my accepting a Peace Corps assignment before Liam. When he received his invitation stating that he was assigned to teaching English as a second language in Lesotho, Africa, and would be gone by Christmas, he asked me if he should accept. That was about as direct or intimate as he could be in discussing our relationship. I heard exactly what he was asking me, which was for me to say that he should decline the invitation. Opening his door for me in this manner and at this time was too little, too late. I found myself saying that there was an adventure waiting for him and he should grab it while it was available. From within I distinctly heard, "And now it is time for you to get on with your life!" Regardless, the part of me that feared being alone was attempting to clamber through the door that he had momentarily opened.

He made it clear that he did not want me around the day he was moving. But I had forgotten that I had his extra apartment key, and thinking that he would have to turn it in to the landlord, I stopped by to drop it off. As I climbed the stairs, my heart pounding from a rush of adrenaline, I understood that I was breaking Liam's unspoken rules of conduct: it was forbidden to drop in on him. When I knocked on the door, he opened it, saw that it was me and then quickly stepped out and closed the door behind him. The door was open long enough, however, for me to notice that, besides his regular friends, there was a woman present whom I had never before seen. Intuition told me it was his old girlfriend. He had little time to say much to me, even if he could have gotten beyond his embarrassment, for I rushed down the stairs trying to keep my hurt contained. I watched my hurt escalate and then consume me throughout the rest of the day. My anger over my reaction was secondary.

That night Liam knocked on my door with a bottle of champagne, an apology and an excuse. I watched myself needing to believe him. I watched my remaining hurt dance around me. I observed how one part of me was tired of dealing with this drama that I consistently magnetized, and only wanted to order him to leave. I watched how a "good fuck" left him thinking, exactly as it had with Carl, that my ruffled feathers were smoothed and that everything was back to normal. I knew that the incident had left me changed somehow, more sober and more cognizant of my own behavior.

For the most part, my lessons with Liam, which I continued to label a relationship, actually came to an end the night before his departure when he invited me to join him at his mother's for dinner. It was an amusing, confusing occasion that after two years he was bringing me out of the closet. I felt stiff and formal around the two of them, watching them drink their manhattans and realizing that mother also was an alcoholic. Despite what had transpired, I tried to subdue my speculation that his insistence that I not see him off at the airport the following morning was because the other woman was going to be there. Instead, I attempted to maintain that it was because he had difficulty handling goodbyes. Was I insecure? Was I jealous? Certainly, I was bewildered. I told myself that I could be confrontational enough to ask him exactly what was going on, but that it was unnecessary to add my problems to his already stressed state. My only real problem was my inability to own my knowing and be honest with myself; Liam's behavior was not my problem.

A day after his departure, I purchased a journal and began to write. I did not know that I would fill countless more journals during my journeying. Nor did I realize that I was beginning to write down my story, which would mostly find its way on the journal pages through a stream-of-consciousness process. My first significant entry read: "Liam is gone. Ask me how I feel and I say that everything is as it is supposed to be. If I am able to love a man honestly, it is Liam. Only through learning to love myself am I able to do this. He is a good man. He tries hard. He must learn to let go of his past, which has a stranglehold on him. His Peace Corps adventure is the beginning of his necessary lessons. He must proceed alone, without me. If the time comes for our paths to cross again, we will know. Before this, we both have much to learn. May he have the strength to learn about his own goodness."

I was unaware of the real meaning of my words, that they had more to do with me than with Liam, and that owning the space of which I had spoken—learning to love myself is learning to honestly love—would be an arduous assignment. Retrospect would be the key to understanding the true meaning of the accounts that I was now being required to chronicle.

Meanwhile, a bout of walking pneumonia guaranteed me time to reflect. Regardless of my obsessive insecurities and sense of responsibility toward Liam, it was a relief to have my life to myself once more. It was painful to deny how dead-ended our involvement had been: how I had once again succeeded in giving myself away, piece by piece; how I had projected my father issues onto him, needing him to do things with me and for me; how he was never there for me. I hated witnessing how needy and temperamental I could be. It was also evident how my ego was unprepared to release the security of believing that I had a relationship. Yet I knew that to join our lives really meant that I would have to sacrifice my life to join him in his.

We exchanged letters...I sent him the obligatory care packages, rationalizing that I would hope that someone would do the same for me if I were far away and isolated from my customary lifestyle...I put myself in his place and imagined how my package would lift his spirits, which had skidded to near-depression. His letters gave minute-to-minute details of his activities, but contained little pith, setting the tone for me to limit my own self-expression. Nevertheless, I convinced myself that I missed him. I would be well on my way into ventures of my own before I wrote to share with him a truth about the surprising turns my life was taking.

7

Spiritual Boot Camp

Liam was removed from my life; Christmas vacation rolled around. Unable to face the quiet it provided, I found distraction by offering to help my parents drive to Arizona where they spent the winter. As if this was not enough, I offered to fly Adam and his girlfriend there and back as a Christmas present. I rationalized this would give me a chance to spend time with Adam that I would not otherwise have had and also provide him a break from school. My generosity thereby assuaged my everlasting guilt over having abandoned him. My manipulation did not end here. I next invited Gertrude (the computer teacher who had come to rely on me to support her with her problems) to join us on her way home from California. She had been hinting for some time that it would be no extra charge to change her flight schedule. In truth, I could not say no to her, partly because I felt sorry for her and partly because she expected me to say yes. The excuse I gave my mother, when I carefully disclosed that there would be yet one more person staying, was that Gertrude had no family with whom to share Christmas. It would appear that I had set the stage for a perfect comedy of errors.

The drive alone portended the coming adventure: my mother, miserable with hemorrhoids; my father, crawling along the interstate at fifty miles per hour cursing roundly and in Scottish blue at whoever had the nerve to pass him. They bickered about one petty thing after another until unable to contain myself another moment, I indignantly rejoined loudly that they were behaving like children. No, worse! When it was my turn to drive, my father, among his many obsessive oddities, continuously sneaked furtive peeks at the speedometer to see how fast I was driving, then mumbled curses as he rolled his eyes. Issues I thought I had long ago set to rest quickly loomed up from their graves.

By the time we arrived, both my parents were imbibing by breakfast. My father attempted to be secretive about the amount of beer he drank by hiding his empty cans in the bottom of the wastebasket; my mother had to dig through the trash to pull them out, giving him hell for not recycling. Otherwise, her hemorrhoids kept her in bed where she whined and complained of her misery as I catered to her. Two days later, when Adam and Mindy arrived, she arose from her sickbed to play the hostess. I was impressed with how decent she was to Adam, much more so than I could or would have expected, although an underlying current of tension was obvious. When I bought Adam some new clothes, my father expressed his disgust that I would actually be financially supporting my son at his age. His criticism reopened my childhood resentments of how self-supporting I'd had to be.

Father displayed his own sense of generosity by unexpectedly announcing that he was taking us all out to eat on my birthday. I watched myself latch onto his announcement as if it was a promise, not trusting, but hoping, exactly as I had done as a child. If nothing else, the situation made me more acutely aware that, even as a child, I had known he was lying to me. I had had to receive his lies as if they were promises; there had been nothing else in my childhood onto which to hold. This had been a matter of survival. Now I was more fully faced with how I had brought my survival conditioning into my relationship with Carl and used his lies as promises, transferring my struggles with my father onto him. I was able to leave Carl because I had moved beyond needing his lies. I needed no more references to begin to understand that the real reasons I had accompanied my parents to Arizona were much different than my original ideas.

The first day together we all piled into the car for a drive to the Sonoran desert. While I was ready to exit the vehicle and begin to explore the vast, wondrous and unique expanse of nature before me, Adam and Mindy at my side, my father's attitude, "we're here, we've seen it, now it's time to go home," once again, only too vividly replayed girlhood memories. I attempted to mentally side-step his antsy display of impatience, but feelings of selfishness got the better of me. A half-hour after our arrival, we were on our way home. I sat in the back seat fighting my sullenness and disappointment just as I had when touring the west with my female relatives as a teenager.

As Mother had been with my friends in high school, she was immediately jealous of Gertrude upon her arrival, and Gertrude's primary concern turned out to be shopping for country western clothing. Before her suitcases were hardly in the house, she had pulled out a phone directory and made a list of stores in the area, and expected me to chauffeur her. I watched myself go through gyrations to make the situation comfortable for both of them. My enabling behavior, while I had no control over it, sickened me.

The following day, Father claimed he wanted to watch the football game and we could go site seeing without him. Then he handed me his car keys. He coveted his vehicle: How could I put miles on it? What if I got in an accident? My exploding anxiety took me back to a memory: my younger brother, then in the service, was using Father's car to drive Mother and my older brother's son, then an infant, to my grandmother's, when he got in an accident. When Father learned of the situation, his primary concern and first question had been: How much damage did you do to my car? I thought about renting a car—that frightened me too. Also, I was not willing to incur such an expense when Father's car was readily available. After all, why shouldn't he share? Without question, one lesson of the day was to override my fear of wrecking his car and having to face his condemnation.

Except for my mother's inability to put aside her concerns about my father being upset over our absence, it was a relaxing and pleasant day for everyone. First thing when we arrived home, however, my father craned his neck through the window to check the odometer as he had done with me as a teenager and muttered his "jesuschrist...goddamn...how...?" under his breath. I turned away hurt, helpless and silent. Anger. He next informed my mother, who immediately informed *me*, that he had been worried about us and waited around *all* day for our return. Guilt. By dinner, both of them were inebriated.

When New Year's Eve rolled around, my father was emphatic about dining out, by my estimation mostly to save face. With him present, dinner was guaranteed to be a perfunctory event, and true to form, forty-five minutes after arrival, he requested the waiter forget about dessert and just bring him the check. Meanwhile, I excused myself to use the washroom. When I returned, the check had been paid, but not by my father. Instead, everyone had contributed. Feeling as dishonored and disowned as in my childhood, I was furious, but the "don't-rock-the-boat/can't-make-father-angry" conditioning kept me silent.

Adam had planned to surprise me with a birthday cake later that evening. However, since being with my parents was such a strain, and they were no longer sober, he decided to present it after they went to bed.

The next morning, my mother accused me of being sneaky and planning activities behind her back. I explained the situation as honestly as possible, trying to contain my anger and not hurt her feelings at the same time. She was more defensive than ever. By now, all the childhood issues of which I considered myself free were running wild and bringing to life all of the guilt and worthlessness that still remained inside me. I felt completely helpless, especially since, once again, I had been an ineffective role model for Adam.

That night, after I drove Gertrude to the airport, I sat both of my parents in the living room and confronted them about their behavior, including their drinking. They responded exactly as they had during the time my two brothers and I, as teenagers, had confronted them about their lack of love for us. They held themselves immobile as I spoke, acting as if they did not comprehend anything I was saying, yet tearfully mewling, "I guess everything's our fault."

Exasperated and hostile, I tore into my mother about her using her cunning "poor-me" routine to manipulate her family. Next, I ravaged my father for the hypocrisy of having the "say no to drugs" bumper sticker on his car. To his long-held defense, "What difference does it make? I'm going to die soon anyway," I retorted, "That may be so, but at your funeral, would you rather have your two sons who are both chemically-dependent themselves, say, 'Wow! We're proud of the old man's strength to beat the addiction. He's an inspiration, especially at his age!' Or would you like them to place a can of your favorite beer in your casket, give a callous laugh and claim, 'You know the old man. He couldn't go anywhere without a beer. At least we're giving him the send-off he deserves!'" To culminate the confrontation, I forewarned them that I would never be around them again when they were drinking.

I knew I had unrealistic expectations of my parents, and also that, at forty, it was ludicrous that I continued to battle with them. I lay awake for most of the night, panicky, ruminating, and desperately fighting my urge to throw myself into the bad person routine. The next morning, my parents greeted us as if nothing had happened. Adam and Mindy departed early. At the airport, my father shook their hands stiffly and wished them a good trip, as he did later that afternoon with me. This pretending that everything was fine, when emotions were as thick as smoke from a raging fire, spotlighted how altogether debilitating my childhood had been. I was certain that rather than ground gained in reconnecting to my family, I had once again put myself on the outs. My emotions being part of the experience guaranteed my being judgmental, and therefore unable to see that there was no right or wrong to this experience; it was, in fact, a Divine lesson enabling me to move further on my path. I was the one who needed to get sober.

A couple of weeks following my return, out of the blue, my younger brother phoned claiming that it was just a spur-of-the-moment call to see how I was doing. His caution was obvious. When I finally brought the conversation around to the Arizona adventure, he claimed that he did not want to talk about the matter because it was between my parents and me, and we would only get in an argument if we opened up the subject. I reminded him that arguing was a choice, whereby his resistance lightened.

The first fact that he brought up was that I had said he had a drinking problem. The self-deprecating character in me wanted to make excuses or put a different spin on my words. I had already tried to convince myself that, since I wasn't sure that my brothers *had* a drinking problem, I was being inexcusably judgmental myself. I focused to refrain from back-peddling and claimed that our parents were not bad, but sick, and full of denial, and that I had worked too hard to acquire a sense of self-esteem to allow anyone, including them, to undermine it. I conveyed that their drinking was symptomatic of their damage, not a problem in and of itself. The longer we talked the more I could feel his barriers diminishing, mine also. I finished the conversation by expressing my gratitude for his reaching out to me. Of all that I had yet to learn how to live, one realization was that acquiring or maintaining self-esteem does not come through struggle or resistance. More than teaching my students about the subject, I had to become a living example.

For six weeks, despite my efforts otherwise, I continued to agonize over my perceived predicament and how I was going to put it to rest (do something so my parents would not hate me and I could fit back into the family). It had been some time since I had gotten myself in such an extremely obsessive state. A part of me was way beyond this, but regardless of how creatively I tried to dismiss the matter, day after day my emotions and thoughts ate away at me. I felt hopelessly stuck and close to going mad.

Not any too soon, I sat down one night to focus again on freeing myself of this cyclopean distraction, when the energy took over instead. Faster than lightening and like an utterance from some unearthly guidance, came a command, "You now have to give up your biological family in order to find your own identity and to give birth to a spiritual family." It burned into my consciousness, frying my senses, and reverberating long after the message was received.

My search for an understanding of family had never ceased. The studying of so-called primitive cultures was the closest I had ever come to identifying a seemingly reliable sense of family: there was no lack, cooperation was the norm, everyone was equally a vital member of the community and, regardless of who gave birth to the children, they were sons and daughters of the community and everyone shared the blessings of guiding the children into adulthood.

Dr. Jennings' history class had provided opportunity to learn about the profusion of grand experiments to create utopian societies during the development of this country. I had been fascinated by the concept and was curious to know the intricacies of how they all had functioned. Visiting a Shaker community that had been converted to a living history museum while traveling with Liam had fed my thirst for more understanding. What most intrigued me about the Shaker community was their advanced understanding of the use of medicinal herbs, their church services consisting of dancing and singing; and that new members were secured by collecting unwanted children from orphanages. Marriage and personal wealth were not allowed. Anyone who decided to leave the community was greatly supported in doing so. The more I learned the more my appetite to know increased. Overall, what had most piqued my curiosity was why the great majority of these utopian societies had failed.

The idea of giving birth to a spiritual family not only baffled me, it triggered an inexplicable level of denial, especially when I was further informed that I could no longer consider myself a part of my biological family—I *had* to divorce them—but if my parents so chose, they could be a part of my spiritual one. With certain disdain, I dismissed the idea of my parents ever understanding the choice, let alone voluntarily entering into my reality. I would gladly step into a spiritual family; I longed to be part of one, but the idea of creating one *by myself* was paralyzing. Who am I to have such a responsibility? And who would think that I was capable? I was unable to even conceive how to approach the idea, let alone how to manifest it. Surely giving birth to a spiritual family meant that as I traveled along my spiritual path, I would simply meet many like-minded people with whom there would be a mutual recognition. Maybe we'd all start living together like a Shaker community.

The only accuracy in my interpretation was how it supported my insecurities. I would live *my conception* of the meaning of this directive, continually searching for like-minded people who were part of "the family," but I was unaware that the crystallization of my spiritual family was already underway. It would be a long time before I realized that what I was looking for, what I needed to attain, what my heart yearned for and what I had to give birth to in order to survive, was not a function of a physical reality. The truth was I had already given birth to my family. Now was the time to prepare to help them awaken.

In the moment, I was required to write two letters, first to my father and then to my mother. The only difference between the two letters was the salutation. I felt an electrifying charge as I wrote that I was no longer a part of the family. Instead, I was creating my own, and if they ever decided they wanted to be a part of it, the door was open. At the same time, I scoffed at the idea that my parents could even comprehend what I was communicating. All I could see was them fighting their reservation to opening the letters once they saw the return address, and then once doing so, emotionally freezing to a lower degree, quickly disposing of the letters, and as best they could, pretending nothing had happened.

After finishing the letters, typed, sealed and ready for posting, I slumped to the floor in front of my word processor. What had I done? My actions felt as if I had written my own death sentence. Sending these letters would leave my fate irreversibly sealed. I was angry, angry at myself, as well as my parents, angry at my guidance for being in this predicament. I desperately wanted to believe that at any moment I would be divinely informed that my task was complete, that I would not have to post the letters. I tried to convince myself that I was not angry, but I was helplessly so and becoming angrier by the minute.

Suddenly, I glanced across the room, my attention immediately falling on the azalea plant sitting on the coffee table. The special reading teacher had given it to me back when we had still been on speaking terms. She had found it in her incinerator, discarded and dying, and knowing that I loved plants, believing that I could bring it back to life, she had brought it to me. I *had* revived it and for some time it had borne a single, pure white blossom. I had certainly noticed it all along, but suddenly I remembered that it had been in bloom from the time I had begun the process of divorcing my family; and now I realized that it was beckoning to me. I crossed the room and knelt, cupping my hands gently around the single blossom and opening to the message of its tender beauty. I knelt there with my hands embracing the flower for quite some time as the message embraced me. It spoke to me then like a benediction, "*You* are my beauty. What you are called to do, you must do in beauty. You must do in beauty and purity. You are called to do this. You have already agreed." With the message complete, I crumbled to the floor stupefied and painfully humbled. I had little cerebral understanding of the importance of this experience, but there was little room for me to feel unworthy, and certainly not angry. It also left me wondering about beauty: what is it really, beyond our definition of it?

Shortly after this, Gertrude stopped by my apartment one day after school. I knew as we sat and talked, that I was being notified, forced in some odd way, to tell her about my sugar-daddy relationship with Charles. The pressure to reveal my secret was met by an all-out, intense resistance inside of me. As I continued to procrastinate, my body began to freeze in utter panic. I observed this inner contest for considerable time until finally, with heart pounding and sweat dampening my sweater, I stammered my shameful secret. Though Gertrude had little reaction, I immediately felt an incredibly forceful surge of relief. I was next required to disclose the conflicts that I had encountered with my fellow female naturalist and the site director at the nature center. My lingering anger was evident, but for the first time I was able to step out of the position of victim. On the contrary, I watched myself own my participation in the drama. This disclosure brought immense relief as well.

After Gertrude left, I spent the evening reflecting on what I was feeling. In revealing my "secrets" to her, I had felt just as when I had picked up the phone to contact Gambler's Anonymous, now several years ago—certain that God would strike me dead. I was beginning to openly acknowledge the shame and pain that accompanied being secretive about my life. Ironically, as much as I had kept Charles a secret in my life, I had also kept most of my life a secret from Charles. He knew nothing about Liam, or vice versa. I had told myself that whom I dated was none of his business. Meanwhile, I attempted to penetrate my own warped need for secrecy. Was I afraid of losing him or the security of knowing that his financial support was available should I ever need it? It was brutal to give this thought much weight, considering my conditioning not to look beyond myself for financial support. What I felt deep inside of me was a belief that if Charles knew that I was sexual with someone else, that somehow obligated me to have sex with him—the thought disgusted me—or he would die or hate me if he knew.

No sooner had I gained enough control of my anxiety when he unexpectedly became ill enough to be hospitalized, re-materializing my sense of obligation. On one visit to the hospital, I crossed paths with his son-in-law. I could feel his distrust of me, and the nature of his questioning hit the mark. The situation left me feeling as if I were living some sort of horrible Payton Place.

One time when he was in the hospital, someone broke into his house and among the items stolen were his deceased wife's jewels. For reasons I could never clearly comprehend, during the time of my early divorce proceedings, he had insisted that I have a key to his house. I had felt too uncomfortable with having it, and therefore, had long since disposed of it. When he informed me of the theft, I instantly convinced myself that the police would, sooner or later, be calling me to the precinct headquarters to be interrogated. In iron panic, once again, I was forced to examine my contorted, maniacal fear of being accused and condemned for a crime of which I was innocent. I hated this. I hated my reaction. I told myself that if Charles suspected me—which of course he didn't—it was his problem. I wanted to get away from this; whatever it took. In fact, it would take exploring a prior memory, a scandalous entanglement, not to get away, but to set myself free.

Months before, my lawyer had phoned to ask to me to come in for a conference to discuss his inability to move the divorce proceedings along. Carl was, once again, the expert saboteur. Even the judge, on the most recent court date, had informed him that if he came to court again without a lawyer, he would find him in contempt. At this point, my lawyer sought my guidance. I knew that if anyone were to get through Carl's defenses, I was the only likely candidate.

I was relieved of having to develop a strategy when Carl phoned unexpectedly, asserting that he wanted to finish the divorce with dignity. More accurately interpreted: one, he knew his manipulations no longer served him, and two, he was finally in a financial position to buy me out. Against my lawyer's advice, I agreed to meet with Carl. I walked into our meeting with jittery nerves and a pounding heart, but I had also come with a sense of determination and clarity, which left little room for my defensive or fixer character to become active.

The fact that Carl hated giving me anything stayed present among my glut of thoughts. I understood exactly why, when our negotiations began, and as an impetus to keep him in forward movement, I presented stipulations. I insisted that, from that moment until the papers were signed, he pay me rent for living in our house. I insisted that he have *his* lawyer draw up the documents this time and, when completed, he could notify my lawyer. I could have asked for more money. In the year and a half since I had moved out, the house had unquestionably increased in value. He understood this; he sold real estate. But regardless of any personal ideas, I was not allowed to alter my initial proposition. My take-it-or-leave-it attitude left him grudgingly agreeing. To get what *he* wanted, he had to play by my rules for once. I walked away from the encounter second-guessing myself; was I taking advantage of him? Nevertheless, a force operating outside my insecurities reassured me. I contemplated my need to have a sense of home and how I, myself, had played as vital a role as Carl in protracting the last chapter of our conflict.

When my lawyer shortly received the papers from Carl's lawyer, he was flabbergasted over my accomplishment. The documents revealed that Carl had, in fact, managed to obtain a loan. When the loan approval was complete and the quitclaim deed was ready to sign, my lawyer expected the four of us to meet. I informed him that the only way to avoid aggravating Carl and complicating matters was for me to meet with him alone. He chafed at this plan, apprehensive of unexpected repercussions of my not being legally represented at the rendezvous, but at this point there was no debate. Besides, I had become accustomed to problem-solving with Carl on my own, and since I was much less fearful of making mistakes, I was that much more confidant in owning the risks, if there were any to be taken. Whatever the reason, I knew I had to do this by myself.

When the time came, Carl arranged for us to meet at his real estate office. He had the quitclaim deed, and a $75,000 check ready for me, but no rent check. When I brought this to his attention, he went off on a "you-don't-trust-anybody" tangent. When he finished, I resolutely responded that I would sign the quitclaim deed when he, in accord with our agreement, produced another check. His growing agitation revealed that he had had no intention of giving me rent money. I watched him pull one trick out of the bag and then another. It would have been so easy to back down, just tell myself I was being greedy and retreat. Something would not let me. He stared me in the eye, his upper lip quivering. I stood firm and strong, bending in the squall of the moment, but not breaking. Finally, he wrote me a personal check. I walked away assuring myself that I was worthy of having this money.

Within two weeks we had our last day in court. Although I was disturbed that I had paid $5,000 in lawyer fees, and felt as if I had gotten my own divorce, I understood that Carl was more than anyone knew how to handle. Besides which, I was beginning to understand that whatever it was I had to do with my life, I had to do it without expecting support from anyone. This was a much larger lesson than I could ever have comprehended.

With my long-awaited divorce finally complete, I was perplexed about not feeling elated. My need to be alone to deliberate on what was happening was so dominant that I declined invitations from friends to celebrate. Having viewed my marriage as too ugly and painful to look at—like rotting waste fouling my life, I had imagined that after digging a huge hole and filling it with my past, my divorce would represent the final shovelful of dirt needed to sever myself from the host of hurtful memories. I had anticipated feeling a commensurate sense of accomplishment when the task was complete, and be able to move forward unencumbered. My fear and anger around Carl had greatly diminished and I knew that I no longer needed to see him as the enemy. Rather, here were two damaged people having played out their issues with each other. What I was unable to release was an inexplicable sense of loss over a seeming potential that had never actualized, as well as a lingering sense of obligation to make his life okay for him.

For weeks I remained unsettled in regard to being unable to obtain a sense of closure to my relationship with Carl. Finally, a journal entry gave me a new perspective. "My past is not for me to bury. Rather, I must embrace it, cherish it, turn it to light so that it can become the foundation for my new life—a carpet of green grass upon which to dance and sing." I had little understanding of the significance of this message. Yet it was clear that I was being required to let go of any opinion that I had wasted my life, especially having stayed with Carl for as long as I had.

That same night, through a "sleep-writing" encounter, came another message, more succinct: "If my past is the darkness, I must walk through it to find the light." When I read what I had written on my diary page the next morning, instantly I exploded, "Don't make me do this! Don't make me go back! If I go back, I'll die!" It took some moments to deactivate my panic enough to approach the message more objectively. Ultimately, my interpretation was rather than burying my past, I had to embrace it, cherish it—accept it for what it has to be—a foundation for a greater reality. I was unaware, but in essence, the message was speaking of the nature of my entire existence. Regardless of how irrational I viewed my reaction— despite knowing I would and could explore my past if I had to—my initial reaction impaled me. Impending experiences were waiting for me to explore my greater past, including the extent of my greater history with Carl, by which I would understand this shadow of unfulfilled potential and my remaining need to make things right. Walking through my darkness—my past—would necessitate my death, the death of my ideas of who I thought I was. Yet, through my death lay my only chance of reaching the light and living my life as a gift.

I had never before had a significant amount of money. Now that I did, it triggered an utterly dizzying array of issues. Some part of me maintained that this settlement money was dirty: I had sold my soul to get it, and therefore I was not deserving and should just get rid of it. Another part, fearful of losing it, was tightening its secure grip. I convinced myself that if I were really a responsible person, I would educate myself about investing money and manage it myself. Consequently, I studied investment literature, but it was way too cerebral for me, and all my effort produced was a tizzy. Also, I knew people who had taken serious losses in recent years as a result of the unstable market. Losing the money was as frightening as being responsible for it. In the end, I came to realize that neither did I know how to have a proper relationship with money, nor did I know what this proper relationship looked like. I only knew how to work hard for money, struggle with it, and hoard it for dear life. It would be a while before I understood the relationship between the consciousness of lack and self-worth.

Simultaneously, my greater awareness conveyed that the settlement was actually not mine, but serving a purpose of which I had not yet been made aware. It was merely in my safekeeping until that purpose revealed itself; and I was reminded of the earlier message—I would need the money—given to me during the storm. Not knowing what else to do at the time, I put a portion of the money in the hands of a broker I had met while I was a naturalist and who had anticipated having me as a client. Another portion I put in a CD, and finally, the rest I put into a savings account, ameliorating my fear of the money not being immediately available should a crisis arise. Obsessively, I placed Adam's name on every account, making sure the money would fall directly into his hands should I come to an unexpected end. Once I finished these transactions, I tried to trust in my decision and get on with my life without the money being overly distracting.

Shortly after, a woman soliciting donations to support a home for abused women approached me. Having no smaller bills, I gave her five dollars. Feeling smug and generous, I walked away hearing, "Someday you will have to give it *all* away." In the truth of the statement was no room for reaction—not anger or fear or denial. This was a knowing. Whatever the meaning, some day I *would* have to give it all away.

For years, I had denigrated myself for wasting my life. However, via my healing, I was realizing this mind set no longer served me. My increased understanding of how our beliefs affect how we see ourselves, as well as how we see and live our reality, was beginning to germinate. It was becoming evident that my *perception* of my life was more a problem than the way I actually lived it. I could no longer simultaneously believe that I was a failure, a bad person *and* a pure, innocent soul of beauty and continue to heal. It was becoming essential that I objectively review my participation in my dramas and take personal responsibility for it. It was time to surrender the victim role. While this principle had a ringing of truth, it was extremely difficult to maintain as a reference. I had to eschew judging altogether, from viewing myself, my life, my experiences, as well as others, as good or bad or right or wrong. If I failed to view my past as a lesson rather than a disaster, I would keep myself lost—lost from the truth. Walking through my past was a key to honoring my life, a key to living my life as a gift.

Healing continued to be my means to advance on the spiritual path. On days when I was not overwhelmed by Divine experiences, I felt bored or abandoned. Even when I had more than I could manage, I felt as if I was not getting enough. I wanted to rid myself of all of my issues—all turmoil and conflict—and move into total understanding. Whatever it took I would gladly do; and I wanted it *now*. My insatiable drive to find my real identity, who I would be *after* healing, was taking on maniacal dimensions. I was unable to explain the urgency to keep moving forward, but I believed that my identity, my destiny, was conjoined to wherever it was I was being led: my destination.

Happiness, I was beginning to understand, played a role of little consequence on the road to wholeness. It is an unreliable emotion, ruled by situations and circumstances. It is impossible to maintain: when you go up, sooner or later you have to come down—like a roller coaster. I sought something more deeply fulfilling and sustaining. This I was finding whenever I was quiet and receptive, open to it. Whatever it was, it sprang simply and naturally from a place deep inside of me and expanded outward. My entire being would hum with this extraordinary energy—as if my heart was singing. Simultaneously calming and energizing, I called this circumstance "my center." When I was off-center or closed down, I could not feel this expansion. Instead, I felt heavy and dead inside. My attentiveness to how external situations and circumstances threw me off-center was becoming a tool to maintaining this connection.

If finding out who I really am necessitated getting in touch with my fears, I had to explore my fear of death. I was beginning to understand the relationship between death and the endless black void of nothingness that had been so intrusive in my inner space for most of my life. My fear of death would uncoil unsuspectingly, without warning and often enough that I had no choice but to address it. Notwithstanding, to comprehend my fear of death in its entirety, I would be required to go into the darkest corners of my psyche where my most painful experiences lay, camouflaged, cloaked, and well-hidden from my conscious thoughts. That would only be the start. Presently, I was unaware that these dark corners even existed. Neither was I aware that the more I relinquished my fear of death, the stronger my inner voice (my guidance) would become. (The void was the source of my knowing, but to get to it I would have to die—that is, my outer reality would.)

Oddly enough, as much as I feared death, I had a weird, insatiably curiosity about it. I wanted to know what death looked and felt like. I wanted to know the relationship between death and life. I wanted to know exactly how and at what point the shift occurred. Throughout my life I had been adept at anaesthetizing myself to pain, whatever form it took. (Even my dentist cringed at my insistence to have crown preps and fillings done without Novocain.) As opposed to a sudden exit, I was willing to endure whatever pain was necessary to apprehend my own death. As a matter of fact, I wanted a prolonged death experience, an encounter through which I could move moment by moment—like Beth in **Little Women**. The idea that I needed to know everything possible about the phenomenon that everyone found so dreadful and attempted to avoid at all costs would remain pressing. Feeling cheated at the thought of a possible sudden death revealed to me how serious I was about this pursuit.

Yet, throughout my life, I had never felt that I would live to a significantly old age. I often thought about the passage of time toward the new millennium and what life would be like once there. I would be pushing into my fifties, which when I was young, had seemed like an impossibly old age. Relatively speaking, reaching my fifties no longer felt impossible, nor too advanced an age to be entering into the coming century. Nonetheless, my earliest perspective that I would not live long enough to step into the new millennium persisted.

In the process of healing, I discovered it was continually necessary to give up something in order to reach a new level of development. However, when we as humans, surrender anything, whether it be an attitude, idea, possession, situation, relationship or belief, healthy or otherwise, the ego only sees loss, which it equates to death. The tip-off of an ego death is that it is in proportion to the value the ego places onto that which it is holding. When I heard that I had to give up something, my ego self invariably attempted to avoid, negotiate, argue, delay or even kick and scream. When I demanded of my guidance why I had to give up this or that, the simple reply was always, "What is given to you is always greater than what you are asked to give up." Knowing this was never especially reassuring, for most often the understanding of what I was being given in return only came as I moved into it or even later. Willingly surrendering to my directives without question, resistance, expectations, or fear of loss required trust. Eventually I would learn that giving up anything was never a loss, only a *perception* kept alive by the ego's seemingly endless list of attachments.

Even given its due, the death process could still be excruciating and the in-between space (between the old reality and the new reality), felt like limbo, but the joy of being reborn into the freedom of a new attitude or awareness justified whatever surrender was exacted. Like having a baby, once the end product of the labor is placed in your arms, the pain is forgotten; it never existed. For weeks I watched how the ego part of me bought into loneliness and sadness over believing that I had lost something when Liam departed. In contrast, without him as a distraction, I was learning to value and trust more deeply in my own self-reliance—trust that I did not need a man to be complete. Without him as a distraction, I had more time and space to make a deeper inner connection. It would take uncountable ego deaths before I was able to see that cumulatively they ultimately supported the death of my personal self.

One day as I left a metaphysical bookstore, I noticed an advertisement for a channeling class. Compelled to attend, I sat alone in a back row, observing the channel and those in attendance. The channel explained that she channeled an entity that used her as a vehicle to be heard on the physical plane. When she began to channel I watched her demeanor and voice change as the entity took over her consciousness. When the shift was complete, the entity began to speak. Only after the entity finished speaking, did I realize that I must have zoned out, or else been made to zone out, for I could remember nothing that had been said. At the end of the program, the audience was allowed to ask the entity questions directly. Most everyone readily asked for information in regard to their personal lives and seemed to trust indisputably in what was supplied. As much as I was enticed and wanted to be impressed, something about the gathering felt agitating. I thought it was arrogance that I was distrustful of information received in such a transcendent manner. Yet my questions overrode my attitude. I questioned the purity of intent of the disembodied spirit: whether its information was accurate or the truth. I questioned the channel's accuracy of interpretation. I questioned her motivations for allowing herself to be used in such a manner. Knowing that my questions would be viewed as a challenge, however, I remained silent.

After the channeling class a woman came forth who read auras. It seemed that we were going to have our auras read as a conclusion to the evening. I was ambivalent about having my aura read: I did, and didn't, want to know what my aura looked like. Going around the room, reading the auras of the twelve or so people who were there, she finally came to me and, after a moment said, "I can see that you have been doing a tremendous amount of spiritual work, but you need a rest." A rest? This I already well knew. I was, in a word, exhausted. But somehow I couldn't slow down: I felt as if I was swimming, swimming, swimming in a vast ocean, reaching out for some proffered life preserver, and whenever I was about to grab for it, it was suddenly pulled away, again out of reach, on some indiscernible current. Yes, I was tired, but due to my unrelenting effort to reach that life preserver, I was becoming a very strong swimmer, and I knew I had to keep swimming: life depended on it.

Returning home with much to ponder about disincarnates speaking through humans, a certain growing awareness had been triggered. I had definitely felt a need, however subdued, to directly question the spirit, to challenge the reliability of the presentation, to reveal its triteness. Some deep part of me had desired to stand right up, to speak loudly and clearly about something else, something outside of the scope of what was taking place in the class—a *real* truth. I could feel this "something else" inside of me that needed to be articulated, but I could not imagine what it sounded like in words. I was not aware that it was my karmic fear of persecution which reduced me to not only be unable to speak this unarticulated truth, but unable to even clearly connect with it.

When my long-overdue divorce was finally brought to a close, I forwarded a copy of the document to my contact at the Peace Corps headquarters in Washington D.C. Subsequently, I was sent one round of forms after another to complete. The status of my health was another hurdle. Peace Corps had previously responded in regard to my allergies that my application would not be further considered until I completed a five-year immunotherapy program and was cleared by my allergist. To date, I was halfway through the program. Since I had already anticipated this being a problem and was willing to abandon therapy and not consider myself at risk for doing so, I thrashed myself for not withholding the information initially.

An incident a year earlier had left me in my allergist's disfavor. Since my allergies/sinus infections had been becoming increasingly worse over the years, I'd had the tests to discover the exact allergens to which I was allergic, which I now knew were dust mites, mold, honeybees and yellow jackets. The doctor had prescribed a nasal spray, as well as a couple of other prescription medications. Regardless of the degree of my discomfort, for some inexplicable reason, taking the medication terrified me. During a follow-up session, he learned that I had not taken the prescribed treatment, as well as declined having an ex-ray. When he asked me why I was refusing treatment, I explained that I had taken the tests only to understand the ailment, but otherwise, I wanted to heal myself. It was at this time that I watched his usually friendly demeanor shift to one of annoyed arrogance. It had been taxing not to cave under the weight of his disapproval, to beat myself for not simply playing by the rules. Until he'd asked, I'd had no real idea of my intention to heal my allergy problems myself. Yet, when this idea surfaced, there was a dogged commitment to it that I was unable to doubt.

Undaunted, I made another appointment. At that time, I queried him about testing me out early. As expected, he adamantly refused. Pushing him further about the medical guidelines, he stated that the program was five years because it was five years, that was the way it was, and many people went years beyond these five before they safely tested out. As many times as I had surrendered to rules that made little sense to me, this time I found a force beyond my understanding transforming my frustration into words. "Look," I focused my attention on making eye contact with him, "My future is dependent on my testing out of this program. Please, let me take the test! I know I can pass it!"

The doctor declared that he could not understand why he was going along with my request, but he finally acquiesced and scheduled me for the next test date a month later. With relentless determination, I went home refusing to be distracted by the odds against me.

During the interim I gave the situation much thought. I had always doubted that I was actually allergic to bees, despite the reaction. Presently I was convinced of this. I felt that somehow the reaction had been a means to prevent me from becoming either lost in a relationship with Kent or from using beekeeping as another distraction in my life. No more keeping myself busy and calling it living my life. Believing that Divine intervention was in action in my life was becoming impossible to deny, although I was as of yet unable to readily share such an idea.

On the designated day, without a shred of doubt in my mind, I walked into a room full of nervous "testers." Since the procedure took the best part of a day, I settled in for the duration. Everyone got his and her first dose of the appropriate venom. I received a shot in each arm by an attending nurse. When the timer went off, the doctor stepped in and, one by one, checked for reactions, dismissing a number of people on the spot. I knew he was anticipating proving me wrong. The second round of shots was administered, the timer went off, and more people were dismissed. The process was repeated once again. I was the only one remaining in the room for the last round. By now the doctor, as well as the nurses, were expectant.

When I noticed doubt creeping into my mind, a deep breath and inner calm allowed me to reclaim my trust. The timer went off for the last time. The doctor came in, checked my arms and then attempted to diminish the results by saying that merely because I had tested out did not mean I was fully protected. Then he continued to stress that no one had ever been tested out early before and therefore, I should proceed with caution—stay away from bees and carry epinephrine with me at all times. He finally signed the papers I needed to step into my future. After I sent these papers on to Peace Corps, I was ready for whatever other roadblocks might be waiting. If it took two or ten more years to be accepted, I was willing to wait. I had no choice. However, I desperately hoped that I would have an invitation in time to avoid facing a third year of teaching.

The more I opened up to new learning experiences in my life, the more I received. Sometimes they came in manageable little packages that I could easily open and assimilate. Other times they were cataclysmic, creating chain reactions that shook the core of my being. One of these major experiences began as an excruciating pain developing in my neck while driving home from school one day. By the time I entered my apartment an hour later, the pain was thoroughly debilitating and I was near panic. Since an epidemic of spinal meningitis had broken out at the university Adam attended, and he had been home the weekend before, my mind ran in that direction.

I phoned Teresa to cancel the evening we'd planned, but she insisted on coming over anyway. Assessing my distress, she again mentioned that I should call and make an appointment with John, her massage therapist. He had frequently come up in conversation, partly because he and her cousin were in the final throes of a rocky relationship. She had previously given me his name and number because she felt the two of us had much in common and should meet. To me, massages were something in which only the elite indulged—like Teresa's family. Besides, I was too insecure to simply call a man in order to become acquainted. What would I say to him? Yet Teresa had shared enough about him—his alternative-lifestyle community and such—that my curiosity had been peaked. I had felt that I had been delaying the meeting partly due to my involvement with Liam and partly due to something less definable—something akin to resistance, although intuition now revealed that our meeting was inevitable.

The pain continued to intensify throughout the evening and Teresa persisted with her encouragement that I give her therapist a try. When the pain reached a point beyond my ability to ignore, I finally dialed John's number and left a message on his answering machine. The moment I completed the call, the pain vanished. Thoughts of calling him back and canceling my massage, however, instantly triggered the pain. I continued to play with ideas of not needing a massage, but to the same end—debilitating pain. Whatever was waiting to happen, some part of me was in dire resistance, yet powerless to change.

8

Crash Course in Confusion

Arriving a few days later for my massage, my energy, which had been rampaging since I had made the appointment, was now ricocheting off the walls. I walked down the long eighth floor hallway looking for John's apartment number. Once found, I stood in front of his door for a moment attempting to center myself, as I had done upon first meeting David, my hypnotherapist. I knew that whatever was waiting, its effect would be beyond profound. Three raps on the door were the thrust that firmly anchored me into this unknown. Bewildered, I stood face to face with John as the door opened before me. Initial eye contact confirmed that there was no going back. Efforts to breathe deep enough to stay in the moment came forth as if I was gasping for air. Worse, my voice would only come forth in a broken whisper as I struggled to respond to his warm welcome.

There was little room to be distracted by concerns of what he thought of me as he quickly ushered me into his tiny, cluttered apartment and showed me where to undress. Not without apprehension, I removed all of my clothes, placed my underwear in my purse and the rest neatly on a chair. Then I quickly slipped onto the table and under the security of the sheet. I was concerned about whether or not I was stepping outside of the boundaries of protocol by completely stripping, as well as concerned that he might consider me bold. But allowing myself to be vulnerable in this way felt like a trust issue. Besides I did not want to deal with the physical restrictions that came with being clothed. I had showered before I departed, as I had always done prior to sessions with David. Certainly, doing so helped quiet the body and become centered. Beyond this, I remained obsessive in regard to being clean, particularly my feminine parts. I ritualistically bathed whenever a situation called me to be in the company of a man, and especially when I knew there was going to be a sexual encounter. Then there was no limit to my need to be "as fresh as morning dew." There was a reason behind my behavior. I could feel it deep within me; it had a life of its own. (Soon enough I would recall the past life embodiment. It was about virgin sacrifices, being bathed, purified and perfumed before being delivered to the altar where high priests, men hiding behind religion, stole my virginity, my heart and my life—all in the name of God.) As I lay chilled, yet nervously perspiring under the sheet waiting for the session to begin, I became worried that John could become put off by my body odor, even when I knew it should be the least of my concerns. This disarming, effervescent little man with his heart-centered laugh, singing eyes and cherubic smile was about to touch, not only my body, but also a place deep within my heart and soul, all at the same time.

As he began the session, and without any apparent impetus, he immediately questioned, "You just don't want to be here, do you?" There was no room to consider him bold or take offense, to say indignantly, "You're just supposed to be giving me a massage." Instead, his words left me quick to shudder at this truth. I did not want to be on Earth. I did not feel that I belonged here. It was crushing to validate just how angry I felt about being trapped in a body. Really angry! The more he massaged my body, the more I got in touch with my aversion to being stuck in human form. I wanted desperately to run off and find a secure place to deal with the distress precipitated by what I was tapping into: John continued with the massage as if he was oblivious of my fragile state.

While working on my neck, he began to explain why I felt such discomfort there. What left me reeling was his claim, "You're a great communicator." Then he went on to clarify that I received incoming messages openly, but my resistance to speak meant that the energy became lodged in my throat; hence, my neck pains. I defended, "I'm just learning how to communicate." As if his intention was to keep me on track, he quickly retorted, "You're way beyond learning. And it's time that you project your voice rather than speaking as ridiculously soft as you presently do." (This confirmed what my kundalini yoga teacher had instructed about opening my throat chakra.) If this was not enough to digest, he further stated that I had to begin to write. Among other things, his words provoked incredible agitation in me. I wanted to rebut, "Who the hell is going to listen to this nobody? And what could *I* possibly say that would be of significance to anyone?"

John continued to work but apparently with my energetic body more than my physical one. He gave particular attention to my heart chakra, which appeared to him to be golden and honeycombed like a beehive, yet quite damaged and full of pain. His words pulled me into what he was seeing—the pain of the beauty and truth. Suddenly, a greater understanding was before me; my heart was waiting to be given voice. I had to speak from my heart. When I did, "it" would be heard. Yes, my shrinking days, my parrying days, as much as my mute days would be coming to an end, but not without a struggle. First, I had to deal with my own resistance. In doing so, I would also come head-on with a greater force that supported it.

John declared the session complete and then disappeared to the other side of the bookcase, which delineated his workplace from the rest of the living room. I arose from the table in a stupor. My experience had been so real; now it felt like a million light years removed. How could I return to the constraints of this oppressing three-dimensional reality? Just the thought of stepping into the restriction of my clothes, in and of itself, seemed too overwhelming.

Despite feeling incoherent, I managed to dress and then, very business-like, I pulled my checkbook from my bag to pay him. Three checks later I remained unable to fulfill my intention. Quite embarrassed, I explained that I had his name clearly in my mind as I started to fill out each check, but as soon as it came time to fill in the pay to section, I found that I had absent-mindedly written my hypnotherapist's name instead of his. I apologized for not remembering his name and asked him to fill in the blank himself. As I departed, we both acknowledged the peculiarity of the situation, and he invited me to phone him when I made sense of it. His words were certainly an invitation, but to what?

The moment I stepped into my apartment and closed the door behind me, still reeling from whatever was happening, I confronted my voice, "Okay! What does writing David's name on those checks mean?" The intense response, "David means teacher," left me scrambling to comprehend. Instead, my mind was made empty, giving the message time and space to sink in: John was my teacher. If this was not enough to own, I was informed that I was to articulate this to him. I adamantly refused. After all, already I appeared odd, and this man was a complete stranger. I insisted that I would not and could not agree to such an outrageous request. My refusal instantly brought back the pain in my neck, this time much more intensely. I was literally wrestled to the floor, flat on my face at the foot of my bed. I told myself that I was going insane and that I should get up and forget all of this nonsense, but I was helpless to overcome this invisible force pressing down on me. Clearly, to be functional required surrendering my willfulness. When I finally agreed to fulfill the directive, the pains, as well as the force were gone just as quickly as they had appeared. I sat up and leaned against the foot of the bed touching my rug-burned cheek. If I momentarily reneged, the pain instantaneously returned. I had no idea why I was so thoroughly fearful of this order, but I was grateful when I was granted an overnight reprieve.

The following morning, I headed for my sylvan sanctuary: I needed comfort; I needed a sense of safety; I needed the lightness of my woodland fairies. Instead, a deep inner pain of an unimaginable intensity began to consume me, breaking forth on a flood of tears. I kept telling myself to breathe, breathe in the energy of the woods and I would be okay. Yes, I knew I would be fine; that did not make whatever death was ripping away at me any more bearable. I prolonged my respite as long as possible, then I dried my eyes, put on my stiff upper lip and headed home, ready to face whatever was waiting.

Once there, I surrendered to the security of my rocking chair. I rocked back and forth, studying the sunlight touching my houseplants and becoming further accustomed to what was being required of me. Disliking my position was clearly a waste of time. I was not being allowed to move from the chair until I made the phone call to John. Not until the afternoon was upon me did I finally muster enough courage to reach for the phone. I desperately hoped that I would get his answering machine.

With the first ring, my body jumped into reaction. The longer the phone rang the more my heart pounded. I tried to hang up; energy moving through me blocked my attempt. All hope of him being away was dashed when I suddenly heard his hearty greeting. Without question, he was glad to hear from me, and he immediately opened the door for me to speak by asking if I had solved the check puzzle. My voice came forth like I was being choked as I began to disclose the facts. The phone call lasted two hours. Rather than calming, my body became more intensely charged as the conversation continued. When it ended, neither of us knew what exactly had taken place, but we both recognized the significance of whatever it was.

As with David, I had informed John that I considered myself responsible for my own healing, and as my teacher, I was looking for his support, not direction or influence. He agreed to play the role, but only if I discontinued with my kundalini yoga classes. He opined that hyperventilating—what he called the deep breathing practice—put me into dimensions that left me in danger and out of control. I felt a truth in what he spoke, and had in fact, already realized the same thing. As John confirmed, I was becoming way too hypersensitive to unnecessarily place myself in risky situations. I had to admit that I knew I had been hanging on to the ancient art when my lessons had been over for some time. Only with minimal reluctance for once, I agreed to desist.

I explained that finances allowed me to have sessions on a biweekly basis—or so I figured—although my next session needed to be as soon as his schedule allowed. Despite throwing cost as a factor into the equation, using finances to create any kind of limitation was about to prove fruitless.

Off the phone, I remained in my rocking chair continuing to rock. My body was shaking as if I was fast into a state of hypothermia. The energy coming through me, as well as the intensity of whatever had been happening between John and me was beyond what it could handle. My head throbbed and I could not collect my thoughts. I wanted desperately to know exactly what all of this was about, assuredly to feel safe. What was impending, however, functioned outside of my ability to define or control it. The only way to truly attain understanding was to fully live the waiting experiences—to fully immerse myself in my life as the character in **Death Comes to the Archbishop** had done with his life. Using my life to hide out was no longer an option. In fact, trying to do so would prove to be deadly.

To my surprise, when my body finally began to cease its tremulous fit and I attempted to turn to my schoolwork, I found myself becoming uncontrollably excited. I began to dance around the living room rejoicing, "I have a teacher in my life, a spiritual teacher! I have someone to listen to me and support me, someone who will consider me special!" Faster than I could contain my thoughts, my mind was off examining potential scenarios. Coming down from my high, I reflected on this outburst, as well as on the degree I had resisted following my initial directive. I was disgusted with myself for having had so little faith, and appalled that I could become so self-intoxicated. I had much to learn: one realization was that no one or nothing was here for me personally.

Teresa curiously inquired about the session during our next regular walk, and I watched myself as I began to divulge all that had transpired. Instantly, I felt guilty, especially since her cousin and John were in the final throes of ending a relationship; if Teresa should tell her husband, certainly word would get back to John. By the time I arrived home from the walk, my guilt had escalated to panic. Consequently, I phoned Teresa and pleaded with her—as if it was a matter of life or death—to refrain from sharing my experience with anyone. When the conversation was finished, I felt in a worse panic. What if I lost my teacher because I could not keep my mouth shut? Of all people, why did I suddenly not trust Teresa? I did not know what it was that I had with this thing called "secrets." If someone were not requiring me to be secretive, I was requiring it of myself. In my relationships with Kent and Liam, the secrets and shame had been nearly as extreme as they had been with Carl. I assured myself that I had been innocently sharing my experience, not divulging information. A scream jangling in my depths, "I'm innocent of any wrongdoing!" echoed for days, forcing me to recognize that this was an issue with which I would have to deal.

When I arrived for the second session, John explained that he had canceled his appointment following mine because he felt that it was essential to leave as much time for me as necessary. Instantly I was enmeshed in a plethora of thoughts. First, his action made me realize how seriously he viewed what was happening while another part of me felt unworthy of such special consideration, such generosity. Second, I desired to know him on a personal level and felt the extra time might allow for that to happen. Further, I felt as if I would have to compensate him for the extra time while another part of me felt elated that I could get my money's worth for once. More deeply, I knew that whatever I was paying or not paying, this experience had nothing to do with money.

Prior to beginning, I informed John that my focus during the session would be on my fear of vulnerability. He said nothing, only shook his head. As he began the massage, I moved immediately into a deep altered state. There was no room to feel embarrassed because he appeared to be in a similar state. The freedom of being so far removed from my physical reality was again extraordinary and I was certain that I never wanted to return.

Nevertheless, as soon as John asked me to turn over, my mood, along with my body became oppressive. I never lay on my stomach, partly due to sinus problems, as well as discomfort in my neck. I reminded myself that these issues had not even been a consideration during the first session. He noticed my reaction and claimed that he could finish the session without my changing position, but my only choice was to fully live the experience at hand. I shifted my position.

As soon as John touched my body, it began to twist and writhe rhythmically beneath his hands. At first I thought that these undulations were a result of something he was doing to me, until he asked me what was happening. What a conundrum! Some part of me stood outside the experience observing while the forceful yet graceful movements intensified. Was a heavenly score being performed through my body? I could not think of being self-conscious. Eventually, stillness encased my body, evidently by the direction of some invisible conductor.

After I was dressed, John unexpectedly asked me if I could dance; that seeing my body in such a state, he would expect that I would have beautiful movement dancing. As much as I wanted to run out the door, I simply responded that I never danced and explained how the two sides of my body did not know how to work cooperatively. I had never before openly shared this limitation with anyone. Even now my voice failed me and my eyes revealed my trepidation as I looked into his. My impulse was to throw my hands over my face. They remained frozen in my lap. I wanted vulnerability and I was getting it: my fear was visible at a core level. As he returned my gaze, I moved into an altered state, my trepidation momentarily relieved. Then, unexpectedly my hands began to extend outward, palms exposed, beckoning him. For a moment, our hands and eyes remained locked in an unearthly exchange. Suddenly, my fear kicked in again. Without a word, he put his arms around me and beckoned me to allow him to take my fear. A part of me wanted to pretend that I was merely being a drama queen, that none of this was real. Instead, my head moved enough to convey an affirmative.

He picked me up and carried me to the couch. Before I knew what was happening, I was laying on top of him. I could feel his heart quietly beating. Despite an unnerving sense of distrust, my body began to relax against his. A deep heart connection was being made. Ever so slowly, I could feel my fear being drawn from my body and into his. From there it seemed to be transmuted, completely gone. On one hand, I was astonished by this prodigious exorcism-like encounter. On the other, it felt like second nature.

With the process complete, we continued to lie on the couch. It was the most incomprehensibly liberating feeling to be without fear. Every part of me felt at peace. I wanted a procedure to follow to make this calmness a permanent state. We conversed for a while, lying comfortably together, that is until he began to touch me. I watched my inner guard stiffen, but juxtaposed to my returning fear, I liked his natural odor, which was unusual; I had always been sensitive to men's body scents, and had never found the scent of any man with whom I had been involved particularly appealing, especially not Carl's. At one point he attempted to kiss me, whereby I immediately pulled away, although I knew that a sexual facet to our relationship was inevitable.

When I was ready to walk out of the door, he requested that I look in the mirror. Where I saw an ash-white face staring back at me, he noted that I looked younger, that Capricorns always held their age well. His final words, "Do you understand that you are an agent of God?" before I closed the door behind me, were like an alarm going off, striking hard at an inner truth. This message, however, was cleanly removed from my thoughts by the time I arrived home. Nonetheless, I assessed the experience inside out, overall trying to make sense of it. Yes, I had been vulnerable, more than I could have ever imagined.

Although I felt fragile after the prior evening's experience and my inclination was to remain at home and quiet during the weekend, as I had committed to doing, I spent the following day with Gertrude. She first insisted that I accompany her to her health club. This was an entirely new experience for me and brought forth a host of fears, the most obvious one being the possibility of having to be around men. Once in the door, I obsessively sought out less trafficked areas while gregarious Gertrude mingled among acquaintances and strangers alike. After a hard workout, we landed in the swimming pool. I pinpointed my mounting edginess as having to do with a number of men being directly across from us in the pool. Before becoming completely overcome, I moved into my sense of distraction. Subsequently, I suddenly began to laugh as I realized—while denying the capacity—that I could manifest my sexual energy and shoot it at the men across from us, leaving them energetically impacted yet consciously unaware of what was happening. Telling myself that I was hallucinating did not temper my ridiculous frame of mind. When I shared my thoughts with Gertrude, we both erupted with a riot of laughter, though I felt I should have been thoroughly humiliated. However, I knew I had rattled something inside of me loose.

After our swim, Gertrude invited me to go country dancing with her that evening. I hedged by claiming that I would have to return home to get an appropriate outfit. She knew that if I got away, I would not return, and said as much. She was right. Going home was an ultimate means to avoid the encounter. There was no question that I was terrified to step into a bar, let alone a country western bar full of men, and on top of it maybe have to dance. What was the big deal? I had managed the bar scene working in restaurants. For no other reason than to face my fear, I had to do this; guidance revealed that it was time.

Gertrude loved to dance, and she had had so many lessons and so much experience she looked like she could have been born line dancing. She spent a couple of hours teaching me a basic step. Once again, I was dealing with my body's inability to take commands from my brain. Clearly, there was some kind of short-circuiting. I had once studied **Drawing on the Right Side of the Brain**, certain that my problem was my inability to access my intuition. Time would reveal that the real issue was my conflict with my intellect. Determination was all that kept me arm-in-arm with her.

I followed Gertrude into the packed, smelly, smoky dance bar to a table where many of her friends were sitting. As with the health club, she appeared so natural here, especially all decked out head to foot in her country-western duds. I reminded myself that I could manage this situation as I carefully observed my escalating discomfort. Within a matter of a couple tunes, a man suddenly appeared before me and reached out his hand for a dance. It might as well been a gun. Before I could think how to deal with the situation, I courteously suggested, "You want to dance with Gertrude. She's a great dancer." Gertrude gave me an annoyed nudge as the man reached for my hand and firmly responded that he was asking me to dance. Again, I deferred to Gertrude, but I could see that there was no graceful way—or reason—to avoid this encounter. I finally rose from the safety of my chair and stepped onto the dance floor. While I felt the song would never end, Gertrude's words, "Don't look at your feet!" kept resounding through my head. At the end of the dance my partner asked me my name. My urge was to say to him that I was not sure, to explain that my present name had become as uncomfortably restrictive as my clothes and I was waiting for a new name to be given to me. Instead, I mentally bit my tongue as my name tumbled out of my mouth. While I had no idea what all of this meant, I could feel a voice inside of me screaming vociferously to be free of the constraints of my birth name.

Later in the evening, I was solicited by a strange, clearly down-and-out, and inebriated young man, similar to my neighbor whom I had taken to court for stalking me. This was in itself a lesson as I watched how, all at the same time, I tried to negate my awareness, take responsibility for his tribulations and not scream at him to get away from me. In the end, I was significantly satisfied with how I had managed myself in regard to his advances. I was all-around grateful for the encounter, but humorously hopeful that I would not be further required to learn my lessons in a country western bar filled with tobacco smoke and twangy voices singing about broken hearts.

Whatever the nature of my weekend encounter, lessons in vulnerability and more, I returned to my "massages" with John more fully committed. Meanwhile, our sessions would become strikingly more intense. Habitually, at some point during a massage, when focus was turned to my heart chakra, it appeared that we somehow merged and together moved off into another reality to carry on our work. Through these encounters, I learned to examine issues from an even greater level of awareness. I was attaining what had been frustratingly unavailable through sessions with David. My feelings that he had been unable to support me where I needed to work were validated.

During a subsequent session, I suddenly felt John set something on my heart—a heart-shaped amethyst. I looked wonderingly at him. He claimed, "You now have my heart." This kind of attention was foreign, romantic no less, and I felt flattered, even embarrassed, and likewise honored. To add to my confusion, a voice inside of me sprang alive screaming, "I won't stagnate! I'm not willing to lose my identity! I won't arrest my growth! You can't have me! No man can have me! I'm not going to sacrifice my sense of self for a commitment! You can't give me your heart; having it is too much of a burden!" John was conveying an expression of love. Since I held an amazingly profound sense of love for him, I felt caught between two diametrically opposing positions. I accepted his heart, not knowing what else to do, but still a sense of distraction remained present.

Working with my new teacher facilitated the continued opening of my heart. Doing so was now a drive, for life felt unbearable with it any other way. Besides my heart, I was getting a feel for my other chakras as well. It was becoming obvious that my three lower chakras were way off kilter and often times completely closed. In contrast, examination revealed that my third eye and crown chakras were commonly spinning wide open and strong. My chakras were like barometers; they revealed the state of my health at an energetic level and at the same time, revealed underlying deeper issues. For instance, feeling heaviness in my solar plexus made me aware that I was perhaps in conflict with someone, feeling guilty or avoiding dealing with a situation. Tension in my chest might reveal I was stepping out of a place of centeredness. Tightness in my throat or softness in my voice could suggest that I was avoiding communicating an inner message or being dishonest with myself. An expansiveness in my third eye or crown chakra, for the most part, was indication of something happening beyond the physical: information coming through, like a "you've got mail" signal. Realizing that my first five chakras were out of alignment with my sixth and seventh chakras signified the minimal degree of my connectedness to my physical self.

It became essential to familiarize myself with all of my chakras and the nature of their energy, as well as my entire energetic body. This was not to be done through studying literature, but first-hand, by actually staying attuned, from moment to moment, to my thoughts, emotions and behavior, and recognizing how they affected my chakras, as well as my entire energy field. When I was off-centered, my energy overall felt compressed, if not absolutely suffocating. When I was centered, my energy felt vibrant, energizing and expansive. For some time already, especially in the isolation of my apartment, my hands, with magnetic force and seemingly of their own volition, were frequently drawn to and held at my heart or crown chakra, as well as to my third eye. Whatever was happening, it was powerfully energizing, as well as extremely comforting.

Of utmost importance, I began to notice that I was beginning to dismiss my first three chakras—those that bound me to the physical—as unimportant and unnecessary. I told myself that I was foolish, especially since it was standard consensus that each chakra, in supporting wholeness and living our spirituality, is as important as any other is. Nevertheless, a divergent part of me remained in stubborn disagreement; it was the part of me that knew that "I" was meant to live like Mr. Spock.

John would articulate what he energetically tuned into during our sessions. The first time he began to speak at length about my having an important purpose, I saw myself attempt to become energetically small, shrinking into myself in a way that would make me invisible. It was then that I tearfully divulged that I was unworthy of anything, that I had lived my life self-absorbed, angry, unmercifully judgmental, resentful, and even actively vindictive. Continuing, I admitted that I had hurt too many people to ever be deserving of having any important purpose. If this was not enough, I suddenly vomited, "And I've taken the life of my own child."

This was decidedly confusing. I was certain that I had worked through this issue for the final time a few years earlier coming home from a Christmas gathering where Adam and I had had much fun playing with the youngsters in the family. In conversation, he had unexpectedly queried me as to why I never had more children since I loved them so much. My sudden shame triggered uncontrollable sobbing. I doggedly held that my actions were none of his concern; yet, subject to his persistence, I found myself divulging my horrible secret. Presently, the anguish of having taken my child's life felt as if it had lain buried deep within the heart of my soul for eternity. Every part of me wanted to push the anguish back from where it had come for I believed I was incapable of handling it.

John's response came forth gently and naturally as he stood before me and gazed into my eyes through his thick glasses, "It's no longer serving you to consider yourself unworthy. You have to release that belief to heal yourself." He then disclosed that souls do not enter the body until close to, or at the time of birth, sometimes even after. The soul that would have entered had not died but lived and had no doubt entered embodiment through another available situation. I was hearing him say that I was not guilty; forgiving myself was not even an issue. This was like a rogue wave overwhelming my established beliefs. Abortion not a condemnable act? Uncertain about readily exonerating myself, I left the conversation to rest inside of me.

After a few sessions, John claimed that he thought it was time to act on our sexual attraction, according to him, to get it out of the way. The attraction, whether spoken or not, had been straightaway recognized by us both. Despite my awareness that such an encounter was at hand and despite sensing the deep bond between us strengthening, I was overwhelmingly concerned about it negatively impacting our teacher/student relationship. Besides this, I remained all the more confused in regard to the ever-present message that I would never have a gender relationship.

Then, too, there was Liam to consider. Fidelity had always been of utmost importance to me. I could not imagine being sexually involved with two men simultaneously; being involved with this many men one after the other (whether sex was involved or not) was already testing my sense of shame. I remained half-holding onto the belief that I still had a relationship with Liam. Further, he was expecting me to visit him in Africa if I was not accepted into the Peace Corps. At some level it was clear that sooner or later it would be essential to share with him the nature of my changing life. I held that my reluctance was based on his emotional frailty. The truth was I was fearful of facing his reaction, and fearful of completely closing that door behind me. I was fearful of being left with nothing, even when I knew I had already left that relationship in the dust. The bottom line read that the sexual door was already wide open and there was no way that either John or I could close it.

The idea of having a sexual relationship with my "teacher" led me back to thoughts of a humiliating encounter with David. Shortly before ending my sessions with him, I had been hearing that we were to have sex. I was horrified by the thought of stepping over professional boundaries (not to mention he was married), of broaching the subject to him and by the act in and of itself. I attempted to dismiss the intensifying messages by convincing myself that I was hearing it all wrong. Nonetheless, the messages continued to pressurize me. As I began one session with him, however, the message was powerful enough that I was unable to move beyond it. At the same time, I was terrified of openly articulating this thought to him. All I could manage was to inform him that I had to tell him something but was unable to do so. Despite his encouragement, I felt that my boldness would cause him to reject me. My resistance left me dumbstruck. At some point he exited to use the bathroom, my signal. When he returned, I took a deep breath and apologetically stuttered, "I have no interest in doing so, but I keep hearing that I'm to have sex with you." His response was, "What's the matter? Is my penis too small?" Despite the fact that the matter was out in the open, and despite the fact that it would never be acted on, my embarrassment never subsided. Now, on the edge of a sexual interaction with my therapist, I was wondering if my knowing had been correct, but only the time and circumstances off. Or perhaps the encounter with David had been a trial run. Presently, I was willing to surrender to the impending encounter with John, at least if it were essential to my growth.

Our first attempt was awkward and confusing, especially when a man with whom John irregularly shared his apartment unexpectedly arrived. At our next try, John had a problem obtaining an erection. When I found the nerve to ask him why, he explained that not feeling in love left being sexual difficult for him. Besides liking his vulnerability, I had no doubt that his predicament would be short-lived. Originally he had stated that sex needed to be gotten out of the way; somehow I felt that sex with John was the way.

Our sessions mainly consisted of working on my heart and third eye, as well as further freeing myself of feelings of badness. It was exhilarating to feel my heart chakra healing. Once I had the signature of an open heart chakra, it became a reference point. Loving myself, being open-hearted and centered resulted in joy and expanded energy, allowing me to go deeper into my intuitive awareness, and thus into a more profound realm of consciousness. If heaven existed, I had found it. Further expanding my heart chakra would continue to be a major area of attention in our work together. It would be the key that would open the way to dimensions presently beyond my comprehension.

Sex came to best fit into our lives in the context of our work together. Habitually, our sessions led to a sexual encounter in which we both transcended to a realm of Spirit. Outside of using sex as a tool to reach this state, our sexual interactions were otherwise of little significance to me, even often distracting. I had explored sex for its own sake enough with Liam to get that out of my system: erotica led to nowhere important. Yes, my body was too often super-sexually charged, and it remained trying to know how to handle that, but experience had revealed that engaging in sexual activity, if anything, only took the edge off of the charge. John, on the other hand, held a regular need to release himself physically through sex and I found myself obliging him. Even so, I began to own that I felt a greater connection, a deeper intimacy, when we were communicating our thoughts and feelings, or simply quietly together, hearts open and flowing, rather than engaging in sex. At times, John would patiently wait for me to wind down, even joke about verbal foreplay, before we moved into him getting his sexual needs met.

There was actually no clear delineation between teacher and student for we had been learning from each other from the moment we met. John shared his abundance of worldly information, his mental warehouse of facts, with me while I shared my otherworldly mind-blowers with him. As much as I valued his patience and support, he respected my obsessive commitment to personal growth and greater insights. Our energetic connection became ever stronger: relating from a heart-centered place was incredible. To talk to him, I only had to put out the thought for him to call me. I could put my hand forth, let the energy flow from it and feel him knowingly receive it. In the middle of teaching school or shopping, I would feel his thoughts enter my mind. I could sense when he was approaching my apartment and recognize his gifts before he gave them to me. I had found myself beginning to use the term "kin" in place of what I considered the meaningless term " I love you." Whenever I said "kin" to John, I could instantly feel both our hearts opening and expanding. In and of itself, this was an extraordinary feeling. Beside this, it left me feeling extraordinarily and deeply connected to John. It was to become our way of acknowledging our truer connection. At some point we would no longer even have to articulate the word. Instead, we each would just place our hand to our heart, or else simply look into the other's eyes.

I wanted to believe that we had the crème de la crème of relationships. In fact, I heard that we were put into each other's lives as a gift. Instead of letting this message define itself, I created a definition that could strengthen my belief that I had found this all-time incredible gender relationship. Our lack of greater understanding of who we were to each other—our naiveté—set the stage for us both to have to walk through impending traumatic lessons.

What was initially troublesome about our togetherness was the separation. Being with him was like being on a prolonged spiritual flight merged as one. When we parted, it was if our spiritual wings were suddenly clipped only to plummet back to the mundane where we suffered separation anxiety. We would soon learn to let the relationship, as it stood, end with each goodbye. Until we reunited again, we would each then focus on our own growth. This allowed us, with every new hello, to step into a refreshing, new relationship.

Outside of our work together, our relationship was less than conventional. Besides being overextended with numerous other financial schemes—by my perspective, will-o-the-wisp—and willing to work whatever hours were convenient for his clients, John most frequently landed at my place at one or two in the morning. I had yet to overcome being handicapped by insufficient sleep. Therefore, it was a problem to adjust to the havoc his lifestyle created on mine. I soon discovered that he was compulsively dedicated to his clients' welfare, habitually six steps behind himself, and relied on marijuana to stay calm.

It took little time for John to invite me to his townhouse retreat in an alternative-lifestyle community a hundred miles from Chicago. I had learned the history by reading an autobiography of the founder. The story deeply moved me, especially the way in which the founder was required to undergo such intense spiritual training throughout his life, and how intense his spiritual guidance had been. Ironically, I wondered what it would be like to have guidance of the nature described in the reading.

It took even less time to begin regularly staying with John at his townhouse on weekends. Here I became acquainted with a vital aspect of his life. This community was his family and he was thoroughly committed to his involvement. It was clear that members were searching for a sense of spirituality as much as he. Some had been part of the community since its inception and had experienced the scandal and intrigue surrounding the malfeasance of the founder and former leader—aspects of the history not included in the book. With this more sobering perspective, I wondered how a person with such guidance and power could go so far astray. Because John had been turned down twice before he was allowed entrance to the community, he valued his position all the more. Presently, there were no restrictions on joining. The out-flux of members had been greater than the inflow for some time. It appeared that its continuing survival was due to a few excessively dedicated members—like John.

The community, itself, had gone through major alteration throughout its history. Although formerly it had not been the rule, for the present, everyone was free to support their spiritual beliefs however they chose. Therefore, much experimentation was in operation. The repressive, as well as sexist, restrictions that had been placed on women had long been lifted. There was a community school as well, which all members were expected to support within whatever capacity their talents afforded. Conservation was a central concern. There were community dinners, as well as other festivities that regularly brought residents together. Outward appearances made a favorable impression, but I perceived something was missing.

On a personal level, ending relationships and creating new ones from within the confines of the community were common. John explained relationship dynamics to such an extent that I could not keep track of who was currently paired with whom. His ex-wife and numerous other women with whom he had been intimately involved lived in the community. His ex-wife was now married to one of his good friends, but neither John nor she had completely severed the emotional ties between them. One woman, with whom he had ended a relationship, was bent on rekindling it. This was not my definition of a spiritual family: this was a collection of insecure people trying to find a place where they could feel safe and obtain a sense of self. I tried to diminish my awareness by labeling it criticism. I wanted to believe that this was an avant-garde new-age community whose residents I should get to know, but I did not know how to relate to anyone.

I had had association with many hoarders throughout my life, but the first time I saw John's place, I was overwhelmed: it looked like a storeroom of the Smithsonian hit by a tornado. He had received many of the items in barter when clients were unable to pay cash for massage. The most recent unfinished project lay against other long-forgotten unfinished projects. He claimed to pay a cleaning woman but I failed to see evidence of her presence. The clutter on the kitchen counters was of the magnitude that preparing a meal was nigh impossible. Food rotted in the refrigerator and cupboards. There was more shit in the cat's litter box than there was litter. Clean clothes were indistinguishable from dirty ones. Many houseplants had long since succumbed to neglect, their skeletal remains hanging over the sides of pots or scattered on the carpet. (In contrast, his marijuana plants were thriving on shelves he had built across his bedroom skylight.) Like the majority of the populace, he embraced the idea of stockpiling survival food in preparation for the perceived imminent planetary upheaval. Much of his supply was used to support his bed, while the rest formed cardboard columns around it.

Being calm and centered under these conditions was impossible. I found myself spending an ever-greater amount of time in our togetherness compulsively cleaning his abode and keeping his life in order, then from a place of exhaustion, becoming annoyed with him. The observer in me watched my caretaking addiction come alive while another part tried to sweep such distracting insights under the rug. I convinced myself that the difference between this and former relationships was that, ultimately, we truly loved each other and were both committed to evolving our relationship to an ever-increasing place of consciousness.

For several weekends, I worked myself to exhaustion helping John indoors, as well as assisting him to manifest his endless landscaping and gardening ideas into reality. I did this while most often he became detained with an unexpected call from a distraught client and such. Thanks to the circumstances, I began to seriously question my compulsive need to put others' environments in order, especially when those I was "helping" undermined my efforts faster than I could keep up. Seizing a modicum of self-control, I was able to reduce the amount of time I aided him. Instead, I redirected my attention to my personal needs: staying abreast of school work, keeping my journal up-to-date, going for long walks along the country roads or sojourning at a cemetery a couple of miles away. Here, I could attain the centeredness that I was unable to attain in the confines of John's community or home. Seeing him caught up in busyness, schemes that consumed his time and energy producing little in return, was a reference point in terms of where I had been much of my life, and also the significant degree to which I had yet to move out of that behavior. He began to somewhat recognize the extent to which he was caught in his own craziness. And I found that when I was strong enough to hold a quiet space for myself, he would often make the choice to join me in that space rather than get lost in his noisy distractions.

Taking John to "my woods" had been another distracting, yet sobering reality. I had given thought to taking him there for some time. Doing so was akin to completely exposing myself from the inside out. Nevertheless, I was excited about sharing this side of myself with him. It was cold, damp and cloudy the day we ventured forth, and John arrived poorly dressed for the occasion. Spring ephemerals that had not been visible on my last visit were popping up everywhere. Rather than excitedly immersing myself in the moment, as was my custom, I remained more attuned to John's discomfort and shortly suggested that we return to my apartment for hot tea. On another occasion, while departing from his weekend busyness to walk in a state park a distance from his community, he complained that he saw no sense in walking or biking somewhere when he could drive his car. I repeatedly reminded myself that, by comparison to what we had in common, these incidents indicated only minor differences in our nature. In truth, they were fundamental.

Knowing John more intimately, I also came to realize that he was an incredible dreamer. His abundance of projects left abandoned in various stages of completion revealed, however, that he was not proficient at manifesting his dreams. He was unable to follow through on much of anything he started. In contrast, it was an obsession with me to complete whatever I started. Even dropping my masters program halfway through remained an uncomfortable thorn in my consciousness. (I was unaware that I had fulfilled my masters, yet not in the context that produced conventional acknowledgment.) I was not a dreamer. With Carl, I had initially lived off his dreams (which translated to promises)—I thought too afraid to embrace my own. I had convictions, and desires, although diminishing. Was having no dreams a shortcoming? I had no answer.

After a few weekends, John declared that we should define our relationship. I was unsure of what he meant, but rather than stay removed and let him deal with what was clearly his issue, immediately my resistance kicked up. He thought that we needed to be honest with each other. I pointed out how we were in the habit of regularly communicating our thoughts and feelings, and asked him what more there was that we could do to be more honest. He seemed satisfied.

Next, he began to talk about money and contributions. (He had disclosed that in prior relationships he had continually gotten himself financially trapped by needing to be the supplier.) This confused me and put me further on the defensive, especially since I habitually took the responsibility to purchase the weekend supply of groceries. Besides this, while I was shopping, I would pick up other necessities, as well as a flat of annuals to plant in the yard, and such. I felt obligated to do the shopping because I came out after school on Friday, whereas John, by dictates of his harried schedule, often arrived in the wee hours of the morning. Further, I rationalized that waiting to get groceries until the weekend was a waste of our personal time and also gas, since the nearest grocery store was forty miles away. And on and on. The greater truth was that I had been taught to buy my way to acceptance. When I enumerated how I was contributing already, then asked him how he thought we needed to work this out, he dismissed this matter also. But some unnerved part of me did not let it go. Once again, I had set myself up to give much more than my share simply to feel worthy to be in the relationship. Worse, he failed to recognize the degree of my contribution. I said nothing to him, however, as I considered my reaction my problem.

Besides this, although John would claim that we were spending a weekend together, or that he was not accepting any spur-of-the-moment weekend appointments, invariably I would discover that, one after another, he had accepted enough appointments to fill a whole day or the entire weekend. I controlled my reaction, understanding that he was over-committed to his clients and had issues with being able to say no. Without question, he reflected back to me just how caught up in busyness I had once been. For this, I was grateful. What disturbed me was that most often I would only be informed of the change in plans when a client knocked on the door for an appointment. When I addressed his behavior, he acknowledged his lack of consideration, and made an effort to change, which he did, but mostly in regard to giving me advance notice as opposed to saying "no" to people who requested spur-of-the-moment sessions.

John freely shared his dreams of marrying me. Unquestionably, my love for him ran deep. I felt honored that he owned our relationship to this extent and had often tried to imagine a man being this committed to me. But try as I would, and as much as I wanted to, I could not imagine being married. Worse, claustrophobia set in the moment I ventured to envision myself as part of this little, rural island encircled by a sea of cornfields. Even the trees that had been planted throughout the community felt as if they were stifled. There was no room for me to be or to grow here. Worse, there were no woods. That eternal inner restlessness had already been stretching around for some time. This was John's life and dream; there was no place to share a life, only to become part of his. It was the same old story only I was unwilling to openly acknowledge it. Instead, I attempted to convince myself that our paths would somehow remain joined.

Despite existing denial, I felt accomplished to realize how much more aware I was in this relationship compared to previous ones, how much more able I was to voice my discontent, and how much less I was sacrificing myself to keep the relationship from drowning. John perfectly reflected back to me where I was or had once been, and I was exceedingly grateful. What I was learning, from what I labeled a relationship, was monumental. However, the true degree of my learning was actually incomprehensible.

I had been receiving information in a plethora of ways since I had surrendered to acknowledging my inner voice. My hands continued to be a main conduit for incoming messages. I did not like this form of transmission, however, for it was overwhelming, if not painful. Further, I had little ability to control it and much difficulty interpreting even with John's assistance.

Energy was now beginning to come more frequently as a pressure or cloud in my head, expanding in a way that left me feeling as if my brain would explode. Relief was produced only when I acquired what information was waiting. Then it came, not in a linear form, but in an odd manner, as if I understood a sentence by reading all the words it contained simultaneously, rather than one at a time, from beginning to end.

Certainly, my third eye was active (and had been for some time, although I was yet unable to comprehend this). Whatever was happening, my physical sight was being affected. Most frequently, whatever my eyes fell upon seemed to lack solidity, desert-mirage like. Often, trying to focus was like having an optometrist adjusting lenses during an eye examination: is your vision clearer here or here? Direct sunlight helped me remain calm and centered, and also aided my visual acuity. In contrast, artificial light was unbearable. I much preferred sitting in the dark or reading by candlelight rather than turning on a lamp. I spent much more time with my hand over my third eye, especially upon retiring. All around, the situation was confusing: Could I see better with contacts? Without them? Or when my eyes were completely closed? I would frequently ask John to see for me whatever it was trying to come through my third eye. Then I had to trust that what he attained was accurate.

Sleep messages were likewise coming more frequently. However, if it was daytime, I would be directed to take a nap, or else fatigue would overtake me so quickly, it was like having narcolepsy. One sleep message, "A memory of ancient times lying dormant inside of you is being awakened," one I was unready to understand, epitomized their nature.

Messages came just as frequently in other ways, like dreams. I would be awakened at the end of a dream and not allowed to return to sleep until I held it in conscious memory or scribbled it down in my diary, which I diligently kept on my nightstand. Other times, yet similar, messages came in the form of automatic writing. I would find myself picking up a pencil and watching my hand move across a sheet of paper, seeing only after the pencil was put down what information had been given to me. Messages continued to come in the form of a song played over and over in my head. Sometimes movement of a body part, my head suddenly swaying from side to side, my finger compulsively tapping, or my arm rocking back and forth would be indication that I needed to pay attention. In conversation, sometimes in the middle of a sentence, all thoughts were removed from my head, as if someone had shut off my brain; nothing came through. I learned that this meant that I was expected to assess my thoughts before being allowed to go on with the conversation, or else I was being prevented from saying anything further. My mind being periodically cleared out made me more conscious of my thought patterns, along with the way I formulated my thoughts. Visions frustrated me because their meaning usually needed interpretation or they came as pieces of a whole given to me one at a time. Each piece in and of itself had little meaning. Where the pieces were taking me did.

I had no clear intellectual understanding that I was actually operating on many levels of consciousness. Nor did I intellectually comprehend that impersonal thoughts were freely penetrating my personal thoughts. Whatever the nature of my experiences, I had to trust in them and in myself in order to understand, as much as live their meaning. I was realizing that all of the inner feelings that I had ever had were merely contact with my greater knowing. By accepting that knowing, I was becoming my own guide. I was getting myself out of the way enough to follow the guidance that was being provided.

By now, I had begun to feel comfortable labeling this greater influence over me my Higher Self. This was reinforced by a message given to me through John one day. He came downstairs to share an excerpt from an article that he had been reading. I had a dire dislike of being read to, and therefore became annoyed that he did not paraphrase. Nonetheless, I was able to subdue myself enough to listen. Of what he shared, I only needed one sentence, which went, "The Super Consciousness, as opposed to outside entities, holds the Truth we need to advance." Before I was completely overwhelmed by the significance within the reading, I heard, "What he says is true. Now own it!" I tearfully stood face to face with John completely overwhelmed by the message. Beautiful John took my behavior in stride; he was accustomed to me. The message left me to reflect first on the significance of my carrying my own truth within me. Yes, I could feel it. Unquestionably, it was there. My test was to learn to trust in it, as much as to follow it. (Unknowingly, the more I trusted in my truth, the more I would be able to follow it. And likewise, the more I followed my truth, the more I would be able to trust in it.) This meant that I needed no one, not even John. Nonetheless, I was unready to whole-heartedly own that realization.

Unquestionably, my healing was moving me into greater understanding of who I am beyond my human self—my connection to expanded levels of consciousness. Although finding Self is a solitary journey, the experiences we need to find the Self involves interactions with others. I was on a solitary journey; yet it could not be done in isolation.

The interactions I needed with others in order to find the Self were coming into my life quickly and in surprisingly varied form. For example, I once envisioned Teresa's denial of child abuse manifesting itself as an energy block in her stomach. As I spoke the words given to me, I could feel the block, like a malignant tumor, loosening up inside of her. With one further directed thought flowing from me, Teresa reached a point of catharsis, emotionally releasing the block.

Another time I heard someone enter my classroom door and instantly felt a sense of turmoil. I automatically checked to see if the turmoil was coming from me. It was not. When Gertrude approached my desk, I asked her what I was feeling from her and she then burst into tears. As with Teresa, the encounter allowed her to come to some important realizations, whereby she later expressed her deep gratitude. These moments created mixed feelings in me. From one perspective, my involvement felt natural; from another, it brought out a self-doubt and strong fear that consistently left me panicked. This was evident when John suggested that I begin using my intuitive awareness in sessions with his clients. Despite my experiences proving otherwise, some part of me adamantly refused to believe that I had anything of value to offer and if I did, it would surely go unrecognized.

Twice during this time frame I had been compelled to make an appointment to see David. Through the nature of both sessions, I had come to realize that I had been required to go not for me, but for him. Both times I was instructed to give him a message about where and how he was keeping himself stagnated. I was extremely uncomfortable during the process, even trying to side-step the message by falling into the "who-do-I-think-I-am-to-be-telling-my-therapist-what-to-do" routine. To reduce the experience even more, but in a diametrically opposed position, my ego self had hashed over the fact that, under the circumstances, my therapist should have been paying me, rather than the other way around. Despite my resistance, I continued to act on the messages and they continued to influence my life.

One incident in particular thrust me into having to more fully trust in my guidance. I was bumping down the steps, hands full of school material, one morning on my way to work when I found myself returning to my apartment to pick up a book entitled, **A Guide For the Advanced Soul**. Believing I did not need the book, I put it down and left the apartment once more, only to find myself returning a second time, and then a third, before I realized that I was being required to take the book to school. Once in my hand, it might as well have been glued there. I carried it with me all day, even bringing it on a field trip to see an opera.

On the return trip, my attention was drawn to the father of one of the students who had come along as a chaperone. His daughter had, through her class journaling, shared her feelings about serious family issues. As I was moving my students off the bus, I suddenly understood that I was supposed to give this man the book. There in the aisle of the bus, I argued with a voice audible only to me, that this man was a stranger and I would feel ridiculous handing him a book for no apparent reason. Nonetheless, the same clear message, only with greater force, came back to me, "Give the man the book!"

While my students waited in the street, I stood in the middle of an otherwise empty bus, continuing to argue against my directive. It was a no-win situation for I could no longer leave my students unattended. I exited the bus, brusquely handed the father the book and mumbled that it was for him. Taken by surprise, he assured me that he would return the book after reading it. I responded, "You can't return the book; it now belongs to you."

Moments before school was dismissed for the day, there was a knock on my classroom door. It was my student's father. Before I could be taken aback, he handed me the book that I had given to him and requested that I sign it. Rather than simply signing my name, I found myself writing a poignant inscription. I then returned the book to him; whereby, he handed me an envelope and then walked away. Later, I opened the envelope, which contained a full-page, hand-written letter. He revealed that his life was a mess and that he had felt lost and abandoned, absolutely hopeless, until I, a stranger had reached out to him in a profoundly caring way. As a consequence, he claimed to have acquired a newfound faith in life. He went on to finish, "Madame Butterfly was not on the stage that day, but sitting directly in front of me in the audience surrounded by her students. And it was obvious that she was committed to all of them."

I was overwhelmed, not simply by his letter, but by the fact that my inner guidance had influenced another—a stranger no less—in such a significant way. I was forced to recognize for myself that my work did have value and it was being acknowledged and there was more at stake than just my own advancement. With this thought present, I was alerted once again, "The seeker is the sought." When I asked for clarity, I heard, "What it is that you seek after, is what others seek from you." The message was then given to me in yet another way, "The awakened must become the awakener." This reminded me of John's words, "You're way beyond learning." Whatever the context, the message felt overwhelming. Besides this, I felt rankled by the word "must." I was a willful person and detested being told what to do. In addition, some part of me remained clinging to the belief that healing myself left me the freedom to do what I chose with my own life.

A few days later, a question pushed its way through my other thoughts and remained boldly present long enough for me to take note: "Is freedom a process, an ultimate position, a state of mind, a state of being, an attitude that's ever changing?" I didn't know. Admitting that I lacked the answer was the first necessary step in finding the Truth. Some trying lessons would eventually take me the rest of the way.

In continuing to sort out my marriage and my participation in its trauma and demise, my confidence that I could create a healthy relationship grew patently stronger. (This was, in fact, true, but not within the framework that my ideas allowed me to comprehend.) Beyond the mental/emotional kinks with which John and I had to deal, I felt an undeniably deep sense of love for him and continued to convince myself that we were creating a healthy relationship. When I heard, during a spring walk in the woods, that I would never have a relationship with a man— that, in fact, I had never had a relationship with a man—I was confounded and decidedly annoyed. Whatever the message meant, I was adamantly unwilling to release the belief that John and I did not have something uniquely special.

Shortly after this, while with Teresa in the woods after a freak April snowstorm, I sat on a riverbank throwing snowballs in the water and eyeing them float along, bobbing one after another, on the fast, vernal current, as if I was hypnotizing myself. All the while I was obsessing over the unfairness of not being allowed to have a gender relationship. I could visualize a small cottage in the country, a huge yard with mature shade trees, a garden and a couple of large dogs. The picture included a man. With the personal work I had done, I felt that I was ready to embrace this scenario and the dictum was otherwise ridiculous. Certainly, I had earned this much in my life; I was not asking for very much. When Teresa reminded me that night was falling, I reluctantly pulled myself back to the moment. I carried my annoyance home with me while a vision of the snowballs remained bobbing in the current of my consciousness. Something was about to be presented.

The following morning, after a fitful night's sleep, I awoke to a distinct perception of a stone lying in the palm of my right hand. Its size, shape and weight were revealed as I found my fingers closing around its energy. Listening, I heard that what I was feeling was the present that I was to give John for his upcoming birthday. Then I heard, like a command, "Get it!" I lay there half-immobilized for considerable time while the message drove home to the point that energy moving in my left hand began to cause my fingers to compulsively thump on the down comforter. In short order, I hopped from bed, reached for a phonebook and thumbed through the yellow pages making a list of gem shops in the area. I was surprised how many there were. Before I embarked on the quest, I deemed it essential to first make a stop at the woods. I had already decided to pick a few pussy willows to give to John for his birthday.

Once I arrived at the woods, I detoured from my normal path and headed toward the wet prairie. I then began to trek from bush to bush absorbed in the task. Although not forecast, it was a perfectly splendid day, perfect enough for me to become sidetracked. I removed my coat, hung it on a tree branch and proceeded to wade around basking in the glory of the energy surrounding me. Birds were everywhere singing: fat robins, juncos, song sparrows, and red-winged blackbirds. And the sun was shining as only it can on a spring morning. I could feel the earth encouraging sleeping plants to awaken. I could feel myself awakening. I wanted to remain here forever. I was too in love with the moment to even care that my feet were soaked and cold from water spilling over the tops of my boots. With great reluctance, I pulled myself away and returned to my car, a bundle of pussy willows in hand.

After changing into dry footgear, I pulled out my list of gem shops and mentally developed a route. I would start in the suburbs north of the city and work my way back. My hope was that the stone would turn up at the first store on my list. However, after several attempts to locate a rock that matched the energy I was feeling, I had only to approach a store before recognizing that my efforts would be futile. By noon, I had exhausted the list and was now certain that this was a senseless exercise. Yet the energy of the stone was still markedly strong in my hand. I stood in the street beside my car exasperated and wondering whether or not to simply return home. What else could I do? I was willing to go the distance, even if it meant a thousand miles, but I needed a directive. As I was beginning to become rattled, I suddenly heard, "Cease your efforts. The stone is already yours." I muttered dubiously, "What the hell does that mean?" The response was a knowing that I had to simply get in my car and drive.

I was subsequently directed to drive across town to the metaphysical bookstore by my school. I felt like a donkey following a carrot dangled in front of it, just out of reach, enticing it to follow. At the bookstore I learned that a psychic fair was taking place. I had never been to a psychic fair and did not know what to expect. I followed signs to the basement and ended in front of a counter where participants were required to register. An attendant explained the procedure to have a reading. Overcome both inwardly and outwardly, my eyes adjusting to the dim, fluorescent light, I scanned the room. It was crowded with card tables and people. I wanted to leave. But the energy of a man sitting unengaged at the far side of the room held my attention. I looked at a list of psychics presented: Without question I knew which name was his. I paid for a half-hour of service, and now thoroughly overwhelmed with expanding energy, I maneuvered through the crowd to finally sit down in front of Paul. Elbow to elbow with other people, I stifled an urge to ask if we could move upstairs or anywhere else where we might live what was waiting to happen with a degree of privacy. Instead, I just sat there in a daze.

Energy overwhelmed me faster than my breathing could manage. I felt sure I might suffocate, maybe implode, I was that overcome with anticipation. I placed an energetic screen around me to isolate myself from nearby distractions. Taking a further moment to settle into a sense of privacy and security, I then focused my attention on Paul. He asked me what questions I had. To my dismay, my voice was gone. I could only squeak that I was unclear as to why I was present, but I had no questions. He then asked what kind of reading I would like. I was unaware of the choices available, but much out of character, I let go of control and requested that he decide. Subsequently, he reached across the table and drew my hands into his. The shock that I felt as he did so revealed that there was no going back.

He first read my palm, describing my life with impressive accuracy. He stated that I had been abandoned and isolated as a child and had learned to rely on myself for spiritual development. He added that I was an exceedingly quick learner, independent by nature and on a spiritual path that would require much travel and change in my life. I could feel my mind attempting to stay abreast of the information as he presented it, but he was moving way too fast. Reading further, he saw a white, fluffy, energetic animal, a young girl and a man. He felt the animal was symbolic of me, stating that I had the power to fly through the sky, swim the oceans, or crawl across the earth—do anything I wanted. Before I could query him, he was on to the girl. He began to cry as he spoke of her, as well as relinquish his hold on my hands. Firmly placing my hands on his, I pressed him for the truth. I knew the girl was a student in my class and asked him if she was suicidal. He claimed that she was put in my path as a lesson and I had to stay focused or I would be in trouble. Following, he described the man as a teacher—tall, extremely thin, curly white-haired, dark complexioned, and light eyes—waiting to come into my life. He further stated that this teacher's name started with an "M" and I would find him on an island of which the location was not clear, perhaps in the Mediterranean. Then with great gravity, he headed in a different direction, warning me about the dangers of evil forces. He claimed that these dark forces were intent on taking me away—there were the fears of my childhood—and if I was going to survive, it was essential to learn to stay balanced. Already John had been subjecting me to such warnings. Coming from a virtual stranger, this warning terrified me to a much greater measure.

When the session concluded, we both remained engaged in the intense energy connection between us. I was on overload, particularly hearing that a new teacher was coming into my life. This felt like a foreshadowing that I had to break my ties with John. If I had had time to react, I would have panicked, but with a sudden charge of energy running through me, I recognized that my session was unfinished.

Paul must have been in tune, for just as suddenly, he inquired if I would like a past life reading. Without hesitation, I stumbled to the front counter, paid for additional time and returned to my seat. The moment he took my hands in his, we both were instantly transplanted to a prior time and place. As he began to describe a character, I realized I was her. Further, I realized I could sense her as much as he could. I had been a Native American woman then—extremely petite, with long, black, plaited hair, clear skin, full breasts and clothed only enough to conceal my loins. I was reserved, maybe even aloof, self-contained and strangely confident, but extremely isolated. He then described a cabin, oaks, hills and a fast-moving stream running down from the mountains and through a virgin forest. He thought it was the western mountains. To me, it was clear that we were in the Appalachians—South Carolina.

As the story of that lifetime unfolded, I was one of three sisters. Playing one day, my younger sister, whom I dearly loved and was responsible for watching, fell into a pit my father had made from digging clay that he and my mother used to make pottery. My sister's fall had been precipitated by a playful push on my part. She eventually died of complications from the accident. My parents held me accountable and, therefore, never forgave me. I was crushed by her death, and coupled with the blame and rejection I received specifically from our father, I continually worked to be accepted back into my parents' good graces. But there was nothing I could do to appease them. My older sister eventually married and left home while I stayed on, supporting my parents, despite their hostility. One day I suddenly left, never to return.

Following the stream, I maneuvered high into the mountains. I found the most isolated spot possible and then set about to make it my home. With much determination, I learned to live off the land in a completely self-sufficient manner. My interaction with nature became profoundly intimate. My closest companions were the woodland creatures who befriended me, especially birds and, in particular, a resident barred owl. Better than a mockingbird, I learned their calls, and freely communicated with them. My physical senses were highly developed and my extrasensory capacity even greater. I was therefore acutely attuned to the spirit realm—forest fairies included—and with my close kinship to plants, it was second nature to extract their secrets enough to create a host of healing concoctions.

My family experiences left me to distrust, and therefore avoid interaction with people. Nonetheless, when I discovered a half-dead man in the woods and nursed him back to health, my isolation became punctuated by visits from those who sought me out for my remedies. My bitterness subsided as years went by, yet I would never have thought to give up my solitary existence, not even for the man whose life I had saved and who encouraged me to return to society with him. More than being in the woods, the woods were in me. I could not have survived anywhere else. Paul added that I did not differentiate between men and women. However, I did cover my breasts when having to deal with others, especially men. Finally he stated that my life had been simple but full and that I had lived to a ripe old age in my woodland sanctuary.

When I questioned him about my name, he claimed that it had to do with something or another floating on the water. I wondered what that something was, but just as quickly, I heard that it was of no importance; I should call her Something-Floating-On-The-Water. I felt compelled to ask how Something-Floating-On-The-Water (Something) had died. With an oddly intense reluctance, Paul disclosed that on a sun-drenched, autumn day she/I lay down on the leaf-covered ground and passed on, her/my forest friends nourishing themselves on her/my remains. Then, with tears streaming down his cheeks, Paul claimed that he was coming back. Again, we sat across from each other, the depth of this shared experience making our connection difficult to break.

I was momentarily more successful than Paul at containing my tears, but I was unquestionably on the verge of becoming unglued. At the same time, I was too stunned to move. Meanwhile, Paul suddenly reached down and hauled his briefcase from under the card table. I tried to hear what he was saying as he rummaged around in the bottom, something about feeling oddly compelled to bring something. He then reached forward and placed "the stone" in my right hand. I closed my fingers around its now-familiar energy. It was the exact size, shape and weight that I had felt when awaking that morning—certainly not a beautiful gem, but a smoothly worn river rock that turned from gray to green when warmed from being held. I had held the likes of it before, way back in the memory. Choking back my sobs, I sat stiff on my folding chair, my gaze on Paul, while my mind zoomed here and there trying to make sense of the situation. Whatever was occurring, it had begun to be revealed to me as I sat on the banks of the river with Teresa the prior evening watching snowballs floating on the water. I expressed my gratitude as best as I could. Then I departed.

Before I was able to get to my car, the flood of tears I had been struggling to contain consumed me. What was this about? Why was it happening? Where was it taking me? I wanted to run back to Paul and demand that he answer my questions. Certainly he knew. I wanted to know if others' experiences with him were like mine. Or were mine special? I wanted to scream I was so riled. Even when I knew somewhere inside that I would never cross paths with Paul again, I could not admit it. I did know that if I tried to reenter the psychic fair I would somehow be prevented. The rock felt glued to my hand as I drove home. I had what I had been directed to obtain for John's birthday. Now, what was I to do with it?

Curiously, John's first reaction to my experience was to profess that it was good that I had chosen not to become a wood nymph, for my spiritual growth would have been arrested in an elemental state. And that it was good that, in my present embodiment, I had chosen to come out of the woods and be part of society again; it was important that I was choosing to grow. I wondered what this had to do with my forest fairy experiences. It was strange to think that, by a different choice, I could have been one of them. Yet, contrary to John's comment, I did not feel as if I had ever come out of the woods. Now, I was beginning to understand. The deeper connection I sought in the woods was actually with *my* Spirit—my own essence.

I explained to John that it was becoming important to me to give someone something special if I were, in fact, going to give a present. Certainly I could give him the stone if so required; nonetheless, it seemed that the stone was meant to be mine. He replied that giving and receiving are the same. Therefore, the stone was a gift for all those involved in the experience. I was unsure what I understood about his perspective; however, I felt there was more to understand than what he had articulated. In the end, I accepted that it was okay to keep the stone, but not without feeling a twinge of selfishness, which took the form of telling myself that he would have little appreciation for an old river rock, and it would only be shortly lost in his clutter anyway. I gave him the pussy willows and a music tape (ironically called **The Fairy Ring**) for his birthday and took him out to dinner. I was disappointed that the pussy willows left no impression on him and sorry that I had failed to find him something exciting for his birthday, something he would value as much as I did the stone.

Regardless, the stone became an important meditation tool for me. Unfailingly, holding it in my hand left me traveling somewhere I was unable to discern—deep into other dimensions—and returning with a clarity that left it hardly necessary for John's interpretations anymore. Consequently, I began to place great importance on the stone, and to my chagrin, I began to rely much less on John's aid.

It only took one encounter, holding the stone pressed just so in my right hand, to realize that it could lead me back to the Something reincarnation. The first time going there I felt Carl's energy suddenly and overwhelmingly clouding the memory; what was the significance? I was held in this cloud for some time—long enough to get the point. Carl had been my father and had raped me. Out of an ever-growing rage over my sister's death, he had finally committed the unthinkable. He had violated me—stealing my virginity, and with it my youth. That was why I had suddenly left home, never to return. The information ripped at me from the inside out, and plowed into deep-seated pain. This single bit of information was a grand "aha" exploding forth further bits and pieces of information. The lights in the closet were going on and I was suddenly rattling among the skeletons.

Realizations came cascading one after another as I examined each available piece of information and then began to put them together. An ever-increasing understanding was waiting. Carl and I had been reliving that embodiment. As my father, he had raped me! So this was why sex with Carl had felt like an act of violation. So this was why we both had felt that my father had sexually abused me. No wonder he had so much contempt for me. No wonder he begrudged me having anything: he had taken everything away from me before. Raping me had been an act of revenge. Or was it? Maybe it had been more than that. He had wanted to break my spirit. How long had he wanted to break my spirit? I was unable to answer that, but it felt deeper than this one incident. He hadn't broken my spirit, however, at least not in that lifetime or this one. Further examination revealed that his action had become his cross to bear, for in the end I was respected while he had lived out his life in deep bitterness and abject emotional withdrawal.

I could actually feel the depth of his hatred for me. Forever posturing in order to stand in his good graces to prove that I had done nothing wrong was only a replay of the memory. I realized how my fear and distrust toward my own sexuality, as much as Carl, were legitimate. I also began to comprehend why I could not feel a sense of completion despite being divorced. My anti-social behavior and obsessive need to be self-reliant—having to learn things, my own way, without asking for assistance—also became understandable as the memory was mirrored in my present life.

When I had felt so overwhelmingly nostalgic during my college field trip to the Appalachian region, I had actually been connecting with what was lost from conscious memory. It was the haunting sense of security, the sense of home, that I had once had, that had been leaving me unsettled and calling me to explore the obscure back-trails, in fact, every animal trail I came upon. I had been fascinated by the haunting, persistent call of a lone barred owl that had remained oddly close during the nights I had slept in my hammock under the stars, rather than in a tent with other female participants. My need to concoct meals rather than follow recipes suddenly made sense. My intrigue with native and medicinal plants, and turning my backyard into a native wildflower garden, as well as conducting field classes on the subject were all responses to an unconscious memory. And there lie the source of my unmanageable urge to drink from mountain streams. The past life also explained my dislike of wearing clothing and the sense of freedom I received from feeling the sun and wind on my naked body. Working at the nature center, I could see, had been an initial step in bringing the force of all facets to that embodiment to life. I had the key—so I thought; there were many more waiting—to explain my idiosyncrasies, my convoluted thoughts, debilitating emotions and my obsessive behavior, as well as all of my knowing.

Further excavation caused me to remember an incident with Adam when he had been about ten. In conversation with him, I had suddenly blurted out with a weird sense of urgency and earnestness, "When I die, I do not want my body wasted. I do not want to be buried or cremated. I want my body dragged into the mountains and left there so the wild critters can feed on it." From where the request had come had been bewildering to me as it certainly had been disturbing to Adam, but once spoken, I had realized that it had been there within me for a long time. In context of the memory, my once seemingly mindless articulation now made sense. This was clearly becoming an exercise in gathering pieces to an ever-expanding picture puzzle. One "aha" shooting here and another there through my mind like a meteor shower.

One most painfully huge "aha" was revealed during a later connection with the stone. The rape had left me pregnant. Although I had aborted through the use of medicinal plants, I had never forgiven myself. Adam's energy became strongly wrenching the more I gained clarity. At first I saw him as the child I would have had. I also saw him as the younger sister who had died. Finally I came to realize that he had been my sister and would have returned to be my child had I not ended the pregnancy. This allowed me to understand the nature of my abandonment issues with him, why I had obsessed over losing him during my pregnancy and through his childhood and why I felt like a failure in regard to parenting. I could now understand why Carl had believed that, through my carelessness, and without his intervention, I would have likely caused harm to Adam. Carl's assertions about my carelessness had always been an effective means to plummet me into a pit of badness. Further, the memory explained why Carl had been annoyed that I was unable to play with Adam when he was young, as if we were siblings. Still I knew that there were more pieces to the puzzle waiting to be discovered.

Awakening to this memory left me conclusively seeing that we die, only to live again. And we bring with us, as part of who we currently are, who we were before: strengths, weaknesses, conflict and a myriad of emotions: certainly all the pain. Going back there was bringing it all back to conscious awareness. I began to understand how the force of my past contributed to my sense of foreknowing that had plagued me throughout my life. Now, I could validate that knowing. With these new insights, I was certain that I could once and for all and with great haste bring resolution/redemption to my life and my relationships. Not so. My present view was a pinhole perspective. I had begun to examine my past—the skeletons in my closet—and I was finding light, which meant that continuing to tap into the resource of my greater history would open to unimaginable dimensions. To continue I would be using microscopic as much as telescopic examination. This was no game. It never is, going back into our history seeking to find who we really are. This was serious business—more serious than I could ever hope to imagine. I was stepping into perilous territory: *how* perilous was beyond my comprehension.

I wrote to Paul to share the further understanding that I had been given through meditating with the stone, to thank him for it and to inquire when he would be returning to the area, for I felt a strong urge to continue working with him. He responded by sending me his schedule. He also stated that he had been disappointed to learn during the reading, that I did not need a teacher for I already had one. I had sensed that he had been attracted to me during our session. I tried to be flattered. I even tried to imagine what it would be like having a relationship with someone who was psychic. Mostly I was annoyed that here was yet another man, a professional no less, who had been unable to leave his sexuality separate from the experience. The value in my irritation was that I would no longer be sidetracked thinking I needed to work with him.

Energy continued to pour more intensely in and out of my hands as my work with John became excruciatingly more intense. I could not keep them quiet. I would regularly awaken in the middle of the night to find my arms stretched to the ceiling, fingers fanning open and closed, charges of energy issuing from my hands, seeming to expand into the depths of forever. On some level, I remembered Paul's warning about forces ready to take me away. His words hit especially hard one evening as I drove downtown to John's place, clearly making me aware that something dangerous and dark was waiting to happen. I looked around: people were bustling about as normal. I bent forward and peered up at the sky through the front windshield. Instantly, an "oh-my-god" reaction overtook me. I had connected to something—a presence? a force—studying me, waiting to make a move. Coming to a stoplight, instinctively my hands flew forth and then moved in circular motion in front of me as if I was wiping condensation from the windshield. In doing so, I felt a huge dome of protective energy surround my vehicle. I told myself that I was acting weirder than ever, yet there was no way that I could have stopped my actions.

Despite Paul's warning and this experience to back it up, I was beginning to have great fun playing with this energy coming through my hands. It was much like a cosmic flashlight. I could turn it off and on, beam it wherever I chose, and heighten or diminish its intensity.

One night, in bed with John, my fingers began to twitch and tingle and my hands became overheated, a sure sign that something was impending. As the energy exploded from my palms, I began to entertain myself with it, beaming it high and low, up and down and around the room. My fun was immediately suspended, however, when a menacing force unexpectedly surged into my hands. Faster than I could react, my hands reached out to touch John. Simultaneously, I heard a sinister voice in my head declare, "You'll have to cut off your hands to avoid harming him." With my hands only a fraction of an inch from his shoulder, my fear manifested into a horrifying scream. Instantly, the malevolent energy sprung out of my hands but remained in the room. Aghast, I leapt from bed and raced downstairs. John was close behind. I collapsed sobbing on the living room floor and attempted to pull myself into a tight ball to protect my energetic field as I explained to John what had just happened. It was one thing getting myself into trouble, but to think that my actions put others, especially John, in danger was horrifying. My trepidation alone caused me to recognize that this experience was real: further, that I must return to the bedroom to face this energy, which was really facing my fear.

John was visibly concerned, but honored my position enough to refrain from interfering. Instead, he gave a few quick tips on how to protect myself. I was so unstrung it took all of my energy to begin to pull myself together. Finally, I made my way to the upstairs hallway where I took a last deep breath and centered myself enough to reenter the bedroom. Paul's words that there were dark forces waiting to carry me away, and my only safety was in staying centered, was now a point of sobriety that kept me focused. My heart pounding in my ears revealed the seriousness of the situation. Upon entering, I could feel the entity waiting for my return. Slowly, I made my way across the room to the bed. There, I lay down, supine, and placed my arms to my side in order to expose my heart chakra. With the greatest purity of thought, I energetically beckoned to the malignant force, uttering, "I only allow that energy in my personal space which serves my highest good." The energy remained strong; so did I. Neither could I be afraid, nor make this a challenge. I simply had to be openly vulnerable and present in the moment. I repeated the phrase again, and then again. When I thought I might be here for the rest of the night, the energy began to slowly dissipate. Even so, I remained alert. When the room felt clear of this foreign energy, and my heart had calmed, I once again made my way downstairs and dropped exhausted into John's lap. His concern would be much slower to fade than mine would.

I contemplated why this had happened and what I needed to understand. I had spent my life feeling unsafe, if not paranoid, in almost every situation—why, I was unsure—and even now, I only felt fully calm either in my or John's abode, or else in the woods. But this force felt like a microcosm of something larger than I could intellectually fathom. I would have liked a guarantee that I had simply been momentarily put through a test and that, since I had passed, I was now exempt from any further testing. On the contrary, this had been only a necessary initiation into another realm of understanding. The lesson in the moment was that foolhardiness came with a price while discernment and appropriate intent were critical for survival within the framework of the reality into which I was being moved. The real lessons had begun.

My receptivity to Universal energy, I assumed due to this experience, soon took a quantum leap. As much as I had previously moved through life with my head tilted downward, closing off my throat chakra, I presently found my head being tilted backward, throat exposed, by a force beyond my recognition. I felt quite vulnerable in this state, but I was powerless to alter it. Further, at times my heart chakra would become activated in a way that left the encounter indescribable. Frequently energy would shoot into my third eye with such intensity I thought I might be blinded. Other times, my crown chakra became so active it felt like my mind was expanding upward like a beam of light, connecting to a realm of endlessness. Shedding tears remained the only successful means to manage the intensity of the energy vibrating inside of me during these occurrences. Also, it became even more trying to wear constrictive clothing—anything that interfered with this all-consuming energy flow.

Being zapped, as I called it, was no longer held to the shelter of the woods or my apartment. It happened everywhere: while driving or riding my bike, in the middle of teaching a class, in the grocery store, while taking a shower, even in the midst of a conversation. Outside of these recurring experiences, I felt empty, agitated or a sense of loss. It was hard to decide whether the high I felt from the experiences was more or less difficult to handle than the subsequent low.

A particular encounter in the woods one day came like a bolt from the blue. While I sat on a fallen log under my favorite matriarchal oak, feeling Amiga's energy, I heard clear and distinct, like an accusation, "You're a teacher!" With certain defiance, I retorted, "That's right! I'm a teacher. I teach school!" Again the accusation came and again I tenaciously repeated myself. Going back and forth several times, my defiance growing, I realized that I was unwilling to own the significance of the statement. The definition I maintained of "teacher" was much different than what was being given to me. Intuitively, I understood what was being asked of me; yet I had never felt this kind of resistance surge from me before this. Subsequently, I felt suddenly energetically wrestled to the ground, flat on my face, arm bent backward, as one of my brothers might have done to me in my youth, forcing me to say, "uncle." Eventually I would have to own the space but, before I could, I would have to walk through the resistance that held me captive from doing so.

As I prepared to leave the woods, certain that I had had all I could handle for the moment, an incredible surge of energy issued from my palms and spread outward like two radiant spotlights. It was explained that the spotlights were wood energy and that it was time to bring that energy into the city. With my arms suddenly stretched downward and palms backward, I could feel in my palms, as I walked down the trail and into the street, that I was pulling the energy of the woods, brought forth like a trailing wedding veil, with me. I continued down the street while the veil of woods energy began to spread forth in all directions, shrouding the city in healing energy. A block from home, I was finally able to move my arms from their seemingly locked position. My hands then moved together in prayer position against my chest. They stayed locked this way until I reached the front door of my apartment building. The message was that I had to maintain a space of humility. I had an intellectual idea of the meaning of humility, but my experience conveyed an understanding that true humility was something beyond intellectual definition. I went to bed physically exhausted, but was awakened periodically by the message that I had been given in the woods, "You are a teacher!"

I was never inclined to review my journal entries. To the contrary, the idea of doing so brought on an intense sense of resistance: it was where all my pain was written down. Later, when I was required to review my thoughts, I would notice a distinct theme in the messages given to me during this period of working with John: Open your heart so John can see you; You have to keep your life simple in order to be in a place of love and joy; The responsibility given to you is to love yourself; Your heart is the key; It is essential that you heal yourself in order to know love; You have to learn about love in order to know the Truth.

I was taken aback, however, by a significant occurrence that had taken place one day when Teresa and I had been on one of our routine walks. She was a continual study in contrasts for, although I saw her as an all-powerful individual, publicly—and especially in her husband's presence—she carried on in a seemingly humorous, but self-deprecating manner. I did not appreciate her devaluing herself in such a way and had, more frequently than not, begun to decline interacting with her when others were involved. Yet she never carried this pretense when it was just the two of us together.

She had begun this walk trying to assess her issues with her mother-in-law, in particular how she trapped herself by needing and accepting the expensive gifts her mother-in-law was continually supplying her. Subsequently, she began to query me about my growth process and how I felt about myself. Unexpectedly, I found myself saying, "The difference between you and me, Teresa, is that I have come to love myself." More than the words themselves, the Truth in them resonated through me in a way that left no room for denial or second-guessing. I felt an immediate and unfamiliarly intense sense of freedom in my articulation—a feeling of enlightenment.

While part of me continued to converse with Teresa, a deeper self danced around with my new understanding. I loved myself! To be able to say this meant that I had come an amazing distance in my healing. The self-loathing was gone; and I knew it was gone forever. I not only liked myself, I loved myself. What a revelation! I could dislike my behavior, even my thoughts, but I loved myself! I truly did! The more I held the knowing, the more empowered I felt. No one could take this away from me. It was mine. I had worked for it. I had earned it. It was the product of my healing, of facing myself head-on, of my opening my heart. I understood that arriving at this point had been a process, but I wondered if there had been an exact moment when it had happened, and if so, why I had not been aware of it as it was happening.

Regardless of my thorough contemplation, what I failed to understand was, not only could I not keep this condition to myself, it had already been moving beyond me and affecting others like Teresa, Gertrude, Carmen, John, and members of my yoga group. This was the nature of their attraction to me. This was the space I was holding for them. This was why they were continually thanking me. The Truth of the power of love would become clearer as I continued to expand beyond the limitations of my linear reality. Meanwhile, considering the struggles that remained to erupt in my life, this Truth would not always be consistently obvious, but the fact that I realized it was a part of my greater consciousness was what was important.

The division between the two realities that I lived was becoming continually more pronounced. Without John as a sounding board, I thought I would go mad. Nonetheless, I realized at some point that his feedback in regard to my experiences often made little or no sense. He espoused lots of ideas; yet I had to admit that they were more a product of being well-read in the latest metaphysical literature, not a manifestation of an inner knowing or personal experience. He did not have my answers any more than Carl or David, my therapist, ever had. Only I did. Therefore, he could not possibly be my teacher, at least in a conventional sense. I could see that sometimes he was uncomfortable with or even threatened by my knowing. I was uncertain whether or not I was using him as I had used David—needing someone to listen to and validate me—but it was becoming increasingly impossible to diminish myself in order to keep a relationship functional. However, if I admitted that John was not where I was on this journey, I would have to face traveling alone. I was too insecure to accept that I was already traveling alone. I was unready to accept that John was placed in my life only to help me come out of the woods and into the world.

John became further distracted after hearing of my successful jump through another medical hoop bringing me ever more close to Peace Corps acceptance. He had already gone through a number of bouts of depression over my leaving—shutting down, distancing himself from me, holding that there was no point in further investment in our relationship since I was leaving. I did not know how to support him any more than I knew how to support my own issues with departing.

His abandonment issue came to a head late one Sunday as I was preparing to return to the city. Unexpectedly, he announced that he simply wanted to call the relationship quits. He went on to explain that it was easier to say goodbye now than drag out the situation. Immediately, all of my rejection issues were staring me in the face. However, I was able to keep them at bay enough to not react. I could do as he requested, walk out the door and never return if that was what he truly wanted. I was not going to bait him; I would not use him as a life preserver. The idea of walking away never to return would hurt to say the least, but I could handle it. I was ready and willing to go; yet I was held in check, listening, waiting for the guidance I could feel coming. Suddenly I heard myself request, "John let me take your fear for you." He emotionally backed away and, with distrust, asked, "Why would you do that?" I told him that I knew how to and that he had once done this for me. He did not say okay, but neither did he resist when I took a hold of his hand and led him upstairs to his bedroom. Contrary to the norm, he slid under the covers fully clothed.

I stripped naked and slid under the covers beside him. It was as if a personal self stepped back while an impersonal self stepped forward. This impersonal self had a confidence beyond comprehension. There was no doubt whatsoever, no questioning, no hesitation, simply utter openness. My body appeared to levitate and then spread over John like a comforting shroud of calm. He felt lifeless; his heart was completely shut down. I was lying on a corpse. Ever so gently, I could feel John's fear (his pain) begin to absorb into my body, like water to a sponge. John made strange, hardly discernable noises as a life force moved into his body and filled the spaces once held by fear. His fear, as it was absorbed into my body, was transmuted, and therefore had no impact on me. If anything, the phenomenon felt extraordinarily natural. Afterward, John claimed that he had been reborn. He looked reborn. He looked as I did the night he had taken my fear for me. I left feeling utterly grateful and enough in an altered state that I got turned around on the back roads. I told myself that I was okay, that there was a lesson in arriving home only hours before I had to head for school. The value in the experience for John was that he began to examine underlying childhood abandonment issues.

We continued to mull over the pros and cons of a long-distance relationship. It was clear that the Peace Corps experience was preordained and had been initiated long before I had met him. I gave thought to the possibility of abandoning my efforts. John had been encouraging me for some time to apply for a teaching position that was vacant in his community school. Some part of me remained stubbornly unwilling to relinquish the impending adventure for any reason. I tried to convince myself that I could have both the man and the experience, while turning a deaf ear on the distant echo that I was beyond gender relationships.

Finally, two years of successful game-playing resulted in an invitation from Peace Corps headquarters in Washington D.C. John had been in my life the last six months of the endurance test. I arrived at his place, so excitedly waving my invitation that I missed seeing his spirits immediately plummet. His words, "Don't you know I don't want you to go?" hit hard at my sense of success and caused my heart to skip a beat. If he could be happy for me, this would be a lot easier, but he could not be, and I had to accept that. I had to accept that no one was happy about my leaving. I had to accept that the only enthusiasm I was going to get was what I could muster for myself. Underneath my excitement, I was scared to death and desperately wanted support. On some level, I knew I was giving up my life as I knew it: I was stepping out of my comfort zone and I was going to be tested in ways foreign to anything I could comprehend.

To my chagrin, of all the host countries available, my country of assignment was that one obscure little island in the middle of nowhere that I had claimed I would never consider. Resorts and telephones erased my dreams of mud huts and elephants. Knowing that this was meant to be, my disappointment was short-lived. For whatever the reasons, perhaps resistance or fear, or perhaps because it was simply not yet time to remember, it did not occur to me that Paul had already foreseen that I would meet a new teacher whose name began with the letter M in an island setting.

When I initially applied to the Peace Corps, I believed that I was doing so to push my self-confidence, independence and austerity to the limits: I wanted rigor. I wanted and needed to test my mettle, although I had no idea why. I was right on target, but not any target I could comprehend. My strength and stamina, my endurance were going to be tested, body and spirit tested. My greatest advantage in the moment was that I was unaware just how strenuous a path lay ahead of me.

I had four weeks to close out my life, two weeks between the last day of school and the day I was leaving for pre-departure training in Atlanta. Going through the transition became an annoying ordeal. I became upset with myself over the attachments I had to my possessions and the difficulty I had letting them go, particularly my clothes. From the first time I had donned a dress, I had proceeded to toss out my jeans and flannel shirts and replace them with a closet full of feminine attire, not necessarily frilly or sophisticated, and certainly not suggestive, but rather earthy and unique. These clothes served as a means to project an identity to which I could relate. The problem was that my identity had been changing so dramatically and quickly, it was impossible to maintain an external reflection. The choices representing the latest identity were at the front of the closet, while the obsolete reflections were subsequently pushed to the far end. Few of these clothes were suitable for the weather or social conditions into which I was entering. Consequently, I felt compelled, even obsessed, to acquire a suitably comfortable wardrobe.

Some months before, Teresa had gotten, what I considered, a sophisticated haircut from an upscale stylist. To my surprise, I found myself now willing to pay sixty dollars for a haircut. For most of my life, I had cut my own hair. Mostly I impulsively chopped away at it whenever a sudden, inexplicable urge overcame me—much like my compulsion to rearrange the furniture. During the time of my breakup and divorce, when I was acquiring an independent, tough-broad image, my extreme impulse was to shave my head. I had never done so, but through repeated "trimmings," I had come close. At the time of the haircut, it had felt necessary to let my hair grow. I had informed the stylist that I only wanted my hair shaped into the style that was already in progress. However, when he was finished, the little that was left was cut sharply at right angles, an amplified, stand-back tough look. I hated it; I hated the stylist for ignoring my wishes. As I paid him and then handed him a big tip, protocol overriding my indignation, he asked me what I thought. As could be expected, I fell into the "gotta-be-nice" routine. All the same, I walked out steaming. I wanted to grab my hair, like one of those Barbie-type dolls, and crank it out to the desired length.

Before I had returned to my car, I asked to be shown my lesson. For once, it was easy to recognize. First, I felt as if I had betrayed John by having my hair cut off, which translated I had actually betrayed myself. Then, only I could give myself what I needed. And although a part of me gravitated to a soft, natural look, another part of me had wanted to have a sophisticated look like Teresa. The stylist had actually given me what I had subconsciously been asking for. I could not be like Teresa or anyone else, and I could not create an appearance, sophisticated or otherwise. I had to be myself. But what did being myself look like?

My hair had grown out somewhat in the passing few months. I decided to get a perm to support the transition stage and also provide me with a carefree hairstyle for my island life. A woman in my yoga class, who was a beautician, made the situation easy for me. I was yet to see that going from butch to long and natural symbolized stepping out of tough and resistant—which had been necessary to exit my entanglement with Carl—and into the feminine. It was about being open, receptive and unconditionally supportive. While on some level I already owned this space, I thought I was clueless as to the nature of being truly feminine. Clothes or hair, I could not remain attached to appearance and continue to move where I was being required to go. This would soon be revealed.

Besides being obsessed over acquiring an adequate wardrobe, I found myself obsessed with packing, unpacking and re-packing, weighing my luggage and contents to see if I was within the weight restrictions and then re-packing again, continually changing my mind about what was essential to comfort (survival) and what was not. I observed my behavior closely. One would think that I was going to the hinterlands and would never be returning to civilization. In this obsessive behavior, I recognized the same paranoia that sprang to life every time I went away from home: I was afraid that I would be trapped somewhere needing something that would be unavailable. My paranoia supported a belief that if I was not prepared for the journey, I would not survive. Even with an awareness of this obsession, I was at a loss to control it.

One object felt vitally important to bring along. A participant in my yoga group gave me a gift shortly before the group disbanded. It was a star sapphire in a handcrafted, silver setting. The front of the setting formed a plain rim holding the raised circular stone in place. However, on the backside, hidden from view, the setting had been intricately formed into a six-sided star design. She told the story of how she had gone to great lengths to choose the stone and find the right craftsman to have it made, after which she dropped the piece, which was attached to a black, leather cord, into my hand. I had no qualms about receiving a gift for once. This was confirmed when she further stated that, although having this "amulet" made was of vital importance to her, she understood all along that she was actually having it made for someone else. When she met me, she knew I was the one. I was unaware of the exact significance of the amulet or the relationship between the woman and me, but it felt powerful enough that I never went anywhere without wearing it and paid great attention to avoid misplacing it.

To my further amazement, John suddenly had a great interest in using much of what furniture I had, including my bed, end tables, lamps and boom box, as well as many other odds and ends. He had consistently appeared to be a generous person and unattached to objects. Suddenly, I was seeing something different. Gertrude took on the same behavior, but I expected it from her. All of this was an important reference point for me. I recognized my own need to acquire things and my unhealthy attachment to the items I kept, and understood that someday they would all have to go. Meanwhile, I stored them at my parents', despite my awkward relationship with them.

While I was sifting through my belongings, I realized that it was essential to return a number of items given to me by Kent, the man who helped me step from my marriage. I was unsure why; although I rationalized that he could use them. We had maintained only minimal contact. Yet there was a genuine mutual caring between us. It was a two-hour drive to where he had moved and started a new business, but it was clearly necessary to fulfill this task. Upon arrival, he walked me around his new retail business, acting unnecessarily humble. The words that screamed in my mind were, "Too small!" as I realized that I could have gotten stuck here, particularly if a greater force had not frozen my efforts to phone him the night our relationship ended. The incident now seemed like so long ago. As we talked over lunch, his normal gay facade had a worn edge. He appeared isolated, struggling in his same old way but in a new context. We both carefully avoided sharing anything of a personal nature. Still, I knew he was involved with one of his employees. For once I did not dismiss my observations as judgmental, for they were too glaring to be able to ignore. Further I saw a reflection of a dysfunctional self from which I was continuing to disentangle. Most satisfying was my disinclination to feel sorry for him. Instead, I accepted him where he was with his life—accepted his pain, knowing it was his by choice. By the lightness I felt as I drove away, I knew I had closed a door to my past.

When my last weekend with John came to an end, and with my eighty-pound suitcase in hand, we returned to the city together. The plan was that he would drop me off at my apartment before he continued on to his appointments. As usual, he was way behind schedule. When we arrived in Chicago, he pulled up to an intersection and unexpectedly stated that, because of his time constraint, he was dropping me off there, where I could catch a train. But he never worried about his tardiness! Surely he must be joking! There was no train that went near my neighborhood. Bus transportation was possible but I would have to make three separate connections to get home. Hailing a taxi was an option but why should I have to pay for the fare? Want for word, and struggling to contain my hurt, I hauled myself out and found myself standing on an unfamiliar street corner with my enormous suitcase, like a ball and chain, at my side. Instantly, I reviewed how that very morning, in order to facilitate John's departure, I had done his laundry, made him lunch, cleaned the house and then made it ready for him being away all week. It was not easy to avoid seeing how little of him, outside of our spiritual work, was there for me.

Salt was added to the wound when I finally phoned Adam for assistance only to have him be uncooperative. I defended that my request to be picked up was not unreasonable considering that he had use of my car for the weekend. He finally agreed but stated that he wouldn't be there until he finished what he was doing. I stood on the street corner feeling like a waif. Anger and guilt snapped at my thought: How could I inconvenience my son? How could I get him involved in my problems? Why shouldn't I ask for help? How many times had I provided taxi service for him? Why can't I ever get support from a man?

My anger and hurt did not subside when I arrived home. I had not been thrown into this kind of a dither for a long time, and I hated it as much as what had precipitated it. I sat in my rocker and rocked, gazing at the trees outside of my window. As I did I was pulled into a memory of when, as a teenager, I had purchased a mirror to hang in my bedroom. I could have hung it myself, but I wanted my father to help me. With great resistance and at his convenience, he did so, but in the process, he dropped it. When I recovered it from behind the dresser, the gold finish on the frame was glaringly scraped. I was furious at him for not being there for me and furious at myself for needing him to be. The mirror incident had only reinforced my belief that if I wanted something done, and done right, I had to do it myself. Nonetheless, my need for my father to be there for me had not lessened. Here I was playing it out with John and Adam. I asked myself, "Isn't it okay to need help? I'm always there for others. Why isn't anyone ever here for me?"

From there, my thoughts shifted to when I first learned to drive. My two brothers contended, whenever I asked them for help, that if I was going to drive a car, I'd better learn how to take care of it. Consequently, I learned to change flats, check tire pressure and oil level and such. I could even change my own oil and was good at overall problem-solving. I valued my self-reliance, valued that I was not a helpless female when it came to cars. However, I had been angry with my brothers for refusing to help me, particularly since I ironed their clothes and cleaned their room and they freely ate the weekly goodies that I was required to bake for the family. The message was that I had to be there for the men, despite them never being there for me. I had served Carl, and Kent, and Liam, and now John. Give, give, give, and what did I get? What would it be like to really have someone support me? And what would that do to my independence?

By the time my review was complete, acknowledging my behavior pattern was unavoidable. I thought that if I addressed the issue with John, it would, once and for all, be finished. If he changed then I would not have to be resentful. When I aired my feelings with him, he apologized profusely. I wanted to be satisfied with his apology. Yet getting it made me realize that that wasn't what I wanted. What did I want? I wanted to understand what was really riling me. I did not want John to have to be a culprit. He was just being himself. He was not my problem. The way I related to him was. Why would I expect something from him—from anyone— which he could not give? Why did I attract men (and women) who were not there for me? How did I continually get myself stuck in the same pattern of behavior? One question led to another and another and I only wanted to scream for relief. Resolution could not be found in my current reality but I would find it, yet not without some serious lessons.

Walking out of the educational institution was the easiest part of closing out my life. Techniques that I had acquired the first year had been ineffectual the second, and as hard as I worked to find new ones, I felt as if I had failed. On top of having so many students with special needs, I had the student about whom Paul had warned me. That situation had been getting darker by the day and the entire class had been being impacted by her negativity. I had walked out of the schoolroom every day carrying all of the day's problems with me, until one day, with my mind back in the classroom, I was involved in my first serious auto accident. That had sobered me enough to withdraw from my over-involvement, but it had not made the rest of the year any easier. When I walked out of the door for the last time, I first breathed a deep sigh of relief and then swore out loud that I would never enter again.

Since the Arizona vacation, my relationship with my parents had remained strained. Without effort on my part, I questioned whether or not there would be any interaction between us at all. My mother's sister unexpectedly phoned one day saying that she would like to have a family get-together before my departure. I was certainly flattered that I would receive this much attention, especially from my family. Just the same, I felt way beyond needing such validation, and being with my family was too distracting considering all with which I already had to deal. In the end, I was stuck between not knowing how to gracefully decline and feeling obligated.

It was a long drive to my aunt's. With John operating in his usual state of chaos, we were the last to arrive. The men hung out in the driveway showing off their new cars to each other, while the women hung out in the kitchen discussing recipes. My mother was cautious and distant with me, and everyone hid their drinking. My discomfort was obvious from my attempt to explain my side of the Arizona incident to my aunt just in case my mother had shared hers. John's charismatic nature allowed him to fit in better than I could ever have imagined doing. The mere fact that I was present at all revealed on some level I remained in need of their approval (or so I thought). However, the extreme dichotomy between my family's and my reality was painful to observe. Articulating anything of value to me would only threaten or confuse them, or create discord. Without question, I did not belong; I did not fit in. Except for John and Adam, I had no family. With Adam fast into his own life and John overwhelmed with his, they hardly seemed like family. I would not let myself get discouraged; there was too little time and I had too little energy to waste. Neither would I let the "you-have-to-create your-own-family" incident surface; doing so, especially presently, would have been too painful.

John had our astrology charts read by a friend of his in an effort to deal with separation issues. When we met her, she had our computerized charts, along with a number of astrology books lined up in which she had marked passages to use to support her information. I knew next to nothing about astrology; yet, to me her approach, reading dog-eared pages from numerous astrology books as if to support her reading, seemed amateurish. I brushed aside my attitude and told myself to simply listen. The crux of her interpretation was that we had to go our separate ways for a while but we would end up permanently together. John's engaging manner indicated that he took her word as gospel. Therefore, I stepped into my conditioned, obligatory courtesy mode, even while my head was spinning. The energy was too heavy in the room and too overwhelming within me. I fought my impulse to bolt out the door.

That night, after John put to rest the preponderance of astrology information, he questioned me about when I felt we would be together again. Before I could contemplate his question, I found myself assuredly claiming, "When our work is complete, we will be together." I was unable to add that I also heard that my work would never be complete. I was frightened to know what that meant, both for our relationship and for me. John talked further about marriage and I agreed to marry him. Being engaged provided comfort for both of us. We also obtained comfort by focusing on his planned visit in the fall, as well as his idea of working at a resort on the island and living with me during my two-year stint. While I agreed to the plans, on one hand needing them as much as he did, I could feel them hampering my impending experiences. Trying to ignore an agitated inner voice, professing, "No man is ever going to get in my way!" only added to an inner consternation.

I had been having a series of dreams that gave warning to my need to remain attentive to where I was heading and avoid sidetracking myself. In one dream I had a dreadful cloud sitting in my head. When I examined it, I saw that its presence, which was maintained by my insistence of hanging onto the belief that I had a relationship with John, was weighing me down and causing me to fly lopsided.

In another dream, I was having the compass on my car repaired. The repairman appeared to be incapable or at least confused about fixing it, and kept asking me to be patient while he found the part necessary to make the repair. While I began to insist that I preferred to take the car home and repair the compass myself, he continued to insist that I be patient while he figured it out. The man was John. The car was my freedom. The compass was my sense of direction. I acknowledged the importance of this dream, at least to the degree that I was able to recognize it.

A baby girl to whom I had given birth and whom I had immediately turned over to family members to care for was the subject of another dream. I was suddenly consumed with the knowing that she was cold and that I needed to reclaim her and care for her on my own. Nonetheless, as much as I continued to look for her, I was unable to remember in whose care I had actually left her. The fact that the female infant symbolized my feminine self, I would not recognize for some time.

One of my most intense dreams occurred one night at John's. As it began, I was wandering through a dense jungle, which eventually transformed into a barren, mucky expanse. Observation revealed that reaching my ultimate destination from there would be of major difficulty. I could see evidence that others had either abandoned the journey or perished on the way, for muddy, rotting backpacks were strewn everywhere. An extremely tall stone fence with an extremely narrow cement slab running along the top—looking like a strange version of the Great Wall of China—suddenly loomed before me. It would be nearly impossible for someone of my stature to climb the fence, let alone walk its distance. Yet, doing so presented the only means to traverse this deadly territory. Further, it appeared to be heading in the direction in which I was required to travel. I decided to sort of hang from the top or straddle it if I could to make my way rather than risk an attempt to stand up and balance myself and possibly fall. Once in the desired position, although awkward,

I was able to see an exhausted array of people struggling over the crest of a hill. Something told me that none of them were going to last much longer. Then I noticed a man being chased by a mad dog. The dog soon changed directions and appeared to be coming after me. I decided to drop down on one side of the wall to hide, but in order to hold on, my hands would still be visible from the other side. I was confident that the dog would be unable to jump high enough to grab my hands, and therefore hung on all the more tightly. But the dog suddenly disappeared somewhere beneath the fence and reappeared where I was hanging on the other side. I looked down and saw his snarly teeth ready to grab my leg. With the "safe" option now out of the question the only way to survive was to stand up and balance myself straight and tall on top of the wall—like walking a tight rope. However, I had little energy left and there was too little time to hoist myself into that position. I was doomed. I awoke sitting bolt upright in bed shrieking in a panic that persisted even upon awakening the following morning. I thought the significance of this dream was readily clear: Not only did I have to get all parts of myself on the path and learn to stay intricately balanced if I were going to survive this journey, I had to go the entire distance. I failed to see that the expansive quicksand terrain, in particular, represented the next segment of my journey.

These dreams bounced hard against my idea that John and I had the prefect relationship, especially when I had had such a strong message, "You and John were put into each other's lives as gifts," to support it. I was yet to learn how dangerous intellectual interpretation could be.

Liam remained another matter. A few weeks after John entered my life, I came home one night to find a message on my answering machine. Liam. He was on leave staying in a hotel in Johannesburg. I was grateful that I had not been at home because it gave me the opportunity to collect myself before he tried again the following day. Without question, I wanted to tell him the truth. What was the truth? It was obvious that he had been both drunk and blue when he had made the call. I was sure that the next day, when he tried again, he would be in the same condition. Was I sacrificing myself again? Was I simply stuck in my old "dessert" routine? There was nothing to go back to with regard to our relationship. Still, he had called for comfort, not for me to dump him. I waited for his call the following day, nervous and distracted. By choice, I would have avoided the situation. When he phoned, he sounded as inebriated as he had the day before and admitted that he was phoning me because he was depressed. It was to my advantage that he was loquacious when he drank and unsolicitous about my life. As much as I desired to disclose exactly what was afoot, to set myself free, all I could say was that my Peace Corps invitation made it impossible for me to make any kind of commitment to visit him in Africa. We continued to exchange letters, however, my enthusiasm, interest and need to write waned—even my "shoulds" were no longer a motivation. My life was moving so full-speed forward it felt as if my experience with him were little more than a distant memory, when really his departure had only been eight months earlier. Now I had to live with my dishonesty.

Five days prior to departure, I handed over my apartment keys to my landlord and my car keys to Adam. Without my personal space and my vehicle, I was left with a "letting-go-of-attachments" sensation that drastically tested my sense of security. No security. No safety. No place to retreat. I did not like this. I was only beginning to learn that true quality of life is measured, not by what we hang onto, but by what we let go of. I had my suitcase full of clothes and a few "essentials": that was scant consolation.

My thoughts ran to my landlord. He first learned of my plans when he knocked on my door two months earlier stating that he was requesting all of his tenants to sign leases. It was divine timing considering I had a valid reason to avoid complicating my life. I had yet to be in a situation where a lease was required, and I was grateful, for the thought of signing one had always felt like a prison sentence, like being expected to tithe when I was a teenager. Without question, I felt all the way around, that I was being watched over. When I divulged my position about signing a lease, the landlord declared, "You're crazy to surrender the security of a job and a dwelling, and to go traipsing around the world as a single woman is sure to get you in trouble!" His words frightened me, some part of me. I could not tell him that I had no choice; my path was calling me and I was in the process of discovering myself. He would not have understood. I dismissed his position as culturally biased; typically, in Middle Eastern cultures, men control and define women's lives. I could not have remained even if I so chose. True, my ego self was trying to have second thoughts about my acting on my intuition and keep as many doors open as possible just in case my plans failed. I took comfort in the landlord saying that he would always have an apartment available for me. Still, my deeper awareness confirmed that the door to my past was being closed. Boredom over my lifestyle, coupled with my relentless restlessness arrested my reservations and prevented me from turning around. So did a resounding message in a song, "You have learned your lesson well."

Teresa and I went for our last long walk together, at which time we hashed over her separation anxiety issues. I assured her that she would be fine without me. However, I knew she would, in fact, have a tough time, for although she had many people in her life, she was unable to relate to any of them in the way she related to me. Better stated, none of them supported her in the way that allowed her to get a sense of her greater self. I was also aware that I needed her much less than she needed me, which was true for my other friends as well. My typical sense of responsibility to take care of others was also noticeably reduced—except maybe for John and Adam.

My relationship with Adam remained troubling. I knew he had unresolved abandonment issues. As usual, I would have liked to fix them. Yet I knew he was responsible to resolve his own issues in his own way. I still had my own issues with him to work out. There was a remaining sense of guilt and failure in regard to him that not even my past life awareness had alleviated. Neither did I know how to be a mother to my child who was now a man, nor did I know how to appropriately support him. I had wanted to more fully financially assist him with his education—somehow, I did not see that he needed me in any other way—but he was continually bailing his father out of financial problems. Consequently, to help him was ultimately to help Carl and I swore that I would never do that again. While David's message that Adam's happiness was contingent on my modeling that for him still held as a reference for me, I remained feeling helplessly confused in the mothering department.

A couple of weeks prior, while John and I were spending a quiet evening in bed, I found myself continually making Adam the center of conversation. It was clear that I was in the process of letting him go for the conversation was mixed with pain and lots of tears, both John's and mine. John's abreaction was based on feeling a loss over never having had children, as much as the unlikelihood of that ever being a reality. He had mentioned on several occasions that he would like to have had a child with me. I had been flattered. But the idea alone, especially at my age and within my circumstances, felt completely alien. Regardless, every time he brought up the subject there was always a confusing pulling on my emotions—guilt over being unwilling to accommodate him.

I wanted to spend personal time with Adam before I departed. I rationalized, however, that he was wrapped up in his own life, had little need to be with me before my departure and would be hurt if I asked to see him without his girlfriend, Mindy, being present. Therefore, I invited them to a dinner planned by John and Teresa. It was our last goodbye. Impersonal and painful! Like most other situations, I walked away with my brain tied in knots by a dozen different thoughts.

One last important effort, one over which I obsessed, was to make sure that my assets were readily available to Adam should I happen to unexpectedly meet my death. I did not know why, but the thought of the outcome being any different would send me in a dither. At the same time, I was reluctant to trust him with my financial affairs, although it largely consisted of someone writing a check to pay for my credit card bill each month and keep my bank statements in order. I had a host of reasons: he was too young; he had enough on his plate; Carl might find out my personal business. I also had considered Carmen, Gertrude, Teresa and John. By my estimation, none of them had good sense when it came to money. I wanted someone as reliable as I would be. At the same time, it seemed like an imposition to ask anyone to take responsibility for my life. In the end, even knowing how thoroughly scattered John was with all aspects of his life, I opened a checking account at his bank and turned matters over to him.

While I was finalizing my finances, John unexpectedly suggested that I invest my money in a duplex for sale in his community and while I was absent he would manage renting it. I did so much as tour the building. The end product was merely to throw myself into doubt. The duplex was rundown and considerable money would be needed to update it. It felt all wrong. Then there was the other side: I'm missing out on a great deal; John expects me to do this; I'm too insecure to take risks, echoes of Carl's brainwashing. In the end, I was able to let the opportunity go. The future would reveal the wisdom of having stayed aligned with my inner knowing.

I stayed with Gertrude during the couple of remaining days before departure, at which time I bid goodbye to Carmen, Charles and whomever else was left. As organized and focused as I had remained in regard to closing out my life, this had been an overwhelming period for me. I was grateful for Gertrude's support. Yet I was aware that her opening her door to me was mostly about her need for final counsel. She had already insisted on having Saturday dinner with John and me during our last weekend together so we could meet with her new beau, and I was unable to refuse. It was becoming toilsome to ignore the fact that she was manipulative, demanding, self-centered, possessive and jealous even of John, not to mention my other relationships. Being in her condominium revealed how much more unbearable it was becoming being in her and other people's spaces. Her place was unkempt and chock full of her coveted possessions. My impulse, which I was able to constrain for once, was to put order to her chaos. Instead, I managed my sense of suffocation by seeking refuge on her balcony. While one part of me was already aware that I had outgrown our friendship, another part of me was battering myself for lacking the appropriate appreciation for her generosity.

John maintained his obsessive busyness to the day prior to my departure before he finally realized our remaining time together was short; then he canceled appointments to spend time with me. As important as our last moments should have been, a part of me had already departed.

The day of departure, I, Miss Punctuality, was ready to leave for the airport fifteen minutes after the alarm rang. (My father had taught me well that it was a sin to be late for anything.) Mr. Disorganization was not. As if he was afraid of depravation or else was marking his territory, he grabbed me for a quick sexual coupling. He got relief; I got a bladder infection. Then he hastily proceeded to catch up on some financial tasks, as well as eat breakfast before getting dressed. Fighting impatience, I reminded him that we had to allow for rush hour traffic. Once on the expressway, we inched along at a snail's pace. My irritation escalated. Making this flight—continuing on with my life—felt like a life and death matter. Here I was setting myself up again—relying on someone else and ultimately getting let down. All told, we arrived at the airport as the last passengers were boarding the flight, and a perfunctory hug punctuated our last moment together. It was not supposed to end this way. As the flight attendant hurried me down the passage to the plane, I turned to get a final glimpse of John. He stood alone on the spot where we parted, staring my way and looking painfully forlorn. I wondered if he could see my hand on my heart. I wondered how many times we had lived this kind of heart-stopping goodbye. I wondered if he would survive my leaving him. I had to go. I wanted this adventure. Still I struggled with an urge to retrace my steps.

The plane door swung closed behind me as I stepped aboard. I shuffled sullenly down the narrow aisle, found my seat and stuffed my bags overhead. As I settled into my seat next to the window, I squeezed my eyes shut in an effort to hold back a flood of tears. I felt as if I was on a spacecraft flying to another planet never to return. Painful emptiness ate away at my stomach. I desperately wanted something onto which to hold, even just a comforting thought, but my mind was numb. An hour later a flight attendant serving breakfast awakened me. Too dazed and distracted to eat, I gazed out the window. The door to my life as I had known it was creaking shut and I was about to land where the new phase of my journey was waiting to begin. The old self, which could do nothing more than get in the way, had to die. Impending encounters would guarantee this process continued.

9

Walking Through the Threshold

I stepped off the plane in Atlanta helplessly confused and utterly disoriented. My condition was tempered by my own words spoken summers before on my first solo vacation in Colorado: "I'm never lost; I'm exactly where I'm supposed to be." At the airport, I boarded the shuttle bus waiting to drive new recruits from the airport to the hotel where pre-departure orientation was being held. Two other women were aboard. I attempted to engage in conversation, but my efforts led nowhere. Once at the hotel I joined my fellow Caribbean-bound recruits, seventy-six in all. Bluntly put, I could see I was going to fit in like Elmer Fudd. The volunteers largely fell into two groups: young adults (mostly newly-graduated college students) and retired professionals unready to surrender to being put out to pasture. I landed in the conspicuous gap in between. I tried to avoid labeling the groups as either "kids" or "old people," and I tried not comparing myself, not feeling less or better than anyone else. I observed just how ingrained this behavior was—like it had a force of its own. I wondered, outside of the experience at hand, if there would be any other common interest among members of the group. It was vividly obvious that reasons for joining varied markedly. Yet I could find no idealists among the crowd. My original thoughts regarding joining—an opportunity to give of myself and also to test my stamina—seemed to have suddenly evaporated, and as the minutes ticked by, I more intensely wondered what exactly my reasons for being in this situation were.

Day after day, that part of me who was terrified of being an outcast examined various ways to fit in. Conversations felt trite. I had little to say that was meaningful to me and, at the same time, non-threatening to anyone else. I wanted to ask, "What does your heart yearn for?" I didn't want to know their work history. Sharing my spiritual side with my roommate, a hyper-tense psychiatric nurse, only resulted in my being thereafter summarily side-stepped. I was glaringly shown how my insecurities habitually came across as aloofness, and that I clammed up and withdrew whenever I felt threatened. Even the manner in which I dressed, which remained distressingly important to me, not to mention my looks, stood me apart. I felt alienated at every turn. My suspicion that the other women had come to certain conclusions about me was confirmed through conversation with my roommate. I watched myself judge them for judging me. My natural impulse was to ingratiate myself. Nonetheless, doing this felt as if I was intimidating them while leaving myself open to further rejection. The best way to deal with my sense of overwhelm was to seek isolation. But if I was in isolation, how could I be a part of the experience?

Contributing to the already formidable challenges at hand, the intensity of incoming energy was stepped up. Sleep was futile, as was simply trying to focus my attention in class. I desperately needed the consolation of the woods. I needed somewhere quiet and secluded where I could focus on opening my heart and making my deeper connection. Within the framework of my free time, I could find no suitable substitute within the proximity to our downtown hotel, so I distracted myself by shopping, eating or wandering around. I understood that phoning John to quell my turmoil was a misuse of our relationship and would only add to his difficulty in adjusting to my absence. He had already informed me that he had been so upset by my leaving that he had stopped his car along the expressway on the way home from the airport to vomit. With my need overriding my ability to resist it, though, I did phone him or whomever else I could to gain a sense of relief. My efforts merely exacerbated my feelings of isolation, and left my heart more tightly closed.

The insecure part of me longed to flee home. However, I had to acknowledge, "Where is home?" My apartment was gone. My belongings were gone. My car was gone. John's community wasn't my home. Having nowhere to return triggered terror beyond my comprehension. I assessed the reality that enlisting as a volunteer was commonplace and reasoned that it should not be so complicated for me. Even so, all that I could fully comprehend was that if I didn't pull myself together instead of trying to escape, I would only be making the situation more uncomfortable for myself than it already was.

For the most part, the week of pre-training included introductions to a seemingly endless stream of procedure and regulations, and more of the endless forms. All the forms came with a reminder that if we failed to be honest in completing them, we placed ourselves in a position to be rejected. This had kept me conscientiously divulging details of my personal life during the course of applying. One morning I realized that I had had enough of this when all the females were required to fill out forms in regard to the nature of their sexual activities within the most recent time period; I lied. I was relieved of my guilt when that afternoon those women who had obviously had unprotected sex were called forward and escorted out to take pregnancy tests. As I watched them walk away, I felt as if I had escaped public humiliation.

My fear of failing to disclose the full truth during the application process was again put into perspective when, by regulation, volunteers with vision problems were required to bring along two pair of glasses with updated prescriptions. It had been stated that all such regulations would be checked during staging to assure procedure had been followed. If it had not, separation was imminent. Therefore, despite the fact that I wore contacts and had not worn glasses for twenty years, I bought the two pair of requisite glasses and brought them with me to class during the first few days of staging, sure that sooner or later the nurse or someone would demand to see them. Instead, there was not one question asked regarding such a regulation. I felt like a robot for having taken the application procedure—exactly following the rules—as seriously as I had, and that I had been so obsessive in my preparation, fearful of being rejected.

My sobriety was tested, at one point, when it was announced that no one would be allowed to pay for luggage in excess of the limit and therefore, anyone having more than the allotted eighty pounds—even one pound over—would be rejected during check-through at the airport. Consequently, almost everyone spent the rest of the day, buying shipping boxes, sorting through possessions and mailing the excess home. I knew my luggage was slightly overweight, yet I was determined that I was not going to invest any more time or energy than I already had on the matter. This was not a show of defiance. Rather, it felt as if I was standing up, proving to myself that I had the courage to withdraw from the games, the bureaucratic intimidation, as well as from my own insecurities; and that doing so would not be the end of the world.

During the course of the week, much class time was spent discussing the issues of drugs, associating with Rastafarians (who are discriminated against in the islands), the difficulties of island relationships and how to avoid sexual assault. It was explained that in an island culture if a woman is seen with a man, she is considered to belong to that man. If this was not enough to rile me, supposedly true examples were given of the difficulties that female Peace Corps volunteers had had in extricating themselves from "Rasta" relationships gone awry. It was severely stressed that white women were the chief targets for sexual attacks. Once again, survival was dependent on playing by complicated rules that prohibited me from freely and comfortably living my life. The more security concerns were drilled into us, the more both my apprehension and anger escalated. With the degree of time and energy I had expended reclaiming myself from the clutches of male domination, I felt as if I was suddenly being forced to operate in a cultural straight jacket.

My overall reaction to our week of staging was that redundancy had to have been a consciously integrated part of the training program. It was interesting to watch how discontent had hit with epidemic force. As volunteers were now in the habit of continually complaining amongst themselves, I watched my own attitude erode day after day the same as everyone else's. The attending officials were carefully monitoring our attitude and behavior, however, so I refrained from openly expressing any reactions.

Completing the first week of training, remaining recruits—two were separated during preliminary training—were then flown to our designated island. My three pounds of overweight luggage had been no problem. My group, consisting of fourteen volunteers, landed on the island where our area Peace Corps office was located. Our arrival was a big event for the Peace Corps volunteer community already stationed on island, and as a matter of course they had a party for us that evening. It was interesting to observe their interactions, as well as the intricate bonding among seasoned volunteers who were all male, except for three females. I found it a test to imagine being friends with any of them, male or female. The two young men who had initiated the environmental program were plainly proud of their perceived accomplishment and expressed their desire for my feedback about the curriculum manual that they had spent two years developing. What they were really asking for was my allegiance. I attempted to stay open and accepting, but my frustration with everything to date was building and intensifying my innate sense of resistance.

Seven new volunteers were currently assigned to take over the environmental program—four to continue the existing program on the bigger island and three (I being one of them) to initiate the program on the neighboring island. My two teammates were a neophyte environmental-major graduate, Brett, and a retired national park director, Jack. None of the other members of the environmental teams on either island had any prior curriculum development or teaching experience. Besides the three in my environmental team, three other young volunteers—two women and a man—were assigned to other programs and would be part of our group.

We six new recruits were required to spend two nights on our sister island prior to completing the last leg of our journey, a twenty-minute flight across the straits to our island. As was customary, various resident Peace Corps members were to house us until we left. I was assigned to stay with a woman who was my age and who lived in a basement apartment with her Rastafarian boyfriend. My natural impulse was to want to believe that my hostess and I could become fast friends. Yet, from the moment I met the boyfriend, I felt disturbingly threatened by him. Almost immediately I found myself trying to energetically cloak my sexuality from his prying glances.

The first night there, I was shown to a sleeping cot in the kitchen/living area. I was relieved that the boyfriend had gone out before I retired and hoped that he would not return at all. Those hopes were dashed when I was awakened late in the night as he entered. In the dark, but with enough light to see, he stood in the middle of the room and proceeded to strip. Once naked, he headed straight for me. Consumed with fear, I quickly closed my eyes and pretended to be sleeping. My desire was to kick him in the balls when, without hesitation, he bent down and gingerly kissed me on the cheek. I did not move however. I did nothing whatsoever as he then stepped behind the partition to his partner; I was not able. His lingering strong body scent made this encounter impossible to deny. I remained in a tremulous state as I dissected the encounter and realized that, by the mere fact that I had not reacted to his kiss, he knew that I had been awake, even watching. I had fallen squarely into his trap. Worse, by quelling my reaction, I had condoned his assault. The next morning he was gone and I said nothing to his partner, mainly because I was afraid of causing trouble or losing the possibility of her friendship—though it remained obvious that we had nothing in common. That evening I breathed a sigh of great relief to hear that he would not be home.

Since another woman was also spending the night, I had agreed to sleep on a bed in a windowless back room, which also served as the passage to the toilet. At some point during the dead of night, I was startled bolt upright from a sound sleep. I was sure someone had touched me. The night was pitch black and what air there was, was humid and heavy. Not knowing whether I wanted an acknowledgment or not, I quickly whispered, "Who's there?" No response. Finally, I lay down again and cocooned myself in the perspiration-soaked sheets, attempting to create a sense of security while telling myself that I had been dreaming. Some time later, I again awoke to the feeling that someone was standing over me, brushing my shoulder ever so slightly. I could discern nothing in the blackness. I only wanted to scream out to my host, "Get your man away from me," but I questioned whether or not I was dreaming, not to mention what trouble I would cause if I wrongly accused her Rasta man. After all, Rastas were too heartily discriminated against already. I slept fitfully for the duration of the night.

The boyfriend was present upon my arising, cool and chatty. My sole desire was to scratch his eyes out. Rather, I energetically distanced myself, as was habit in threatening situations and abided the mindless etiquette while attempting to accept that my imagination had gotten the better of me. I would later learn from other women guests, that this man was nondiscriminatory in his sexual harassment. Greater understanding—which is characteristically accompanied by greater confidence—was necessary to address such issues, which he had not created, but only triggered. My "real" Peace Corps experience was beginning to come to light, and as I had wanted, my mettle was being tested. Meanwhile, the encounter had me definitively generalizing about men in the culture. I was annoyed enough that it was continually necessary to be wary or protective of myself in the presence of men, and now, in this culture I had to be hyper-vigilant.

A female relative of the couple with whom I would be staying was waiting at the airport to drive my two female associates and me to the families—home-stays, as they were called. I sat in the rear seat during the drive unable to participate in the lively conversation going on around me. Anxiety and doubt about belonging or ever fitting into such a foreign environment added to the level of my general discomfort. I was certain that I would never adjust to the climate. I had always hated being in damp or sweaty clothing, annoyed that my body had difficulty adjusting to extremes in temperature. Besides having to become accustom to the heat, I was going to have to overcome my dislike of perspiring, as well as my paranoia of having offensive body odor.

Beyond my aggravations, my curiosity had immediately awakened to the abundance of new stimuli as we drove along. The island consisted of a thirty-five square mile volcano, old enough to have acquired its own lush ecosystem, but active enough to have geothermal areas and periodic, noticeable tremors. The copious effulgence of the vegetation, the cacophonic birds, the salty smell of the air, virtually every aspect of this environment was foreign and I was profoundly aware of how far away I was from the familiarity of my woods. Be that as it may, my binoculars and field guides were the first items that I unpacked.

My host family was waiting for me when I arrived. The Remy's, a gentle, reserved elderly couple, lived in a roomy (by island standards), whitewashed cement block cottage with a rusty red, tin roof. Their home was adjacent to the only main road, which circled the island, in a little village called Morning Star. It was homey inside, but cluttered, run-down, and moldy smelling. Regardless, I was grateful to have a semblance of personal space in a back bedroom I shared with their storage. This would be my home until I completed the remainder of training, part of which would take place on my island, the other part on St. Lucia, where the entire group would again be brought together for four weeks of technical training. In the interim, the search for my own place to live was of primary concern.

Mr. Remy was a retired head teacher who now found his calling as a lay minister and poultry farmer. Mrs. Remy was a housewife through and through. One of their three adult sons still lived at home, although he was off island when I arrived. It was not easy to relate to the Remy's, for we had little in common, particularly their degree of involvement in established religion—such as getting up at five in the morning to read together from the Bible. It took very little on my part to reveal myself as a "heathen." Though my customary impulse to escape from unfamiliar circumstances remained intact, I had immediately felt a warm place in my heart for this gentle couple. Somehow, I felt as if I was the daughter they never had. This made me even more serious about conducting myself in a manner worthy of their approval.

Events continued to reveal that it would take time to adjust to almost every facet of the island environment: The sun setting at 6:30 on summer evenings. Fuzzy donkey spiders (tarantulas) scurrying across the porch at twilight. Goats, sheep, and donkeys tethered to bushes or ambling loose through the neighborhood, not understanding that a newcomer lacked appreciation for their endless nocturnal dialogues. Waking with a start when geckoes, frogs and cockroaches plopped onto my bed from unscreened windows, which I refused to close upon retiring. Palm fronds rattling on a breezy night giving way to roosters crowing reveille. Sudden, frequent but abrupt soakers (downpours) causing islanders to scurry for cover for fear of catching a cold and causing the skies to ribbon with rainbows. All of this was on top of becoming accustomed to the cultural dynamics of the island.

Mr. And Mrs. Remy bestowed on me the full cultural charge of hospitality due a guest. In fact, I felt doted upon, even protected—both foreign experiences. It was a challenge to sit, doing nothing—my "being-useful" syndrome coming alive—while Mrs. Remy, who was clearly accustomed to serving the family, cooked meals and kept the house in order. I explained enough times that I felt much more comfortable participating as a family member. She finally began to allow me to set the table, clean up afterward or wash and box the chicken eggs when Mr. Remy gathered them.

The most difficult aspect of home-stay life, however, was the lack of personal space and time. Every attempt to go for a quiet walk in their back field or across the street to an old plantation site was foiled by my hosts who perpetually had timely plans for us to drop eggs off down the road, take a ride to town or meet relatives. The times I did escape their protective kindness, seeking shelter under an unidentifiable, but winsome-looking tree across the street to write in my journal, I found an ever-increasing circle of bare-foot, bright-eyed village children surrounding me. When I stayed long enough, the circle would expand to include curious mothers as well. They would squat next to me, less self-conscious than I would have expected, satiating their curiosity by asking innumerable questions. Their odd, English dialect had been passed down generation to generation from slave ancestors brought to the islands from Africa. It might as well have been a foreign language to me. In weeks to come, the children would become my students. They would demonstrate their curiosity by running their fingers through my red hair, peering into my ears, tugging on my earrings and examining my freckles as they discussed whether or not they were a sign of AIDS. And, in more ways than I could imagine, I would come to find them incredibly beautiful.

My young colleagues were forever going off on their own, hitting the tourist spots, dancing and drinking, and having a lively time. I was disgruntled that they never invited me to join them. In contrast, I told myself that I was being ridiculous for feeling left out since I only really wanted to be with them to relieve my own sense of isolation and because I did not feel safe going out on my own. Besides, I alleged, I would never sacrifice my relationship with Mr. and Mrs. Remy or my position in the culture by carrying on like a tourist. I did want to explore the natural environment, however, and go to the beach to swim. Even if the Remy's allowed me the time, training had left it ingrained in me that doing either alone was putting myself at risk. My recourse was to remind myself that I was here to fulfill a responsibility, not indulge my own needs and desires.

The second weekend, after sitting on a hard pew through a three-hour church service, the Remy's announced that they were giving me a tour of the island. It was clear that this was a grand outing for them and I appreciated their efforts. The drive reminded me, though, of the time when my grandmother and my aunt had taken my cousin and me on the trip west. The Remy's would stop at one historical site, explain a bit of history and then drive on to the next. I wanted to request that they park in an isolated spot somewhere along the coastline and wait for an hour or two while I scouted on my own.

As I could find no solitude in the neighborhood and was in dire need of exercise, I decided rather than to be chauffeured to town or classes by Mr. Remy, I would walk the five miles despite feeling vulnerable being out by myself. Broaching the subject to them, they discreetly insisted that the distance was too great. Mr. Remy was happy to drive me. I accepted the ride. All the same, as my need for exercise and solitude increased, I became more persistent about walking, and Mr. and Mrs. Remy became noticeably more reluctant to agree to my request. I finally honored my own needs. Despite the unrelenting heat, it felt wonderful to be out and free, to move spontaneously—not be dependent on anyone. Nonetheless, I felt a pang of selfishness and guilt, for getting my needs met, I could sense that I had violated some undefined social propriety. The feeling intensified the second day when after class, I stopped for a swim with the kids before I returned home, only to then have my caretakers express their concern over my tardiness.

Later on, in a quiet moment with Mrs. Remy, I broached the subject of my walking. She carefully explained that poor people walked, less poor people took the bus and people of means drove their own car. Also, she was concerned that the neighbors, observing me walking, considered me unwilling to pay bus fare and Mr. and Mrs. Remy inhospitable for not chauffeuring me. Their dilapidated car clearly revealed that they were not people of means, but it appeared important for them to maintain an overall good standing in their community. Thereafter, I bade their wishes.

I was prompted to further scrutinize my own behavior. There was a truth that it was difficult for me to accept being chauffeured, to accept being catered to, to receive anything at all. But some part of me *did* find walking, besides avoiding the discomfort of having to receive, and addressing my need for exercise, also a means to pinch a few pennies by avoiding public transportation. In fact, while the meagerness of our Peace Corps allowance was a major issue with almost every volunteer, I had been watching myself compulsively conserving my allowance from day one—what with not partying or drinking it away—and subsequently obtaining a sense of security from the expanding size of my wallet. Living within my means, regardless of how minimal, I was reduced to admit, was an obsession.

Beyond all of this, I was left to face the fact that I was afraid to step onto one of the island buses (really a modified van). I did not relish the thought of subjecting myself to the sexual scrutiny of the bus driver, or being squashed in among sweaty-smelling strangers, and then to have to call attention to myself when it came time for me to exit. I was, in fact, terrified to be in public at all and, oddly enough, feeling terrified for my very life. Wherever I went, I found myself trying to make myself invisible, to take the back streets in order to be unnoticed, or otherwise putting up an energetic protection around myself.

My first venture to town alone only sharpened my survival impulses. I had come upon two men conversing as I walked along a side street. While my immediate urge was to ignore them, I side-stepped my discomfort and instead took great effort to give them the best proper greeting, exactly as I had been taught in training. One of them, however, after I had passed, picked up a large rock and threw it in my direction. "White American bitch! Too good to speak to us?" I turned around as the rock rolled passed me and then realized that it was me at whom they were yelling. Then, without thinking, I offered them somewhat of a cross between an apology and a defensive assuredness that I had properly greeted them. They proceeded to pay me no mind but resumed their conversation, as I stood in the middle of the street stunned. Once I finally collected my thoughts, I berated myself for kowtowing to them, and for diminishing myself by having acknowledged their rudeness at all. I could only accept that I had a long way to go. Yet my survival felt dependent on my playing by their rules.

This incident provided me with the nerve to pull out the can of mace that Adam and John had insisted I bring with me. Rules or not, I was determined to survive this experience. Wherever I went, I had the mace ready, tight in my hand concealed in my pocket or purse, my finger on the trigger ready to use it if necessary. I hated being in this predicament. I was constantly tense with fear, afraid of being attacked, afraid that I would hurt my attacker if I maced him, afraid of having the trigger backward and spraying myself instead, leaving myself completely wide open to being attacked. Worse, I was afraid of being laughed at as my brother used to do when, as an adolescent, I tried to defend myself against his provocations with my spray bottle of perfume. The more fearful I became the angrier I felt. This was too much like being back in my apartment during the time I was dealing with my predator neighbor whom I finally had to take to court. I watched my two female cohorts. They went anywhere and everywhere with whomever they wanted—one local man after another around them like mosquitoes—seemingly unconcerned for their safety. We represented two extremes in operation. But, somehow, I was certain that their behavior would catch up to them.

My next trip to town alone fared no better than the first. This time, however, the perpetrator came in the form of a big, black Doberman Pincher tight on my heels coming seemingly from nowhere. It was unusual to see anything but mangy curs on the island, not that this one looked particularly well cared for. In fact he smelled as offensive as all the rest. This Doberman, as I was quick to realize, had an odd, relentless interest in me, profusely sniffing me up and down with tail-wagging excitement, then attempting to hump me right among passersby. I tried to inconspicuously shoo him away, yet he only became all the more persistent. To escape, my only recourse was to bolt into a store. After a few minutes, I left, certain that I was free of the annoying canine, but hardly out the door, he pounced on me. Pushing him away had no desired effect. As a white woman walking down the street being trailed by an oversized, black canine, I was already drawing attention and feeling the first tinges of humiliation. I again quickly slipped into a store and wandered around distractedly checking out all the tourist paraphernalia, feeling furious and trapped. More than anything, I wanted to race outside screaming bloody murder and kick the annoying cur in his big, dangling balls. Instead, I cautiously exited a door on the opposite side of the building emerging on a different street. Before I could take a breath of relief, to my chagrin, the fetid creature, as if he was able to predict my moves, was at my side, now excitedly barking at me, clearly loving the game. I quickly ducked into the next available shop despite knowing it would be to no avail. I was correct. Consequently, I hustled down the street to the bus stop, hopped into a waiting bus and took refuge in the rear where I watched the beast from the window. He also kept his eye on me. The bus finally took off down the street and out of town, the dog now coming to the attention of commuters as he ran barking alongside and then attempted to make his entrance each time the bus stopped. Even a couple miles out of town, tiring, but still persistent, the dog remained darting along behind. If anything, I thought I had stepped into a living nightmare. I exited the bus in front of the Remy's fully expecting the maniacal thing to come bounding on me from somewhere as a bloodhound would a runaway slave. With great relief, I found that I was on my own. I wanted to believe I was finished with this. I wanted to never go through a degrading occurrence like this again. It would be a long time before I would be able to laugh about this experience or the one he was foreshadowing.

My first two weeks of on-island orientation were akin to an endurance test. We six new recruits would arrive at the designated time for class, only to wait for at least an hour before the facilitator showed up. Typically, when she finally did appear, she would realize that either the person assigned to open the building had not done so, she had left her materials at home or some other matter had unexpectedly arisen. We would be asked to bear with her while she addressed the matter at hand.

On top of this, my menses caused me trouble in this new environment. When rest rooms were available, the toilets, as well as the water system were typically not functioning. The thought of soiling my clothing in public horrified me. The thought of leaving evidence of my condition in a public facility was equally terrible. The best I could do was to carry a plastic bag around with me to stow my used paraphernalia and then secretly dispose of it as soon as the opportunity arose. This, in and of itself, was a major task since waste receptacles were seldom available, and when they were, were overflowing and picked apart by stray dogs. Trying to convince myself that my behavior was obsessive proved fruitless. If I were going to survive the next two years, it was clear that I was going to have to find a way to take the charge out of my inhibitions.

Most often, training class got started at ten and lunch was eleven until one. Therefore, out of an entire day, perhaps three hours would be spent in instruction, which seemed to be taught from a hurried moment of contemplation rather than an organized format. When I approached the facilitator about my intention of coming to class an hour after the designated time, knowing I would still arrive early, she refused to honor my request, insisting that we Americans must set an example for islanders in regard to punctuality. I wondered for whom we were setting an example when no one was present to realize that we were punctual in the first place. Eventually, I too would adjust to the many facets of the pace and approach of island living, particularly "island time"—functions started when they started. This was about much more than having patience. It was about learning to be in the moment.

Finishing the two-week orientation on my island, we were flown to St. Lucia for technical and cultural training. The fashion in which further training was conducted shaped my impression of what my two-year commitment would be and also how seriously I wanted to take it all. For instance, although the environmental teacher trainees were expected to use the curriculum manual that had been created by the two exiting young male volunteers who had sought me as an ally, it was not made available to us during training. Therefore, much of our technical training involved creating our own lessons and practice teaching them to local children who volunteered to participate. As easy as this was for me, my two inexperienced teammates, Brett and Jack, were floundering, disheartened and ready to quit. Fearing facing the assignment solo, I took great efforts to shore up their confidence, especially Jack's, and supported them in whatever other ways necessary to keep them from dropping out. The greatest benefit of my technical training was that all environmental teacher trainees got to go on numerous field trips as opposed to spending the entire four weeks sitting in a classroom.

All the recruits who endured the total six weeks of technical training had similarly critical opinions of the experience. I had not only survived, having learned the game quite quickly, I had passed whatever tests—some defined, some not—I needed in order to live the forthcoming experiences. Having had the experience of my educational classes—how to not take academia too seriously—was paying off. When my final interview with the area director took place, it only took one awkward moment before I realized that he was only interested in canned responses to his questions. For example, he asked me how my parents felt about my decision to join the Peace Corps. "What the hell do my parents have to do with this? I'm middle-aged!" I responded mentally, while my audible response, "My parents are really proud of me and support me in every way," was exactly what he wanted to hear. A number of recruits, who voiced personal views, were not considered Peace Corps material in the final evaluation and were consequently dismissed.

On the other hand, one man, who even a half-wit could immediately recognize as an imposter, slid through. Right from the start, he had incensed most recruits and outraged a number of others. His deviant behavior had no end: He came to class habitually late and half-inebriated, addressed female volunteers as "babes," begged money from most everyone, refused to involve himself in assignments and was openly belligerent toward anyone who was not black. He had already crossed me and I had struggled from doing battle with him. His roommate, Timothy, had phoned me for counsel on a number of occasions when this character had breached cultural propriety with their host family and Timothy had been left scrambling to make amends. It flabbergasted volunteers that those in charge had failed to respond to the numerous complaints about him. (It was believed among volunteers that Peace Corps officials had turned their back on the situation because they were unwilling to deal with the possibility of him crying discrimination, and also because there had been significant effort taken to obtain minority volunteers.) To make matters worse, this troublemaker was a part of my two-island team, which meant that there was no relief from him, no relief from him entirely fouling Peace Corps' reputation.

I questioned myself as to why this man so riled me. At the same time, I was forced to examine why I took my Peace Corps' reputation so seriously. Our trainers had impressed upon us, one way or another, that Peace Corps was like a family with a code of honor, but to myself I looked as obsessed as some seasoned volunteers who had worn themselves out by worrying about their standing in the community. Was I projecting my biological family issues onto this situation, trying to look good and avoid rejection? All I knew was that my behavior baffled me as much as the con artist's did.

All volunteers in my group were noticeably relieved when, within a matter of weeks—yet, not before the police were involved, Peace Corps' image smeared and volunteer morale smashed—the belligerent chap was separated from the program and returned to the States. I did not feel good that I had accurately labeled him, but I was thoroughly relieved that he was gone, for I was certain, whatever it meant, that none of the volunteers in my group would have survived if he had remained with us. Thereafter, I more soberly observed the politics and power of the institution I represented, as well as those in command. Staying alert, more than doing my absolute best, was what was going to get me through the next two years.

Returning to my little island, I felt fully ready, despite my apprehensions, to take on the challenge of what I believed was merely developing environmental curriculum, training teachers and teaching elementary students in three different schools about the natural wonders of their island and how they might protect them.

First, we had a few more days of so-called training with the same inept local woman who had headed our first weeks of island training. My view of her was unchanged, although I had tried to alter it. When it came time to fill out a written evaluation of her job performance, I was stumped. My fellow volunteers were ready to hang her. I was not. I felt compassion was somehow in order, however I was unable to define how to apply it. I thought that it had to do with being sensitive to others' feelings, empathy, but I was unable to comprehend where that fit into this situation: what it actually was like to operate outside of judgment, where accountability appertained, for her and for myself. (I was unwittingly seeking resolution.) Neither being lenient nor taking her to task seemed to work. There was no doubt in my mind that the results of our reports would get back to her, in one way or another. Since we had to answer to her to some degree for the next two years, I wondered what price or benefit would come by openly voicing our dissatisfaction. Further, this woman was a relative of the Remy's. Was I compromising myself by censoring my response? And what was speaking? Was it my fear? I hated having no solution with which to feel comfortable. In the end, I decided that there was no benefit to anyone by giving her the scathing evaluation that I might have. Though I struggled to produce a fair and appropriate summary, the matter felt unfinished.

Since island life is infused with ceremonies, we volunteers were unable to avoid the honor of a swearing-in ceremony at the Governor General's mansion. Educational officials, host families, as well as our area Peace Corps director would be present, and I was chosen by my teammates to give the vote of thanks. As this was a significantly important part of every ceremony, a part that was always of explicit interest to the guests, I took my responsibility seriously enough to spend an entire day writing and rewriting my speech, making sure not to exclude anyone. By evening, I was tense, exhausted and dismayed with my never-ending obsessing.

When I awoke the following morning, much to my mortification, I heard that I had to throw away my notes. When I caught up with my panic and managed to put it aside, I was aware of a sense of abiding confidence taking its place. Despite being nervous, I would be fine. When the time for the vote of thanks finally rolled around, signaling relief from the hot, crowded room was at hand, I was ready to step forward. To begin, I gave a big vote of thanks to Mr. and Mrs. Remy, extending my heart open and warm, and then I appropriately acknowledged all others who had supported our experience. I returned to my seat feeling relieved and smugly accomplished, especially hearing the resounding round of applause.

As our Peace Corps director was in the middle of bringing closure to the event, I suddenly realized that I had forgotten to express gratitude to our local trainer, the woman whom we had all found to be inept. How could I rectify my egregious error? In a flurry of panicked thoughts, my impulse was to slink out of the door. Abruptly, however, I stood up, stepped forward and then unhesitatingly interrupted the director in mid-sentence. It went against protocol to cut short the figure of authority in a former British colony steeped with pomp and circumstance. When I explained that I needed the floor again, the director stepped back and extended his arm as if to say, "It's all yours." The audience, taken aback, was clearly eager to know what was afoot. I felt in a fog as I spoke, and when all was said and done, I had no idea what exactly I had communicated, but the audience's reaction revealed that I had been entertaining. I did not feel smug as I returned to my seat; I felt free. In the end, I had given what turned out to be a special vote of thanks to our local trainer.

Later the Governor General approached me to say that putting people to ease during the vote of thanks was extremely important and advocated that giving the vote of thanks should become my official job. The thought of me putting people at ease was momentarily amusing. But more importantly, a sense of peace I felt in my heart suggested I had lain to rest something between the trainer and me. The vote of thanks acknowledging her had emerged from my heart where compassion operates, where judgment has no influence. I did not need to expose her weakness. I needed to honor her greatness, which is true accountability. Only retrospect would reveal the true extent of the healing that had then and there taken place—my healing.

The recent demand for workers at the island's first resort hotel caused an influx of people to the island, which resulted in housing shortages, and rent increases of two, three or even five hundred percent. As it followed, living on an allowance comparable to the local average, made it a challenge to find affordable housing. The four younger volunteers had decided to live communally in town, although Peace Corps officials had sanctioned the arrangement only temporarily. Jack, the elder of my two male teammates, had landed himself use of an entire, spacious guesthouse on the far side of the island in the district where his schools were located. It came replete with a huge, fenced-in yard, wrap-around veranda, hot water, washer and dryer, and four bedrooms with attached private baths.

My concerns about permanent living quarters ended when I visited a departing volunteer, Drake, who lived in the capitol and only town on the island. His landlady, Miss Huff, complained about renting to him, he being friends with Rastas and such, and claimed that she would no longer rent to volunteers. Still, with the same kind of knowing that had precipitated my ex-husband placing a bid on our house, I was certain that I would be living in his cottage upon his departure. It took my tenacity, but Drake reluctantly agreed to make introductions with Miss Huff, another retired head teacher. Before the scheduled tea, Drake coached me on how to deal with her cantankerousness. I was to let him do all the speaking. It was evident that he had cottoned to her so-called authority during his two-year stint. In fact, it looked as if he was another who had sold his soul trying to be an integral part of this culture. He was clearly in need of rest and relaxation. Notwithstanding, during his remaining few weeks in service, he would serve as my Emily Post, keeping me abreast of correct behavior, as well as safety factors.

Much to Drake's amazement, directly after introductions were made, Miss Huff offered to rent me a room in her guesthouse where she also resided. Her ailing aunt, she demurred, for whom she had cared had died two weeks earlier. To date, she had never lived alone. She wanted companionship. My intuitive feelings about her, which I refrained from questioning this time, were she was miserly, cunning and used to getting her way by whatever means necessary. I did not trust her. Thanking her for her generous offer, I explained, "I've lived alone for years. That is what I am accustomed to and need. Perhaps you would consider renting your cottage to me when Drake leaves." I sensed that she was acutely dissatisfied with my response, but she jumped at my suggestion, and doubled the price of the rent. Acting on my sense of distrust, I explicated that in my culture when we shake hands after a deal has been made, it is a commitment to honor that deal. Then, before we departed, I took great effort to shake hands with her to acknowledge our business deal. Still a strong inner discomfort that I was want to shake off revealed that something was amiss.

The next day I returned to Drake's on business only to be set upon by the beast that had plagued my second visit to town. It took Drake to put him at bay. I was furious. It was going to be complicated enough, I thought, having a landlady with Miss Huff's personality: snoopy, gossipy and conniving—too much like my mother—living on top of me, but to learn that the beast actually belonged to her was almost more than I could handle. I could not understand why everything in my life seemed to come with such an extreme price. Did I really have to have this canine plaguing me for the next two years as if I was perpetually in heat? I contemplated backing away from the entire situation, yet I knew adamantly, beyond a shadow of a doubt, that I was meant to live in this doll house-size cottage in town where I felt I could at least get out and about, especially after dark, with at least some degree of safety. I wanted to believe that this was what I was feeling was amiss, but I knew it wasn't; there was something else, something eating away, leaving me feeling tense and off-centered.

By invitation, I stayed with a British volunteer, Lee, for the first few weeks after my training was complete. Her invitation relieved me of my only other available option, which was staying with a middle-aged, widowed American schoolteacher who had been married to a local man. She was determined to find another woman to live with her mainly because she wanted to reduce her living expenses. The way she complained about everything and then clearly tried to convince me that her offer was generous made me nervous right from the start. She was noticeably disturbed when I notified her that I would be staying elsewhere and would play out her grudge toward me in many different ways during the next two years. Lee, on the other hand, refused to take any money, was glad to have the company, and did what volunteers do—support each other. I soon learned that Lee, like Drake, appeared to be de-energized, as well as disillusioned by her circumstances, both personal and professional. Lee and I had little in common; aside from being vulnerable white women attempting to effectively fulfill our assignments in a culture whose views of females made our attempts seem futile. Even so, I respected her and closely followed her example in proper deportment. As I observed her, I was aware that a part of me was attempting to latch onto her for a sense of security.

It was through Lee that I met beautiful, young Myla, with whom I felt an immediate affinity. Myla had originally come to the island from Scotland to work as a physiotherapist in the hospital while her local counterpart was in England completing her training. The underlying motivation for her to take the job was her life-threatening eating disorder; she had been under the mistaken impression that laxatives or other purgatives would not be available in a third world country. She had decided to stay on after she had completed her work assignment, and when I first met her she was carrying the child of a Rastafarian named Gavin. At best, their relationship was rocky.

A few days before I was scheduled to move into the cottage, Miss Huff alleged that repairs were incomplete and that she expected me to stay in her guesthouse with her during the interim. Interestingly, she was aware that my stay with Lee was coming to an end due to Lee having visitors coming from abroad. Already feeling manipulated when she informed me of her expectations, she then introduced me to her cousin, a lawyer, who had recently arrived from the United States and was residing with her during his stay on island. My dislike of her arrangement intensified, especially when shortly after introductions, he announced from out of the blue that I would have to pay a security deposit (a foreign concept to islanders) for the cottage. He was physically a big man, and used his size to make it clear that he, like his cousin, was accustomed to having his way. I was instantly taken aback and, as usual, at a loss to think of a response that I could and should have used to put him in his place: tell him that this was none of his business since Miss Huff and I had already made a deal and had even shaken hands. I walked away feeling traumatized, if not demoralized. Was this the pressure I had been feeling earlier when I thought something was amiss? Since my nerves were in a constant knot about one thing or another, it was difficult to discern.

I contemplated ways of handling this situation. Wanting the cottage, *knowing* that I was supposed to have it, I nevertheless feared losing it, if for no other reason than through my stubborn willfulness. The most logical solution was simply to give her the money. I phoned my area Peace Corps director for guidance; he thought I should give her what she wanted and let the situation go. I realized I would rather have died than give her anything, especially my money, and especially since it took little savvy to know that it would never be returned. Further, it was obvious that I would be spending money out of pocket upgrading the cottage myself regardless of what repairs she claimed she was having done. So when she cornered me a few days after her cousin's departure, afraid to simply say "no," half-cowering, half-defiant, I handily reminded her that I had shaken hands on the deal with her, not her cousin, and a security deposit was not part of our original deal.

During the two weeks that I lived with Miss Huff in her guesthouse, I tried to calm my agitation and center myself, to get to know her, not judge her or be on the defensive. Inasmuch as my feelings of entrapment only increased, I sought out avenues of escape. One such tactic involved checking up on the motley father/son team of repairmen; that is, when they were not off getting supplies, quitting early because they had run out of something or when they succeeded in showing up for work at all. Never in my life had I seen such a relaxed work ethic as in this culture.

Elmer, Miss Huff's dog, remained another issue. The crusty, foul-smelling thing—flies buzzing around his head, and who knew what creepy crawlies moving around in his fur, leaving him to continually scratch—never let me out of his sight. Like the stalker I had taken to court, he anticipated my every move, to the extent that Miss Huff had to chain him so as to keep him from following me whenever I went out, at least if she could catch him. Especially, he liked to show up at the beach and swim out after me when I was in the water. By now, it was becoming a common sight having him trailing me around. Miss Huff found the attention he gave me amusing. As aggravating as they were, I had to admit that I was fond of them both.

Miss Huff's cousin had given her money and a list of improvements he deemed necessary for the upkeep of the cottage. (It was never clear who actually owned the property.) From day one, she complained about how the allotted money would not cover the improvements her cousin had enumerated or how the workmen were misusing her money. Afterward, she would add to this mix her most recent adversity. As for myself, I would have been content for her to simply get out of the way. It was easy to see that with a little effort, I could have the place comfortably livable in a short time. Without my woods, the cottage was the only apparent means to find a sense of solitude and regain my centeredness, and I was feeling more and more desperate as each day slipped away with little or nothing accomplished.

I was grateful when the workmen, claiming that they were finished, finally walked away. I had been able to move beyond my judgment of them, and even felt comfortable interacting with them. It was obvious, that they had taken a respectful liking of me. In fact, they took to airing their frustrations over Miss Huff's continual accusations that they were wasting her money, and generally taking advantage of her. (This would be no novel experience.) Before I moved in, of necessity, I had first to undo or redo almost everything this duo had so ardently "repaired." Among other things, this included attaching the new drain pipe beneath the sink to the drain opening, so water drained through the pipe rather than onto the floor. After scrubbing and painting the walls, I repaired the odd bits of furniture and then shuffled them around until I created a balanced sense of space. Miss Huff even gave me a semblance of a day bed—a piece of thick foam on a five-foot long platform. I then began to look for affordable touches that would provide a sense of warmth and personality to my tiny (two hundred square feet), three-room abode.

The cottage, set on the backside of a large piece of property, provided a wonderful view of the volcanic peak that formed the center of the island. It provided a pretense of privacy while allowing accessibility to the benefits of town life, as well as a swimming beach within walking distance. My little front porch, fit with a table with one leg shorter than the others, a couple of chairs that collapsed when not sat upon just so, and a string hammock I brought with me, provided the means for me to live closer to nature than I ever thought possible. In fact, a colorful, little lizard had taken up residence in my bedroom and often watched me in bed at night from its perch on the rafters, while birds freely flew in and out taking advantage of the fruit I kept on the kitchen table.

To my delight, Drake was an avid gardener and had planted the area around the cottage with flowering bushes—hibiscus, crotons, bougainvillea, and frangipani—affording me the delight of having fresh bouquets regularly. I began to spend an endless amount of time cultivating and weeding the shrubbery, growing vegetables that the insects or chickens got to before I had a chance and exhausting myself before realizing that my only accomplishment was saving Miss Huff the cost of paying a gardener. When I finally gave up investing my time in yard work, as well as aiding her in a host of other ways, the first instructions she gave the gardener, while I was away for a day, was to cut down the vegetation around my cottage. I took this as a personal affront and also a means for her to have a less obscured view of my private life, although she asserted that she had it done for my safety.

Even after moving into the cottage, I was subjected to her regular overtures about my owing her a security deposit. I consistently used our handshake as a reminder of our agreement and then ignored her. Unrelenting, she reduced her request to half of the deposit. One day I became so uncontrollably annoyed by her protracted harassment that I informed her that I did not appreciate her manipulation. Her response was, "How dare you talk to me this way!" She then added that I might be required to move. Still having a strong knowing that she both needed and wanted me in her cottage and I was meant to live there, I retorted, "And I'm prepared to do that!" Although it was the last time she mentioned the subject, an unidentifiable tension continued to fester between us.

The close proximity of my cottage to the guesthouse (she had only moved from her old house on the property to the guesthouse at the time her aunt died) enabled her to keep a more disapprovingly watchful eye on my comings and goings than she had been able to with Drake. She gossiped about me, as much as she had with Drake with her cohorts in the community. Waiting to catch a word with me, she would declare, "The neighbors say you were out too late last night." Or a fellow professional would discreetly inform me that Miss Huff had divulged that I had too many male visitors. I was livid that once again I was in a position where I had to prove my innocence.

Mr. and Mrs. Remy, who had a long-standing feud with Miss Huff, had diplomatically shown their concern over my being involved with her from the beginning.

In fact, they would occasionally stop by with information about other places available to rent. As much as it made sense to remove myself from my predicament—and a number of times I would follow-up on leads to no avail—I was resistant to leaving. I thought that I was being either stubborn or practical. Actually it was something else, although thus far, it was well beyond my understanding.

Elmer continued to hound me after I moved in. He took to hanging out on my porch during the day, sleeping there at night and giving me a great greeting in the morning upon arising. I soon discovered that if he could not get close to me, he would make do with a piece of my clothing. Failing to be vigilant, I would discover my bathing suit, hung to dry on the porch, somewhere off in the yard, dirty and chewed with holes. Miss Huff found this humorous also. His presence did provide a sense of safety; local men were known to peep into the windows of white women, but locals were generally afraid of dogs. Without Elmer, I would have been inclined to sleep with my shutters closed, which would be like sleeping in a crock-pot. On the other hand, his barking at my coming and going gave Miss Huff clear signal of my whereabouts, despite my efforts to shush him. I would attempt to coax him from my porch, or from my living room when he took the opportunity to sneak in, except he would snap at me, as he did with Miss Huff when she attempted to constrain him. He was certainly unruly and unpredictable and I did not trust him, even when I wanted to believe that he was actually sweet, great company—he liked me so I had to be nice to him syndrome—and I was misjudging him.

For a few weeks I had been observing on a regular basis a catastrophe waiting to happen. Before and after school, Elmer, with great sport, would chase the younger students, who were temporarily housed in the church adjacent to Miss Huff's property. He would chase them up the ghaut, scattering them in all directions, and terrifying them enough that they would scream bloody murder. Each time I had observed I had taken a deep breath, fearful of the potential repercussions. Miss Huff always found humor in the situation, which strengthened my belief that she was heartless.

One day, my sense of foreboding manifested. Jack and I stopped by the deli—also part of Miss Huff's property—to pick up snacks during a lunch break. I liked going at this time of day simply to observe the preschool children dressed in their plaid uniforms, girls with hair plaited and held in place with a variety of colorful hair baubles, boys with just as colorful homemade tops in hand, faces shining, coming to buy penny candy. On this occasion, Elmer appeared from nowhere and out of the blue lunged forward toward one of the little schoolgirls in front of me in an attempt to nab the candy from her hand. Startled, the child took a step backward only to land flat on her back, the dog leaping on top of her, snapping and growling as she hysterically struggled to get free. In a split-second, as if Jack and I had rehearsed the scene to perfection, he reached down and grabbed the dog by his collar jerking him forcefully backward, while I reached down and scooped up the terrified, screaming youngster into my arms and headed for the entrance to the store. The moment the child was in my arms, she locked her arms and legs around me in a vice grip so strong I was literally choking. Wild-eyed and frantic, she impulsively looked down over my right shoulder and then my left, expecting another attack. Surprisingly, within fifteen minutes or so, the girl was recovered enough to rejoin her friends.

Following her out the door, I discovered Jack sitting at the picnic table nursing a bite on his hand. His response to my concern was, "By God, if he were my dog, I'd shoot him in the head!" His comment was enough to cause us to head directly to Miss Huff's. She laughed when we disclosed the situation, as much as she always laughed when the children would scatter in all directions screaming whenever her dog would catch them off guard. Jack took her to task then, telling her that a dog that snapped at its owner should be put to death, and if she could not keep him under control, she should think seriously about keeping him chained. She did after that, at least when the children were about.

It became my routine to walk to the beach late every afternoon to have a swim and then a quiet communion with the sun as it slipped into the horizon. I accepted that my only viable means of exercise in this culture was swimming, although I didn't particularly like it. Neither did I like the saltiness on my mouth or skin, nor the waves splashing in my face. Ocean swimming was an entirely new experience, and I had to admit it unnerved me. I could feel my childhood fears of disappearing in deep water, never to be seen again, being awakened within me. The ocean was so enormously endless, magnifying my insignificance in comparison. All the same, I was aware that there was a certain powerful attraction between the sea and me. My wariness would have to be short-lived.

A more difficult detail of swimming was the bathing suit. I did not mind so much wearing it; it was *being seen* in it that had always been the problem. For me, a bathing suit was a vehicle of seduction, an advertisement of my sexuality. Local men ogling me intensified my discomfort. We had been informed in training that island men were not attracted to thin (meager) women; therefore I had initially attempted to deceive myself into believing that I would be exempt from such attention. I was entirely wrong. I would walk to the beach in a beach wrap that hid most of my body. Once there and ready to swim, I would quickly shed the wrap and hop in the water, immediately slipping it back on the moment I stepped out. I hated my inability to be casual, but I hated the attention even more. Most of all, I hated being so distracted by the issue, especially when I observed the carefree attitude of my young, female co-volunteers.

For a good number of years I had been involved in reading self-help books written by such authors as Wayne Dyer, John Bradshaw, Mary Summer Rain and Dan Millman. I had become captivated by, even envious of these authors' experiences, and sometimes wished that I could have experiences of such magnitude. It was my habit to underline, highlight or make notes, and even espouse certain passages. Although unknowingly, this was why, at some point, I was suddenly no longer allowed to read much at all: I was no longer being allowed to adopt or adhere to anyone else's philosophies. I had to find my own Truth. The material that I was allowed to read revealed itself to me, rather than me choosing for myself. It was no longer about gathering ideas, but more a means to obtain a reflection, a mirror, of my own Knowledge. If I attempted to read "unsanctioned" literature, my mind went blank or the words just seemed to be scrambled and I was unable to absorb the material. It took only a few experiences to recognize that my efforts to override this condition were a waste of time and energy.

I was allowed to bring a few select books with me, but hardly the type that would keep one lost in an evening of reading. One was, **The Prophet,** given to me by Teresa. The passages from this book seemed to run very deep within my soul, touching some deeper awareness. Another was, **A Handbook to Higher Consciousness**, a collection of quotes by various famous people. When I became broody or was seeking comfort or answers, I took to the habit of randomly opening the book and reading the quote at hand. I did not know that I was divining, but I did realize that whatever quote I happened upon consistently provided a moment of needed comfort or clarity. One quote, "You can't reach new horizons unless you let go of the shore." was a constant sobering reminder that unless I fully let go of my life as I had been living it, I could only get more of what I already had.

John had given me a deluxe copy of **Tao Te Ching**. I read it through and through—sometimes randomly—mostly absorbing the information, not intellectualizing it. The passages that struck a deeper cord in me I underlined. These included: "Practice not-doing, and everything will fall into place." "The Master leads by emptying people's minds and filling their core." "Can you remain unmoving till the right action arises by itself?" "The Master does not talk, he acts. When his work is done, the people say, 'Amazing, we did it all by ourselves!'" "A good traveler has no fixed plans and is not intent on arriving." "If you realize you have enough, you are truly rich." "When you realize there is nothing lacking, the whole world belongs to you." "True mastery can be gained by letting things go their own way, not by interfering." "If you stay in the center and embrace death with your whole heart, you will endure forever." "Thus the Master is content to serve as an example and not to impose her own will." I could recognize that I was being required to understand these quotes at a deeper level. I was yet to understand that I was being required to live all of these highlighted passages to the fullest.

John had also supplied me with a manual provided by his community. Included in this material were the twelve virtues—charity, courage, devotion, discrimination, efficiency, forbearance, humility, kindliness, patience, precision, sincerity, tolerance—which were influenced by the Brotherhoods: secret organizations of scientists-philosophers who, over time, had studied the laws of cause and effect enough to recognize which actions bring about the best results. Using the virtues as general rules or guidelines in daily living were purported to lead to happiness and serenity. John, himself, had considered them important enough to memorize them, as well as their established definitions. Further, he had often explained them to me or selected one or another to focus on during our sessions. Regardless of feeling that I should adapt these seemingly lofty principles into my life, another part of me felt as if I was an adolescent again struggling to prepare for my public confirmation exam. Once I became more mature and confident in my knowing, I would see John's material for what it was or was not—as with all reading material, and whatever else came into my life—a timely reference point, triggering or confirming what, within me, was needing to be awakened or else released. When I tired of reading, I turned to my journaling. It was here that I was free to express my pain, confusion and loneliness.

The sun set around dinnertime throughout the entire year, and at that point, community activities wound down, except for the men's drinking and carousing. It proved taxing to continually keep myself occupied for the duration of an entire evening. Besides, my sinus/allergy symptoms affected my eyes, making them puffy and irritated, and next to impossible to even keep open. Added to this, my certain, strong dislike for artificial light was intensifying to the degree that I would rather sit in the dark than turn on a lamp. Often, I gave into the struggle to stay awake and simply retired early.

Although each time I had to find the courage to run the gauntlet of men who loitered at the rum shop outside of my gate, periodically, in the evenings, I would make my way across the street from my cottage to the museum courtyard. There, I sat on what I called my Philosopher's Stone (actually boulders used as fill to prevent shoreline erosion), a name John had suggested for my rock. Thus positioned, I had a full view of the lights of the sister island twinkling from across the channel, bioluminescent creatures aglow in the surf, as well as a Milky Way-streaked sky abundant with pony-tailed shooting stars, from where, I imagined, the tiny light critters originated before making the ocean their home.

On the Philosopher's Stone, beneath the expansive Caribbean night sky with the evening breeze gently caressing my body, waves of unidentifiable yearnings beset me. Here, once again, I was torn between Earth and heaven: Earth and something greater, not here or there, stuck somewhere in-between—and I felt furious about it, furiously helpless. I longed to call it quits and simply go home, home always feeling in these moments as if it was way up there in the heavens, far, far from Earth. My heart wanted to go home. As much as I focused on the path I was traveling and felt driven to continue forward, I had continually felt as if a deep inner-exhaustion was working equally hard against me. Furthermore, I remained as unclear as ever in regard to who I am and whether or not my life had value. Whatever home it was toward which I wanted to reach, intuition told to me that there were no shortcuts. There was only one direction, the one that I was facing, and continuing forward, step by step, letting go of my resistance and fear along the way. For now, sitting upon my Philosopher's Stone, being one with the heavens above and the ocean at my feet, I was momentarily able to transcend the weight of my existence, the pain, loneliness and frustration. I was able to breathe deeply of something that sustained me at a deeper level.

John had an oddly intense interest in alchemy. I thought the idea a bit strange—changing base metals into gold. But energetically there was something that became triggered inside of me whenever he had brought the subject into conversation. Therefore, it was ironic that I had actually adopted his name for "my" rock, not knowing that on a broader scale alchemy has to do with accelerating the natural workings of nature to produce supernatural results (that is, to reveal the ultimate source of life, a transmutation of the human soul in spiritual perfection, able to express Divine or God-like attributes.) To touch a person alchemically was to transform into a perfect state, to transcend death. All of this was way beyond my time to embrace. Sitting on the Philosopher's Stone was further preparation however.

Thumbing through the astrology reading that John had had done prior to my departure, my attention had been drawn to two statements that I had previously missed. One was, "your challenges are to learn to use authority wisely, to find your own personal power, and to accept and express yourself." The other was, "your real issue is finding your power within." Because this information came from a computerized print out, I minimized its legitimacy. Now, this information echoed earlier messages and, unbeknownst to me, spoke of many lessons waiting to be lived. Learning to use my authority wisely would be one of the toughest. I was a Capricorn, which meant a take charge, get things done, "pick-up-the-slack-wherever-necessary" person. Allowing experiences to manifest, to unfold, in their own time required trust, focus and living in the ever-present now—attributes difficult to maintain—and I first had to learn to stay out of the way.

My cottage was in a location that attracted many mosquitoes and, as much as I tried, it was unbearably difficult to keep my doors or windows closed, even with the danger leaving them opened presented. Therefore, it was a notable blessing to have inherited a mosquito net, despite it significantly blocking air circulation. I was never certain what was happening to me within my gauzy, white shroud, except sleep was no longer about sleep, any more than it had been for some time. Each night as I settled into bed, I routinely centered my star sapphire directly over my heart chakra. Then I placed my left hand over it. The reason for this habit was unclear, but it was intensely soothing to my heart and extremely centering—extremely peaceful. Whenever I altered my position during the night it was as if a force watching over me immediately returned me to my original supine position, hand over the star sapphire on my heart.

In addition, disturbances intense enough to awaken me, were continuing to occur to my body, especially in my legs, loin and abdomen. Thus awakened, I would become alert to the room filled with many presences. I might be surprised or even stupefied, but I never felt afraid for I could discern no malignancy to this energy, only a strange, enveloping sense of love.

It took only a short time to realize that the Peace Corps, as an enticement, unabashedly glamorized its job descriptions. Despite what I had been initially informed, there was no operable plan or procedure for how to develop or implement my environmental program. Furthermore, as I soon learned, the host country officials, rather than having requested Peace Core assistance or having vital interest in an environmental education program, had been solicited by Peace Corps about the program's implementation. Fundamentally, beneath the showy diplomacy was an attitude of non-commitment and indifference. Having talked to prior Peace Corps volunteers, I understood that this was nothing new. However, it was a sobering reality that I was in circumstances that, largely, no one took seriously.

Worse, once I was finally given a copy of the curriculum, I deemed it as little more than a collection of information, not readily usable by teachers and certainly not designed for use in primary classrooms. My position was risky considering the two seasoned recruits who had authored the curriculum placed a high value on the product of their efforts, as well as had expectations of it being published and widely used throughout the Caribbean. Regardless of how I approached it, they were going to take my opinion of their work as an attack, but I was unwilling to frustrate myself working with something that did not work for me. I obsessed for days how I could address the situation without hurting anyone's feelings or alienating myself. Finally, I realized there was no way around this. So I honesty shared my perspective with my area director. He recognized my position as legitimate, but two years of supporting his recruits in an effort that had produced little of value put him in an awkward position. Nonetheless, he gave me his blessings and free rein when I informed him that I wanted to develop my own teaching material independently. In the end, I feared that I had taken on more than I could handle and felt intimidated by the idea of creating a program that might perhaps earn only the disapproval of my superiors.

I prepared to rise to the challenge, which was considerable. I had no resources and knew little about a tropical ecology; further, venturing out to explore on my own was a safety issue. Since my fellow team members, Brett and Jack, were by now floundering and contemplating dropping out, I called a meeting to suggest working together. It appeared logical that making environmental lessons uniform throughout the eight elementary schools on the island would be more successful than the present haphazard, individualized efforts. I suggested that we work cooperatively to develop lessons one day and instruct the remaining four. They readily accepted. I understood, on some level, that I would be the glue that kept the production together; Brett was unable to take his own initiative on almost everything, and Jack, having been in management his entire life, was largely only qualified for giving orders and delegating responsibility. Besides this, prior experiences had taught me to be self-directed, adept at problem-solving, work without the benefit of resources, develop concepts into lessons and bring blueprints to culmination (although I was not fully aware of this). Beyond the practicality of working together, the team provided me with a sense of support that I thought I still needed and relieved me of having to deal with my life all by myself. I could not see then that my serving the situation as a means for me to be secure would backfire on me.

During the opening days of the school year, my educational advisor informed me that I was to attend a teacher's meeting to become acquainted with my host country counterparts. I punctually arrived at the designated place while, one by one, teachers ambled in. An hour after the meeting was scheduled to start, the participants sat around chatting with each other. I wondered who was to lead this meeting until a male teacher asked me when I was going to start. Suddenly, it dawned on me; *I* was the meeting. Thrown off guard, I thought it best to first discuss my credentials and background experience to let my new co-workers know that I was qualified to handle the assignment. However, before I hardly began, I felt a wall energetically rise between the teachers and me. I even heard a teacher suck her teeth, a distinct sign in that culture that the person is upset. It took me a while to realize my blunder. On the island, only a few months of training is required to become a teacher. I had made myself appear superior to my counterparts, thus alienating rather than endearing them to my cause. Appraising my egregious error, I realized that, since the circumstances did not allow me to shut down, I had fallen into my secondary mode of survival in social situations, which was to try to present myself in a favorable way. Although I had not consciously tried to toot my own horn, that was what I had done, nevertheless. I had little energy for self-flagellation, but I was now all the more insecure in relating to my counterparts, as well as scrambling to find ways to make amends.

My second noticeable blunder (lesson) came through classroom teaching. The educational system on the island was modeled on the old British system meaning that pedagogy took the form of competition, class recitation and rote memorization. Worse, corporal punishment remained inculcated into the system. I quickly learned to cringe silently, to never show any reaction at all, less I weaken my fragile position in the institution whenever I saw a child take his/her "licks" with the sharp edge of a ruler or with a belt, sometimes conveniently carried around a teacher's neck. Arrogantly, I decided that I would turn this antiquated system upside down!

The first day, I went to school with a creative lesson plan in hand, confident that I could and would be the one who turned these kids onto a whole new and exciting way of learning. It would start with an open discussion and end with small group problem-solving. Beginning the first class, I asked questions and encouraged students to openly respond, whereby they merely sat in silence looking at me like I was speaking Russian. Group work resulted in students fighting with each other over who had the correct answers. I thought they did not get it, but I was the one who did not get it. I went home feeling like a total failure.

Undaunted, I returned the next day with my arrogance in control. First I wrote information relevant to the lesson on the chalkboard, then had the students stand and repeatedly recite the information in unison until they were familiarized with it, as they were accustomed to doing. Finally I had them copy the information into their notebooks. Slowly, day after day, week after week, I would wean them away from the conventional system on which they had been raised and would lead them to an exploratory, cooperative learning adventure that we all found exciting. In regard to living my purpose—my real teaching—this would be one of my most pertinent realizations: I had to start where the students were, rather than where I wanted them to be. My students would come to anticipate my arrival in their classes as much as I would come to cherish all that I had to learn from them.

Their trust would become a vehicle for me to experience the culture in an intimate manner. Wherever I traveled, I would be greeted with big-eyed, bright smiles and warm greetings. Sometimes I would hear my name called out from behind a half-shuttered window, sometimes from high in a Tamarind tree, "Meez Stawnlee!" other times from behind a mother's skirt when I was in the market. There was an innocence about these children that was not as easily recognizable in children of my own culture. They were untainted by materialistic excesses or television. They interacted creatively with their environment and each other—obtaining snacks from trees and bushes, playing games, making dolls, kites and tops from bits and pieces of paraphernalia and natural materials. They were active, energetic and healthy. Except for when in school, they ran barefoot through life. Frequently, tourists would drive into the schoolyard or along the road, pull out their cameras and start snapping pictures of the children. This ignorant invasiveness would never cease to anger me.

Within a short time, I had made plentiful acquaintances, yet none with whom I could freely and openly be myself. Because the culture was tightly knit, outsiders were not lightly admitted; neither were their own if they had gone abroad and returned educated, successful or polished. There were many expatriates on the island. It appeared that they spent their lives involved in the cocktail circuit and small talk. Then there was the volunteer community, which consisted mostly of Americans and British. They, too, relied heavily on alcohol to support social interactions. I'd had a taste of all the groups but none of them seemed to provide the kind of nourishment for which I hungered. Once again, I either had to ignore my awareness, or choose isolation. More often than not, I attempted to fit in.

Watching myself within the context of my new experience found me more deeply reflecting on the meaning of "friend," as well as my need for friends. I never had many (none during my marriage), and the majority of them had quickly come and gone. They all had come with a price. I mostly thought of friends in terms of female relationships. Men, from my experience, were ultimately looking for sex. Typically, I was the one who ended the relationships, once in a while through confrontation but mostly through avoidance or simply letting them wither. Clinging to the idea that if I had no friends then there must be something wrong with me, I had convinced myself that the remaining ones were important. It was the part of me abiding in limitation who sought friendships, ultimately to avoid being alone—as with all of us—while my deeper awareness revealed another perspective: I was already way beyond the linearly-minded concept of friendship.

As I convinced myself, Jack and I had become friends during our training. I was impressed that such an old cowboy had come out of retirement to volunteer two years of his life to service overseas. From the start, however, he had been overwhelmed, highly unadaptable and homesick, and still grieving for his wife who had died a few years earlier. After we started working as a team, the three of us would meet at Jack's to work on curriculum development. Brett would spend the day while, at Jack's invitation, I would settle in for the weekend. Having this weekend retreat provided relief from Miss Huff's unrelenting scrutiny and from loneliness, as well as safety in exploring the island in ways that would have been impossible without the security of a male escort. I convinced myself that I enjoyed Jack's company. That is, until, among other things, he began to repeat the same old stories, endlessly reminiscing. Reminiscing for its own sake had never made sense to me, and I had barely gotten beyond the point of outrage having had for so many years listened to Carl endlessly and pointlessly recounting to anyone who would listen moments in his life which he considered high adventure.

After Jack retired for the night, I got in the habit of wandering around the expansive grounds. There I felt free of having to listen to him, free to be *me*, free to take in the medley of nocturnal sounds, the humid, tropical breeze, the stars, and most especially the energy that enveloped me. Before long, however, I was unable to avoid the uncomfortable reality that my weekend sojourns were leaving me ill at ease and all the more restless. Beside Miss Huff, Jack's neighbors were beginning to speculate on his and my relationship. I half-succeeded in convincing myself that the gossip was harmless. Without my support, I reasoned, Jack would soon be on a plane back to California, especially since he had been receiving notices that a number of his friends' health was failing. In fact, he had been recently notified that one had passed on. All in all, I was avoiding my own isolation.

The cultural dynamics of relationships drilled into recruits during Peace Corps training continued to butt against my hard-earned belief that I was an independent female. In the island male-dominated, black culture, to be seen with a man indicated that you belonged to that man. To be seen, a white woman, anywhere alone and off the beaten path, was an open invitation for getting raped. "If she didn't want it, she wouldn't have been where she was," was a standard defense for sexual assault. Whether by force or consent, to "have" a white woman was a status symbol. There had been a number of such attacks on white women immediately prior to my arrival. Being red-haired and light-skinned, my presence was conspicuous, and even my age was not a deterrent for a teenage boy who boldly solicited me on the street. I responded that I was old enough to be his mother, at which he smiled sheepishly claiming that I would not be disappointed. It was aggravating that every move I made was scrutinized and that I had to be bombarded with, "Come on baby, you want some good lovin'? You want some black lovin'? You ever had good, black lovin' befo'?" If I gave an acknowledgment at all, it was my standard line, "I think you're talking about sex, not love." Their crooning sally, "No baby, I mean lovin', real lovin'!" was standard also. I walked a cautious, fine line: living the cultural code of sanctioned behavior—dressing properly, only being seen in proper places, attending church—in order to be as effective as possible in my work and safely meet my own needs.

One evening the entire volunteer contingency was invited to a cocktail party hosted by the Governor General, whose seductive bearing bestowed upon him a lascivious reputation, at least among the female volunteers. To me, he carried himself like some weird, over-sexed Willie Wonka character, talking in a nonsensical manner and leaving his listeners ill-equipped to know how to respond. Despite him having praised me for having given such a fine vote of thanks at our swearing in ceremony, my distrust of him was instinctive. Still, for whatever reasons, I was inclined to participate in this function. After initial efforts at small talk, I retreated to the veranda of the mansion, which was perched on a hill on the outskirts of town. My position provided a spectacular view of the volcanic peak magnificently aglow in the rays of the setting sun. Lost in the magic of the moment, out of body and far away, the Governor General suddenly approached me, and asked directly that I share my thoughts. There, in the moment, I struggled to find my voice. He scrutinized me for the time that it took me to take a breath and separate from both parts of me, the one that felt special that he gave me this attention and the one that was intimated by him. Not knowing what to say, I blurted out, "I'm thinking about when I can climb to the peak again." Without only a moment of hesitancy, he dramatically broke into singing, "Climb every mountain/Ford every stream/Follow every rainbow, 'till you find your dream." The message given to me through this creepy character was so powerful it made me queasy and ready to break down in tears. The Universe was telling me to maintain my faith; I would find what I was seeking. What was I seeking? Myself? A reliable reality? Home? His mention of the word rainbow pulled me into a favorite childhood song, **Somewhere Over the Rainbow**. I walked home with the words, "there's a land that I heard of once in a lullaby...if birds fly over the rainbow, why then oh why can't I?" streaming through my mind and body, quickening something to life within my heart, convincing me that what I was looking for lay somewhere over a rainbow. Never again, for the remainder of my time on island, would I be able to observe a rainbow—almost a daily occurrence—without the words to this song flooding my mind and heart.

Before completing Peace Corps training, I had been directed to write a letter to Liam. The reason, I had been told, was the time had come for me to close that door. Keeping my need for regrets, apologies, excuses, and especially guilt at bay, I had honestly explained the turns that my life had taken. A few weeks later, I picked up a letter from my mailbox and immediately recognized his tidy penmanship. I accepted his harsh reaction, not taking it too personally, and mindful that (knowing him as well as I did) he had more than likely already found another woman to keep him from becoming blue. Closing this door was the impetus needed to open the next. It was of great value to me that I was still oblivious to exactly what was in the womb of time. I was not lost; I was exactly where I was meant to be.

10

Dying to Live

My attention on adjusting to a new culture came to a hairpin turn a couple of months after arriving on island as I lay in bed on a typical, sultry night, soaked with perspiration and unable to sleep. I tossed and turned, listening to noises outside while watching the linear designs made across the wall from the streetlight entering through open shudders. Suddenly, I was aware of a presence in the room. Simultaneously, the all-too-familiar shifting of my energy pulled me into a heightened state of consciousness. In this state, my body felt immobilized except for my left arm, which unexpectedly I found ever-so-slowly rising, hand first, above my chest toward the ceiling. By the same token, my attention was riveted on this extended appendage. I had done nothing; it simply rose. All too soon I realized that my index finger was straightening while my other fingers were folding into my palm. Subsequently, my arm began to move, once again, in slow motion, this time downward toward my body, my index finger landing directly beneath my left breast. My finger remained tightly rigid in that position, as if waiting for my brain to comprehend the significance of the action. Then it began rotating in a small circle directly over a rib. The message finally sank in: I had a tumor. Attempting to convince myself that this was an unrealistic concern left waves of energy surging through my body and my finger pressing more tensely into my rib.

I had not thought that my life could be any more overwhelming than it already was. With this revelation, I felt stunned. More than anything, I wanted this to go away, but the presence in the room held firm. The exasperated self was already silently wailing, "What do you want me to do with this information? Can't you see I'm on overload? How much do you think I can handle?" Ultimately knowing that if this was being given to me, it was for a reason; and that whatever was in store, I was ready, came as some consolation. I continued to feel around the area below my breast long into the night, checking and rechecking, until my rib was sore. Unquestionably, I had a tumor. Undeniably, I had felt it before, but I had continually concluded that I was feeling my rib. I had to admit that somewhere in the back of my mind I had known about this aberrant little cell cluster, known that it was not what I wanted to believe it was.

At a loss to know what step to take first, I simply sat with the revelation for a few days. It was a major challenge to keep it from becoming an obsession. When the opportunity arose for me to ferry over to the sister island, I proceeded to gather information from the Peace Corps library. Even without reading pertinent literature, there remained no doubt that my little lump was a tumor, not a cyst or anything else, and it had to be removed. The horror stories that I had heard about the lack of medical professionalism among the island's practitioners made me exceedingly distrustful, more so than I normally was toward allopathic medicine. I thought about the chances of having cancer. And how would John react? Was this, in fact, my time to die?

My school principal in Chicago had convinced me to refrain from formally resigning in case the Peace Corps did not work out, stressing that I would also be maintaining my benefits if needed. At the time, I had cudgeled myself for being so insecure as to follow her suggestion. Now, I was seeing it as one viable avenue to financially handle this issue if it were necessary to side-step Corps medical procedure. My brain continued to dance from one possible scenario to another, while I missed the truth hidden behind the smoke screen of my agitation and insecurity. The truth was that everything was laid out. All I had to do was stay in the moment and out of the way, and let the experience define itself.

As one day passed and then another, I found myself reviewing the state of my health. I was exasperated that regardless of my life-long effort at choosing a healthy lifestyle, one more issue was now stacked atop the rest, particularly encircling my sexuality. Years before I had been diagnosed as having an abnormal breast condition, which had been extremely painful. After taking expensive medications for a time, I decided to research both the problem and the medications. Reading about the possible long-term side effects, I had immediately dispensed with their use, and the symptoms had gone away without further treatment.

My uterus was another issue. For years I had unknowingly hemorrhaged during menstruation. I had been treated for anemia—another diagnosis I had made on my own—but no doctor had ever asked me the nature of my menstrual flow and connected my anemia with my menstrual hemorrhaging. I had never considered it abnormal, since I'd had nothing with which to compare it, that is until I put two and two together after reading a doctor's column in the newspaper. Immediately I made an appointment with my gynecologist. She informed me that the fibroids on my uterus were the likely cause of my hemorrhaging and insisted, that if I refused to have a hysterectomy, I should immediately have a D&C.

I knew that when I was a teen, my mother had had a "non-essential" hysterectomy (it being considered among the medical community as a fashionable elective surgery for any cancer-fearing woman past child-bearing). My mother was terrified of cancer to the degree that she had taken out supplemental cancer insurance many years earlier. I believed that she would have had her breasts cut off too if a doctor would have suggested that it was the "safe" thing to do. In contrast to Mother's relationship with her body, I had sworn that no one was ever going to cut out my female parts if I had anything to say about it. Consequently, I had refused the hysterectomy, but had opted for the D&C knowing that I could no longer afford to live in a perpetual state of exhaustion.

The day of the D&C procedure I told the prep nurse that I was going to place myself in a hypnotized state as an alternative to anesthesia. I had easily done this during dental procedures, including crown preps, and never had a problem. When the anesthesiologist arrived, she wholehearted supported my request and assured me that she would stay on hand in case I changed my mind. I had felt completely at peace with the situation, and with Carmen, Carl's sister, at my side, I placed my focus on altering my state of awareness. Before I knew it, I had fallen into a profound hypnotic state.

The nurse brought me back to consciousness when she returned to inform me that the doctor, a woman, did not approve of my plan and was therefore insisting that I have the prep for anesthesia. I resisted the request and she left the room stiffly. An hour went by and then another and another. Since I had been scheduled second for surgery, I was certain that the postponement was a deliberate attempt to break me down. The more I thought about my female gynecologist not supporting me as a female, the angrier I got. Consequently, I became off-centered, which led to anxiety, and then doubt about being able to pull myself back together. Finally the anesthesiologist returned to relay that the doctor had requested that I have the IV inserted just in case I changed my mind. Both of us were aware that I was being set up—she was a bit chagrined—but by this time I only wanted it to be over. The gynecologist felt the same, for I had already disrupted her assembly-line mentality. When I was wheeled into surgery, she crooned patronizingly that I would not want to experience any pain.

At my post-op check, I wanted to give her an earful about being unsupportive of women having power over their own bodies. I did not, however, for as usual I became confused and tongue-tied, and fearful of retaliation. When I left I was angry with myself for failing to be assertive, not only for myself, but also for other women who would come after me. I was no longer able to defend myself by claiming that, as usual, I was simply being contrary and causing trouble. Yes, I was angry, now more at myself than her. I walked out knowing that I would never return. Be that as it may, walking away does not equate to standing up or to resolution.

A short time later, a different gynecologist informed me that my pap smear was questionable and scheduled me for a procedure that required removing several chunks of tissue from my vagina to be biopsied. The results proved negative—no cancer. However, because I had an infection from the procedure, she accused me of engaging in sex during the recovery period despite her warning to abstain. I assured her that I had not, but she insisted that I had. I was hurt and defensive; when I wanted to bellow that I was not the sex-addict she insinuated, I instead shut down.

Adding to my distrust of medical professionals, Lee, the British volunteer nurse, provided me with important perspectives on the ineptitude of medical conditions on the island. If anything, her disclosure only increased my desire to forget that this was happening. I found relief, however, in finally having disclosed my situation to someone, and with her encouragement, I felt more ready to take the next step. Besides, I knew that I could not avoid the inevitable: contacting my Peace Corps nurse.

As I considered my options, I remembered that Teresa had had a breast tumor shortly before we had become friends. She had confided that she had been hysterical from the point of being informed until learning that the tumor was benign a week later. This recollection was a message that under no circumstances was I to let my emotions get the better of me.

The weekend arrived, and I headed for Jack's, as usual. At the present, I had been unable to make that definitive move: phoning my medical nurse. I knew I was pushing my luck by not yet having proceeded, and that there would, no doubt, be a price to pay.

I remained distracted throughout the long weekend, but did not think that Jack would notice since he was in the habit of chattering on, self-absorbed, whether or not I was engaged. By Sunday evening, however, he had definitely noticed that I was out of sorts. As a result, he suggested having a glass of wine to cheer me up. I accepted. He joined me, and after his third glass, in an unguarded moment, he candidly asked permission to kiss me. With this advance, I felt as if he was another Charles poised to devour me. I was incensed. Never had I given him any indication that our relationship was anything other than collegial. I was able to quickly rebound from my indignation to state that I was flattered; then I demurred by reminding him that I was in a relationship. It was obvious that my words were taken as a rebuff, and that we both were uncomfortable. I went to bed wondering why my life consistently took such complicated turns. But, somewhere, somehow, I had to admit that I had seen this coming. He was way too glad to have me around on weekends. His serving me up breakfast, once even in bed, was not just him being a nice, generous guy, as I had tried at the time to convince myself despite my overt discomfort. He was enamored. And I was, once again, disgusted that a man always had to bring his penis to a situation. For the moment, I was wondering if I needed to lock my door. Just the same, what if he tried to open it and found it locked? He would think that I distrusted him. But I did distrust him, even while I assured myself that he was a gentleman and would never force himself on me. This situation was suddenly as much as a distraction as my health issue—another Charles entanglement with which to deal.

The following morning, half because it was time and half to create a diversion, I divulged my circumstances to Jack. He immediately insisted that I phone John. Once done, John heartily urged me to come straight home and forget about everything else. He tried once again to convince me to take the vacant teaching position at his community's school. His viewpoint suddenly and instantly triggered my equally strong, willful, but silent declaration, "No one's going to tell me what to do!" Adding John's reaction to the mix struck hard at my self-possession.

When I got off the phone, feeling desperate and in tears, I walked down the road to a pay phone and called my school principal. She was taken aback to hear from me. But she, too, suggested that I return to the States to get the proper medical care needed. My insurance remained in tact, as well as my teaching position. Ending the phone conversation, I only wanted to curse to the high heaven. It all seemed safe and guaranteed, just return to my life as I knew it. But it was gone, dead, and somehow I knew I would not be able to—and did not want to—revive it. I returned to Jack's in a more turbid state than ever.

Later in the day, I stood with my snorkel, mask and fins on a beach on the windward side of the island where the shallow, offshore reef created interesting problems maneuvering in the surf. The other times I had stood here I'd had an odd sense of personal challenge at the idea of swimming out to the reef and back. Doing so seemed formidable and I had asked myself how one could manage this feat unscathed. Then there was the energy of the ocean itself with which to deal. She (as I had begun to refer the sea) could consume me and without a thought I was sure. Thus far, I had only swum around the quiet waters on the leeward side of the island near town, and had had only little opportunity to become familiar with snorkeling. Today, I understood that I had no choice other than to swim alone all the way to the reef and back. It seemed like it could be as much as a mile each way. The longer I stood procrastinating, the farther that distance became. Going the distance symbolized moving through my fear of dying, as well as through something else I was unable to discern.

While Jack chatted with Lee and her boyfriend, I took a deep breath, mustered an undaunted spirit of resolution, and slipped into the water. One more deep breath and I donned my equipment; then I began to swim. With a mask and snorkel, it was impossible to maintain my silly-looking side stroke. I had to brave the ocean straight on and whole-heartedly, face full in the water, eyes wide open, arms and legs moving in synchronized motion.

Before I was far, Lee's boyfriend started to come after me, but I could see Jack drawing him back as I turned for a moment to gage my position from shore. By Jack's action, at that moment, I understood that there was a deeper connection between us. I was thankful, especially that he let nothing interfere with me testing my mettle.

The waves tossed me to and fro and filled my snorkel with water until I was gagging on the salty liquid, but I continued forward, tenacity maintaining my intention and keeping my fear at bay. One thought crashed against another as one wave after another crashed against my body, shoving it back and forth. I did not like this. I did not like feeling out of control, being at the mercy of this hydrosphere. I would learn how to comfortably swim however. I was determined. Doing so had to become second nature. Sooner than I thought possible, I was on top of the reef. This was the most dangerous part of my endeavor because if the waves caught me just so, I could be impaled on the jagged coral lying barely beneath the surface. I swam far enough and long enough to swim the fear out of me and then, upon volition other than my own, I reversed direction and headed back toward shore. It was irrelevant that I had broken the rules of safety as well as left my companions on edge.

Jack said nothing to me about my bold venture—my unsound behavior. I was grateful. The last thing I needed was a lecture. When the day was over, I gladly hitched a ride back to town with Lee and her boyfriend. Despite feeling stunned with all that the weekend had brought forth, I spent the night suddenly brought face to face with a word I had heard an island woman use in conversation: nixie, which meant female water spirit. The word, first hearing it, had stung at my consciousness. Now, I had no idea what I was being shown, but I knew it had something to do with John continually referring to me as "sprite" from the moment we first met. I gathered that sprite was akin to what I called my "forest fairies" but I did not relate "sprite" as having to do with water—water spirit. I had no idea that I would have to become one with the ocean of consciousness, a "nixie"—no idea that I was already one with the ocean of consciousness, that all-around I was on a benthic adventure.

The following morning, feeling clear and resolute, I phoned the Peace Corps nurse. After making the necessary phone calls, she got back to me. My medical evacuation to Washington D.C. was being delayed because the processing of volunteers presently being evacuated from a politically volatile country in Africa had priority. I was being sent to Barbados for a mammogram instead. Based on hearing further horror stories in regard to island-style medical treatment, I was only convinced that this action was a thorough waste of time. I contained myself as best I was able, and at least looked forward to the opportunity to travel to another island.

I had just enough confidence by now to feel a modicum of security traveling on my own, but to my dismay, I discovered that Barbados had little of the quaintness of my island. In fact, it was a major tourist island. My hotel room was in a huge complex sandwiched between other huge complexes lining the beach for considerable distance. I was saddened by the exploitation of the natural environment. Still, it was a relief to be away from the confines of my restrictive code of conduct and be where no one recognized me, where I could relax.

By sunset, however, I was antsy to escape the tourist scene. I wandered down the beach a safe distance. Then I made my way to the far end of an abutment and sat quietly, feeling embraced by the gentle breeze, the sound of the waves and the last rays of the setting sun. Suddenly, I felt a strange, intrusive energy coming from somewhere behind me. From my peripheral vision, I noticed a sturdy-looking local man, in colorful shorts, jogging along the beach. Without question his energy lingered, disrupting my meditative state. Later, returning down the path to my hotel, this same man suddenly approached me and immediately initiated conversation, assaulting my general guardedness. When I flatly informed him that I was uninterested in being picked up, he protested that I had him all wrong, and was insulted by being stereotyped. I told myself that Peace Corps training truly had prejudiced me and that I should be ashamed of myself for doubting this good-looking man's intentions. He must have noticed my defense weakening, for before I knew what had happened, I had agreed to have a drink with him later in the evening.

I sat in my hotel feeling disoriented. Although seduced by the opportunity to experience this island culture firsthand, the situation smelled of trouble. Yet breaking my word was uncharacteristic. Besides, somehow I felt the choice was not mine and so somehow squelched the idea that I was putting myself in real danger. At the designated time, I directed my course to the pool to wait for this local man. After a half-hour, I breathed a sigh of relief and then made a quick beeline for my room, feeling at liberty to read the rest of the evening. I had no idea from where my pursuer made his entrance, but suddenly he intercepted me as I reached the door. He was now freshened up and smelling of cologne like only an island man can. Without a doubt, I was cognizant that I had been trying to deceive myself by thinking I was going to spend an evening reading.

He drove us, in his taxi, to a quiet seaside restaurant where he had a beer and I had a Coke. I shared with him what I had been taught about island men's view of white female tourists. He claimed that there was a degree of truth to this, but that he was, again, different. Falling into my patterning of needing to view him as understanding and engaging, I let down my guard a bit more even while inner alarm bells clanged. Then I carefully began to disclose my metaphysical interests. When he finished his beer, he invited me to his favorite neighborhood establishment, where I envisioned I would get a taste of the island outside of the tourist circle.

When we arrived, however, the place was closed. I thought it strange that he would have been unaware of this since it was in his neighborhood, but again, I dismissed my doubts. Before I could think about what was next, we were walking into his cramped apartment. He showed me around and then pulled a bottle of wine from the refrigerator. He encouraged me to sit and relax. Instead I shuffled around his tiny quarters, waiting for the opportunity to ask to be driven back to the hotel. Before the moment presented itself, he caught me in a tight "embrace." I struggled to break free, threatening to walk back to the hotel if he did not immediately drive me there. He balked until I got as rough in keeping him at bay as he was rough at his attempts to grab me. Without a second thought, I would die before I would surrender to being raped. (I failed to see that we, in fact, had played this scene out before; I was killed resisting being ravaged. Unfinished business had brought us back together. Once again, I had tried to get him to see me for who I really am as a means to avoid being killed when experience told him that I was subject to his will. Ingrained behavior on both of our parts: only greater awareness could set me free.)

He stopped twice on the way back to the hotel in an unflagging effort to get me to succumb. When push came to shove, I told him I was on island to be checked for cancer. He subdued himself enough to admit that his mother had recently died of the disease. I recognized that some part of me was grabbing for a last-ditch effort to change the dynamic—maybe as I had attempted with Jack—although his interest remained one-pointed. In a moment of sobriety, I jumped out of the car and headed toward the hotel. He blurted that he was going to pick me up the morning of my departure to drive me to the airport, but as certain as I was that that would be unlikely, still I noticed that some part of me wanted to believe him.

By the time I was in my room, humiliation had overtaken me and I felt that the only thing worse that could happen was someone who knew me would find out about my disreputable conduct. Outside of berating myself, I felt befouled and hopelessly angry. I stood in a scalding shower until my skin was blood red and I was feeling decontaminated. Quite defensively, I reasoned that I had given this man no more indication that I was available to meet his needs than I had the crazy young man whom I had taken to court, or Charles, or Jack or any other man who had made advances. But, somewhere outside of my sense of victimization, I questioned that there had to be some participatory action on my part, or these situations would not keep occurring. David, my hypnotherapist, had told me that it was difficult for men to leave sexuality outside of relationships; I had not wanted to believe him. Now my certainty that platonic relationships with the opposite sex were possible was faltering.

The following day, I went through the sham of having an x-ray taken. As much as I had found medical professionals stateside callous and varying in degrees of ineptness, this first-hand experience produced a new reference point. Without question, healthcare in the islands has a meaning onto itself.

Afterward, adamant about not making this experience be a waste and therefore eager to see the island before I departed the next day—and willing to do it on my own—I walked to town to determine the logistics of taking public transportation. When I approached one of the many cabbies hanging out at a downtown cab station about where to make bus connections and the logistics of getting to the sites I had in mind to experience, I was in my cautious, tough broad, no-nonsense mode. No one was going to get through this time. The cabby politely communicated the impracticality of attempting to cover by bus the sites I had in mind in the remaining daylight. His words triggered my stubbornness, but I realized that beyond trying to work a few dollars out of a tourist's pocket, his rationale was valid. I also realized that, under my present circumstances, the serried conditions that came with using local transportation were more than I could manage. I desperately needed to be alone. Consequently, we haggled a moment until we came to a mutually agreeable price and my day of private exploration was under way. He wasted no time in hitting on me. It was evident that he was acting within the context of his cultural norm, but he lacked the slickness of the character the night before. I liked him. That did not mean in any way that I was ready to abandon caution.

Barbados is a coral island, unlike my island of assignment, which is volcanic. Therefore, it has an entirely different ecological flavor. I found it grossly overpopulated. In fact, I had read that it is the most densely populated country in the world. Nonetheless, it is endowed with unique, ancient caverns, a tropical garden, and dotted with beautiful beaches. A number of historical sites add to its interesting features. My driver was well informed and had a good feel for my interests. He gave me an idea of how much time I would want to explore a given site, told me where he would meet me and then left me alone. Most of all, being able to wander freely among the gardens and the preserve in solitude allowed me to rebound from my previous evening's nightmare, not to mention my Peace Corps experience in general.

My favorite moment of the day, however, was the time spent on the way back from sightseeing. The driver was acquainted with the woman who was in charge of the last historic site we visited. When I returned from surveying the sunset from the steps of an old stone windmill, the driver hesitatingly asked if I would consider allowing the woman to ride with us back to town rather than her waiting for a bus. To his surprise, I responded, "I'd be delighted." Returning me to my hotel, the cabby made one last pass for dinner. I declined, handing him a big tip and expressing my appreciation.

The following day, I picked up my x-rays and returned to island. What most struck me was the amount of shame that I was unable to leave behind—my bad-person syndrome had never been so alive. I might as well have been raped I felt so bad. It would take months before the fear of someone finding out about my encounter subsided. It would take considerable more time—when my shame subsided—to comprehend the significant value of this jaunt to Barbados. Meanwhile, I would have to keep a vigilant eye on my mushrooming jaundiced attitude toward men.

A week later, I learned that the x-rays were over-exposed and virtually useless. Next I was sent to a local female gynecologist who asserted that I had only a cyst which needed to be drained—a simple procedure which she would be glad to perform on the spot if I so chose. When my nurse phoned me with the next move, I wanted to scream, "Enough is enough!" I finally took the advice of a seasoned volunteer who had already traveled this route; I phoned my area director and pressured that he do whatever necessary to get me on the right track for it was time to remove this distraction from my life. Three weeks from the time I discovered the tumor, I was on my way to Washington, D.C. I refused to believe that I had cancer. Nonetheless, without question, I could sense that I was already in the clenched jaws of some sort of death.

John had driven all day in order to meet me at the airport when I arrived. Being midnight when the plane landed, we were both exhausted and disoriented. Immediately after an initial embrace, and right there in the middle of the airport, face to face, before I was aware of it happening, I decisively announced to him, "I'm not dying of cancer, but I am dying, and if I'm to survive, I have to go to the woods immediately!" Much to our mutual dismay, I then added, "And whatever ideas you have of me staying, you can forget about them. I'm here only until my health issues are put to rest and I fulfill any other requirements. Then I'm returning to island." I refrained from saying that I had no intentions of letting any man get in my way.

The next morning, we drove to my beloved deciduous woods. Walking the Appalachian Trail, in my favorite season of the year, I felt the security and comfort of a familiar home; this was Something's territory. I could breath again. I could open my heart. We meandered down the trail, hand-in-hand, casually conversing. Even so, I anxiously anticipated some special, secluded spot waiting to be presented to me. "The spot" was not as secluded as I had expected; it was only a short distance off the trail, readily observable by anyone who happened by and scattered with poison ivy. I assured myself that there would be no passersby, as I definitively understood what my next step was. John asked no questions as I stripped naked and carefully lay down in the freshly fallen leaves. He remained silent as I breathed in the scent of old memories and released my fatigue and anxiety to the warm rays of the autumn sun. These northern rays could not tan me, but tanning at that moment was superfluous. The Caribbean rays had provided me with a golden bronze Indian tone.

Lying there in the gentle breeze, I recalled how long ago on a beautiful day like this, Something had died. Feeling her energy brought my discontent to light. Why did I need to search this world, as well as what was beginning to feel like other worlds, driving myself forward like a *Don Quixote* chasing windmills? What was I looking for? Why couldn't I be content in my relationship with John? Why did I feel as if I was hurting him because of my need to go on? Why could I find no satisfaction in my life? I did not know why I simply did not stay in the woods where I felt comfortable and secure. Mostly, I wished I could be locked up until I recovered from whatever was creating this turmoil.

Suddenly, a bolt of energy took my breath away. Just as fast, there in my third eye was a vision of Something looking exactly the same as when I first "met" her while searching for "the stone" for John's birthday. I closed my physical eyes to better see. She was solemnly studying me. Making a profound connection with her, we knowingly eyed each other. Likewise, I was listening intently to her silence. There was a message for me, but what? At some point, I finally beseeched, "What do you want from me?" Clearly, without any shift in her expression, her appeal penetrated my mind, "Take my virginity for me." I was not rattled or confused; I turned to John and asked him if he would consider making love. He asked no questions, only removed his clothing. His fears had inhibited our intimacy the night before, but in the ensuing encounter, he consummated his role with great energy and grace.

This was not a sexual encounter, regardless how it might have appeared. Somehow, I/she had been purified. I could feel the cleansing energy still running through both my vagina and my uterus, and my heart as well. I was so overcome I wanted to break into weeping just to get relief. She remained strangely and strongly visible in my mind's eye. However, she was presently following a zigzag trail of switchbacks leading up the side of a mountain. As I realized this, I tearfully exclaimed, "John, she's leaving!" John said nothing, only put his hand gently on my shoulder. Too caught off guard to be analytical, I simply observed the unfolding scene. Something moved deliberately, but effortlessly, like an apparition. Yet she was so real to me. I studied her further as she continued to distance herself. Her entire energy bespoke a predetermined intention that I was powerless to comprehend. At each turn on the path, she'd pause a moment and gaze at me. Resolute, her farewell permeated her silence—I understood just how few words she had spoken from the moment her father had violated her. Her leaving me felt worse than any possible death. With one final turn, she stepped out of sight and then the vision faded. I longed to beseech, "Don't leave me!" but she was gone, and I was just as quickly overcome by an intense aching void in my heart.

I tried to believe that this was only a painful delusion. (A bout of poison ivy would guarantee the impossibility of doing so.) John was unable to understand, although he tried. I sat in the car, simultaneously feeling numb, frazzled and confused, while my dear, gentle John drove us to a motel where we would spend a fitful night.

Previously, I hadn't been able to make sense of the significance of Something's and my connection. My bewilderment from this present encounter left me obsessed to obtain clarity. It seemed that she had to release me so *I* could "*get on,*" whatever that meant. However, she was unable to support me until she received what she needed, which was letting go of her fear of her feminine self, as well as her life of isolation. The tender act of John's and my deep sexual intimacy had transmuted her sexual violation. Further, through her/my healing, she had freed my voice. She had been a powerful healer, albeit self-taught. Her healing power remained a part of me. When she bade me farewell, my instant concern was that I had lost her hardly before becoming reacquainted with her. But she *was* me. I/she was *coming out* of the woods—*out of hiding* so I could use my voice again. I was bringing the woods energy with me—as part of us. In her healing, her knowledge was freed for my use. As much as I felt a stronger sense of direction and a further confirmation of prior messages—healing myself, reclaiming my femininity, owning my voice, teaching, bringing the energy of the woods into the world—the enormity of what it meant to step out of the security of my own woods remained elusive. From one perspective, my understanding felt as solid as a rock. From another, it felt fragile and newborn. Impending experiences would gradually allow me to embody the understanding. For now, it was enough to face the situation at hand.

This I was presently able to do with unquestionable confidence. The tumor was a vehicle to transport me to where my greater understanding awaited me. It was not a problem; it was not an issue in itself. Even my medical experience was a refreshing antithesis from prior ones. My doctor, a male no less, was amiable, showed interest in me beyond my tumor, and had thoroughly explained my case to me, the possible courses of action and expected me to make as many decisions myself as circumstances allowed. He also explained that, due to the location of the tumor, local anesthesia would not necessarily eliminate discomfort. It felt appropriate that I allow myself to be fully anesthetized, that I could feel safe regardless of my unconscious state, and that I was not a coward for doing so. In fact, it was essential that I surrender control and simply trust. My last words to the doctor, uttered as the anesthesia quickly moved up my arm from where it was being injected and stole consciousness from me were, "Don't make any mistakes. My work here is not yet complete." He laughed while I wondered what my words meant.

John stayed in Washington D.C. only long enough to deliver me to my hotel room following surgery. Our brief time together had been bewildering for both of us. Between my encounter with Something and my surgery, there had been too little time to delve the depths of our evolving relationship. We were accustomed to saying goodbye, in little and big ways. This goodbye was challenging for both of us however. Such a bittersweet reunion! And now we were both on our own again.

Shortly after he was out the door, I followed. The golden-leafed season remained, calling to me; I knew that I only had a short time to enjoy the magic it brought forth in me. Besides, I could not stay indoors if I wanted for I had become accustomed to living outdoors.

The edge that remained in regard to the possibility of having cancer was relieved when my doctor presented me with a red rose and the biopsy results. Most confusing, nonetheless, was a remaining inner certainty that I was in the process of dying. The doctor engaged me in conversation, asking me about the nature of the island culture and how I was faring with my assignment. He had dealt with other Peace Corps volunteers. I liked this man, not just because of the rose, because he treated me as an individual. I stayed present in the conversation even while another part of me was concerned about taking up his time and wanted to proceed to a place of solitude in order to contend with inner shifts taking place. I finally bade my farewell, took my rose and headed out the door. If I were free of cancer, why did I still feel this strong sense that I was dying? What could I do? Was I free to carry on with my life? Or was something else going to kill me? The answer—both—was not yet within reach.

I walked the several miles back to my hotel, stopping to rest in an outdoor seating area at a McDonald's restaurant. No one was around, so I was free to have a much-needed cry. "God," I thought, "this journey is tough and lonely. And something really, really hurts." Outside of my moment of self-indulgence, I knew that wherever I was heading I would follow through to the end. Energy surging from within validated my conviction. As if this wasn't enough, my attention was suddenly pulled to a speck of white in one of the fruit trees planted around the area and acting as a buffer from street traffic. I was compelled to examine it more closely. To my astonishment, I was eye-to-eye with a single cherry blossom. I blustered as a deeper connection between it and me manifested, "This is impossible, a cherry bloom at the end of October?" Instantly, its purity took me back to the single white hibiscus bloom that was given to me when I had been directed to divorce my biological family to create my own spiritual family. The same purity and the same message: "You are my beauty." Now, what could I do with this message other than crumble to tears?

John was noticeably disappointed when I phoned him with the "good news." He had envisioned me returning home to him and faithfully caring for me to my last painful breath of life. He had admired his brother who recently had played the same role to his wife's death. Test results altering his fancy, he was forced to examine what insecurity had seduced him to this fantasy. His reaction afforded me insights; the most prevalent being his need to be needed, even when he was unable to keep his own life together.

Due to a delay in post-op care, I was further detained from my return to island. Consequently, John decided that he would drive back down to D.C. to snatch me home for a few days. We ended up driving all night, playing music, talking and being wildly sexual, as best we could under the circumstances. Although John loved our lustful, crazy moment, I was wondering what was really transpiring.

Wondering too, why, when not being erotic, I continued to play the soundtrack to the movie **Glory** over and over until I was in a trance state. The movie had had a shockingly intense effect on me when I initially saw it. I had no idea why or even how the soundtrack still took hold of me. Assuredly though, even now the music twisted and yanked me deep into the heart of the story. Here was an idealistic, young colonel who had the capacity to see the intrinsic value of men and, therefore, was not distracted by class, color or circumstance. Collecting seemingly ragtag rogues, rascals, indigents and other social misfits, he supported them in excavating their latent potential and transforming themselves into dignified, disciplined, focused and committed soldiers. They became vital members of a cohesive greater something and marched to music that only they could hear, and therefore only they could believe in. They were marching to freedom, not for freedom. Regardless of what happened to them along the way, they would all, every last one of them, reach their destination. This incident was a piece to a puzzle, and related back to my recent McDonald incident with the single blooming cherry blossom, the hibiscus incident the spring before, and even to the "failed" Daniel Boone/graduate paper now three years ago—all various pieces to the same puzzle. I was being shown, via the movie, how I would bring my army of family members forth.

By the time we arrived at John's, I felt completely detached from being in this place that held so many incredible memories. Just the same, I was unable to be calm and centered. The garden I had planted was choked with weeds and the fruits of the season were rotting on vine and bush. I wondered why John would not have at least invited the neighbors to help themselves. The house was as overgrown with chaos as the garden was with weeds, but I was not inclined to fix it this time. We attempted to pick up our inner work where we had left off. To my astonishment, the connection was gone: gone too was the spiritual bliss that we habitually achieved through sex.

Instead of letting go, we held on to each other all the more tightly. My confusion lay in the misunderstanding of our true bond. Lacking this vital awareness, my confusion was about to escalate. The stage was being set for that confusion to be played out at Christmas when John would be visiting me for a week. Not only had I booked the reservation, I had paid for the ticket out of obligation for his recent support and because he was suddenly bemoaning his financial issues.

I spent two days in Chicago visiting Adam, Teresa and a few others. Almost everyone remained uncomfortable facing another painful goodbye. Further, I spent an afternoon with my family. I was unable to share important matters, so I showed them photographs and chatted about my adventures, but their interest was only minimal. What I most realized from my trip "back home" was the apparent and significant changes that had occurred in me during the short time I had been away. If no one could understand me before, they were certainly clueless now—for those unable to hear the music, they'd have to think the dancer mad. Nevertheless, I remained unready to face that I had left my life as I knew it when I entered the

Peace Corps.

I returned to Washington D.C. and to my hotel room, which now felt more a home than anywhere else did. It was with great gratitude that I discovered that I had no roommate, at least for the time being. I was doubly grateful for the privacy when I learned that I would be staying on to have a cracked tooth repaired. Subduing frustrations over having again been foiled at getting on with my life, I donned my walking shoes and took to the streets. Having no autumn on the island, like I knew it, made me exceedingly appreciative of another unexpected interlude. I enthusiastically headed out to explore the capitol. First, I hit all the parks and old, secluded cemeteries. I ambled about freely wherever I chose, sometimes far off the beaten path, where no Miss Huff's could scrutinize my every move.

Due to my abhorrence to violence, I found my attraction to the war memorials extremely odd. I spent hours walking through the Arlington Cemetery, studying the tomb of the Unknown Soldier and watching formal ceremonies in progress. The Vietnam War Memorial, in particular, held an energy that I was unable to escape. I was mesmerized by the constant flow of middle-aged vets running their fingers down the line of names inscribed on the marble, by the tears they shed and the mementos they left behind. Not usually a television watcher, I was compelled to turn it on whenever I was in my room. Every channel seemed to have a special on war: the Civil War, the First and Second World Wars, the Korean War. With a morbid unfamiliarity, I watched them all.

On the way to visit the Smithsonian one day, a phrase from a song, "Whatever I do, I do for you," began to resound through my head. This was unquestionably a message that needed translation, so I began to decode it. First, I asked if the message meant that I was supposed to do something for someone. The response was a psychic slap across the face, "try again." So, I tried again and again, only to hear each time that I was wrong. Finally, I broke the code. The message was that whatever happens, it is done for me. The message indicated that everything in my life was put there for a reason, affording me the lessons I needed to advance spiritually. Nothing was a coincidence. Nothing! This felt beyond even my Higher Self in operation. Confused, I asked, "What are you doing for me? And who are you, that you speak in the first person?" My questions went unanswered.

Arriving at the museum, my intent was to visit an exhibit on old growth forests. The exhibit was tucked in a corner of the second floor, and took some effort to find. Upon arriving, I looked around for a moment, bewildered, while I began to inwardly vibrate so intensely I felt I might disappear. The moment I collected myself, my attention was drawn to a video playing in the middle of the area. I watched closely. The camera panned across an ancient forest in the Pacific Northwest in the process of being clear-cut. As one tree fell, and then another and another, I was suddenly energetically drawn into the event. Like a hologram on the screen, I witnessed all the trees in existence toppling to the ground—Mother Earth completely destroyed! My heart cried out. I was the only one who saw this holocaust; the rest of the audience retained their placid demeanor. When I refocused my attention, I was instantly redrawn into the experience. This time, hysteria overcame me. I bolted for the stairs, out the museum and down the mall, toward the setting sun. The incident throbbed in my head. The Earth Mother was raped, devastated—gone forever! As the song had indicated, this message had been given to me for a reason. I was reluctant to understand why it was being shown to me or who was doing the showing. I wanted this agonizing prophecy erased from my awareness.

I ran until I was out of breath, landing in front of a tent far down the mall. The hum of the generator lighting the tent distracted me out of my horror. The light was too dim to see clearly the pamphlets strewn across the counter, but my attention was drawn to a middle-aged man attending the tent. I attracted his attention as well. It was tough to tell which of us found the other more puzzling. When I finally inquired about his purpose for being there, he replied that he was a Vietnam veteran and he was there because men had yet to heal from their war experiences. I knew there was something about war that was being conveyed to me. Was I unwilling to understand? Or was I unable to understand?

I headed toward the Vietnam War Memorial with the idea of further observing the soldiers that made their way there. As I neared the monument, a statue of Albert Einstein caught my eye. I stood on a street corner distractedly torn between the two. I chose the war memorial. Before I could move, however, a force literally stepped inside my shoes, turned me around and delivered me, willy-nilly, straightaway across the street to Einstein. All I could manage to do was breathe as I stood staring at the scene before me.

The bronze Einstein was casually dressed and half-reclining on three semi-circular cement steps, his head bent forward as if lost in a daydream. The statue appeared unfinished, as if the creator had more defining to do. Beyond Einstein's feet the Universe expanded out on what could have been a small circular dance floor. I studied him in the shelter of surrounding trees, out of the view of other onlookers. His gaze appeared to go nowhere. When the last observer moved on, I read the marker and learned that significant astronomical events during Einstein's life had been commemorated on the Universe dance floor. After reading the information, my brain exploded with questions. The more I contemplated the questions, the more riled I became and the more I challenged the information given on the signage, indignantly hearing myself claim, "How do they know that?" At the same time I asked, "Well, what do I know?"

I was exhausted. It was dark and I had already been warned by a police officer about the risks of traipsing around Washington D. C. unescorted, but momentarily, something unidentifiable kept me detained. The longer I stood there, the more I realized that I was being directed to step onto the dance floor. That meant stepping out of the shelter of the trees and into a shower of floodlights. I opted to leave. Before I could take a step, I was immobilized. Then, with no time to wonder what was taking place, a sudden, insatiable urge to make eye contact with Albert overpowered me.

As if possessed, I cautiously looked around to see if anyone else was nearby.

Momentarily assured, I quickly stepped forward into the illuminated circle hoping to complete whatever was being required of me with great haste. Before I could concern myself with fears of being apprehended for my misconduct, my eyes were drawn directly to Albert's. I was not satisfied to merely see them; suddenly I *had* to see *into* them. With no time to ask myself what that meant, my feet began to shuffle about, here and there upon the Universe—the strangest sort of dance—looking up into Einstein's eyes every time my feet landed on a different cosmic event marked on the circle. My need to make "real" eye contact possessed me. I positioned my feet and looked into his eyes, repositioned my feet and looked into his eyes, again and again, an otherworldly determination keeping me in motion. Suddenly, it happened! I was gazing, telescope-style, directly into the hollow pupils of Einstein's eyes.

The return gaze felt like a bolt of pure energy. It penetrated into the depths of my vision. As my gaze converged with Einstein's, I was drawn into a realm of consciousness far beyond the realm of imagination. My feet no longer seemed to touch anything; I felt impaled, suspended by his gaze. Here, without any sophisticated technology whatsoever, I was experiencing the cosmos. I did not know if I was moving into it or it was moving into me. I was in a state somewhere between no longer existing and being all of existence. The words, "Akashic Records," pervaded my consciousness.

Eventually, the chatter of approaching tourists thrust me back into linear reality. I retreated again into the seclusion of the surrounding trees. Dazed and disbelieving, my only impulse was to return to my hotel; yet the demand for confirmation overrode my inclination. When the tourists departed, I returned to the cosmic dance floor with determination, stepping and gazing, over and over, until I relocated the power spot. I experienced for a second time a connection to infinite consciousness, Einstein-style. Time was lost to me, once again, as I became transfixed by this "other" reality, until the babble of voices also again drew me back into linear existence. Confirmation accomplished, I now felt like an appliance whose surge protector had failed.

Although well after dark, I proceeded to walk the entire distance to my hotel in Arlington, Virginia, feeling turned inside out and ruminating until my brain felt like a firecracker. Question after question ignited in my mind. The most disturbing was, "Why me? Who am I to be worthy of such an inviolate encounter?" I had little knowledge of Albert Einstein, other than he had been a famous scientist and had developed the theory of relativity. John had talked of the Akashic Records on a number of occasions. To my recollection, it was a vast cosmic library holding all the thoughts, actions and events that has ever taken place in all of existence. Most mind-boggling, John claimed that everyone has access to this library in the sky. Now, in the midst of my confusion, I believed him. The longer I was back in the limitations of the physical, the more I attempted to define the encounter. I needed to have a comfortable relationship with it, as well as with Albert. I believed that the affinity created between us defied explanation. Further, I deduced that he was now a mentor who would assist me in understanding "what is." I wanted to share all of this with someone. Who would understand? Who could relate? Who would not think me mad? Or a self-possessed braggart?

In my naiveté, the truth eluded me. Through this cosmic experience I was being prepared for the gift of what Einstein's genius had missed; I was being shown how to avoid the same mistake that Einstein, himself, had made during his embodiment. My knowledge to me was as plutonium was to Einstein. Only pure intent, maintaining my focus on a greater purpose, one that functions outside of the human dimension, could prevent me from misusing the power into which I was tapping. Until I reached a place of solid maturity, that is, freed myself from the hold that my past had on both me and my understanding of who I am—until I could manifest my true identity—I remained in grave danger of doing so.

And now I was back in the air, appearing to be returning to island to continue forward with my Peace Corps duties, but really being delivered to where further lessons were waiting. I was just as confused in regard to where all of this was leading, as I was confused about the events themselves. From the tumor transporting me stateside, to dealing with John, to Something saying goodbye, to a cherry blossom in autumn, to being bombarded with images of men and war, to seeing the world destroyed, to Einstein's bestowal of cosmic consciousness—how were all these events connected? I understood that when something was "given to me" I was ready for it, but actually assimilating these new experiences seemed preposterous. I only knew that I was functioning on overload, deeply exhausted and solely desired to return to island for solitude and rest, and then get on with my life. Getting on with my life, however, was not what was in store for me, for my life no longer belonged to me. I had turned my life over to something greater the moment I had agreed to let the world see me for who I really am. I had not escaped death. I would be continuing to die, that is to die in order to live—live my life as a gift.

11

Lessons in Gender Reality

    I arrived back on island well after dark. A young taxi driver, the first to grab my attention as I exited the airport, was so intent on wrangling a promise for a date that my last minute efforts to center myself during the drive to town were lost to frustration. Then, upon reaching my cottage, he not only refused to take my money, he snatched my luggage from me and careened down Miss Huff's lane ahead of me. His attention was redirected when he ran headlong into her barking, "Drop her luggage, young man! *Right here!* And get on your way!" He dropped the bags on her porch and skedaddled. For once, I was grateful for her interference. Lee and Myla, and I realized Miss Huff too, were waiting to welcome me back. That felt good. I selectively updated them on my ventures and they updated me on island news. I went to bed feeling as if I was in a time warp, splintered; one part of me was still in the U.S., one part was here and other parts were scattered in unidentifiable locales.
    At the time I left, I wasn't sure whether or not I would be returning; the area director had instructed me to box up my belongings to be shipped to me or passed on to other volunteers, whichever I should decide. Oddly, Jack had insisted that certain items be stored at his place—Miss Huff was "mistrustful." I had questioned his motives, but at the time told myself that I was too preoccupied with other issues to be concerned with what seemed to be a distraction. This was much easier than acknowledging that I was attempting to assuage my own discomfort over having rejected his advances. Jack had the only key to my cottage and had assured me, when I phoned him from Washington D.C., that he would have the key and my belongings at my cottage when I arrived, but when I began to reorganize my dwelling, I found a number of items missing. I phoned him to discuss my discovery, only to have him admit, with no excuse or apology, that he had kept what he needed for himself. Knowing that he had a host of friends and family supplying him with whatever he requested and had huge care packages frequently coming to him, I was certain that he was nursing his grudge over my rejecting his advances. My inability to demand the return of my belongings compounded my annoyance. I side-stepped confrontation by claiming that I would not argue over trivialities—I had done that too many times before—but I knew that I harbored resentment.
    During my absence, I had taken the time necessary to observe that I had an un-

equivocally unhealthy relationship with Jack. I had latched onto him during training, and *I had created an idea* that we were colleagues who worked on curriculum and enjoyed time together; the same sort of platonic interaction I had attempted to create with Charles and Kent. Even as I proceeded to examine the relationship's dysfunctional dynamics, I had maintained contact with him from the States, worrying whether or not he and Brett could manage our program or even remain in the Peace Corps without my encouragement. I was deeply terrified of his rejection, as well as terrified of having singular responsibility for our program...terrified of being a leader.

Meanwhile, my original perception of Jack as being a sweet man continued to erode as I witnessed the extent of his gibing cynicism, and how flatly abrasive he could be with women, particularly Miss Huff and the curator of the museum with whom we coordinated our environmental program. Despite my insights and need to step out of the game, the part of me that became paralyzed by another's anger, especially a man's, would remain attempting to make amends for my perceived blundering.

My initial priority, as soon as I returned to island, had been to sort through my most recent experiences. I was more than ready to gain clarity in regard to my relationship with John. Above all else, I felt an urgency to find a new point of centeredness, which I figured would allow me to readily pick up my life where I had left off, and to resume my focus on this strange spiritual path I was following. Intellectually, it was impossible to understand that it was my path which was focusing on me—defining me—or that my efforts could only be fruitful if I maintained my focus right where I was at. It did not serve me to try to figure things out. My ideas about how to proceed on my path got in the way of recognizing that the next step was already taking form.

A few days later, as I sat in conversation with the museum curator, we were rudely interrupted when an unfamiliar man burst through the office door. In a self-important manner, he brusquely demanded to get a chapter of a book he was writing printed off. He thrust a computer disk into the curator's hands. The curator promptly abandoned our conversation to respond to his need. While he pursued the oddest sort of congenial—I thought controlling—conversation with her, I found my attention riveted to him. More odd, I was equally enthralled and unnerved by his deportment. On his way out, he off-handedly requested that the curator introduce us; I suddenly felt bushwhacked. His first question was, "Where are you from?" When I replied, "Chicago," a sour expression twisted across his affable front. Simultaneously, he condescended, "Oh, I'm so *sorry* for you!" Although I remained smilingly composed, my immediate inclination was to retort, "You pompous bastard! Who do you think you are?" He stayed for a further moment of small talk, but before closing the door behind him, he gave me a backward glance. At the same time, he invited the curator and her husband to come to his house for a cocktail gathering that evening, adding as an afterthought, "And make sure you bring your lovely friend along. She'll certainly enjoy the sunset from my hillside balcony."

Then he was gone. I sat there in a daze, feeling hit unexpectedly by a williwaw, and wanting to scoop up my scattered thoughts and forget about him and his cocktail party. Still, I was curious enough to ask the curator what she knew about this expatriate.

I momentarily returned to my cottage, but rather than concentrating on further lesson plans, uncomfortable memories of a number of other cocktail parties to which I had been invited since arriving on island consumed my attention. Undeniably, I had attended for a variety of reasons: being a mere Peace Corps volunteer, I felt flattered; I needed to be noticed; I feared missing out on something; and I avoided spending an evening alone. On these few occasions, I would watch my awkward attempts at social banter as some part of me remained bent on being included. Feelings of ineptness would sooner or later overtake my sensibility, and then I would shrink into some obscure corner to spend the rest of the evening observing. Each time I returned home, I felt more and more profoundly that all I had accomplished was to violate myself, not to mention waste my time. Nevertheless, some aggravating part of me remained persistently hopeful that, sooner or later, there would appear—like magic—a chance to spark a meaningful conversation or even a meaningful friendship. Here I was, once again, vacillating between a sense of flattery to have another opportunity to be hobnobbing with the expatriate elite and a sense that I should not be climbing up to a rung of the social ladder on which I had no business.

The most influential tug this time, the irresistible bait, was a chance to be in the country, as well as the novel opportunity of viewing a tropical sunset from high on the mountainside, and something else...something indefinable. Despite having the willies, I knew I would be attending the function.

After the curator and her husband picked me up, they drove to the hotel near my swimming beach to pick up a native author/environmentalist from an adjacent island who was also joining us for the occasion. It was certainly a treat to be away from the bustle of town, despite feeling obligated to engage in parlor talk. We drove through one colorful little community after another, a few now fairly familiar to me. I would have been content to have simply driven along observing the locals engaged in their daily routines, but suddenly we made a sharp left off the main road. We headed upward straight toward the mountain, presently looming in the fading sunlight, through Gingerland, a village where one of my schools was located, and then through another village higher up, called Hard Times. Further along we entered Rawlins, where a steep, ribbon road led us even higher into the mountains. Thus far, the view was spectacular enough that I wished I had eyes on all four sides of my head. The ribbon road ended among a cluster of makeshift dwellings impossible to imagine withstanding hurricane winds. Making a sharp turn, we then dropped completely off the pavement into a pasture where several goats were tethered, and proceeded along two rain-rutted tracks following a ridge running perpendicular to the mountain itself. Before us stretched a panoramic vista of sky and sea, and at last we drove through a line of dense vegetation into a secluded estate. The newly-built, fortress-like dwelling stood on an outcropping at the end of the ridge in a manner that provided the most amazing view of the ocean and countryside extending below, and behind, the jade-green covered mountain. The heavy, humid air dense with titillating scents, the energy of the jungle tangibly close at hand, the mysterious sounds of the night coming to life, monkeys scurrying from surrounding trees disturbed by our presence, as well as the intensity of what was left of the day's light totally captivated me. We had arrived at Max's. More than anything, I wanted to be alone to explore and commune with the overwhelming beauty of my surroundings.

Tagging along behind the curator, her husband, and the other guest, I entered the impressive, yet-to-be-finished abode. The curator's husband introduced me to a British couple seated in the living area. The wife, as I soon learned, had authored a book about the history of the islands. I should have been thoroughly engrossed but all I could do was rue that social dictates necessitated my being in one place when I wanted to be in another. While Max mingled, carrying on what seemed like the most disjointed, trite conversation imaginable, I felt him studying me. I was also aware that my own energy was uncontainably responding. I finally sidled out of the room to a spot on the veranda that allowed for a breath-stopping view of the setting sun. Conclusively, Max had told the truth.

His energy, even at a distance, lingered as penetratingly as the last rays of the sun. Shortly, he joined me. First, he made an overtly conspicuous point of conveying how beautiful I appeared in my red dress and red hair, framed by a red sunset. I felt simultaneously wiled and apprehensive as he chatted on. Yet he was too intensely familiar with me and gone too long from his other guests to avoid drawing their attention. When I reminded him of his obvious disregard for his host duties, he promptly rejoined his guests.

As the get-together came to an end, however, and I was ready to hop into the curator's car, Max informed me that he was driving the islander and me back to town. His explanation for this unexpected arrangement made no logical sense to me, and I wondered why I had not been consulted; however, the islander was already in the back seat of Max's jeep waiting, so I climbed in as well. Adding to my confusion, before we were even off the mountain, I began to matter-of-factly and succinctly relate my D. C. experiences, in particular, the Wall and the old soldiers who had not healed. I was much relieved that I was not required to disclose my Smithsonian happening or Einstein encounter. After dropping off the islander, Max casually declared that he was starving and suggested that I join him for dinner. Since I was neither hungry, nor relaxed about accepting dinner from him, but unsure how to gracefully decline, I agreed to join him while he ate.

We sat on a second-floor balcony of a wharf restaurant—Max's favorite. I chose a seat nearest the water and farthest removed from other patrons. I was acutely aware of every detail: the lack of breeze, waves lapping against the rocks below, sweat causing my dress to cling to me, my fear of being seen in public alone with a man, an urgent impulse to flee while I still had a chance, my energy becoming more overwhelming by the minute. Under these conditions, he shared with me the effect that my story had had on him: the tears he had been unable to stifle, but had managed to keep silent. There in the oppressive darkness of the night—in the darkness of my own resistance—I recognized that my soldier story had touched a chord deep inside him, exciting his own inner war zone.

Our next discussion focused on the behavior of island men and issues surrounding being a white woman in a black culture. I disclosed the precautions we had been coached to maintain in our Peace Corps training. He thought the entire situation ridiculous, claiming that island men's behavior was innocuous, that my carrying a can of mace was an excessive precaution. He assured me that I would soon find out for myself. So contrary to my training and experience to date, and despite my Barbados episode, I was suddenly second-guessing myself. What if I *was* wrong? How could he so easily cause me to doubt myself? I thought only Carl could do this to me.

Next he proceeded to direct attention to himself, which I found a curiosity, especially since the curator had told me that he was known to be secretive about his life. Quite candidly he disclosed that he was a Vietnam Vet who hated war enough to have sought citizenship in Canada afterward, was in a failing marriage, had three dependent children, was a journalist and lived on a ranch in northern British Columbia. He further elucidated that he and his wife took turns going on extended vacations. This was his turn. He did not mention his wealth.

When he suddenly turned the tables and inquired about my life, inexplicably, my mind went blank and my throat began to constrict until I could hardly swallow, let alone speak. Panic shot through me like a jolt of electricity. Laying his hand atop mine with an air of understanding, he professed that it was fine with him if I did not want to talk about myself. I stared at my hand, which felt as if it was frozen beneath his. I desperately wanted to jerk it free. This was becoming too much the color of my Barbados experience. In mounting confusion, I began to assess the best possible way of making a quick, inoffensive get-away to my cottage, which was only a short walk down the street.

To my bewilderment, just as swiftly as I had lost my voice, I found myself divulging my past life as Something, as if to distract him from making any further advances—just as I had used divulging my health issues in an attempt to keep the local from Barbados at bay. The more I divulged, the more I wanted to push myself away from the table and dash down the stairs. I thought this moment would last forever, but as suddenly as I had begun, I was finished. Clearly I was to say no more, although the need to take it all back somehow, or soften it by going on to speak of some silly incident or another from my present life was pressing. Whether or not he believed me was unclear for he showed no reaction. Again, I sat there second-guessing myself, trying to dismiss the idea that I had sold my soul by "going public" with Something. Nonetheless, I also felt as if my disclosure had somehow been a challenge, a "let's-see-how-far-you're-willing-to-play-with-fire" game: or a "you-want-to-know-me-well-here-it-is" game. More than anything, I realized that

I still carried shame in regard to how I had lived my life and still feared rejection because of it. If nothing else, I concluded that my revelation would squelch his interest in me.

On the contrary, he insisted on walking me to my cottage. He stood there idly chatting, oblivious to my discomfort. I did not know how I would react should he try to kiss me, but without question there was some part of me anticipating a kiss. Added to my momentary discomfort was a sudden thought of Miss Huff staring out the window, open-eyed and burning with curiosity—much like my mother when I was a teenager going out on a date. She had already taken the liberty to inform me to stay clear of Jack if I knew what was good for me—that had been when, although unplanned, I had told her about Jack's overture. She had been pressuring me and I thought that this disclosure was meant to get her off my back. In retrospect, I had to face that most assuredly my underlying intent had been for her to see that I was not as loose as I believed she considered me to be. Suddenly I sensed a stubbornly willful outburst in my myriad of already charged thoughts: "I'm-an-adult-not-a-teenager-out-on-a-date-who-has-to-answer-to-her-mother!" Ill-equipped in bringing closure to these awkward moments, as had been the case when I had been a teenager returning from a date, I waited impatiently for him to unwind and depart. But before that happened, to my stupefaction, I found myself agreeing to have dinner with him on another evening.

I went to bed assuring myself that I was under no obligation to follow through. Next, I tried to convince myself that, especially since we lived at different social levels (I was a mere Peace Corps volunteer), he would forget about the engagement before the night was over. Quite the contrary, as if his touch had cemented some indefinable attraction between us, I was powerless to deliver myself from his energy. And when he called a few days later to settle the details, I had still not found a way to extricate myself without lying or fearing that I would upset him. When the day came, I was waiting for his arrival in the shadows, well away from Miss Huff's prying eyes, as well as away from the attention of the men who hung out at the local rum shop immediately outside my gate. Despite my reservations, I had to admit that there was a charge, a certain excitement to be going out with Max, an excitement that bothered me as much as he did.

He had lived on island with his wife and family for a year during the building of his house and had, therefore, made many local acquaintances, so after he made a showy entrance at an out-of-the-way restaurant on the opposite side of the island, he immediately got chummy with the employees as if he expected them to treat him as a valued customer. I sat alone at a corner table for some time observing him and pondered whether they were really on as familiar terms as he believed. Once he had coaxed all the juice he could from his conversations with the bartender and waitresses, he turned his attention to me.

I found him glib and pretentious, seductive and self-absorbed. Instead of a meaningful conversation, after asking me a question about myself, he would acknowledge my response by revealing something about himself, as if to one-up me. By the end of the evening, I was convinced that no events in my lackluster, little life could compare to his high-thrill escapades. When he was not rivaling to present the best story, whether his own or one of a friend's, he was off on some convoluted philosophical tangent. In particular: how my attitude toward local men was tainted by Peace Corps training; how I had it all wrong about them; and how they were not the hell-bent, sexually-predatory monsters I believed them to be. He was too much a clone of Carl—always trying to talk me out of my beliefs. I was certain that I wanted nothing further to do with him. When we parted, I breathed a sigh of relief, confident that I would never see him again. He was little more than a power-flaunting, wealthy man accustomed to acquiring whatever he wanted. I walked away from the evening deadly determined that he was not going to acquire *me*. *I* would not be his trophy! Outside of my willfulness lay an invaluable understanding; Max was in my life to help me find my way home, and I could not get there without him.

Throughout the following day, and then the next, as determined as I was, rather than continue routinely on with my life, an odd, but growing sense of panic began to overtake me. I lay awake at night obsessing over what I had revealed about myself to Max; I looked to avoid running into him in public; certainly it had been a deadly mistake having gone out with him. Knowing that my reaction—any reaction—was ultimately about facing my fears made neither understanding nor managing my behavior more effective. Dodging a chance meeting in a country with a population of 10,000 people, one main road, and one town, was a difficult and exhausting, if not a ridiculously futile, exercise.

Still, I obsessed over being taken by surprise, as if I might be condemned to wear some kind of scarlet letter on my breast if further interactions were to occur. Even with that thought, I failed to understand that I was living from a memory; we both were. In fact, there was a whole Pandora's box of shared memories, one in particular that would in time take me all the way back to my Adam and Eve moment of entrapment into the duality of gender. If anything, I desperately desired someone with whom I could reflect. I needed to move my thoughts and feelings outside of myself in order to get a clearer understanding of them. There was absolutely no one whom I considered able to help me understand the nature of this humiliating affair.

Almost a week after our dinner date, as I was cautiously exiting the post office, Max took me by surprise when he pulled his vehicle to the curb along side of me and stuck his head out the window giving me a conspicuous greeting. Face to face, my body and voice stood frozen, nowhere to escape, no way to avoid the situation, while my resistance to being seen as belonging to him beset me. Rebounding quickly from my wordless rebuff, he accused, "You could at least have the courtesy to explain your attitude!" Triggering my bad-person character, I pleaded, "Not here! Not in public!" I watched him drive down the street giving his "howdy partner" greeting to every passerby, and realized that my agreement to explain myself had become another dinner date.

Any attempt at exorcizing the spell under which I felt I had been placed resulted in my feeling all the more enmeshed. His energy permeated my body, my emotions, my mind; I was aware of him in the depths of my soul. As had been the case with Carl, some force, somehow made it impossible for me to refuse his attention. My life was not supposed to become more complicated. I wanted it simplified. Nonetheless, the second dinner date led to further interactions, as well as more confusion. Beyond recognizing the degree of my resistance, I knew that a sexual component to our relationship was imminent, just as it had been with Carl, Liam and John, upon first meeting them. With them, however, I had not experienced this intense of resistance.

Inexorably, the magnetic force of our past, as well as the Divine guidance that was bringing us together, were exponentially more powerful than my limited awareness allowed me to grasp. This was about purging and purifying. This was about radical review of the nature of my karmic patterning in order to take my rightful place to support a greater purpose. From my greater awareness my understanding was perfectly intact—Max was nothing less than a great gift supporting my evolution—but on a human level I was in for another roller coaster ride.

During a marathon work-weekend stay with Jack (I was still making intermittent weekend sojourns there based on infelicitous reasons) the nature in which I had been informed that John was my teacher began to repeatedly run through my head. I was learning that my teachers came in many disguises, but I found it a test to accept, as I recognized I was being informed, that this power-flaunting man was the tall, thin teacher whose name started with an "M" and who I would find on some island that Paul had predicted at the psychic fair. My first impulse was to try to believe that I misunderstood what was being revealed. If this was true after all, where did John fit in? Rumination took on new meaning as I overlaid my life as I knew it with what I was being shown. My life would be impacted, changed, altered, possibly destroyed. Intuitively, I knew that to surrender to my directives was to give up my life as I knew it. Intellectually, I was certain that I was unready for such a preposterous-looking move.

However, as with John, the message only intensified, pushing and pulling at me and pressuring me to the point of immobilization whenever I went into full resistance. Still I maintained my fruitless rebelliousness. Without question, I was being forced to phone Max to share with him the nature of my insights. I argued that it would be more appropriate to wait until I was sure of the message or at least until I returned home. I defended that it was dishonest to address the matter in Jack's space, and especially due to what had transpired between us, but prior experience had made clear what price I would inevitably pay to be in rebellion to my guidance.

I withdrew to the solitude of the yard and gave free rein to my tears, thereby facilitating the ego death that was upon me. I was as uncertain of what I was giving up as I was of what was being given to me. The degree of pain involved revealed the size of the death. Shedding tears would ultimately lead me to a place of equanimity, a place of deep, inner quietude, a deeper connection with my knowing, a place of absolute trust. Whether my trust was presently in my guidance or in myself, I would be unable to proceed without it. I knew I wouldn't back down now. I wouldn't quit. I couldn't. I had to go on. I had committed myself. There was no going back to living unconsciously again, not unless I wanted to waste my life.

I returned to the house focused and committed to following through on the directive, following through on this lesson wherever it was leading me. Despite the continued tension between Jack and me, the substantial reserve on either of our parts, he was decidedly pleased to see that I had returned from my isolation and he now had a willing ear. (If anything, I remained grateful that Jack had always remained respectful of my need for solitude.)

After he retired and I could hear him breathing heavily, with as much stealth as possible, I moved the phone as far as the cord would allow and sat on the cool, tile floor at the far corner of the sofa, away from his bedroom door. Then, with some hesitation and as quietly as possible, I dialed Max's number. His phone rang once and then again while my pulse raced and sweat trickled down my body despite the coolness of the night. My heart began pounding so loudly that I thought Jack would surely be awakened. My jaws clamped, my throat muscles tightening and my breath was labored; I remembered playing this scene with John not so long ago. If Max were in his office, separate from the rest of the house, it would take him a few moments to answer. As much as I hoped that he was out, I knew that if I were being required to phone at this time, doing so would not be in vain. My perception was accurate.

I responded to his typical, lively greeting in a raspy whisper. He was thrilled when he realized to whom he was talking, but I was intent on completing my directive and retreating to my room before Jack should happen to awaken. Max became serious when I informed him that I had not phoned to engage in an idle conversation, but was being guided to convey a message to him. Therefore, as best as I could, I set my reservation aside and focused on articulating what was required. I wanted to speak with the greatest of clarity, save for thoughts tumbled out on top of each other landing in all directions: there was no room to check if Max was getting the gist of the message, no pauses in the flow of verbiage to check for signs of approval. To bring closure, I added that I considered our relationship as nothing more than platonic. (I wanted to believe that.) The silent space between my finish and Max's reply was a killer. Finally he responded, admitting that he was awed by, as well as ill-equipped, to live the role being asked of him. Yet there was a trifling to his sincerity. After the conversation, I remained on the floor, dazed, in disbelief of what had transpired and disturbed as to where this was all going.

I laid awake most of the night with my unsettled thoughts, continually distracted by a voice inside of me screaming, "He just wants to have you! You've opened the door for him to have you!" Unquestionably, and regardless of whatever resistance or fear would crop up from moment to moment, I was just as committed to following through on this lesson wherever it would require me to go as I had been with John. Yet an uneasy sense of confusion overshadowed my anticipation of whatever was about to transpire.

John phoned unexpectedly the following day just as Jack, Brett and I were settling down to develop our weekly lesson plans. Despite serious reservation, I found myself relating my understanding about Max being my new teacher. John was threatened enough by my news to insist that I make an on-the-spot choice between Max and him. I was baffled and unnerved. (In my naiveté I thought that nothing had changed between us.) I assured him that I was not interested in having a sexual relationship with Max, but merely following Divine instructions. Regardless of not understanding why John should be jealous, guilt over my behavior was now added to my stew. I hung up the phone in tears and returned to Jack and Brett to face their concern. Neither would be privy to what was transpiring as far as I was concerned, especially Brett, whose sharp-edged cynicism made his propensity for gossip deadly.

John phoned again the following day insisting that I define our relationship. I tried, but I could feel nothing except consternation. I asked him to give me some examples in order to have a reference point to build on. He gave me three. Each centered on sex and exclusivity. I was confounded! Never had I viewed our relationship as fundamentally sexual. Then, not content to simply let him own his own issues, I trapped myself into trying to make the situation comfortable for both of us. I was miffed, with myself as well as him. My life was becoming more complicated and rife with strife just when I had been taking such efforts to bring peace to it.

My first meeting with Max, after sharing my guidance with him, took place on his favorite beach where we met prior to sunset. Max liked to body surf here. I did not like to body surf at all. It made no sense to me, like being on a crazy Six Flags ride. I just could see no thrill in subjecting myself to being battered, knocked about and ground into the sand. I preferred the placid leeward beaches, where swimming was meditative. Max suggested that we take a walk along the beach before riding the waves. I agreed. Yes, somewhere, somehow, for some important reason, I agreed to ride the waves.

As I nervously walked beside my "new teacher," I remembered telling David, my hypnotherapist, at our first meeting, that I was in charge of my own learning, John also. With both of them, there had been a context from which sessions had taken place. Telling Max that he was my teacher did not give him power over me, but suddenly I realized I was waiting for some kind of cue from him, some formal something from him to acknowledge that our work together had begun. I was edgy as we left the sandy area and began to traverse a more removed rocky terrain. My energetic wall was up, which was the best I could do to let him know that I did not want him to take my hand. When he did reach out and take my hand, I felt frozen, again unable to slip it free of his, unable to say, "Please, let's keep this clean." He knew I was uncomfortable. Why did he do this then? Why didn't I just tell him that his forwardness was uncomfortable and unwelcome? I was certain that Max was interpreting what was happening as an open door to "having" me, and as we walked on the beach that late afternoon, I wondered how many times he had used the beach approach to hit on a woman, and also just how many notches were on his pistol. The minute he had taken my hand the context from which we were to work had been set. There was no right or wrong or good or bad about it. It was simply what it was.

My commitment was to following my guidance, while my desire was to completely forget about Max and return to the familiarity of John. A sleep-writing showed me the way, "You have a responsibility to not let his life be wasted. He can live through you if you have the courage." On another page I read, "It is time that you take his ancient pain." Both messages seemed ominous and I wanted to ignore them, but that evening as I picked up the phone to call Max I was overwhelmed by an intense foreboding of death. Deliberately, I replaced the receiver. No more than a moment later my phone rang: Max was calling me to share that he had just learned that a friend from Canada had been killed. His pain was evident. The moment the conversation ended, the second sleep-writing message began to pulsate in my mind. With reservations, I phoned him back to relate that I was being told that I was to comfort him. True to my expectation, he claimed that he could manage his pain by himself. I hung up the phone feeling ridiculous, but the directive remained strong in my consciousness.

The following evening he phoned to say he was ready to release his pain, and again I waited in the shadows for him to pick me up. We got down to business shortly after arrival. Even with a mind full of doubts, I did not question the nature of my role for I had done this before with John. Max retreated to his bedroom, which came replete with a spectacular panoramic view of the ocean. I observed from a corner as Max lay on his bed while I, all business, prepared to blanket his body with mine. Before he got seriously comfortable, he reached down and removed his shorts, which happened to be all he was wearing. I took a deep breath as I averted my attention from his nakedness. As I was telling myself that I could go through with this and that I was safe, he just as suddenly requested that I remove my clothing also. When he saw the magnitude of my recoil, he assured me that he had no intentions of being sexual, but my distrust and my discomfort were now difficult to mollify. As much as I liked being nude, being exposed and being nude were two entirely different states. I wanted to run. Was I immobilized by my fear or my guidance? Whichever it was, I finally followed his lead.

Providing the security required of me, he slowly moved further and still further into an ancient pain, which appeared to be imbedded in the depth of his soul. Once anchored to it, he began to weep it loose. It came in waves, ebbing and flowing, ebbing and flowing. I remained spread across his body as best I could, riding the surges as they came, all the time wondering if I was doing this right. With John it had felt so natural that there was no room for questioning. I thought perhaps it was because sexual matters hadn't been a distracting factor. Finally, Max lay curled up against my body, soaked with perspiration and limp—fully purged and at peace, much as John had. The degree that one part of me had participated in the experience—even obtaining a sense of importance from my role—balanced the degree that another part of me had stayed watchful and removed, making sure to not come into contact with his private parts. Afterward, I returned home grappling to grasp our actual roles to each other.

Contrary to the curator's view of Max being a secretive person, with me he never shut up. He particularly relished talking about the times of his youth spent on his grandfather's dude ranch in Wyoming. Hearing him repeat his stories—more greatly embellished with each telling—evinced that he was living in his past. One evening he shared a new aspect of his history: during the long evenings alone in the back country, sitting by a campfire, he habitually envisioned a woman whom he called "the lady of the night." As he went on to describe his encounters with her, I knew intuitively that I was this lady. When he eventually acknowledged that I was the woman in his vision, my head was spinning. What was the meaning of all this? It was certainly a romantic idea, some part of me easily swooned; destiny had finally brought us together.

Soon after, I shared with Max my experience of a few years prior in Wyoming at an Outdoor Leadership seminar for teachers: climbing a famous peak behind the lodge; being the only female willing and ready to tackle the trek; being discouraged by the director who questioned me about my hardiness; being angered that I had been the only one in the group of eight whom he had questioned, when I had given birth to the idea in the first place; having made it to the summit, sleeping in the open, lined up in sleeping bags between male bodies beneath a star-jeweled sky so soul-energizing that sleep became virtually impossible; wandering off to the back meadows whenever possible to listen more closely to whooping cranes; rafting a nearby river after a surprising, sudden summer snow the night before, cold and wet enough to think that I was beset with hypothermia; feeling the sexual charge from lying in the warm waters of nearby hot springs with nature surrounding me in all directions. It was then that we realized that it was the same ranch, once owned by his grandfather, where he had spent much of his youth and where he had encountered his lady of the night. My head was again reeling as I labored to comprehend the significance of what appeared to be much more than a serendipitous moment.

A few nights later, I was awakened by a Divine force and guided to write down this story:

I met a man. He was full of pain. He was searching, but he hadn't found a path suitable to make his search a journey. He was a beautiful man, full of love, passion and kindness. But because "his search" hadn't been transformed to a journey, his passion, kindness and love were wasted—strewn carelessly along the way as he fearfully maneuvered through his life's experiences. As full of goodness and wisdom as this man was, he couldn't see that he already had the answers he needed to be on his journey. He didn't believe in himself.

One day the man crossed paths with a woman. It was not a coincidence. It was the Universe touching him. He saw this woman's beauty. He didn't know it was his own. He saw her compassion. He didn't know it was his own. He saw her strength. He didn't know it was his own. He loved her. He didn't know that he loved himself for the first time. The woman was merely a mirror for the man to see the essence of his own being. What did he do with his experience? Until he trusted himself, what could he do?

Intense energy infiltrated my body and seared my nervous system during this experience. I had barely enough vitality left to respond to many more of these occurrences, as well as little idea of how to act on them. I watched that character that needed to feel important attempt to use this information in a personal way. This felt dangerous enough to scare me, but not enough to keep me fully sober. Full sobriety would have also revealed more clearly that I was beginning to feel responsible for Max's well-being.

One day he invited me for dinner, adding that I should consider staying overnight since the following morning I was teaching in the community and he would then be free from driving me home later in the evening. I thought this was a horrible idea: Miss Huff was sure to discover my absence and I was sure to have to explain myself, lie, if not to her, then to someone else. A dozen reasons made this a stupid move, not to mention placing myself at his service. All considered, I could not say no. Worse, I was not sure whether or not I wanted to, or was suppose to, say no. Between logic, guidance, knowing, fear and resistance I could not discern right from left. Yet the mere fact that I was proceeding was indication that this encounter was waiting to happen.

The evening was uneventful, even tedious and distracting. Mostly I wanted to go home to connect with that which was available only in solitude. When the evening ended, with relief, I withdrew downstairs to the security of the guest bedroom ready for sleep. It was a room that provided no air circulation unless I left the bedroom door open to create a cross-ventilation from the sliding glass doors on the opposite side of the small room. I closed it but refrained from locking it in an attempt to discard my reservations; also I feared that he might discover that I did not trust him. I shucked my clothes and crawled beneath the sheet. My knowing told me that only shortly I would be dealing with his advances. I thought about getting up and locking the door, then pulling the sliding door closed and locking it also. The thought alone was suffocating. I lay there, nervous and distracted, thinking that if I were a sophisticated female, I would not consider this situation a problem. I could casually laugh it off, politely and non-reactively put him in his place. I heard his footsteps on the stairs. When he entered, I wanted to pretend I was sleeping—the Rasta nightmare all over again. I could hear him doff his clothes before he lifted the sheet and slid in beside me. I stiffened at his touch. His invitation had included a promise that he would make no advances. Now here I was, getting that for which I had set myself up. He proceeded to give me some nonsense about his wife not being there for him. I asked him about being sexually involved with her. His affirmative was no real surprise. Nonetheless, suddenly I was furious, with him, with feeling trapped, with myself and what else, I was unsure. I did not scream at him to get out. Just the same, I turned my back on him, energetically placing an insurmountable wall between us, as I had often done with Carl. Within minutes he departed. What made the situation absurd was, somewhere in another awareness, I still understood that being sexual with Max was an event waiting to happen.

The next morning, I arose and readied myself for teaching. He was in the kitchen preparing breakfast like nothing was amiss. I wanted to be indifferent to the idea that my drawing a line might have been the end of our relationship. I wanted to at least duck my head in order to not be seen when he drove me down the hill and dropped me off in front of my school. Mostly I wanted to disappear. I wanted to forever forget about him, but his estate was visible from the windows of all the classrooms in which I taught. Contrary to my desire, I could not resist stepping close to one window or another, and then gazing upon his place, abandoning the moment to some weird inner yearnings, sabotaging my efforts to maintain my attention on my class. Now I was seriously angry, even more when a student asked me why I kept looking at Mr. Gamble's house. Already a couple of students had queried, "Who be he to you?" To make matters worse, when I arrived home, Miss Huff was standing on her veranda, most assuredly waiting for my arrival, claiming that Jack had been around early in the morning to drop off my newly-issued Peace Corps bicycle and found me absent. Currently, I was sure that the entire world was privy to my indiscretions, my secret life.

I remained committed to living whatever purpose had brought us together as I continued to resist Max's further attempts at seduction. At first I thought—rather I tried to convince myself—that it was fun, even exciting, to do things together, to adventurously explore the island, especially since I was otherwise restricted. I quickly realized that our activities were mostly on his terms and time schedule. As had been the case with most everyone who had come before Max, I was soon surrendering bits and pieces of my life to be there for him.

One night we drove to a secluded beach where there were the remnants from the era when thriving sugarcane plantations brought black Africans into slavery. Within the walls of what still stood of an old, brick limekiln, he placed mats for us to lie upon and built a roaring fire. As if he was going mad, he stripped naked and began to dance around the flames, screaming and howling. He was thrilled that I would participate in his escapade. I was afraid to tell him how uncomfortable I was: I felt unsafe on a deserted beach in the middle of the night; I feared the authorities apprehending us for trespassing; or someone of ill-intent sneaking up, knocking Max unconscious and then forcing himself on me (after all I must have wanted it or else I would not have been there). I was overheated from the blaze, fatigued, and wanted only to return home.

Sometimes I felt his antics were a means to measure the degree that I would accept him, or more correctly, accept his outrageousness. This was epitomized late one afternoon by his naked frolic on his favorite beach, which was also a hangout for neighborhood fisherman, or, not to mention, sometimes for my students. He was defying me to be reactive, while he openly dared me to follow suit, calling me a coward when I refused. Embarrassed, I watched, on guard for a bunch of local men I suspected were "spying" on us from the cover of the bush. Although I wanted to be naked as well, I tried to convince myself that I was too inhibited to be that carefree, too caught up in conventionality to be frolicking naked on a local beach. Yet it seemed that our motivations were different: his desire was to be in rebellion, making a social statement; mine was to acquire a state where I could more easily connect to something (Something) outside of the limitations created by being clothed.

Often, when he was running late, he would phone to ask me to take a bus to the country instead of his having to come to town to pick me up. Then he would most often ask me to purchase an item or two at the hardware or grocers for him. Once I arrived at his estate, he would insist that I enjoy his place while he finished up his business. How could I enjoy myself when the air was full of dust and noise from weed whackers, power saws, cement mixers and the like? Further, I was thoroughly uncomfortable with his work crew suspiciously eyeing my every move and surely wondering what I was doing there with the lady of the house absent. My inclination was to wash the sink full of dirty dishes or sweep the floor, anything to be busy. Max would take the broom or dishcloth from my hand, pushing me away from my chore, and insist that I enjoy the place. Thereafter I would wander around the yard, thinking about all that I could be accomplishing at home.

He presented himself as understanding the dynamics of auric energy and chakras, yet I felt he was placating me more than he was really participating in working together energetically. Trying to make the moment work and rid myself of doubt was challenging, especially with the contradictory messages I was receiving—I did not see how *he* could be *my* teacher while *I* was being required to be there for him. As far as my definition of teacher went, my mistaken and arrogant position was that he had much more to learn from me than I did from him.

One day, Max gave me a chapter of his book to read and afterward asked me what I thought. Unexpectedly frank, I responded, "It's too noisy!" Obviously, this was not what he expected, for he went on to defensively justify that he had to write in such a manner if he were going to make money. His comment was one I would not forget. When I examined what I meant by "too noisy" I saw too many adjectives and adverbs—too much description, too many far-fetched analogies. As a reader, I felt manipulated, even controlled, as if there was no room for personal experience or interpretation. There was no question that he was talented (this could also be seen in his photography), although I thought he could be much more effective if he wrote from his heart rather than from his intellect. He continued to ask me to critique and edit his material. I learned how deeply enmeshed his identity was with his writing, exactly how far he was open to suggestion and how to give him a perspective without triggering his defensiveness. Time would reveal the personal value of playing this role to him.

Max's mother arrived a week before Christmas, the first of his family to arrive for the holidays. He had already spoken of their conflict, his wife's dislike of her and her interfering nature. My first impression of her, when we met, was that she was a thoroughly insecure woman who excessively relied on her only child for a sense of security. Max invited me to join them for dinner the day following her arrival but appreciating the likelihood of her detecting that something was afoot, I declined.

On Christmas Eve, his wife and children, along with John, arrived at the same time. When we ran into each other on the wharf, it was implicit that we had withdrawn from our mutual sense of familiarity. I watched him greet his wife and three daughters one by one as they stepped from the ferry and walked down the wharf, strung apart among the dwindling crowd. It did not appear to be a happy reunion.

Moments later, John stepped forth from the crowd. My initial guilt-laden reaction was that I was not going to allow my reputation to be tarnished by being seen in public with him either. My second impulse was that I wanted him to go away. Butting against this reaction were both my compulsive need to confess something and my need to swear that I had done nothing wrong. Was I using my belief that my relationship with Max was none of John's damn business as a means to avoid being honest? My "defense" that I had not been sexual with Max was only a technicality. If I were open about what had been transpiring, would John hate me forever? Was I avoiding hating myself? Regardless of where I put my thoughts, I was unable to avoid their stickiness.

John had brought a suitcase stuffed with Christmas presents. I tried to feel flattered by such generosity, but his "gifts" were burdensome. Still I felt selfish having so little to give him in return...that is after dismissing the fact that I had paid for his airfare. He fell into his familiar habit of expressing how well he was planning to provide for me when I knew he had little capacity to keep even himself financially organized, let alone solvent.

We had already run up an astronomical bill trying to iron out our issues by phone, but mostly our sessions merely circumvented the issue, ending where they started, with us articulating our love for each other. During his eight-day stay, I attempted to retrieve the deep connection that had been the foundation of our relationship. Simultaneously, I found it troublesome being sexual with him. But I was never quite able to say no. My bed was exceptionally small, so I had an excuse to sleep separately. Overall, the best I could manage was to be in resistance or avoidance, leaving John all the more threatened and persistent. I told myself that I was never sexual with two men at once, and continued to maintain that I had not been sexual with Max. The worst of my dilemmas was my inability to keep my attention away from Max. I was half convinced that some determined force was implanting thoughts of him right into my mind.

I took John to the local volunteer hangout to meet the Peace Corps family the night of his arrival. He made a good impression, casually joking and even talking within a spiritual framework, which done so naturally and in such a situation took me by surprise. I wondered what the group thought, my having always referred to John as my fiancé, yet was sure that they were all by now aware of my acquaintance with Max, despite my efforts to keep it secret. I had planned a party in John's honor for the following evening, giving him further opportunity to interact and make acquaintance with my circle. Since I had borrowed a couple of coolers and other items from Max—maybe because I needed to prove to myself that nothing was amiss—I felt obligated to invite him and his wife. Considering they were of a different social stratum than the Peace Corps community, I thought the likelihood of them showing up to be slim.

Jack was thrilled about the party. He even whipped up a couple of chocolate cake mixes, two of many he had received in his care packages and had been gleefully stockpiling. Because of his enthusiasm regarding the party, I thought that he would be a fun element. Instead, his abrasiveness and immediate jealousy toward John set me off-center right from the moment of his early arrival. My belief that I would find relief when other guests finally began to arrive was short-lived. Brian, who worked for a British agency that provided overseas technical aid to third-world governments, arrived accompanied by a woman who kept him at heel, steering him explicitly clear of me. Then a number of young men from the volunteer community arrived inebriated. I overcame one little annoyance after another, determined to not appear the novice hostess.

Late in the evening, just when the party was winding down, Max burst through the door in the same manner as when I had first met him, this time trailed by his wife. Without any hesitation, he ceremoniously presented both John and me with a Christmas package, and encouraged us to open them on the spot. Mine was a coral skeleton obtained on the windward side of the island in proximity to where he had done his jumbie dance only a short time before. John's was a seashell stuffed with locally grown marijuana. My discomfort now knew no boundaries—breaking the numero uno Peace Corps regulation by having an illegal substance in my dwelling. I did not protest however; I was too fearful of making a scene.

Max's wife remained standing awkwardly at the door. If I had been on my toes, I would have reached out my hand to her, but I was overwhelmed by Max's attention-grabbing entrance, as much as being together with Max and his wife. Maintaining formalities only for a moment, Max quickly honed his energies on Lela, a Dutch woman, completely abandoning his wife. She looked as uncomfortable as I felt, while I was suddenly overtaken by a surge of jealousy toward Max and Lela. To add to the absurdities, John moved to the bedroom to privately counsel Amos, the local man with whom Lela had come to live, and who needed feedback on personal problems.

With all that was going on, I had no choice other than to mix with Max's wife. Typically, my first thought was that she might be someone with whom I could develop a friendship. I watched my compulsion to divulge all that was transpiring between her husband and me, to prove to her that I was merely following guidance, and innocent of any wrongdoing. Instead, I struggled to maintain small talk. At the conclusion of the party, I sat on the front steps attempting to get centered; my clouded thoughts of having to go to bed made that a ticklish task.

Until John massaged Miss Huff's bum knee, relieving her discomfort, she was initially curt with him. Thereafter he was *wonderful*. At the Christmas Eve church service, she invited us to have Christmas dinner with her. In response to her admonition, "You should always give in order to guarantee that you get something back," I asked if she had taken that notion from the **Bible**. I was surprised about the invitation, particularly because, not only had Miss Huff become aware of my interaction with Max, they had crossed paths on my front porch, and she had communicated, without being direct, her disapproval of "that pony-tailed man." Appropriately responding to challenges of this nature remained arduous for me, and my growing silence in the matter of my personal affairs fed the growing tension between us. Fortunately, John and I had already made plans for Christmas day.

First, we arose well before daylight, for John had decided that it would be an adventure to see the sunrise from "the source." I had been there several times and had found it a truly magical place. It was high in the mountain (the trail head located adjacent to Max's estate) where natural spring water was channeled into catchment basins and then piped down to local communities. Partly because I had a strong dislike for starting a day in the dark, as much as spending the day running on a sleep deficit, I was resistant to making this trek. But, since this was John's vacation, and this was what he wanted, I agreed to go anyway. Even arising with a urinary tract infection made no dent in my obligation. So, I was there but not there: creating a travesty and hating myself.

During the Christmas volunteer gathering, when I thought I could not possibly be more uncomfortable, a new face appeared in the crowd: Bob. A biology professor from Canada, he was involved in environmental studies. As I was to learn, he came to island three or four times a year to carry out field studies, both aquatic and jungle. He also regularly brought his students along on field trips. I could not believe the immediate, obvious attraction between us. It was as if a part of me stepped forward, crossed the veranda, and made a connection with this stranger that could not be broken. John, attuned to what was transpiring, was as visibly hurt as he was jealous. All I wanted to do was lock that obnoxious part of me in a cage and throw away the key. How could my behavior be any more humiliating than it already was? Here was my maverick energy now split between this new character and Max, while I attempted erstwhile to aright my situation with John.

Max had earlier announced his belief that we could just be one big, happy family. And although I had voiced my objections, he still phoned to invite us to join his family for the annual horse racing event in which he was proudly involved. I turned the decision over to John who unhesitatingly accepted the invitation. We were to first meet at Max's house for refreshments. The closer we came, bumping up the hill, my students calling out to me from among the throngs of people streaming down on their way to the racetrack, the more stupid I felt, even while telling myself that I had done nothing wrong and did not have to feel guilty. John and Max were noticeably at odds with each other from the start, vying underneath the hood of my rented car to get it running smoothly. Max's wife was running in circles trying to get the family galvanized; his mother was huffy about something or other; and his three daughters were indifferent about going anywhere. Again, I wanted to spill my guts to Max's wife, with a kind of "kill-me-and-get-it-over-with" attitude, or else run for dear life. Thankfully, my discomfort was momentarily allayed when I was asked to cut the youngest daughter's hair; she in her nervousness, habitually pulled on it enough to have created bald spots. I had never overcome my anxiety-motivated habit of pulling on my own hair. I was aware enough, however, to watch myself, knowing that doing so was like a barometer measuring the level of my anxiety. Obviously it was not as extreme as this child's.

John loved the races, which Caribbean-style, made the word "unique" an understatement. He effortlessly mingled with Max and his wife's crowd of friends who were all focused on picking winning horses. I enjoyed watching him so casually engaged as if he was among long-time friends and wished that I could follow suit, but my demophobia was running rampant. Once again, I was freed from my discomfort when I agreed to take Max's youngest daughter swimming at a nearby beach. Shortly after returning, Myla, the very pregnant ex-volunteer from Scotland, who had thought she was strong enough to participate in the big, holiday event, immediately tired and asked me to take her home. With the heavy traffic delays, I returned with perfect timing, minutes after the final race.

Myla gave birth the following day. An interesting bond had developed between the two of us in the short time that I had been on island and she had been a frequent visitor, sometimes bringing Lee along with her. Conversing with her came naturally and I had found myself, when alone with her, communicating at a deeper level of awareness. To my consolation, she had never backed away. Her son, Bairen, captivated both John and me. John maintained his deep yearning to have children, often expressing his regrets that we had not met early enough, and held his serious fatherly liking to Adam. I was intrigued and very much touched to witness how gently and genuinely he interacted with Myla and her newborn. Being a handy photographer, he soon had mother and child posing before the camera. The birth of Myla's baby became a sweetly shared moment of John's stay.

As he boarded the plane a few days later to return to the States, he turned around and gazed back at me. I put my hand to my heart and directed my energy to him. He did the same. As dishonest as I felt, the love between us was, without question, real. Beyond deeper kinship, we were both in great pain and confusion. All I could do was chastise myself for my insensitivity toward a person that I loved so deeply. Strengthening my self-reproach was the feeling that I had to release him so I could get on with my life. In fact, while some stubborn part of me kept refusing to let him get in my way, another part was in total resistance to separating from him. Why should I? I loved him and whatever was happening with Max, I had no personal interest in him. Besides, I could love two men if I wanted. I could love a thousand! Love did not have to do with making choices, sex or ownership, I defiantly maintained. A deeper disparity to letting go of John was an innate awareness that he would be devastated and I was unwilling to face feeling responsible for that.

New Year's Day. My birthday. Since leaving Carl, it had become a tradition to spend this day alone and in reflection. I was compelled, however, to first deal with my laundry duties. I pulled out the hose and buckets and began the process, scrubbing away as I sat on my front steps. My energy had been going haywire since awakening. As I began hanging the first round of laundry on a line strung between two Coconut palms behind the cottage, an odd impulse led me to dart around the building to check if something was amiss. I found no one. Yet I had distinctly felt that someone had been there. Stepping onto the porch, my eyes fell on a large envelope with my name conspicuously scrawled in Max's trademark calligraphy. I made a dash across the front of the property to see if I could catch him. He was already pulling from the curb, but from his rear view mirror he noticed me hailing him. He said he had no time to talk, but encouraged me to examine my birthday present.

Unable to wait until I returned to the house, I greedily opened the envelope and pulled out a poem that he had written to me. When I was finished reading it I was at a loss to know what to think. Certainly I felt flattered. When had I ever received this kind of attention? I sat on my steps and insatiably read the poem through a few more times. A sense of alarm began to overshadow my initial reaction. Max had taken the entire experience at Coconut Walk, the night he did the naked jumbie dance around the fire, and placed a distortedly romantic twist to it. Just when I had hoped that the "student/teacher" relationship was complete and I would bid him riddance; just when I had decided that I was free from whatever it was that held me captive, the poem, even the paper and his handwriting, cast a voodoo spell over me. I could not rip my thoughts away from him.

He phoned the following day to ask if he could stop by that night for a haircut. He would be departing with his family in two days. I could not say no, nor did I want to even when I attempted to do so. Since I had cut his daughter's hair and otherwise had a reputation among the volunteers for giving good, free haircuts, this reason for a trip to town was a reliable a ruse as any. As the pressure that I sensed mounted, the day wore on. I was fully aware that something "big" was waiting to happen. While I trimmed away at what little hair he had—fringe around his ears and a tiny thing of a ponytail at his nape—I watched myself half-submit to, half-resist his fondling. The tension between us felt as if I was trapped on a wild carnival ride. Before I realized it, I was the one who made the first move that ended our sexual cat-and-mouse chase. He liked what he got—what he had been trying to acquire all along. He exited the situation as smug as Liam had been when I had taken him by surprise after having shared a bottle of champagne. My emotions as he departed vacillated between anger over having again been submissive—surrendered my virginity, my purity somehow—and a disconcerting sense of conquest, even retaliation.

Contemplating the situation, my ruminations fell on a conversation with David, my former hypnotherapist. He had told me about his wife's friend and him. Although there had been no sexual facet to their relationship, he had labeled it an affair because the intent was there. The message was clear, but I hated having to own it.

Max had intended to stop by to say goodbye before his final departure. In the end, he phoned to say he had no time. I was not surprised, and for many reasons was relieved that our interactions had ended so abruptly. Whatever had happened during the holidays—with John, Max, or even Bob—I persuaded myself that I could put it all aside and move on with my life. It was time to place my attention on the business of lesson plans and making further cultural adjustments. My narrow perspective shadowed my awareness that my Peace Corps experience was much more than something in and of itself, and, rather than me defining it, it was defining me.

No sooner had Max and John made their exits than Bob found his way to my door. Thereafter, he spent considerable time exhaustively elaborating about his island projects, his work and his life in general, much like Max had done—only he was not married. It was readily apparent that he needed someone to listen to him, just as Max did, and that he got a sense of importance through his island involvements, again, just as Max did. Since he also worked in conjunction with the museum and coordinated his projects with the curators, it was inevitable that we would frequently be crossing paths.

I could not identify the force behind the attraction between us. I assured myself that I had no personal interest in him, that dealing with men was wearisome to say the least, and most assuredly if he were not sniffing around me, he would be sniffing around someone else. Besides, it was unimaginable how tarnished my reputation might become if I were seen with a third man. Nevertheless, for the week he remained on island, he continued to seek me out, to the point that my annoyance began to outweigh my sense of flattery. Among further insights gleaned from watching my involvement in this escapade, was a need, an intense longing, coming from deep, deep inside of me that he would listen to me at least a smidgen as much as I listened to him.

In the meantime, my determination to forget about Max and focus on my relationship with John was continuously challenged by Max's efforts to keep the door between us open. A first effort came immediately after his departure in the form of another poem of similar ilk to the first. I hid this one away under lock and key, along with the other, horrified by the thought that someone, Miss Huff in particular, might read it. However, like the initial poem, some warped enticement left me to continually sneak it out, read and reread it, half-striving for a deeper understanding and half-getting a high. From a conventional place, I was feeling like one of the many uncountable island she-dogs, victims to the scent of being in heat, and plagued by three determined curs, four including Elmer. I could not raise myself out of the limitations in which my sexual body held me, which was a prerequisite to living who I really am. Not through resistance, but only through understanding. Continuing experiences would be required and provided before I could fully realize the limitations that our past holds on us through our sexuality. More than rising out of my environment, including the sexual body, I was in the process of rising out of the confines of my physical reality. I was setting myself free. Although in the moment, to me, it looked like I was stepping back into prison.

12

Reflections on Limitation

The most intense opportunity to learn to trust in my own knowing would come through my connection to Myla and her partner, Gavin. Shortly after the Christmas holidays, I stopped by their dilapidated, two-room board house down the hill from Max's for a visit. Pails of water that she had hauled from the community spigot to use to wash diapers sat amongst the weeds, revealing the nature of the new mother's domestic chores. Upon my arrival, Myla was at the door, with Gavin, to whom I had not yet been formally introduced, hovering behind. Although she was embarrassed by her situation, she was genuinely glad to have me visit and, after introductions, she quickly led me into the back room to see the baby. I sat down on the fusty mattress and pulled aside the mosquito netting in order to draw him into my arms. The combined sense of love and pain once again sprang alive in my heart, as it had each previous time I had held him. There was little time to become distracted, however, for immediately upon carrying Bairen into the sitting room, I was besieged with a barrage of questions from Gavin.

He reminded me at once of Carl, manipulative and overtly on the offensive. I refrained from second-guessing myself. In particular, I was taken aback when he asked me about the significance of my star sapphire amulet. Myla noticed my hesitation and indicated that it was okay to speak openly with Gavin. Nonetheless, I was compelled to reveal as little as possible. As if he realized that he was going to get nothing from me, he suddenly began to expound some philosophical gibberish. As time passed and he continued in his self-absorbed vein, I felt threatened in a way that I had not been since the night at John's when that maleficent energy had penetrated my hands. The more he carried on, the more compelled I was to escape. Finally, when I found an apropos moment to depart, he insisted on giving me a ride. I did not know if it was common sense or a warped sense of protocol that left me accepting his offer rather than walking the five miles back to town.

I cautiously straddled the rear seat of the motorbike, avoiding making bodily contact with him. This was an interesting exercise considering the size of the vehicle and the pathetic condition of the roads. Despite my efforts, halfway to town, I found my hands being placed squarely and deliberately on his muscular, broad shoulders, jolting him in an undeniably intrusive manner the moment contact was made. I was at a loss to know how to deal with the instantaneous rush of energy that surged through my hands and into his body for there was no removing my hands. I made a futile attempt to believe that the situation was a product of my imagination, but when he pulled to the curb in front of my dwelling and I climbed off, my eyes, as if they had a mind of their own, riveted on his, emitting energy in the same manner as my hands. My behavior appeared to be a direct challenge, yet I had no idea why or from where it was coming. We stood facing each other, like a showdown, neither of us able to break the mutual glare. Just when I thought we must be forever locked in this exchange, the energy subsided as suddenly as it had manifested. Neither of us mentioned a word about what had occurred, but whatever the nature of this power, I was certain that he desired it for himself. As I walked the path to my cottage, two thoughts permeated my awareness: I was frightened, and he would soon be back.

It took him two days to phone to ask if he could visit and added that he wanted to work with me and to learn from me. I had heard stories from other volunteers regarding how Miss Huff had played out her contempt for Rastafarians. Fearing her discovery, as much as being unwilling to be seen with him in public, I requested that he meet me after dark in the museum courtyard across the street from my cottage. As dusk descended on the town, I made my way to a bench in the courtyard away from the streetlight. I could see him, even in the dim light, swaggering forward. Hardly before acknowledging my presence, he placed his hand firmly to his bulging crotch, proud of what was under his hand, and claimed in his odd, Caribbean dialect, "I can't understand why I get an erection around you." I resisted any sort of reaction while he again absorbed himself in spewing metaphysical froth. As I observed him getting high on his own warped sense of veracity, I began hearing, over and over in my head, "You've made a commitment to work with him." On one level I could acknowledge this statement. On another, I only wanted relief from the man.

He clearly had the capacity to drone on and on throughout the night. At one point, ready to pull out my hair, I found myself abruptly interrupting his discourse and insisting that he listen. The message poured forth from a place far removed from my capacity to control, "If you want power, if you want true power, if you want the power that you see coming through me, you have to completely surrender your need for control. You have to learn to be quiet. You have to completely silence yourself. Then you have to learn to listen. I mean really listen—listen to your heart. This is the only way. There is no other." Some part of him recognized the truth, but there was no pith to his commitment. He did not want to learn anything, and especially not from me. He did not want to work to come into his power. He only wanted power. He wanted *my* power.

A few days later, he phoned to ask if he could begin to work with me. This time I overrode my fear of Miss Huff's reaction enough to allow him to come directly to my cottage. We sat across from each other in my tiny living room. I was tense and sweaty. He was cool. I tested, "Are you ready to listen?" He nodded, but his effort to remain silent was monumental. Again, what I was to convey to him came through me, not from me. As this was taking place I recalled a time when I had vowed that I would never allow a disembodied entity to operate through me. Despite my lacking a true reference point, I was certain that this was different. Certainly this was not a novel experience. Yet, never before had I been used with this intensity. I did not have proof, yet I was convinced, as I heard the truth and conviction of my words, that a Divine presence—beyond my Super Consciousness—was using me to call Gavin out of the depth of his own darkness. He did not interject or intervene during this torrential message: he did not dare. Afterward, it took a few minutes for us both to recover from the impact of this Divine edict. Once he did, he immediately went off on a tangent, trying to regain lost footing. The more vociferous he became the more it became clear that he was attempting to make it look as if the fiat had come from him. If I had not considered Gavin's behavior alone reckless enough, I myself would have speculated that this endeavor by the Divine was an exercise in futility.

Later, Myla phoned me to say that she and Gavin were having a christening ceremony at their house. They had attempted to have the baby christened at the Methodist church, but were told that, since they were not members, their request could not be granted. My thoughts were that the real issues had to do with Gavin being a Rasta.

Lee and I arrived on the day of the occasion not knowing what to expect. The Governor General was there, along with another Rasta friend of Gavin's whom I had not met. Right from the start the whole circumstance made my skin crawl. The Governor General had a reputation for womanizing, with a special interest in female volunteers. Lee had already revealed that he had made overtures on a number of formal occasions. It was difficult to dismiss the feeling that we were unsuspecting females, or at least, misled females, being duped by the darkest, most devilish and vile of male energy. I wanted to turn and run but I told myself that I could not desert or disappoint Myla. After all, without Lee and me, she had no one.

Before the beginning of whatever ceremony was planned and while the host and hostess were preparing refreshments, the Governor General unexpectedly broke the silence by conveying his views to Lee and me about women who indiscreetly engaged in sex in front of their children and how damaging such exposure was to the children. I had no idea what his point was except that it functioned way outside of etiquette. In fact, it was a clear assault on us as females, as if we were so sexually addicted that we were beyond any kind of self-constraint. I knew the Governor General knew we were both uncomfortable: I was certain that he wanted it that way. I wanted to blast him with, "Who do you think you are you aggressive bastard, that you can conduct yourself this way at this precious child's christening? Who do you think you are that you can project your own deplorable tendencies onto females?" I didn't say anything. Just as with the Rasta the night my group first came to the islands, my silence gave him license. I didn't like my behavior anymore than I liked his, but there seemed to be no way to find my voice. All of what I had heard about the Governor General only added to my distress, especially that he was involved in some sort of secret occult organization called Rosicrucians.

When it came time for the ceremony, Gavin took the baby from his mother's arms and held him up in the air, naked and vulnerable, and then mouthed a spray of mumbo jumbo that triggered something in me that made me want to vomit. I attempted to tell myself that it was great that these parents were not letting convention or religion restrict their child from being christened, that it was beautiful and original that parents could make their own statement about raising their child. Then I noticed that Myla was not involved in the ceremony, only Gavin and the Governor General, although at some point we each were given a momentary opportunity to contribute a thought. At a deeper level, I felt as if this child was being sacrificed to the devil. Devil worship. Baby sacrifices. The ceremony ended as quickly as it had begun.

This was not a novel experience. All involved had lived it before. Being together in this manner was awakening the original memory, causing me, all of us, to relive the experience once again. Without a greater awareness, we would be further doomed to relive this experience again and again, over and over, until we did remember. My gut reaction, my inner knowing, indicated the exact nature of the original experience.

A couple of weeks later, Lee phoned requesting that I come to her house immediately. Once there, I found Myla collapsed in a chair and Bairen wailing in her arms. A number of other women present appeared as distraught as Myla herself. I drew the baby from her arms and queried her. She explained, through fits of crying, that she and Gavin had been fighting and, although he had refrained from taking the advice of his friends to give her a good beating (as a true Rastafarian man would to get his woman in line), he *had* threatened her severely.

When Myla completed her story, the other women present proceeded to analyze how Myla should deal with her problem. I sat quietly in a corner and listened while something else was happening inside of me. One local woman insisted, "You are going to take yourself right back to your cottage, tell Gavin that you are sorry and ask for his forgiveness, and feel fortunate that you don't get a good beating." Her words manifested a weird shift of energy within me, and in response to the woman's advice, I heard that same powerful force that had spoken to Gavin say silently, adamantly, "No, she's not going anywhere!" The force continued to settle into my body as I sat there present, but separate from the unfolding experience before me. Suddenly, I found myself standing up and moving to kneel in front of Myla, taking effort to make direct eye contact with her. My eyes, burning with such intense energy, reminded me of my experience with Albert Einstein. Another woman, who had proceeded to give her opinion, stopped short.

Once eye contact was made, words sprung forth with strong conviction, "You listen now, Myla. You're not going to run back to Gavin. You're not going to apologize. You're not going to get beaten. And you are not jeopardizing your child's safety. You're going to stay right here. Lee will take care of Bairen tonight while you get some sleep. When you wake up, you're going to take the responsibility to look inside of yourself to resolve this issue." Eye contact between us held firm. And, as the message sank in, Myla began to sob. Outside of her weeping, there was dead silence in the room. The other women took Myla's sudden request that I stay the night with her to sort things out as a cue that it was their time to depart.

Thereupon, Myla retreated to Lee's bed. Within the security of the mosquito net, her long, slim body naturally curled in a tight fetal position. She was exhausted. Still, her shame spilled forth on a rush of tears. The more she divulged about her messy situation, the more I saw shades of my life with Carl. Confusion, pain, secrets and humiliation had defined her life. When she was momentarily drained of tears, we sat quietly together. Though her stability was fragile, I had to refuse her further request to stay the night. There was no room for pity here, not even room for sympathy. I was being called to stand back, to stay out of the way in order for her to reach inside of her fear to find her strength. This was a new space for me: not fixing, not feeling sorry, and not getting sucked into someone else's pain. I felt strong because I was centered and connected to that which worked through me, not tripping over circumstances.

I walked home from Lee's in the wee hour of the night. For once I was not afraid of being out alone. Unable to sleep upon my return, I randomly opened the book, **Tao Te Ching.** One highlighted passage immediately spoke to me: "True mastery can be gained by letting things go their own way. It cannot be gained by interfering." Energy surging through my body revealed that this was an important message. Without question, I had lived this message in the moment. My question now was, "How do I live this message on a permanent basis?" I did not need an answer. Neither did I need to read any further. I intuitively knew that mastery had to do with practice.

Returning the following day, Lee expressed once again that Myla regularly put herself in extreme circumstances and then looked to others to rescue her. I took her statement as a reminder to remain appropriate. Myla was in bed with the baby, still weak, in tears and ready to rely on me now that I had returned. I took a deep breath, at the same time acknowledging the challenge at hand: it was a perfect setup for a co-dependent relationship to manifest. First, I drew the baby from her arms and held him close to my heart. Then, with great sobriety, I requested that she begin to take some deep breaths. From there, I helped her move deep inside *herself* to a place in consciousness where she could look at her issues in a more empowering way, as I had learned to do with myself. So many times I had read the passage in the book, **The Prophet,** "Pain is the cracking of the shell that encloses our understanding." Here I was again witnessing the truth of that statement. I also understood the value of the flood of tears springing forth from Myla, understanding that once the floodgate was open, the tears would flow as long as necessary. I felt incredibly honored to play a role to Myla reaching for empowerment—deeply humbled also.

Afterward, she inquired if I would continue to work with her. I was required to comply, but at the same time, I was also required to make clear under what conditions I was allowed to do so; she had to draw her strength and her answers from

Reflections on Limitation 293

within herself. I did not have her answers. Neither was I to be used as a crutch, only a support. (I had no idea that I was setting a precedent to work with many who would follow.) Most assuredly whatever this was about, it was meant to be. That did not make a strange inner disconcertment any easier to handle.

I allowed Gavin to continue to enter my personal space when he came for a couple of subsequent visits. From encounter to encounter, our interaction increasingly took on the nature of a psychic battle, reminding me of the sci-fi novels that Adam had always found so enticing. While Gavin babbled ideologies, he sent out his energy like a weapon, and as unfamiliar as I was with this kind of behavior, this seeming warfare, I would put up my energy as a defense, always intuiting his strikes in time to thwart a hit. Indeed, I was terrified of him. Yet I knew that somehow this time—whatever "this time" meant—I had the true power, the strength to use it, and he was not going to get it from me, regardless of his tactics. The more effectively I met and neutralized his challenges, however, the more aggressive and power-hungry he became.

Prior to one of his visits, I was instructed to give him my meditation stone, the old river rock, which had led me to Something, and to a clearer understanding of myself. The stone was no longer essential for me to make a deeper connection, but between my remaining attachment to it and my feelings toward him, I was disinclined to surrender it. When I finally did acquiesce to directions, I was further instructed to tell him that he was to pass the stone to Myla, along with the message that she was to tell him who I was before he handed the stone over to her. I thought these were strange instructions, and also an absurd means for the stone to get to its new owner. Nevertheless, with the opportunity to obtain information about me, Gavin would certainly pass the stone on to her. He readily took the bait. Once in Myla's possession, the stone became an important meditation tool for her and, from that point, for reasons I neither understood nor questioned, I was no longer required to work with Gavin. In fact, he mostly avoided me.

Myla's work took the form of her walking through deep-seated childhood issues—an alcoholic father who sexually abused her from the time she was an infant to the time she began her menses, and a mother who condoned the predicament by begging ignorance, sacrificing her daughter to avoid having to meet her husband's sexual appetite herself. I focused on staying removed from judging her. Rather, I sought to understand how these situations occurred, and how we, as females, were so susceptible to behavior patterns that did not serve our growth: how situations related to the patterns feeding into them lifetime after lifetime—like my relationship with Carl being influenced by a previous shared lifetime. More than I could imagine, working with Myla was allowing me to see much more clearly what Carl and I had been acting out. All told, into whatever understanding I was tapping, it left me with a certain inner-nausea.

For myself, I wanted to believe that I was close to closing the door on my childhood issues. I knew people who had been working on such issues for most of their adult lives and appeared to be no better off for their efforts. After a while, reading the host of inner child self-help books on the market had put me off. Enough was enough. I saw no value in forever coddling the inner child, attempting to meet its needs or maintaining a focus on keeping it in control, when life was about more important matters. Neither did I see a point in maturing the child within me. From the start of my therapy, my focus had been to simply transcend childhood issues—transcend my human limitation altogether. Along with reaching further into understanding relationship issues, a pertinent personal benefit of working with Myla was the opportunity to obtain a more coherent perspective as to how childhood issues affect and influence our lives.

Myla's strength began to blossom as her fears began to wane. I was clearly seeing that I personally had to do nothing, nothing but keep myself out of the way and let my role to the moment define itself. I was barely aware, however, that as I worked with her I was learning "my work"—barely aware that I was beginning to live the message in the Aboriginal woman's quote that had so attracted me: "If you have come to help me, you are wasting your time. But if you have come because you know your liberation is bound up with mine, then let us work together."

Working with Myla was natural. I began to realize the depth of my capacity when Lela was present during a session. Afterward, she kept querying me how I had learned to do what I did, how I knew what to say and when to say it. I had no answers, but just the fact that she wanted me to teach her made me feel important; it was more obvious than ever that such a need was dangerous, especially when following the path that I was on. It was also frightening to assess how this need influenced most aspects of my life. I began to consciously attempt to side-step this chronic need for importance—recognition. Yet, more glaringly than ever before, it seemed to have a life of its own.

Myla had found the overall strength and courage to take a job as a massage therapist at the lavish resort hotel on island that attracted many celebrities. Since she trusted few people with the baby, I frequently took care of him when she was unexpectedly called to work. The considerable money she made helped lift her out of her squalor, both physically and emotionally, as well as spiritually. In every sense of the word, she was ready to move. As greatly as her fears had diminished, however, she believed that she lacked the courage to face Gavin. He would certainly not easily relinquish the advantages he gained by being involved with her: a continual supply of gambling and drinking money, personal access to her vehicle, as well as a white woman and a "clear-skinned" child to give him status in the community.

The day she definitively decided to leave him and move into a rental cottage in a neighboring village, she beseeched me to inform him. Her request immediately took me back to the moment when David, my hypnotherapist, had reflected back to me my need to extricate myself from the quagmire that I had gotten stuck in with Carl. I had had to address the situation alone. Without question, doing so had been terrifying. I could still readily make contact with that seemingly horrific moment when I had stood face to face across the kitchen from Carl, my throat restricting while a surge of energy bursting from my hands had pushed forth the words that would move me toward freedom. Viewing the situation from hindsight, I could clearly ascertain the advantage of having had to go solo through that experience. Unquestionably, it had been a rite of passage. Without it, I might never have been able to launch myself into this wondrous, albeit often excruciatingly intense, reality that I was living. How could Myla find her own strength if I intervened? Also, I could feel my blood almost curdle at the thought of coming between Myla and Gavin. Something about doing so felt deadly. I applied logic to the situation, inside and out, backward and forward, and over and over again. Regardless, how I attempted to find objection to my involvement, that I was to respond in the positive to her request held firm.

At the time of this discussion, Myla and I had been at Lela's, who now lived in a cottage at the bottom of the road from Gavin's and adjacent to my Gingerland school. It was from there that I initiated the task that was divinely put upon me. With my damp clothes clutching my body in the afternoon heat, while the rushing of my adrenals added to my discomfort, I climbed the steep road, the same one that took me to Max's. My impulse was to turn around and return to Lela's, to tell Myla to take responsibility for her own damn life. Instead, I put my attention on centering myself and separating from my fear.

As I had suspected, Gavin was absent when I arrived at his ramshackle dwelling, but I sensed him coming up the road on Myla's motorbike and knew he would appear shortly. Even before he got sight of me, he knew I was there; and I knew that *he* was aware of my presence. Once in contact, he asked no questions, as if it was natural for me to be there, but suggested that I wait for him in the house. My inner guard stood markedly ready to take action as Gavin haughtily strode in and claimed he had to bathe before we talked. Disappearing behind the curtain for a moment, he reappeared naked, his erect penis proudly displayed. I stood seemingly frozen as he stepped outside to wash. As I listened to him splashing water on himself, my mind flashed to my teenage cousin who had exposed his erection to me in the cow pasture so long ago. There was no room for the rage I felt wanting to take over. Nor was I going to step backward in fear as I had done as an adolescent, for I was unwilling to ever again return home soiled and shamed. I would not embrace helplessness. Instead, when Gavin returned, I stood tall and confident, and looked him deep in the eye, talking soul to soul where he could do nothing except listen. With great vehemence, I declared "Put your clothes on, Gavin, and your sexuality away; it has no influence over me." Our eyes remained locked. Without any warning, he moved again into the bedroom. When he returned wearing a pair of jeans, I continued, "Myla has rented a cottage and wants to live on her own. She needs to do this for her own growth except, as of yet, she lacks the necessary strength to inform you herself. I trust that you understand that she needs your support to make this important move."

These were the words that came out of my mouth, but coming from somewhere else, we both heard, "If you fucking mess with her, you'll have me to reckon with this time." (There was that "this time" again.) I did not understand from whence these challenges issued, or why I was so fearful of Gavin. I did know my fear gave him power. He agreed to not interfere but I did not believe him.

Without incident, Myla collected her possessions and moved safely into her own cottage. However, a certain inner tension, a haywire sense of suspicion, left me continually on edge. With serious commitment, she worked on her personal growth, actually day and night, until she became exhausted. She phoned or visited regularly. I continued to make it clear that I never gave advice, but I would always be there for her on the condition that she was coming from a place of her own strength—looking for perspectives from me, not answers or to be rescued. This required us both to walk a fine line. On occasion, when I did not hear from her for a number of days, it was clear that she had gone into resistance. She knew this also. It was not me to whom she was in resistance, rather what I reflected back to her, her own truth.

Initially, Gavin showed little interest in Myla or his offspring once she moved out. Free to maintain his own lifestyle unencumbered, he visited only sporadically—mostly when he was in need of money or sex, both of which Myla was unable to refuse him. Still, her inner strength continued to grow. Consequently, she was gradually acquiring clearer boundaries, as well as focusing her attention on leaving the island to begin a new life elsewhere. Gavin, sensing her changes, began to show up at unexpected times and then hung around more often, leery and apprehensive over his faltering grip on her and less self-constrained than ever before. Myla was becoming unnerved by his behavior despite her continued efforts to become a healthier person. More than ever, I felt I was reliving my divorce.

13

Scrutinizing the Nature of Human Relationship

In the meantime Bob, the Canadian professor, to whom I had admittedly been so attracted during the Christmas get-together, was shortly due to arrive on island. Since his departure, he had kept me abreast of his itinerary, and he made it clear that he considered me, as well as the rest of the environmental team, an asset to his work. It was evident that his real focus was on initiating a relationship with me. I believed that I had come to terms with the initial attraction between us and that it no longer held an influence over me.

All the same, making his way to my cottage first thing upon his arrival, it was apparent immediately that a force to the attraction remained. He was staying with a British volunteer on the far side of the island and, therefore, asked if he could store his gear at my place. He rationalized that this arrangement was much easier than dragging it back and forth via the bus. With only 200 square feet to my personal space, this left me walking around or over his belongings. I, in turn, rationalized that because of the opportunities he was providing for me, and because that's what people do: "help each other," I could not refuse him. He was soon spending more time at my place than away, expecting a free meal or use of my shower, interrupting my quiet and making it quite obvious that he was anticipating a romance. Further, it had come to my attention that I was far from the first female on island to whom he had taken a shine. It was unquestionably essential for me to establish clear-cut boundaries, regardless the cost: or else I only had myself to blame.

One night, escaping the noise of a volunteer get-together, we two sat together on a huge rock watching the stars glistening down on us from the heavens. Contrary to what he thought the moment was going to bring, I firmly stated that I had no interest in creating any kind of relationship with him beyond platonic or professional. His disappointment was visible as I spoke, but I managed to remain detached. Whatever the charge had been between us, at least for me, it dissolved the moment I articulated my truth.

I was more fully recognizing that every action I took came with a price. Still, I had not explained, softened, tried to fix, or concerned myself with his reaction. I was willing to accept whatever the outcome, whether or not it meant losing certain opportunities, even his friendship. Having spoken honestly, from a place of truth, I walked away with a sense of integrity, which accompanied a sense of empowerment, a sense of freedom and certainly a sense of relief.

Despite the brush-off, Bob remained intent on recruiting me to assist him with his field projects. I welcomed the idea for it allowed me to be in nature more intensely, to learn field techniques and more fully explore the jungle, beaches and ocean. He was obtaining his diving instructor's license and, needing practice-teaching experience, he offered me, as well as others, the opportunity to learn to dive. I rationalized that the cost was manageable and knowing that I retained an intense fear of deep water, I had no choice but to accept. The class ended up consisting of a young local man, Timothy, the third male Peace Corps volunteer on island, and me. The cost was significantly more than originally quoted, however, for Bob and his instructor were at odds, and we students became the scapegoat upon whom they acted out their issues. Besides this, I quickly learned that Bob was much better at creating ideas than carrying them out, and many of his outings were ill planned, delayed, something far from what he claimed they would be or just simply a waste of time. The lesson for me was to see that some part of me lingered in need to take men's words at face value—the old "a-promise-is-a-promise" syndrome.

Max, too, had maintained contact with me following his departure. His letters were noisy and newsy, or else reminiscent of the wonderful time spent with me, along with adulations of how wonderful he thought me to be. Once he sent me what he called a care package. He phoned ahead to tell me to expect it and made a big deal about taking good care of a poor Peace Corps volunteer. When it arrived, I found his care package actually consisted of an old satellite view poster of clear-cut areas in a wilderness track that he had proudly participated in bringing under protective laws, a hand-made belt and bolsa left from a trip that he had taken to Peru with his wife twenty-five years earlier, and photographs of his northern estate. Although I attempted to be appreciative, the fact that he sent me merely odd bits of extras from his life and photographs as a means to impress me with his adventures and wealth left me nonplused. Further, when he phoned, he would talk for a few minutes and then say, "I'm going to hang up so you can call me back. We'll talk on your nickel for a while." It seemed quite strange that he viewed me as needing care packages, but expected me to pay for international phone conversations that he initiated. When I questioned him why he phoned and wrote, he responded that he did not want me to forget him.

He need not have worried. As much as I tried, I was having great difficulty succeeding with that effort. In fact, to my dismay, I had begun to hear that I had to leave John for him. Being directed to move from one man to another made absolutely no sense considering that I was also continuing to be reminded that I would never have a gender relationship. My resistance to acting on the dictum had been steadily mounting as it continued to be given more and more strongly, and regardless of my opposition, the message was the same. The thought of leaving John so horrified me that I would weep in resistance until exhausted. After all, I loved him from a place indefinably deep within my heart, and try as I might, I could not dismiss my certain dread that he would die if I left him.

John and I were forever on the phone trying to manage our relationship. After going around for hours, we inevitably came to the same conclusion: we loved each other. Partly because I was unable to be unequivocally honest and partly because I thought it none of his business, I had withheld from him what had transpired between Max and me. Neither had I shared the nature of my guidance. I wanted to sugarcoat the entire situation to protect him from pain, which also enabled me to avoid feeling guilty or dealing with my fear of ending up with nothing. Actually, I was keeping him in limbo and myself in prison. Avoiding the dictum and trying to find a comfortable position, I continued to convince myself that I could love both men if I chose, and willfully contended that love had nothing to do with sex or relationships.

During the fall, the lead volunteer of our group had called a meeting. There had been general concern among all of the volunteers on island, not just Peace Corps, that the conduct of the two young women in our group was leading them into some serious problems, as well as possibly creating problems for the rest of us, particularly the women. Instead of valuing the concerns that fellow volunteers had for them, they both tore into us as if we were meddlesome gossips. We were stunned. Feelings of guilt clouded my certainty that one of them would soon be facing serious danger. For the moment, it was enough that one of the two girls had barely escaped two sexual attacks in two days—one in her home and one on the beach. For her safety, Peace Corps officials were reassigning her to another island. Although she'd had nothing to do with me during the course of our service and feared receiving an "I-told-you-so" from me, she landed on my doorstep when she learned her fate, hoping that I would act as an intermediary between her and Peace Corps officials in an effort to dissuade them from their decision to transfer her. I did what I could, and amazingly without judgment, but her fate had already been sealed. The entire situation left me with much on which to reflect. Certainly I needed more practice standing in my knowing and remaining detached from however it is received—and not go into the "I-did-something-wrong" routine. I could see where, in the end, I had acted maturely. I could also see how far I had to go in that regard. Most significantly, I realized that, despite my premonitions, some scenarios are meant to happen just as they are played out, even seeming tragedies.

Due to these incidents the entire female volunteer community was more than normally concerned for their safety. I was put off by my increased apprehension, as much as by my lack of freedom to go about on my own without the risk of harassment or harm. The other female volunteers were content to hang out together at their homes, in a restaurant or a safe beach. I needed the freedom to range and roam, and especially on my own when the urge struck. Lacking the freedom to explore the island my way or to seek solitude in quiet places off the beaten path often left me feeling like I was living in a box. I wondered, in my anger, if there had ever been a time or place on this planet where women could be safe from male aggression—safe to simply be.

Lela, my neighbor, would become an all-around reference for me in terms of male/female issues. Her recent move from Holland to live permanently with Amos, the man John had counseled at my party, was taking on dynamics that were more than interesting. She arrived on island accompanied by a man whom she had recently met and become romantically attached. She believed that she and her two men could create a life together, albeit she had not beforehand sought the views of either of them. Now both men were up in arms, and she found herself caught in an uncomfortable love triangle. I watched to see what my lessons were as she came face to face with what she had created. To my surprise, when she requested a perspective, I asked why she thought she had to sleep with either of them—a question that I had been dealing with personally.

Lela had not extricated herself from this dilemma when she was in the throes of yet another entanglement. Her situation provided the opportunity for me to witness the intensity of her sexual energy and how it magnetized men. I soon realized, as I observed her move from man to man, that her energy was a reflection of my own. Owning this was painful and humiliating. My unwillingness to accept myself as a sexual character or even to watch that part of me in operation was noteworthy. I did not know exactly why, but when I looked around me, whether locals or expatriates, what I most consistently saw was sexual energy running rampant. I rationalized that Lela and I were different though. The difference being that I did not fall into bed with every man that was attracted to me (or to whom I was attracted). However, the lengthening string of men sniffing at my door belied my rationale. Like a broken record, I prefaced every acceptance of an invitation with, "You understand I'm only interested in a platonic interaction?" Further, I insisted on paying my own way, hoping to diminish the possibility of my companion thinking we were on a date. I soon recognized my strategy did nothing more than sabotage my savings and leave me deflecting sexual advances anyway.

Amos had returned to island some years before, after having spent his adult life in Canada. He was a gifted poet and playwright, and had turned his backyard into a social center, where on weekends he provided entertainment. Occasionally, when I could no longer handle the isolation of the long, tropical evenings, I made my way across the street to seek distraction. His garden, with its tangle of mature tropical trees and bushes, seemingly always in bloom, provided breathing room, fresh air and a sense of safety otherwise unavailable away from the confines of my cottage. Most often, however, I isolated myself in front of Amos' television, watching CNN news to catch up with the happenings outside of my little Alcatraz, and also to avoid social interaction, especially when only men were present.

Sometimes Amos joined me at a table where I did my journaling. It took little time for him to begin using me as a sounding board. One evening, instead of his normal discourse, he unexpectedly disclosed—like Kent, my beekeeper friend—that he was in love with me. My first defensive thought was, "No! I haven't done anything wrong. I did not create this. I have only been supporting him in his efforts to sort out his life, and I fail to see how he could possibly confuse this with love." When I finally escaped the situation, I had little memory of how I had responded, other than I had tried to talk him out of his feelings, telling him he was still in love with Lela and projecting that onto me. Still, I berated myself, certain that this was what I deserved for seeking relief from my loneliness instead of staying home where I belonged. Struggling to avoid fixing the situation, knowing I would only end up compromising myself all the more, and not knowing how to bring resolution—not knowing that I only had to see the lesson for what it was and let it go—I thereafter avoided retreating to his garden.

My original justification to learn to dive to overcome my fear of disappearing in deep water was replaced during my initial dive by an odd familiarity with this liquid dimension. I quelled my impulse to strip off my cumbersome diving gear and swim as free as I felt I remembered—like the dolphins. Timothy, my diving partner, had reservations when our dives took us to sixty and seventy, even ninety feet; but for me, doing so only fed my urge to go still deeper, and solo, just me merging with this energy-transforming world.

When Bob returned to Canada, we diving students were left to complete our dives with his instructor. This man previously had a dive operation with a local, but the two of them had parted company, so the instructor had recently struck out on his own. Considering that he was a hard-core alcoholic and a pothead, I questioned the safety of completing my dives under his supervision. Even so, somehow, I felt driven to become certified.

With my certificate in hand, along with the stipulation that I contribute to the cost of gas, the instructor invited me to join him when he went lobster diving. I considered this a rare opportunity; while he was off scouring the reefs for lobster, I got to explore on my own. I only had to stay within sight of the anchor line and to surface at the time he designated. Swimming in the deep allowed me to be one with my thoughts, and also one with my breath, a part of myself with whom, under these unique conditions, I acquired an incredibly more intense relationship. The thought of diving any other way than alone was repulsive. I became attached to diving, and put out hundreds of dollars to have John purchase my own diving equipment for me. Yet I knew, at some level, it was not something in and of itself, but only a lesson, a reference to something much greater than the physical experience.

The real price I paid to have this adventure, once again, went significantly beyond dollars and cents. This man who gave me license to dive my own way was totally chaotic and unpredictable. Our plans were often delayed or canceled. He frequently set anchor at a beach bar on a neighboring island to imbibe between dives. Before long, he was knocking on my door, wanting to hang out or borrow money, although he lived on a once-impressive estate on the hill (obtained after he divorced a wealthy woman). Here I was bailing out another man, or more aptly put, feeding his habits. To top that, he was edging his way into becoming personal with me, even when I had clearly articulated that I was already involved. Then there was the annoying issue of being seen as his woman. The cost of saying no to him was to sacrifice my unique diving opportunities. The cost of not saying no was to sacrifice my integrity. I had myself trapped once again.

My gender lessons continued when the owner of a day-sailing operation approached me about assisting him with chores in exchange for having time to snorkel during the sail. I had already been informed that this man was a salty, old Brit with a reputation as a womanizer. Nonetheless, I ignored this and focused on what a great opportunity this would be to learn more first-hand about the environment and what I was required to teach. It took little time to learn the routine. I was also aware that he felt that an attractive woman onboard was good for business. I would arrive at his house early in the morning to help him prepare the lunch he would serve on board and then clean up the prep. Next I would help him trim the boat, pick up his guests, get the lunch ready at the given time, serve it, clean up, and then maybe for an hour, I would be free to snorkel. By the time the sail was finished, the day was gone, but not my duties. He would then expect me to join him for dinner and I would feel obligated because of the opportunity he had provided for me. Invariably, after a few drinks, he had difficulty hearing me say no to his advances and I would become furious that I had to risk sacrificing myself to get something for myself.

At a musical performance one evening, Lela introduced me to a British writer whose acquaintance she had just made. He unexpectedly appeared at my door the following afternoon, asking to spend some time with me. His presence made me uncomfortable and I wanted him to leave, but, for the sake of propriety, I did the opposite and invited him in. Not far into our conversation, he claimed to be feeling ill and asked to lie down. Within a few moments he was asleep on my bed. I stood on the porch, listening to his heavy breathing and wondered how this could have happened. It was a normally hot day. Still I closed my shutters in fear that Miss Huff would appear on my porch wanting to share some mindless gossip, and would be provided, instead, with more fuel for her fires. Rather than asking him to leave when he awoke, as I wanted to do, again protocol reduced me to maintaining enough distance for him to get the hint by himself. When he finally did depart, I wondered why I was unable to simply enjoy his company, rather than being in resistance. More blunt than usual, the following day when he returned, I queried him about what he wanted. He claimed he wanted only to be friends, but I had become too cynical to believe that the platonic relationships with men I perpetually sought were possible. The next morning, pushed under my door, I found a poem from him that he had scribbled on a piece of notebook paper at sunrise on the beach before departing island.

I seethed with indignation as I read through the poem. How dare this man think that I was not a whole person unless I had a man! How dare he think I had my head in the clouds! How dare he see my body as fertile, ripe for men desiring to sow their seeds! How dare he try to define me! How dare he! How dare he! Within my outrage, I could feel deep inside of me a sense of being ravished—being eaten alive, piece by piece—along with an obsession to protect myself. I had no idea what any of this meant. I stuffed the poem in my bookcase, along with Max's, under lock and key, thankful that I would never have to show this poem to anyone.

My gender lessons now took a different twist when a professor with whom I had become friendly during the time I had returned to college, and who often used me as a confidante, especially in working out his complicated family issues (one of his adult daughters was suing him for allegedly sexually molesting her as a child) came to visit me as part of a personal journey he was undertaking. Prior to his arrival, I had informed educational officials of the potential opportunity awaiting. They, in turn, invited him to participate in an educational workshop occurring during his stay. Being of black ancestry himself, he welcomed experiencing a black culture in this manner. Disregarding a nagging annoyance over eating up my allowance to rent a car in order to make his stay comfortable, I felt his visit was beneficial for many people. But, to my chagrin, before he departed, he declared that he was returning to the United States to clear out his life in order to pursue a relationship with me.

Considering that he knew that I was involved with another man, I was flabbergasted that he did not think to ask me how I felt about his plans. I suggested that rather than sorting out his life to pursue a relationship with me, he might consider sorting out his life to develop a relationship with himself. That was not what he wanted to hear, and it became patently clear that whatever relationship I had thought we had was over. I indignantly dismissed the belief that I had led this man on or done something wrong to create this situation. I knew I was attractive, at least in an earthy sort of way, but I was certainly no bathing beauty, nor a fresh "pickin." And now I was desperate to know the force behind my sexuality.

One male encounter turned out to be the antithesis of all the others. Brian, the middle-aged, British man in charge of one of the foreign aid projects on the island, "Father Protector" of the British volunteers (the one whose date kept him away from me at my get-together for John) took considerable effort to become friends with me. He was a hard-drinking and adept socializer who, underneath his facade, was quite shy and isolated from his feelings. The way in which he managed his British sense of protocol to mask his feelings toward me was a marvel. However, he did claim that I never had to worry about him, for he was impotent, at least at the moment. I consciously focused on accepting him right where he was, yet continually challenged him on his beliefs. He often stated that he shared things about himself with me that he never divulged to anyone else. I had an inkling that part of my lesson with him was to relate to the person behind the alcohol—lessons I had failed with my parents. Further, as easy as it was for me to judge alcoholics, I owned that I had my own addictions.

An inner knowing gave some clue that, as much as I was reluctant to deal with myself as a sexual being, my male encounters were a vehicle for a greater understanding waiting for me. I was being required to examine the nature of sexuality in general. It appeared that people were, to varying degrees and regardless of gender, in bondage to their sexuality, whether by denial or, more commonly, using it inappropriately—to manipulate, entice, intimidate, subjugate and so forth. I did not understand why men and women had to relate to each other through gender lenses.

And I certainly did not understand what truer purpose sexuality, as well as relationships, were meant to serve. However, observation left me more than ever certain that gender relationships were little more than destructive.

Lela's and my interactions provided the opportunity for me to look closely at the dynamics of female relationships. As much as we professed to support each other's growth, and as much as we did, we also were often at odds, particularly in terms of how to live who we were as females. For instance, one minute Lela was chastising me for being too outspoken with my beliefs. In the next, she was pressuring me to speak to one or another of the lost souls she attracted. Yet, whenever I made a definitive statement, her typical response was a flat, "No, that's not right!"

It was a challenge to know how to respond to a person—much like Carl—who dealt in absolutes. I viewed Lela as a powerful female and encouraged her to live that power. As much as I encouraged her, however, I struggled with my need for her to live her power in order for her to be where I could obtain a reflection of myself from her. Also, there was a part of me, a stranger until now, that I recognized was jealous of her. This came out especially in social situations, when I watched how naturally engaging and charming she was—almost seductive. I recognized that it was no more my nature to be jealous than it was to be angry. But the jealousy was undeniably present at times.

Overall, I was seeing that as long as women operated through gender identity as opposed to feminine power—between which I was only beginning to discern the difference—they could only compete with, rather than nurture and support, each other. The minute I put on make-up or perfume, or wore an outfit for reasons beyond my own comfort, I was putting myself in competition with other women. Instead of focusing on presenting myself, I needed to learn to be myself. It was time that my appearance became of little importance to me. More than ever, whatever the situation, I began to more closely observe the dynamics of female behavior and interactions, wondering how we had all lost sight of who we really are.

One day, during a routine pre-dusk visit to the beach, I met a local woman who was the president of an adult education organization. As we exchanged pleasantries, she asked if I would consider teaching a yoga class. I told her that I was too busy but would give it some thought. I walked away telling myself that I was already writing a monthly environmental newsletter for the primary schools, and so had fulfilled my obligation to have a secondary project. Underlying my position, as I could see on some level, was a certain fear of this undertaking. What if they did not like me? What if I said something wrong? I ran into this woman again shortly after our conversation, and she informed me that she had the women lined up. I accepted her unilateral actions as an indication that this "opportunity" was primarily about walking through my fear.

Sobered, even disheartened, describes how I felt after the first class. The participants were unfit, unconditioned, overdressed, giggly and self-conscious (not to mention easily distracted). Sensing their first negative reaction to terminology I used, I carefully monitored my words. For instance, we did not "meditate," we went into "deep relaxation;" we did not "breathe in life force energy," we "breathed deeply;" we did not move into "higher consciousness;" we simply moved deep "inside ourselves." I taught the class, week after week, in the heat of the late afternoon, and became accustomed to their tardiness, their children playing outside, and to passersby who unabashedly stuck their heads in the door or windows, disrupting the class freely to give curious greetings to one or another of the women.

Yet, in an amazingly short time they shifted from their kindergarten-like demeanor to being self-confident, and committed to further wellness and self-understanding. Beyond the yoga experiences, they asked me to teach them to swim, which for them was a giant step in trust since, some years before, a ferry running between islands had sunk and fatalities had left few locals unaffected. (Ironically the incident had not been a strong incentive to learn to swim.) Miss Huff assured me that because people had not forgotten, there was scant chance that interest would be sufficient to maintain a swimming class. Even without the stigma of such a mishap, it was not a cultural norm to swim, especially for women.

Fortunately, the other female volunteer, Jane (who in the past had had little to do with me unless she wanted or needed something) was a physical education and swimming teacher, and at my behest, agreed to participate in teaching the women to swim. As with yoga, the first meeting revealed what we were actually up against, for most of them had never been in water deeper than their ankles—"sea bathing," as it was called. On top of this, wearing bathing suits was culturally unacceptable. The weight of their apparel alone—dresses over pants and tee shirts over dresses—if they should happen to fully submerge themselves, was obstacle enough. Since Jane had never dealt with such circumstances and I had no idea how to teach swimming to anyone much less fear-laden (albeit committed) women, my first suggestion was that they take off as much clothing as they felt comfortable doing. Then I began coaxing them into water deeper than their ankles, then on to deeper than their knees and so forth. So, again, I learned to do by doing. By the end of the first session—we beheld a miracle—every participant was floating on her back! This had been accomplished by my first holding them, one by one, supine in the water, and then instructing them to relax and take a big yoga breath just as they were accustomed to doing in yoga class. Much to their surprise, as well as mine, they would automatically become so relaxed that I was simply able to remove my hand without their notice, while they continued to remain relaxed as well as afloat. Jane was amazed by the experience and asked me how I knew how to do this, but I was as amazed as she was. I did know that having had the trust of these women (and honoring that trust) was a considerable part of the success. I had successfully rebounded from my first failed efforts at teaching in a Caribbean classroom; I had learned that success was dependent on working with my students at their level. I had tuned into these women and started to work with them exactly where they were at, not where I wanted them to be or where they wanted to be, and that had been the primary key to this moment of success. And I had done this naturally. I could have cared less if they ever became good swimmers. I cared about them being comfortable enough in their environment to explore it.

Next, they wanted me to teach their children to swim. Then they wanted a walking club, which I finally informed them that they could handle on their own. One wanted me to teach her to ride a bike, while another wanted to learn to drive a car. They were an inspiration and I was getting a taste of what it was like for women to truly support one another. I also was clearly beginning to recognize that once I had mastered a situation, I became restless (even bored). Up from within me came a relentless yearning (for fulfillment, for the next step) that could not be set aside or avoided, but demanded realization. I could have easily let someone else take over my classes, and on one occasion was actually convinced for a moment that someone had been provided to take my place.

In spite of needing and valuing my solitude, I still confused it with isolation and loneliness. When I had quiet space, I continued to run from it, characteristically ending up in noisy, meaningless social situations where I felt more isolated than if I had remained alone. I needed someone with whom to converse, someone who shared my expanding metaphysical insights and who could help me validate these phenomena that I was increasingly experiencing. I painstakingly continued to subdue my urges to seek distraction, but too little avail.

My diverse messages continued to arrive from all directions. One came through a conversation with Timothy, my diving partner, with whom I had developed a close connection. He explained that a psychic friend of his, an elderly man, had told him that his soul mate lived in the vicinity of his home. The psychic even gave him his soul mate's name and address. The fact that Timothy was in his middle twenties and this purported soul mate was then fourteen left him to do little more than satiate his curiosity by driving around the block where she lived a few times in an attempt to get a look at her. He questioned whether he should forget this matter and get on with his life, or abstain from further relationships until his soul mate came to an appropriate age for him to approach her. I thought his story was bizarre, and I had no idea how to respond. Yet the discussion had greater significance, made known to me by an energy hit occurring during its course.

The little I had read about soul mates indicated that a soul mate was the penultimate in gender partners, a celestial coming together of a man and woman to live in perfect love and harmony. I had remained in the struggle to hang onto John, despite all indication that I was meant to do otherwise, and hoped, as I owned the message coming through the exchange, that John was actually the one who was my soul mate.

Another "you are a teacher" message came through a book that John had sent to me. The only part of the book that I was actually required to read was the title, **The Reluctant Shaman.** Although I did read the entire book, I found it to be a replication of other such books popular in the new age circles. I argued that I was *not* a reluctant shaman. I was forging ahead in my lessons, whether as fast as was expected of me or not. The message continued to taunt me, "Reluctant shaman! Reluctant shaman!" I persistently responded with the same defense. The message came back, "Have you claimed your voice? Are you speaking your truth? Are you living your power?"

It took little examination to find the truth. I remained afraid of being seen or heard, of standing up in a crowd. I had even initially cowered from teaching a simple yoga class to the locals. My voice came out in a whisper. I still lived in resistance. Although less often and with less impact, some part of me still thought I lacked the strength, as much as the self-worth to fulfill whatever was being requested of me. I did not want to be this way. I was healing and growing as fast as I could. I wanted to be open to my lessons, however endless or challenging they felt. Nonetheless, my growth did not seem fast enough for the Divine force that perpetually held its steady bead on me.

Timothy loaned me a book, **Mr. God, This is Anna**, wherein was contained yet another message. This book was one man's true account of a little girl named Anna who had come into his life and turned it upside-down during the short time she was with him. This little girl appeared to have a direct connection to God. This came through in her insatiable curiosity, her endless sophisticated questions and her close connection to nature. Reading her story proved to be excruciatingly painful for me, enough so that every page was tear stained. I did not quite understand the story's true impact. I did, however, keep sensing myself as this little girl, as if I had merged with her at a deep level, even by simply holding the book in my hands. The message that my connection with her was an indication that I also could speak to God increased chapter after chapter. But my relationship with "God" was so troublesome; I was unable to know how to respond to this message. Still, when I went to sleep at night, I found it a comfort, as much as a necessity, to keep the book, with a sketch of Anna on the cover, next to my bed.

One sultry night lying secure inside my mosquito net—my own sacred shroud—I listened to questions as they formed in my mind: "If I ask why this power, this Einstein power, is given to me, can I have an answer? If I ask where my experiences are taking me, will I be given a response? Is it simply that blind faith is required of me? What happens to me in my sleep? Am I being rejuvenated? Am I being prepared? Am I being restructured? Is the love now quietly radiating from my heart the same force that moves me through my lessons and on to a greater truth not yet fully revealed to me?" The acknowledgment was provided through an intensification of energy. Whatever the nature of what I was feeling, with a flow of tears welling forth, I humbly gave thanks—which had become a routine each morning before I arose and each night before I entered sleep. On some level, I understood that the regular charge of gratitude was more coming *through* me, through my heart, than from me. Clearly, my ego self could never get an inkling of the nature of this humility, this gratitude, which seemed to be almost one and the same.

The ocean became a substitute for my beloved woods. Because I felt a certain strong feminine energy from the ocean (like the woods), I referred to her as she. Like the woods, in whatever state I was when I came to the ocean, being immersed in her consistently returned me to a place of intensely quiet balance. I mainly swam by myself. When I did go with someone else, I felt disconnected and restless, even cheated. Unlike most other Caribbean islands, the beach was sparsely populated, especially during the weekdays or during non-tourist season. Sometimes, I had it all to myself; and I was always annoyed when "intruders" were present on "my beach." It felt necessary and it became my goal to become a strong swimmer. I never swam parallel with the shoreline, rather straight out and then back, and if any sailboats were anchored off shore, swimming out to them was my goal. Up to the present moment, I was intellectually unaware that the ocean symbolized cosmic consciousness, and my need to swim strong and far from shore or into her depths represented immersing myself in that consciousness.

Another obsession that overtook me, and which I took seriously beyond belief, was to teach myself to swim using both sides of my body in a synchronized manner, instead of being stuck doing only an awkward left-handed side stroke. My efforts took me back to my childhood when I was learning to skate and such. No more scooter reality for me. Only with great effort, concentration and time, was I able to master a right-handed sidestroke. I came to literally be able to feel my brain struggling—I called it brain cell confusion—as I worked to coordinate movement between arms and legs. Once I could swim almost as equally strong on one side as the other, I turned to practicing a regular swim stroke, moving one arm and then the other. Then I added the breathing, overcoming my fear of having my face flat in the water. This proved the most difficult. Put a snorkel on, however, and my fear vanished completely.

During one of Bob's (the Canadian biologist) visits, I lay stretched out on the beach absorbing the last rays of the day's sun while listening to him expound on the nature of commercial development taking place on the peninsula of our sister island. He spoke matter-of-factly of the destruction of natural salt marshes and inland lakes and the reconstruction of artificial ones in locations more convenient to a burgeoning tourist population. He went on in the same manner about the future of the entire planet being completely man-altered and artificially managed—no natural areas left. He rambled on, oblivious to what was happening to me as I lay beside him.

His words at first triggered an anxiety inside of me, and I found my hand mechanically tapping the sandy beach as he continued idly elucidating the rape of the local area. The force moving my hand increased until I was pounding the sand with my fist and searing pain shot through my head and eyes. I struggled to control the sobs silently racking my body. I was reliving my Smithsonian encounter: watching the violation of the earth. The more he talked the more deeply I moved into the agony of experiencing all the trees—all of nature—destroyed. I wanted to scream at him to shut up. Instead, I struggled to contain my tears enough to merely politely request that he change the topic. He was astonished that so seemingly casual a conversation could disturb me to such a degree.

That night, Einstein energy permeated my consciousness and electrified my awareness. I loved it. I hated it. It was dreadfully painful. When the energy subsided and

I lay limp and soaked under my mosquito net, I wondered what the parallels were of seeing again, first the Earth destroyed, followed by an infusion of Einstein energy. I pondered what he wanted from me, what I was meant to do with this energy, with his awareness. Operating from my linear mind I was unable to realize that my perspective was skewed, that while I was seeing Einstein as instrumental in my guidance, it was actually something greater using him as a reference point.

As energy continued to move through me to an ever-greater extent, I became that much more attuned to the energy of others. The shift in my energy began to manifest in the dynamics of my local yoga class, especially during my two yoga/meditation classes that started up through the request of a number of expat women who were keen on expanding their spiritual awareness. For example, I was told to place my hand on the back of one participant. As I did, I heard myself say, "This large lump here (in her energy field) leaves your body all twisted. See if you can straighten up." Hearing my words, she burst into tears. When her abreaction was over, the lump had dissolved. She then found herself able to stand straight and even touch her toes for the first time in her adult life.

The guided meditation phase of my yoga classes also began to intensify. More than ever, these meditations defined themselves as I was taken through them. They were invariably appropriate to the moment, and I knew I was deeply attuned, on a collective level, to all the participants. However, I mostly understood the importance of the moment when participants shared their personal experiences following the meditation. I could only minimally understand that the situations and experiences being given to me were reflecting back to me a sense of my own value. Because I had not learned to keep myself out of the way of what I was called to do, or out of the way of needing validation, I was as yet unable to distinguish between personal and impersonal value, that I was only an instrument, and nothing more.

While I was being bombarded from all directions with lessons, Max's late spring visit neared, and I grew anticipatory and nervous. I had previously written to him telling him that I was not his answer, that his answers were not to be found here, but inside himself. I further shared that I was a completely changed person. So, if he had expectations of picking up where we had left off, he should prepare for disappointment. I added that, in looking at him, I had seen a host of aspects of myself that needed attention. I also reminded him that I was uninterested in a relationship, only in living why we were brought together, this was despite still hearing that I was leaving John to be with him. According to him, his marriage was faltering to a standstill and a divorce was imminent. I accepted that I could have been a stimulus for the divorce, but I was certain I was not the cause. Besides this, I maintained a weird idea that I was little more than a sweet distraction from his problems.

Max phoned me from Puerto Rico, the last layover before he arrived, to ask if I was planning to see him; if not, he would avoid putting himself in a position to be rejected. I was half-amused, half-surprised that a man who had previously exuded such confidence could be so openly insecure. I assured him that we would be seeing each other whether or not either of us desired it. While I was clearly aware that our unfinished business together was only beginning, being seen with him in public remained a monumentally distracting concern, partly because he was still married and partly because I abhorred being viewed as belonging to any man.

We met for dinner the first night he arrived, at which time he claimed that he wanted to spend as much time as possible with me in order to get to know me. Although he had a host of adventures planned for us, he also spoke of a friend who was due to arrive within a couple of days, and a new project to complete on his unfinished house, as well as further work on his book. I observed that I was being shelved.

In order to give him the chance of walking away while it was still easy, I informed him of the nature of how I had lived my life. At the same time, I took note that there was much less force behind this habit. I also told him that I was uncomfortable receiving gifts. Giving had always been the easier part. Receiving remained trying for me. I had to admit, however, that a new understanding of giving and receiving was, although not in hand, at least coming into view. Besides having read literature on the subject, John had explained, when I received the stone from the astrologer at the psychic fair, that giving and receiving were the same. If I was unable to receive, I was unable to give and vice versa. I had never seen anyone living this giving reality, including John. I understood that there was a difference between giving and giving myself away. I also knew that my giving myself away was compulsive behavior. By the inner cringe I felt upon telling Max that I was not good at receiving gifts, I was aware that I had set myself up for some interesting lessons.

Since I shared the story of my life with Max, he shared his story with me. And on and on he went, in detail far into the night, until I struggled to remain awake. Among the many things he told me about himself was that he had a doctorate degree, and that his father had been a successful lawyer with his own law firm. Paradoxically, in the same conversation, he mentioned that his father had been an alcoholic who went on periodic binges, disappearing for months at a time. When I asked him how he had maintained this behavior and a successful law firm simultaneously, he suddenly began sputtering. I dismissed further questionable variables of his story, except when his friend arrived and I jokingly referred to Max as "doctor," he brusquely informed me that he had no doctorate, as if to quickly and unarguably settle the matter. In confusion, I pushed the matter, however he expediently defended that I had misunderstood. It was a challenge to doubt myself, to doubt that I had heard incorrectly, but I had always been a poor listener.

After initially meeting Max's friend, I mostly declined Max's invitations to join them. It was easier to say I was giving them time together than to own the fact that I felt thoroughly out of place and bored with them while they smoked marijuana and talked about how wonderful it would be to relive the sixties. When his friend finally departed he was ready to spend time together, or so he called it. Characteristically, he would phone two or three times to explain why he was running late before he finally arrived to pick me up. Other times, due to his lateness, he would request that I meet him at his place. This remained particularly awkward for me because his work crew usually remained on duty at the time of my arrival. Knowing Max's wife, they were as much unable to know how to respond to me as I was unable to relate to them. Habitually, I put aside my annoyance that I had taken public transportation and then had to walk a mile uphill, only to hang around for a thoroughly uncomfortable hour or more while he ran circles in his chaos. It would have been at least bearable if he had allowed me to help him straighten up or do the dishes, but he remained insistent that I just "enjoy myself."

The first time he invited me to spend the night, somewhere in the middle of the evening, he became noticeably moody, and without a clear explanation, excused himself, disappeared into his private study and closed the door. What amazed me more than his odd behavior was my sense of rejection as I waited for the door to open. What the hell was I doing there? Yet, when I readied myself to leave, he reappeared, just as suddenly as he had left, as if he had a timely sixth sense. He rationalized that since he was a writer, when he was inspired to write, he had to follow that directive. And I would come to learn that, while I spent much of "our" evenings on my own, in truth, he was most often smoking his pot.

The marijuana was especially an issue with me since, as a Peace Corps volunteer, I was under continual scrutiny, and already there had been a scandal around its use among some of the volunteers on our sister island. It was an accepted fact that the police, not only focused on the expatriate community, but also were known to plant marijuana as a means to make arrests. The police were rightly motivated since a cut of all money collected was given to them and expats could afford to pay the fines. Max was concerned, not that he was placing my welfare in jeopardy, but for his own welfare. These circumstances never deterred him, although he sought security by being especially friendly with his village's policeman, assuring him that he was clean, erstwhile purchasing the substance from the village Rasta, from whom the police most likely bought their own supply.

When it came time to be sexual with Max, I did not hide my reservations. And when I finally surrendered to his bed, I found little consistency in the way we came together. Sometimes our interaction was simply incredible raw eroticism. Sometimes I was sure that I was only meeting his momentary needs. At other times our coming together could be incredibly otherworldly. At such moments, I was certain that I was being cosmically impregnated. I could literally feel something being implanted and almost instantaneously springing to life in my belly, something that I began to refer to as star babies. Max loved the concept. He even claimed to be able to feel the conception as if it was taking place inside him also. These experiences were awesome and, for me, a reference point with regard to feeling a meaningful connection with him.

Little else about our connection, however, felt "right." Yes, we could have great fun, but how far could fun go? I wanted substance. I continued to try to convince myself that I was caught in some kind of temporary, mindless infatuation. I examined the enticements over which I thought I was allowing myself to be sidetracked.

This became a study in contradictions. I was impressed by his uninhibited lifestyle, and I loved his passion for life, but a deeper awareness told me that he was confusing his turmoil and his grasping for life for passion. As much as by his "passion," some part of me was seduced by his romantic notion of adventure, although I was aware that it was based on something lacking in his life. His wealth was also an enticement, although it was becoming apparent that he used it mainly to impress or control others. Further, I was also lured by the flattery and attention I received from him, even when I was aware of his fawning flippancy and ulterior motives. Exploring parts of the island with him that were otherwise unavailable to me was also alluring. Yet doing anything with him, more than not, was an ordeal. Some part of me thought I could gain a sense of importance being with someone who moved freely among the upper strata of society, even when I was unimpressed with the upper strata. I was unable to come to terms with the discomfort of being seen in public with him and I was becoming aware that he was not especially liked. The product of intellectualizing the situation—of dismissing my awareness in order to create a semblance of comfort—left me further removed from the real reason that we were brought together.

I greatly cherished one advantage of being involved with Max. Due to the nature of his estate being thoroughly removed from the larger community, I could doff my clothing whenever the urge hit, which was most of the time, and ramble around his house comfortably naked. He relished that I was so uninhibited. This came to haunt me early one morning when Max forgot to close the gate the night before. We were sitting on the veranda in conversation, he naked, me stripped to the waist, when I looked up to realize that a local man had walked in. Right there, I felt as if I was caught red-handedly engaged in the most God-awful sin possible. Knowing this culture was suckled on gossip from birth, I thought there was no way this incident would not be splayed across the island tabloids. Max quickly donned his shorts to reach the local before he was out of reach. When he came back, knowing that my concern for my reputation was of dire importance to me, he heartily disclosed that this would go no further than where it was now; he had taken care of the matter. I asked him what he said that was going to keep this man quiet. He gave me the lowdown but I was skeptical. I knew the man. He was a carpenter and had a shop adjacent to one of my schools and not too far from Mr. and Mrs. Remy; and he knew that I was a Peace Corps volunteer. I wanted to die. I could not imagine ever again walking past his shop without him, and all the local fellows who hung out there, talking under their breath. This incident would leave me traumatized for months, defending in my own mind that I had done nothing wrong, and at the same time telling myself that I got what I deserved.

When it was time for Max to return to Canada, he claimed to be madly in love with me. I certainly felt a deep sense of love for him, but I was too serious about something else to be blinded by romance. Following his departure, I realized how much personal energy was required to be with him and how glad I was to have my life to myself once again. I also noted that it was much easier to feel close to him in his absence than in his presence.

I hadn't told John about Max's visit, which felt exceedingly misleading. I had no idea what to think or feel. I questioned my honesty (or lack of it) and the guilt that followed close behind, which compelled me to examine the meaning of honesty itself. I had been taught to believe that honesty had to do with telling the truth—like a confession, coming clean regardless of the discomfort or guilt produced in the process. The concept of guilt and dishonesty rolled around in my brain and I played with the idea of which came first and which triggered the other. Most important, I was beginning to understand that honesty had more to do with how I related to myself than how I related to others. Honesty has to do with seeking a greater understanding from a situation, not trying to avoid anything. Honesty does not produce guilt or shame; it frees me from them, that is if I am able to remain non-attached to outcome. I had no idea why even the thought of being detached from outcome seemed like such an impossible position to maintain, why I manipulated to produce desired results, or why I still fell into a space of guilt about most of my actions, or lack of them. Ultimately, I was unable be honest with myself in this instance. My thoughts, feelings, desire, inner guidance and emotions were all knotted together with fear—fear of persecution. Only continued greater awareness could bring me to a place of living unequivocal honesty.

With my summer break coming on, John wanted me to return to the United States and travel to California with him to visit his family. This felt thoroughly uncomfortable and nonsensical since I could travel in the United States at any time. Neither was I inclined to explore the islands any more than I had already. I did not know what I wanted to do or where I wanted to go. Many volunteers traveled to South America, partly because it was inexpensive. I was interested in visiting Venezuela, but, since John had grown up there, he was disinclined to accompany me. Therefore he suggested we meet in Central America. That made no sense to me either, since the most viable way to get there was to first return to the United States. Going around and around, we were both confused. More than not knowing what I wanted, I did not know what I was *meant* to do with my summer, until one day while Timothy was debating where to spend his vacation, I unexpectedly asked him if he would like to travel to Venezuela with me. With little consideration, he agreed. I immediately berated myself for being too needy to travel alone and asked myself what I was doing traveling with someone, a man no less, who was close to my son's age.

John was angry when he heard about my plans, especially that I had made them without discussing them with him. We came to a truce when we agreed that he would come to island for a visit in the fall. I remained feeling out of sorts with my life, as well as with the idea of traveling with a youngster, as I considered Timothy. With so little enthusiasm, I failed to ascertain why I was considering vacationing at all. Yet I could no longer handle the claustrophobia of living on an island—rock fever as the phenomenon was called.

Adding to my distractions, my Peace Corps director unexpectedly called me in for a meeting prior to my departure. As habit, my impulse was to think that I had done something wrong. On the contrary, he presented me with a letter he had written commending my accomplishments, dedication and commitment to service, and added that a copy had already been placed in my files. How could I be flattered? If he knew the circumstances that actually supported the actions for which I was receiving his praise, he would change his mind.

He then proposed an offer, which he gave me the summer to think over. He was asking me to relocate to the sister island, to teach at a college for the upcoming year. I had known of this vacancy because another volunteer had shared with me the extent of his efforts to acquire the position himself. When I asked the director about the potential discontent that was being stirred up, he told me to give it no thought. But I did, for I was aware of the problems this volunteer had already created and I knew that he would likely turn the situation around when he found out, if I took the job, and make it appear to the volunteer community that I had, in some underhanded way, insinuated myself into the position he wanted.

Without regard to an annoying part of myself that was always looking for greener grass, I would have given no thought to refusing the offer. Now, pros and cons bumped against each other until I was entirely annoyed. First, there was the old force that claimed that if I did not grab onto this opportunity, I would be missing out on something over which I would later regret. Nonetheless, a part of me was afraid of the challenge. Further, I did not like that island. I had never felt safe there and living arrangements were difficult to find and would, more than likely, be double or triple what I was paying for my cottage, if available at all. This would put a dent in my allowance and, therefore, minimize other opportunities that my frugal lifestyle made possible. Also, the swimming beaches were located on a peninsula that experience had already shown were next to impossible to reach without a vehicle. That meant that I would never be able to just up and go swimming and, otherwise, the only other opportunities would be on weekends, which were when the beaches were most crowded. Further, on island I had a circle of acquaintances with whom I felt a semblance of comfort, something I did not have with the volunteers—American or British—on the sister island. There was my work with Myla, my yoga classes, my interesting contacts through the museum and my connection with Max. Overall, moving felt much more like a loss than a gain, although a part of me, admittedly, was becoming bored with most every aspect of my circumstances. In regard to this annoying part of myself that was always looking—for a challenge—for something more, I told myself that I needed consistency in my life, not further change. At the same time, I labeled myself a chicken, hanging as I was onto my fragile sense of home rather than opening the door to opportunity. Ultimately, the offer only added to my mounting frustrations.

A number of volunteers from other islands were on our plane to Venezuela. Timothy dodged considerable hazing from them about the nature of his sleeping arrangements with me during the trip, and such. I reminded myself that they were only kids and that I was here for reasons beyond their understanding. Still, I continued to struggle to dismiss my feeling of being out of place.

Even before I knew I would be traveling to Venezuela, I was compelled to learn Spanish. Both Brian and I had been taking lessons for some months from an American woman who taught Spanish and French at the high school level. She was the same manipulative, needy whiner of a woman who had made a seemingly generous offer for me to temporarily stay at her house while I was waiting for my cottage to be "readied." Further experience with this woman had revealed that she was a clone of my mother; and I was certain that in taking lessons from her, our involvement would become more cumbersome than it already was, but there was no one else who taught the language. My apprehensions proved true. As usual, I thought, "My God, I'm paying for this class, what more do I have to give to get what I need?" In the end, both Brian and I ended our tutelage.

Upon our arrival in Venezuela, Timothy and I soon learned that few Venezuelans spoke English. To make matters worse, when I tried out my newly acquired skills, instead of Spanish, to my great dismay, I discovered my words spilling forth in French (which I had taken for three years in high school). In public, even the simplest greeting came forth in French, while, when I was alone, Spanish wasn't a problem. Timothy had claimed all along that he had taken Spanish in high school, so I assumed that his skills would compensate for my limitation. When we found ourselves in a plight that revealed his handicap was as significant as mine, he admitted that he had barely passed. Feeling like a stranger was frustrating enough. Learning this left me feeling ready to explode. Nevertheless, what with combining our skills and carrying my pocket dictionary, we effectively, if not humorously in many cases, met whatever communication challenges came our way.

I quickly acknowledged my incorrect assumption that being off the rock and in a country the size of Venezuela would allow me space to be alone. Caracas, where we first landed, was a congested, bustling city and because there had recently been an attempted coup, armed soldiers were virtually everywhere. The pressure of sudden messages ready to be born became so unbearable to ignore at times I thought I would break out screaming right in public. As dangerous as it was, I sought out quiet spaces in remote corners of city parks where I could open myself up to receive them. One of the most disconcerting was, "No past! No connection! Nothing! You go with nothing." This message frightened me and made me want to go home; odd, considering I had no home to go to. Now ready to suck my own teeth, I asked if I was expected to wander the planet alone, surviving on little else than my self-reliance. I received an affirmative.

Traveling with Timothy afforded the opportunity for us to get in touch with the spiritual connection between us that I had earlier been unable to define. And I had a disconcerting and growing feeling that I owed him something. Also there was an understanding that I was to support him in finding a greater truth. My understanding proved accurate. Sometimes he would come to me to obtain a deeper clarity of a concept, such as doubt, after which we would intensely explore together to obtain a greater awareness. Other times, I would be given information to pass on to him.

After a week in Caracas, we took a bus to Merida, a city in the mountains. En route armed soldiers stopped us, entered the bus brandishing their machine guns, and demanded to see passengers' identifications. I was unruffled and, on the contrary, stifled a strong impulse to confront them for intimidating people who were merely going about their business. My impulse was ludicrous if only considering the language barrier. The benefit of being detained in such a manner was to become more fully aware of this confrontational character inside of me. The twenty-hour drive, otherwise, was uneventful. Timothy and I sat in the very front of the bus where we were able to observe the changing terrain, the rampant pollution and environmental destruction, as well as the comings and goings of passengers. The bus driver played an Anna Gabriel tape over and over during the entire trip, and the young woman sitting across the isle sang along, totally uninhibited, when she was not dozing. I liked that.

I felt freer and safer and able to breathe more easily in Merida, although, it too was a bustling place. I immediately checked out the parks. Whether there or elsewhere, I spent considerable time studying passersby. More than young people hanging out, there were numerous parents and children, and quite often grandparents, taking afternoon or evening strolls together. On my island, rather than families being together, the women mostly hung out in church together managing the children, while the men hung out at the domino table or rum bar. My observations made me profoundly aware of how my childhood propensity to study the nature of family had never slackened. Deeper, it reminded me of the time I had written the passionate letters to both of my parents saying that I no longer considered myself a part of their family, that I had been divinely informed that I would create my own. All told, I exited this moment feeling more than ever intensely alone in the world; but this sense was creating much less discomfort than I would have imagined. On the contrary, it was somehow reassuring to be given note that being without a sense of family was no longer as painful for me as it had been in my past.

One day we took a tram up into the mountains to an elevation over ten thousand feet, then hiked twelve miles through cold drizzle to a remote village where we stayed at an inn, abundant with warm hospitality, however lacking creature comforts. While I addressed my backpack of rain-soaked clothes, thankfully a German woman, who was also a guest, provided me with a couple of warm sweaters to wear. It was freezing cold at night with wind sailing through open spaces around doors and windows and hot showers were unavailable. My allergies flared, but I refused to let my condition interfere with my urge to explore the open spaces here in this remote location.

Wandering aimlessly along the foot trails worn deeply into the mountains by generations of local inhabitants, I was perpetually amazed and even more distracted over the dire extent of environmental degradation—sides of the mountain literally slumping away—that had occurred from long-term, excessive and thoughtless agricultural practices. As was my habit wherever I traveled, I tried to imagine the appearance of the area when it was still pristine. The dearth of trees bespoke that such a condition had been long absent. Regardless, I pushed aside any sense of sadness and embraced a sense of gratitude for having been given this time to roam.

Sitting on a hillside above the village where Timothy and I had hiked one day, I moved into the energy that was calling to me. Once removed from my linear mind, I first heard, "You will do no more traveling in your life. You are giving up everything, as you know it, for the love of God." Instead of waiting for a deeper understanding of the message, I reacted. It seemed that I had been giving up so much as I moved deeper into what was calling me, but to no longer travel was incomprehensible. Besides, I was unable to decipher what the love of God had to do with my life. I was fighting furious and screaming with resistance. "I've just found the courage to come out in the world and be open to adventure, and now you're bringing my life to a standstill?" I demanded. If I had been able to remain open, I would have understood that I was being told that currently my only necessary travels were to be internal, inward—traveling through Cosmic Consciousness, Einstein stuff. My ridiculous abreaction to this message confirmed that I was at present unready to own that space. Yet I had already moved into it on another level, and on that level I was already aware that I was bored and distracted with physical travel. The greater truth was that I did not need to go anywhere or do anything to be okay with myself. At a human level, however, I was still maintaining a tourist mentality.

One night the inn owners invited their guests, a group of a dozen people from around the world, to join them at a community get-together. It was enjoyable to watch the activity from my corner of the room. Young and old alike danced about in the middle of the room as ethnic music blasted from a boom box. At one point, a young man approached me to dance with him. I immediately felt myself freezing up and shutting down. He pulled on my hand with kindly encouragement. Timothy smiled encouragement from the middle of the dance floor. Even when some part of me desired to join in, I was unable to budge. He finally surrendered his efforts. I wanted to find a quiet, safe place to hide. Not knowing though how to gracefully depart, I stayed in my corner. The walk home under a glittering night sky provided time for reflection. Why had I been so afraid? I could have never felt more welcome and safe in a situation. No one there would have cared that I danced with two left feet.

The next morning, as I stepped out into the sun to find warmth, I watched the community converging on a central location below me. With curiosity, I joined the crowd gathered alongside some sort of a barn. Here a large, healthy-looking bull was tethered on a very short rope to a post in the ground. Men were busy sharpening knives and gathering buckets, obviously preparing for the slaughter of the bull. My first impulse was to turn around and walk hastily away. A greater force deemed it necessary for me to stay. As two men held a container beneath the head of the animal, another deftly slit a vein in its neck. The creature appeared to be in no pain as it stood there in an immovable position slowly bleeding to death. I connected to its energy. It was calm and free of fear—far different from slaughterhouse situations about which I had read or experiences I had had growing up on the farm. I stayed to the end, watching the young and old alike who were involved in the event and I was enticed by the definite cohesive bonding in this community. I walked away feeling grateful that I had put my own potentially self-limiting attitudes aside.

After returning from the mountain village, we rented a car to explore an area of national parks farther along in the mountains. It was then and there that certain of my aggravations with Timothy, that I had been stuffing, came to a head. For instance, when I was buying a snack or drink, I felt obligated to ask him if he would like one also, at which time I paid for both. However he rarely reciprocated. Besides that, he borrowed money until he went to the exchange, but sometimes failed to reimburse me. I kept telling myself not to make it a big deal, that he was a poor young man and the least I could do was make his trip a bit easier. Or I would assure myself that I had misread him, that he was not actually taking advantage of me at all. Rather, I was distorting the situation and setting myself up for trouble. I was unable to ignore my mounting annoyance at his letting me take care of him. I was aware that his mother and sister were continually sending him care packages and had come to the island on vacation. At that time, I had seen first-hand how well they took care of the man of the family. Now, by the time we rented the car, he had only enough money left to get back to island, so I paid for the rental and further sleeping accommodations, as well as the cost to repair a dent he put in the car. He was keeping a running list of how much he owed me but, by my estimations, his accounting was in his favor. Finally, I began to keep tabs myself. As usual, I was caught between feeling used and feeling like I was making a big deal over money, when it was not that important. This time an inner force was requiring me to be adamant about being reimbursed. It would take him a year to pay me off and he was visibly annoyed over his indebtedness to me. Although it would have been easier for me to simply say forget about it, in the end, I neither felt justified nor guilty for my actions. It was merely what I had to do to continue reclaiming myself from my own debilitating patterning, and in this case, money was the vehicle. Nothing more. Nothing less.

During the mountain drive, we toured an observatory. It was refreshing to have an English-speaking tour guide who was actually from the United States, for he agreeably answered my endless questions about the area and its people. When the tour was complete, Timothy and I wandered from room to room observing the displays, while I kept hearing that I was to understand more about the Universe. I was clueless to what this meant until my gaze fell on a painting of Einstein. His energy instantly beckoned me. I was grateful that no one was around other than Timothy, for once again, driven to make eye contact with Einstein, my feet began to move from square to square, not stopping until I finally located the magic tile. Much to my curiosity, however, I found Einstein's eyes out of focus. Puzzled, I whispered to Timothy to stand where I stood and also look into his eyes. He saw the same: one eye looking one way, the other another—a strange binocular, bird-like vision.

Energy frying my senses indicated I was to stay alert to further understanding.

Again I found my feet moving around on the square tiles of the floor, continually looking into Einstein's eyes with each move. Finding the exact location necessary to view Einstein's eyes in focus, it happened—another dance with the Universe! Einstein's message was that I was out of alignment: my compassion went in one direction, while my understanding went another. In order to live my true power, I had to bring them into balance. Beyond my ideas of the significance of this experience, I would be taken through myriad experiences before my compassion fell into alignment with my understanding—before I was living from my heart.

Shortly after, while wandering along a mountain trail shrouded in dense mist, I was informed, "You are a catalyst. Being a catalyst is your talent. It is your gift to the world." Although the magnitude of the energy the message contained made clear that it was of great consequence, I questioned its meaning. Contrary to my beliefs, I was being told that I *did* have a talent, if being a catalyst could be considered a talent. My definition of catalyst was something that affects change or produces a reaction. How could *I* affect change and what was the change? As with all information given to me, full understanding would only come through living it. If I was unable to understand the message, I certainly was unable to grasp that I had already been living the message my entire life.

One night I was drawn from sleep to write down my dream messages. I was told that now I was acquiring a greater sense of self, I no longer had to struggle to be me. "Me" is not static. "Me" is dynamic and I must constantly be open to change. I was further informed that John was not my enemy. He was to help me move to a place beyond my present understanding, to a place closer to Max, which would be a means to move closer to myself. Max was a part of the process; he was not the end. This made me aware of the triangle, the corners representing Max, John and I, which had been manifesting in my dreams. Beyond my bafflement and apparent resistance, I thanked the Universe for communing with me.

After spending a week on the coast, where it was unbearably hot and I became ill, I was ready to leave. We returned to Caracas, however, and stayed a few more days before returning to the island. For me, the trip was complete at the time I received the last of my messages. After that, I was merely biding my time, wrestling with my restlessness and wanting a Coke (which was unavailable, at least wherever we had ventured). Besides being given a barely manageable amount of information, my vacation to South America forced me to further assess my insecurities.

There was no question that I returned from Venezuela a different "person." Although I was incapable of discerning how different, I was at least able to grasp that I was more detached from "my" life than I had been when I had left for vacation. I had made a commitment to know who I am. At that point I was hardly able to remain abreast of understanding myself—a constantly changing concept.

14

A Race for Understanding

Immediately upon our return from Venezuela, Timothy informed me that there was a Terry Fox Run to be held on the island in three weeks. The ten-kilometer marathon was a charity event to raise money for the hospital. Being a jock, there was no question whether Timothy would sign up, but he caught me off guard when he kept insisting that I join him. I had many excuses: I was out of shape; my running shoes were worn out; it was not customary for women in the culture to run; my running shorts and top were too skimpy to wear publicly. Besides, three weeks was too little time to train. Timothy would have none of it. Instead, he continued to apply pressure.

His persistence brought to mind a powerfully vivid and detailed dream that I'd had a few months prior. In the dream I was in a so-called "primitive," African culture, a young and willowy girl who loved to run, mostly for the sense of strength and freedom—to run like the wind. Due to cultural restrictions, however, running was only acceptable for men. The men tolerated my foolish inclinations until I reached adulthood and could outrun them. Then, while I was out one day, they hunted me down. Collapsed from the chase, they circled me, cursed me for breaking tribal tradition, for shaming them and then, without second thought, speared me to death. I silently studied them as I took my final breaths, which angered them all the more. I died deeply regretting having been born a female.

Presently, I was realizing that the dream was actually a past life memory coming to light. The message coming with the realization was, "Do not forget that you are a running woman!" With these words resounding in my head, I understood that there was an important understanding waiting for me within the context of running the race.

Hitherto having been discreet about being on the beach, undressing and redressing in careful modesty whenever I went for my swims, I now trained for the race wearing only my bathing suit and perhaps a tee shirt, running like the wind, barefoot on the sand. I felt incredibly free wearing so little and running so fast. Feeling the sand absorb the impact of my weight reminded me that I had run barefoot before. When I became overheated, I had the advantage of simply jumping into the water to cool down. Initially, my running caused a riot of attention—which I hated—with the local men who hung out on the beach. However, once they learned of my intentions, they began to encourage me.

Feeling that I could not accept pledges until I was confident I could finish, I set out to practice run the course ahead of time. Brian, my British friend, agreed to drive me to the starting point, which was the airport, and then drive ahead of me, stopping at significant points to keep me abreast of my speed and distance.

At the crack of dawn the day of the race Brian again drove me to the airport, where I stood in line to receive my number. Afterward, I took my expected place on the edge of the gathering. I was surprised, but pleased to see that many locals were participating. My attention was quickly drawn to a lanky, adolescent local girl. What most impressed me was that she was running barefoot.

Another focal point was that my period suddenly started. My first reaction was to curse the untimeliness of the circumstances, along with the annoyances that came with my gender. Determined that I had come too far to let a bit of blood deter me, however, I proceeded to the airport washroom where I stuffed the tissue that I had brought for my allergies into my underwear. The end result was a precarious sense of security and an uncomfortable lump between my legs. I headed to the starting line more than ever motivated to be successful.

As the signal sounded, a charge of ebony, bronzed and ivory-skinned bodies sprinted off ahead of me. Knowing my most important advantage was to pace myself, I hung back rather than push to be in the initial rush of runners. The barefoot teenager charged ahead also. It was a beautiful sight to watch her lean, dark-skinned body in motion. She reminded me of whom I had been in the memory. In contrast, I plugged along as fast as my stubby legs could carry me.

The sun had been up for only a short time, but it was already sultry. Sweat ran down my face and glued my shorts and shirt to my body. I made an effort to run in a manner that would not disturb the lump between my legs, but still compulsively reached down to feel the inside of my legs for blood. At the one-mile marker, I had my one and only chance to stop at a bathroom. Despite my fear of a mishap, I convinced myself to keep going.

As others continued to surge ahead of me, I surrendered obsessing over my condition and focused on maintaining my pace. Brian informed me that I had two miles under my belt, then handed me a cup of cold water and words of encouragement as I passed where he was waiting in his car along the side of the road. I would see him again in another two miles. I watched my mind dance from one thought to another as I continued on and took in now familiar sights along the way.

Somewhere down the pothole-riddled, curvy road, I realized that, instead of being passed, I was now beginning to overtake a number of runners who had initially been in the lead. Turning a bend, I further realized that I was approaching the young barefoot runner, who was now clearly running out of energy. I gave her a few words of encouragement as I passed her and maintained my stride while trying to ignore the sudden impulse to slow down and wait for her. Realizing that I was being given a directive, I argued, "I've put much effort into preparing myself and I want to beat my personal time. I'm not waiting for anyone." The response came as a pain in my side. I had a choice to ignore the pain, as well as the directive, and keep going, but having connected to the girl's energy, I knew that I had to detach from personal motivation. Therefore, I slowed my pace and waited for her to catch up. Initiating conversation, I learned that Lydia was thirteen, from a country village, and running the race because she had promised her mother she would bring her a trophy.

Competition was and still is a vital facet of the cultural mind-set and greatly supported in the educational system, particularly in sporting events. I had witnessed students sabotage each other's successes as a means to win. I had also seen parents wrangling over official outcomes of races and beauty contests and other competitions. Nevertheless, this girl's focus was less on winning than on fulfilling a promise to her mother, and suddenly, I felt committed to supporting her.

As Lydia's energy slowed, I saw that her chance of fulfilling her promise was slim. Her drive was waning and she was contemplating dropping out, while the pain in my own side remained present but manageable. I attempted to assess the situation. Instead, I found myself professing, "Lydia, we'll run this race together. Simply set a pace and focus your mind on crossing the finish line. *We* can do this." My encouragement became her belief. Yet she was unaware that she was my encouragement, as much as I was hers. We continued on, side by side, engaging in conversation as best we could through labored breath. Meanwhile, her male cousins drove ahead and then periodically stopped, waiting for us to catch up. When we did, they would give encouragement to Lydia and then drive off, waiting a bit further down the road.

Realizing our success was in sight, we quickened our pace as we approached the resort hotel where the race came to a finish. We then joined hands, half-laughing, half-crying, as we ran down the lane between rows of hibiscus and coconut palms. Our joined hands were raised in triumph as we crossed the finish line. Women from my local yoga class, Timothy and Brian, were all there to cheer me in. Within the confusion of bystanders, Lydia and I hugged each other while Timothy enthusiastically informed me that my timing was great, and he was sure that I had come in first place for my age category. Whatever the nature of the joy I was feeling at the moment, I was sure it had little to do with coming in first place. I excused myself and headed straight for the bathroom to remove the bloody wad from my shorts—akin to a pebble in my shoe—and freshen up. In the quiet moment I realized how far I had come since my adolescent years to be able to take this situation so readily in stride. There was nothing any longer serving in viewing my gender as a curse.

After the last participant had crossed the finish line, officials began to announce the winners, who then stepped forward and received their prizes. Timothy received a first place trophy. I did also. Lydia's name was not called. Hoping to offer consolation, I pushed through the crowd to reach her, but before I could do so, an official returned to the stage to announce an oversight. Lydia's name rang out. She had, indeed, won a trophy for her mother. I was the oldest female to win; Lydia was the youngest.

I was high on my accomplishment—on the entire experience, but the attention that came with winning was accompanied by a certain unshakable discomfort. I stood in the background watching the crowd milling around, my eyes finally coming to rest on the woman who had come in second in my category. I followed through on my impulse to congratulate her, but when I extended my hand to her she indignantly recoiled. Then she asserted that the only reason I had won was because she hadn't counted on any competition and, therefore, had taken her time. I was dumbstruck. Eyeing her second place prize, a tee shirt, which I considered much more useful than a trophy, I suggested we swap. It was a fair trade since she was certain that she could have beaten me. She sucked her teeth at this, claiming that the only way for her to accept the trophy was for the two of us to run the race again. As if she was joking, I laughed courteously, and then eased myself from the situation as graciously as possible.

I departed the experience contemplating the real rewards. I had run, even competed. Unlike the memory, rather than being condemned by the men for running, they had supported me. And as much as many fellow females had supported me, I had been unsupported by one. Fooled by the gender of the woman who had taken second place to me, I failed to see that she had been the first man in my past life memory to plunge a spear into me. And when I had congratulated her, historically speaking, I was actually adding salt to the wound. It was the memory, the unconscious, cellular influence, which left her certain that she could have bettered me and left her reacting as she did. It was also the memory—fear of persecution—that left me trying to make amends, however it might have come across. In contrast, through encouraging Lydia I had vicariously supported the runner in me who had previously been put to death.

The race, as much as winning it, and beyond the broader lessons, also reflected my need to be noticed as important, or special. Some part of me was thrilled when I heard that my picture was displayed at the resort hotel along with the other winners. That same part of me was also thrilled when I was recognized on the street as "the woman who won the race." Intuitively, I knew that I could not live a greater purpose while maintaining a need to be recognized. Neither could I support a competitive streak, no matter how small, and live a greater purpose.

With summer coming to an end, I half-heartedly turned my attention on preparing for the new school year. In the end, I had declined my Peace Corps director's offer to teach at the college on our sister island. I had given much thought as to whether or not to accept, from "shoulds" to desires and needs, to my perceived lack of responsiveness to my director's expectation. Eventually, I set aside my ruminations long enough to get in touch with my deeper knowing which revealed that I was not meant to relocate. Whatever the price for my decision, I was willing to pay it.

Our environmental team's first year was considered a success by both the school and our area Peace Corps director. Jack had acquired a grandfatherly approach to teaching that worked for both him and his students. As for Brett, he had gained confidence through his experiences despite his thoroughly negative attitude. For me, it had taken much energy and effort to keep the program functional and our team together. An inside view would have made it clear that there was only a thin veneer to our success, and I was the thin veneer.

Our local counterpart teachers and head teachers, as well as my team, were taken by surprise during a meeting when our area Peace Corps director announced suddenly that Peace Corps officials had decided that our environmental team would no longer be working directly in the classroom. He asserted that our efforts were not supporting a sustainable program. There was no question about the validity of his position—that had been obvious from the start. Yet, although we were being told what we could no longer do, we were given no directive as to what was presently expected of us. Teachers in attendance, as well as head teachers, articulated their support for our present program, as well as their dislike of the change. Jack and Brett were up in arms as well. I was largely indifferent. A hot debate ensued until our director finally declared that the directive would not be changed.

It was a major complaint among the volunteers that programs were not designed to be sustainable and it had been clear from the start that ours would be no different. This was reinforced by the fact that, local people went into teaching mostly as a stepping stone to a more lucrative career position. Further, the majority of local teachers saw our value only in terms of the amount of time they were free of responsibility when we took over their classrooms. It was not unusual for a teacher to nap, paint her nails or leave to visit a neighbor while we conducted class. Adding fuel to the impossibility of a successful program, many teachers retained a belief—despite a year of us teaching otherwise—that being environmentally conscious was largely about not littering.

From the start, I relinquished the idea that the goal of our program could be accomplished. Instead, I focused on doing whatever seemed realistic in terms of making a difference with my students and then gaining whatever experience I was meant to personally receive—practical or spiritual—from the situation in general. This included my involvement with various environmental efforts supported through the museum. In fact, I already had a job offer following my Peace Corps commitment from a woman who spearheaded an endangered sea turtle reclamation program. As for my Peace Corps assignment, I was unquestionably bored.

After the formal meeting, Jack, Brett, and I met. Both of them were reconsidering quitting. I could understand Jack being disheartened over the change in circumstances, yet since Brett avoided the classroom anyway, and had continually criticized our program, I had more difficulty than usual tolerating his complaints. Unwilling to go at this alone, still holding on to a need for our team to appear cohesive and successful, not to mention being a sucker for a challenge, I took it upon myself to pull this matter around.

"Our" plan, for which we were given the blessing of both our supervisors, was to meet on a daily basis to develop curriculum material, which we would transfer to the teachers during a series of teacher training classes and field trips. One week a month, as we had done in the past, we would take our monthly environmental newsletter into the classroom. Our Peace Corps director and our educational supervisor reconfirmed they would be in regular contact with us. Since they had seldom done so before, I knew they would not do so now, although the second floor of the museum was designated as our central work location.

I did not want to tackle the curriculum alone, nor did I want to abandon working on the other more exciting projects—my babies—which I felt would not be done well without my continued involvement. Therefore, I suggested that we all work on each project, starting with the curriculum, and once that was developed we could begin to introduce the supplementary materials to the teachers. From there we would develop the field trips. In between, we would create the monthly newsletter. Since neither of my colleagues knew how to initiate any of the projects on their own, they readily agreed to the arrangement. At my suggestion, Brett agreed to take charge of illustrating material to supplement the curriculum and Jack agreed to research needed information, which left me to create a format and develop the study units. By comparison, I had about eighty percent of the responsibility. Brett remained disgruntled and mostly sat around harping, when he showed up at all. Jack was committed, although he was more a bother than an asset since his chatter interfered with my focus as he threw pages of hand-written material (lifted verbatim from resources) at me faster than I could keep them organized. Besides this, given the heat, the regular interference of visitors, and having to work without a computer, productivity was, at best, slow and arduous.

Regardless of the many Divine messages informing me that I had to leave John for Max, forgetting about Max was what I adamantly attempted to do since his last departure. It made no sense to me that I had been told that I would never have a relationship with a man only to be told that I had to leave one man for another. From first receiving the dictum, my resistance continually mounted. Thoughts of leaving John continued to fill me with horrific pain. I would weep and beg to have the directive withdrawn. All I ever accomplished was to exhaust myself.

John and I continued to try to iron out our relationship even while I knew there was nothing to resolve; I merely had to let go and face head-on whatever was waiting. This door had to close, but how? Why couldn't I let go? It had to be more than simply my fear of being left with nothing. If I let him go, it felt as if I had to let the love between us go. I couldn't do that.

One night, meditating on the Philosopher's Stone, I found myself energetically placed directly inside of John's body. From this position, I experienced him making love to another woman. Before I completely went to pieces, I heard, "How many different ways does the dictum have to be presented before you surrender?" My only request was to be removed from the situation. First, however, I would have to say, "I release him." I was unable to honestly say that. Therefore, the matter continued on and on until I wanted to scream for relief. Instead, I raged in anguish, "You want me to do what I can't do. I don't want to be responsible for his death. He'll die if I leave him." Finally the demands lifted, but I was aware that I was only being given a grace period. I had been shown that John was ready to pursue other relationships, and our relationship, as we had known it, was over.

Another night, all alone on a hill overlooking the ocean above where I was house-sitting, the message came again, this time gentle and embracing, yet very firm, as if from a loving parent, "Let John go. You have to get on with your lessons. Your lessons are with Max now." I crumbled to the ground sobbing, again full of anguish and confusion, wondering why I was unable to relinquish what was already finished. Being drawn deeper into my anguish, I distinctly began to hear the words to the song, **Amazing Grace**. I could never have felt more like a wretch than in that moment, and certainly more lost and blind than found. Standing outside of my emotional dilemma, I knew John's charm would make attracting another woman easy; he'd already had many women in his life. Yet I remained unable to rid myself of the deep inner feeling that he would be unable to live without me, and that I was responsible for his well-being. In my present state, I was ripping us both apart and sabotaging my forward movement. Rising above my emotional drama, I focused on lovingly releasing him from my life. On some level I was successful; on another I was not. My confusion was created by my misconception that I had to sacrifice the love between us to release the relationship when, in fact, what was being asked was that I step out of my history in order to step into the truth about relationship, as well as love. There was nothing to sacrifice: sacrifice is a human concept. There was much waiting for me however.

While I was in this state, Lela pulled into the drive on her motorcycle. On one hand, I needed and wanted someone there to support me. On the other, her support was limited, as well as limiting, even annoying and distracting. Beyond surface appearances, she had little awareness of what I was experiencing. What she had to offer was what she most often had to offer, which was "drop all this emotional stuff, calm down and pull yourself together." Ultimately, I had to move beyond a need to be comforted (or any need at all). I needed to be self-reliant, to totally, without question, rely on my own guidance and learn to fully accept whatever was happening, knowing that when I was ready I would have whatever understanding I needed.

Once I had myself together, Lela pulled from a bag a wall hanging I had requested she make as a gift for John. Although she was an accomplished seamstress and acquired extra income from making dolls, this had been her first attempt at such an undertaking. I had given her no directive other than to follow her heart. The product of her effort was a baby being born from a lotus blossom, stars shooting across the sky like firework, and a mosaic of greenery all around, reminding me of a tropical Garden of Eden. The imagination and detail that she had put into it was amazing, though I thought it an odd theme to give to a man as a gift. Lela and I speculated about the significance of the baby and the nature of the birth—we failed to recognize it as an omen—but came to no conclusion. Just as interesting, from the commission, Lela's creative focus moved from making dolls to elaborate wall hangings, many of which would be an overt expression of her inner healing process.

John's late summer visit provided the opportunity for me to formally finalize our relationship. Nonetheless, as strong as my intent was, I still could only dance around it. I remained unable to definitively say "no" to his sexual interest; yet neither could

I surrender myself. Instead, I avoided the inevitable by maintaining a busy schedule. My continued lack of integrity horrified me, but I remained powerless to be honest. John recognized my position anyway and began flirting with other women, which I took as a show of hurt, as well as a show of preserving his footing in the circumstances. Whatever it was, I watched my attitude, knowing that I could not keep him hooked and release him at the same time.

Coming home from dinner with him one evening, I began examining the messages that had recently been coming to me, messages that, in the past, I would have needed his assistance to decipher. Without missing a step as he walked along beside me, he bluntly interjected, "I think you're a fake." I knew he did not mean this, that it was his pain speaking. I felt more anguished than angry as I turned and looked him squarely in the eyes. Our gaze held strong, while a sense of determination overtook my anguish. Then the message came tumbling forth, "You don't have to believe in me. But I do. The whole world is dependent on my believing in me." I had no idea what my words meant. However, John was impacted enough to feel faint and he dropped to the steps of my porch. Under a starry Caribbean sky, with the sound of the ocean hitting the shore across the street, I drew myself behind him and wrapped my body around his. The deeply held connection between John and me was suddenly alive. As if this was a setup for something else to happen, my hands were abruptly lifted upward, landing on his shoulders, where they were then held firmly. Energy began running through them full force, filling his body with vital energy. He melted against me murmuring, "I'm not usually the one to receive the healing." Silence held us for a moment as he moved more deeply into the energy being provided for him. Then I stated, "Now you can sense for yourself the energy that moves through me. I am powerless over it. It dictates my life. I accept this as best as I can." I wanted to ask him not to hate me, but I was unable to bring the request forth. Overcome, we remained sitting on the front steps of my little cottage, Miss Huff a stone's throw away and probably listening. I only knew that I loved this being more than I could ever fully comprehend; much like a cross to bear. It was in this space, and on some level, that we both understood that I was not leaving him for Max; I was leaving him for something else. This knowing did not make the situation any easier for either of us.

He had to be at the airport long before sunrise to catch his flight. Putting aside protocol for once, I declined accompanying him. I thought it was because it would be too painful to travel back to town alone. I made arrangements for a cab, and then set the alarm to make sure that he arose on time. Returning to my cottage after seeing him to the waiting cab in the predawn, I observed the trail of his presence: a half-eaten cookie left on a chair, a tee shirt under it, the refrigerator door ajar, his bathing suit and cologne in the bathroom. I wept free deep anguish as I put my little cottage in order, working through the ego death that was upon me. He had played such an integral role in supporting me healing my damaged heart. Now, the damage seemed irreparable. As best as we could further release each other, we would do so through an exchange of letters. Yet a deep sadness, a shadow somewhere over my life, held John in my every thought.

Shortly after this, Bob, the Canadian biologist, returned. He had fallen out of the good graces of the museum curators and their supporters due to certain indiscretions with a female intern, and he was now mostly trying to keep his research and educational programs alive on his own. He had confided to me the entire situation as it played itself out and forever sought my feedback. He was realizing to what extent his sexual behavior impacted his life, but he failed to see that his professional services were no longer being sought. During one of our conversations, I listened to him making decisions regarding his future. His plans, however, were incongruent with what I was hearing at a deeper level, "Traveling on a dead end road." Whatever that meant, it felt foreboding.

Max had wanted me to meet him in Puerto Rico for two days in the spring on his way down to the island. As the time approached, however, his life became too complicated for that to happen—thankfully, for I was uncomfortable with his request. Currently, he was asking again. He claimed that he wanted to introduce me to his favorite hotel in old San Juan, about which he was writing a story; it was a romantic place to stay. I tried to convince myself that I should be thrilled to have such adventure in my life. Except my reservations were strong, especially since getting permission to leave island, even if for a weekend, required a formal written request given in advance, and since time was short, I would have to sneak away—not an easy task. Nevertheless, setting aside my reservations, I agreed.

I soon learned that nothing was much different being there with him than on island. He spent much of his time in a helter-skelter shopping mode, buying building material here and there, and then proceeding to the shipping yards to make certain the handling of his goods was all in order. When that was out of the way, his focus turned to interviewing the hotel manager, as well as taking photographs for his article. Impatient with his distractions, and feeling wretched about being with a married man, I ventured out on my own in an effort to find a place to make my deeper connection. The old walled fort, a historic site down the street from our hotel, proved to be the perfect place.

When I went shopping, an ingrained sense of obligation moved me to purchase a thank you gift for Max, when actually the hotel stay was free for him and I had paid for my own airfare to meet him, as well as my share of the meals. Meanwhile, my irritation was tempered by an intense, but odd moment of coming together that was precipitated by him divulging a personal moment from his past. The act appeared to be a sexual encounter, but was really about something that I was clueless to identify. Even Max was taken aback by the profundity of the experience.

When I returned from my get-away, I learned from John that Gertrude, the computer teacher who had taken efforts to befriend me, was planning to visit me over the Thanksgiving holiday. I found it curious that she had made such plans without my knowledge or agreement and felt that having her and Max around simultaneously was more than I could handle. Max was already incensed that she would arrive just a few days after our return from Puerto Rico and that I would allow such a disruption in our personal time.

Gertrude was not a person who adapted easily, and for that reason I let her sleep in my bedroom, while I slept on the cot in the living room. Even before she had been there one day, her two large suitcases brimming with clothes and other travel necessities were scattered throughout the cottage. It rained every day that she was on island, and she was changing clothes as quickly as they became damp. She complained about having to take cold showers and disliked the limited variety of food that I could provide, but was disinclined to eat out or go to the grocery store. She was disinterested in learning about the island or my life there. Further, she disliked Max the moment they met and was not discreet about it. Next, she claimed to be broke and on a strict budget. Yet her main focus was to shop, even if it meant flying to St. Thomas. When I asked her why she had come, she responded that she had nothing else to do during the holiday. Despite this being a sobering slap in the face, I still was ensnared enough by obligation that I spent a couple more days expending time, energy and money catering to her needs and desires before I let enough be enough. At this point, she changed her itinerary and left a day earlier.

The long overdue reckoning occurred the night before her departure. By choice, I would have gladly let her walk out the front door with no further ado and consider the issue over, burying my resentment. No distractions readily available for either of us, we sat across from each other in my tiny living room. The tension between us was heavy. I could feel myself squirming inside, my throat chakra painfully restricted, as I wondered what exactly was being required of me. Direct honesty remained unfamiliar, as much as uncomfortable territory for me. Nevertheless, there was no way out of this coming-to-terms, for guidance was watching closely, asserting that I had to reclaim the parts of myself that I had abandoned to the situation.

Finally I opened the door by asking Gertrude if she was ready to discuss the issues at hand. She began by attacking Max and then me, and the way I had changed. I held firm to my boundaries, adamantly unwilling to play counselor or get entangled in her criticisms. Each time she articulated one of the many ways I had disappointed her, I merely asked her to tell me what was behind her issues. Over and over, she relentlessly shot verbal bullets at me while I steadfastly deflected them, until finally she admitted that she was jealous of me. She added that having seen Max and me together made her realize what was lacking in her own relationship. Our friendship—better stated, our co-dependency—ended when her stay ended. I found it interesting that I willfully refused to feel guilty or try to fix her discontent. Still, an unsettled feeling signaled that something between us was unfinished. After borrowing Max's vehicle to drive her to the airport, I returned my cottage to a state of order and focused on continuing with my life. I was not overly pleased in regard to how I had handled this encounter, but I was able to abstain from berating myself, for I knew I was getting better at living from a place of integrity.

I now had Max's visit with which to contend. He claimed to want to make up for lost time, but when I was with him, as usual, he spent more time communing with marijuana than with me. He accused me of interfering with his writing, his building projects or else he accused me of taking him away from spending time with his local friends. Because he was chronically late for everything, plans were frequently modified, rushed or abandoned or took a back seat to visiting a friend or returning early to receive an important phone call. Rather than our relationship being a priority, he fit me into his schedule. When he felt guilty for believing he neglected me, being with me became an obligation. When I finally came to terms with my fears of being seen with him, he suddenly made rules about how we were to interact in public, and then acted as if we had come upon the rules by mutual agreement. Adding insult to injury, I soon learned that his rules were meant only for me. When he did not want me around, he was clear about that also. He romanticized our relationship and objectified me, professing, "With a beauty like you by my side, I can be the envy of every man."

Yet, even in my presence, he was brazenly philandering with women, particularly the locals. A number of women had warned me about his womanizing tendencies. Once, I told him that the owner of a plantation inn, whom I had gotten to know, informed me of his behavior, as well as a description of the explicit advances he had made toward her. He claimed that she had taken his friendliness incorrectly and before I knew it, he was on his way down the hill to put her straight. I had no question that he was covering his trail. Nonetheless, I felt guilty that I had "opened my mouth" and provoked his discomfort, and most likely the innkeeper's too.

Any expectation I may have had of a free ride was brief. Max claimed to be a self-made man, but more than rumor told me he was living off his wife's wealth. He carried with him pictures and journal articles he had written about his two estates and pulled them out to impress visitors, yet professed to me to live from hand to mouth. I could not take this as anything less than a means to finagle or communicate to me to have no expectations of him. He regularly asked me to pick up supplies for him on my way to his house and frequently borrowed money until he went to the bank and such, but seldom reimbursed me. One way he conveyed that I was expected to foot a bill was for him to find he had forgotten his wallet or misplaced his credit card when a dinner check or the like was presented to him. When I put aside my insecurities enough to ask why he failed to return to me the money he borrowed, he argued that it was my responsibility to remind him that he owed me money. His behavior was not specific to me. As much as he presented himself as a magnanimous character, he manipulated almost everyone to get his needs met.

If anything, he had me scrutinizing my own behavior, and finding a part of myself that addictively sought to get something for itself, regardless how insignificant, even for nothing, if possible (despite my fear of receiving, despite my belief that nothing was ever free). "Why?" I asked myself. I did not need to dig deep to find an answer. That part of me was ultimately seeking a sense of worth—Daddy issues: if you give me something, then I know I'm loved: the greater the value of the gift the more I know you love me. In truth, "I" did not need anything from anyone, but "I" was at a loss to know how to subdue that lesser part of me that was in need of being validated. Once again, whether or not I liked it, Max was reflecting back to me aspects of my own dysfunctional nature.

Much of how Max painted his life and the adventures he planned for us were, at the least, distortions. Consequently, any enticements I may have entertained or cherished dissipated the more I was with him. One condition that had completely turned around from when we first met was that he was not only willing, but expecting me to support him in his many projects, as opposed to insisting that I enjoy the environment while he got around to having time with me. At first I was flattered by the opportunity to feel as if we were sharing an experience, but I was soon reduced to following him around taking orders as if I was a member of his crew. At sunrise, he would say that if I helped him all morning, then we would spend the afternoon at the beach. Most often, an hour before sunset, with both of us exhausted and hungry, he would tear recklessly down the mountain in order to keep his promise.

One day he informed me that he was having a cocktail party that weekend, but I was not invited, he demurred, because some of his local friends who were invited would feel uncomfortable with me present. If I had ever felt rejected, this left me feeling worthless. I attempted to stifle my hurt, except it was uncontainable. Subsequently, he softened his attitude, saying I could come, but I had to promise that I would refrain from assuming a hostess position. So, my choices were to stay away or stay in the closet. The more he tried to rationalize his point the more I fumed. I proceeded to keep my distance after that, sulky and off-center, claiming that if he wanted to see me, he knew where to find me.

Outside of struggling to not disturb the peace, my anger was reaching the explosive stage. I recognized that I had to more fully learn to openly express my anger, to allow it to have a voice without believing that I was breaking the rules or being bad. Max was a perfect vehicle for me to practice anger expression because almost everything he did made me angry—more appropriately stated, triggered my anger. It took only an initial encounter to get my footing. I forewarned him about my intentions, and was sure to add that I considered my anger my problem, not his. He hated having to deal with me in this context, with me openly saying, "Now! I'm angry and here's why..." Habitually, he would ask me how long I was going to be angry. And I habitually replied with great huffiness that I intended to be angry for as long as I needed to be—maybe a few minutes, or all day, or perhaps until the end of the week. With all the practice he provided and having become accustomed to my routine, we both often ended up laughing in comic relief.

Sometimes my anger was less easy to diffuse, and occasionally, I would storm out of his dwelling swearing that I was finished with his manipulations. Yet, a force greater than my understanding would consistently push me, in one way or another, back into his life. Once after having called it quits and not having seen him for a couple of days, I was pushed to the window of the classroom where I was teaching. Experience had already proven that if I glanced out I would see his house conspicuously overlooking the village. All it took was one quick glance to be sucked deeply enough into his energy to become frozen in space and time, and abandon my classroom responsibilities. I was powerless to refrain. This time I heard, "Take him the tickets that you bought for the two of you to go to the school function." I argued, "He can go buy his own damn tickets!" Each time the message was repeated, I argued. As could be expected, my students were keeping an eye on me, and one brought me suddenly back into the moment by asking me why I was staring at Mr. Gamble's house. As the school day ended, I heard, "It is now time to complete your duty." I ignored the message and headed for the road to catch a bus to town. My efforts were wasted when a Divine force literally turned me around and pushed me up the steep hill, past braying donkeys, my school students, the rum shop and gawking men, across the field and onto his property. When I arrived, he was sitting on the veranda smoking a cigarette and appearing to be lost in thought. I quickly pivoted on my heels, hoping to exit before he turned around, but he was already aware of my presence.

Our intermittent cosmic sexual encounters where I felt like I was being impregnated were what persisted as a reference point. Sex but not sex; I could not explain what was happening. I only knew that I consistently walked away feeling locked in what seemed to be a weird time warp. Max often played a song from a tape I had given him that went, "When I grow up, I'm going to marry me an old man. We're going to have a hundred and one babies..." He loved music in general, however this song triggered something inside both of us, and left him animated and joking about us having lots of babies of our own. Somehow, this song about having an endless string of babies had something to do with these moments of cosmic conception.

At other times, there could be a great chemical exchange between us, and I could be deeply erotic—"pleasures-of-the-flesh" erotic—and physically engaged. This was great for a while, but I wanted and needed something more—a deeper intimacy. When I was not fully engaged, Max would become upset with me, demanding, "Do I have to dance by myself?" One day I erupted with, "Sex is always on your terms!" To my surprise, he became irate, retorting, "Don't think that I'm going to be a John to you." Rather than holding my ground—looking more deeply into the nature of his response, seeing that I had caught him off guard and exposed—I slunk off to examine what *I* had done wrong. Then seeing that I had done nothing wrong, I berated myself for cowering beneath his wrath instead of standing in my knowing.

Nevertheless, above my exasperation over my emotional state, above my turmoil with John, above the fact that Max was not yet free of his marriage and impossible to understand, I committed myself to live the reason that we had been brought together. My commitment did nothing to make what was happening any easier. I struggled between sexually surrendering myself to make the relationship operable, and resisting giving him anything. If I thought the tough broad stance was all I needed to be around men, presently it only served to confuse me as much as surrendering myself did. The anger I projected onto Max was really the product of my sense of helplessness. If I could not escape this relationship, at least I wanted to fix it—bring it to a higher level of functioning—so I could be comfortable being in it.

However, this was not about fixing anything; it was about living something all the way through to the understanding.

Adding to my confusion, as I walked down the beach one evening after a sunset swim making my cosmic connection, I was presented with a vision of a skinny cowboy. When the vision persisted, I moved into it. I realized this was a replication of the vision of a skinny cowboy that I used to have in my adolescence. As I watched, Max's energy gradually overlaid the cowboy vision—right down to the English Leather cologne. I was being shown that he was actually the cowboy I had envisioned in my youth, the one who would gallop up on his white steed and free me from my mundane life by carrying me off into a world of great adventure. I dropped to the warm sand to get a grasp on the meaning of what was at hand. All I could think was, "What a wonder. Way back in my youth, I was somehow cognizant of Max coming into my life?" The truth was that "way back" went further back than my youth. I was in a memory, one in which the promise of fulfillment had never been attained.

My feelings of wonderment over this awakening were suddenly cut short by yet another vision. This one was of the numbers six and eight dancing in my field of inner vision. Puzzled, I played around with the numbers. A date? No! An age? No! Years? Yes! Years until something? Yes! As I understood the vision, the numbers had to do with Max's death. He had six to eight years left to live. How I could be shown a vision of the man who was waiting all these years to enter my life and then—wham—be shown that he had six to eight years left to live? Suddenly, anguish consumed me. I sat on the warm sand, pulling my body into a tight ball, and cried and cried. Unknowingly, a memory had again overtaken me. It was dark before I returned to my cottage. My mind felt crazed with questions. Primarily, if emotions were so useless, why was I unable to get rid of them?

When I further contemplated what I had been exposed to on my beach walk, I realized that Max perpetually engaged in a dance with death. He managed to live always on the edge, going out of his way to put himself in danger, addicted to an adrenaline high. Stories of his fist-fighting youth and his war experiences revealed much in this context. And one night I saw how his killer instinct surfaced and was ready for action when an unexpected vehicle disrupted our privacy on an isolated beach. His naked, jumbie dance around the fire, screaming into a full-moon night; his hunted/hunter, tormented dark side come alive, unconcerned of my presence, was a further revelation. He rodeo clowned with bulls and participated in search and rescue missions. He had witnessed countless acquaintances meet death living a life in the harsh north.

Prior to my beach revelation, and on a number of occasions, Max had already spoken of his belief that his number would soon come around, much like Jack was in the habit of doing. Then, oddly, he would consistently ask me if *I* knew when his time was up. My response was always to ask him why he thought that I would be privy to that information. Soon after my revelation on the beach, he again asked me if I knew when his time would be up. I assuredly stated that I had no idea, but somehow this time he knew I was lying. My secret, that really was not a secret, soon became a form of torment. I was clearly getting the message that I was to tell him what I knew, but I resisted with a vengeance. It was more than simply a fear of being seen as evil or being scoffed at that reduced me to hiding the truth from him. I felt that if I spoke of his death, I somehow would be supporting or guaranteeing it.

Shortly after my beach experiences, the soul mate conversation that I had with Timothy, now many months previous, flashed into my mind. Focusing on the message, I realized the conversation was once again overlaying the vision of a skinny cowboy. It appeared that I was being informed that Max was my soul mate. It was challenging to accept, as my understanding went, that he was my ideal partner and that we would be living the ideal relationship, especially at a spiritual level. I took this Divine disclosure as a further confirmation that we, through destiny, were being brought together. I was correct, but not for the reasons I thought. I was learning about the nature of love, although unlike the kind of which romance movies are made.

Sitting on Max's veranda, communing with my guidance one afternoon, I was suddenly given a directive, "Stand on the railing and announce to the world that you are in your power." Horrified, I responded, "*What?*" The message came again, only this time with greater punch. I attempted to ignore the message, but it pummeled me all the more. Experience revealed that there was no way around following this directive. Overcoming my reluctance, I finally stepped onto the railing and, laboriously, with great distaste, fearful that the villagers below—Gavin included—might hear me, I surrendered to a greater will. My words stumbled forth in a broken, raspy whisper. I tried again. My efforts were still not met with approval. I tried again, and then again, each time with more clarity, certainty and force. I was being required to wake the community below. Finally, taking the plunge, I filled my lungs with air and then exhaled "I-am-in-my-power!" The words scraped my throat as they shot forth. To my surprise, a sense of empowerment filled in a space within me that had been emptied out through shouting. My test was complete. Max remained quietly in the background. Subsequently, stepping from the railing and suddenly feeling as silly as empowered, I found myself looking toward him for validation. His response, "Don't look to me for support," perfectly supported the moment.

Before I could begin to regain a sense of composure, I next heard something about writing a book, a story about my life it seemed. In my instant resistance, I tried to give meaning to what I heard. This message must be about Max's book. *He* was the writer. The message most certainly had to do with *his* life, his bold adventures. A greater truth overrode my attempt to give personal meaning to the message. Rather than surrender, however, I attempted a different twist. Was it Max who would be required to write about my life? After all, he was an expert at colorfully painting a story. I was left simultaneously scoffing and feeling flattered and self-important over the idea that my life could be important enough to be written about. However, as much as I attempted to reduce or call it by another name, I was being told that the book would be about *me* and *I* would be the author. What, if anything, was there for me to convey about my life that would be of interest or value to anyone? This entire experience, especially with Max as a witness, left me feeling exposed and disconcerted. Whatever was happening, it seemed to be much more than I could absorb. That night, alone in my own bed, under my shroud, I was directed to shorten the cord on my amulet so that the star sapphire hung directly over my throat chakra. I failed to recognize that my action was a show of commitment on my part and evidence that the book was already in the process of being written. But the intensity of celestial energy inculcating the moment made it obvious that a great deal was afoot.

There seemed to be a consistency in the messages coming to me: facing my sexuality, getting my voice back, being in my power, owning my femininity, opening my heart, understanding male energy, teaching. And now a book! What did it all mean? Until I was capable and fully willing to own the messages given to me for what they were, I was in for some rough times. Nonetheless, if it took rough times for me to get where I was meant to go, that was okay, for it did not matter under what conditions I traveled, through struggle or acquiescence, maintaining momentum was all that was important.

Max's departures from island were no less chaotic than his arrivals. He would be awake late in the night, tying up loose ends, packing, attempting to locate his misplaced passport or something or other of importance. Perturbed or not, I would consistently remain my helpful self. After driving him to the airport in the predawn, I would then return his rental car and complete a list of errands he had given me. Thereafter, I would refocus my energy on returning to my own life. All the while I would see shades of John's and my relationship—all of my gender relationships— coloring the moment.

I attended church on the island largely as a means of integrating into the culture. I remember sweltering mornings, drawn out sermons, and ministers haranguing the congregation about hell and damnation, the "heathens, change your ways!" mentality. One Sunday, however, I intentionally attended service to hear an American minister speak. He was staying in Miss Huff's guesthouse, along with a number of other church members. We met when he became lost taking a shortcut home from the church and ended up in my backyard. I listened intently as he delivered his sermon in a gentle, personable and humorous manner. When he stated, "We cannot hear God speak to us until we know who we are," his words resonated deeply into my psyche and triggered a rush of energy so strong I frantically struggled to hold back my tears. Questions tore at my mind: Do I know who I am? Could my inner voice be connected to God? Is God speaking to me? Why would he speak to me? Why does this overwhelm me so much? My impulse was to pounce on the minister in an effort to pull from him any secret understanding he had.

By the end of the service, I knew I would ignore protocol and corner him with an invitation. Miss Huff happened to be along side of me as I approached him at the door. For once, I cared not a whit. Within the privacy of my cottage, I proceeded directly to the purpose of my invitation and openly explained to him about my commitment to know who I am, my inner voice and the message I had heard in his sermon. I inquired if he thought the force behind my voice and God were one and the same. My intenseness was apparent, even to me, and the minister was noticeably on edge. However, after some thought, he stated, "I believe it is God speaking to you." He then added, half-enviously, "I wish God would talk to me so clearly." His comment left me confused, even disappointed. I thought to myself, "If anyone can hear God speak, surely it is a man who has dedicated his life to serving God. And surely it was God speaking to me through him that morning in church." I deemed it inappropriate to question a minister as to his perceived limitations, but by his words to me I realized that he was unable to understand where I was at, although I desperately wanted him—anybody—to understand. Since I was obviously becoming too ardent for the minister, and I perceived that he felt uncomfortable being alone with me in my house, I made a big pan of popcorn, and we moved to Miss Huff's veranda and chatted until our snack was consumed.

That night, within my gauzy shroud, I focused on my own revelation. So, it was God talking to me—as with Anna—God talking to all who learned how to listen inside of themselves, to all who came to know themselves. This should have been another joyous awakening, except something inside felt perturbed. I knew that beneath my strong sense of wonderment, sat a feeling of distrust. It had to do with my unwillingness to use the term God—that omnipotent he-being whom as a child I had believed only lived to take bad girls away forever. As I began to awaken to a larger reality, I found that I used the word Universe or Divine and to a lesser degree, Spirit, to define my belief in a higher power—never God. The Universe was all encompassing and epitomized my Einstein experiences. I was part of the Universe; the Universe was part of me. I trusted in the Universe. Now, I wondered where "God" fit into my beliefs.

Teresa's visit was a bright moment during the holiday season. Sharing time with her was like a refreshing respite. Unlike Gertrude, she showed an avid interest in every facet to my island life. She loved being outdoors as much as I did and was open to whatever adventure came along. One by one, we created beautifully close moments. I often thought if she were a male, she would make a perfect partner. However, our relationship had gone through serious adjustments since my move to the islands. The most evident challenge was when she had phoned me immediately after my return from surgery a year earlier. She was having difficulty and she claimed to know that I would always be there for her even if no one else were. In her words I could feel the weight of her neediness, for which I was unwilling to take responsibility. In response, I claimed that it did not matter if I was there for her or not, her always being there for herself was what was important. She had stepped back from me after that and I had refrained from mitigating the moment. I saw her as an amazingly powerful person, but she habitually put herself in a box, especially around her husband. If nothing else, the situation forced me to further examine the role I played to needy people.

It was difficult for me to admit that my health had been poor during my stay on island. And it was difficult to admit that, in some way, I was supporting it. I disliked cooking, as much as eating, in the unrelenting heat, and most of the time my refrigerator was inoperable—Miss Huff refused to have it repaired. Also, I was little willing to sacrifice the time or cost to invest in a healthy diet, as well as fearful of gaining weight. Fresh milk and yogurt were unmanageably expensive when they were available. It was impossible to buy a bag of rice without worms in it. And the concept "fresh produce" had a meaning onto itself in the Caribbean. Carrots, mangoes and hunks of pumpkin that did not sell at market one day lay out in the heat for another day, and another, becoming limp, pathetic looking and covered with flies. As a naturalist, I was also aware of just how many "poisons" farmers used on their crops. All in all, outside of my stash of packaged falafel, couscous and beans that John and Teresa had brought with them, I was in the habit of living on mostly cheese and crackers, fruit, and my daily allotment of Coke.

I continued to convince myself that I was healthy. Yet I was consistently limited in energy and required an inordinate amount of sleep. Since I was allergic to dust and mold, the environmental conditions kept my sinuses on red alert, my head pounding and my eyes swollen and itchy. I fractured a toe on one occasion and was perpetually coming down with stomach problems, I presumed from some tropical beastie or another, that left me periodically laid up. It took a while to realize that my incapacitations were not random happenings or something in and of themselves. Rather, if I was too noisy and distracted or, otherwise, ignoring incoming messages, my illnesses became the means to provide the amount of quiet time necessary for me to receive those messages. Once a waiting message was acquired, I was invariably, if not nearly instantaneously, recovered. Overall, this was an indication that it was essential that I keep my life simple and quiet. Still, I was a conditioned "doer," so solitude and "just being" remained trying states to maintain.

Besides all of these minor problems, since I had begun to dive, an odd pain plagued me in my right ear, and it was getting worse day by day. I saw a number of doctors and was given eardrops, nosedrops and a host of various antibiotics, but the pain persisted. Worse, a couple of the prescribed medications left me with allergic reactions. The problem was now severe enough that I had difficulty equalizing pressure in my ears after riding up a hill with even the slightest elevation. Consequently, I was sent to Antigua to a specialist who, after taking x-rays, asserted that the problem was in my left maxillary sinus and surgery was required. It was beginning to look as if I would be medivacked to Washington D.C. again. I could no longer be fooled into thinking that the visit was about surgery. This was about "more lessons." Was I ready? I didn't think so.

15

Believing in Me

Bob, the biology professor, had agreed months earlier to teach a daylong field class to a group of students who were spending a semester at sea. Now that the time was at hand, he approached Timothy and me about assisting him. He painted the situation so colorfully, seemingly only a fool would refuse the offer. As a final incentive he offered us monetary compensation. Experience had already taught me to have no expectations when it came to any situation that Bob spearheaded, regardless of how he presented it, but in the end, both Timothy and I finally agreed. As we loaded up our camping gear readying for the trip to the adjacent peninsula, where the vessel was scheduled to dock, Bob, as usual, chatted on and on about the project as if we could feel nothing less than privileged to be involved. I only felt as if I had once more put myself in a compromising situation simply to keep someone else's life together. After we set up camp, we spent the rest of the day making final preparations for the vessel's arrival.

Enough being enough, and the need for solitude consuming me, I excused myself and left the two men readying a campfire. The sun hot on my shoulders told me I had a couple hours left of daylight. I walked along the shore, aimlessly combing the beach for treasures and letting the sound of the waves wash over me. I was ever so grateful to be alone. Finally, I was free to breathe deeply enough to become centered. The thought of being unsafe, alone off the beaten path, was present, but the transformation taking place within me kept it subdued.

At length, my eyes were drawn to the skeleton of a sea fan lying beneath a palm tree. Sea fan skeletons were plentiful and, as was habit, I had many among my nature treasures that I used to decorate my cottage and for teaching. Yet this one appeared different than any other I had seen. It was the barest of skeletons, looking like—I imagined—the trunk and main limbs of an ancient oak tree with all other parts removed. It was smooth, and black, and shiny. However long ago the force of the sea had bit-by-bit worn the rest of it away, what was left looked as if it could last forever. I dropped to my knees to examine it more closely, but it seemed to pull me down into a prone position—to pull me into it—until my face pressed against it. What exactly was transpiring, I didn't know, but when I was finally free to sit up, I held the skeleton in my hand. It reminded me of a Cabala, a tree of life or, perhaps, a family tree. Rather than having the capacity to live forever, I thought conceivably it had already lived forever—or maybe both. After a while, I was brought back to my linear mind. Thereupon, I began to cry. From where these tears sprung forth was unfathomable. Was this a manifestation of gratitude? Of understanding? The intensity of holding this Cabala was akin to my experience with Einstein. I was certainly transformed—in a quieter way this time however. I wandered farther along the beach hoping to anchor back into my body, if not regain my composure, before I returned to camp. It seemed that the Cabala was a gift, something to do with Max, and therefore necessary to bring home with me. I could not have dropped it anyway, not even if I so chose.

As I returned along the beach, following the path by which I had ventured forth, I felt the energy of the sea fan moving from my hand into my arm and throughout my entire body. Since it was all I seemed able to do, I sat down once again, holding the sea fan in front of me. Suddenly, I heard the word "marriage" resounding in my mind. My first thought was Max. Feeling my energy merge with the fan's, I saw myself as a pivotal point, a fulcrum, with an incredible past on one side and an incredible future on the other, as if I was holding the two in the balance, or perhaps, bringing them together. Overlaying this was the same word—marriage. Max's energy was infused in this entire experience. As the rays of the late afternoon sun began to leave its impression on my freckled skin, I was finally returned fully to the moment.

By the time I arrived in camp, I realized that this trip was hardly about supporting some wealthy American kids' education as they traveled the Caribbean on a sailing vessel. (In fact, a week later we would learn that, due to miscommunication, there was a discrepancy in scheduling, and the ship of students had arrived a day after we had given up on them and gone home.)

My reasons for being there did not end with the sea fan experience. That night, after returning to our camp, I was again compelled to go off on my own to make a waiting connection. After I found a quiet spot high on a hill, just off the road and in full view of a spectacular night sky, I was quickly put in review of the time that Carl, in a fit of rage, had burst into the bedroom and attacked me. This memory kept playing, condensed fashion, over and over in my head with the words, "but I survived!" Finally, I realized that there was a message in this memory. When I opened to receive it, the words to the **23rd Psalm,** "Yea, though I walk through the valley of the shadow of death, I will fear no evil. For thou art with me…" immediately came to mind. The psalm had already been pressing into my awareness for some time, and to the degree that I had borrowed a book from the church intending to copy the psalm in my diary. With intense mixed feelings, I asked further what I was to understand. All I got was an overwhelmingly intense sense of Myla's energy, nothing more. While the night sky beckoned to be observed, I sat in a dazed state, the **23rd Psalm** running through my mind, wondering again—always wondering—what was afoot.

My puzzlement ended when the phone rang before sunrise the second morning after my return. It was Myla. There was a sense of urgency, if not alarm in her voice, as she requested that I come and help her with the baby as soon as it was daylight for she was ill. From the time of the call to the time it took to catch a bus to her village and walk up the ribbon-road to her cottage, I could sense her illness, whatever it was, becoming more severe. At the same time, the words to the **23rd Psalm** echoed through my mind.

The door was open when I arrived. One of my young students, whom Myla had befriended, held Bairen in her lap. The house was messy, which was typical. I asked the youngster where I could find Myla. She pointed to the bedroom. Myla lay on her bed in a fetal position, half-clothed and half-conscious. I left her for a moment to phone Lela to come, then phoned my doctor. He expressed that he would make a house call only if I came to his house to show him the way. (It was confusing to comprehend his request since he lived in the same village as Myla, a short distance down the road and had a car.) I stifled my frustration, grabbed Bairen and ran down the hill to his place. When we returned, Lela was with Myla whose condition had worsened. Being in the medical profession herself, Myla understood that whatever was happening was serious.

Lela pulled me aside for a moment to explain what Myla had shared with her in my absence: Gavin had shown up unexpectedly the previous evening, and totally out of character, had a freshly-cooked fish he claimed to have brought just for her. He had insisted that she not even share it with the baby. She had eaten a small amount before refrigerating the rest. Shortly afterward, she became ill and took to her bed. Gavin stayed the night but arose before sunrise to leave. When she asked him to stay and help her, he asserted he had more important things to do and left. That was when she had phoned me for help. Lela's words brought to mind the vision that I'd had of Myla while camping, as well as a sense of overwhelming panic. Whatever was happening, it felt like my first step into the valley of the shadow of death.

There was no time to react, however, for dealing with the ramifications of island healthcare was about to demand all of my attention. After asking Myla a few questions and then assessing her condition, the doctor made a phone call for an ambulance and disappeared. I assumed that he would be waiting for us at the hospital. Lela and I got Myla into the ambulance, which was hardly more than a transport vehicle, and then whisked off to the hospital. Myla was placed in a private room where her condition continued to deteriorate more rapidly than imaginable. A nurse unsuccessfully attempted to administer an I.V. A number of other nurses gathered in the room, engrossed, as if they were watching their favorite soap opera. Since Bairen was traumatized and screaming for his mother, I stepped out of the room with him, hoping to calm him down. But I knew I was not supposed to leave Myla. I returned to the room to ask Lela to take him away awhile. Then I waited for the doctor's arrival.

Waning encouragement was all I could muster for Myla as I watched her. A numbness that had started in her feet moved steadily upward, and her long, thin body was atrophying before my eyes. A young physiotherapist, one of Myla's colleagues, came to see what the commotion was and stayed to help. Under her guidance, we massaged Myla's paralyzed limbs, while the other nurses simply gawked and a thousand thoughts collided in my mind. The two most prevalent were that this was a nightmare from which I must soon awaken, and that I had to muster enough energy to properly deal with whatever was happening. At some point, Myla mumbled through her limited consciousness that the paralysis was presently moving into her diaphragm and she would die if she were not immediately put on a respirator.

Beyond warding off hysteria, I ran out of the room and down the hall screaming for a doctor, only to run blindly into the head nurse, who calmly explained that there was no doctor on duty. No doctor would be there for hours and the nearest respirator was an island away. She then placed her hands squarely on my shoulders, looked me straight in the eyes firmly emphasizing, "You have to understand. We do things different here." There was no mistaking her message. She was saying, "We let people die." I stood there for a moment, in a fog, while the message sunk in. No help was on the way.

Thrusting aside my mounting sense of helplessness, I raced back to Myla's room where the group of nurses still huddled, engrossed in what was taking place. Taking hold of Myla, I informed her that we had to say goodbye. She understood. I wanted to scream at the nurses, "Get out of here! This is a private moment!" I didn't. Instead I focused within, groping for what I was to say to Myla. As we expressed our love for each other, she faded further from consciousness. Suddenly, feeling possessed by an unidentified impetus, I began to shake her forcefully. Through my sobs, I ordered, "Say it, Myla! Say it now! You have to say it!" We both knew what she was supposed to say: she had to name me Bairen's legal guardian. While I asked myself how I could possibly incorporate a baby into my life at this time, with determined effort, Myla uttered the words on her last breath. The nurses were witness.

I sat on the bed next to her body, perspiration-soaked and stunned. Nonetheless, at another level, I was being told that Myla's death was untimely. I was jolted into primal alertness. Before I could contemplate my actions, I was slapping her beautiful face, shaking her girlish shoulders fiercely, and sobbing an anguished command, "Wake up, Myla! We've worked too hard for you to end this way! You still have work to do! Wake up! Wake up!" Beholding a miracle, her eyes fluttered slightly and then finally, in very slow motion, opened. Although laboriously, she was breathing again! I was certain though that at one point she had died. Was this a miracle?

If this encounter were not confusing enough, Myla would later explain to me what had been taking place in her own consciousness through all of this. As I was telling her to "say it," she was seeing the Angel of Death asking her to give up her child and come with him. She initially refused, but the Angel was adamant, so she finally acquiesced. Then, when I was slapping her, telling her to come back, the Angel of Death informed her that she could return, that her lessons on Earth were not yet complete. I truly loved Myla from a deep soul level and I knew I could accept her death. I could not, however, accept the timing because I also knew that she was not finished here. This was the most intense experience I had ever had with death and a severe lesson for both of us, one that was far from being played out.

Not only was Myla now immeasurably weak, she also had great difficulty speaking. She labored and choked to form words and get them out. Even before she attempted to give voice to her thoughts, I could feel her difficulties in my own throat. The more she fought to speak, the more I was affected. My first reaction was, "This is all too crazy, choking on my own words." I remembered John having said that my problem with my throat chakra was my refusal to express my inner knowing, but I was not doing this to myself. It was happening to me.

Gavin arrived at the hospital shortly after Myla's initial recovery. He was wielding a forced air of surprise over her state, which gave way to a scowl when our eyes met. Until now, Myla remained in denial, insisting her poisoning was accidental—fish poisoning, not poisoned fish. Gavin showed little concern for her malady or recovery. Instead, he demanded to know where his child was. His rage erupted when she refused to tell him. He lashed out and virtually incriminated himself with every word he spoke. When the head nurse threatened to kick him out, he quieted down and made a show of concern for Myla. She was deathly afraid of him, but found her voice enough to enjoin that he not threaten me in any way, and that he could see Bairen at the hospital when she was feeling strong enough. He sweetly agreed, hovering around her and kissing her face. I could see Myla's conviction weakening as she requested to be left alone in order to rest.

Gavin and I exited the hospital room simultaneously. Once outside, he instantly dropped his facade and cornered me, his hatred flaring, demanding to know where I had hidden his boy. Although I was unaware of exactly where Lela had gone with Bairen, and could honestly tell Gavin that I had no idea as to his whereabouts, I hoped that she would not suddenly appear. Seeing that he was getting nothing from me, he went on to claim that I was the she-devil in disguise and had stolen Myla's mind. I was certain that his holding me responsible was his way of taking the heat off himself. I was also certain that he hated me as much as I feared him. To my bewilderment, for a moment, I had my voice back. In that moment, my cool, removed, if not arrogant, response to him came as, "I do not judge you, Gavin, but your karma is catching up to you. You will define for yourself the price of your actions." Instantaneously, I heard myself inwardly ask if I understood my own words. I wanted to say "no," except it hit against a strong affirmative feeling. There was no time to wonder, for the significance of what I said was even then in the process of revealing itself.

My sense of danger and feelings of responsibility for Myla and Bairen were overwhelming. After listening to me choke out the story, Brian insisted that I bring the baby and stay with him at the guesthouse that he rented directly across the street from the hospital. Preparing meals for Myla and taking them to her would be simplified. There was also space to take care of an extremely stressed Bairen and laundry facilities. I let go of my habitual fear of being an imposition, as well as my fear of what others, including my landlady, would say about the arrangement, and welcomed the opportunity.

That night Jerry and Janice, acquaintances from Chicago, who had phoned from Puerto Rico a week earlier, arrived. Their first reaction to seeing me sprawled on the couch was that I looked near death. They were even more surprised to see Bairen asleep on top of me. After they heard what was underway, they were beside themselves. Compared to their mundane life, ironically, they saw mine as high adventure. It was amazingly fortuitous that Jerry, who owned an import/export business, having just completed a diaper deal in Puerto Rico, had a whole suitcase of disposable diapers with him. Although my guests were willing to support me in any way possible, I felt reluctant to draw them into something I felt was potentially volatile. Nevertheless, for the few days they were on the island, they provided relief in many significant ways.

Gavin began to phone or appear at the hospital at all hours checking to see if Myla was still there and demanding to know where his son was. The hospital staff became annoyed with his incessant disturbances and Myla, succumbing, began to own her fear. It was clear to me that Bairen would be used as a pawn in whatever struggle was about to ensue, for it was only a matter of time before Gavin discovered that I was hiding the boy right under his nose.

Intuition evinced that I had to get Myla off island if she were going to survive. I tried to convince myself that I was overreacting, except my sense of foreboding only escalated. It was tougher than I could imagine to unquestioningly believe in myself. I assumed that Lela would be a support, and she had agreed to retrieve Myla's money and passport before Gavin got the same idea. When I ran into her and queried her about obtaining the items, she contended that her partner had convinced her that her doing so, as well as my reactiveness, was unnecessary. My first response was, "When did you start letting your man do your thinking for you?" My retort caught her by surprise but I did not back down, "Why didn't you tell me you changed your mind? I could have gone myself to get her things. The chances of them being there now are slim."

I turned and walked away struggling with my sense of utter betrayal. In a reactive state, I later borrowed Brian's car and took my two Chicago guests with me to stay with the baby and keep watch, while I went inside Myla's house to retrieve her valuables myself. I really expected Gavin to have been there already and taken her money and passport. Since nothing appeared to have been touched, Lela's words of my over-reactiveness became like a reality check.

I remained convinced that Myla's only chance of survival lay in getting her off island, away from Gavin. She had agreed to my arrangements for her to take a night boat, a short distance to an adjacent island, where a friend of hers and Lela's would shelter her until she was strong enough for further travel. This plan was foiled when, again under the influence of her male companion, Lela called the friend assuring him that I was out of control and should be ignored. Now there was nothing that could dispel my sense of betrayal. When I pointed out her behavior this time she flung at me, "Well, you let Max dictate your thoughts and actions!" Rattled, my focus became thrown from the issues at hand.

I knew that this entire situation was the talk of the island and that more than just Lela's man was viewing me as crazed. I could imagine Miss Huff in her gossiping glory. But the vision of my near-death at Carl's hands continued to play through my mind. I perceived this as a reminder that I had to take whatever was happening seriously. If I ever felt alone, it was in this moment, but I would not allow myself to take comfort from the words of the **23rd Psalm**, that God was with me. As much as I wanted someone to hold my hand, trusting solely in myself was proving easier than relying on anyone else for support—as it always had. I was fired up and ready to battle anyone who got in my way.

My faith in myself was further tested when Brian came home from work and announced that his friends had urged him to get rid of me, as well as the baby, if he knew what was good for him. In tears, I responded that I would take the baby and return to my cottage so as to waylay any potential community backlash on him. After all, he had an influential position and a reputation to protect. And he had already done more for me than I could or should expect. In his response that he would never consider asking me to leave I understood how overly defensive I had become.

After the failure of the initial plan, I conversed with Myla about how to best serve the situation. We agreed that staying in the hospital would allow her to gain strength and keep Gavin at bay, while further plans for her safe departure from island were arranged. The plan looked more viable after the doctor agreed to allow Myla to stay as long as she felt necessary. While Myla was in circumstances where she could focus on regaining her strength, however, my health was deteriorating. Sleepless nights taking care of Bairen, cooking meals for her, keeping up with my work, my ear problem and the lingering effects of having been ill with some tropical microorganism, coupled with the anxiety of the situation, were taking their toll.

I thought the matter was under control until, under Gavin's influence, Myla began to believe that everyone had misjudged him and that I was over reacting. Watching her make this about-face consigned the "bad character" in me to sabotage my beliefs. Yet, regardless of my efforts to view the events differently—that perhaps I was over-reactive and transferring my own issues onto Gavin—a force beyond my own will was keeping me committed.

I also learned that the doctor's first impression was that Myla had overdosed on drugs and that this, and his prejudice against Rasta's and mixed relationships had resulted in his ambivalence to fully provide medical assistance to her. However, **Bible** quotes taped on this East Indian doctor's office walls were evidence that he considered himself a Godly man. My first impulse was to confront him about his attitude, but I managed to keep myself in check for I knew that outrage was no more serving than prejudice.

A local man came to visit Myla one afternoon to share a dream he had about Gavin poisoning her. Through his tears, he kept insisting, "Skate fish don't poison," and avowed that if he had the fish he would feed it to his puppy to prove that the fish had been poisoned. Myla claimed that, as far as she knew, the fish remained in the refrigerator. In their conversation, I clearly heard that I had to retrieve the fish and, before I knew I was speaking, I had blurted out that I was on my way to do just that.

My heart was pounding. What if I ran into Gavin? I put my fear aside as I stopped by the guesthouse to inform a friend, who was watching Bairen, of my actions and then headed to the bus stop. Oddly, I suddenly felt that I had to first obtain something from my cottage, although I had no idea what it was. Miss Huff was there, waiting as I approached, as if she had been informed of my arrival. Everything she was thinking came through in her icy greeting. I walked passed her, grabbed my key from where I kept it on the porch and entered my abode. I had not been here for a few days and it no longer felt like my place at all. Standing in the living area, breathing in the hot, musty air, I pleaded to know what was being asked of me here, for I only wanted and felt the urgency of getting on with my task before my courage failed.

Suddenly, I dialed Max's number. Hearing the phone ring once, and then again, I told myself that this was an unlikely time for him to be home. Three rings later, I heard his standard cowboy greeting. He was thrilled by my surprise call. Dismissing superficial chatter, I explained, in my broken voice, what was transpiring and then, oddly, I interjected that if I did not return, he would know the truth of what happened; nevertheless, he was not to blame Gavin or take revenge in any way. I was confounded about where my diametrically opposing thoughts were coming from or what they were about. As concerned as he was for me, still he kept insisting, as he had done during our previous conversation, that a father has a right to his child, regardless of the situation. I wanted to scream at him, "No, he doesn't, you stupid idiot. You don't know what the hell you're talking about!" I had not called looking for his support. I had no idea what was happening, but suddenly I was deeply enraged that his support was absent. I left the house steaming, stomped by Miss Huff again, shooting her a bloody look, and headed down Main Street toward the bus stop, ready to flatten anyone who even appeared to challenge me.

On the way I ran into Timothy. In a no-nonsense manner, I asked him if he trusted me. Hearing an affirmative, I further asked him if he would, without explanation, come with me. His only question to me was in regard to my voice, which presently was especially raspy and guttural. I told myself that I was simply afraid to handle this on my own and, because of this, I was putting Timothy in danger. However, he appeared to have no issues with my request, and came with me with no further questions asked.

When we arrived at Myla's cottage, the door was wide open. Only something more powerful than my fear allowed me to step through the threshold. I first glanced into the side room where Myla kept her money and passport; it now was obvious that someone had rifled through her belongings. Before I could react, Gavin stepped out of the kitchen. My bowels churned as he volunteered that he had acquired a key from the babysitter and then professed to be looking for some things that were his. Further, he asserted that if I had come for the fish I would find it in the refrigerator. It was as if he was either daring me or tactically discouraging me to follow through with my mission. My knowing told me that he was there for the fish, the money and the passport, but suddenly my intellect left me doubting and fearful of being wrong. I was now my own greatest foe—my doubt immobilizing and deadly. I stood before him, eye-to-eye, for a split-second, a sizzling silence. Neither of us moved, neither of us wanted the other to know why he had come. Suddenly, without waiting for a response, he slipped out the door, hopped on Myla's motorcycle and drove off. In an instant, I saw that his not staying to see if I took the fish was necessary for him to maintain an appearance of innocence. Without hesitation, I took the fish and returned to town. Although Timothy had stayed in the background, I thought I understood why his presence had been needed.

Once in town, I requested that he take the fish home with him, put it in his freezer and tell no one he had it. When I realized that the puppy would die regardless of whether the fish was poisoned or was poisonous, I felt foolish for having put either of us through the ordeal. Yet, having the fish would at least leave Gavin with the impression that I had leverage, for he had no way of knowing whether or not I actually would have the fish sent away to be analyzed. I wanted to believe that I was not going to these lengths to get revenge, but I would do whatever necessary to save Myla.

Running into Gavin created an unshakable sense of foreboding, which actualized a few days later when I left Bairen in the care of a friend while I went to work. Gavin entered the guesthouse unannounced, grabbed Bairen from my friend's arms and ran. Minutes later, after receiving a call from Myla, I arrived at the hospital. She was on the balcony, half-resisting, half-supported by two nurses, shouting as best she could for me to get her baby back. ("Tel-a-person" has always proven to be the fastest form of communication on island.) I knew that this could be the critical point in her survival if the situation turned out unfavorably.

I focused to stay calm and look at my choices. My first response was to call a local businesswoman whom I had heard worked with abused women (and who also happened to be the same woman who had taken second to me in the run). Hearing my story, she felt this incident fell into the category of kidnapping and warranted police action. She was acquainted with the chief of police and voluntarily phoned ahead to inform him of my arrival. Having personally witnessed the behavior of the men who called themselves police, as well as having heard about the liberties wearing such uniforms afforded them, I had little faith in this being fruitful, but I saw no other route to take.

Walking the few blocks to the police station, my thoughts were drawn to when a number of times Myla and I had been swimming with the baby, and Gavin had unexpectedly shown up. Consistently, he had taken the baby and begun to play conspicuously with his penis, laughing and saying, "Come on, you got to get it up, boy. It's time you start knowing what it's like to be a man." All the time he had watched for a reaction from me. I had never known what to do besides ignore his intimidations. Myla had always done the same. Presently, this seemed to be a tit-for-tat game. I had taken the fish. He had taken the baby. The next move was mine.

I expected to be ushered into the police chief's office immediately. Instead, I was casually escorted to a folding chair in a stark, dirty room that looked like a jail cell. Moments later, a police officer ambled in, sat down across from me, and began to scratch my words on a crumpled scrap of paper. After I finished telling my story, he excused himself. The look on his face, when he reappeared a few minutes later, revealed his message: the father could relinquish the baby if he chose, but the police could not otherwise force him. I fought back tears as I began again to explain the seriousness of the situation. He was unaffected. As a last ditch effort, I asked him to consider taking me to Gavin in the police vehicle, so that I could safely talk to him. Hearing me out, he excused himself again and I, with Myla's last words ringing in my ears, found that I was being drawn into another dimension.

Unaware of exactly how long I had been in this state, a tap on my shoulder brought me back to the moment. Dazed, I opened my eyes and stared at the policeman who stared back at me, a puzzled expression on his face. I had not returned to my body enough to feel uncomfortable with my behavior or the silence in the room. Nonetheless, the policeman hesitantly requested permission to ask me a question. When I shook my head in the affirmative, he blurted out, "What were you doing? Meditating?" Phrasing my words in a way that I thought this island man would accept, as well as focusing beyond my damaged voice so I could be clearly understood, I explained, "I was asking God to show me the way; a woman's life is in my hands. I don't know what else I can do." Our eyes locked, soul to soul, an inner connection strengthening. He excused himself once more, but this time, on his return, he announced that his superior had agreed to have me driven to wherever I thought I would find Gavin.

I gave the driver instructions as I sat in the backseat feeling too overwhelmed to even give snoopy on-lookers a second glance. The two officers in the front seat conversed in their odd dialect and called "hello" to familiar faces along the way. A jumble of thoughts left me out of touch with time as we traveled the now-familiar road toward Gingerland. Gavin was waiting for me exactly where I envisioned him, conspicuously sitting beside the road leading to his village, holding Bairen in his dark, muscular arms. Momentarily forgetting the officer's assistance, I jumped out of the police vehicle and stepped directly in front of Gavin, reaching out my arms and calling to the baby. As I was Bairen's most recent figure of security, he began to cry, struggling to come to me. I felt Gavin's resistance weakening. Suddenly, appealing to a caring place that I believed lay dormant inside of him, I queried, "Do you really want Myla dead? You weren't successful the first time around. Taking Bairen will finish her off for sure, and it's even legal. Is this really what you want?" He requested that I take a walk with him up into the bush so we could talk. Instantly I was thrown into doubt. Yes, I should go with him for no other reason than to hear him out, but hadn't I learned my lesson when I gave into the request of the crazy Chicago neighbor who had stalked me? Simultaneously, another side of me was screaming, "Why? So you can kill me?" I ignored his invitation, as well as my doubt and fear, and focused on getting the baby to struggle more to come to me. With my arms stretched out, I coaxed, "Let's go home to Mommy now. You want to see Mommy?" Feeling a crack in Gavin's opposition, I quickly reached forward and snatched Bairen from his arms, but not quickly enough to avert his grabbing hold of Bairen's foot.

Thus far, the two policemen who had escorted me remained distanced from the situation. With Bairen caught in the middle, they readily intervened. While they scuffled with Gavin, I drew Bairen, now wailing, safely into the backseat of the police vehicle, rolled up the windows and locked the door. Gavin struggled to get at me even as the police were pulling away. The hatred on his face was indelibly pressed into my mind as we drove to the hospital.

The energy upon me when I awoke the next morning told me something was amiss. Seeing Gavin sitting with Myla on the veranda of the hospital as I approached clarified what I was feeling. He had a triumphant glint in his eyes as he dismissed himself. Meanwhile, Myla mustered her courage enough to be honest. First, she rationalized Gavin's presence. Then she explained that I really needed to go somewhere and rest, I was taking this situation far too seriously and she could handle it now. I responded, "I honor your position. However, it is not mine. The entire island, at this point, including the police, is aware that Gavin has been sitting here with you. If there is any more trouble, I will no longer have police support—anyone's support—for no one will take you seriously." I went on, "I love you deeply, but I will not interfere in your living your own beliefs." I returned to the guesthouse exhausted, disheartened and struggling to maintain my own knowing. I was without a clue as to how this episode in my life was going to end, but I wanted it finished.

That evening I brought Bairen to the hospital for a visit. It was clear that Myla had been crying for most of the day. Through her sobs and her broken voice, she stated that she understood that I never gave advice, but she was presently asking for it. She confessed that she was addicted to Gavin and had no idea how to break free of him. She begged me to help her. Focusing on Myla's greater truth, I asked her what she would do if she were an alcoholic. She responded, "I would take it one step at a time." Myla had her answer. In fact, her admission of her addiction was her most important step. Acknowledging my deep sense of love and responsibility for this young woman, I wondered about the true nature of our connection.

With fresh support from unexpected sources, including Jack, a week later Myla and Bairen made a safe, covert departure home to Scotland. My sense of fear defined that when Gavin discovered his loss, he would come after me. There were many people, besides me, presently concerned for my life.

As Myla and I sat on the balcony of the hospital the night before her departure, I had shared with her what I had been hearing: once she left, except through letters, I could have no further contact with her. Because of my deep sense of love for her and her child, I felt that this was one of the most challenging requests ever made of me. Not knowing whether I would ever again see this woman or the baby for whom I had spent uncountable hours caring, who belonged to both of us, but believing there was a purpose to this directive, I obeyed the edict given me. Myla had much working against her and remained physically and emotionally fragile, but she knew how to find her strength and that she must rely on, not me. She was returning to her family to further come to terms with the trauma of her childhood. Bairen was acting out the stress as well. My focus now was to understand how to face Gavin's wrath.

I learned two important lessons in my experience with Myla. The first one had to do with believing unequivocally in myself. The other had to do with God. I knew that it was no coincidence; rather it was Divine will that had led me to relate to the island policeman in terms he would accept. "God," I had stated. I had asked for God's support. I thought my long-standing fear of asking for help had stemmed from my upbringing. Even with the Universe, I only asked for the information I needed to establish my own understanding, nothing more.

The day after Myla departed, I attended a Peace Corps meeting pertaining to Brett's conduct. Due to the nature of the situation, our director was requiring the lead volunteer, presently Timothy, to participate. I was resistant to having anything further to do with Brett, and at the time of this meeting I remained ill and concerned over Myla's welfare and my safety.

Brett was another matter. When he came to work at all, it had usually been shortly before lunch. Then, from the time of his appearance, he would sit around and bitch about the changes in our program, or whatever else he could criticize. If and when he returned after lunch, it was only long enough for more bitching. It was clear that he used his complaints, as well as his illnesses to mask his habitual absence and irresponsibility.

Ever since he had become involved with a British volunteer, a psychiatric nurse, his negativity had taken a quantum leap. I had been struggling for a long time with whether or not to blow the whistle on him, but I told myself, among other rationales, that I was not his babysitter. The truth was that I was unwilling to be seen as having been covering for Brett. I was also unwilling to present our program as less of a success than it actually was. Further, on some level, I knew that, until the meeting, I had been willing to pay the price of Brett's behavior rather than being left on my own without any team at all.

At the end of one working day, my frustration with his behavior snapped when he abruptly appeared with no other focus than to read his mail. I lashed out, "For the little good you serve why don't you forget about coming to work at all. In fact, you need to contact the director to make other arrangements." Without a word, he walked out of the door. I struggled afterward to refrain from taking on the "now-look-what-you-did-to-poor-Brett" routine or seek out Jack to defend my stance. I was determined to let the chips fall where they may.

The following day, Brett returned excitedly claiming that he had permission from our director to do whatever he wanted, and he decided that he was going to return to the classroom. His position was ludicrous, especially since we had been given the directive that we were *out* of the classroom and he had been uncommitted when we were in. That night I phoned the director myself to ascertain what had actually transpired. His version was much different than Brett's.

The meeting now being called was held in my tiny cottage. After living in the spaciousness of Brian's guesthouse, the cottage felt suffocating, and sitting a mere arm's length from Jack and Brett felt all the more oppressive. Somehow, I felt Jack was feeling sorry for "the lad," as he referred to Brett. Though Jack could be tough as nails with almost anyone himself, I sensed that he did not cotton to my being so with his lad. After the director formally called the meeting to order, he proceeded to turn the floor over to Brett. As could be expected, Brett did little else than beat around the bush.

When we had first received our Peace Corps identification cards, the area director's signature was missing on the back of Brett's. Rather than go through the appropriate channels to resolve the problem, he chose forgery as a quicker solution. His actions got back to the area director and Brett had actually been flown to island headquarters to be held accountable. In the end, he received a slap on the wrist; but his reputation had been sullied, and then further tarnished by his preoccupation with discovering who had squealed on him.

The more he presently justified his behavior, the more juvenile he appeared. When it was my turn to respond, I took a moment to set aside my growing irritation, and then struggled through my damaged voice and exhaustion to present the facts. They were enough, in and of themselves, to incriminate him. However, the manner and thoroughness with which I stacked them up left him, not only incriminated, but also pulverized. It was apparent to everyone that I had gone far beyond the point of necessity to display a clear view of Brett's irresponsibility. He walked out totally deflated. Part of me was stiffly indifferent, even justified. Another part of me was horrified by my unexpected, inexcusable conduct. Where was my compassion? Certainly it had not been in alignment with my greater awareness. Was Einstein watching?

What had happened to true accountability? What had happened to my supporting another's greatness rather than exposing his weakness? At the end of Peace Corps training, when I had been inclined to lambaste our local trainer's unprofessionalism, I had instead managed to support her greatness by giving her a special vote of thanks at our swearing-in ceremony. Doing so had cleared the air and put something between us to rest. Why had I not been able to apply that same lesson to Brett? And what price was I about to pay for my baffling behavior? Unquestionably, I was reluctant to know.

All I wanted was to simply wash my hands of what had transpired but the director, as he departed, suddenly informed me that I was to keep a watch on Brett and report back to him on a daily basis regarding his behavior. I was flabbergasted; he might as well have handcuffed the two of us together. I defended that it was against Peace Corps protocol to place me in a position to oversee a fellow volunteer's behavior, and if it were to be done at all, it should be done by the lead volunteer.

The director was adamant. In the end, feeling guilty over my behavior and realizing the fruitlessness of further protest, I agreed to his request although only on the condition that it be put in writing and placed on record. Worse than handcuffs, I went home feeling as if a noose had been placed around my neck. As for resolution, it felt beyond reach. (This was because my history was infiltrating the moment. Outside of my judgment, I was living this lesson exactly as divinely planned.)

I returned to my cottage the next day to face moving back in. As I reached for the key, I discovered a letter tucked under the door. It was purportedly from Miss Huff's lawyer stating that I was to vacate the cottage in a month's time. She claimed that she had put her old family house up for sale and needed the cottage to store her furniture. However it was presented, the truth was that she was evicting me. I knew why. During the time Myla was in the hospital, Miss Huff had cornered me on the street one day and informed me condemningly that Gavin had come, masked and armed with a stick, to my cottage in the night, attempting to break in. She wanted me, and my Rasta connections, gone.

From the first time that she had seen Myla at my place, she had been incensed that I was friends with a Rasta's woman and that I cared for a Rasta child. In fact, I had one day tested the degree of her prejudice after Bairen's birth, by dropping him into her lap as she criticized my involvement. Even the innocent beauty of a newborn could not weaken her prejudice. The stage had been further set for animosity when I had declined to care for her property and pets while she went to the United States for two months. So as not to look like I was doing *her* a favor, she had approached me one day claiming, "Elmer (her Doberman Pincher) says he wants you to take care of him while I am away. He knows you will take good care of him. He says you can also watch the guesthouse." My only response to her novel approach to getting her needs met was, "If you want a favor from me, you can ask me directly." She departed without another word to me. Even following her return she spoke to me only in snips.

As much as her continual manipulations and accusations about my personal life had annoyed me, her eviction left some part of me not merely devastated, but ready for revenge. I had done nothing to deserve this and I was unwilling to give her the upper hand. Instead of staying the month she allowed, I moved out the following day, taking her by surprise, especially over losing a month's rent. Brian made this easy by opening the door for me to remain with him until my stint was complete. Miss Huff stood in thin-skinned silence on her veranda as Jack and a friend of his loaded my scant remaining possession onto a waiting pickup, making sure that I took nothing that belonged to her.

Further annoying her, I decided to wait until the end of my current month's rent to return the house key to her. When she had originally given me the key, she made it clear that it was the only one she had and she expected me to have duplicates made. Since this was only one more way that she was trying to get something for nothing, I had taken the risk of having no extra key rather than feed her manipulation. Now, even with my moving out, she was at my mercy to enter her own property. Any concern of her reprisal was overshadowed by my sense of indignation. If I were being required to play a bad person role, I was going to go all the way with it.

February was coming to a close, which left only a few more months of service. Some part of Jack was already gone; that was obvious by his continual talk about what activities would be taking place on the ranch and how he felt he had to get back for calving. Brett had never been present. He had often come to me seeking perspective with his trials and tribulations and his endless traumas with the numerous girlfriends he simultaneously juggled. He had spoken of his childhood, specifically his father's alcoholism and his mother's bitter unhappiness. He did not share that he was also an alcoholic, but that was obvious. Many of the men in the Peace Corps were chemically dependent. I knew the extent of his damage. However, as Einstein had proclaimed, my compassion was not in alignment with my knowing and ultimately, I remained confounded by, as much as ashamed of, my behavior. My big question was, "When will I ever learn?"

What really frightened me was that there was a dark side to Brett, a side of him that was a merciless gossip. There was a side of him that could shake your hand while holding a knife in the other ready to stab you in the back the moment you turned around. I could not explain it, but there was a part of me that feared for my life, as if I had revealed the imposter for whom he was and his wrath was sure to descend. I tried to convince myself that whatever the outcome, I had set myself up for it and had to pay the price. I could have rationalized that it had been my exasperation over his behavior that had pushed me to act inappropriately. Yet there was another force, something beyond intellectual comprehension that had provoked my seemingly tasteless behavior. Even so, I took the blame.

Contrary to Brett's original belief, he was not given free rein to do what he wanted. Instead, the three of us were instructed to find a way to work together. With little thought, I was aware of what I had to do, and that was what I had been resistant to doing all along. I suggested that Brett, knowing that was within the framework of his capability, take sole charge of the production of the monthly environmental newsletter—my pet project—as well as take over my classes when it came time to take the newsletter into the classroom. I then suggested that Jack organize the teacher field trips while I continued with my present focus on curriculum. As I sat in the room, in isolation, and developed the curriculum material, I was aware of how hard it was for me to surrender doing what I liked most, and leave Brett and Jack to sink or swim and know that it was not a reflection on me.

The plan was for the three of us to meet once a week to review our efforts and coordinate whatever was necessary, but it would soon became a perfunctory exercise. Whatever work they were producing, it was obvious that the two of them had joined forces against me, and now even Jack was as belligerent to me as he was with Miss Huff and the curator of the museum. While I struggled with my hurt, I told myself that I got what I deserved.

Five days after Myla's departure, I was medivacked to Washington D.C. This time it came as a relief, despite the fact that I was facing surgery again. Although I only had a few more months of service left, I knew for certain that I would be returning; whatever my lessons here, they were not quite complete, especially matters with Gavin. He was out for the kill, and I was terrified. So far, I had been holing up at Brian's or at the museum, only going out in public when necessary, and then avoiding places where I might expect to cross paths with him.

I was no longer so naïve as to believe that I was simply headed to the United States for surgery. Whatever the circumstance into which I was moving, I was expecting an opportunity to rest, address my health issues and get away from the predicaments that were overwhelming me.

16

Illness: A Gift Supporting Awakening

It was a relief to be off the rock and somewhere with space to move around, albeit scrambling to acquire adequate winter clothing. It was also a relief to be where I was unknown, where I could simply be alone and recover from my confusion and exhaustion, where I could plant my feet on terra firma. In contrast to my previous medivac experience, I had little drive in me to use the free medivac phone to call anyone—a sure sign of maturation.

As I had been through the Peace Corps medical routine before, there were few unforeseen adjustments to be made in that regard. Nonetheless, the nurse was visibly concerned during our initial interview and proceeded to interrogate me as to why my health was so deteriorated. I knew I appeared a wreck: my voice remained a problem, I had lost considerable weight, a pain in my hip left walking or sitting difficult, a rash covered my face, and whatever had attacked my intestinal tract hung on tenaciously. She obviously directed her questions to get a handle on my mental state, but it felt unwise, if not unsafe, to volunteer more information than necessary. She had already scheduled an appointment for me to see an Ear/Nose/Throat specialist, as well as a dermatologist and a specialist to examine my hip. I was fed up with my illnesses, which I had largely ignored, and downright annoyed that I was relying on doctors rather than manifesting my own wellness.

I brought to the Ear/Nose/Throat specialist the x-rays taken by the specialist in Antigua. After his exam, the specialist concluded that the infection was in my right maxillary sinus. I told him that although this made sense, since the pain was mostly in my right ear, the island doctor had insisted that the problem was in my left sinus. The x-rays brought with me confirmed this. To clear the matter, the doctor had another set of x-rays taken again denoting the problem to be on the right. (The x-rays taken in the islands had been inadvertently reversed, revealing that surgery by the local doctor, if I were to have had it, would have been for naught.) The final diagnosis was complications from recurring acute sinusitis. Surgery was required, which included the removal and biopsy of some abnormal growth discovered in the sinus. The doctor picked up the phone to explain the situation to my nurse and then scheduled a surgery date. Hanging up the phone, he caught himself, and then half-chagrined, turned to me and asked if surgery was acceptable to me. I wanted to say, "Why the hell are you asking me at this point?" Instead, I nodded politely. I had a week until the surgery to address my other health issues. I walked away refusing to buy into another cancer scare. No, this trip was about more important matters than my health issues.

John and I had kept in contact after our separation. He had blessed my relationship with Max, and further, had revealed his involvement with a twenty-year old woman. At some deep level, neither of us had been successful at bringing closure to our relationship. He maintained that I had run from his love, while I felt that I had abandoned him. Presently hearing that it was time to reclaim my possessions—the many he had been inclined to use in my absence—in order to further extricate myself from the relationship, I phoned him.

The lack of energy in his voice when he answered the phone dismayed me. I questioned him about the state of his life, but as could be expected, he gave a glowing report. Seeking the truth, I continued to probe. He sounded relieved when he finally revealed that his young partner, Ann, was pregnant. It was a situation, he went on, that they had both consciously worked toward and were elated over their success. No sooner were his words out than I felt a sharp pain in my belly, which became more intense by the moment. At some point the pain was so overwhelming that I doubled over in my chair, held my abdomen and struggled to contain my tears. It felt as if I was in childbirth and something was going awry.

In my peripheral vision I could see that a couple of other volunteers, waiting to use the phone, were aware of my distress. John was quickly alert to my inattention and began to question me. Unhesitating in sharing my dilemma, as odd as it was, in turn, he confessed that he had to regularly remind himself that it was Ann who was pregnant with his child, not me. I hastily ended the conversation and sought a secluded spot in a nearby cemetery. It took the rest of the day for me to pull myself together. However, the significance of the experience eluded me.

I took a cab to the hospital the morning of surgery. It felt strange, but comfortable, going through surgery this time with so little support—no John by my side. When I had been medivacked the first time for surgery, neither of my parents had kept in touch, not even to inquire as to the state of my health, although I had phoned them from the island prior to leaving. Adam had called, mainly to find out if I would loan him money for a new car. I was hurt by what I had then perceived as their lack of concern. Presently, that view seemed childish, but it was a critical reference in terms of how I was now willing to be self-reliant.

The surgery was routine and the biopsy came back normal, but the recovery was unpleasant. I needed to be alone and was grateful that I'd had a roommate for only two days thus far. I made a comfortable, cocoon-like resting place in the windowsill of my fourth floor bedroom, which allowed me to feel as if I was outdoors. From there, I watched snowflakes wafting through the bare tree branches and caught up on my journal-writing, at least for the two days I was able to stay put.

During that time, a sense that I had to retrieve all of my possessions from John hit full force. I was not particularly attached to these items, and not particularly inclined to put myself out to obtain them, but I was definitely being directed to collect them and store them at my parents' with the rest of my belongings. Feeling I needed more time in the States, I phoned my area director to ask for an extra week after being medically released. I thought that this would be no problem since I had accrued more than six weeks of unused personal time, which I would be unlikely to use otherwise. My real motive felt too personal, so I simply told him that I felt that I needed extra time to recover, as well as to complete some necessary business. He was resistant to the idea and asserted that he could not afford for me to miss an upcoming, weeklong educational workshop being hosted by Peace Corps in Dominica, which included our local teacher counterparts. I felt it necessary to hold firm to my request and he obviously felt it necessary to hold onto his position, for he insisted that if I were to have any extra time, I would have to get permission from island headquarters. This seemed unjust, and I did not want to go to the workshop, nor did I see any value in going. I saw little value anymore in the entire environmental endeavor; it was all a game, and I wanted out. My sudden sense of resentment unnerved me. I reminded myself that I, too, had been uncooperative: I had declined my director's offer to relocate to the sister island to teach at the teacher's college; I had been egregiously inappropriate concerning the matter with Brett; and I had challenged his authority by insisting that he put his requests in writing and in my file. I set aside my frustration and trusted that if I were to have the extra time, it would be there. In the end, it was not granted.

Thoroughly piqued, nevertheless undaunted, I turned to the medivac personnel for permission to leave between my scheduled doctors' appointments. The Peace Corps person assigned to keeping track of medivacked volunteers readily granted me the leave, especially since from the moment it was approved, I was financially on my own. More than this, even during my initial medivac experience, I had felt a special bond with this man, and on a couple of my numerous appointments, we had communicated on a level beyond the perfunctory. Besides beginning to see synchronicity in operation, I was beginning to trust it. I did not have to struggle to make things happen, but I did have to keep myself removed and accept, from moment to moment, whatever was transpiring.

I phoned John to make arrangements to pick up my belongings and then booked a flight to Chicago. I was to stay with Teresa who was thrilled to have me with her for whatever time possible. I found her in the midst of packing; she was moving to Colorado upon completion of the school year, with her husband already departed to start a new job. When I entered her apartment, I immediately felt as if I had entered a much-needed sanctuary, but shortly I was forced to realistically acknowledge our relationship for what it was. Her visible disappointment when I told her I was not well enough to go on one of our typical long walks along the lakefront indicated how I had supported her needs. I would have liked to have believed that she and I were still as close as we had ever been, but cooking, watching a movie and talking until the wee hours of the morning jilted me into further realizing that our relationship was actually warped.

I took note of how I was compelled to compensate for being in her space, especially now that she was giving up her high-paying teaching position and abandoning her well-heeled lifestyle. I watched how easily it had been to sacrifice myself while dismissing her insecurities, and beat myself for remaining caught in my own insecurities. I watched her put substantial but unsuccessful efforts into understanding. The observer in me was becoming so sharp, it was more difficult for me to dismiss my awareness to maintain my own personal needs or avoid facing my own issues.

When I met John, he drove us directly to his in-town apartment. Upon entering, he pulled the couch out into a bed. Gently, I asked him if his intentions served our highest good. Thereafter, to smooth the awkward moment, as well as to take advantage of having someone with whom I could communicate at my level, I chatted for a while. However, hearing my own jabber, I stopped myself short, shifting directions one hundred-eighty degrees, and declared that if we were to have an honest connection, it was time that he openly shared where he was really at in his life. In the moment, he opened to his pain.

He was thin and haggard looking—not the gay-spirited man with smiling eyes that I had once known. My love for him was so deep and intense it was painful. Instinctively, I put my arms around him and held him as he had so often done for me. He absorbed the much-needed energy that my embrace provided. Afterward, I assured him that I would support him in whatever way was appropriate, through whatever was in store for him.

Teresa invited John to dinner that night. He did his best to be his charming self with the other dinner guest present, while I attempted to subdue my need to be removed from the pretentiousness of the evening (which was supported by wine and marijuana). When the evening came to a close, I walked John to his car and, before he left, I handed him a birthday present. One more candle would hardly leave much of an impression on him, however I knew he would value the thought. He attempted to kiss me, but I reminded him that there was no way I would dishonor what he had created with another woman.

The following day John drove me to his community. During the drive, he revealed that he had told Ann about me, divulging to her that he still loved me. Even if he had revealed nothing, I would have felt intrusive coming into her space and laying claim to what was mine. Already she had her hackles up and I wanted to back out the door, and I would have, if I could have gotten away with it. I made an awkward attempt to converse with her, mainly focusing on the state of her pregnancy, but anything I said came out condescendingly. Feeling suffocated by her negativity, I was certain that she had been putting John through an emotional meat grinder.

John had not collected my possessions prior to my arrival, as I had hoped. Therefore it was necessary for the two of us to move from room to room, among the clutter and chaos, locating what belonged to me. It was unbelievable to see the substantial quantity of my goods that John had been inclined to take. I could not shake the thought that his desire to use my belongings reflected Jack's behavior, although it was not within the nature of our relationship to fight over possessions. I continued to hear that I had to take every last item. The longer I stayed, however, the more volatile Ann became. In the end, I gave John the items to which he was attached, including my bed, their only bed. After the distractions were behind us, John and I stood at the gate of the loaded truck, dazed and silently apologizing to each other. His dread of his return to his townhouse and the waiting Ann was written all over his face. I drove away hoping that I had taken what was required of me and would not have to pay too big a price for what I felt obligated to leave behind.

Driving a vehicle for the first time in months and having the luxury of wide-open spaces, I embraced the familiar sense of freedom I invariably received from being on the road. I was alone, but this solitude felt wonderful—me, my deeper connection, the brilliant sun brightening the cool day, the wind blowing my hair in all directions, and music lightening my heart. An expanding energy emanating from my heart revealed the depth of my centeredness. I was in tune with the moment. How could I ever think of myself as being bereft? How could I ever think of my life as other than full of abundance? I was compelled to rewind a music tape I was playing to listen repeatedly to a Shaker song, **'Tis A Gift To Be Simple**. The words ran through my head. "'Tis a gift to be simple. 'Tis a gift to be free. 'Tis a gift to come round where we ought to be...When true simplicity is gained, we bow and we bend; we shall not be ashamed...By turning round right, we will be in the valley of love and delight." The song took me back to the time when I had visited a restored Shaker community. I had been struck by the simplicity and resulting ease and efficiency of a Shaker lifestyle, full of abundance and beauty. The message in the song was obvious: there is freedom in living simplistically, freedom in trusting in abundance. (I still failed to recognize that my great interest in the Shakers was founded on having once lived a Shaker lifetime, as an herbalist.)

Contemplating simplicity and its relationship with abundance drew me into an incident that Max had shared with me. One Christmas, he had asked Miss Jensey, a village elder, what Santa had brought her. Her wise reply to such a foolish question was, "Me no ask de' Lord for what me no have and me grateful for what me does." She lived in a one-room, rotting, termite-eaten shack, precariously supported by rocks and set on the edge of a steep hill. There had once been another room attached, but it had fallen off recently during a storm. Miss Jensey had never known the luxury of running water or electricity. She cooked her meals with charcoal on a tire rim, and washed her clothes in buckets of water that she carried from a community spigot up the road and then hung them on bushes to dry. Even knowing Miss Jensey as little as I did, I had no doubt that she knew God well.

Stepping into my parents' house became another reference point. It appeared more like a rental storage space than a home. Attachment to objects was an addiction in my family, an addiction from which I had not fully extricated myself. Therefore, I pushed my boxes in among others that filled an upstairs bedroom, knowing that, in time, I would be forced to deal with them.

My mother was, as usual, dissatisfied with, among other things, the limited time we had together. Ludicrous, considering she had maintained merely a sporadic correspondence with me, and that was initiated by me. My visit was unquestionably a blessing in the sense that it revealed to me what I had yet to resolve. There was no way that she could comprehend that this was purely a business trip—spiritual business.

I returned John's truck the following day, and even from the parking lot, I could hear Ann's screaming. I cringed knowing he had too little strength to handle this kind of stress. After knocking on the door to announce my arrival, I returned immediately to the parking lot where I waited for him to join me. He approached the truck looking paler and even more exhausted than the day before.

On the return drive to Chicago, I was compelled to press him more deeply about where he was in his life. He tried to be nonchalant when he asserted that if the relationship failed, he could raise the baby on his own. I pointed out the problems he had managing his own life, the probability of Ann willingly giving her baby to him and the great responsibility and commitment that comes with raising a child. He then heatedly exclaimed that perhaps the two of us could raise the baby. I took this as an opportunity to corner him about loving Ann. He spontaneously blurted out, "No!" then quickly attempted to retract his word.

Sitting next to him on the drive, as I had done many times before, words, working outside of my broken voice, were suddenly put into form faster than I could realize, "I see a noose around your neck, John. The cord to the noose is attached to a post. Instead of focusing on moving to the post, creating slack and removing the noose, I see you running in circles around the post trying to get away. Your behavior is creating a tension on the rope that is tightening the noose. You're going to strangle yourself." I withheld that I also saw a dead-end road. What I had said already was enough to leave him visibly shaken.

When we arrived in Chicago, he suddenly claimed to be running late and dropped me off at Teresa's as if our plans to have lunch had never been discussed. He added, as I stepped from the vehicle, that he would phone me before I left. As I stood on the curb watching him turn onto Lake Shore Drive, deep in my heart I knew that I would never see him again. Both thoughts left me disjointed and I would have liked to dismiss their ominous overtones, but the best I could do was curse myself for what I perceived as extreme bumbling on my part.

I sought respite from my fatigue and fidgety thoughts on the window ledge of Teresa's condo, gazing in my normal trance-like state out over the park and across the vast stretch of Lake Michigan—the closest I could get to a connection with my ocean. Energy flushing through me fed a growing surliness. If John had not wanted to use my possessions during my absence, I would not have had to put myself through this painful reunion. I would still be in Washington D.C. wandering around the zoo, parks or wonderful, old cemeteries. "Okay," I said to myself, "I can see that John was meant to take my things because I was meant to be experiencing what I am experiencing, whatever the reason, but this does not mean that I have to like the situation." I thought I would find relief talking to Teresa when she arrived home for the day, but trying to explain myself only heightened my discontent.

Later, she rented the video, **Thelma and Louis**, a story of two women whose vacation unexpectedly becomes an increasingly convoluted quandary with every turn in the road. I watched with rapt attention; the message to me—once you get caught in the momentum, there's no going back—made me sick to my stomach.

Max phoned as the movie was ending. He had seen it before and had a great laugh comparing me to the two outrageously colorful and gutsy characters. I could not imagine sharing my thoughts with him in regard to what had happened with John. Yet, as he did whenever we conversed, he alleged to be supporting me all the way. He spoke for a moment about how much he missed me and how many days were left before we would be in each other's arms, having great fun, great sex and more star babies. Then, with great enthusiasm, he stated that he had sent me a large, framed and autographed photograph of himself that would appear on the back of his book jacket. What I needed least with my life in flux was one more possession to haul around. I told myself that I was flattered by his thoughtfulness and attempted to convince myself that this gift had significant meaning, especially since he and his wife were now separated. Despite fully knowing that I had to be self-reliant, it was a momentary challenge to refrain from seeking support from Max.

He had been obsessing for months over moving his book through the publishing process and was presently preoccupied with preparing for an impending book-signing tour. I was happy for him, but was unable to muster the kind of excitement he expected. His book was a fictionalized version of his family history, embellished with cliff-hanging events and other thrills—much adventure and romance, as well as some poignant moments, yet overall short on substance. Regardless of my perspective, I was committed to supporting his experience in whatever way I could.

He also informed me that Myla had phoned him in an effort to locate me. This explained my dream two nights prior where a teacher, me, was admonishing a student, Myla, for being reluctant to graduate. It was clear that this message meant she was returning to the island. When she phoned the next morning, she was broken down, weeping and half-frozen with fear. She believed that, in spite of her fear of doing so, she had to return. I insisted that, before I respond to her, she move into her center. She took her deep breaths, as she knew how to do, and found her place of strength inside. I stated that she must do what she needed to do, but if we happened to be on the island at the same time, I would be allowed to have nothing to do with her, to the point that if we met on the street, I would walk passed her as if she were a stranger. She understood. Hearing that was all the time I was allowed to give her, we said goodbye. Brian phoned two days later to say that he had seen Myla and that her arrival was the talk of the island. After I had gone through hell to get her safely away, there was a part of me feeling like a complete fool. I presumed that this was a further test of unconditionally believing in myself.

Returning to Washington D.C., I received another call from Myla. She explained that she had flown back to island, and after contacting Gavin, proceeded to wander around in the bush above the village where she had lived. There she connected to what was calling her back. Feeling a great sense of danger from Gavin, she departed the day after she arrived without informing anyone. She was calling to alert me that Gavin had made it clear to her that he wanted to harm me, but his fear of jail had kept him in check—so far. Already a fire had destroyed the co-op run by the British man who had assisted in her initial departure. Gavin was the prime suspect, however, the police were unable to obtain enough evidence to press charges against him.

Myla had learned during her return to the island that it was a past life memory that had drawn her back. In the past life, she had been brought to the island from Africa as a slave. Her baby had been ripped from her arms, never to be seen again, when she was sold to a plantation owner. Gavin had been her baby. This explained her addiction to him, her need to take care of him and his need to sustain himself through her. (But it did not explain her, or my, fear of him.) She was living out her guilt and he was living out his abandonment issues. Now that she had again inexplicably disappeared without a word to him, we both understood that he would hold me accountable.

The following day, after a meeting with my medivac nurse, my plans were to spend a quiet afternoon at the Smithsonian. In the lounge, after the appointment, a fellow volunteer initiated a conversation with me. Todd was a middle-aged man just medivacked from Russia. I wanted to punch the energy that caused me to suddenly invite him to join me for the afternoon. I tried to convince myself that it was really simply me being needy again, and after I returned from using the washroom, I decided that I was going to excuse myself in some way or another...except that I lost my voice the moment I attempted to articulate an excuse.

Despite our original intentions of visiting the museum, we never got further than walking in circles around the front of the building absorbed in conversation. It was Peace Corps protocol to not ask medivacked volunteers about their health issues, but instinct told me that he was an alcoholic. After he left me for his doctor's appointment, I was able to calm myself enough to tour on my own the exhibits I had planned to see.

For reasons I found hard to rationalize, I heard that I had to stop at the Peace Corps office before going to my hotel room. I wanted to believe that I was surprised when I ran directly into Todd as I turned the corner of the building, but I wasn't. In a business-like manner, he proceeded immediately to declare that he was looking for me and needed to talk. A cowering inside of me indicated that something "big" was at hand. I sidestepped an urge to run the other way, and instead focused my attention on his story. He'd had a lifelong dream of going to Russia. Therefore, when that country opened its doors to Peace Corps aid, he applied, stipulating that he would only accept an invitation to Russia. Meanwhile, he began to learn the language. When the invitation came, he resigned from a law firm in California and closed out the rest of his life to live his dream. He survived the months of training in conditions that seemed amazingly trying compared to what I had been through. Yet his commitment had not faltered. It was over the course of this time that his drinking problem became undeniably out of control. Consequently, he offered the information to his Russian Peace Corps superiors. They assured him that he would be treated and then returned to duty. He had just learned that he was being medically discharged, not returned to Russia. Peace Corps was providing him with thirty days in a drug rehabilitation center and further therapy. His life-long dream had been dashed in an instant. Especially considering he had no life to which to return, it was remarkable that he was handling this so stalwartly.

I asked him when he was scheduled to enter rehab. Unhesitatingly, he declared that that was dependent on me. He then disclosed that his therapist wanted him to make an immediate choice of rehabilitation centers offered to him and be ready to leave the following morning. His therapist's rationale was that, considering the situation and without immediate professional support, odds were against him staying sober very long on his own. He requested that his therapist give him the weekend, after which he would surrender to his treatment. He was now saying that he needed me to be a part of that time. I reminded him that he did not know me. He responded that he had already told his therapist about me and the therapist was withholding a final decision in order to give him time to talk to me. I said to myself, "I don't believe this." As I heard that old, familiar voice of panic inside of me declaring that he was just another man who was going to hit on me and I would spend two days fighting him off, I was told squarely, "Follow through with this lesson."

I explained cautiously to Todd that I would honor his request, but only on the condition that he understand that I was involved with someone else and wanted to keep our impending experience free of any complications. His expression of relief was as if he had just received a stay of execution. He was a gentle man and honorable. I could see this. I was forced to accept that my distrust was coming from my conditioning and tainting the moment; it was not because of him.

This distrust had a force beyond comprehension. This was evidenced by the fact that I spent much of the night second-guessing what was happening. On one hand, I was feeling trapped, which provoked my anger. I told myself that Todd was avoiding the inevitable and should just get on with facing his fears. On the other hand, some annoying part of me was feeling a sense of importance and responsibility. Both positions were dangerous, for either way, I was in the way of living the moment. Adding further fuel to my mix of emotions was a sense that Max would be put off if I were to tell him about this situation. Experience had proven that he was able to make me feel as dirty as Carl had the time I had told him about my wondrous night-long canoeing experience with the man I had met at the Audubon Camp. Thinking this, alone, left me knowing that I would have to let Max know about whatever was waiting to happen, if for no other reason than to prove to myself that I no longer had to feel bad about my actions; that, in fact, it was necessary to know that I didn't.

Todd and I met in the lobby at the designated hour the following morning. Our time would be spent touring museums, nosing through bookstores, going to movies and conversing over dinners. I knew this man. He was another Carl, another Liam, another Max, another Brian, even another Brett—completely isolated from his feelings and a greater sense of self; living from the intellect is even more debilitating than alcoholism. Perhaps I was being given the opportunity to give him what I had not been able to give to the others—compassion. I focused to keep myself—any possible annoyance, impatience, judgment, defensiveness, questioning—out of the way, to remain in the moment and carefully listen inside, sensing, from moment to moment, what role I was to play to him. During pauses in his incessant talking, I found myself continually required to interject tidbits of "spiritualness." Characteristically, he gave little acknowledgment to my comments. And when I stated, "If you don't embrace your addiction from a spiritual space, you'll be nothing more than a dry drunk," he dismissed me altogether.

I returned home from the evening convinced that I had made little impact. I did not know what I was expecting, but I recognized that I was in need of some confirmation—some kind of sign from him that I was successfully fulfilling my responsibilities. My problem was that I was looking to the physical for a response. I was mostly unaware that, although we were interacting on the physical, the real interaction was not visible on the physical. If I were to know the true significance of the situation, I would have to place my attention upon a greater dimension. The truth was that as much as I was playing a role to his advancement, he was also playing a role to mine.

The next day, I was divinely instructed to go to a metaphysical bookstore and purchase a daily meditation book to give to him as a departing gift. I could see no point in the exercise, especially since he had previously informed me that he was not allowed to take reading material with him. Further, I could envision him giving the book a glance, stuffing it in his coat pocket as if it had little value and then giving me an obligatory show of gratitude. As directed, I purchased the book anyway. Our final scene together unfolded just as I had foreseen in the bookstore and I felt as if I had wasted fifteen dollars on top of my time and energy. Afterward, Todd presented me with a woolen scarf that a close friend had hand-woven and given to him as a gift. I had no need for a woolen scarf, but I recognized that it was a heartfelt show of gratitude. Then we shared our goodbyes, my responsibilities complete, or so I thought.

Two days later, as I arose, I was told that I had to phone him. Again, I viewed this as a fruitless maneuver since he had already disclosed that he would not be allowed personal phone calls. I set aside my annoyance and dialed the number he had given me. Further guidance revealed that I was to ask him permission to send him a letter that I was being directed to write. Whoever answered the telephone informed me that he would be with me as soon as he was located, whereupon, he relayed that I had caught him minutes before he was to go before his group to tell his personal story. He was scared to death and openly grateful for the timely support. He eagerly continued, recounting his initial experiences in the rehab program and how he was associating with people from walks of life whom he never otherwise would have met. Every word he spoke was of miracles. Further, he informed me that the only reading material he had been allowed to keep, and which he had been fervently reading, was the daily meditation book I had given him. His words stung my lack of unquestioning faith. When I explained the reason for my call, he responded that he was flattered that I would write. I knew he might feel differently when he read what I was being directed to convey; that he had to give up the sense of false-security of his intellect in order to live a productive life; that he had to be more than simply a dry drunk. Thereafter, I spent the entire day receiving the message, a tough enough challenge in and of itself, in addition to the formidable task of finding the most appropriate words. Thus engrossed, I failed to see that I was learning how to use my voice.

My perspective of this trip to the United States was that it had been as much as I could handle. The Universe knew differently, because for a considerable time I had been receiving numerous clues that I had to write a letter to Max—a love letter. During my time in Washington D.C., and above everything else on my plate, the Divine forces had been pressuring me to complete this task. I had written many letters to Max, certainly they were personal and ardently expressive. Why wasn't that enough? The mere thought of a love letter made me uncomfortable: romantic mush and sex stuff was not my style. But the soul mate conversation with Timothy began to pressure my mind. Attempting to compromise, I tape-recorded a message. It did not suffice. Putting aside my undefined resistance, I finally opened myself up for the letter to be written.

Much to my surprise, when I reread the letter it had nothing to do with romantic rhetoric. Instead, I expressed our love as having a purpose and if we sought that purpose with abandonment, we would know the essence of Divine love: Our love was not something unto itself or an end in itself, but a beginning that was beyond either of our understanding. I declared I was willing to risk who I am to join our spirits. I talked about living from a place of trust, using our past life experiences as a foundation to live a conscious connection and embracing the work that lay before us. As a new woman, I had made this commitment, which came from deep within me. It came from the Universe, strong and glowing, permeating who I am. While I attempted to get a truer perspective of my words, my ego, with its own understanding, raced off this way and that trying to put the matter into a conventional relationship paradigm. Yet our coming together was conclusively preordained, and with this understanding I resolutely renewed my commitment to living whatever was required of me. It was to my benefit that the import of my commitment remained intellectually out of reach.

Max and I had frequently conversed during my stay in the United States. In fact, the phone had become our most productive means of communicating. I thought that during our most recent conversations we had successfully expressed our feelings and created a more solid common ground on which to further explore who we were to each other. However, my thoughts invariably fell short of my greater understanding.

Outside of the surgery for my sinusitis, I considered all other examinations and treatments a waste of time, money and energy. Whatever this trip was about, it felt complete. Still, I had a sense of foreboding about returning to the island, and some part of me was heartily resistant to facing the unfinished business there. And again, the me who had left was not the me who was returning. My energy was becoming expansive enough that most of the time I felt as if I moved with my feet no longer touching the ground. I had no idea who I was or how to obtain a sense of self. Any thoughts of remaining in the United States were checked by the awareness that there were little more than shreds of my former life remaining.

No one told me that understanding who I really am was going to be so utterly challenging. Nor did anyone tell me that understanding who I really am necessitated examining and understanding, layer by layer, illusion by illusion, who I am not. In essence, I had to discard all of my ideas about who I am in order to reach the truth about who I am. In discovering my own truth, a Universal truth would then be available, a truth about who we all are.

17

Winds of Change

Whatever the nature of my experiences in the United States, I was once again returning to the islands a new me, but with little awareness of how the new me was going to manifest. It only took a moment to realize how stifling my volunteer adventure had become; my heart was no longer where my physical experiences were taking place. Nonetheless, I arrived with only one short day to get grounded before flying to Dominica, along with the rest of the environmental team, and our local teacher counterparts, for the weeklong educational workshop.

The morning after my arrival, I marched down the hill to town to obtain my mail and be brought abreast of the latest happenings at the museum. As I ambled back up the road toward the guesthouse poring over a letter from Myla, I heard a vehicle heading toward me. I glanced up to find Gavin springing out of Myla's Mini-Moke. Blocking my path and seething with rage he demanded, "Tell me what you've done with Myla! Have you killed her and buried her in the bush?" The fear that engulfed my body whenever I was around him once again left me at a loss for words. Impulsively, I handed Gavin Myla's letter, for what she revealed was enough to answer his questions. Before I could explain that I wanted it back, he stuffed it in his pocket. Next he demanded to know what I had done with the stone.

Having seen it on Myla's hospital bed shortly before her departure, I was aware at that time that it was about to "disappear." My impulse had been to reach out and grab it, discreetly slip it in my pocket and say nothing, but doing so was clearly forbidden; I had to let it go. And so I had, but not without a bit of grieving. Thus, it came as no surprise when Myla disclosed during her phone call from Scotland that it was nowhere to be found. I informed Gavin that I had no idea, but his expression revealed that he did not believe me. With an end to the questions, we stood glowering at each other, while the inner battle between us raged full force. The silence was stark, electric.

Sharply-conveyed words coming from a place I was unable to identify abruptly broke the deafening silence. "How is your resentment toward me going to manifest, Gavin? Perhaps you are going to sneak up on a dark night, bludgeon me from behind, rape and then strangle me." The truth stunned us both. As suddenly as the words had come forth, I was that suddenly freed to step around him and continue up the hill. The force of his hatred pressed me from behind and distress pressed me from within. Back at the guesthouse, I fell apart and, as much as I felt like an overreactive drama queen, I was unable to regain my composure. When Brian arrived, he was beside himself to know how to deal with me.

I paced to and fro along the fenced boundaries of the yard for much of the evening, continually weeping and feeling a ghastly tightness in my throat chakra, as well as an appalling sense of fear worming around in what felt like every cell of my body. After retiring, I lay in bed, unable to readjust to the tropical heat, or manage my fried emotions and maddening thoughts; where and when was Gavin going to accomplish his goal?

The following morning, I arose before sunrise to prepare for the trip to Dominica. I had a different foreboding. What if Brett had spread vicious rumors about me throughout the volunteer community, and now I was about to witness just what kind of an outcast I had become? Brett and Jack were already at the airport as I arrived. Even before my departure to Washington D.C., it had become clear that they had joined as allies against me. Now, as before, I vacillated between believing that their distance was a figment of my imagination and that I was deserving of what might happen, considering my egregious behavior. Yet, I wanted to find a solution—mostly to ease my discomfort—and then get on with business. As usual, I was unable to see that nothing was wrong, nothing needed fixing; I was merely reacting to our history. The situation was simply what it was—an opportunity for greater awareness. Nevertheless, I was limited from the information that would definitively free me from the energy still bound up in the situation; free me of my emotions and sense of culpability.

Being in the workshop proved to be immediately unbearable. Whenever I walked into the conference or dining hall, I unfailingly felt certain that I was being scorned. All I wanted to do was escape to the security of my room. During an interview with an official who was under the island director, I disclosed at length the entire situation, after which she informed me that Brett had already spoken to her. This confirmed my suspicions. Having heard Brett many times articulate nothing but contempt for this woman, I could see the absurdity of his attempt to now get her sympathy. Still, regardless of what I said or how I said it, it felt as if I was merely justifying my own position and trying to acquire her as my ally. Now I was forced to realize that my behavior was anything but novel. Seeing exactly how I was using her to play savior to my martyrdom, I was all the more disgruntled with myself. Besides, if I needed an ally, why focus on a woman who struggled to maintain her own effectiveness? Anyway, this was not her problem. It was mine. My obsession was a waste of time, energy and emotion. Instead of doing something to make it okay for me to be there, I simply needed to come to terms with my fear of being an outcast. I needed to remember one of my highlighted quotes from **Tao Te Ching**, "True mastery can only be gained by letting things go their own way. It cannot be gained by interfering." I needed to simply be. Only through further understanding the influence that my past has on my behavior and more practice would this be possible. Until then, I resorted to standing back and observing situations and also my reactions.

In short order I noticed an older man directing his attention toward me. I soon learned that he was a new volunteer stationed on Dominica. He was adept at socializing, but seemed to seek me out for more serious conversation. His trials during training were not out of the ordinary, except that he had become involved with a younger female volunteer. And although they had decided to live together during their two-year stint, at the end of training she was labeled unsuitable for service. Still, she planned to visit him during the summer and they hoped after that to live together permanently. I listened carefully. At the same time, I felt a certain strong inner disturbance.

As it turned out, for reasons not explained, Brett's, Jack's and my return flight was a day later than everyone else's. The thought of being around the two of them for twenty-four hours felt unbearable. The alternative was to go off on my own. But, besides not wanting to incur additional expenses (my trip to the States had set me back financially), I also remained fearful of taking off on my own, being a white woman in an island culture. Therefore, when the local volunteer offered to give me a tour of a number of unique island attractions during the time that was left, I elected to accept his invitation. As a result, logistics required me to stay overnight at his place and then take public transportation to the airport the following day. It all seemed too complicated and I had my qualms, but I recognized the push-pull force between staying in my safe zone and stepping into whatever it was I could feel waiting. I opted for the tour.

In the end, my "friend," once we reached the capitol, suddenly had a list of must-do's on which he directed his attention. By the time he checked his mail, signed in at Peace Corps headquarters and bought groceries, the day was gone, and we did little more than tour the community around where he lived, rather than the waterfalls, the river or the jungle, as I had desired. I could not let go of how his preoccupied behavior mimicked both Max's and John's. Whenever I had played the tour guide, I had done it to the fullest extent and with great earnestness. Why would he extend an invitation and then not follow through on it? Had he been insincere all along? Or had he simply overextended himself? I remained tense, distracted, and wondering why I had gotten myself into such a situation, not to mention what I thought Brett and Jack must be thinking about my going off with a man. In contrast, intuition left me certain that I was exactly where I was meant to be—comfortable or not.

Later that evening, I suddenly began disclosing to my host my trials with Jack and Brett. This time, however, I articulated the circumstances, not as a victim, but owning fully the role I had played in the dilemma. Afterward, I felt noticeably relieved, as if a weight had been lifted. Subsequently, I began revealing myself on a deeper level and at one point, a number of messages, much like a warning, came forth. One particularly odd one was that this man's life was not going to unfold as he was anticipating. Neither of us was particularly comfortable with the disclosures, but consequently my host began to further elaborate about issues in his life.

The following morning, we continued to converse, and predictably, at one point, he became obliquely forward, saying that he gave fine massages and offered me a shoulder rub, although I would have to remove my blouse for it to be done properly. Once again I found myself caught in my same old mind set: being afraid to say no and trying to convince myself that I was misreading his motive; but this time, I was able to stay with the situation without reacting or succumbing to fear or shame. I departed knowing that this encounter was another milestone. I also felt intensely agitated—something was about to happen.

Immediately upon my return, I ran into a woman with whom I had become friendly. She, along with her retired-minister husband, had come to island to do volunteer work for a year: he, with the church, and she, with the education system. The original plan had been that she would volunteer at the preschool, which was her area of expertise. I had been compelled to invite them over for tea shortly after their arrival, and during our conversation she had asked me about the nature of the education system. I gave her a frank and honest view—corporal punishment and all. She expressed her gratitude for being provided with this awareness, but it had made her experience no less trying. In the end, she was unable to handle the way the preschool children were treated, and therefore, abandoned that focus to work one-on-one with older students who had reading disabilities. We often crossed paths at the museum or on the beach and had been a mutual support, yet I was becoming alert to the fact that I kept the real me under cover while I used her to vent my frustration. I was also realizing that her life was no more together than mine. Consequently, I was determined to elevate my interaction with her to a healthier level.

Presently, with her husband having returned to the United States for a conference, she was inviting me to dinner to meet Valerie, a woman who had arrived on island during my absence and whom she thought I would find interesting. What was happening? I did not want to wait until the following evening to meet her; I had to meet her immediately. My energy was so overwhelming me, I was reminded of how whacked out I had become prior to meeting John. Since my friend and her husband were staying in a tiny, efficiency room in a local beach hotel complex, I took the opportunity, as was my habit, to swim and then commune with the setting sun before my dinner engagement. Straightaway, I was in an altered state. Before I was able to pull myself together, my friend and Valerie had joined me on the beach.

An instantaneous and severe energetic connection between this "stranger" and me revealed that this was no random encounter. I managed to stay collected during dinner, but when the hostess stepped inside to prepare dessert leaving Valerie and I alone, I suddenly began spilling out the past life experience of Something. Just as quickly, I apologized for my behavior, for being so intense and sabotaging the dinner.

With Valerie comforting me, I dried my eyes and then, as she began to speak, my attention riveted on her words. She first claimed, "You came as a light and you're like the sun; you're so, so bright. You have a great purpose. And you are exactly where you are meant to be at this moment." I sat across from her, stunned, while she went on, "You no longer have to carry the weight of the world on your shoulders." Except for this final statement her words had a solid ring of truth. There was no way I could dismiss them. Nor did I want to. My mind was traveling faster than the speed of light. While one long-held question was being answered, dozens more were slamming at me as if I were suddenly in the middle of an asteroid belt. Above all, Valerie's words pounded in, not only how utterly lonely this island experience was for me, but how overwhelmingly lonely my entire life had been. As unfathomable as the depth of my loneliness felt, the longer we interacted, the deeper I was carried into it. It was then that I knew that it was part of my soul consciousness: to be on Earth was to be alone. She also could see, as clearly as John had the first time we worked together, that I had never wanted to be here.

As she drove me home that night, uncountable thoughts jumbled my mind and I wanted to share all of them with her, to obtain her perspective (or more accurately stated, her validation). I had never felt such a high or this fortunate to have someone with whom I could so freely converse, at least not since my initial interaction with John. Pulling in front of Brian's guesthouse, we looked into, no, through each other's eyes, to a space deep in Einstein consciousness where thought transfer replaces conventional communication. Moving deeper into this state, I found myself beginning to repeatedly blubber, "I don't remember your name. All I hear is Mary, my mother. My mother, Mary...You speak my language! I know you speak my language!" I had no idea what I was wailing about, but I wanted to prolong our teary embrace and depth-defying eye contact for as long as possible, for I had a strange, fervent feeling—a feeling of finally being home.

Valerie was temporarily working in a bookstore that I had to pass going to and from town. Therefore, maintaining contact with her was easy—too easy. I found it a trial to stay away from her. Many people did, for she had a magnetic personality, and even locals, faster than I could imagine, were seeking her out. I watched my neediness blossom, even some jealousy, and hated it. I would step into the store and wait around, browsing if she was occupied with business, or someone else wanted her attention. Although I would invariably walk away with a new understanding, I felt that my behavior was dangerous: seeking from someone else what I was capable of finding for myself. It was uncomfortable to own that Valerie was in my life only for a moment, and only as a reference point—no different than John. Hanging onto someone as a means to avoid my own isolation had already proven to be futile, if not dangerous. And then there was my astrology reading: my real issue is finding my own power within.

One important reference point was Valerie's habit of addressing me as Sunshine whenever she greeted me, she claimed because of the expansiveness and brightness of my auric energy. In fact, she delighted in getting charged from my energy, and I delighted that she did. Already I felt my energy expanding in ways that could no longer be contained or concealed. And in response, I needed more than ever to change my name. I had toyed around with many options, but always seemed to return to, in some form or another, the name Sun, which for me signified a source supporting life. Yet I was unable to definitively find a comfortable variation. John, on the other hand, had believed that I should call myself "Montana Skye." Oddly, I resonated to that name; it felt exceedingly luminous and expansive, but also way, way too big to wear. Valerie's continual reflection, besides making me clearly cognizant that my energy was becoming highly luminous, was the encouragement I needed to begin to be unafraid of it. (More than acquiring a name, I was in the process of giving up my identity, and being attuned to a higher vibration, an IA dimension. To embody Ia, would first require incredibly more maturity.)

Meanwhile, Brian was off island when I returned and would be gone for a week. My fear of Gavin's potential actions had not subsided and consequently, staying at this huge, open guesthouse with doors on every side, on my own, was downright horrifying. Originally, Brian had insisted that someone stay with me during his absence, but there was no one I could think to invite or feel comfortable having around, not to mention put at risk. Also, I knew I had to find a way to address my fear, not use someone else to keep it at bay. Nonetheless, I found myself unwilling to step out after dark without a companion. And contrary to normal behavior, I would walk around the spacious abode each night before dark, closing and securing the multitude of doors and windows, despite closing off ventilation, then retreat to my bedroom, like a cornered animal. I was continually all eyes and ears. I even phoned Timothy and entreated, that if something happened to me, he must convince Max not to seek retaliation. As much as Max had claimed initially that a man had a right to his child, he had recently expressed his intent to put Gavin in his place the minute he returned.

Three nights into Brian's absence, an intense storm blowing through provided a disheartening perspective. I lay huddled in bed under a sheet, sweaty and wired, feeling fear rage through my body, while I worried that the roaring storm would obscure any sounds of an intruder. At one point, a loud bang echoed through the house. Instead of getting out of bed and checking out the matter, I hunkered down, all the more petrified. The following morning, I discovered that the wind had blown open the door immediately outside of my bedroom. It had been wide open for most of the night, and anyone could have walked right in, but no one had. It was then that I understood that my real problem was not Gavin, but only my fear. From that moment on, I vowed that I would separate myself from my fear and if, in fact, Gavin was meant to kill me, I was ready to accept my fate.

Having taken this vow, I immediately felt my throat chakra restricting to the degree that I was certain that I would suffocate. Since the tightness persisted, and not knowing what else to do, I resumed wearing a long, blue scarf loosely wound around my neck, as I had been doing intermittently for a while, and especially since the episode with Myla when my voice had become broken. For some time I had been unabatedly more sensitive to color. Blue, in particular, seemed to be an important healing color and I began to wear it to the exclusion of other clothes in my wardrobe.

A day later, when I stopped on my way from town to give greeting to Valerie, she queried me about my scarf. She had once had a color therapy business, and was keenly attuned to the dynamics of color, as well as to the fact that my wearing the scarf was not happenstance. I explained to her my endeavors of healing my throat chakra, as well as what had happened to my voice as a result of my encounters with Gavin and Myla. Her only comment was, "His energy is in your throat chakra." That was enough to send me reeling. She began to swish her arms around and behind me, saying she was cutting energetic ties to him. For me, outside of feeling important receiving this attention from Valerie, something about this felt "wrong." Most assuredly, the only way out of this situation, whatever it was, was to take full responsibility and follow my own guidance. Consequently, I excused myself and sped up the hill, trying to keep myself together long enough to pass through the gate and into the security of the yard before I broke into hysteria.

Brian was at a loss when he returned from work and saw my condition. I relieved him of his quandary by removing myself to the rear veranda. Once again, I paced back and forth, carrying on way into the evening, continually gutturally muttering and mumbling to myself through my damaged voice. The more I paced the more I moved into the frenzy, the horror, with total willingness and determination, cracking deeply through the shell that enclosed the memory that was being replayed—living it physically, living it emotionally, embracing whatever pain necessary. An observer would have unquestionably deduced that I was an escapee from a psycho ward, but I was way beyond such concern.

The record was not coming through intellectual recall. I could not see it, nor obtain any details. I was feeling my way to the essence of the memory, a process that was extremely taxing to the body. I could feel my terror. I could feel Gavin's hatred and rage. I was intuitively reliving being stalked, bludgeoned, raped and finally strangled, exactly as I had articulated to him on the street. I was open to reliving whatever pain was necessary to free myself from my past. Therefore, I kept moving deeper and deeper, opening to the extent of the hold the record had on me...he had killed me when I had attempted to save Myla from the same fate I was experiencing. I wanted details. All I could attain was that Myla had been my younger sister, Gavin had destroyed her to get my power, and when that failed, he came after me directly. I had taken an overwhelming sense of fear to my death, as well as an overwhelming sense of failure for not having been able to save my sister.

Finally I had my understanding. This memory explained the entire phenomenon that was being played out among us. Every facet could be explained, right down to my having told Gavin that his karma would define his restitution. If I held onto any fear or emotions, we were doomed to replay this experience, again and again, in one form or another, until one of us finally acknowledged that we were merely trapped on stage. I realized that I needed to know how I could discontinue living in my history, as well as the exact extent that my history defined/controlled my life. This felt like an impossible feat; at the same time I knew I had to do it. I had to learn how to live my life outside the influence of my past. There was no way, at this juncture, to understand the feat I was taking on.

Yet my wondering/wandering mind yearned for answers to the questions that persistently mired my thoughts: Were all events in my life merely unfinished replays of past life business? Where were my experiences taking me? What was their purpose? Ultimately, what did I need to understand? How was I changed? My connection to Myla was love, to Gavin fear, to Bairen an overwhelming sense of motherly responsibility. Are our first responses to people in our lives based on past life memories? What are we all "really" doing here on Earth? Could this entire conflict with Gavin have been avoided if I had been experienced enough to recognize the true nature of our initial attraction? The answers to these questions were waiting for me. Nevertheless, beyond the revelation, beyond the knowing, the fear maintained its grip on my body, and I was helpless to understand why. Despite this, with my greater awareness, I was able to tip the scale enough to lessen its hold.

This was evidenced a couple of days later, when I found Gavin selling cabbages on the main street corner in town. I stood at a distance watching him while monitoring my reaction. Under these circumstances, I focused to get out of the memory and into the moment, for I knew that I had to approach him, not with fear, rather with an open heart. My efforts took me back to the experience I had had in John's bedroom toying with the energy in my hands, and that menacing force had entered: my greatest danger was my fear. I took a deep breath, centered myself, and proceeded to walk through the crowd to the opposite side of the street. Gavin noticed me even before I stepped onto the curb. Unwavering, I approached him and reached out both of my hands, which is a show of formal greeting on the island. As we engaged eye contact, the only energy coming forth from me was from my open heart. Shortly, he let go of my hands and beckoned me to sit and talk. I first asked him how he was handling his pain. For a moment, he acknowledged that he had some. Thereafter, he shot questions at me without waiting for answers: Why did Myla return in my absence? What evilness was in the stone and how did I use it against Myla? Where did I get my power? What did Myla mean to me?

How could I explain to this misguided man that when I watched the plane disappear in the distance, carrying mother and child, a part of my soul went with them? How could I explain the pain that their absence had left in my heart? How could I explain that I would give my life, if so required, to keep her safe and alive? I did explain that there was no power, evil or otherwise, in the stone itself. It was simply an old river rock. I did not know if my position was true, although it appeared to put his mind to rest. I finally explained that I had no power over Myla; she was learning to take charge of her own life. After buying a cabbage, I rose to leave, but before I could take a step, he declared in his thick, island accent, "We need to talk more." I requested that he state his comment more correctly. He clarified, "I need to talk to you more." As much as he thought he hated me, I was the only one from whom he could get an understanding of the power for which he quested. With my open heart subduing my fears, I could perceive that I loved this soul as much as I loved his partner and offspring. Despite what had transpired, I was unable to totally rid myself of my fear, which yet had a hold on my body, or my annoyance for being unable to do so.

Only time and retrospect would enable me to recognize that I had begun to step out of my persecution syndrome—my karmic patterning—and that being in my power is not a function of struggle, resistance, surrender or forgiveness. Embodying empowerment is accomplished through moving out of limited understanding and into unlimited awareness, which is naturally accompanied by the release of the karmic vise-grip our past has on us. Viewing myself a victim is a choice, one that, if embraced, leaves me separated from the Truth, my past alive and me powerless. Our past, in fact, does not follow us, but drags us into and defines our future, locking us within the limitations of our human-ness (our suffering), an emotionally/mentally reduced state and preventing us from living in the moment, which is living our true greatness. As of the moment, although barely cognizant, I was deep into the process of reclaiming/disentangling myself from my past.

One morning, I heard through the Peace Corps grapevine that the partner of the Dominican volunteer, the man who extended an invitation to be my tour guide, had made it to island for her planned visit. Shortly upon arrival, however, she was washed off a cliff by a rogue wave; days later, fishermen found her body on the shore of an adjacent island. I was hardly taken aback. On the contrary, the message I had been required to give this man the night I stayed with him, "Your life is not going to unfold as you expect it to," ran through my mind. I could not deny the relationship between the occurrence and the message. "But why?" The message for him had done little more than make him squirm. So, it had to have been for me, for me to learn—what? Pay attention? Trust fully in myself? Again, I had more questions than answers.

A few days later, the museum curator called me into her office and suggested that I sit down before she conveyed what she wanted to say. She finally disclosed that she had just received word that Bob, the Canadian biologist, had unexpectedly died of a brain tumor. My thoughts instantly zoomed to his last visit when he had been conveying to me his plans for the future, but all I could hear was, "Traveling on a dead-end road." I had received a postcard from him, only days before, reminding me of his impending visit. It would have been in a couple of days. When I had read the postcard, I was unable to sense his visit becoming a reality, as if the idea would not fit into my mind. Now, I understood why.

I did not know how to feel about Bob's passing, but more perplexing was my undeniable feeling that something further was impending—something extremely disturbing—especially having Max's queries about his number being up, as he put it, continually besetting my thoughts. When he heard about Bob, he kidded that being attracted to me could end up deadly. I saw no humor in the situation. Nor did I want to entertain the feeling that perhaps someone else was about to exit the physical.

The woman who spearheaded the sea turtle reclamation program funded by the United Nations returned for her seasonal round of field studies and public lectures. Since she typically stayed with me, Brian was open to maintaining that routine. During a previous visit, she had offered me a job that had sounded exciting and adventuresome, too difficult to refuse. Or so I told myself. I would be traveling from island to island on a regular basis giving presentations on the efforts to save the endangered species of sea turtles. The primary target would be the educational institutions. What I tried to convince myself was most appealing about this job was that I could remain living in the islands. This was despite my knowing that the restless part of me was bored with the entire Caribbean experience and ready to move on to whatever new challenges awaited.

When she approached me during this visit about getting down to business, she presented the proposition entirely differently. Now she was asking me to develop curriculum material which would require me to do exactly what I was doing presently, except that the job would be short-term, lower-paying than I had imagined, and I would be working in a designated office in California instead of traveling around the islands. To make the situation even more unappealing, she first had to write a grant proposal to acquire the funding for my position and she expected me to support her efforts in accomplishing this task. If this was not enough, she was also making a position for herself in the proposal, which would give her two-thirds of the grant money, leaving only the remaining third for me.

She had stayed with me whenever her work brought her here, and I had valued the opportunities having her as a guest had provided. But on this occasion, the longer she stayed, the more reservations I had. Then, when she expressed that her entire life evolved around her environmental work and, without that as a focal point, she would not know what to do with her life, I abandoned all illusions.

Watching her interact with the museum curator the next day, I suddenly saw myself in the curator's place. The curator was attempting to make flyers for my would-be boss. Numerous times she brought a revised copy of the flyer to her, only to have it rejected and be given further instructions on how she wanted it done. This incident made it clear that creativity would not be part of the job description and the only challenge would be trying to figure out how to please her and, at the same time, maintain a sense of self. I was certainly in no need of another tumultuous nature center experience—not another Kerry struggle in my life.

Facing the future head on with no agenda, plans or even ideas of the form it was going to take was frightening. Therefore, I was reluctant to decline her offer, especially since it was my only solid job lead. However, I knew I had to stay open to my inner prompting rather than recreate myself in another similar situation—that is grab onto an illusion of security—which would ultimately lead nowhere other than to more conflict.

Nevertheless, after all of this time and show of interest, it felt awkward to reject her offer. I spent a good deal of time, therefore, mulling over ways by which I could present the situation for it to be comfortable for both of us. I came up with none. I had to simply speak the truth, regardless of her or my discomfort, and regardless of losing a "great" friendship: honesty speaking, we both had been using each other. Among other reasons, I had been using her to feel as if I was a part of something important, which also included getting a sense of importance. Coming face to face with the same old story hurt. Before me was yet another opportunity to heal my damaged throat chakra. After all, my astrology chart had read that I not only had to own my personal power but also express myself. Being honest always came with a price; so did being dishonest. At the same time, being honest was a wise investment; it paid off in the long run, especially in regard to self-esteem. Silence was a form of dishonesty also—that is if I was using it to avoid addressing a matter. I had the understanding, now I had to find the courage to speak.

That evening, while we sat on the veranda after dinner, she pulled out a notebook and began to outline the proposal and list the responsibilities she was expecting me to assume. My stomach churned at the thought of trapping myself in this situation, while I tried to convince myself that I was only feeling incapable of handling this great opportunity, and was going to be sorry for backing out. Simultaneously, I could feel that I was on the verge of rocking the boat, and that what I had believed to be a friendship was now coming to an end. My resistance mounted as an inner prompting to take action began to pressure me. Finally I surrendered my ideas of the future, as well as my need for security, and spoke. But I did not simply say "thank you," or "no thank you." Rather I articulated my observation of her and the curator's interaction, and how I saw that if I worked for her there would be no room for me to breathe any individual life into the project; in fact, there would be no room at all to breathe.

She was stunned by my unexpected revelation and heartily defended that she was asking me to do this only because she had no time to do the work herself, and further, that there were plenty of competent graduate students who would be happy to have such an opportunity. The old part of me felt guilty for making her feel uncomfortable, and would have liked to do something to make amends. However, the new me felt a sense of relief all around. I failed to see that handling the situation the way I did freed me from playing out our shared tumultuous past. By speaking my truth, I had set myself free, not from her, but from my own disconnection.

Before I could even begin to worry about what I was going to do or where I was going to go from here, I clearly heard that, once I closed the door on my Peace Corps experiences, my journey would be taking me to Alaska. I was hardly surprised. Little surprised me anymore. Besides, going to Alaska, especially seeing the aurora borealis, had been a puzzlingly strong consideration if my Peace Corps experience had not materialized. Nonetheless, I found myself suddenly side-stepping this directive by convincing myself, as well as my area director, that if my environmental program were to survive, it would be essential for me to stay an extra few weeks in order to personally hand over the program to the new, incoming recruits when they completed their basic training. This request was despite the fact that any interest in my project was a struggle to keep alive. My only necessary focus should have been to clear out my life in order to embrace whatever was waiting, not finagle, not grasp for security, not stall my life or waylay myself, or in any way make my life more complicated. Any effort to do so was an indication of a fear of moving forward.

Valerie was gregarious, and soon knew more people on island in the couple of months she had been here than I had come to know during my entire stay. She and a couple of younger women, who lived and worked on island, had begun a women's group and Valerie asked me to join. I was skeptical, especially since this had already been attempted: the previous group had degenerated immediately to a gossip circle, and I had walked away, but not without a degree of condescension. While I questioned my motives, I accepted Valerie's invitation. This time I found the women focused on hashing over their issues with men, as well as male bashing, yet avoiding any deeper exploration. Without judgment or feeling angry that the situation did not meet my needs, I honestly articulated my perspective to Valerie, and then walked away.

A number of American women, who lived and worked on island, had asked me to teach a yoga class in the morning, which I was motivated to do. These women were keenly interested in spiritual growth and every one of them had had some sort of background experience. It was in this setting that I was beginning to feel a sense of stronger purpose.

Jane, the other female Peace Corps volunteer, phoned me when she heard about the class, although until that point she had wanted little to do with me. The feeling was mutual. We had had words a while back and to my bewilderment, rather than letting her squirm away, I had kept her cornered to the point that I told her that I found it necessary to have nothing further to do with her. Now she was asking permission to be in my class. I explained that the class consisted of a group of serious women mutually sharing a larger experience and if she were able to come for the "right" reasons, rather than coming to be a part of what she might perceive as "the in-group," she was welcome. She made it; she worked hard, and worked with everyone else. It felt as if it had taken the two of us a long time to be where we were meant to be with each other in the first place. She confided that my telling her I would have nothing further to do with her was the first time that anyone required her to have to be accountable for her behavior; and as disconcerting as it had been, she was grateful that I had taken this stance. I was equally as grateful for the opportunity that she had afforded me. It had been painfully difficult to "cut her off," and I recognized that to do so some part of me had overridden my inclination to feel sorry for her. Indeed, I had maintained a position of uncompromising integrity.

In addition to the women's yoga class, Timothy had asked me if I would resume teaching him yoga. I had, at one time, traveled to his house to teach Brett and him. Brett retained too little interest to participate regularly, but Timothy was keenly interested. As it ended up, Valerie and he both came in the evening for class. This proved to be particularly interesting and set the stage for me to realize that I had some sort of obligation to complete with Timothy before we left island. The purpose of this class expanded to be about much more than deep breathing and asanas. In fact, it seemed that both Valerie and I, each in our own way, were being required to play a role into whatever space Timothy was presently being required to move. Week after week, the feeling increased until I began to feel frenzied and overwhelmed with a sense of responsibility that I was unable to identify.

At the same time, Jane, along with a friend of hers, Rosa, a beautiful woman of Mexican descent, had started a journaling group and asked me to join them. A few other women had come and gone, but only the two of them remained committed. Setting aside my usual skepticism, I attended a meeting. They were using as a guideline a book on how to keep a spiritual journal, which suggested weekly writing assignments. Although I felt the structure was too restrictive, I found it necessary to attend, partly due to my odd interest in getting to know Rosa better. We actually had made an initial connection when she had approached me about playing a role to Myla's recovery, and had provided the vehicle to deliver Myla and Bairen safely to the airport. I was impressed with how expressive both Jane and Rosa were in their journaling, but was aware that my efforts would be of an aberrant nature to theirs. The first assignment that I attempted was on the topic of loss of innocence. I went home to write and found, as much as my thoughts carried me in and out and through myriad facets on the concept, they characteristically came back to sexuality and virginity.

The following week, they each took turns reading the two or three page product of their efforts, which I found poignant and beautifully expressive. When it was my turn, I read the only thoughts that I had been able to put on paper: "We never lose our innocence. Innocence is impossible to lose. The most we can do, which we all do, in one form or another, is lose sight of our innocence." I was unsure of the true significance of what I was expressing, but having done so left all of us in a transformed state and conversing long past the allotted time of the class. Rather than either of them seeming to mind, they accepted my non-conforming approach—spontaneously articulating my thoughts rather than reading from a paper created beforehand—and, thereafter, our interactions took on new dynamics.

New lessons arose for all of us when Timothy showed interest in joining our all-women group. For me there was no question that he was meant to be part of the experience. It took little time for the other two to agree. What I most noticed about him was his extreme difficulty articulating his thoughts that began and ended, as well as were interjected with, "ums" and "ahs." I was clueless to understand why, but I was upset with his behavior. In fact, I felt that he was putting himself in danger by not communicating proficiently. Further, I felt a sense of responsibility to assist him in learning to do so.

During one class, I was compelled to share my Einstein experience. I had never shared this with anyone except John, not even Max, and immediately felt thoroughly vulnerable. My first thought was they would think that I was merely trying to impress them, and Jane had only recently moved beyond feeling inferior to me. Finally, I got beyond my resistance, and let the words come forth. It was evident that the dynamics of the class made another intense shift as a result. Like it or not, I also saw the leadership responsibility that came with it. In some obscure way, I recognized that this was a testing ground in regard to letting the world see me for who I really am. Still, I tried to dismiss the idea that I was playing a role to them, rather than this simply being a shared experience. But the dynamics of each subsequent meeting made it laborious for me to doubt my greater awareness. A part of me was even intrigued, if not delighted, that they noticed my "spirituality."

My yoga classes had already been providing the opportunity to move into a more deeply intuitive place, especially in terms of tuning into another's energy, whether collectively or one on one. The meditations, which culminated each yoga class, also took on a dynamics that I had never before experienced. There was suddenly nothing routine or predictable about them. I simply seemed to be moved into a heightened state of consciousness—more than normal—and then, before I knew it, the meditation was over, and all involved were relating the profundity of their experiences. Again, participants were reflecting back to me the form" my work" would be taking. I was privy to only limited understanding, however, for I was not prepared enough to know fully. Nonetheless, for the first time ever, I was beginning to feel a sense of truer self. Among other things, this had the potential to be a serious problem, for I still had little understanding of how to get myself, my personal self, out of the way. If, in fact, I were going to live a greater purpose, this would be absolutely and unequivocally essential.

While in Washington D.C., I had been compelled to phone Liam's mother. I was unsure as to why, but I knew that Liam's two-year stint was close to completion. To no surprise, he was visiting when I phoned, and informed me that he would be returning to Peace Corps as a staff member once he concluded his vacation. He was on his way to Florida to visit a friend in a couple of weeks and queried me about visiting. I did not particularly want to see him, nor did I need to. However, I had phoned him, which meant that something between us was unfinished. I informed him that I had mixed feelings and he understood, adding that he would phone me later from Florida to assess where we were at then. In the end, I agreed to his coming for a visit, which coincided with the time that Max was due to be on island.

Prior to his arrival, and once again, Max phoned to ask whether or not I were going to dump him, for if I were, he was not going to seek me out only to be rejected. He was much relieved when I reassured him, but again I was reminded what little understanding he had of the commitment I had to our relationship. Consequently, he went on to let me know that he had a huge surprise for me and could not wait to see me.

Since he was only able to catch the resort ferry, I waited for him on the hotel wharf among the well-to-do tourist crowd. Out-of-character, as well as out of line with the rules he himself had established about our public interaction, he grabbed me as he stepped off the ferry and, in the midst of a rush of tourists, proceeded to give me a long, exaggerated kiss. Minutes later he explained that he had used this greeting as a means to thwart the attention of a bothersome woman with whom he had become acquainted on the plane. Then, seemingly to redirect my attention, he began to encourage me to guess the nature of the surprise he had for me. Since it was unusual for Max to present anyone with a surprise (which I mistakenly interpreted as a gift), I had no idea what he could be giving me. With great drama, he kept insisting that I guess. Disappointed over my failure, he finally disclosed that he had quit smoking. I did not consider this a surprise—certainly not personally for me—since he had not really quit, he was only on the patch, and he had already attempted to do this a number of times. I sat across from him in the cool lobby of the lavish resort hotel, at a loss for words. After not seeing someone who was supposedly so important to me for five months, anticipating his arrival, and then having his stay begin in this manner, I was more than let down. Max was certainly aware of my reaction, for he suddenly dropped his gay facade and asked me if it had been appropriate for him to use me to keep another woman at bay. I thought it was a rhetorical question.

On the drive to his estate, we passed Gavin, who was walking along the road near his dilapidated cottage. Max thrust his head out the window and spewed, "If you want to come after someone, you puny coward, come after someone who can provide you with a challenge. Otherwise, you mess with my woman and you're in trouble!" As much as I had dealt with Gavin, and as often as I had witnessed him publicly spouting his militant, Rasta verbiage in front of a microphone, at the moment he was even too insecure to make eye contact with Max. I did not feel sorry for Gavin, nor did I think that he was getting what he deserved. Mostly I thought that Max was using a situation that had nothing to do with him to vent his aggression. I attempted to explain to him that his actions were unnecessary, that the issues between Gavin and me were finished, and I was not in need of protection, nor was I his woman, but I went unheard.

As if this was not enough, Max next informed me that he had invited the wife of a friend, as well as her friend, to stay with him for two weeks, despite his seething that I would invite Liam down for three days and interfere on our personal time. He alleged that inviting them was his way of returning a favor to his friend who had done some legal work for him. He added that the wife, who was to arrive in two days, was recovering from her husband having had an affair, and he, Max, felt obligated to support her. He then assured me that, due to her spiritual nature, I would have much in common with her.

It became obvious the moment I was introduced that his houseguest knew nothing of his relationship with me. Furthermore, when she realized that I was staying the night she was openly furious. The following morning, bright and early, addressing Max directly, and in front of me, she complained that she had been expecting to have him all to herself during her visit. Max proceeded to try to make the situation work for everyone, but the more bizarre his behavior became, the more disgusted I felt.

What pushed me over the edge was an occasion when Max decided that we should all go for a swim. By the time we arrived at the beach, a wicked-looking storm was blowing through. Max and his houseguest suddenly decided to brave the storm and go skinny-dipping. My tenuous position in the community did not allow me such a luxury, nor did I think, considering the weather conditions, swimming a wise move. Moreover, all I could accomplish by participating was feeling trapped between embarrassment over their frolicking together and competing for Max's attention. In the end, I stayed in the car with the houseguest's friend, who was far too inhibited to join in the moment.

I spent the evening telling myself that Max's behavior was abnormal, while some part of me was trying to convince myself that I was the only one who had a problem. When I approached him about the real nature of his and his friend's relationship, he claimed that he had no idea why his friend would think that she was going to have an affair with him, other than that was what women did—abandon their inhibitions—when they came to a tropical paradise. I fumed from the scene. He phoned later, amused, and claiming, "When there is a little competition, you run. You're a coward." I wanted to say, "And you're crazy," but I kept silent. I did not need to compete. Nor did I further need to be used as a vehicle to keep his swooning sweeties at bay. I informed him that when his company departed, he should give me a call. He phoned a number of times, whining about how complicated the situation had gotten. Yet his guests had agreed to pay for the cost of his car rental for the time they were there, and also regularly took him out for dinner or cooked for him. For those reasons alone I knew his complaints about them were mostly a means to soften my angst. He finally encouraged them to spend a few days touring off island in order that he and I could have some time together.

When Liam was about to arrive, Max informed me that he wanted to know nothing about what went on between us, he only requested that I make sure that Liam wore a condom. He had already questioned me as to whether or not I was having sex with Brian (as well as whether or not I had engaged in sex with every other male with whom I was acquainted). As usual, I was caught between being stunned, hurt and furious, for his statement only further confirmed the differences in our realities. Most infuriating was his wondering over why I was upset.

It was patently evident that I was no longer the character who had once been involved with Liam, and the thought of having been sexual with him was close to sickening. Worse, I felt unsafe with him. Not knowing what else to do, I energetically distanced myself. Any concern over potential advances proved to be a waste of time and energy, however, for his routine was to dabble at seizing the day and then head for the local bar for refreshments. The more rum punches he guzzled, the more he repeated his Peace Corps stories, until he was slurring his words and losing his train of thought. He had not changed, and I was as bored as I ever had been with him.

Liam's visit confirmed once and for all how sick I was of playing hostess to the string of visitors who had stayed with me, not to mention Peace Corps volunteers and associates of the museum whom I had put up during their travels. I felt accomplished that I had left Liam to rent his own car, as well as a motel room, rather than chauffeuring, housing and feeding him. Further, I left him on his own more than my rigid sense of protocol would have normally allowed—I refused to travel off island with him to visit another battle site. I was sick of living beyond my means to provide someone else a good time, sick of playing the tour guide and trek leader, sick of sacrificing my personal space and time, and sick of having to put my life back in order once I was alone again. Already I had told a couple of other people—Carmen, my ex-sister-in-law included—that a visit was impossible.

Before Liam departed, he made an off-handed comment about the suicidal woman with whom he had broken off a relationship prior to becoming involved with me. I acknowledged to myself that this was his way of communicating that he had been unfaithful to me during our relationship and a means to address his discontent over the distance that I had been keeping. I was grateful that he had shared this with me for it allowed me to drop any lingering guilt for not having been straightforward with him upon my becoming involved with John. I took his words as a sign that whatever was between us was being brought to a close and I would never have to see him again. No, regardless of the nature of this visit, it had not been a mistake.

Still, I believed that if I had been more together, I could have brought more grace and dignity to this closure. But I was learning that perfection is a matter of living each moment to the fullest of my capacity and that each lesson, every experience, was moving me into an ever-greater capacity to live fully in the present.

After Liam's departure, I redirected my focus on whatever was meant to happen between Max and me. Somehow, when it came to Max, living each moment to the fullest of my capacity was habitually reduced to getting the situation "right." Despite his having professed his longing for me during our separation, during his stay, he was compelled to relegate an obligatory amount of time to fit me into his schedule. Habitually, after departing, he would mew his regrets for having failed to spend significant time with me when he was on island. He expected me to sit at home and wait for his call, to be available when he needed me, then bristled over my unwillingness to alter or abandon my agenda when he felt that it interfered with his plans for us. He continually accused me of divulging sides of himself to others that he wanted kept secret. Worse, he did this in a manner that stopped me in my tracks, as if he had suddenly cut off my head—cut off my head because he was threatened by what I might have revealed. If this was not enough, he continued to interrogate me in regard to my fidelity. He would criticize my hairstyle, my sunglasses and hiking hat. He even bought me a bikini to replace my "industrial strength" bathing suit. Of greatest concern to me, however, was his growing disapproval of my "spiritual mumbo jumbo," as he labeled it, as well as his disapproval of my growing involvement with the many women coming into my life.

The Universe declared that Max was my soul mate and required me to live that connection while he made a mockery of it. And despite my commitment, he was becoming less and less tolerant of whom I was becoming, while I became more resistant to his incessant manipulation and capitulated less to his expectations. I was tired of being diffident. I had watched the fixer in me make numerous attempts to address the growing rift between us, but he either accused me of making trouble when none existed or told me he was sick of my negativity. Our star baby encounters became fewer and farther between and my need for so-called intimacy, or an illusion of it, diminished. Max continually claimed he loved me. But, as I gained further clarity as to the meaning of love, I realized that the difference in our perspectives was immiscible—like oil and water. Yet I knew there was a love for him that ran deep from within my heart, and despite our differences, it was unshakable.

Adding to the confusion surrounding our connection was an unnerving message that had begun dogging my thoughts more and more frequently. It had to do with him being my Judas. I wondered how someone could simultaneously be my soul mate, as well as be someone who I was possibly meant to marry, while being my Judas. Whatever this message was about, it caused my jaws to clench, a sure sign that I was on my way to a trying lesson.

My recourse, whenever I reached the limits of frustration with Max, remained to charge out the back door and head for town. But such efforts continued to be quelled, in one way or another, by whatever the force that kept me there. I wanted to get on with our relationship or get out, not remain in a senseless state of struggle. When he departed, I was, as usual, in total confusion, drained of vitality and scrambling to regain a sense of self, as well as replenish my drained bank account. Assessing the situation from a distance, it became clear that he was running scared and did not know what to do with me, now that he was separated from his wife and I would no longer be tucked neatly away as a sweet, little island benefit, and not only returning to the United States, but heading for Alaska. He was scared that I was going to land at his place on my way and, instead, consider it the end of the road.

Throughout the late winter, I had been spotting between my periods. With my tour of duty coming to a close and facing no ready medical benefits, I found myself moving into a strange sort of panic. Finally I phoned my Peace Corps nurse to inquire about the best course of action. Being this close to the end of my tour of duty, it was most likely that I would be sent back to the States for good, and earlier than my original closure date. I was presently waiting for the final word.

Two months after returning from my most recent health care adventure, I received a thirty-two-page letter from Todd, the Peace Corps volunteer from Russia. He shared all of his experiences to date—none of which were less than miraculous. He had decided not to return to California, but instead stay in the D.C. area where he planned to start a new life. He stated that he now understood the meaning of being a dry drunk and was addressing his life from a deeper place of consciousness. He further claimed that he had fallen in love with me during the two days we had spent together. I returned a letter sharing my glad feelings over his success story and explaining that, perhaps under the circumstances of the two days we shared, it would be understandable that he had misconstrued feelings, both his and mine. I would never hear from him again. Among other realizations, his letter left me cognizant that I was not inclined to feel responsible or trapped or ashamed, or be reactive to a man claiming his love for me. However, I failed once more to make a vital connection: that coming to terms with my sexuality was linked to coming to terms with my struggle with men and opening the door for me to understand the truth about love.

Shortly after, I received a letter from a young man, a student of Bob's who had come to island as a member of one of his field study programs. That was almost a year and a half earlier. To my amazement, he explained in his letter how much of a profound impact I'd had on him. He also included a tape of music he and fellow musicians had composed and recorded. I stretched back in my memories to even remember him. Yes, we had met, and he had come to my house to check out my music and ended up staying the evening. We had talked. Then he had returned to make copies of some of my music. But what had we discussed? What had I said that had impacted him enough to remember me, of all people, someone old enough to be his mother? For the life of me, I was clueless. I remember him being sensitive and gentle and not so much of a party-person as the other students. His music was wonderful, mystical, with an eastern flavor. I was all the more touched, in fact, deeply honored. At the same time, I knew there was more to this than met the eye. So what was this young man's acknowledgment showing me? My question was answered in a sleep message: "I can not always know when and how and where I will be used as a gift (a catalyst), and I do not have to necessarily know. I only have to be present in a situation." This was a profoundly important message for me, I knew this, if not by any other reason, than by the intensity of the energy moving through me, and by the intensity of presences in the room.

In April, those volunteers who remained were brought together a final time for a close of service held on Antigua. The most important point of reference in my participation was the assuredness that I had nothing in common with fellow volunteers. This was not arrogance speaking. Nonetheless, I stayed abreast of my reactions, as they cropped up, especially for a sense of rejection. At least, for once, I was holding a balance. Most of the time I went my own way, seeking places of solitude where I could make my necessary deeper connection. The couple of women who were attracted to me I opened up to, allowing for intense interactions. Clearly, two years of service had left me better able to handle these events in a healthier manner.

A number of women on island had clearly not liked me. Rather than remaining indifferent, I had habitually become sucked into my own reaction. One woman in particular had certainly held me in contempt, although, from my perspective, I had never given her any reason. Brian had related to me that she had aggressively sought out a relationship with him, but the nature of initial encounters had led him to shy away from her. This information confirmed my position that he was a factor in the issues that she had with me.

I watched how initially I had periodically stopped by her business, nervously cautious, and under the guise of wanting to see her latest collection of artwork, but really posturing. Lela was friends with her and it was obvious that the two of them talked about me. Many times I asked Lela to explain to me why this woman hated me. One moment Lela was wishy-washy, acting as if my imagination had gotten the better of me. The next moment, Lela was giving one of her high-handed lectures, or insinuating that she knew the exact reason but would rather keep me guessing. It took the course of my two-year stay to desist from seeking this woman's approval, as much as be unaffected by her attitude toward me.

Another was Brett's most recent girlfriend, the British psychiatric nurse. When she first arrived on island, she regularly came to me for haircuts. I never got to know her well, having little in common. However, once when we spent an evening together, we both shared much about our personal lives. I wanted to believe that this was a meaningful encounter, but I noticed that I felt an increasingly growing tension between us as the night progressed. During the walk home, I heard my critical self claim that I had been too intense, too prying, had stayed too long and now I was in trouble. After that, she kept a distance, and when we next landed together in a social situation, she seemed to have had her barbs up. Since she had become involved with Brett, her wall grew higher. I had to confess both that she deeply triggered the "I-must-have-done-something-wrong" character in me and that she frightened me in a way that I was unable to identify. Further, regardless of my efforts otherwise, I could not talk myself out of the growing feeling that she was crazy and would kill me herself if she could get away with it. It became impossible to ignore her acrimony. Yet I was learning that I could handle not being liked, that not everyone had to like me and that being alone did not equate to being rejected or being an outcast. It was an ultimate lesson to learn to be unaffected by others' dislike for me, for persecution would become a continual greater reality as I continued on my journey.

When I listened to Timothy give a public speech one day, I realized to a greater degree than before how his throat chakra was closed, and heard that if he did not open it, he would not survive. I left in a panic. That evening I discussed my feelings with Valerie. Her feedback allowed me to understand that it was more of the Gavin memory coming to life. Timothy had also been my younger sibling and had met the same fate at Gavin's hands that Myla and I had. As with Myla, I had failed to save him. However, the death I was sensing seemed more in the future than in the past. I kept hearing that if I failed to assist Timothy in sufficiently getting his voice back, he would be killed. Particularly challenging was that I had to aid him without revealing the situation to him. That meant I could provide no motivation for him to come and work, no communication of the memory or hint that he was in danger. Even when none of this made sense, my sense of responsibility and fear for his welfare became obsessive. Whatever was being asked of me, I had to get it "right." I listened from moment to moment, when he came for classes, exactly how I was to relate to him. I saw significant changes, miracles, in fact. Still, whatever I was called to do at any time never felt enough. Sometimes I only wanted to shake him and scream, "This is serious. Open your throat chakra now, so you can survive this time." Without Valerie being there to temper my anxiety, I would have driven myself crazy.

Due to illness in the family, Timothy unexpectedly departed a month earlier than planned. It became an extremely tough dictum to follow when I was directed to give him my amulet to wear until we met again. The star sapphire had always felt like a protection, especially wearing it against my throat chakra; I never went anywhere without it and became obsessed if I misplaced it. Whatever its significance, it was essential for Timothy's welfare that he be in possession of it now. I had to appropriately relinquish it. Further, I could not hope that he would be okay, for hope no longer seemed appropriate; I had to trust, which meant that I put no further thought into his safety—a new challenge. In passing the amulet on to him, I realized that it had never been mine, only in my possession for as long as it served me.

Jack departed next. This was no surprise as he had been having health problems himself, even some skin cancer. Thoughts of him departing put me in intense review of an incident that had occurred about a year after our arrival. After Jack continually told people that he had already climbed all the mountains he was going to climb, he unexpectedly showed up at a planned climb that a newly-hired, young employee of the museum had asked me to coordinate. Even in the best of conditions climbing to the peak was a tough venture. When I assessed the ill-prepared members of this particular party, including a pregnant woman in sandals and her out-of-shape husband, dressed in their tourist best, it was obvious that the group was unaware of the true nature of the hike. After having taken a number of groups of people to the peak, I had made a commitment that I would not take anyone who was inexperienced and had informed the museum employee of that when he had asked me to participate. I presently turned to him with a "how-could-this-have-happened" look. The most positive note was that Brett appeared at the last minute. Nonetheless, an anxiety that I was unable to suppress kept me on constant alert.

The ascent necessitated following a razor-back ridge, hacking along with machetes through vegetation that cut and sliced at bare skin like razor blades, and stopping periodically, besides to catch a breath, to evaluate whether or not we were still on the trail. The climb down the opposite side was equally torturous but for different reasons: hikers had used this same trail to the extent that it was now eroded into a virtual vertical gully. Consequently, hiking down required hanging, monkey-style, from vegetation to establish solid footing. Many hikers, after a while, found it easier and more expedient to surrender caution and slide down the muddy trough on their behinds.

I kept tail end during the upward climb, encouraging stragglers and assessing time. Jack was struggling from the start. Three-fourths of the way his stamina was near depleted. He was extremely embarrassed considering that he was an old trooper who had lived a rigorous outdoor life. But he figured that if he could get to the top and eat lunch, he could get a second wind. I continued to pep him up, telling him whenever he asked, that we only had a short distance before we reached the peak—that is until he demanded that I stop bull shitting him. By the time he and I reached the summit, perspiration-soaked and out of breath, the others had already eaten and fallen into a state of rest.

When it was time to depart, Jack claimed, as if he were an elder Indian recognizing that he was at the end of his days, that he could go no further, and we should leave him behind. His legs had become shakier, despite having eaten and rested, and he now was having difficulty standing. To make matters worse, he was openly thrashing himself over his foolhardiness. The other guide looked to me for direction. I wanted to make this a shared decision, mainly as a means to avoid having to take total responsibility should this turn into some sort of calamity. Intuition revealed that I did have the responsibility, whether or not I wanted it. I quickly assessed the situation as I kept my doubt at bay.

Because of the amount of recent rain, the descent would be a more intense challenge than normal, certainly for Jack, and especially for the pregnant woman and her husband. In the end, I suggested that we split up; the other guide could continue on with the main group while Brett and I remain behind with Jack. However, Jack was dead set against anyone staying behind with him. For a moment I was ready to blurt, "Drop your pride you old fool." Never, under any circumstance, would I allow him to be left behind. I also knew that I was the only one he would be unable to bully out of leaving him. How could I stay by his side without denting his dignity? How could I avoid making this a battle of wills? Didn't he know that, despite the conflict we had endured between us, I loved him deep within my heart? With Jack now beginning to bellow up a storm, the other guide gave me a desperate sideglance; I gave him a quick hand motion that said, "Just get going." As the others moved through the bush and on out of sight, Jack continued with his blustering. I pulled an extra large candy bar that I had been compelled to purchase before leaving town from my backpack and tossed it to him. Then I handed over my water bottle. Surprisingly, he accepted both. My hope was that the sugar would give him the spurt of energy he needed to complete this trek. Outside of that, even for two people, he was too huge a man, and the nature of neither trail would allow for him to be physically supported. Even after downing the candy bar, he continued to order us to leave him behind while simultaneously castigating himself for being the old idiot. Brett shortly followed suit when I began to joke with Jack; my doubts were suddenly vanished and all I could relate to was the humor in his sour carrying-on. After a half-hour, fortified by the sugar, Jack was on his feet and moving, although still quite crankily. I followed along, listening to his humorous muttering, and feeling much relieved. At some point in the descent, he began to desist from beating himself for attempting the hike, and instead began to joke himself, as he slipped and slid—muddied from head to foot—his way down from the peak. When we arrived in town, he jumped out of the bus and proceeded to proudly display his mud-caked clothes to whomever he met as if they were his red badge of courage.

That night he phoned me, and in all sincerity, he thanked me for saving his life. I subdued the part of me that attempted to gain a sense of importance, responding that I had only stayed with him and supported him; I had not saved his life. Again we argued, until I finally accepted his gratitude. Later, as the argument revolved on in my mind, part of me thought that if I had left him alone, he would have simply rested until he recouped his energy and then descended on his own. Another part of me was adamant that if I had not been there to encourage him forward, he would have given up and died.

Why this review? And why now? Without question, whatever our ups and downs had been, however we had rubbed each other the wrong way, I had a great fondness for this old grizzly. What we had gone through in these two years felt more than I could actually conceive—and I was correct. As his departure neared, I invited him to lunch, at which time he presented me with the belongings that he had refused to return to me after my first return from surgery in D.C. I had no idea why he was returning them now, especially since I had no need for them. In an instant, some part of me was ready to take insult, to feel used and abused. Except for that reactive character in me, it now all seemed so amusing and inconsequential. All of it!

As Jack had done so many times before, he once again reminded me of how many friends he had lost to death during his absence. One time he has asked me to accompany him while he spread the ashes of a recently deceased friend into the sea. (Upon the dying man's request, his daughter had sent the ashes to Jack.) It was obvious that he had an inclination of where he stood in line. In less than two years, his turn would come. But whatever was happening, I felt our luncheon date had brought some kind of indefinable closure to whatever disharmony we had been playing out. I was grateful, for I was not inclined to go our separate ways on a note of discord.

Jane was next to leave. She had become pregnant by a local man, and although he was ready for a commitment, she was not. Beneath her layers of damage lay a powerful, powerful being to which she was also unable to commit. She was not afraid of me, as she thought; she was afraid of my mirroring back to her the truth about who she really is. She had already overcome drugs and alcohol; however, she had yet to overcome depression. Still, I had no doubt that, whatever she did with her life, she was going to make it. She was another for whom I felt a deep sense of love.

Ironically, now only Brett and I were left. Weeks before, I had invited him to lunch as a means to make one last effort to bridge the rift between us. I even took responsibility for my inappropriate behavior. It was evident that he also wanted to clear the air, but there was still something about his girlfriend, as if she had a spell over him, that kept him distanced from me. It was not difficult to see his greatness also; that is what I had nurtured for so long and with such great commitment. And what did I get for my efforts? I knew the most important question was: Why did I expect or need something in return? At the time of my departure, I would leave him a note in his mailbox, giving him opportunity to say goodbye, but he would not respond. I felt confident at the time that I had done whatever I could to bring closure to whatever was between us, and I would be at peace, that is as long as I stayed in my heart, not in my emotions.

It would be some time before I realized that this, as well as all other conflict in my Peace Corps experience, was merely more replaying of unfinished past-life situations. The psychiatric nurse had killed me: I had asked too many questions and consequently threatened her covert effort to destroy a community of lepers when she was employed to care for them. Under her spell, Brett joined forces with her, despite his disinclination to do so. The fear that I felt when I was around her and Brett, as well as around others, was all a product of experiences from prior embodiments.

One vital realization of my growth began to be more evidenced as my time on island was coming to a close. As I worked with others in helping them discover their own power, I realized that at necessary moments, and as a means to give support to an understanding or to more significantly convey a message, I was sharing, not simply incidents from my life, but what I had considered personal aspects—shameful aspects. I was using my past as a foundation for a new reality, not simply for myself, but for others as well. Doing so felt good, occasionally even natural. It was a revelation that I no longer had to struggle to keep my past a secret, that I no longer had to view it as shameful, that I no longer had to present myself in an acceptable way in order to feel safe. If owning my feminine power/being who I am was what this was about, I was learning to trust. Yet, indisputably, I had a great distance to travel before my past was transformed to the foundation used to support a new reality.

I brought closure to an issue that I had been avoiding when the woman who initially hosted me my first night in the Caribbean, called to ask if she and her Rasta partner could stay with me for a weekend visit. They were coming to island for a British volunteer bash. Mustering my courage, I informed her that she was welcome to stay, but her partner was not; I then explained why. She wanted to know why I had said nothing before now. I had already explored all of my excuses and had come up with one conclusion: I was afraid to be honest. The woman declined to stay with me. That weekend, however, she and her partner confronted me about my accusations. I responded that I could give them a list of names of women who had been systematically victimized by this man while having been a guest in her home. Nothing could convince me, that on some level, this woman had not been aware of what had been happening. The position of silence that all of the women involved had taken had supported this man's continued aberrant behavior. I was disgusted to think how my silence and self-doubt had left the women who came after me subjected to his whims. We were all guilty. I watched him squirm under the truth; his game was finished. I noted my own sense of self-righteousness. Intuition revealed that it was dangerous and would have to be released. I was far from seeing myself as a feminist; but, for now, I could only feel that if all women would stand up, being subjugated by men would be over forever.

My relationship with Valerie had continued to grow and I had learned much from her. The insecure part of me would have liked to stay on island and hitch myself to her in some way or other, finding strength in her encouragement and insights, as well as possibly becoming involved in her "spiritual" endeavors. Her grandest scheme—I would learn that this would be one of many—was to turn the old bathhouse hotel, that had been abandoned and in a state of disrepair for ages, into a health spa. Just considering island politics alone, which were like quicksand—I knew from experience, as well as having continually heard about Brian's challenges—I could not imagine how she could possibly manage this. She assured me that the officials with whom she had already made contact were showing support. I told myself that I was no one to doubt, after all, I had no courage to take on that sort of project myself. As much as I wanted to deny it, I was able to see sides of her that limited the effectiveness of her awareness. Further, much of what she revealed about her children and family relationships told me that there remained many unhealed facets to her life.

Most confusing, Valerie continually talked about the importance of doing things to have fun and being happy with our lives. Sometimes, I became annoyed with her silliness and the childish way she expressed herself—all in the name of having fun. I was way beyond thinking about my life in terms of fun or happiness—in fact, now I could see that I had entered embodiment with a focus on something other than temporal matters. I only needed my life to be meaningful, in whatever form that took. Nevertheless, I tried to maintain that Valerie must be aware of something that I was not.

Another point of confusion with Valerie was the conflict that she seemed to create, here and there, with various people—not everyone adored her. Besides this, she was in some sort of White Brotherhood group of which she claimed her father, an advanced soul, had been a member. Like John, she had literature, teachings and such, from the organization. Upon initial exposure, I watched some part of me want to latch onto her folder of material, as I had done with John's group's philosophies. I refrained from going for the dessert, however, knowing that, in truth, I was missing out on nothing. I was currently aware enough to own that my power came from my heart, not from dogma. It was with noticeably great effort that I attempted to dismiss my knowing in order to keep Valerie in my life and myself free of facing being alone.

One of the most vital reflections that I received from Valerie was, one day, when I was assessing my situation with Brett and Jack, she suddenly interjected, "Over-involvement is a form of control." Her statement, stirring a sense of deep inner truth, made anything else that I might have said look ridiculous. I did not like this message, but it had come my way because, without it, my forward movement would be hampered. Ever since then, I assessed endless situations throughout my life where I had been over-involved, which translated too controlling. Most difficult was to see exactly how much I had been my mother's daughter, especially with Adam when he was a child. Undeniably, my behavior had to change.

One matter in particular confused me in regard to Valerie. She made mention one day about her relationship with the Governor General. I thought it incomprehensible that she could want to have anything to do with him. I understood that he had some involvement in a secret society called Rosicrucian; Gavin too, which was particularly odd since he was a Rasta. Now, Valerie seemed to also know about the sect. I couldn't understand why I was suddenly so perplexed, or that I somehow felt betrayed by Valerie. Making my head swim, a few days later, like a rampant plague, the word that the Governor General's body had been pulled from the ocean by a fisherman earlier that morning spread across the island. It was known that the Governor General went every day at sunrise for a swim. There was much speculation: Suicide? Accident? Murder? Fueling the theorizing, the day before he had been accused of financial misappropriation, while at the same time, he had his Doberman Pinchers put to death. The entire situation greatly distracted me, as if the Governor General, although dead, remained close at hand, lurking about, watching and somehow influencing unaccounted-for matters. Regardless how I approached my discomfort, one resounding thought stood firm: he is not gone. I said nothing about my impression to Valerie. After all, she thought highly of the man, going to the point of defending him when I attempted to convey to her his indiscretions with various female volunteers.

During an afternoon swim with Valerie and another woman, the question about my health and my need for health insurance came into our conversation. Peace Corps was providing volunteers access to health insurance, as well as encouraging us to take advantage of the opportunity. The application procedure, which for days I had been attempting to complete, seemed unnecessarily complicated and confusing. I knew it was "what ifs" and "shoulds" that were motivating my efforts. In discussing this with my swimming companions, I realized that the only time I had ever needed insurance was when I'd had it. Did this mean that if I obtained insurance I was inviting health problems into my life? Yes! Choosing to have no insurance, on the other hand, was like taking a leap of faith. I wanted that faith. The greater understanding was, instead of relying on an external system for health, it was time to create my own wellness. Obviously, my worry was the most detrimental force working against being healthy. As much as I hated to admit it, I was too much like my mother: somewhere inside was a character obsessed with trying to stay alive. A sense of relief overtook me as I thought about abandoning filling out the insurance forms. I laughed in joy as I declared that my real issue with my health, like any other part of my life, was my attitude. Still, this was a new step, and scary, but I saw no other reliable choice. All I needed to do for now to ground myself into this new mindset was dispose of the application. I had no idea how, but I was going to be healthy. Valerie understood and encouraged me to follow through on my insights. Yet her friend, whose ex-husband was a medical doctor, spent the rest of the swim trying to convince me otherwise. For once, it was easier to hold firm to my belief, instead of allowing someone else's position, particularly a powerfully persuasive and highly educated woman's, to weaken my own resolve.

The following morning, I awoke feeling as if I was gagging. When I attempted to speak, I went through the same gagging sensation. Whenever I put my hand to my throat, it felt like my head was missing. When I closed my eyes, I could see my head being severed from my body. These sensations continued throughout the morning. Later, half-miming my sensations, Valerie confirmed that I was awakening to another memory in which I had been beheaded for voicing thoughts that were contrary to the accepted common belief. Unknown to me, Valerie's friend had been the instigator and my interaction with her the day prior had triggered the memory. Once I emotionally moved through the trauma of the experience, my throat chakra felt much more balanced and open. Reflecting on how many other similar experiences I had encountered left me with the understanding of why we remain content to be ignorant in regard to exploring our greater history.

I had not realized the degree of my connection to the island culture until it was time to depart. I knew I could never be an islander and, unlike Max who desperately tried to believe that his community embraced him as one of their own, I had never tried to fit in. Yet I oddly felt more of a kinship to this culture than I did my own, even when many aspects of the island dynamics bothered me. One that had gone unchanged was the men's view on sexuality and females. I had already witnessed how men responded to the AIDS programs being implemented on island. The general consensus was that it was the woman's problem, not theirs. I had acquired a more holistic perspective, however, realizing that on some level women were really more participants than they were victims to the sexual/gender dynamics of the culture; and if change occurred, the women would have to be the ones to initiate it: they would be the ones to establish a new mindset. At this point, I was little able to understand how this philosophy would apply to my own life—women have to be the change that is essential for a new reality to blossom. All my lessons in this regard were closer than my present reality allowed me to understand.

An aspect to island living that troubled me was seeing a slave quality in the culture still intact. About ten percent of the island population were expatriates; they came to the island for a variety of reasons. It was largely their money, along with foreign aid, that kept the island fiscally afloat. In whatever way the expatriates presented themselves, segregation was a reality. In fact, the locals served in positions of servitude to the white expat community—maids, cooks, and gardeners. Many of the plantation inns, all owned by white foreigners, displayed murals or lithographs depicting plantation life. Looking beyond the walls of the inn property, one could see that a great number of local people lived in much the same conditions that were depicted of their ancestors in the fine arts displays. Beyond this, I could see that the beliefs and attitudes of the local people themselves left them in a subservient, if not a welfare state.

With great interest, I studied the island environment and environmental issues during the time I had spent on island. What most disturbed me was the catastrophe waiting to happen. Over-cultivation and overgrazing (much caused by feral donkeys and goats) of the land had left the island, particle by particle, being washed into the sea. Exacerbating that, the coral reefs that provided the island protection from relentless assault by the sea were being destroyed by the sediment washed into the sea through erosion. Excessive sand mining caused coastal regions to be continually more vulnerable to erosion and wave assault. To compensate for increasingly poor soil conditions, uneducated farmers carelessly applied massive amounts of pesticides and chemical fertilizers. Water resources were stressed by the advent of the resort hotel complex and threatened by a waste dump located directly over a major aquifer. There was little space for the expanding population, not to mention the increased amount of solid waste. Waste oil from the electrical facilities, about which I had harassed Brian, was dumped directly into a wetlands habitat. Fishing regulations had been established, but lack of funds made enforcement virtually nonexistent. Through tradition rather than necessity, sea turtle eggs were dug from nesting sites, resulting in sea turtles precariously perched on the endangered species list (thus the sea turtle reclamation project).

I was aware that one part of a whole cannot be affected without all parts being affected—the state of one aspect of society reflects the state of all aspects of society. The precariousness of the environment was related to the precariousness of the economic, political and social facets of the society. Just as when ill health manifests in the body, without being addressed at the source, it eventually invades all parts of the system. I asked myself what was the real purpose of developing and teaching environmental education? I did not have the power to bring about change. Change comes from willingness. Willingness comes from awareness that something needs to be changed. Education—dispensing facts—makes awareness possible, but it is not awareness itself. Something must be done with the facts for change to be made. When change does not occur by choice, however, it often takes place by circumstances. For instance, I recognize that there are few fish left in the sea, so I choose to find an alternative food source; or the fish population has been depleted so I now am forced to seek another means to feed myself. The environmental program into which I had put so much effort was not sustainable because it was not valued enough by my local counterparts to invest time or energy into it. Holding onto an old way of being would itself bring about change—both personally and collectively. I found it greatly revealing thinking in terms of this island as a microcosm of every country in the world—our planet heading for serious trouble. One thought always led to another and then another; never was my mind at rest—not so much seeing, but being shown.

A month before my Peace Corps experience was to come to completion, I left work abruptly, compelled to return to the guesthouse. It was a long trek up a steep hill in the middle of a hot day and I was caught between being annoyed and bewildered. Once there, I was drawn into a spacious hallway closet adjacent to my bedroom. Next, I found myself sitting down in front of the large suitcase that I had been using for storage. I followed my inclination to open it, and then began to rummage randomly through the contents. I withdrew a small photo album containing pictures of John and me, that he had compiled and given to me as a gift, and then I leaned against the wall, half-dazed and opened the cover. As I was drawn to move from photo to photo, I was pulled directly into a gut-wrenching past life memory. John and I were married, middle-aged and heading west by wagon train with our two grown sons. The baby (Adam) I was carrying and I both died in childbirth gone awry along the way. John and our two sons completed the journey, but because John had loved me so deeply, he had never recovered from his sense of loss. With a broken heart, he could only live a dead life. But what form had that taken? (Understanding only leads to more questions.) I remained sprawled on the floor of the closet, uncontrollably sobbing, while John's words, prior to my departure for the Peace Corps, "Don't you know I don't want you to go?" pierced my mind.

Finally, I understood why it had been so impossible for John and me to end our relationship: why he was so attached to me; why he thought of Adam as his son; why he called me by my middle name (same as my first name in that life); why he wanted to have a baby with me; why I felt so responsible for his welfare at the time of our breakup. My feeling of pregnancy complications, when he had initially informed me of his impending fatherhood and why his life was in such a disastrous state, now made sense. The understanding lay hidden in the memory. Our emotional attachment had left us to play out the unhealed aspects of a previous life together. At my death in that lifetime, we parted—me feeling that I was abandoning him, and him feeling irreconcilable loss. John had lost me again and was trying to vicariously recreate what he had had with me by his involvement with his young partner (who also shared the same name as me). Now I understood why there had been little more to his and his partner's relationship than a mutual focus on producing an offspring. (Only time would give me a fuller picture: John had buried me under a Montana sky; he had gone on to try to recreate with another woman what he once had with me; all he managed to create were enough regrets to seek relief through death; I would eventually be taken to Montana, partly to reclaim a part of myself lost in that memory.)

Healing all of this seemed urgent enough that, when I finally pulled myself together, I found a quiet spot under a welcoming Mango tree adjacent to the back veranda and wrote John a letter requesting permission to share this information with him. He phoned a day later and we talked briefly. Concerned that his partner might intercept his mail, especially knowing it was from me, I mentioned that a letter was on the way and that it contained important information. He stated both that he would watch for it and that he had only recently sent a letter off to me. He sounded forlorn and exhausted, and I hung up the phone fighting an intensely deep concern for him, reminding myself that we were leading separate lives, and mine alone was more than I could manage.

Having had this memory surface, along with the conversation with John, I began to feel more convinced that I would be leaving a week earlier than my scheduled departure date. I could feel something impending. It felt onerous and distracting and I wanted relief from it. When Valerie asked about my departure, I unexpectedly gave her the date that I was feeling, caught myself and then explained to her what was happening. She too felt that my parting was closer at hand than scheduled. Feeling a pressure of my exit mounting, I focused on continuing to bring closure to my island adventure.

I had already given away a significant quantity of my clothes. I could hardly wear anything anymore. My wardrobe was all the wrong color and energetically no longer fit. I had given many articles to Max during his most recent visit to distribute among members of his community. Much to my dismay, he had rather ceremoniously carried out the exercise. I should not have been surprised. He had already mentioned that at Christmas he would routinely buy a fifty-pound bag of rice, break it into smaller portions and then distribute them to various community members as Christmas presents. I thought that he was being insulting treating his neighbors as welfare recipients. If he were going to give then let him give, not just make a show of it. His behavior had forced me to acknowledge the deceptions and dishonesty that had frequently accompanied my own "giving." Among many considerations, I took note that I had been irresponsible in having passed this task to him in the first place. What clothes I had left (besides the new articles—all blue—that I had brought back with me from D.C.) I kept, only because I was too insecure to be left with "nothing."

I had given a television that I had inherited and many household items to Max, again for mostly the wrong reasons: a sense of indebtedness, obligation, feeding his tacit expectation, buying into his crying poor. Many others I left for incoming Peace Corps volunteers, to make their experience easier for them. A few items: a blanket, pillow, towels, I dropped off at Miss Jensey's, the elderly matriarch of Max's community to whom I felt a strong connection. In ways that I was yet to define, I knew that I had learned much from having made her acquaintance. A few special items—like a glass prism shaped like an obelisk which made beautiful rainbows when the sun shown on it—I dropped off by Mr. and Mrs. Remy, the couple with whom I had initially stayed during my training process. (It did not go unnoticed that Mr. Remy's vital energy was low. Within a year, he would exit the physical.) There was definitely a close connection between us. They had continued to drop off fresh eggs and such every once in awhile, and their son came to borrow my camera whenever a special occasion called for its use. I knew that if I were truly generous, I would give him the camera to keep. Overall, it had become much easier to dispense with my possession, but I had many miles to travel before I reached a place of total non-attachment, total trust in abundance, living from my heart, which all tied together allows us to live true giving.

In the end, my suitcase contained a few clothes and my scuba gear, and otherwise, mostly mementoes of my island experience: lots of shells and coral fragments, photographs, baskets woven by area artisans, Max's eight by ten framed picture of himself that Teresa had had to forward to me and gifts from local participants of my yoga classes. Of vital importance were gifts from John, which, yet unbeknownst to me, I would soon have to relinquish.

Miss Huff unexpectedly cornered me one morning as I made my way to the museum to work. Elmer, her dog, had been missing for a few days and she, without mincing words, asked me if I had poisoned him. A year earlier, or even a short time earlier, I would have been consumed with hurt and seething with rage to have been jabbed with such an absurd allegation. I struggled to remain non-reactive, to not take this as a personal affront. I did not need to be in conflict with Miss Huff any longer, not with anyone, including myself. As she continued to eye me suspiciously, I searched for my inner balance, to let my heart speak—maybe my last chance to do so with her. I wanted to say, "Miss Huff, why don't we just drop all of this? You know you like me. And I know I like you. Let's take it from there." Those words would not come. Instead I claimed, only somewhat indignantly, that I knew nothing of her dog's whereabouts, but hoped that he was fine. Without question, I had always been aware that Miss Huff, much like my mother, was desperately lonely, and had acted out her jealousy, as much as her disappointment in regard to my failure to personally support her. I felt traumatized walking away, and did not know why, but I wanted to know. Why my aversion to her when I felt a deep sense of love for her? Why the urge to avoid her? Why, oh why, couldn't I live from a place of harmony? Certainly I was meant to do so.

Little more than a week before my scheduled departure, in the middle of the night, unable to sleep, I found myself digging into the same suitcase where I had previously found the photo album. This time I singled out two glass paperweights that John had made for me while visiting his brother, who owned a glass company in California. The first paperweight was simple, sky blue with ribbons of white running through—which reminded me of the wind—and a couple of pink flowers, as well as one white one moving on the wind. John and his brother had experimented with unusual material to make the second paperweight, successfully creating the appearance of a coral reef in a rich, blue ocean of waves, a long-haired mermaid swimming through. John had given that paperweight to me during the time I had learned to scuba dive. It had become symbolic of my initiation into another reality, along with the awakening of a prior memory of having experienced life in an ocean environment. He had impressed upon me at one time, "Don't give these away like you do everything else." Knowing the love that was instilled in the two paperweights, I cherished them. But as I held them in my hands, which were suddenly pulsing with a most dreadfully intense energy, I kept hearing, like a strange foreboding, over and over, "Too heavy! Too heavy!" Finally I retreated to bed, taking with me the framed photograph of Max and the two paperweights, which I arranged on the nightstand close at hand. I resorted to trying to fall asleep, but I could not keep my eyes closed; I could not keep my gaze from the three "gifts" given to me by these two men whom I so dearly loved.

The following morning, distractedly agitated, I prepared to attend a meeting with the educational director. I was just about to lock the door when the phone began to ring. Even before I reached for the receiver, the sense of foreboding I had felt during the night sprang forth, full force. The female caller identified herself as John's neighbor from his community. Struggling to hold back a storm of tears, I vacillated between beseeching, "No, don't tell me, I already know!" and "Go ahead and tell me, I can handle it!" John had a flair for living his life with pizzazz, so it came as no surprise that he made his exit from the physical dimension by way of a fiery car crash. The accident had taken place the preceding morning, about the time I had precipitously departed the museum and scurried up the hill needing to dig into my suitcase and pull out the photo album.

After the conversation ended, I sank into Brian's favorite chair on the cool corner of the veranda. I thought that the only situation that could be more devastating was to hear that Adam had been killed. "What do I do now?" I asked myself. Holding myself together I phoned my educational officer to ask permission to postpone the meeting. Then I phoned Lela. She arrived shortly.

Lela had become friends with John during his two visits and had even stayed with him for a month in his community townhouse the prior summer. Despite John and I having, as best we could, gone our separate ways by then, refraining from being suspicious had been a challenge, especially since she had no boundaries with men. She had assured me during the course of her stay, when John would phone me and she would end up conversing also, that his focus of conversation was habitually about our breakup. Since oftentimes the two of them gave conflicting perspectives of their time together, I was never certain what had transpired, and I told myself that it was none of my business. More than being jealous over the possibility of their being sexual, I had found myself more jealous that Lela had participated in John's sessions with clients. I was never exactly sure as to what form that had taken. I told myself that it was ridiculous to feel left out, especially considering that I had previously declined John's offer to do the same.

When I informed Lela of the nature of the memorial arrangements—a formal Catholic ceremony arranged by his family from California and then the following day a community memorial event—she unexpectedly claimed that she wanted to attend the latter. On my own I would have never considered attending. Thoughts of setting foot in his community alone unnerved me, although I failed to understand why—why I shouldn't be part of the experience; why I was suddenly feeling like an outsider and would stir up trouble if I should suddenly make my appearance. After all, his neighbor had phoned to inform me. Lela's position left me to realize we would be sharing the experience. Consequently, I immediately made the necessary phone call to my Peace Corps director. The sign that I was meant to attend John's memorial service would be his sanctioning an early departure. I explained the situation as honestly as possible, although my inclination was to create an edge by stating that John was a family member. Doing so proved unnecessary, for with hardly a second thought, he agreed. Lela quickly departed to make necessary preparations for the trip.

Since news on island moves with hurricane wind velocity, within an hour, the phone was ringing nonstop. When Brian heard the news, he left work early, and as best as he could deal with such emotionally wrought situations, he asked me how he could support me. Without hesitation, I requested that he drive me to the beach. We conversed little along the way. Yet his strong, familiar euphonic British accent and, non-intrusive mannerism were comforting enough. I had certainly been aware of his deep fondness for me, aware that with only as much as a signal from me, he would have heartily pursued closer contact. I was aware of his dislike for Max, as much as Max's treatment of me. I was aware of how trying it had been for him, having me so close, yet so far. I had thought how unfair it was for him to have to live under such limitation, but I had always been ready and willing to move from his premises if so called to do. I never doubted, however, that we were brought together under these conditions for certain reasons—reasons I was unable to fully define. There was no question of the love between the two of us, despite my disinclination to step into a sexual relationship. More than a rigid sense of British protocol, he had always demonstrated a deep consideration and thoughtfulness in whatever situation he encountered. His integrity was impeccable. These were only a few of his many attributes.

This did not mean that I missed the fact that he was an alcoholic, painfully lonely and had issues with women, as well as self-esteem. As he had often taken me into his confidence in regard to all facets of his life, I probably knew him better than almost anyone else. In contrast, he hardly knew me. I understood that this was because my reality was of an uncommon nature, that no one could know me. It was comforting that, for once, I had been able to refrain from imposing my need to be understood onto this relationship. Nonetheless, I was also aware that there was reluctance to openly and freely reveal my true self to Brian. Why? Incontestably, my fear of being viewed as crazy, translated to, my fear of rejection.

Once at our destination, Brian left me to myself while he sought out the beach bar. I was grateful that the beach was deserted. Perhaps for the last time ever, I was here communing with my reliable source of solace—the ocean. All the same, her power had little healing effect this time, or perhaps I was not ready for comfort, for suddenly a sense of helplessness began to fuel my growing anger and distress as the thought, "He died of a broken heart—and it's all my fault!" echoed painfully through my psyche. I assured myself that if he had only received my letter in time he could have avoided death. I cursed my premonitions. I cursed having had to tell him that he had a noose around his neck and he was going to kill himself if he did not get a grip on his life. I screamed. I wept. I hated myself for the wrong I believed I had done to him. I was angry and I wanted to stay angry, to hate myself forever if possible, to die in my own pain, just as I perceived he had; die, because doing so seemed easier than letting go of my sense of culpability. He was gone, and just as I had known when he dropped me off at the curb in front of Teresa's condo complex, I would never see him again.

Through my franticness, I suddenly felt a wish beginning to permeate my consciousness. It took me by surprise and caused me to become quieter. It was uncommon for me to make wishes. To me, wishes were for people who had difficulty managing their own lives: wishing was akin to praying. But the wish was there, becoming more prominent in my thoughts. I was wishing on the stars in the heavens to see John just one more time, to tell him how utterly sorry I was for how I had treated him, and that leaving him had not been my choice, rather a choice which was required of me. I desperately needed to let him know how heart-felt my love for him was.

As I further calmed myself, I realized that my wish was being granted, for I suddenly felt John's laughing, carefree presence, exactly as he had been when I first met him, there with me. My wonder was so great I burst into tears anew. Instinctively I knew that an abreaction would interfere with our communication, so I once again calmed myself and then listened carefully. He implored that I not mourn, that he was fine, happy and free. Energetically, we continued to communicate for considerable time. Feeling his presence so close momentarily offset my weight of guilt. Still, many "what ifs" kept running through my mind, especially the "what if," besides dying of a broken heart, he had died as a means to avoid dealing with his relationship with his partner.

When we returned to the guesthouse, I phoned Max. He conveyed his condolences. It had never set well with him that John and I had maintained such a strong connection, despite my assurance that he had nothing to worry about. Before we said our goodbyes, trying to appear like a jest, he once again articulated the dangers of being attracted to me and then asked if he might be number three. Even without this conversation, I was already beginning to feel as jinxed as I had in my youth. I hung up the phone struggling to avoid such a backward step.

Meanwhile, John maintained close contact. This situation validated the feeling I'd had about the Governor General sticking around after his death, but, conversely, it was comforting having John hereabout. However, all too soon he began to talk non-stop, shooting his thoughts directly into my mind. To my utter amazement, he shared that he would be reincarnating through the body of his unborn child. I wanted to share the memory of our westward journey with him, yet I knew that from his vantage point all this information was readily available to him: he already knew I was remorseful; he knew I loved him, that I would always love him; he knew our heart connection was too strong to sever. I shortly realized that he was becoming a nuisance. I even felt as if he was thrilled having the opportunity to be in my room while I changed my clothes. I did not want to lose him, only for him to be less intrusive.

Valerie was visiting the next day when he again blew in like a disorderly little whirlwind. At first, she too was charmed by his behavior; but when he persisted in being distracting, she questioned me about the nature of his calling. Understanding the repercussions of a deceased being holding onto the Earth plane—he holding onto me and I to him—Valerie made clear the necessity of my assisting John in completing his transition. Understanding the truth in Valerie's message—this did not mean that it was easy or that I wanted to do it—I connected to John through my heart, as we had done so many times before, and then proceeded to inform him that it was time that he move on. Both Valerie and I could feel his departure, the final stage of his transition process. At the moment, I thought this was the end of our interaction, but it was not. He would continue to make contact with me, although less frequently, and with great maturity.

I understood that John completing his transition now attuned him to a larger scope of awareness. Yet something holding my mind captive made it impossible for me to fully release the belief that if he had understood our shared past, he could have avoided many of his problems, and ultimately his death. I was my own heartless God condemning me to a sentence of life burdened with guilt. I was compelled to eliminate all the ties I perceived linked me to him: all gifts, photographs, mementoes, all except a few items, most especially the two paperweights, which I had promised to never give away. Ridding myself of memories was a covert effort to rid myself of the pain, which I could not separate from the love we held. Time constraints did not allow me to begin the elimination process before my departure, but it would be a priority upon return to the States.

My last night on island! Goodbyes were behind me. Brian was asleep. I sat alone, my bags packed and ready, and began to examine my conspicuously spacious bedroom. This one room was larger than my entire cottage, and here I even had my own private bath, going from stark and simple to almost posh by my standards. Yes, I did feel worthy to end my stay in such luxury. Yet I felt a sense of longing for my mosquito net shroud—shaped like a pyramid wrapped around the corners of my tiny bed—pyramid power! All those unseen beings surrounding me during all those nights of sleep work! More than I could imagine—or ever want to imagine—had taken place within that gauzy embrace there in that cracker-box bedroom. If Miss Huff only knew all that had transpired in her rental cottage.

The raging wind rattling the palm fronds nearby made it obvious that a storm was a breath away. That was how I felt—stormy. Although I well knew I was finished here, so much felt unfinished. There was my "work," my classes with the women. Such incredible new spaces were opening in that context. Was I really meant to walk away from it all?

Then there was Max. He felt so far away, like a strange dream. Yes, he had expressed his condolences. Regardless, he was not here to comfort me in the way that I had comforted him when people in his life had died. He was not here to blanket me and take away my pain. I had to admit that some part of me wanted him to be here for me. I wanted a shoulder to lean on. All things considered, I knew that Max could not, and would most likely never be able to be supportive. How could he? He had yet to learn to support himself. I loved him—yes! But what did that mean? I unzipped one of my packed suitcases and pulled out his eight by ten photograph. He was photogenic all right, poised there in his well-developed manufactured image. "Being around him can be so exhausting," I said to myself. I reached beyond the surface to his core self. I could feel support there. My teacher! I could still not comprehend that intellectually. Only time and more lessons would reveal just how invaluable he was in regard to my awakening. He was a key. Without him, I would be unable to follow the thread of my existence, and not only discover the tapestry of consciousness, but acknowledge my place in it.

I pushed aside the bedspread and curled up on the cool sheets. The wind was gusting through the three sizeable windows, and through every cell in my body, my mind, and my consciousness, bringing change. The situation reminded me of when, seemingly so long ago, I had hiked to "my woods" in the aftermath of a storm, and had been compelled to wrap myself around a sapling Maple, feeling its calm, even while it was being wrenched to and fro in the blustery weather. Sleep would not come to me this night: more review was at hand, and much information was ready to be downloaded into my psyche—Einstein matters again.

Two days after John's death, my dear and faithful Brian drove Lela and me through a pre-dawn soaker to the resort hotel ferry. It would deliver us to the sister island where we would catch our flight. After dealing with glitches that came with living in the islands, we strapped ourselves into our seats for the flight to Puerto Rico and then onward to what I once called home. Disregarding all of the highs and lows in Lela's and my relationship, it felt good to have her sitting beside me. We were departing on the exact day that I had been sensing.

Always an obsessive need, I managed to get a window seat. The sun was only minutes above the horizon but already brilliantly luminiferous. I pressed my face against the tiny window, straining to obtain a permanent mental picture of my beloved, verdant gem set in an endless, glistening ocean, merging into a sky of exquisite shades of healing blue. I had no idea whether or not I would ever lay eyes on her again. I tightened my blue healing scarf around my neck as I greedily strained all the more, incising the moment, intaglio-style, into my mind. What irony that I had once claimed, "The last place I will ever consider going is to some obscure little island in the middle of nowhere!" My island affairs had teemed with as much experience as there was life in the ocean. What I would have missed had I maintained my arrogance! It was scary to think that I could have gotten in the way of my own growth—my own Divinely-planned adventures. Minute by minute, my only sense of home—my life as I knew it—became smaller and smaller, then only a dot, and finally lost from sight. My heart felt empty and I needed to cry. This mourning would have to come later.

Among other topics brought up during the flight, was the significance of the wall hanging that I had commissioned Lela to make for John. I could not ignore a resounding certainty that it had been a premonition, a representation of an impending phase in John's life. He was the baby in the lotus blossom. Lela had used the wall hanging as a prototype, and now had a number of refined versions. Despite this, she was suddenly bent on getting the original back if at all possible. For a moment, I thought that if she were generous and understanding, she would be offering me an opportunity to have it. But I knew ultimately that I was not to have it, whatever the reasons. There was no room for me to indulge in pettiness.

When not in conversation with Lela, I brooded over the challenges of moving on with my life. Going to Alaska seemed so unreal, so far away. Returning to the United States seemed challenging enough. I didn't know why I so desperately wanted John's last letter to me. Perhaps moving on would be easier if I could hold his last thoughts in my hands. The letter should have arrived already, but mail service in the Caribbean was like most every other service, hit or miss. Tenaciously, I clung to the belief that his letter would reach me in some way or another, even if it took a miracle.

If having to deal with all this wasn't enough, I was suddenly put in review of the uncountable times during my island adventure when I had felt that I had bungled situations and relationships. My ego self still tried to hold onto the belief that I was too judgmental and controlling, too self-centered, needy and compassionless. My ability to see inside of people, to identify what they denied about themselves—both strengths and weaknesses—remained bothersome to me. This present review, however, confirmed that I was learning to hold a healthier view of my behavior and involvement with others, that my many varied island experiences had been a further means to free myself from my limiting beliefs, and especially from my addictive need to be accepted.

One of my most important understandings grew out of hypnotherapy sessions with David. He had continually explained to me, through my bouts of impatience, that I could only fully and accurately comprehend what was happening to me in retrospect, not while in process. This meant that at some point I could look back on a particular time or situation in my life and comprehend what had actually happened, what I had relinquished, what I had received in return, the healing and growth that had occurred, the greater awareness I had attained, and the distance I had traveled since then. Sort of an "Oh yes, now I get it."

Despite frequent bouts of anxiety, confusion and overwhelm, my life was becoming more meaningful than I could ever imagine. I was learning to live in the moment (which is a function of a greater reality, while patience is a function of linear, time-related reality). I was learning that where I was at any given time was exactly where I was meant to be. Yet, much like a mosquito caught in my mosquito net during the night, that restless searcher in me continued buzzing me to distraction.

Many years earlier I had vowed that I would learn the truth about who I really am, and live my life as a gift. Shortly after taking that vow, I was given the dictum that I had to let the world see me for who I really am. Retrospect would reveal that my vow and the dictum were one and the same, and that I was in the throes of manifesting that reality.

If I thought that my lessons to date had been painful, or tough, or impossible, if I thought my mettle, my strength of spirit, had been tested, a revelation was waiting. I was about to take a further step into my purging and purifying process, a course of action that would continue to rip me free from the limitations of my past and bring me face-to-face with who I am—who we all are. It was a guarantee that the winds of change would continue to gust through my life. I had traveled an immeasurable distance since declaring my vow. Yet this journey of journeys, this quest for understanding, had hardly begun.

An Invitation

Yes, there is another IA story coming to fruition, and then another.
The next book may be yours, for our stories must be shared.

Your story is no less valuable than mine.
Word by word, experience by experience, begin writing your own story.
Live it consciously.
Believe in its importance.

Trust in your own intuition.
Trust in your own guidance.
Both are waiting.

It takes only one first step to begin your own incredible journey.
Follow your own thread and you will find yourself—and me.
Join me.
Your home is waiting for you.

It is time to acknowledge our true identity.
Only then can *peace* reign.

ISBN 155369025-7